Writing Dylan

Writing Dylan

The Songs of a Lonesome Traveler

LARRY DAVID SMITH

Westport, Connecticut
London

Library of Congress Cataloging-in-Publication Data

Smith, Larry David.
   Writing Dylan : the songs of a lonesome traveler / Larry David Smith.
      p. cm.
   Includes bibliographical references (p.   ) and index.
   ISBN 0–275–98245–9 (alk. paper)
   1. Dylan, Bob, 1941—Criticism and interpretation.   2. Popular music—United States—History
and criticism.   I. Title.
   ML420.D98S56   2005
   782.42164'092—dc22   2005013519

British Library Cataloguing in Publication Data is available

Library of Congress Catalog Card Number: 2005013519
ISBN: 0–275–98245–9

First published in 2005

Praeger Publishers, 88 Post Road West, Westport, CT 06881
An imprint of Greenwood Publishing Group, Inc.
www.praeger.com

Printed in the United States of America

The paper used in this book complies with the
Permanent Paper Standard issued by the National
Information Standards Organization (Z39.48–1984).

10 9 8 7 6 5 4 3 2 1

To

William R. Brown
Jack E. Douglas
Joseph Foley
and
James L. Golden

Buckeyes All

Contents

Preface

What would I do without Eric Levy? Eric's my editor and dear friend. He and the fine folks at Praeger have dutifully supported all of my studies on songwriting. *Thanks everybody*. It's been quite the journey. In the early 1990s, before Eric arrived, Pamela St. Clair and I initiated this research program with our exploration of Pete Townshend's career. Thanks to Pete's and Nicola Joss's generosity and kindness, I was able to embrace the details of my subject matter by reprinting each song's lyrics as needed. Discussions of individual songs or other materials featured their specific details. If I advanced a particular claim, I had the evidence to support it. It doesn't get any better than that. Afterward, Eric and I gave birth to the "twins" that are my comparative analyses of Bob Dylan's and Bruce Springsteen's work (and their respective contributions to the Woody Guthrie celebrity-singer-songwriter tradition) and Elvis Costello's and Joni Mitchell's work (and their respective contributions to the torch song tradition). The twins were frustrating in that I was unable to achieve the depth I obtained with Pete's art. Without the space necessary to reprint the details of individual songs, the artists' work rushed by in eras with selected exemplars offering hints of what was actually there. The artists and their representatives kindly gave me everything I asked for; I was simply following a different critical strategy. The plan worked in that the comparative approach generated insights that only a macroscopic argument could yield. As such, they represent invitations for further study. Here, I'm able to return to the Townshend method and present Robert Allen Zimmerman's lifework in all of its glorious detail. Thanks to Lynne Okin Sheridan and Jeff Rosen of Bob Dylan Music, I'm able to offer the data necessary to support my claims about the artist the world knows as "Bob Dylan." Consequently, I'm in a position to build upon the foundation that was *Bob Dylan, Bruce Springsteen & American Song* and advance my research program on songwriting. None of this would have transpired without Eric and Praeger. Like my professors at Ohio State listed in the dedication, they're responsible, but not to blame.

The first question any *reasonable* person should ask about another study of Bob Dylan's art is "What could you possibly offer that's not available elsewhere?" I mean, as we'll see, Dylan has been discussed from every imaginable angle—often in *tremendous* detail. His biography, his musical lineages, his poetic associations, his day-by-day activities (amazing), and his role in the history of the world have been massaged repeatedly with varying results. I'm truly humbled by this body of literature. Honestly. But I have a twist that has, somehow or another, been overlooked in those projects. Here I separate the artist, Bob Zimmerman, from his public persona, Bob Dylan, as I argue that Zimmerman systematically pursued a series of creative *missions* through strategic applications of his Bob Dylan persona—a character that consists of two distinct dimensions: Bob Dillon and Jack Fate. As Zimmerman marched through his career, he deployed Dylan in a calculated manner, applying Dillon's rebellion or Fate's encyclopedic knowledge of music to his current ends. For this study, Zimmerman's biography ends rather early. This is an account of the man's art, not his persona's celebrity history.

What would I do without Eric? He digested my idea and gave it this title. He understood exactly what I wanted to say before I had written the first word. This book is about how Zimmerman *wrote for* Dylan, created the auteur "Bob Dylan," and built an oeuvre as impressive as any artist's from any time in any field. I aspire, then, to present an argument that not only complements what others have to say, but also takes us inside a formidable body of art. The oeuvre is diverse, extensive, innovative, provocative, and, in every sense of the technical term, historic. It's quite a story.

Before turning to the specifics, I feel compelled to share a personal take on this Bob Dylan thing. This has been my job for some time, and I've traveled and read, listened to, watched, and considered all sorts of materials. There's no shortage of information on this topic! One important source involves Dylan's live performances. This man performs one out of every three nights a year. It is a vital aspect of his career—and his current mission; therefore, I saw as many shows as possible over the past few years. One moment was telltale. In the summer of 2004, Dylan and the legendary Willie Nelson toured the United States by performing in minor league baseball parks. The show admitted children under twelve for free. A family atmosphere blended with the usual activities associated with outdoor music events. After a brief opening act, Nelson appeared before his adoring—I mean *adoring*—crowd. People openly wept. The rapport was quite emotional. Nelson tossed his hats into the crowd. They tossed their hats onstage and Willie wore them—much to the delight of his fans. He blew kisses. He tossed bandannas. He threw guitar picks. Willie and his audience had themselves one mighty fine public sharing. It was a sight to behold. Then Bob Dylan and his band came onstage. This band dressed formally, acted in an extremely professional manner, and never *ever* interacted with the audience. Dylan never said a word outside of introductions. They may have seemed detached, but this band was as good as any musical ensemble that you'll ever see. They're simply stunning in their virtuosity. When the group accepted applause at the show's end, they stood motionless—arms by their sides, expressionless. This show was about the music, not the performers. During the South Bend, Indiana, show, drummer George Recile lost a drumstick while playing and it laid before Dylan as he walked across the stage at concert's end. He picked it up, looked at the audience, and the audience went nuts, screaming and begging him to toss the drumstick into the crowd. Dylan gazed back at them, looked at the drumstick in his hand, glanced back at the crowd (showing no expression whatsoever), and walked off the stage carrying the drumstick. *That* is Bob Zimmerman of Hibbing, Minnesota, as I have come to know him through his art. I hope you enjoy the book. Thanks, Eric.

Introduction

Sam Peckinpah's 1973 film, *Pat Garrett and Billy the Kid*, opens with scenes of 1880s male bonding as the Kid and his entourage relax around the old corral and shoot chickens for fun. When a rifle shot blasts from behind (and another bird bites the dust), the boys celebrate the arrival of old pal and soon-to-be-lawman, Pat Garrett. Once the Kid and Garrett nestle in a local bar, the lawman announces his intentions to his former comrade. The two men part with their new understanding in place. Next, the movie takes us to an abandoned farmhouse, a gunfight between a portion of the Kid's gang and Garrett's overwhelming official forces, and ultimately, the Kid's arrest. Once in custody, the Kid and his captors enjoy a game of cards (while Garrett makes his rounds), then the Kid makes his move, kills everyone, and parades out of town as a shy, unassuming shopkeeper observes. The shopkeeper is clearly captivated by what he has just witnessed. The young man rips off his apron, tosses it down, and contemplates his new situation. After Garrett returns and discovers the wreckage, he ventures over to the barber for a drink and a shave. The young shopkeeper follows. During his shave Garrett turns around, faces the shopkeeper, and asks his name. The nervous, young man with bright blue eyes acknowledges the question's validity. Soon, the youngster joins the Kid's gang and we learn his name: "Alias."

In January 1978 Bob Dylan's four-hour celluloid adventure, *Renaldo & Clara*, premiered in New York and Los Angeles. The film—based on scenes and characters associated with the 1975 vaudeville caravan "The Rolling Thunder Revue"—is an intriguing blend of fact and fiction. Concert footage, travelogue scenes, interview segments, scripted and unscripted fictional episodes, and a host of chaotic visual sequences unfold in unpredictable, nonlinear fashions. Characters wear masks and assume new identities. Noted celebrities take on new names (e.g., Bob Dylan is "Renaldo" and Ronnie Hawkins plays "Bob Dylan"). Questions of identity, celebrity angst, and relational confusion float in and out of scenes that vary with regard to their complexity and focus. That stagehands wear shirts with "Who is Bob" printed across the front contributes to the identity theme. The film is, in a word, cryptic. The critics formed a chorus of negativity; consequently, Dylan had his brother edit the film down to two hours, that version was released and ridiculed as well, and Dylan quickly pulled his creative and financial investment away from public view, leaving his intense, probing statement in the hands of an international cult following that would treasure and distribute the film within a tightly knit circle of devotees. To make too much of *Renaldo & Clara* is as formidable a mistake as to ignore it. The film is a powerful—and passionately private—work of art. "Who is Bob Dylan," indeed.

In 1986, Robert Shelton issued his long-awaited biography of Bob Dylan. Shelton was the *New York Times* reporter who discovered Dylan, and his review of the youngster's September 1961 performance at Gerde's Folk City facilitated his signing by Columbia Records' legendary producer, John Hammond. Shelton's relationship with Dylan enabled the definitive biography. His interviews with the artist's family and friends, his visits to the entertainer's hometown and schools, and his unrivaled access to his subject made *No Direction Home: The Life and Music of Bob Dylan* the most substantive source on Dylan's life to that point. Shelton opens the book by wondering where he should begin his story. For him, Dylan's entire life seemed like one performance after another. As Shelton awaits Dylan's arrival for yet another interview, he wonders which of the artist's various characters will appear that afternoon. Will that day's performance involve "Elmer Johnson" or "Tedham Porterhouse" or "Bob Landy" or "Blind Boy Grunt" or someone else? Who would come through that door? Which of Dylan's many characters would submit to that day's interview? Who is Bob Dylan?

Although "Alias" is Peckinpah's invention, "Renaldo," "Elmer Johnson," "Bob Dillon," "Blind Boy Grunt" (my favorite), "Bob Dylan," "Jack Fate," and the other characters are creations of one Robert Allen Zimmerman of Hibbing, Minnesota. As young Zimmerman gazed across the frozen tundra that was the early 1950s Minnesota landscape, he converted it into a magical movie screen full of rebellious bikers, roving bluesmen, and provocative poets. An avid movie fan, a sonic sponge, a natural performer, an assimilative reader, and an imaginative practical joker crystallized into an inventive personality that would synthesize any and all influences in service of a given day's creative imperative. You see, Bob Zimmerman is an artist who applies his talents in a systematic manner. When and if a particular mission requires a shift in public persona, the resourceful Minnesotan has always been quick to respond. His creativity knows no rules; therefore, it's free to do as it wishes—borrowing, stealing, redirecting, or inventing whatever he needs to respond to that moment's agenda. The key word here is *assimilation*. With each new influence or idea, Zimmerman integrates that knowledge with what came before it, never completely forsaking or abandoning one idea for another, but always *building*. Subsequently, Zimmerman created a family of interrelated characters who deliver his art to the world. Let's take a moment to explore their evolution.

We begin with young "Bob Dillon," Iron Range biker. This leather-clad teen integrated the sartorial styles of film stars Marlon Brando and James Dean, the quintessential 1950s symbol of rebellious freedom (a Harley Davidson motorcycle), the underground sounds of an emerging—equally rebellious—musical movement, and the name of a famous television character (*Gunsmoke*'s Marshall Matt Dillon) into a photogenic, image-conscious teenager with a single ambition: to get the hell out of Minnesota. He associated with friends who shared his interests and followed his leadership, he listened to faraway radio stations that fed his musical orientation, he absorbed films that propagated his rebellious worldview, and he used it all in service of his emerging creative agenda. Bob Dillon provides the characterological foundation for Bob Zimmerman's lifework. The rebellious blend of Brando, Little Richard, Elvis

Dillon's image-conscious rebellion is the genesis of Bob Zimmerman's career.

When Zimmerman enrolled at the University of Minnesota in the fall of 1959, his Bob Dillon character experienced a series of modifications. First, he immersed himself in the folk music scene that emanated from the Dinkytown art district near the Minnesota campus. At this point, Zimmerman's musical taste continued its evolution from its rock-and-roll roots to the trendy platitudes involved in White college student adaptations of traditional rural music. Here our sonic sponge absorbed *everything* he heard. Library of Congress recordings of American roots music, surrealistic beat poetry, and the emerging hybrids of pop, folk, country, and blues sounds fed the youngster's artistic education. Second, he shifted his last name's spelling. Dylan Thomas's role in all of this is uncertain. Some sources claim that "Dillon" never existed and that young Zimmerman modeled the poet's name from the outset. Robert Shelton reports otherwise and cites his subject's insistence that the Dillon origins be acknowledged. In his 1978 *Playboy* interview, Dylan admits the Dylan Thomas influence but backs away from any inspirational connection. Finally, in Bob Dylan's autobiography, *Chronicles*, the author reports it all came down to the way "Dylan" looked and sounded. Third, Woody Guthrie's book, *Bound for Glory*, provided a creative anchor. In Guthrie's persona, Zimmerman discovered an inventive force that revised and extended his public persona. Now, Dillon's rebellion would find a home in the hard-traveling, socially conscious, anti-establishment Guthrie model. It was a natural extension of Dillon's relentless rebellion. He traded his motorcycle for a boxcar.

When Bob Zimmerman hitchhiked to New York City in the winter of 1960 to visit a dying Woody Guthrie, he set the scene for another characterological evolution. At first, he would co-opt the Guthrie style and apply its approach to his new situation. His visits with Guthrie and his affiliation with the Oklahoma bard's friends and family provided a depth of understanding that facilitated his emergence in the Greenwich Village folk music scene. His harmonica playing, between-song antics, vocal intensity, and ever-present attention to image quickly made young "Bob Dylan" the talk of the Village. Dylan began writing his own material and slowly introducing the new songs into his stage act. Once he received his break in the *New York Times* and obtained a contract with Columbia, that writing exploded into something that transcended his newly acquired folk roots. With original songs such as "Blowin' In The Wind," Bob Dylan quickly obtained the title "the voice of his generation." The more he wrote, the more famous he became. The more famous he became, the more difficult it was to hide the fact that he was really Bob Zimmerman of Hibbing, Minnesota. The fall of 1963 featured a world-famous Bob Dylan, his official recognition as a force for political change, a *Newsweek* article that exposed his real identity, and yet another major shift in artistic direction and Dylan's evolving character.

(Note: I must acknowledge at the outset that Bob Dylan flat-out hates the label "the voice of his generation." Occasionally, he pokes fun at it. More often than not, he attacks it by noting the restrictive qualities of these media-driven characterizations. His 2004 autobiography and related media interviews get downright angry about the description. Throughout this study, I'll refer to Dylan by this label and the name he gave himself in his 2004 *60 Minutes* television interview: "the Archbishop of Anarchy." When I do this, I do it affectionately. I mean no disrespect whatsoever.)

Word is that labeling rebels is a bad move. With his rise as the voice of his generation, Dylan shed what was left of his Okie poseur persona and leaped into the antihero role. All those nurturing political messages that massaged the anxieties that engulfed the times were replaced by enigmatic expressions that stonewalled any attempt to penetrate their meanings. Tales of societal victimage, political unrest, and youthful ambition dissolved into strange blends of surrealistic poetry, quirky imagery, and dark musings. "Blowin' In The Wind" and its accessibility yielded to "Highway 61 Revisited" and its cryptic moralizing. The political aggression of "Masters Of War" gave way to the blistering imagery of "Gates Of Eden." When the new Bob Dylan moved from his folk posturing period into his Newport Mod era, he called upon the leather-clad rebellion of Bob Dillon, the exclusionary word games of teenaged Bob Zimmerman, and the outlaw qualities of his celluloid heroes to shape a new, more defiant character. The so-called voice of his generation spat on his situation like a James Dean character. It was Bob Dillon's greatest act of rebellion.

The Newport Mod Bob Dylan of 1965–1966 burned the candle at both ends. His manager overscheduled him. His creative pressures overwhelmed him (e.g., songwriting and film and book projects). His public demands disgusted him. Perhaps his greatest creative achievement occurred when his audience booed him, an irony that surely pleased this rebel. When it all crashed and Dylan exited the public stage for seven years (thanks to the motorcycle's unsuccessful return), he changed characters once more. At first, he was the consummate family man, photographed time and again with his wife and growing family in the serenity of their Woodstock, New York, home. His return to touring and the gigantic "Tour '74" spectacle set the scene for his evolution into the vaudevillian character that occupied the center of the Rolling Thunder Revue. Although he may sing the antihero's songs, his presence—and occasionally his articulation of those songs—adjusted that image in unpredictable ways. Pancake makeup, exotic clothing, crazed schedules, and a cast of thousands (well . . .) transformed the Iron Range biker turned Okie poseur turned political hero turned antihero into a roving minstrel with an outrageous troupe. The craziness of 1975–1976 resembled the madness of 1966; only the characters had changed. Like the tumultuous 1966 campaign, this too would have to end.

And end it did. In the late 1970s, during a private moment in a private location, Bob Dylan accepted Jesus Christ as his savior. With that, yet another Dylan appeared. A wave of religious songs poured from his pen and a revived artist preached his gospel in a dedicated manner. His act resembled an old-time Black gospel show with its sincere testimonials, emotional deliveries, and passionate playing. Like Bob Zimmerman's hero, Little Richard, Dylan had survived his excesses only to preach of their evils through the fire-and-brimstone rhetoric that, in many respects, birthed the rock-and-roll spirit. Dylan reached back to his roots every bit as much as he publicly reached out to his Lord. The topical songwriter who was the voice of his generation now applied that voice in Service. The defiant performer who once absorbed his audience's bile now faced the devil's army. The vaudevillian actor shifted performance venues. It was all a systematic synthesis—and extension—of Zimmerman's characters.

What was not a natural product of this characterological evolution was the Bob Dylan of the mid to late 1980s. As the religious fervor faded, Little Richard's fire exited in favor of the cool detachment befitting a cultural icon of Dylan's stature. Once

Dylan's Christian period passed, a wayward character emerged and roamed from musical platform to musical platform via tours with Tom Petty, the Grateful Dead, and other acts. He also adopted contemporary recording practices and abandoned his traditionally spontaneous method of music production while he randomly sampled his historic musical catalog for songwriting themes and sonic inspirations. This Bob Dylan offered flashes of his creative past as he performed around the world, but those performances were increasingly lackluster, uneven, or uninspired. Bob Dylan seemed to grow tired of being Bob Dylan. Consequently, Bob Zimmerman made yet another character move: He unveiled Jack Fate.

Jack Fate—the star of Dylan's 2003 film, *Masked & Anonymous*—is the ultimate Bob Zimmerman character. Jack Fate may be Bob Zimmerman's longest-running act, or he may not be an act at all. He—like Bob Dillon—is an authentic manifestation of Zimmerman's personality. You see, Jack Fate represents Bob Zimmerman's love of music. Thanks to his teachers on the radio, in Dinkytown and beyond, with Guthrie, and in the Village, Zimmerman is a walking encyclopedia of American roots music. Jack Fate is a direct manifestation of that knowledge. He looks like a Bob Wills–era country swing musician. He sounds like the wizened bluesmen that dominated Gatemouth Page's radio program. He sings Bob Dylan songs. He bleeds in those songs like Hank Williams. His passions flow like Little Richard's. He plays an average of 100 shows a year. His band is as good as any in the musical world. Jack Fate is the perfect character to carry Bob Zimmerman's art into its final era.

What a cast of characters! A rebellious biker, a sincere activist, an insincere poet, a dedicated traditionalist, a crazed vaudevillian, a repentant believer, a detached professional, and a reborn rounder. What a cast. Behind it all is one Bob Zimmerman of Hibbing, Minnesota. Though we know little of his personal activities since the early 1960s, Zimmerman created a series of provocative public personalities through his music, films, poetry, and fiction writing. Then he hid behind them, using them as shields to protect his privacy and deflect attention from his personal affairs. Those characters may change names or appearances, but their *voice* flows from a magical synthesis of biography, creative influence, artistic philosophy, and stylistic tendency. That *voice* flows from Bob Zimmerman's talent.

That *voice* changed the world.

Here we integrate auteur theory and narrative synthesis to explore how Bob Zimmerman *wrote* for his various characters and created the "songs of a lonesome traveler." Through narrative synthesis we examine the characters, values, and plots evidenced in the respective songs and interpret how they serve specific storytelling functions that flow from the diverse missions that represent the songwriter's career. When Zimmerman wrote for Dylan, he pursued precise agendas that influenced the content and style of the subsequent offering. Such an interpretation unveils "the auteur." As noted above, Dylan's voice emerges from Zimmerman's *art* and that art renders the *auteur*—a composite of biography, influence, philosophy, and style. We may only get to the *auteur* through the *art*. What Zimmerman's characters may say is always of interest, but in terms of this study, the *truth* comes from the *art*. Remember: Trust the art, not the artist! Through narrative synthesis we disassemble the art, chart its internal workings, note its strategic functions, and reassemble that work in terms of an *oeuvre* that exposes our auteur, "Bob Dylan."

Allow me to further establish the ground rules for this exploration. As I noted in the preface, this research is an extension of my previous examinations of Pete Townshend's, Dylan's and Bruce Springsteen's, and Joni Mitchell's and Elvis Costello's careers. The synthesis of auteur theory and narrative criticism deployed here is a direct reiteration of that previously established methodology. The emphasis is on the oeuvre, its stories, and the stylistic trends that yield the auteur. Consequently, the details of "Bob Dylan's" biography may be found elsewhere. His celebrity is also well chronicled in other sources that explore his various public activities. This project is a systematic interpretation of the oeuvre in order to appreciate the auteur, "Bob Dylan," and the stylistic principles Bob Zimmerman deployed on his behalf. Therefore, biographical matters are addressed only as necessary (dictated by their perceived relevance) and the myths surrounding the celebrity are, hopefully, restrained. Finally, the *Bob Dylan, Bruce Springsteen & American Song* study chronicles the broad range of critical responses to Dylan's work, and readers are encouraged to consult that volume for those insights. The biographers do a thorough job, the journalists follow their prescribed agendas, and the mythmakers do whatever it is that the mythmakers do. Here, my friends, we concentrate on the art. My aim is true.

One last procedural comment is in order. As all Dylan fans realize, there is a substantial difference between "songs written" and "songs performed." There are times when the "official" lyrics represent unique versions of songs in that *no performance* seems to use that particular arrangement. Dylan may change lyrics for a specific occasion, for a given tour, or in response to some whim. At times, these revisions are substantial. For example, the 1984 European tour version of "Tangled Up In Blue" represents a serious revision of the original—shifting characters and scenes and shaping a new story. Many times, these revisions go beyond omitting verses or shifting their order as Dylan recasts the song (instrumentally, lyrically, or both). Since there *is* an "official" version of the song (provided by Bob Dylan Music, listed on his official website, and cited in his book *Lyrics 1962–1985* and *Lyrics 1962–2001*—when controversies emerge regarding lyrical changes, the website "made the call"), I shall rely solely on those artifacts—as per my legal obligation.

That Bob Dylan has inspired a legion of academic, journalistic, and popular writing is beyond question. He may be the most discussed artist in history. Mark Jacobson's colorful 2001 *Rolling Stone* piece considers the science deemed "Dylanology." He interviews a madman who sifted through the artist's garbage in pursuit of god-knows-what, he describes an unbalanced fan who managed to secure Dylan's used cigarette butts in order to obtain the DNA necessary to clone the artist, and the author submits his repentance for a review of 1978's *Renaldo & Clara* (in which he wished Dylan were dead!). For support, Jacobson notes the activities of music critic Paul Williams and cites that writer's motivations for his work on Dylan's career: "If Shakespeare was in your midst, putting on shows at the Globe Theatre, wouldn't you feel the need to be there, to write down what happened in them?" That statement reveals the intensity, the reverence, and the dedication that make Dylanology an all-consuming passion.

Any consideration of Dylanology necessarily begins with the biographers. The biographers have interviewed anyone and everyone with any connection to their subject as well as combed through studio records, public documents, financial statements, and—predictably—each other's work in their dogged pursuit of their topic. Chronologically, we begin with Anthony Scaduto's (1971) *Bob Dylan: An Intimate Biography*, then Robert Shelton's (1986) *No Direction Home: The Life and Music of Bob Dylan*, Bob Spitz's (1989) *Dylan: A Biography*, Howard Sounes's (2001) *Down the Highway: The Life of Bob Dylan*, and Clinton Heylin's (2001) *Bob Dylan: Behind the Shades Revisited*. Heylin's work also includes the indispensable 1995 chronology of Dylan recording sessions from 1960 to 1994 and a 1996 account of his daily activities from 1941 to 1995 (oh my!).

Complementing the biographers are academics and their attempts to generate systematic interpretations of Dylan's work. Though theoretical mischief occasionally raises its partisan head, these writers more often than not state their case and systematically pursue it. Several examples include Betsy Bowden's (1982) *Performed Literature: Words and Music of Bob Dylan*, Aidan Day's (1988) *Jokerman: Reading the Lyrics of Bob Dylan*, William McKeen's (1993) *Bob Dylan: A Bio-Bibliography*, Christopher Ricks's (2003) *Dylan's Visions of Sin*, and Richard Wissolik and Scott McGrath's (1994) *Bob Dylan's Words: A Critical Dictionary and Commentary*. Academic periodicals also offer considerable yield for Dylanologists as critics/theorists from a host of disciplines apply their trades to various aspects of Dylan's lifework (such efforts are far too numerous to list here; please consult McKeen for a thorough account of the academy's output to that point).

Journalists contribute to Dylanology in a variety of fashions. Journalistic periodicals not only serve the commercial, informative, critical, and promotional needs of a complicated international industry, but also produce writers who bring their craft to book-length accounts as well. We begin with Michael Gray's impressive 2000 analysis, *Song and Dance Man III: The Art of Bob Dylan*; Paul Williams's multivolume set (1991's *Bob Dylan, Performing Artist: The Early Years 1960–1973*; 1992's *Bob Dylan, Performing Artist: The Middle Years 1974–1986*; 1996's *Bob Dylan: Watching the River Flow*; and 2004's *Mind Out of Time*); Greil Marcus (1997's *Invisible Republic: Bob Dylan's Basement Tapes*—since renamed and reissued); Tim Riley (1999's *Hard Rain: A Dylan Commentary*); and edited volumes by Carl Benson (1998's *The Bob Dylan Companion*), Elizabeth Thomson and David Gutman (2000's *The Dylan Companion*), and Craig McGregor (1972's *Bob Dylan: A Retrospective*).

Finally, we must acknowledge the Internet's impact on the science of Dylanology. Starting with Dylan's official website and extending around the globe, the flow of All Things Bob is consistently impressive. To offer addresses for these sites could be misleading, since these things change for a host of reasons; nevertheless, allow me to pause to mention a few. The "expecting rain" site (from Norway) lists every Dylan article that appears in any publication around the world. (That claim was put to the test in 2003 when I gave a lecture at a small Midwestern university. The lecture was on the Dylan-Springsteen book, and the school's student newspaper dutifully reported the happening. I was shocked when I saw that article listed on "expecting rain" *the next day!*) "Bob Links" (out of Wisconsin) lists every set list from every show along with vital tour information (regarding locations, tickets, and so on). That Dylan's official website links to "Bob Links" demonstrates the tightness of their association. "Still on the Road" (from Sweden) maintains set list and band information for decades of shows. "Sky's Corner" offers unofficial recordings of *every* Dylan show (there are very, very few omissions) for a dollar and uses any profit to support Third World families. Sky's Corner transforms service to Dylanology to service for humanity. It is an amazing project. The list goes on and on from sites that broker information to sites that are individual hobbies and offer idiosyncratic readings of specific Dylan activities (e.g., there are sites specifically on Dylan's religious period, 1966 tour, and more). The World of Dylanology, then, is a focused, interlocked, and dynamic blend of scholars, journalists, advocates, and friends. It is a most impressive phenomenon.

Amongst all of this is that special category that I deem "Applied Dylanology." Here, specialists from diverse fields bring their skills to the World of Bob—often with startling results. Michael Gray is relentless in his historical interpretations of Dylan's musical influences—real or perceived. The man traces every vowel or bar to somebody somewhere at some point in time. Christopher Ricks brings his unparalleled knowledge of poetry to the Archbishop of Anarchy's writings. He, too, is thorough beyond belief. Clinton Heylin's knowledge of the music industry's history, Dylan's recording sessions, and his day-to-day whereabouts take Applied Dylanology soaring beyond where humans normally travel. A lot of this stuff is truly impressive.

While Dylanologists chart every move their subject makes, the musical world has also paused to appreciate the artist who transformed songwriting. Dylan was inducted into the Songwriters Hall of Fame in 1982, received the "Founder's Award" from ASCAP in 1986, and was inducted into the Rock and Roll Hall of Fame in 1988; he has been honored with the French Ministry of Culture's "Commandeur des Arts et des Lettres" (1990), the Kennedy Center Medal (1998), numerous Grammy awards and nominations, the Polar Music Prize from the Royal Swedish Academy of Music (2000), the Golden Globe (2001), and the Academy Award (2001); and Dylan has been nominated for the Nobel Prize in Literature in every year since 1997. He has also received honorary doctorates from Princeton University (1970) and the University of St. Andrews (2004). That the auteur's is a distinguished career is beyond question.

That magical movie screen that was the frozen fields of Minnesota yielded a series of characters who captured the tenor and tone of their times. Bob Zimmerman applied his talent to weave tales tailored for specific characters and their scenic conditions: The Okie complained, the hipster cajoled, the loyalist celebrated, the servant condemned and celebrated, the icon conciliated, and the bluesman committed. They were all travelers of one form or another, and they all traveled alone—free spirits absorbed in their individual milieu. When Bob Zimmerman wrote for Bob Dylan and his various incarnations, he wrote the songs of a lonesome traveler in pursuit of a specific destination. The following pages chart those artistic missions and the art that flowed from those creative imperatives.

The Bob Zimmerman Story

Sitting here in front of my computer, I find myself some twenty miles from Fairmount, Indiana—birthplace of James Dean. When you drive west down Indiana Highway 26 and enter Fairmount, you instantly gain a feeling for why the young actor assumed such a rebellious, enigmatic, and mysterious public persona. With no offense to the fine people of Fairmount, there is absolutely *nothing* there. From the American Legion Post to the farm suppliers to the small shops around this agricultural community, the town is a quiet—seemingly uneventful—rural community. To be sure, the fastest track out of town for young people living in Fairmount must be their imaginations, for to look out at the cornfields and bean fields is to stare into the interminable Hoosier Abyss. No doubt, the youngsters of Fairmount frequently rebel against their circumstances—at least you'd *think* they would. Rebelling against *nothing* means rising up against *everything*. Mustering the internal resources necessary to reject your hometown is a formidable challenge for a teenager. It requires an instinctive understanding of what you despise, a firm belief in what you are, and a fearless dedication to what you will become. That kind of teenage rebellion demands uncommon faith—the kind of faith that flows from a deep sense of desperation. The kind of desperation that accompanies growing up in quiet rural communities like Fairmount, Indiana—or Hibbing, Minnesota.

Tradition requires that all Bob Dylan biographies open with some account of his native Minnesota's Iron Range and its history. Assuredly, it is a harsh environment. Minnesota winters are nothing less than incredible. But for many of those northern Europeans who settled there, the dark, dreary, desolate winters are reminiscent of the Old Country and propagate the provincial nostalgia that relieves immigration. One immigrant, Franz Dietrich Von Ahlen, departed his native Germany for the New World, changed his name to Frank Hibbing, landed in northern Michigan, and moved to Minnesota after hearing of its vast natural resources. The story has it that one morning Mr. Hibbing emerged from his tent to temperatures around 40° below zero and declared that he felt iron ore in his bones. How he could feel anything in 40° below temperatures is formidable in and of itself. Still, that intuition prompted his men to dig, and dig they did, as did the men after them, and the men after them, and the men after them. For some fifty years, the men around the location called "Hibbing" used whatever means were available to unearth the iron ore Frank Hibbing felt in his frozen bones. When they determined more ore existed beneath the town named after our intuitive minerals speculator, they placed Hibbing on huge logs or wheels and *moved* it. Their efforts provided the high-grade ore that supplied the victorious armies of two world wars and, in so doing, made Hibbing, Minnesota, the self-proclaimed "richest village in the world." By the mid-1950s, that ore—and those riches—disappeared. The subsequent economic downturn was severe. New mining techniques were deployed with minimal-to-moderate success, although they inflicted moderate-to-maximum environmental damage. Those efforts yielded an open-pit mine that covered 1,600 acres and extended some 500 feet into the ground. Frank Hibbing's original intuitions ran deep and, eventually, ran dry. Unemployment was unnaturally high. Community spirit was probably unnaturally low. The huge open-pit mine was unnatural—period.

In 1978, the celebrity-singer-songwriter "Bob Dylan" offered his recollections of Minnesota's Iron Range to Ron Rosenbaum:

> Well, in the winter, everything was still, nothing moved. Eight months of that. You can put it together. You can have some amazing hallucinogenic experiences doing nothing but looking out your window. There is also the summer, when it gets hot and sticky and the air is very metallic. There is a lot of Indian spirit. The earth there is unusual, filled with ore. So there is something happening that is hard to define. There is a magnetic attraction there. Maybe thousands and thousands of years ago, some planet bumped into the land there. There is a great spiritual quality throughout the Midwest. Very subtle, very strong, and that is where I grew up.

Dylan's convinced that Minnesota's Iron Range plays a central role in his personality: "I got something different in my soul. Like a spirit. It's like being from the Smoky Mountains or the backwoods of Mississippi. It is going to make you a certain type of person if you stay 20 years in a place." He reinforced that perspective in a 2004 *Newsweek* interview about his autobiography: "I had no idea of what a city was like. And I think it probably made me who I am today. The country where I came from— it's pretty bleak. And it's cold. And there's a lot of water. So you could dream a lot. The difference between me now and then is that back then, I could see visions. The me now can dream dreams. . . . What you see in 'Chronicles' is a dream. It's already happened." That dream started in the mining town of Hibbing, Minnesota.

Little doubt that May 24, 1941, was a relatively normal spring day with residents busily preparing for the summer months by planting gardens, manicuring yards, and doing their ritualistic spring cleaning. Yet, those seasonal activities occurred under unusual circumstances: It was wartime. The war in Europe was raging just as the eventual war in the Pacific was percolating. The Pearl Harbor attack was just over six months away. The world was in a serious state of uncertainty. It was as dynamic and perilous a time as the world has ever known. The resolution to these conflicts would both end the vicious hostilities that engulfed the planet and threaten the Earth for the next fifty years in a fashion no one could imagine. The power harnessed to end a second world war soon haunted the generations that followed.

That weird yin and yang of life extended to the literary world as well in that 1940–1941 witnessed the deaths of legends James Joyce and F. Scott Fitzgerald. At around nine o'clock on the evening of May 24, Beatty Zimmerman delivered her first child at St. Mary's Hospital in Duluth. The birth was difficult due to the size of the child's head; nevertheless, the procedure was successful and Abe and Beatty Zimmerman were now the proud parents of one Robert Allen Zimmerman. What the early 1940s had taken away with Joyce's and Fitzgerald's deaths was replenished that May 24 with the man who would become known as "Bob Dylan."

Bob Zimmerman was born into a Jewish family with strong Iron Range roots. That family apparently prospered over the years. All evidence indicates that they were an industrious lot. Hard work, commitment, and a sincere belief in the American Dream delivered prosperity for Abe's and Beatty's families as they had for countless other Americans. The 1946 addition of David Zimmerman rounded off what became known as the "nuclear family." The Zimmermans socialized, consumed the goods of the day, and participated in civic activities with regularity. They were as normal as they could be. Derek Barker's *Isis* anthology cites Abe Zimmerman's comments to Robert Shelton about his family's environment. He noted that the family used "two rules" of governance: "One, don't come and ask me for anything unless you are prepared to hear me say no, and two, do things for us because you like us, not because you are afraid of us." Beatty added, "We were more like friends. We'd tell [the boys] that they would have children of their own and they would want to be friends with them." Simple rules for a simple life in a simple, but demanding, environment.

The biographers indicate that Abraham Zimmerman was a hardworking guy. Shelton befriended Abe and, as a result, offers the most insight into his character. He reports that Abe entered the workforce when he was seven, and that he worked hard throughout his life. Young Abe spoke Yiddish at home (to his family of eight) and English elsewhere. He shined shoes, sold newspapers, and, by the time he was sixteen, obtained a messenger boy job with Standard Oil in Duluth. He prospered at Standard Oil, rising through the ranks to various supervisory positions. Abe was also athletic and played semiprofessional baseball. He was a serious young man who matured into a serious older man. When he lost his job with Standard Oil in 1945 and was stricken with polio during the 1946 epidemic, he endured a series of events that contributed to his stern demeanor. Although he recovered from the polio, it left its mark physically and psychologically. When he settled into the electrical appliance business with his two brothers, Abe brought a life of hard work, ethnic pride, and personal perseverance to the job of raising his middle-class family in the consumer-oriented world that was 1950s America. As his two house rules indicate, Abe Zimmerman kept it simple.

Beatty Stone of Hibbing was a genuine complement to her future husband. We are told that she was a bubbly, vivacious, outgoing teenager with an intense desire to escape her circumstances. Although her family had done well on the Iron Range, Beatty's ambitions were elsewhere. Her father (Ben Stone) owned a general store, and her mother's family (Florence Edelstein) owned a series of movie theaters. Their family of six prospered as a result. Her father had a reputation for generosity among the area's working class. If times were hard in the mines, Ben Stone cut his prices for his ethnically diverse clientele. When Beatty came of age and used her father's car to travel to Duluth in pursuit of her social agenda, she maintained a firm image of the life she wanted to lead. According to Shelton, she sought a solid, secure life with a hardworking Jewish lad. Looks and personality were important to Beatty, but she also wanted a young man with a *job*. She found it all in Abe. They married in 1934. She moved to Duluth. She escaped Hibbing—for the moment.

Many things changed during the volatile year that was 1946. That year opened with David's February arrival, but that joy was soon challenged by Abe's bout with polio. For support during these difficult times, the Zimmermans moved into Beatty's parents' home in Hibbing. Since Abe's brothers were in business there, the move had possibilities. The family eventually bought a home on Seventh Avenue. Beatty re-counted their life there in Shelton's biography. She described attending local weddings and graduations, living alongside people of different faiths and ethnic backgrounds (they were, however, the town's only Jewish family), and the respect everyone had for everybody. Never did a neighbor call with a complaint about her boys. She proudly recalled that Hibbing's residents had nothing but respect for her children. The Zim-mermans fought through life's challenges as any family must with Abe's and Beatty's parental strategy leading the way. By all accounts, these people were normal beyond belief.

Although reporters and writers of various types have recorded the many thoughts of Abe, Beatty, and other Hibbing residents, there is little available from David Zimmerman. The biographers describe the quiet little brother who experi-enced a typical familial relationship with an older sibling, but never do they cite David directly. Andy Gill and Kevin Odegard spend considerable space discussing David's role in the making of his brother's album *Blood On The Tracks* in 1974, but David has virtually nothing to say about his formative years with Bob. It would appear that Bob Dylan's request for familial silence has been honored by his little brother in a way that his parents could not. As we proceed, the reasons for this will become abun-dantly clear. I conclude that Bob and David Zimmerman's youth resembled any other brotherly relationship. There is simply no substantial evidence to the contrary.

Chronicles says little about its author's formative years. He talks about his par-ents from time to time and, occasionally, he references some youthful experience. Dylan describes his father as "plain speaking and straight talking." He claims that his father "was the best man in the world and probably worth a hundred of me, but he didn't understand me." He speaks with pride about his sixteen-year-old father risk-ing his life to pull a stranger from a burning automobile. He recalls his mother's undy-ing devotion and never-ending support. He describes his live-in grandmother as his "one and only confidante." Although it's implied more than it's overtly stated, I con-clude that the Zimmerman family was essentially nurturing, usually supportive of one another, and generally tolerant of young Bob's rebellious ways. One thing is certain: When the author speaks of his family, there's affection in his words.

So Bob Zimmerman grew up in a middle-class family in a dying mining town. His dad may have been angered over his inability to join the local country club (no Jews!); however, as Beatty's remarks indicate, the neighborhood's melting pot was in-clusive. Economic issues pounded *everybody*, and Bob Dylan has consistently stated how his youth endured a stifling socioeconomic uniformity. He told Cameron Crowe that Hibbing "was not a rich or poor town, everybody had pretty much the same thing and the very wealthy people didn't live there, they were the ones that owned the mines and they lived thousands of miles away." Nevertheless, Abe kept the bills paid and provided many of the traditional and emerging comforts associated with America's new middle class. There was a piano in the house. Young Bob had a record player and a radio. A family television quickly appeared. Teenage Bob had a motorcycle and access to funds that provided leather jackets, mail-order record purchases, and other popular teenage consumer items (reportedly, Bob worked for his father's business from time to time). One may easily imagine young Bob Zimmerman racing his Harley Davidson around a 1600-acre, 500-feet-deep hole in the ground or posing in the mirror in his new leather jacket as the sun set on a 40° below zero Minnesota afternoon. It must have been a life of contrasts: The serenity of a comfortable middle-class upbringing coexisted with a harsh physical environment populated by people enduring all sorts of socioeconomic struggle.

When we pull back to examine the information the biographers have assembled, several patterns quickly emerge. Zimmerman's early interest in performance, his creative inclinations, and his tendencies toward self-indulgence stand out. Feeding each of these qualities is his unrelenting commitment to *image*. The rebellious 1950s movie characters portrayed by Marlon Brando and James Dean inspired a social orientation that was reinforced by the raucous sounds of southern bluesmen, the plaintive stories of country singers, and the outrageous gyrations of rock-and-roll performers. When these influences were assimilated into Bob Zimmerman's personality, they generated the quintessential 1950s teenage rebel. He may appear to be quiet and withdrawn in school. He may appear to honor his parents and their traditions. But not so deep inside, a fire was sparking, and that fire was fueled by motorcycles, leather jackets, race records, and the various influences that flowed from an emerging mass media that specifically targeted youngsters like Bob Zimmerman of Hibbing, Minnesota. The media created an *image*, and teens everywhere flocked to those inventions—often, with little to no regard for the consequences. Perhaps we should take a moment for a closer examination of Zimmerman's formative years and contemplate their relationship to the characterological inventions that followed.

We begin with young Bob Zimmerman's penchant for performance. Shelton reports the child enjoyed hearing his recorded voice, so the two-year-old played with his father's Dictaphone at work and Abe used those recordings to tease his colleagues at Standard Oil (e.g., by interrupting a report or order with a quick sound bite of Bobby's voice). At a Mother's Day gathering in 1946, various family members performed for Bob's grandmother. When it came time for Bob to sing, he stomped his foot and declared that he would perform once everyone was quiet. After commanding his audience's attention, he launched into "Some Sunday Morning" and, after receiving his audience's praise, he concluded with "Accentuate the Positive." Beatty told Shelton that she received numerous congratulatory telephone calls after her son's fine performance. That praise inspired another gig, as Bob donned a new white Palm Beach suit (which his mother preserved) for a performance at Beatty's sister's wedding reception two weeks later. At first, the kid was reluctant to perform. An uncle offered him $25. His father pleaded with Bob to relent and perform. Young Bob acquiesced to his father's request. Once he quieted his audience (again!), the two-song set was performed to everyone's delight. His uncle dutifully paid the bill. Later, the youngster returned the money. From this, two lifelong traits may be noted. Bob Zimmerman has, from day one it appears, maintained a rather cantankerous relationship with his audience and uncertain ties to his benefactors.

The die was cast on Mother's Day 1946. Abe Zimmerman's response is cited in the aforementioned *Isis* interview:

> [Everyone] would laugh; they really loved him. He was, I would say, a very lovable, a very unusual child. People would go out of their way to handle, to talk with him, to ask about him—they just loved him. I think we were the only ones who would not agree that he was going to be a very famous person one day. Everybody said that this boy is going to be a genius, he was going to be this or that. Everyone said that, not just family. When he would sing "Accentuate the Positive" like other children would sing "Mary Had a Little Lamb," they would say that this boy was brilliant. I didn't pay too much attention to this, because I figured any kid could learn it if he heard it often enough. He learned this from the radio: he was four years old.

With a fine blend of parental pride and Midwestern modesty, a father recalls his successful son's early years and how they set the scene for what was to follow.

Not only did the child perform, but he was creative as well. His parents treasured the poems Bob wrote for Mother's Day and Father's Day in the early 1950s (Shelton reprints portions of them in his biography). They note how the youngster spent more and more time alone, reading or drawing. He eventually turned to a variety of musical instruments to channel his urges. Abe purchased a piano, and lessons ensued. Very quickly, the precocious lad quit his lessons and declared his ambition to play the instrument his way. He toyed with the saxophone and other instruments before he settled upon the guitar as his weapon of choice. From there, the young man further isolated himself and concentrated on his ambitions. He described this portion of his youth in Shelton's biography. Dylan recalled that he didn't hunt, fish, or play basketball; rather, he played his guitar and sang his songs. He shared these traits with his friends as well. They weren't class leaders or star athletes or industrious students. No, all young Bob wanted to do was write, sing, and draw. He wanted to "dissolve" until he was "invisible." For Bob Zimmerman, "invisibility" meant self-indulgence. It appears that once he concentrated on his guitar, he initiated a lifelong self-education in which he isolated himself and systematically fed his interests. This personal education occurred on two levels: the public and the private.

On a public level, Zimmerman was a frequent patron of the local movie theater. Film stars Dean and Brando appealed to his introverted rebellion and played a central role in his personality's formation. Bob Spitz explains the impact of Dean's film *Rebel without a Cause* within this developmental process: "If ever the term 'born-again' applied to Bob Dylan it was then, following this celluloid revelation. He had gotten a glimpse of the future up on the screen in the form of James Dean, teenage rebel, and it appealed to his sensibility. He was inspired by the whole package—the defiant posturing, the attitude, the mumbling, and especially The Look. The Look established a state of mind that allowed you to slip into the role with relative ease." In the *Isis* interview with Dylan's parents, Abe recalled that his son "must have" seen *Rebel without a Cause* "twelve times" and collected all the information he could about James Dean. Abe claimed his son "wanted to live like Jimmy Dean."

Privately, Zimmerman was an avid consumer of late-night radio, as his musical adventures via high-powered southern radio stations influenced his understanding of blues, country, and their offspring, rock and roll. The mail-order record business allowed the teen to purchase what he heard on the radio; consequently, he was able to accumulate—and assimilate—a vast array of music. It is not surprising that Bob Zimmerman emerged from this blend of media influences with a keen awareness of and appreciation for artistic *image* and its direct relationship to a given artist's work.

Zimmerman's enactment of "The Look" sharpened with the acquisition of a motorcycle, the requisite leather jacket, and biker attitude. Shelton writes of brotherly art where David photographed Bob riding his motorcycle or posing with props. The teenager was consumed by the Dean/Brando image, and that perspective informed all facets of his life. Zimmerman's identification with Elvis Presley, Little Richard, and Hank Williams reinforced his image-laden musical ambitions. He may have entered this world with artistic proclivities, but Zimmerman developed those abilities through a rebellious image that he projected *through* those activities. That is, his initial creative motivations did not respond to his muse as much as they channeled his rebellion. As Shelton wisely observes, the young man played the guitar whether he was plucking it or carrying it about town over his shoulder. *Everything* was a performance. *Everything* served the carefully contrived image of that moment. For a guy that desired a state of invisibility, he certainly paid a great deal of attention to his public persona.

Like most teens, Zimmerman surrounded himself with people who shared his interests. As his comments to Shelton reveal, his friends mirrored him. In A&E's *Biography* of Bob Dylan, school friend John Bucklen recalls that the group of friends who associated with Zimmerman all shared the same interests, and those pursuits centered around, you guessed it, *image*. To join the group, you had to display a love of the blues, the emerging rock-and-roll movement, and the celluloid biker attitude—and do it all in a quiet, almost secretive, fashion. The group apparently followed Zimmerman's commitment to not talk about what you're going to do, but to use the element of surprise whenever possible. When Zimmerman began to join bands, the plan was not to go around boasting of your intentions; to the contrary, the teen formulated performance tactics that he would spring on unsuspecting audiences.

The biographers chronicle Zimmerman's life with teenage friends and creative cohorts during his adolescence. They were, without question, thorough in their interviews (e.g., Bucklen, Larry Fabbro, Echo Helstrom, and Leroy Hoikkala), and their findings are instructive. Though the details occasionally differ, their research suggests that Zimmerman was an imaginative young man with a penchant for storytelling. His ability to recast the popular songs of the day (Hoikkala remembers Bob's lyrical revisions of current songs, often asserting his authorship over the results), his capacity to weave tall tales (Helstrom recalls a particular concoction about a large, threatening snake wrapped around a tree, even though Minnesota and such snakes are an unlikely combination), and his propensity for word games offer concrete evidence of a mischievous wordsmith in the making.

Of particular interest is the Bucklen-Zimmerman word game "Glissendorf." Sounes and Heylin describe the "mind game" (Sounes) or "word game" (Heylin) the two teens played at the expense of their audience. Heylin provides an example of a Glissendorf exchange between the boys: "I see it's raining. / It isn't raining. / You say it isn't? Okay, if you wanna be difficult, it isn't. So let's move on. What's the next first thing to come to your mind? / The what? / The what? Just what I thought. I won! You won! / I don't understand. / That's exactly right. You don't understand. You don't understand." The game's purpose was to confuse the observer, or, as Sounes concludes, "It left the other person wondering if they had missed something." The biographers report there were occasions when a Glissendorf victim became angry or hurt by the game—a response that concerned Bucklen and delighted Zimmerman. In any event, the youthful experiences involved in creative revisions of existing songs, imaginative (and occasionally off-the-wall) storytelling, and word games designed to confuse/exclude their "victims" represent the creative foundation of a personality that would one day apply those traits in other contexts.

Zimmerman's musical maturation featured a host of happenings ranging from his participation in singing groups (e.g., The Jokers), in rock-and-roll bands (e.g., the Shadow Blasters, The Golden Chords, and Elston Gunn and the Rock Boppers), his attendance at concerts (e.g., the Winter Dance Party in January 1959 just nights before the show's participants—Buddy Holly, Richie Valens, and the Big Bopper—were killed), his encounters with area radio personalities (Jim Dandy from nearby Virginia, Minnesota), and, in the summer of 1959, a brief stint as Bobby Vee's piano player (sources differ regarding Vee). Of these musical experiences, two stand out: his bands' performances during his high school's "Jacket Jamboree" and at the "St. Louis County Fair" in the late 1950s. Both events featured hostile audiences with rude responses (booing, laughing) to the sound and fury of Zimmerman's rocking, Little Richard–inspired act that apparently disturbed everyone but Bobby Zimmerman. During the Jacket Jamboree, the piano-playing Zimmerman broke the instrument's foot pedal and a school official killed the P.A. system in order to quiet the sonic assault. Reports indicate that after this public explosion, Zimmerman returned to his seat in the back of the class, silently satisfied. Even at this early point in his life, Zimmerman displayed a quiet resolve to express himself that could not be shaken by external factors. It was as if the teenager performed for himself—an inner, unshakable audience fully cognizant of and devoted to his personal mission. This creative self-indulgence would one day support an artist with an uncanny ability to withstand public attacks on his personal ambitions. Like a fine game of Glissendorf or a musical assault on an unsuspecting high school audience, Zimmerman played to the satisfaction of an audience of one: himself. This simple trait enabled a creative career that never suffered from the strain of audience expectations. In fact, the opposite occurred.

With regard to Zimmerman's early songwriting, the biographers differ in their reports. Howard Sounes reveals that Zimmerman's first song was written about actress Brigitte Bardot (Bob Dylan confirmed this in his 1978 *Playboy* interview), Clinton Heylin indicates his first tune was a revision of Jimmie Rodgers's "A Drunkard's Child" (entitled "The Drunkard's Son"), and Bob Spitz claims the first composition to be "Big Black Train." Whichever it was, Zimmerman played with words throughout his youth. He wrote poems, told outlandish stories, aped record lyrics, and used it all to toy with people. How interesting. By the time he was sixteen years old, the future Bob Dylan displayed all the qualities that characterized his career. For the next fifty years (or more), the talented wordsmith would deploy these traits in service of private agendas that may have little to no relationship to *anybody* other than himself. Just as he might take a popular record from 1954 and make it his own through whatever means suited him, he would take scenes from Junichi Saga's book, *Confessions of a Yakuza*, and transform them into the stories that populate his 2001 release, *Love And Theft*. He would take a true story from a newspaper, twist the events around, and produce a factually inaccurate but compelling account of elitist judicial abuses ("The Lonesome Death Of Hattie Carroll"). He would deftly deploy the "folk process" (i.e., the songwriting tradition of freely borrowing melodies or scenes from previously established songs in service of a "new" song) to create original songs that followed an acknowledged tradition or to invent adventurous songs that break down, recast, or dismiss those traditions. Such abilities emerged from the unique combination of two factors: Bob Zimmerman's personality and his private musical education, a topic to which we now turn.

Zimmerman's artistic education occurred in three installments: the Hibbing phase, the Dinkytown period, and the Greenwich Village/New York era. In Hibbing, the aforementioned media influences complemented his tutorials from Black disc jockey Jim Dandy to establish the foundation for his life's work. Gatemouth Page's late-night radio show may have led the way. Sitting up late at night—often using his pillow to shield the music from his sleeping family—Zimmerman absorbed the sounds of the South: cutting-edge blues, rowdy honky-tonk tunes, and the Memphis concoction known as rock and roll. What he heard at night, he ordered through Page's clever mail-order program. According to Shelton, Zimmerman's record collection began with a series of Hank Williams 78s and, once the 45 rpm singles came into vogue, extended to recordings by Little Richard, Buddy Holly, Hank Thompson, and Johnny Ray. A high school graduation gift of Leadbelly 78s was a major influence on the sonic sponge, who steadfastly assimilated everything he heard. After hearing a ripping Little Richard tune, the youngster could be found attacking the family piano, banging away on the instrument while dancing and screaming in classic Richard mode. With time, the haircut, performance style, and general wildness of Little Richard's unique style culminated in Zimmerman's ambition to "join the band of Little Richard" once he graduated from high school (such was the inscription featured below his senior portrait in his high school yearbook).

Zimmerman's visits with Jim Dandy reinforced those inclinations. When John Bucklen accompanied Bob to Virginia to visit the only Black family among the town's 12,000 residents, a new world unfolded before them. Dandy would drop his "White" WHLB radio voice in favor of a more hip, Black slang that he used to educate his young friends with a keen interest in rhythm and blues. For those who say the "blues" is more than a musical genre in that it embraces a way of life, Bob and John learned those lessons from the generous benefactor that was Dandy. Page and Dandy provided the musical foundation that supported the other aspects of Zimmerman's artistic education.

Young Bob Zimmerman was also a reader. Girlfriend Echo Helstrom noted her old boyfriend's love of John Steinbeck. His parents recalled the hours upon hours their son spent upstairs in his bedroom, privately absorbing various print media that fed his understanding of the world and his emerging desire to write. Beatty Zimmerman offered a detailed account of her son's artistic maturation in Shelton's biography. She claimed her son was "upstairs quietly becoming a writer" for over twelve years. She maintains he was a voracious reader. Even his comic books were substantive. He enjoyed going to the library. He was constantly drawing or painting. She encouraged him to consider architecture in order to earn a decent living. She discouraged his poetry for fear that he'd die and be discovered afterward. Beatty argued that he couldn't "go on and on and on and sit and dream and write poems." She feared he would end up the kind of poet who had "no ambition" and "wrote only for himself." She begged him to attend college and learn a meaningful vocation. Beatty certainly understood her child. She understood very early what her son would do with his writing career: write for *himself*. Fortunately, she was wrong in her conclusion that such practices would lead to destitution. The youngster who would one day be "Bob Dylan" did rather well "going on and on and on" sitting, dreaming, and writing.

All of which began in Hibbing. From the movies, he learned how to act. From his readings, he learned how to write. From his poetry, drawing, and painting, he learned how to express himself. From his radio, he learned what he liked. From his record player, he integrated what he liked into a personal repertoire that would support his protracted career. From Jim Dandy, he reinforced all of these things and expanded his understanding of the culture that spawned it all. And from his circle of friends, he gained the practice necessary to bring everything to life. What an education! Bob Zimmerman's education in Hibbing was based on a private curriculum involving media unique to his time. The youthful rebellion of the 1950s manifested in the movies, songs, and literature of those times—content that the future voice of his generation incorporated into a private agenda that supported his creative inclinations. His parents may have discouraged those tendencies in favor of more practical ambitions; however, they never prohibited their development. That house on Seventh Avenue in Hibbing, Minnesota, represented a private school with but one student, and that student would apply that education to do more than earn a living—he changed an art form.

While he graduated Hibbing High with the ambition to join Little Richard's band, he acquiesced to his parents' wishes and enrolled at the University of Minnesota. But first, Zimmerman's private education received a few lessons from a brief stint as Bobby Vee's piano player in Fargo, North Dakota, and a summer trip to Denver, Colorado. The stay in Denver was instructive for several important reasons. First, the Denver trip offered an opportunity to work on his emerging stage act. He may have performed at off times or in seedy venues, but nevertheless, he gained valuable stage experience from those shows. Second, his music shifted from the Little Richard–inspired rock and roll to the emerging folk sounds that used traditional blues or protest songs as springboards to a new form of popular music. He briefly lived with Black musician Walt Conley, who taught Bob old Pete Seeger tunes and furthered his musical education through his vast record collection. Furthermore, Zimmerman's exposure to Jesse Fuller introduced the harmonica into the sonic equation, and Fuller's use of a "necklace" to hold his harmonica while he played his guitar inspired the youngster to do the same. Subsequently, the opportunity to perform, the shift in musical styles, and the introduction of new performance techniques made the brief stay in Denver an important part of Zimmerman's musical maturation. With all of that in place, Denver afforded one more innovation: the opportunity to reinvent himself. Stories about rail hopping, carnival troupes, and historic musical encounters slowly—but surely—displaced tales of 500-feet-deep strip mines, Minneapolis girls, and playing with Bobby Vee. The mischievous imagination that supported games of Glissendorf now turned to biographical matters that recast the Minnesotan in a more romantic, sensational fashion. Denver was, assuredly, a brief but useful period.

In the fall of 1959, Zimmerman enrolled at the University of Minnesota, moved to Minneapolis, and entered the bohemian world of the university's art district, Dinkytown. Bob Dylan described the situation to Cameron Crowe: "I came out of the wilderness and just naturally fell in with the beat scene, the Bohemian, BeBop crowd. . . . I had already decided that society . . . was pretty phony and I didn't want to be part of that . . . also, there was a lot of unrest in the country. You could feel it, a lot of frustration, sort of like a calm before a hurricane, things were shaking up." He explained how Dinkytown's inhabitants were "poets and painters, drifters, scholarly types, experts at one thing or another who had dropped out of the regular nine-to-five life." The writings of Jack Kerouac, Allen Ginsberg, Gregory Corso, and Lawrence Ferlinghetti affected Zimmerman more "than any of the stuff I'd been raised on" such that "everyday was like Sunday, it's like it was waiting for me, it had just as big an impact on me as Elvis Presley." That impact was exacerbated by Zimmerman's lifelong capacity to absorb influences, pick and choose what was of value to him, and synthesize those materials into new forms. It was a skill that served our ambitious youngster well.

The Dinkytown musical environment stressed folk music, and Zimmerman's Denver experiences allowed him to fall in easily. Since his musical background was diverse thanks to teachers such as Gatemouth Page and Jim Dandy, he proved to be a quick study. The biographers note that a Dinkytown girlfriend's father's record collection fed the shift in musical genres. Whatever was around, Zimmerman absorbed. The fire of the rock-and-roll spirit remained ever-present; the performer merely applied that intensity to the musical task at hand. You just cannot underestimate the significance of this time period on the new "Bob Dylan." When combined with the lessons gleaned from Walt Conley's record collection, his Dinkytown colleagues' musical knowledge, and the opportunity to practice what he learned, these experiences represent Zimmerman's postsecondary education. He would consistently draw upon these resources for the rest of his life.

When a Dinkytown friend provided a copy of Woody Guthrie's memoir, *Bound for Glory*, Zimmerman's ambitions discovered an anchor in Guthrie's hard-traveling, hard-living, man-with-a-message persona. With his name change in 1959, the ingredients were in place for the first incarnation of the "Bob Dylan" characters. Zimmerman would combine bohemian biker-poet attitude, American Song's blues/country traditions, and the Guthrie image to produce an unprecedented musical hybrid. David Hajdu explains Guthrie's significance: "In Guthrie, Bob found more than a genre of music, a body of work, or a performance style: he found *an image*—the hard travelin' loner with a guitar and a way with words, the outsider the insiders envied, easy with women, and surely doomed. An amalgam of Bob's previous heroes, the Guthrie he found in *Bound for Glory* was Hank Williams, James Dean, and Buddy Holly—a literate folksinger with a rock and roll attitude." Spitz concurs, "If Bobby had an idea of 'Dylan' before, then *Bound for Glory* provided him with a blueprint from which he could build his identity."

Many colorful stories circulate about the impressionable young man with a new hero. Zimmerman had people call him "Woody." His language shifted into a new "Okie" vernacular and accent. He invented stories that placed him on the road with his hero. He changed the way he dressed. He learned all of Guthrie's songs. He *became* Woody Guthrie, and his Dinkytown cohorts laughed at the results. At parties, the kid would be summoned to the telephone by someone shouting that Woody was calling. It was all a big joke to everyone but Hibbing's Bobby Zimmerman. In *Chronicles*, Dylan speaks of Guthrie with the highest reverence. He calls him "an epiphany." He reports that Guthrie was like a flash of blinding lightning going off in the dark room that was his life. Ultimately, he's proud of his affiliation with Woody Guthrie—darned proud.

There is some controversy over the motives behind Bob Zimmerman's new persona. People debate whether he wanted to shed his past, romanticize his present, or solidify his musical future. Several biographers suggest that Abe Zimmerman's relationship with his son had deteriorated so much that Bob rebelled against the family name. Others argue for a rejection of his religion or his community. While I don't necessarily dismiss these conclusions, I suspect this imaginative young man was focused on image building of one sort or another, and, as his creation gained a voice in Dinkytown, he continued to embellish that persona in a fashion that enlivened its marketability. Nevertheless, as Bob invented stories about being an orphan, living a poor but exciting life riding the rails (or whatever), and more, he hurt his parents. With time, their desire for the "truth" would intensify. The parents who raised their children as their "friends" were no doubt injured by the publicity that cast their friend as an orphan (or whatever).

The Dinkytown experience was instructive but short-lived. The University of Minnesota had nothing to do with anything. He seldom attended classes, much less studied. Like his initial piano lessons, Zimmerman did not respond well to formal instruction. Instead, he submersed himself in Guthrie's world, and that inspired him to visit his hero. He, indeed, left Minneapolis "bound for glory." After hitchhiking his way across the country for several months, "Bob Dylan" arrived in New York in December 1960 or January 1961 (depending upon the source). The new Dylan entered New York's folk scene in an impressive fashion. He moved to Greenwich Village's MacDougal Street in February, he achieved his dream and visited Woody Guthrie in early February (in a New Jersey hospital) and developed a relationship with the dying legend, he played for Guthrie and met his friends during weekend visits to Guthrie's home, he was billed on a show with John Lee Hooker in April, he played harmonica for a Harry Belafonte recording session in June (his first professional session), he performed throughout the folk community and received a favorable review from *New York Times* music critic Robert Shelton on September 29, he played harmonica during Carolyn Hester's recording session for Columbia Record's legendary producer John Hammond the next day and signed with Hammond/Columbia that afternoon, he delivered his first major performance at Carnegie Chapter Hall on November 4, and on November 20 and 22, he recorded his first album for Columbia (*Bob Dylan*, released in March 1962). That is one full year! His ascendance angered as many as it pleased. For some in the Village, the kid was an opportunist, robbing and using whatever he could for his private crusade. To others, he was a genius, a budding talent with unlimited potential. Any indiscretions, therefore, were excusable. To all, he was a musical force of surprising depth.

Initially, it was his performance that gained attention. Scaduto cites Miki Isaacson's recollections of the entertaining style that charmed New York folk circles:

> He used to do all these kooky things, and they never seemed like a routine. He could even make a comic act out of tuning his guitar, get up on stage and fiddle with the guitar strings and pretend he wasn't able to get it right and cursing under his breath, and we would all be in the aisle with the joy of it. And I'll never forget the thing he did with his harmonica. His eyes were so bad that we didn't know if it was a joke or real, but he'd begin taking harmonicas out of his pockets and laying them down on the table, pulling out one and saying, very *sotto voce*, "Now where is that E flat harmonica?" then pulling out another one, and not being able to find it. And saying, "Who's got that damned harmonica?" And it broke us all up. It was so Chaplin-like.

Dave Van Ronk agrees in the *Biography* video when he describes Dylan's initial stage act as "excruciatingly funny" with its "Chaplinesque mannerisms" and between-song monologues.

Bob Dylan's 1961 was a dynamic—even explosive—period in which he created and refined an image that was part Guthrie, part Chaplin, a little James Dean, and, somewhere in the mix, a portion of Little Richard. The result was a countrified, self-effacing folk singer with an intense drive to express himself. He wore ruffled Okie outfits and displayed the hygiene of a homeless person. He was "the kid" to Woody, and was adopted by the community. In less than *one year*, he managed to enter the New York folk family, master their musical style, and place himself in a position to surpass his mentors. *Bob Dylan* featured two examples of the means through which the aspiring artist would transcend his newly acquired peers: his songwriting. The album's two original songs, "Talking New York" and "Song To Woody," demonstrate Dylan's understanding of folk traditions through their humor, topicality, and musicality. Soon he provided additional proof of his songwriting skills as he penned "Blowin' In The Wind," "The Death Of Emmett Till," "Masters Of War," "When The Ship Comes In," and "A Hard Rain's A-Gonna Fall" (among many, many others). Had Zimmerman merely created a character to mimic the words and mannerisms of others, the act probably would have died out. But when he delivered these strong compositions in support of that image, Dylan introduced a new, refreshing act that could cross over from folk's narrow constituency into broader, more commercially viable audiences.

Although the songwriting was certainly impressive, *image* continued to drive Zimmerman's art. How successful were these public relations strategies? Consider music historian David Ewen's description of "Bob Dylan's" biography:

> Dylan attended the public schools in Hibbing and was graduated from Hibbing High School, no mean achievement for a boy who was more often away from Hibbing than in it. Between his tenth and eighteenth years he ran away from home seven times, traveling by any means of locomotion available—by foot, boxcars, by hitching rides—and covering a wide area from the Dakotas to California. He was learning at first hand the meaning of personal suffering and want, as well as inequality and injustice. He was running away from the domination of his parents and the constrictions of a small town, but actually he was being helplessly driven by a nervous restlessness, an inability to stay put anywhere for any length of time—a trait to which he was addicted all his life. But these years of *Wanderjahre* were not without their blessings. As has already been described, it enabled him, when he was ten, to get his first guitar. (Later on he learned to make music also on an autoharp, harmonica, and piano.) A year later it made it possible for him to meet Big Joe Williams, and recognize the importance of the blues. And when he was thirteen, it brought him a job with a traveling carnival, an experience during which he met all sorts of people—from roustabouts and day laborers to gamblers and prostitutes—and to sing songs for them to his own guitar accompaniments.

Now, Ewen's not writing for a pop music magazine or some celebrity tabloid; rather, he's a music *historian*. This is the biography that he uses in his *1972* book on the "great men" of "American popular song." That the periodicals and books of 1963 would fall for these inventions is a bit more understandable; however, for a historian to step into this trap some ten years later speaks volumes about Zimmerman's image machine's success (among other things). Little wonder Abe and Beatty longed for the truth to be told.

The Bob Zimmerman story pretty much ends here. He made it to New York. He successfully established himself in the music industry. And he dropped the curtain on his private life. Whether Bob Zimmerman shared any of the views that supported Bob Dylan's protest songs is uncertain. Was he on the motorcycle that wrecked in 1966? Was he anywhere to be found within the Rolling Thunder Revue? Did Zimmerman accept Christ with Dylan? No one knows the answers to these questions, and Zimmy's not talking. Dylan's autobiography and corresponding commentary also skirt over these matters. Rare is the brilliance displayed by the Bob Zimmerman image machine. Once he created the Dylan character so diligently propagated by Ewen and many others, he was staggered irreparably by a November 1963 *Newsweek* article that exposed him as Bob Zimmerman of Hibbing, Minnesota. When journalists realized and reported the facts, the wall of fiction evolved into a wall of silence. The confrontational personality that once demanded silence before he would sing for his grandmother now counterattacked with a vengeance. Ask a stupid question, Mr. Journalist Man, and get an answer that transcends stupidity and challenges your sanity. Probe a personal matter, Madam Reporter, and prepare for a "truth attack" that may eclipse even the greatest game of Glissendorf. Regardless of the encounter's tone, you will *never*, ever find Bobby Zimmerman. In his 2004 *60 Minutes* interview promoting his autobiography, Dylan claims he never was "Bob Zimmerman." He always has felt like he was somebody else. I think Sam Shepard describes this phenomenon well in his book about the Rolling Thunder Revue. In a segment called "The Inventor," Shepard offers this take on Zimmerman's invention:

> Dylan has invented himself. He's made himself up from scratch. That is, from the things he had around him and inside him. Dylan is an invention of his own mind. The point isn't to figure him out but to take him in. He gets into you anyway, so why not just take him in? He's not the first one to have invented himself, but he's the first one to have invented Dylan. No one invented him before him. Or after. What happens when someone invents something outside himself like an airplane or a freight train? The thing is seen for what it is. It's seen as something incredible because it's never been seen before, but it's taken in by the people and changes their lives in the process. They don't stand around trying to figure out what isn't, forever. They use it as a means to adventure.

Ultimately, Shepard sees this process as they key to the artist's longevity. He writes, "If a mystery is solved, the case is dropped. In this case, in the case of Dylan, the mystery is never solved, so the case keeps on. It keeps coming up again. Over and over the years. Who is this character anyway?" Yes, who is Bob Dylan? Who, indeed.

Nevertheless, Bobby Zimmerman remains a central part of the auteur. The biography that supports the public artist is his. The influences that shaped the artistic philosophy that guides the auteur's pen were his. The personality behind it all is his. Bob Zimmerman's connection to Jack Fate and Bob Dillon is genuine. The man is a walking musical encyclopedia. He probably told stories like a ninety-year-old rounder when he was ten. Bob Zimmerman's relationship to Bob Dillon is natural. These Bobs are rebellious guys, always have been. The cantankerous little boy who refused to sing before an inattentive audience matured into a cantankerous man who takes his best songs off of an album if he thinks they make the recording *too* good. Mix a rebellious personality with a musical encyclopedia and you get the subject of the following chapters. Watch this unsolved mystery evolve. Watch Jack Fate dominate one period, Bob Dillon another. Watch them adjust to the various missions that "Bob Dylan" engages. This is, my friends, *exactly* what Sam Shepard says it is: one wonderful mystery. And it all started on Seventh Avenue in Hibbing.

I think I'll cruise down Highway 26 later this year and attend the James Dean Festival in Fairmount. You know, just to look around, feel the rebellion, eat some corn on the cob, and get mad about the future.

The Folk-Posturing Period

Our musical story begins with some foreshadowing. When Bob Zimmerman left the Midwest and brought his "Bob Dylan" character to New York to meet his dying hero and pursue his destiny, he previewed the end of his career before it actually began. We now enter Jack Fate's postgraduate education. It was young Jack Fate who roamed the streets of New York looking for work, who traveled to New Jersey to sing for Woody Guthrie, who was adopted by the New York folk community, and who was systematically educated by the musical veterans at the Folklore Center. It was young Jack Fate who mastered all the folk classics and refined his skill as a "Woody Guthrie Jukebox." It was young Jack Fate who quietly absorbed all of the musical and poetic influences that floated through that magical air around Greenwich Village. The young artist called himself "Bob Dylan." But that character was actually gestating in the background, allowing his unique characterological combination of James Dean, Little Richard, and Hank Williams to complete his education. Before the voice of his generation emerged to confront the world through his innovative poetry and celebrity charades, the Jack Fate portion of Zimmerman's public persona gained a foothold in the New York music scene, educated himself for his life's work, and opened the commercial door for the man the world would know as Bob Dylan.

New York was more than an artistic opportunity for our budding auteur; it was a storytelling playground. Stories were everywhere: in the songs, between the musicians backstage, with journalists anywhere, during performances, and in the various writings that circulated within the community. Whether he was writing an autobiographical piece for a folk magazine, posing before an interested journalist, or enriching a show with a lively tale, Bob Dylan was a relentless storyteller. Moreover, when our Glissendorf Master initially plied his trade in the Big Apple, there were no Hibbings or Iron Ranges in the background to dilute his fantastic tales of wanderlust; to the contrary, his was a clean narrative slate—free to roam where it wished, inventing scenes and creating characters that served his not-so-carefully-planned public relations agenda. He was a carny one day, a singing barfly the next, or a roving gambler the day after that. His professed influences ranged from the legendary bluesmen roaming America's highways to the luckless outcasts riding America's railways to the freaks populating America's cheesy circus circuits. He may appear as the quiet student in one setting or the obnoxious stage hog the next. While his stories changed with his audience and its perceived needs, the one unwavering aspect of his public identity involved his *talent*. Whether he was passing himself off as the veteran road warrior, a savvy rounder, or a loyal patron, Bob Dylan's *talent* was self-evident. While it will take thirty years for Jack Fate's public emergence, the folk-posturing period of Bob Dylan's oeuvre laid the foundation for Fate's occasional appearance (e.g., during the Basement Tape period) and his dominance of the 1990s and beyond. If there's one thing to remember about this artist's career, it's this: The songs are his creative currency. That catalog of material may have been introduced by Gatemouth Page, reinforced by Jim Dandy, and refined by the Dinkytown experience, but it was solidified as the lifework's artistic foundation during this portion of Zimmerman's career.

The four albums that comprise the folk posturing period (*Bob Dylan, The Freewheelin' Bob Dylan, The Times They Are A-Changin'*, and *Another Side Of Bob Dylan*) represent but a portion of Dylan's output from this era. His liner notes for albums (e.g., "11 Outlined Epitaphs" for his *Freewheelin'* and for Peter, Paul and Mary's *In the Wind*) and his "open letters" and commentaries (published in *Hootenanny, Broadside*, and concert programs), along with his poems celebrating Guthrie ("Last Thoughts On Woody Guthrie") and his fabricated autobiography ("My Life In A Stolen Moment"), join a considerable list of songs that were omitted from album projects to create a diverse creative period. No phase of Dylan's oeuvre contains the narrative diversity of this initial segment.

As with every period of the auteur's lifework, this era involves a clear-cut mission; in this case, it was discovery. The folk-posturing period features the eager student's evolution into the accomplished young professional. Here he meets his musical teachers and absorbs their respective lessons. He refines his stage act and attracts a dedicated audience. He enters his chosen profession and encounters the music industry's long-standing, dogmatic prescriptions. He expands the scope of his thinking through new friends, enlightened girlfriends, and talented acquaintances. It is, indeed, a dynamic time full of romantic dreams, idealistic principles, and enterprising art. But all of it—from the political posing to the feigned musical allegiances to the contrived publicity stunts—served a dedicated mission. During this timeframe, Bob Zimmerman may execute a careful plan, react to a raw impulse, or seize an unpredictable moment; in all cases, he pursues an ambition that is nothing less than his life's calling. All those frozen mornings on the Iron Range with their hot dreams of celebrity pleasures fueled an artistic/commercial drive that would not be satisfied by anything other than success—whatever that may involve.

Yes, the Jack Fate dimension of Zimmerman's "Dylan" character received his postgraduate education during this timeframe. He refined his musical knowledge. He expanded his narrative approach. He explored his chosen industry. He temporarily accepted his professional role during this crucial formative period. His mission of discovery was accomplished in no uncertain terms. What's so fascinating about this initial era of Zimmerman's protracted career is the fact that when all is said and done, "Bob Dylan" emerged at the *end* of this opening period. So relax and enjoy young Zimmerman's rise through the ranks of the 1960s folk music scene. He learned so much. He assimilated his lessons in his own joyful manner. And on October 31, 1964, he said goodbye to it all.

Bob Dylan

First albums are intriguing creations—especially in protracted careers. Does it foreshadow the future? Does it betray what follows? You never know. For instance, the Bruce Springsteen appearing on his first album used an impressionistic writing style that got him labeled "the next Bob Dylan," even though the songs are nothing like Dylan's. Springsteen quickly departed from that writing style (*never* to return) as he turned to the articulation of the musical world's first—and only—extended soap opera. Pete Townshend's career opened with pop ditties that reflected the musical times but undermined his heartfelt commitment to "art." His early songs were masterpieces of that particular style; however, his interest in that approach was short-lived. Elements of Joni Mitchell's and Elvis Costello's first albums provided foundations for extended careers and, in turn, previewed their respective lifelong pursuits in no uncertain terms. Of these various artists, only Bob Dylan initiated his professional career with an album of cover songs. These versions of established songs not only positioned Dylan within the folk song tradition, but also demonstrated Jack Fate's dedication to his musical heritage as well. *That's* the news from *Bob Dylan*, and it would take thirty years to fully appreciate its significance.

The biographers carefully chronicle the story. Robert Shelton's review in the *New York Times* set the commercial table, a scheduled recording session with Carolyn Hester at Columbia Records offered the vital opportunity, Dylan's appearance and harmonica skills provided the musical ingredients, John Hammond's direction of the Hester session introduced the innovative chef, and music history feasted on Hammond's intuitions. Bob Dylan was certainly committed to his personal mission, but the magical combination of Shelton's review (in the *Times*, mind you!), Hester's timely session (at Columbia, no less!), and Hammond's presence (oh my!) *had* to go beyond the ambitious youngster's wildest dreams. Although Dylan used the Woody Guthrie sound to present traditional folk music that appealed to an established audience, Hammond unleashed a talent that he perceived as extending way beyond that starting point. Hammond's prescience complemented Zimmerman's talent in a manner that guaranteed both men's place in music history.

Released on March 19, 1962, the thirty-seven minute, thirteen-song album entitled *Bob Dylan* cost $402 to produce, as Hammond's production style reinforced Dylan's emerging penchant for minimalist recordings to render two efficient sessions. Everything about *Bob Dylan* suggests a controlled commercial enterprise. This first album must make Jake Fate proud. The budding auteur may sound like a hillbilly, but he sounds like an *authentic*, hard-working, dedicated hillbilly. "The Kid"—as Woody deemed him—works *hard* on this record. Gut-wrenching vocals, leather-lunged harmonica playing, deeply emotional stories, and the first glimpses of Zimmerman's pen work in harmony to initiate something that would blossom in ways only John Hammond could imagine. Assuredly, the "folk process" (i.e., the practice of taking established melodies or story lines and recasting them in various forms) dominated this creative venture. As I state in *American Song*, that Bob Dylan revised and extended the celebrity-singer-songwriter tradition established by Woody Guthrie is clearly evident in this opening offering.

Bob Dylan explores three topics: love, the traveling musician's life, and death. The album contains six songs about death ("In My Time Of Dying," "Man Of Constant Sorrow," "Fixin' To Die," "Highway 51," "Gospel Plow," and "See That My Grave Is Kept Clean"). The remaining songs celebrate love ("Pretty Peggy-O" and "Baby, Let Me Follow You Down"), lament love ("You're No Good" and "House Of The Rising Sun"), describe the musician's life ("Talking New York" and the Guthrie tribute, "Song To Woody"), and portray life on the move ("Freight Train Blues"). The first person death narrations invoke Christian values in predictable ways as characters cope with the present as a path to redemption ("In My Time Of Dyin' "), endure the projected pain of leaving loved ones behind ("Fixin' To Die"), contemplate their funeral arrangements ("Highway 51"), and seek respect for their resting places ("See That My Grave Is Kept Clean"). Little metaphorical mischief appears through these straightforward yarns. Dylan tells us who's doing what, why, and to what end in a direct manner as the singer sticks to the Guthrie script through a regional dialect that would control this era.

The opening track, "You're No Good," sets the tone for an entire career with its portrayal of the faithless woman and the trouble she brings. Dylan wails against Evil Woman in a direct, forceful style that would soon be his personal trademark. "House Of The Rising Sun" is less personal but equally compelling as Dylan assumes the woman's perspective in this traditional tale of love gone wrong, the gambling lifestyle, and the oh-so-predictable consequences. Complementing those songs are the tracks that celebrate loving relationships and the ever-present urges that accompany that wonderful, albeit wacky, state. This is the genesis of Bob Dylan's oeuvre. He may examine societal issues, explore spiritual matters, or weave fantastic accounts of unlikely situations in his songwriting; however, his preoccupation with affairs of the heart is firmly established on this first album. While that topical focus does not separate him from his songwriting peers, the intensity of those expressions most certainly will. That intensity is most apparent in the singing on this record. These may not be "Bob Dylan" songs, but they are presented through his personality—a trait that returns thirty years later when Bob Zimmerman embellishes Jack Fate through two more albums of cover songs, *Good As I Been To You* and *World Gone Wrong*.

The two original compositions established narrative orientations that reappear throughout the lifework. "Talking New York" demonstrates Dylan's sense of humor, his capacity to recast events, and his application of the folk process. That Dylan borrowed lines from Guthrie tunes and musical phrases from a variety of sources created little controversy at this point, since such practices embodied the folk music songwriting tradition. As he assembled his story, Dylan engaged in another practice that would one day cause frustration; he interjected his persona into the narrative and elevated the author's role in the story. The other original song ("Song To Woody") reveals Dylan's ability to sharpen his pencil and produce a story about a specific set of circumstances. These "topical" narratives not only articulate some view on some subject for some audience, but they, too, create a context for attribution. Much like "Talking New York," "Song To Woody" speaks to a broader topic from a subjective point of view. Both in their thematic orientation and musical enactment, these two original compositions foretell the future. Let's examine the specifics.

Our hard-traveling, Colorado-born (according to "Man Of Constant Sorrow"), veteran bluesman with his vast experiences with love won and love lost offers two excerpts from his weather-torn diary on *Bob Dylan*. The first, "Talking New York," tells the story of his arrival in New York City. The opening stanza captures the song's narrative style:

> Ramblin' outa the wild West,
> Leavin' the towns I love the best.
> Thought I'd seen some ups and downs,
> 'Til I come into New York town.
> People goin' down to the ground,
> Buildings goin' up to the sky.

The sort of slapstick pun about witnessing life's ups and downs is a trademark Dylan tactic. He may borrow the idea from a Guthrie song, but his use of this type of goofy observation recurs throughout the lifework and offers a counterbalance to the heavy-handed lines upon which his songwriting reputation rests.

The eight verses (four to seven lines each) of urban wonder continue with observations about the record-setting New York winter, our central character's journey to Greenwich Village, and his search for work in Village coffeehouses. After singing for one club owner, he's cast away with the admonition "You sound like a hillbilly / We want folk singers here." On his very first album, Dylan fearlessly attacks the superficial qualities of a musical movement that he's exploiting. Here Bob Dillon's rebellion reveals itself for the first time on record. The story continues with our persistent character's search for work that extends from playing his harmonica for "a dollar a day" to obtaining a better job in a "bigger" venue with a "bigger" paycheck. From this experience, our roadwise rural bluesman has evolved into a streetwise urban musician who cites Guthrie's famed observation (from "Pretty Boy Floyd"): "Now, a very great man once said / That some people rob you with a fountain pen / It didn't take too long to find out / Just what he was talkin' about." With that, the bluesman takes off for "Western skies" and exits the Big Apple for East Orange, New Jersey. That he is wiser for his stay in New York City is beyond doubt. The blend of insightful wit and sarcastic commentary yields a classic Bob Dylan song presented through the sonic strategy of that creative moment.

That tone lightens considerably with the tip-of-the-traveling-hat that is "Song To Woody." Here, too, we witness the wise road warrior who plies his trade a long way from his home. This time, he walks Woody's path. He sees what Woody saw. He meets the people Woody met. From those powerful experiences, he wrote a song for his hero:

> Hey, hey Woody Guthrie, I wrote you a song
> 'Bout a funny ol' world that's a-comin' along.
> Seems sick an' it's hungry, it's tired an' it's torn,
> It looks like it's a-dyin' an' it's hardly been born.

Hey, Woody Guthrie, but I know that you know
All the things that I'm a-sayin' an' a-many times more.
I'm a-singin' you the song, but I can't sing enough,
'Cause there's not many men that done the things that you've done.

The five-verse tribute continues by acknowledging Woody's mates and other like-minded travelers who make the sacrifices necessary to sustain the traveling life that yields the depth of understanding that underpins a bluesman's musical wisdom. In its own simple way, the song is an anthem for a celebrity character and his infamous lifestyle.

"Talking New York" and "Song To Woody" are intelligent, witty, and committed songs. Operating from an established stance—the road-weary bluesman—the songs chart the suspicious fascination of a first trip to the dog-eat-dog world of the New York City entertainment industry and contrast that experience with the tranquility of life on the road with the boys. The traveling life may be hard, but it's honest—an honesty that is nowhere to be found among the "authentic" folk singers in Greenwich Village. Thus, to the extent that Dylan praises Woody and his life's work, he damns the New York establishment and its money-hungry hypocrisy. Jack Fate's musical knowledge may have enabled this sonic trip through the Dust Bowl musical library, but Bob Dillon's rebellion fueled the venture. Our first recorded "truth attack" (a Dylan term for a confrontational conversation or statement) reveals that on Record One, the auteur already knew the score.

While *Bob Dylan* is occasionally dismissed as a group of cover songs presented through an obvious imitation of Woody Guthrie's established style, this analysis suggests the recording represents much more than that. First, the performance displays a signature passion. The vocals, the guitar and harmonica playing, and the songs' contents unveil a musical intensity that controls the auteur's work, regardless of the mission at hand. Whether he's screaming over the Hawks' instruments during the 1966 tour, shouting his way through a Rolling Thunder set, or sarcastically moaning his way through a Jack Fate song, Bob Zimmerman performs with an unmitigated passion—and that presentational style controls *Bob Dylan*. Second, the record conveys Jack Fate's commitment to his musical heritage. All of those Gatemouth Page purchases, all of those conversations with Jim Dandy and in Dinkytown, all of the Sunday afternoon gatherings at Woody's house, and more were carefully assimilated into Fate's musical repertoire. As we shall discover, whenever Bob Zimmerman's characters seem to lose their way or wander off the mission's course, Jack Fate's encyclopedic musical knowledge restores the necessary equilibrium. That commitment is the artistic anchor of Zimmerman's career. And third, Bob Dylan's eventual writing style is in evidence on this record. The humor, sarcasm, and attention to detail that would guide the protest songs, support the satires, and inspire his impressionism appear within the two original songs from *Bob Dylan*. As Zimmerman's creative intensity deployed Fate's musical knowledge and used it for guidance and inspiration, the results produced a series of songs that forever changed the art of songwriting—and that evolution began with Bob Dylan's first record. So, while music critics and historians may dismiss *Bob Dylan* as a cheaply recorded album of covers, this analysis indicates that it is, in fact, a remarkably representative starting point.

The Freewheelin' Bob Dylan

By the time *Bob Dylan* hit the record stores, Bob Dylan had moved well beyond that album. A little over a month after his first album's release, Dylan and Hammond were in the studio for their second and final project, *The Freewheelin' Bob Dylan*. From that initial session on April 24, 1962, until the second album's official release on May 27, 1963, a whirlwind of events unfolded around the emerging auteur. He secured the services of one of the industry's most aggressive managers, Albert Grossman (known as "the Bear" for a variety of reasons); he switched music publishers for a more profitable deal (for Grossman, anyway); his participation in the Civil Rights movement and its political spin-offs intensified; he legally changed his name to Dylan; and his talent attracted the attention of people living beyond New York. As he appeared on radio programs and in the folk music press, the enterprising youngster continued to build the Dylan Myth via tales of the rails, famous musical encounters, and his outlaw lifestyle. Meanwhile, the songs poured from him. "Blowin' In The Wind" was a major success for another of Grossman's acts (Peter, Paul, and Mary); his protest songs were printed in *Broadside* (e.g., "The Ballad Of Emmett Till"); his commentaries—crafted through his own approach to phonetics—added to the developing legend; and in virtually every way imaginable, Dylan seized his moment. Those around him may have considered him to be the darling of the folk-protest movement, but something else was brewing. During this moment in his career, the Iron Range's original biker-poet was creeping out from Woody Guthrie's shadow. The young man who entered New York Town on the heels of Woody, Cisco, Ramblin' Jack, and the rest of that Okie entourage was, in fact, *nothing* like those mythical characters. He could write songs like them. He could perform songs like them. He could carry himself like them. But *they* couldn't write songs like the ones that were about to emerge from *him*. With Bob Dylan's *talent* established, it would be but a matter of time before Bob Dillon's rebellion surfaced.

It is impossible to overstate *The Freewheelin' Bob Dylan*'s significance in popular music history—or, for that matter, within the history of art. Much to the author's eventual chagrin, the personalization of this project's content set the scene for the avalanche of celebrity worship that was to follow. The many crowns that "Bob Dylan" would soon wear were fitted during this timeframe. He lights the torch, gives it his moniker, carries it, and sells it in a fashion that invited the world to stand in its glow—absorbing the light that emanated from his wit, wisdom, and wide-eyed wonder. The man said things that had never been said before, and this would bring him wealth, fame, and critical acclaim.

He would quickly learn to hate it all.

Originally entitled *Bob Dylan's Blues* (and totally revised just weeks before its release, making original pressings quite valuable), *Freewheelin'* represents but a portion of Dylan's songwriting from this incredibly productive period. Songs such as "Emmett Till," "Who Killed Davey Moore?" "The Halls of Red Wing," the provocative

"John Brown," and the colorful "Talking Bear Mountain Picnic Massacre Blues" and "Talkin' John Birch Paranoid Blues" were available yet omitted from the album. That John Hammond brought in Tom Wilson to produce the record's final session on April 24, 1963, signaled the growth Dylan demonstrated since the *Freewheelin'* sessions began one year earlier. Hammond opened the door for Dylan and it was time for Dylan to step through it. At the heart of it all were Dylan's topical songs, his personalized messages, and their hybrid: the personalized topical song. He even gave these songs their own label: "finger-pointing songs." Here the celebrity songwriter placed a personal stamp on the perspective advanced in a manner that elevated the role of authorship: The work was more than a *song*—it was a *statement*.

"Hammond's Folly" (the name Columbia executives gave their most famous producer's unprofitable project) turned the musical corner with this fifty-minute work containing thirteen compositions that emphasize elegiac accounts of romantic and societal issues. Joining that theme is an expression of personal nostalgia ("Bob Dylan's Dream"), a personal celebration ("Bob Dylan's Blues"), and two satires ("Talking [or "Talkin' "] World War III Blues" and "I Shall Be Free"). Controlling the album are the nine songs of complaint that embrace love (the traditional "Girl From The North Country"; "Down The Highway"; "Don't Think Twice, It's All Right"; "Corrina, Corrina," an adaptation of a Joe Turner tune; and "Honey, Just Allow Me One More Chance," an adaptation of a Henry Thomas original) and contemporary society ("Blowin' In The Wind," "Masters Of War," "A Hard Rain's A-Gonna Fall," and "Oxford Town").

As I note in *American Song*, three stylistic tendencies control the work: the continued use of personal references, the advent of surreal imagery, and the intensity of the emotions portrayed. While Hank Williams used his "Luke the Drifter" character to convey musical editorials about public events, Bob Dylan would have none of that. That two songs use his *name* in their titles advanced this unprecedented personalization of song content. Dylan may not have aspired to become the voice of his generation, but he surely positioned himself for that role. Furthermore, "Down The Highway" refers to Dylan's girlfriend (Suze Rotolo) in such a direct manner as to call attention to such matters in virtually all of his songs from this period. The writer baited the hook of attribution, audiences took that bait, and Dylan would regret this invitation into his private world.

Balancing that trend, *Freewheelin'* introduced another storytelling signature: the use of surreal imagery. Whether he was hiding behind these opaque renderings or revealing his propensity for word games, Dylan deployed a free-form writing style quite outside the folk tradition. "A Hard Rain" and "I Shall Be Free" feature an internal logic that prohibits their consideration as narratives. Instead, they involve bitter ("Hard Rain") or playful ("I Shall") value-laden expressions with minimal characterization or plot progression. Still, when construed with the highly personalized commentaries of the other tracks, one instinctively searches for the "message." After all, these songs are presented through a musical genre that stresses authenticity. By co-opting the folk tradition's posture, Dylan invited his audience to search for something that may not exist—even though he directly ridicules folk songwriting and its Tin Pan Alley style in the introduction to "Bob Dylan's Blues." "I

Shall," in particular, foreshadows the Newport Mod's chaotic wordplay and its irreverent, no-holds-barred imagery. It is all one big laugh (or cry).

The third narrative trait once again reflects Zimmerman's personality through its intensity. At this point in the artist's career, this intensity goes beyond the vocals, harmonica playing, or guitar playing. Here the lyrics display a controlling anger that fuels the expression's power. "Masters Of War" is overwhelming. "Oxford Town" is humiliating. "Don't Think Twice" is subtly mean-spirited. "A Hard Rain" is frightening. On the other end of the intensity scale is the humor from "Talkin' World War III" and "I Shall Be Free." These are not your run-of-the-mill pop love or protest songs. They're fierce expressions that use biblical characters to communicate the sin portrayed in the song ("Masters") or take everyday activities to relate the stupidity of living under the threat of the nuclear nightmare ("World War III"). There is an edge to these songs, the *Dylan Edge*, and that trait makes these songs unique.

We begin with the lifework's bedrock narrative form, the love complaints. In "Girl From The North Country," (cited as "Girl Of The North Country" in its copyright—whichever) Dylan laments the passing of a beautiful love though a simple, straightforward story that uses minimal instrumentation to support the account. The narrator addresses a traveler bound for the "north country" and implores him to give his regards to the wonderful woman who lives there. The five verses recount the north country's harsh weather, the love object's impeccable beauty, and the narrator's anxieties over the loss. The simple story closes with a simple plea: "So if you're travelin' in the north country fair / Where the winds hit heavy on the borderline / Remember me to one who lives there / She once was a true love of mine." Those nostalgic feelings gain a much sharper edge in the blues-driven story, "Down The Highway." Here, too, our narrator pines for a lost love; this time, *she* has departed for a "far-off land," leaving her wandering partner behind. He's "walkin' down the highway," traveling from coast to coast, gambling and fighting off trouble. His ambition is without mystery: He hopes to gain the "luck" necessary to leave his traveling days behind and settle with his love. Consider this pivotal verse:

> Well, the ocean took my baby,
> My baby stole my heart from me.
> Yes, the ocean took my baby,
> My baby took my heart from me.
> She packed it all up in a suitcase,
> Lord, she took it to Italy, Italy.

First, notice how Dylan uses a standard blues structure to tell his story. Heavy lyrical and instrumental repetition is used to drive home his point as each of the six stanzas opens with a two-line comment, repeats that sentiment, and closes with a two-line summary. I'm not surprised that *Freewheelin'* was originally entitled *Bob Dylan's Blues* when I listen to this—you can smell the Delta when you hear this tune. Second, notice the age-old fear of all romantic blues songs and the narrator's regret over his woman's trip to *Italy*. This is a clear interjection of autobiographical commentary since Rotolo—who graces the album's cover, walking arm in arm with Dylan—was in Italy, and Dylan used the song to lodge his complaint. This would not be the last time the songwriter uses personal information in the context of a romantic complaint or celebration. No sir, the man is just getting warmed up on that measure.

Dylan's adaptations of "Corrina, Corrina" and "Honey, Just Allow Me" are standard romantic complaints. In the former, the narrator just can't get his love interest off of his mind, and that leaves him in a sorry state; in the latter, the narrator is pleading for the standard second chance. Using transportation metaphors to state his case (i.e., requests to ride in her "aeroplane" and "passenger train"), "Honey" is a fast-paced account that focuses on the title's request to the exclusion of all else. Both songs follow tried-and-true blues formulas that stress simple imagery communicated through heavy repetition. "Corrina" contains three verses that replicate the "Down The Highway" strategy, while "Honey" expands the tactic through its three ten-line verses. There is news in "Corrina," however. This track contains the first backing band for a Dylan song (i.e., bass and drums). Although several outtakes feature similar sonic strategies, this is the only cut to make the final record.

Our last romantic complaint opts for a different storytelling technique. With "Don't Think Twice, It's All Right," we witness a synthesis of the songwriting strategies evidenced in the previous songs, but with a specific twist. Three of the four stanzas open with the repetition that characterizes the blues songwriting tradition as the narrator urges his lover not to "sit and wonder why" or turn on her "light" or call out his "name," since it is just too late in the romantic game for those activities. While he wishes "there was somethin' you would do or say / To try and make me change my mind and stay," he surrenders to the realization that he gave her his "heart but she wanted" his "soul" and resolves his situation in this manner:

> I'm walkin' down that long, lonesome road, babe
> Where I'm bound, I can't tell
> But goodbye's too good a word, gal
> So I'll just say fare thee well
> I ain't sayin' you treated me unkind
> You could have done better but I don't mind
> You just kinda wasted my precious time
> But don't think twice, it's all right.

Traces of autobiography exist through references to Rotolo's age ("I once loved a woman, a child I'm told"—Rotolo was seventeen when she started dating Dylan); however, the news here is in the strength of the narrator's response to his deteriorating situation. He may deploy a simple blues structure to articulate an autobiographical complaint, but his view that the relationship squandered his time adds a dark twist to the story. This is classic Dylan. Just as he attacked the coffeehouse owners for their musical hypocrisy in "Talking New York" (e.g., the line about preferring folk singers over hillbillies), he now used the tactic in a love song. He may wish things were different or that she'd try to persuade him to stay, yet once the dust begins to settle, he dismisses her as a simple waste of his *precious* time. That sarcastic edge transforms the song. What began as a traditional romantic complaint evolved into a personal statement with Bob Dylan's signature stamped firmly in place.

That songwriting strategy controls the societal complaints. Although "Blowin' In The Wind" follows more traditional prescriptions, the Dylan Edge dominates the other songs. "Blowin' " is a pop-protest masterpiece. Although Dylan claims to have written the three eight-line verses in ten minutes, this track showcases his ability to co-opt an established songwriting structure to a personal end. The song opens with these poignant lines:

> How many roads must a man walk down
> Before you call him a man?
> Yes, 'n' how many seas must a white dove sail
> Before she sleeps in the sand?
> Yes, 'n' how many times must the cannon balls fly
> Before they're forever banned?
> The answer, my friend, is blowin' in the wind,
> The answer is blowin' in the wind.

The song continues with more simple questions that frame complex observations: How many "deaths" will it take before we understand that "too many people have died," or how long can "some people" exist before "they're allowed to be free?" No polemical resolutions are offered. No answers of any kind are provided. Instead, Dylan raises his questions, applies them to recognizable contexts, and leaves us to identify with those concerns. What an anthem! What timing! Yet, something seems to be missing. Something seems to be lacking.

The answer, my friend, is that Bob Dylan Edge. When Peter, Paul, and Mary sing this song, you can hear "Puff the Magic Dragon" singing along in the background, waving his tail to the song's rhythm, urging everyone's participation while he places another marshmallow over the campfire. Very few *Dylan* songs assume such a passive stance. The song lacks the blazing core that typifies this writer's work. Consequently, "Blowin' In The Wind" is a one-shot deal. The other societal complaints on *Freewheelin'* follow a totally different strategy.

The Dylan Edge is the controlling factor in "Masters Of War," "Hard Rain," and "Oxford Town." "Masters" opens by identifying the enemy:

> Come you masters of war
> You that build all the guns
> You that build the death planes
> You that build the big bombs
> You that hide behind walls
> You that hide behind desks
> I just want you to know
> I can see through your masks.

(If anybody can see through a mask, it's Bob Dylan.) The eight-verse diatribe continues by denouncing the enemy's lazy ways, their manipulative strategies, and their cowardice. Dylan aligns the enemy with Judas as he decries the transparent qualities of their self-serving, harebrained belief in a winnable world war. He continues with additional attacks about how the masters pad their wallets by abusing innocents, the unforgivable qualities of their despicable acts, and his heartfelt promise to stand over their grave until he is certain of their deaths. This situation is so awful, Dylan tells us, that people fear to bring children into such a horrible world. Why? Why is this situation so bad that Jesus refuses to grant forgiveness? The masters have made a serious miscalculation, as the songs' penultimate verse reveals:

> Let me ask you one question
> Is your money that good
> Will it buy you forgiveness
> Do you think that it could
> I think you will find
> When your death takes its toll
> All the money you made
> Will never buy back your soul.

Few songs in the history of popular music display the anger conveyed through "Masters Of War." The song is staggering in its invective. The use of biblical characters not only invokes widely held American values, but also leaves little doubt about the nature of these characterizations. By identifying the "Masters Of War" with Judas, Dylan advances the highest form of betrayal, a treachery so complete it is unforgivable. Since the Christian story of Jesus Christ is predicated on "forgiveness" and the central character's martyrdom for that principle, to suggest that Jesus would not absolve these characters is to cast considerable damnation. Dylan used clear language and a recognizable story to tell a tragic tale of societal victimization and ultimate revenge. The intensity of the retribution unveils a storytelling signature that would at times dominate Dylan's writing. The Dylan Edge is ablaze in this masterful song that refuses to go away; each decade seems to offer another layer of significance to the auteur's initial observation.

To the extent that "Masters" overwhelms you, "Oxford Town" embarrasses you. The song chronicles James Meredith's attempt to enroll at the University of Mississippi, located in Oxford, Mississippi. Even the residents of Oxford walk around town with "their heads bowed down" over the shame of rejecting a citizen's enrollment in a state university because of his race. Once the song establishes the absurdity of the situation, it warns of the dangers that surround those conditions. Consequently, the narrator wonders why in the world he, his girl, and her son bothered to visit such a dreadful place, and concludes with a promise to return home soon. The song is simple, clear, and compelling. No mystery here. People die in that awful town, "All because his face was brown / Better get away from Oxford town." The song may be simple, but the Dylan Edge sharpens that simplicity.

There is absolutely *nothing* simple about our last societal complaint, the impressionistic "A Hard Rain's A-Gonna Fall." Robert Allen Zimmerman of Hibbing, Minnesota, transformed the art of songwriting with this Bob Dylan song. Assuredly, it is a societal complaint. Things are bad, man. Yet, the song is much more. Its surreal imagery takes songwriting where it had never before been with each line, as Dylan told Studs Terkel in 1963, representing the first line of a new song. The five verses (featuring between nine and sixteen lines each) establish different scenes as one character asks another—his "blue-eyed son"—where he's been, who he's seen, what he's heard, who he's met, and closes with the question, "What will you do now that you've done all of this?" (my words). After those queries are posed, the blue-eyed son replies through images that are in turns fantastic, frightening, fascinating, and fearful. When asked where he's been, the blue-eyed respondent recalls stumbling along the "side of twelve misty mountains," walking and crawling along "six crooked highways," stepping into "seven sad forests," standing before a "dozen dead oceans," and traveling "ten thousand miles in the mouth of a graveyard." The stanza ends with the tag line: "And it's a hard, and it's a hard, it's a hard, and it's a hard / And it's a hard rain's a-gonna fall."

Next, our blue-eyed one recalls what he's seen. These images are startling. He saw "a newborn baby with wild wolves all around it," an abandoned "highway of diamonds," a "black branch" that was dripping "blood," "ten thousand talkers" with broken "tongues," and heavily armed young children (wielding guns and swords). When asked what he's heard, he replies that he listened to "thunder" that issued a "warning," "the roar of a wave that could drown the whole world," 100 drummers, 10,000 people whispering without any listeners, a person starving while others laughed, the "song" of a "poet who died in the alley," and the sounds of a clown crying. Conjuring images of Dante's *Divine Comedy*, the dread continues with the blue-eyed one's account of the people he met along his way: a child with a "dead pony," a "white" man with a "black" dog, a woman whose body was aflame, a "young woman" who offered him a "rainbow," and two men—one "wounded" by love, the other by hate. Finally, after experiencing all of this mayhem, the blue-eyed traveler is asked what he intends to do now. He replies,

> I'm a-goin' back out 'fore the rain starts a-fallin',
> I'll walk to the depths of the deepest black forest,
> Where the people are many and their hands are all empty,
> Where the pellets of poison are flooding their waters,
> Where the home in the valley meets the damp dirty prison,
> Where the executioner's face is always well hidden,
> Where hunger is ugly, where souls are forgotten,
> Where black is the color, where none is the number,
> And I'll tell it and think it and speak it and breathe it,
> And reflect it from the mountain so all souls can see it,
> Then I'll stand on the ocean until I start sinkin',
> But I'll know my song well before I start singin',
> And it's a hard, it's a hard, it's a hard, it's a hard,
> It's a hard rain's a-gonna fall.

With that, the practice of songwriting changed forever. On his *second* album, our Glissendorf Master, Bob Zimmerman, transformed his childhood game into Bob Dylan's signature method of writing. The extent to which the writer was influenced by symbolist poets is a mystery. At times, he says he was; at others, he denies their influence. In any event, this technique revolutionized the art form, and it would never be the same again. (As a quick aside, it is often assumed that the "hard rain" in question is nuclear fallout. Dylan denies this. In his interview with Studs Terkel, he is adamant that all he means is a hard, perhaps cleansing, rain. Though written during the time of the Cuban missile crisis, Dylan's stance is unambiguous.)

In *American Song*, I deemed this songwriting technique "narrative impressionism" due to its use of recurring opening and tag lines as a means of creating the illusion of a storytelling structure. The song seems like a story, but it's not. Instead, Dylan introduces a form of impressionism that operates within a specific structure. With time, he'll introduce songs that abdicate any structure whatsoever, as his words frolic in their own symbolic playground. What I find so amazing is that it all started on his *second* album with "Hard Rain." *That* is startling.

From the demanding, and at times terrifying, world of relational and social complaint, we turn to the two satires, "Talkin' World War III" and "I Shall Be Free." Here we note blends of the old and the new. The old involves the campfire tomfoolery that dominates both songs as they play with silly rhymes, disjointed images, celebrity or product names, and general chaos. That "General Chaos" could easily be the name of a character in these two songs says it all. Dylan is playing in his songwriting playpen with these songs, and they balance an album featuring such weighty works as "Masters" and "Hard Rain." In "I Shall Be Free," our crazed narrator offers a litany of opinions on a host of unrelated matters that leap across topics as we move through the song's eleven verses. He loves to drink (he walks "like a duck and smells like a skunk"), he advises presidents (telling John Kennedy that all the country needs in order to "grow" is, of course, "Brigitte Bardot"), he associates with wonderful women (she's a "humdinger" and a "folksinger"), copes with Cold War politics, questions the value of television ads featuring football players, and enjoys the humor of the "funniest woman" he's ever seen, the "great-granddaughter of Mr. Clean." The song closes with this revealing verse:

> Well, ask me why I'm drunk alla time,
> It levels my head and eases my mind.
> I just walk along and stroll and sing,
> I see better days and I do better things.
> (I catch dinosaurs
> I make love to Elizabeth Taylor . . .
> Catch hell from Richard Burton!)

While "Talking New York" affords a glimpse of this type of writing, Dylan takes the approach to new levels with "I Shall Be Free." How could it be that this song is on the same album as "Masters Of War"? As these songs demonstrate, Dylan's pen cuts a variety of ways, and the folk-posturing period features them all. No other era offers such wide-ranging material.

Falling somewhere in between "I Shall" and the album's more melodramatic tracks is the campfire satire "Talkin' World War III." To the extent that "Masters" damns those who build and sell bombs, "WWIII" toys with the aftermath of their insidious efforts. The song's subtext massages those Cold War anxieties that render end-of-the-world nightmares, while its surface reading plays with those very same emotions. The track's logic is evident in its opening verse:

> Some time ago a crazy dream came to me,
> I dreamt I was walkin' into World War Three,
> I went to the doctor the very next day
> To see what kinda words he could say.
> He said it was a bad dream.
> I wouldn't worry 'bout it none, though,
> They were my own dreams and they're only in my head.

(That last line is often sung, "Those ol' dreams are only in yer head.") From the outset, Dylan places the tale firmly in the tongue-in-cheek mode with the doctor's response to his experience: It's a bad dream and nothing more. In performance, Dylan really stresses that point. Eleven more stanzas follow in which our dream-drunk narrator emerges from the "sewer with some little lover" only to discover a war has transpired. He wanders about, smoking a cigarette, checking things out. He's turned away by a stranger with a shotgun who refuses to give him food, rejected by a stranger who fears he's a Communist, ignored by a woman who turns down his request to "go and play Adam and Eve," cruised the area in a Cadillac ("Good car to drive after a war," we're told), played "Rock-A-Day Johnny" on his record player, and listened to the operator repeat the time for an hour in order to secure interpersonal stimulation. Suddenly, the doctor interrupts the story to complain that he has the same dream with a slight twist: *He* was the only person alive after the war. The fun concludes with this timeworn wisdom:

> Well, now time passed and now it seems
> Everybody's having them dreams.
> Everybody sees themselves walkin' around with no one else.
> Half of the people can be part right all of the time,
> Some of the people can be all right part of the time.
> But all the people can't be all right all the time
> I think Abraham Lincoln said that.
> "I'll let you be in my dreams if I can be in yours,"
> I said that.

The *Bob Dylan Live 1964* release demonstrates just how effective this song was in concert. It bounces along to a simple tune with Dylan's joking delivery adding levity to the story. Nevertheless, the tale clearly operates on two levels; underneath all the fun and games is a probing fear of the thermonuclear nightmare. How interesting that the author who penned "Let Me Die In My Footsteps" (a song about preferring to die above ground rather than resorting to a fallout shelter for protection) wrote that song's opposite by poking fun at someone who pops out of the ground (a sewer, no less!) after the nuclear dust has settled. I guess we may conclude that the auteur has examined all sides of this particular issue.

My treatment of *Freewheelin'* concludes with the two personalized editorials, the nostalgia of "Bob Dylan's Dream" and the celebration portrayed in "Bob Dylan's Blues." As I mentioned earlier, "Blues" opens with Dylan's denunciation of Tin Pan Alley–driven folk music and its commercial orientation before launching into yet another fantastic account of the celebrity's life. Here, the "Lone Ranger and Tonto" are in town "fixin' ev'rybody's troubles" but the narrator's. He concludes someone must have told them that he was "doin' fine." And that sums up the song. From there, the narrator just celebrates his life. He doesn't need sports cars; walking is just fine. As long as he has his hat and his boots, he'll be happy as can be. The five-verse song closes, "Well, lookit here buddy / You want to be like me / Pull out your six-shooter / And rob every bank you can see / Tell the judge I said it was all right / Yes!" The Logic of The Rails is alive and well in "Bob Dylan's Blues."

The last song we'll look at from this album, "Bob Dylan's Dream," is a seven four-line verse account of days gone by, when life was simple, the music was everything, and friends existed without complication. Unfortunately, those days have gone. "The world outside" has overcome those youthful friends who laughed and sang the night away. They've aged. They've parted. The narrator is left with his nostalgia: "I wish, I wish, I wish in vain, / That we could sit simply in that room again, / Ten thousand dollars at the drop of a hat, / I'd give it all gladly if our lives could be like that." This wistful tune seems out of place on this album. To be sure, like all Bob Dylan songs, there must be some agenda associated with this solemn song. Placed between "Don't Think Twice" and "Oxford," it offers neither relief nor depth. It seems odd that this track was included with so many songs available. In any event, "nostalgia" is an instrument that is rarely pulled from Dylan's narrative toolbox; consequently, let's appreciate its appearance and move on.

The Freewheelin' Bob Dylan ranges from the sublime to the ridiculous. From the stark devastation of "Hard Rain" to the intense vitriol of "Masters" to the craziness of "I Shall Be Free" to the simple beauty of "Blowin' In The Wind" to the madness of "WWIII," this record roams the storytelling spectrum in its own idiosyncratic fashion. Zimmerman's Dylan is in his element here, that is certain. What I find most fascinating is the raw qualities of the writing. Zimmerman has always been a prolific storyteller. When we consider the biographers' accounts of his playful lies to his girlfriends, his sophisticated renditions of his fictional musical experiences, his diabolical portrayals of his personal history, and on and on, we note a steady stream of inventive storytelling. Then, of course, there is that marvelous game, Glissendorf. Here is where Zimmerman's stories gain the Dylan Edge. An agenda seems to guide the narrative process, a *secret* agenda. All of this is on display on *Freewheelin'*. The record is nothing less than a raw manifestation of a natural talent. Give the man a topic and stand back.

A colleague once told me that writers only get so many words in their lifetime, so they'd better use them wisely. If that's true, Bob Zimmerman's word count must be based on his various characters since the *Freewheelin'* portion of the artist's career features a lot more than the songs on that record. He wrote essays for liner notes, for folk publications, and for performance. He wrote song after song deploying a variety of genres. Some are simple blues songs that stress repetition (e.g., "Standing On The Highway," "Poor Boy Blues," "Baby, I'm In The Mood For You," "Ain't Gonna

Grieve," and "Walkin' Down The Line"); others involve more sophisticated character profiles (e.g., "Ballad Of Donald White" and "Rambling, Gambling Willie"), portray characters as they endure specific situations (e.g., "John Brown"), feature situations that involve certain characters (e.g., "The Death Of Emmett Till" and "Who Killed Davey Moore?"), or offer scenic assessments (e.g., "Hard Times In New York Town" and "Walls Of Red Wing"); a few preach (e.g., "Long Ago, Far Away," "Quit Your Low Down Ways," "I'd Hate To Be You On That Dreadful Day," and "Whatcha Gonna Do"); and others just tell stories (e.g., "Man On The Street," "Long Time Gone," "Bob Dylan's New Orleans Rag," "Farewell," and "Seven Curses"). Before moving on, we would be wise to pause and consider some of these songs since they demonstrate the maturation of Dylan's pen in various ways.

The "Talkin'" series is a fun group of songs. Why this songwriting approach is so quickly abandoned is beyond me, if for no other reason than the fact that he is so good at this type of storytelling. His ability to take a news report, a political movement, a scenic location, or fictional scenario and develop it is impressive. The results may emphasize a character, a moral, a situation, or any number of things. Whatever the case, the writer is thorough. Take, for example, the splendid "Talking Bear Mountain Picnic Massacre Blues." Told in the first person, the nine-verse story opens with a man reading an advertisement about a family boat ride/picnic to Bear Mountain. The character responds, "Yippee!" and dashes off to get his tickets. The story continues,

> Took the wife 'n' kids down to the pier,
> Six thousand people there,
> Everybody had a ticket for the trip,
> "Oh well," I said, "it's a pretty big ship.
> Besides, anyway, the more the merrier."

The results are predictable, aren't they? Once all the people start piling on board, the boat begins to sink. Our narrator soon loses sight of the wife and kids, all the people and their pets fight for their lives, he questions the validity of this particular idea, and he winds up laying on the shore, abused for his trouble. Afterward, he collects himself and his family (and his picnic basket) and heads home. He resolves to have his next picnic at home in his bathroom. The tale closes with this moral:

> Now, it don't seem to me quite so funny
> What some people are gonna do f'r money.
> There's a bran' new gimmick every day
> Just t' take somebody's money away.
> I think we oughta take some o' these people
> And put 'em on a boat, send 'em up to Bear Mountain . . .
> For a picnic.

With that, our story ends. Dylan weaves his clever tale of commercial exploitation via his personal adaptation of the satirical songwriting genre. While the story is funny, and its moral is oh-so-clear, the news here is in the auteur's language. Notice the phonetic spellings that populate the writing. This is the language Dylan uses in his essays such as "My Life In A Stolen Moment" and his liner note pieces for Joan Baez and Peter, Paul, and Mary. He takes his feigned Okie accent and transposes it into the written word. And it works. It creates a vernacular that is specifically suited to the image he's creating: a wisecracking Woody Guthrie. By the time we get to *Tarantula* and the Newport Mod's image, this writing will adjust accordingly. Zimmerman is behind it all, but his characters guide the particulars.

Another example of the "Talkin' " series is a marvelous number with a charming history. You don't believe that the Iron Range's rebellious biker-poet was lurking in the background during his critical point in Bob Zimmerman's career? You don't think Zimmerman restrained the "Dillon" portion of his character's personality in order to facilitate his "discovery"? Well, then, consider the story of "Talkin' John Birch Paranoid Blues." As the Beatles will tell you, one way to make it BIG in America is to appear on the *Ed Sullivan Show*. From the mid-1950s to the late 1960s, the *Sullivan* show was as big as a television show gets. His Sunday night audience was huge, and an appearance there could make a career—or, as Elvis Presley learned, solidify a legend. The biographers tell us that Albert Grossman booked Dylan on the Sullivan show for Sunday, May 12, 1963. Dylan rehearsed "Birch" for the show, played it for Sullivan and his producer (it met with their approval), and dramatically walked off the set when the network refused to air the song. When asked to play another song, he refused and left. What a coup! He may have lost a national audience, but Bob Dylan gained a national reputation. Presley allowed the show to do as it wished; Dylan didn't. Sometimes the things we reject can become bigger than the things we accept.

Since "Birch" aligns its subject with a Jew-killing Adolf Hitler, well, it's not hard to imagine why the CBS officials balked at the song's inclusion. The song is fun. The story is comical. The moral is beyond question. Our mischievous folky is having a real go at the Cold War paranoia that swept through his times. The ten-verse song opens with our central character's anxieties over the Communists' success in infiltrating American society. To our narrator, the Communists are everywhere, so he has to join the John Birch Society in order to do his civic duty and thwart the Red Threat. He offers his philosophy in the third verse:

> Now we all agree with Hitlers' views,
> Although he killed six million Jews.
> It don't matter too much that he was a Fascist,
> At least you can't say he was a Communist!
> That's to say like if you got a cold you take a shot of malaria.

(So, you still wonder why the Sullivan people canned the song?) With that, he's off in pursuit of those "gol-darned Reds." The guy is thorough. He looks under his bed, around his sink, in his automobile, up his chimney, and in his toilet. The Reds proved to be evasive, but our narrator is not to be deterred. His search continues:

> Well, I wus sittin' home alone an' started to sweat,
> Figured they wus in my T.V. set.
> Peeked behind the picture frame,

Got a shock from my feet, hittin' right up in the brain.
Them Reds caused it!
I know they did . . . them hard-core ones.

Once he recovered, he marched on. He quit his job to focus on his prey (changing his name to Sherlock Holmes). He discovered there were red stripes in the American flag and questioned Betsy Ross's patriotism. He searched the library. He questioned the patriotism of Dwight Eisenhower, Thomas Jefferson, and Theodore or Franklin Roosevelt (he's not that specific), and concludes that the only "true American" is "George Lincoln Rockwell." The madness closes with the character's decision to investigate himself, and his paranoid response to that conclusion. What a ride!

The "Talkin' " series is a funny, insightful, and clever group of songs. Some—like "Birch"—display that patented Dylan Edge. Others—like "Bear Mountain"—toy with their observations. Regardless of their focus or intensity, they offer evidence of a master storyteller at work. When we get to the Newport Mod period of the auteur's writing, remember the clarity of expression involved in these songs. They are, indeed, a special part of the oeuvre.

Another important dimension of the folk-posturing era involves "name songs" that either examine a specific situation through a particular character or explore a character as he or she deals with a situation. Regarding the former, let us turn to "The Death Of Emmett Till." Dylan opens by setting the scene:

'Twas down in Mississippi not so long ago,
When a young boy from Chicago town stepped through a Southern door.
This boy's dreadful tragedy I can still remember well,
The color of his skin was black and his name was Emmett Till.

From there, Dylan's seven four-line verses recount the horror: Local men take Till to a barn and beat him while people laugh outside. Their motives, according to the song, were recreational—they killed for fun. In order to defuse a federal investigation, two brothers accept responsibility for the murder and are dutifully acquitted by a genuine jury of their peers (in this case, unindicted co-conspirators). Our narrator is furious. He denounces all those who fail to understand the heinous qualities of this racially motivated atrocity. His language is powerful:

If you can't speak out against this kind of thing, a crime that's so unjust,
Your eyes are filled with dead men's dirt, your mind is filled with dust.
Your arms and legs they must be in shackles and chains, and your blood
        it must refuse to flow,
For you let this human race fall so God-awful low!

The final stanza encourages an understanding of the evil that inspired such an act, just who the perpetrators were (he mentions the Ku Klux Klan by name), and how the nation must do its best to make America a safer place for everybody. It is a powerful song about a despicable act from a dark, violent period of American history.

The Dylan Edge is evident, and his outrage appears sincere. It is a testament to this portion of his songwriting career.

To the extent that "Till" uses that sad situation as a means of discussing racial prejudice, "Who Killed Davey Moore?" uses Moore's demise as a vehicle for probing the brutality of boxing. The track opens with a simple, two-line chorus that is repeated between verses and at the end: "Who killed Davey Moore, / Why an' what's the reason for?" Three stanzas follow in which the referee, the "angry" audience, and Moore's manager absolve themselves of any responsibility for the incident. Consider the referee's response:

> "Not I," says the referee,
> "Don't point your finger at me.
> I could've stopped it in the eighth
> An' maybe kept him from his fate,
> But the crowd would've booed, I'm sure,
> At not gettin' their money's worth.
> It's too bad he had to go,
> But there was a pressure on me too, you know.
> It wasn't me that made him fall.
> No, you can't blame me at all."

The song continues with the crowd's excuses ("We didn't mean for him t' meet his death. / We just meant to see some sweat") and the manager's rationale that if Moore were "sick" he should have reported it, but he didn't, so he's off the hook. The track is simple, straightforward, and thorough. The moral is equally clear: No one cares enough about the fighter to take any responsibility for his death. Like "Bear Mountain," the moneychangers grab their loot and don't look back. Somebody dies, somebody drowns; who cares? Dylan takes his subject, examines the particulars, and points his finger at the transgressors.

"Till" and "Moore" explore racism and violence through the examples of the respective cases. Dylan uses a different strategy in "John Brown." Here a young man is sent off to war, does his duty, and returns home horribly maimed. Interestingly, the central character of the song is neither John Brown nor the war, but Brown's mother. She naively endorses a "good old-fashioned war" and a form of comic book bravery she believes to be associated with men in battle. Brown stands tall in his uniform and his mother is so very proud:

> "Oh son, you look so fine, I'm glad you're a son of mine,
> You make me proud to know you hold a gun.
> Do what the captain says, lots of medals you will get,
> And we'll put them on the wall when you come home."

Ma Brown is so proud, cheering his departure, showing letters to neighbors. Then the letters stop. After many months, she receives a notice to meet her son at the train station. She joyously travels to the station, but her son is nowhere in sight. When she finally locates him, he is unrecognizable. His face is mangled, his hand is amputated,

and he speaks in an unknown, "slow," voice. When she asks what happened, he can
barely reply. He tells his mother that what she thought was so glorious was not. When
Brown arrived on the battlefront, he questioned why—especially the fact that the
people he was there to kill looked just like him. He declares,

> "And I couldn't help but think, through the thunder rolling and stink,
> That I was just a puppet in a play.
> And through the roar and smoke, this string is finally broke,
> And a cannon ball blew my eyes away."

John and Ma Brown turn to leave. She is in complete shock. He calls her over to him,
and places his medals in her hands. With that, the song ends.

These three songs demonstrate Dylan's capacity to take a situation, explore its
details, and delivery a story with a clear and precise moral. In these examples, violence is everywhere. Racism, sport, and politics produce violence, and violence takes
victims. If it hadn't been Till, Moore, or Brown, it would have been somebody else.
Evil judicial systems, enterprising entrepreneurs, and corrupt politicians allow mur-
derers to go free, athletes to be abused, and young men to return home mentally and
physically destroyed. These songs demonstrate the *consequences* of social injustice in a
fashion distinct from "Blowin' In The Wind" or "Oxford Town." The answer may
be blowing in some wind, but while we're sitting around the campfire humming along,
people are dying. To tourists, Oxford may seem like a weird town to be avoided, but
to those who live there, danger abounds. Dylan's narrative sword, then, cuts both
ways. He may choose to elaborate on a principle or to focus on a specific manifestation of that principle. In these songs, he pursues the latter in a fashion consistent
with folk songwriting traditions.

The folk-posturing period of Dylan's career contains more than his songwriting. He wrote all sorts of things in the early 1960s: copy for concert programs, articles for folk magazines, and liner notes for albums. His second book of lyrics (1985's
Lyrics, 1962–1985) offers several examples of his "proetry" (to use Clinton Heylin's
term), and we would be wise to spend a moment with them. "My Life in a Stolen
Moment" is a biographical sketch that was prepared for inclusion in a 1963 concert
program. Robert Shelton reports that Dylan often denounced the work as something
he was forced to do for a promoter; nevertheless, the fact that he included it in *Lyrics*
suggests his ultimate acceptance of its value (an attitude that apparently changed with
the 2004 release of *Lyrics 1962–2001*, since it deletes these essays). "My Life" is part
fact, part fiction, part gibberish. In all cases, it is classic Dylan from this period. The
piece opens with references to Minnesota (his parents' home), Hibbing (with its open
pit, movie house, bars, and more), his "first song" (for his mother, he says), and his
adolescence. Next, he takes us to the University of Minnesota and his life there. From
what we know, much of his commentary seems accurate. Once he concludes, "That's
pretty much my college life," the plot thickens considerably. He describes trips to
Texas, New Mexico, and Louisiana, and his hard traveling life on the road:

> With my thumb out, my eyes asleep, my hat turned up an' my head turned
> on

I's driftin' an' learnin' new lessons
I was making my own depression
I rode freight trains for kicks
An' got beat up for laughs
Cut grass for quarters
An' sang for dimes
Hitchhiked on 61-51-75-169-37-66-22
Gopher Road–Route 40 an' Howard Johnson Turnpike
Got jailed for suspicion of armed robbery
Got held four hours on a murder rap
Got busted for looking like I do
An' I never done none a them things

The piece continues with references to learning the guitar, singing, and writing; more expressions of wanderlust; and his arrival in snowy New York. More travel tales follow (back to Madison, to Florida, to South Dakota, Cincinnati, Kansas, Iowa, and finally back to New York), and he explains how he signed with Columbia. He refuses to list his creative influences for fear of leaving someone out, although he mentions Guthrie and Big Joe Williams. He closes with these lines: "Hibbing's a good ol' town / I ran away from it when I was 10, 12, 13, 15, 15½, 17 an' 18 / I been caught an' brought back all but once." What can you say?

The liner notes to the first edition of the *Bootleg Series* offers an account of another writing entry that not only appears in *Lyrics*, but also was performed in public on the night of April 12, 1963. That seven-minute performance appears on the first disc of the three-disc set and, according to John Bauldie's liner notes, represents the only time Dylan ever performed his poetry in public. The piece, entitled "Last Thoughts On Woody Guthrie," is extraordinary. The 293-line "valediction" (in Bauldie's words) is a stream-of-consciousness expression that flows from one line to the next in a seamless fashion. Ultimately, "Last Thoughts" describes a search for meaning. It addresses places, people, and things that may *appear* to offer something meaningful, but ultimately fail. Consider the work's opening lines:

When yer head gets twisted and yer mind grows numb
When you think you're too old, too young, too smart or too dumb
When yer laggin' behind an' losin' yer pace
In a slow-motion crawl or life's busy race
No matter what yer doing if you start givin' up
If the wine don't come to the top of yer cup
If the wind's got you sideways with one hand holdin' on
And the other starts slipping and the feeling is gone
And yer train engine fire needs a new spark to catch it
And the wood's easy findin' but yer lazy to fetch it
And yer sidewalk starts curlin' and the street gets too long
And you start walkin' backwards though you know that it's wrong
And lonesome comes up as down goes the day
And tomorrow's mornin' seems so far away

The imagery goes on and on and on and on and on. Each line seems to build toward some resolution to this search, but it keeps churning onward, issuing layer after layer of imagery. Occasionally, the march pauses for a question, such as "Who am I helping, what am I breaking / What am I giving, what am I taking." Lines appear that suggest song lyrics: "And no liquor in the land to stop yer brain from bleeding" (shades of "Hard Rain"). Lines appear with not-too-subtle agendas: "And you can't find it either in the no-talent fools / That run around gallant / And make all rules for the ones that got talent." Finally, a resolution is offered. For an answer to it all, we're told we may go to the "church" of our "choice" (and find God) or to the "Brooklyn State Hospital" (and find Woody Guthrie). Dylan closes with these lines: "And though it's only my opinion / I may be right or wrong / You'll find them both / In the Grand Canyon / At sundown." Ultimately, it boils down to nature's beauty—a major piece of foreshadowing.

This stream-of-consciousness writing style is absent in our final entry, "Joan Baez In Concert, Part 2." This is an even *longer* piece (295 lines) that doesn't challenge the reader's attention span as much as "Last Thoughts." In fact, "Part 2" is darned coherent. Dylan opens with a scene from his character's childhood, then moves through that person's teen years and into adulthood. The sincere curiosities of a child follow that person into adulthood, where they continue to plague him until a female friend helps him resolve them. *Everything* about this piece suggests autobiography. But this is Bob Dylan, and care must be exercised in *any* attribution about *anything*. Still, references to the Iron Range, New York, and Joan Baez (referring to his friend as "Joanie" is one major hint!) lead the reader down the autobiographical path. The phonetic writing continues (albeit in a tamer mode) and the imagery maintains its edge; however, there is something different about this statement. Something distinguishes it from the writing we've observed thus far.

The difference is that "Part 2" is a touching story. It traces a lonely child's search for beauty. At first, he thinks that nothing is real unless he can touch it with his hands; moreover, he teaches himself that "beauty" is actually "ugly" ("An' I'd judge beauty with these rules / An' accept it only 'f it was ugly / An' 'f I could touch it with my hand / For it's only then I'd understand / An' say 'yeah this's real' "). This journey starts with the child playing by the railroad tracks, pulling up hunks of grass, gazing into his hands, and feeling guilty ("I'd taken an' not given in return") over the "empty patch" he left behind. This child is lonely, and Dylan establishes this with a line here, another there. At one point he writes, "An' I asked myself t' be my friend," before he describes his isolated world:

> In later years although still young
> My head swung heavy with windin' curves
> An' a mixed-up path revolved an' strung
> Within the boundaries a my youth
> 'Til at last I backed so far away
> From the world's walls an' friendless games
> That I did not have a word t' say
> T' anyone who'd meet my eyes
> An' I lock myself an' lost the key

An' let the symbols take their shape
An' form a foe for me t' fight
T' lash my tongue an' rebel against
An' spit at strong with vomit words
But I learned t' choose my idols well
T' be my voice an' tell my tale
An' help me fight my phantom brawl.

This is revealing stuff. Read it again. Can it be true, or is it yet another game? Is the auteur sharing how he felt about his life, or baiting us once more? Indeed, Glissendorf is a "friendless game." Assuredly, his "idols" paved a careful path for him to follow. Obviously, his rebellion is his fire. Fascinating.

"Part 2" continues by announcing that his "first idol" was Hank Williams and his "first symbol" was "the word 'beautiful' " before declaring, "An' I walked my road an' sung my song / Like a saddened clown / In the circus a my own world." Next we're taken to his adult years, where he "rebelled twice as hard an' ten times as proud" as he continued to struggle with his beauty-ugly symbolic war "like a lonesome king." "Time traveled an' faces passed" until he met a girl "who like me strummed lonesome tunes." At this point, the conflict sharpens since his new friend sings with a beautiful voice that he couldn't comprehend since beauty is ugly. Our "scared poet" sticks to his guns, believing that if he "can't feel it with my hand / Then don' wish me t' understand." The account turns with a story from his new friend. She told him about growing up in an "Arab land," where people apparently beat dogs to death in the street for fun. The poor thing tried to hide a dog in her house but failed. Suddenly, his mind drifts back to that hunk of grass and his guilt returns; yet this time, his feeling are not for the handful of grass, but for the poor dog. He resolves his life-long quandary:

I did not begin t' touch
'Til I finally felt what wasn't there
Oh how feeble foolish small an' sad
'F me t' think that beauty was
Only ugliness an' muck
When it's really jus' a magic wand
That waves an' teases at my mind
An' knows that only it can feel
An' knows that I ain't got a chance
An' fools me into thinking things
Like it's my hands that understand.

This intriguing account then goes back to the place where we began, by the railroad track in the grass. This time, he has new knowledge and comes to peace with himself. Instead of pulling up a hunk of grass, he resolves, "I'll jus' pet it as a friend." He accepts his rebellion. He accepts beauty. And he resolves to relax and let life come to him: "An' I'll sing my song like a rebel wild / For it's that I am an' can't deny / But at least I'll know now not t' hurt / Not t' push / Not t' ache / An' God knows . . . not t' try."

When taken as a whole, these three pieces of "proetry" represent the author's unfolding, complex, multifaceted personality. We see the bragging—occasionally lying—Bob Dillon ("My Life"), the true-believing Jack Fate ("Last Thoughts"), and the architect behind both, the vulnerable, sincere Bobby Zimmerman ("Part 2"). "My Life" opens with factually accurate statements and drifts into an insincere game of Glissendorf. It reads like what it is: a publicity ploy. It directly contributes to a myth that would one day—very soon—haunt its author. "Last Thoughts" reads quite differently. It is more sincere, more genuine. It builds and builds and builds, and in many respects, grows tiresome for that reason. Yet, it delivers: God, Woody, or a beautiful sunset. Choose your god. And "Part 2" is so revealing. It displays the sincerity that controls *Chronicles*. It traces a lonely search for understanding beauty. Unlike "Last Thoughts," it pauses for sincerity. It builds empathy. It evokes feelings. The "grass" and "dog" spins make the whole thing sympathetic. "Joanie" opens a door, and more importantly, he willfully steps through it. The narrator proves that by returning to the opening scene. We go full circle: A lonesome, curious child evolves into an accepting, self-contained adult. Fascinating. Like *Chronicles*, it challenges the Dylan Myth, opening doors that may—or may not—lead to the truth (whatever that means). I find significance in the story's placement. By attaching it to a Baez album, Dylan's essay gains a sense of independence that seems to suggest authenticity. But then, you never know, do you?

To suggest that Bob Zimmerman's vast talents were on display during the *Freewheelin'* period is to understate the case in a potentially reckless manner. Just look at what we've seen! From "Blowin' In The Wind" and its folk platitudes to the harsh imagery of "A Hard Rain's A-Gonna Fall," from the jokes about the John Birch Society and life after a world war to the symbolic landmine that is "Masters Of War," from "My Life In A Stolen Moment" and its carefree account of a rounder's life to the heartfelt search for personal equilibrium of "Joan Baez In Concert, Part 2," this phase of the auteur's oeuvre exhibits a raw manifestation of his considerable talent. The stories just oozed from him. The man was in his element.

Dylan emerged from the *Freewheelin'* adventure a national celebrity. Just four days after the record's release, *Time* described him this way: "Beardless chin, shaggy sideburns, porcelain pussy-cat eyes. At 22, he looks 14, and his accent belongs to a jive Nebraskan, or maybe a Brooklyn hillbilly. . . . At its very best, his voice sounds as if it were drifting over the walls of a tuberculosis sanitarium—but that's part of the charm. . . . But he has something unique to say, and he says it in songs of his own invention that are the best songs of their style since Woody Guthrie's." From there, *Time* advances Dylan's "Stolen Moment" mythology of runaways, circuses, and hall of fame musical encounters. (How interesting that a national newsmagazine would print such propaganda.) The trend gained momentum that summer when Dylan performed at the Newport Folk Festival on July 26–28, 1963. According to Robert Shelton's reporting, Dylan traveled to Newport 1963 as a curiosity and left the event a star. He claims the young man's "apprenticeship" ended in Newport in that the Greenwich Village pet was about to become the voice of his generation.

"Joanie" (Joan Baez) played an important role during this portion of Bob Dylan's career. She allowed him to perform during her shows (often to her audience's chagrin). She encouraged his writing. She facilitated his emergence at Newport 1963. Though Dylan delivered the goods, Baez provided opportunities to get those songs before a public that would come to worship the work. Correspondingly, Dylan's protest singer public relations initiatives gained serious momentum through the photo opportunities that were voter registration trips to Mississippi and his historic appearance at the August 28, 1963, march on Washington, D.C. Joining noted protest singers such as Baez, Harry Belafonte, Odetta, the now-popular Peter, Paul, and Mary, and others, Dylan performed before 200,000 peaceful participants who absorbed the music just before hearing one of history's most accomplished speakers deliver perhaps his most famous oration. Bob Dylan *must* take great pride in the fact that he performed on the same stage from which Martin Luther King Jr. delivered his "I Have a Dream" speech.

By Labor Day 1963, Bob Dylan was America's foremost protest singer.

The increased attention generated a shift in the media's treatment of the newly crowned king of the American protest song, and this change in reporting would affect the king's world. The November 4, 1963, edition of *Newsweek* features the aforementioned report on Bob *Zimmerman's* youth on the Iron Range and quickly dispelled all of the talk of runaways, broken families, and earthy musical contacts. The change in publicity gained momentum on December 13, 1963, with Dylan's appearance before the Emergency Civil Liberties Committee and his acceptance of the organization's Tom Paine Award for social activism. Whether Dylan's intoxication or his general discomfort inspired his response is irrelevant; what's important is the public reaction to his identification with John Kennedy's alleged assassin, Lee Oswald. By saying that he identified with Oswald's motivations, Dylan not only alienated his immediate audience, but also provided additional fuel for the fire ignited by the *Newsweek* article. Dylan's intuitive publicity machine now faced a formidable challenge.

When Dylan and Tom Wilson entered Columbia's Studio A in New York on August 6, 1963, they set about the task of recording one of musical history's most impressive protest records. On this record, the raw manifestation of talent that generated *Freewheelin'* evolves into a calculated application of those same abilities. The results, *The Times They Are A-Changin'*, is a *programmed* response to the *urges* that float throughout the *Freewheelin'* project. What blows through the wind on the second record carries the sound of seven shotgun blasts on the third album. The above-the-law rednecks from Oxford, Mississippi, move to Maryland, adorn their finery, and throw their canes at old women. The masters of *Freewheelin'* now overtly play with their pawns on *Times*. What *Freewheelin'* has a tendency to talk around, *Times* heads straight though as it articulates the *consequences* of the societal ills that threaten the world. Having made his statement and understanding that the *Newsweek* exposé is about to expose his little biographical game, Dylan returns to the studio on October 31, 1963, to record but one song, the album's capstone statement: "Restless Farewell." Bob Dillon is about to push young Jake Fate aside and introduce a new Bob Dylan.

Released on January 13, 1964, *The Times They Are A-Changin'* contains ten original compositions (running 45:37). Recorded in six sessions, *Times* presents a seasoned folk veteran carefully articulating the hopes and fears of his constituency through the use of protracted examples. Just look at the photograph on the album's cover. The smiling youngster of *Bob Dylan* and the strolling lover of *Freewheelin'* give way to a *very* serious man on *Times*. His face is firm. His eyes are downcast. One look at that photograph and you just know what's inside. Yes, the times, they were changing—and *serious* times require *serious* responses.

Times is a one-dimensional concession to the musical genre that birthed the budding auteur. This is a solemn record: no jokes, no puns, no fun anywhere. Two songs aside, it is a dark, brooding, pessimistic project. After the pain flies from every angle, the author dusts himself off, says so long, and exits. The five songs of societal complaint ("Ballad Of Hollis Brown," "With God On Our Side," "North Country Blues," "Only A Pawn In Their Game," and "The Lonesome Death Of Hattie Carroll") convey the victimization of decent folks by coldhearted oppressors whose day of reckoning is coming. These tragedies portray suicide on the farm ("Hollis Brown"), domestic abandonment ("North Country"), sociological manipulation ("Only A Pawn"), historical atrocities ("With God"), and judicial elitism ("Hattie Carroll") through a direct, understandable narrative style. The two songs of societal celebration ("The Time They Are A-Changin' " and "When The Ship Comes In"), Dylan's last-second tale of personal transition ("Restless Farewell"), and the two love complaints ("One Too Many Mornings" and "Boots Of Spanish Leather") round out an album with a purpose. Interestingly, the optimistic title cut that opens the record is merely a flash in the topical pan. A brief reprise appears via "When The Ship" and its eternal optimism; otherwise, we sink into the societal/relational abyss on *Times*.

The darkness emerges from multiple angles: the thrice-abandoned woman of "North Country"; the sad exchange between the romantic couple of "Boots"; the introspection of "One Too Many"; the compassionate reporter of "Hollis," "Pawn," and "Hattie Carroll"; the challenged patriot of "With God"; and, finally, the author himself ("Restless"). *Times'* themes are certainly without mystery. Dylan wants his audience to know why Hollis Brown killed his family, why William Zanzinger should be punished, why victims must understand their situations so they may respond accordingly, and how history may be rationalized. Though he may occasionally shift perspectives ("Boots Of Spanish Leather" and its male-female narrators, and the female narrator in "North Country"), "Bob Dylan" is taking a stance against these perceived injustices. Once more, these are not merely *songs*; they are *statements* from an accomplished messenger. To the specifics, we now turn.

We begin with the minority and the social celebrations. For the second album in a row, Bob Dylan opens an album with an anthem, the title track: "The Times They Are A-Changin'." From answers that blow in the wind, we turn to times that change. Just as the key to understanding "answers" is to acknowledge their evasive qualities, the essential element in accepting change is to recognize its inevitability. Dylan establishes this principle at the song's outset:

> Come gather 'round people
> Wherever you roam
> And admit that the waters
> Around you have grown

> And accept it that soon
> You'll be drenched to the bone.
> If your time to you
> Is worth savin'
> Then you better start swimmin'
> Or you'll sink like a stone
> For the times they are a-changin'.

Alas, change is inevitable; so, accept its natural qualities or prepare to suffer a natural fate: Stones don't float. From this starting point, Dylan addresses three audiences. He implores the country's journalists, politicians, and parents to get with the program, to understand that the person who suffers today will overcome that problem tomorrow, to not delay and to act now, and to realize that the old ways don't work anymore. The five-verse song is simple, direct, and without equivocation. The final stanza reiterates the argument:

> The line it is drawn
> The curse it is cast
> The slow one now
> Will later be fast
> As the present now
> Will later be past
> The order is
> Rapidly fadin'.
> And the first one now
> Will later be last
> For the times they are a-changin'.

The moral of the story is more than self-evident; it's impossible to avoid. To reinforce the inevitable change that occurs as the weak evolve into the strong, Dylan offers the title cut's companion piece, "When The Ship Comes In." With these two songs, Dylan speaks to the folks on both sides of the metaphorical fence. Just as "Times" addresses the journalists, politicians, and parents who need to embrace change, "When The Ship" is an eight-verse pep rally for the oppressed. Be patient, this song tells its constituency, for your time is coming. Dylan deploys the traditional "there's a storm brewing" analogy to set his scene:

> Oh the time will come up
> When the winds will stop
> And the breeze will cease to be breathin'.
> Like the stillness in the wind
> 'Fore the hurricane begins,
> The hour when the ship comes in.

Get it? Everyone and everything will stand up and take notice on that glorious day. The sea will open, the fish will laugh, the birds will smile, and the rocks on shore will stand—all in praise of the much-deserved victory of the oppressed over their oppressors. Not only will "the sun" respect "every face" on the ship's deck, but the moment will transcend social acceptance and embrace victory. The final verse is telltale:

> Then they'll raise their hands,
> Sayin' we'll meet all your demands,
> But we'll shout from the bow your days are numbered.
> And like Pharaoh's tribe,
> They'll be drowned in the tide,
> And like Goliath, they'll be conquered.

Well, we're moving just a little bit beyond the acceptance of social equality here. From pleading with journalists, politicians, and parents to embrace the inevitable or suffer the natural consequences of their obstinacy, we've moved into the realm of serious threat. Has the argument shifted from the acceptance of equality to a warning of dominance? Is retribution overtaking mutual understanding? It seems so. The battle cry for patience has been replaced by one stressing victory, or at least the enemy's submission. From the rhetoric of "Move over and make room for everybody," this song takes us to the rhetoric of "Get thee behind me, Satan." That's a pretty substantial shift. Why would the story shift so forcefully? The answer, my friends, is in the songs of social complaint that dominate this record.

The social complaints on *Times* are extraordinary in their depth and scope. We move from a history lesson regarding how it all works, to a specific discussion of the nature of the elitist game, to three precise accounts of the *consequences* of this evil phenomenon. The songs are not arranged in this fashion; however, it doesn't take a Communist rocket scientist to figure out this narrative sequence. So, let's take a little stroll down memory lane and refresh our memories about how the bad guys go about justifying their actions.

"With God On Our Side" is a slow, prodding account of the age-old prescription for justifying any conceivable act: It's God's Will. The nine-verse story opens with the author declaring that his name and age are irrelevant; however, what *is* important is the fact that he's a Midwesterner who was raised to "abide" by the God-inspired laws that govern the land. We next move through four stanzas that delineate how different military operations functioned by the grace of God. The American cavalry defeated American Indians, Spanish American and Civil War "heroes" were immortalized, and World War I was accepted to be a just cause since in each of these instances, God was on the victor's side. Unbelievably, Dylan continues by describing how the Germans were forgiven for their horrible atrocities during the Second World War, and now they too stand with God. The song takes us to contemporary times and the Cold War. The narrator relates how he was raised to hate the Russians and, in order to preserve God's will, must accept any means necessary to combat the evil they propagate. The plot thickens with the final two stanzas:

> In a many dark hour
> I've been thinkin' about this
> That Jesus Christ

Was betrayed by a kiss
But I can't think for you
You'll have to decide
Whether Judas Iscariot
Had God on his side.

So now as I'm leavin'
I'm weary as Hell
The confusion I'm feelin'
Ain't no tongue can tell
The words fill my head
And fall to the floor
If God's on our side
He'll stop the next war.

This is powerful stuff. With God on your side, you have a license to kill. You may commit genocide. You may use whatever technology that's necessary to vaporize your enemy. You may even do things that you don't really understand. It's all good—if God is on your side, that is. Yet, an element of doubt remains, and our narrator leaves it to his audience to determine the verdict. He spends all those dark hours trying to figure out God's right from God's left, he emerges tired and confused, and he prays that the hostilities will end. The answers are not blowing in the wind here. But the questions are reaching gale force.

Or maybe it's all just a game. Maybe people use God. Maybe God is yet another unindicted co-conspirator. After establishing how the Lord's name is taken *more* than in vain (it's corrupted), Dylan takes aim on the corruptors. "Only A Pawn In Their Game" lays it out on the proverbial line. Everybody's being used. When that ship comes in, there'll be pirates on board who were cleverly placed there by the supposedly defeated system. Is life a vicious game in which the elites just use everybody? That is the question posed here. The song begins with Medgar Evers's shooting and the narrator's belief that the killer was not to blame, since "they" put that gun in his hands and urged him to fire it. The second verse identifies who "they" are (Southern politicians) and describes how poor Southern Whites fear Southern Blacks because they've been manipulated by the political system. The third stanza explains,

The deputy sheriffs, the soldiers, the governors get paid,
And the marshals and cops get the same,
But the poor white man's used in the hands of them all like a tool.
He's taught in his school
From the start by the rule
That the laws are with him
To protect his white skin
To keep up his hate
So he never thinks straight
'Bout the shape that he's in

He's only a pawn in their game.

The track continues with more descriptions of White poverty and the violent responses that flow from that condition. The five verses end with Evers's burial and the realization that "when the shadowy sun sets on the one / That fired the gun," his grave will be marked by the epitaph "Only a pawn in their game."

I wonder how Bob Dylan felt when he stood in front of the Lincoln Memorial during the 1963 march on Washington and sang this song. I wonder if his audience listened to him. This is a compelling, controversial statement. To look behind the curtain and see elites manipulating people through jealousy and fear is a frightening observation. Don't blame the ignorant reactionary, we're told. The same people who justify their every whim by asserting that it's God's will have another plan that flows from that spring well. By teaching people to hate one another, "they" keep the pot stirred, protect their interests, and maintain the status quo. And they do it all, they insist, with God's blessings.

Just in case you don't grasp that the world is a mess in abstract terms, how about a dose of good old-fashioned concrete evidence? Elites kill their servants, women are recklessly abandoned, families get shot, and I'm just not certain if God is on *anybody's* side in these scenarios. The fun starts with Hattie Carroll's lonesome death. Here, we observe the extent to which the elites who use the masses to do their dirty work (i.e., maintaining the desired social order) aren't very nice people. Supposedly, Dylan convoluted the facts in his story, but since it *is* his story at this point, we'll stick to his scenario. William Zanzinger, a wealthy Baltimore socialite, killed a Black servant, Hattie Carroll, at a social gathering at a local hotel. He was arrested for first-degree murder. The author describes Zanzinger and his response to his crime in the second of the song's four verses:

> William Zanzinger, who at twenty-four years
> Owns a tobacco farm of six hundred acres
> With rich wealthy parents who provide and protect him
> And high office relations in the politics of Maryland,
> Reacted to his deed with a shrug of his shoulders
> And swear words and sneering, and his tongue it was snarling,
> In a matter of minutes on bail was out walking.
> But you who philosophize disgrace and criticize all fears,
> Take the rag away from your face.
> Now ain't the time for your tears.

Dylan next describes the victim. Hattie was fifty-one years old and the mother of ten children. She was a hardworking servant who never sat at the tables she labored over. Zanzinger threw his cane at Hattie (for some unknown reason) and hit the poor woman, and she died as the result. The final verse reveals society's response to the murder:

> In the courtroom of honor, the judge pounded his gavel
> To show that all's equal and that the courts are on the level

And that the strings in the books ain't pulled and persuaded
And that even the nobles get properly handled
Once that the cops have chased after and caught 'em
And that the ladder of law has no top and no bottom,
Stared at the person who killed for no reason
Who just happened to be feelin' that way without warnin'.
And he spoke through his cloak, most deep and distinguished,
And handed out strongly, for penalty and repentance,
William Zanzinger with a six-month sentence.
Oh, but you who philosophize disgrace and criticize all fears,
Bury the rag deep in your face
For now's the time for your tears.

When our ship comes in, people like Zanzinger will, no doubt, get The Chair; yet, until then, enjoy American justice. That anyone would receive a six-month sentence for throwing an object at, and killing, a defenseless person is the kind of injustice that fuels revolutions. Dylan tells us that we should be patient with poor White people who are manipulated to do despicable acts against their Black brothers and sisters, but that sympathy is nowhere in this story. The elites are out of control and doing more than playing with their pawns: They kill with smirks on their faces and get their wrists slapped for their public indiscretions.

Down the social food chain, people suffer from the socioeconomic consequences of this corrupt political system. "North Country Blues" and "The Ballad Of Hollis Brown" communicate two examples of this sorry situation. With "North Country," we witness the sad plight of a poor woman from the Iron Range who suffers from the awful combination of economic instability and faithless men. Her father, a miner, deserted his family. Her mother died. Her brother, a miner, raised her, but one day he just didn't come home. She quit school and married a miner. (Bad move.) She had three children, and things were fine until the mining companies cut their shifts in half and soon shut down completely. It seems the company can obtain the ore cheaper from South America, where the miners work for slave wages. The next two stanzas describe her new situation:

So the mining gates locked
And the red iron rotted
And the room smelled heavy from drinking.
Where the sad, silent song
Made the hour twice as long
As I waited for the sun to go sinking.

I lived by the window
As he talked to himself,
This silence of tongues it was building.
Then one morning's wake,
The bed it was bare,
And I's left alone with three children.

The final stanza (of ten six-line verses) relates how the town continues to die and her understanding that, soon, her children will grow up and leave. She is destined to live a luckless life, standing by the window, looking out over the Iron Range, and enduring her loneliness. By these standards, maybe Hattie was the lucky one.

But, as they say, things are always worse somewhere else. And on *Times*, that's no joke. "Hollis Brown" is a classic blues tune that uses heavy lyrical and instrumental repetition to drive home its sad, sad point. Hollis lives outside of town in a rundown cabin. He's married with five children. He's without work and, it seems, with no prospects of finding any. His kids are so hungry that they are unable to smile. There are rats in his food, his horse is sick, his baby won't stop crying, and his wife won't stop screaming. Goodness. Hollis spends all of his money on seven shotgun shells. Here's what happens:

> Your brain is a-bleedin'
> And your legs can't seem to stand
> Your brain is a-bleedin'
> And your legs can't seem to stand
> Your eyes fix on the shotgun
> That you're holdin' in your hand
>
> There's seven breezes a-blowin'
> All around the cabin door
> There's seven breezes a-blowin'
> All around the cabin door
> Seven shots ring out
> Like the ocean's pounding roar.

Interestingly, Dylan closes the eleven-verse song by noting that while seven people are dead on this sorry South Dakota farm, somewhere else seven people are born. Life, then, goes on.

These five songs of societal complaint reveal a master storyteller at work. From the justifications of "With God" to the applications of "Only A Pawn" to the manifestations of "Hattie," "North Country," and "Hollis," Dylan weaves a strong, compelling tale of a social system that victimizes its populace with impunity. Those "masters" do what they want, when they want; and until that mighty ship comes in, that's the way it is. No wonder the occupants on our corrective vessel have more than a little bit of revenge on their minds. With innocents killed for no reason, abandoned women coping with empty lives, and fathers shooting their families, the times, well, they *need* to change. Bob Dylan articulates that case by way of these songs.

The joyful experience continues with *Times'* two songs of relational complaint. "One Too Many Mornings" is a simple tale of love lost and the pain that ensues in its aftermath. It's a soft song delivered in a plaintive fashion. Dylan begins with the sights and sounds of the neighborhood, turns to the silence the evening brings, and describes his inner turmoil. He stares at the bed he once occupied with his lover. His remorse is consuming, and the final verse states his case:

It's a restless hungry feeling
That don't mean no one no good,
When ev'rything I'm a-sayin'
You can say it just as good.
You're right from your side,
I'm right from mine.
We're both just too many mornings
An' a thousand miles behind.

The song is short and bittersweet (three eight-line verses). The conflict is honest, but devastating. The long, pleading harmonica solo that closes the track communicates the narrator's angst and allows us to share his misery.

"Boots Of Spanish Leather" is a classic. The song is a conversation between two lovers, with different verses representing the respective parts of the conversation. The story is an old one: He's sailing away to distant shores and wondering if he might bring something back to his abandoned lover. She says no, just return safely. He persists. She responds,

Oh, but if I had the stars from the darkest night
And the diamonds from the deepest ocean,
I'd forsake them all for your sweet kiss,
For that's all I'm wishin' to be ownin'.

Again, he persists—arguing that he's going to be gone for a long time and he wants to send her something to remind her of him. She wants only his safe return. He departs for his journey. One "lonesome day," he receives a letter from her. She's off on a trip of her own. She's uncertain when she'll return, since "It depends on how I'm a-feelin'." He acknowledges that her mind must be "roamin'" and her thoughts must focus on where she's going. The song closes with a line from the man in which he asks *her* to send him a gift from her voyage: "Spanish boots of Spanish leather."

Unlike our tales of societal complaint, these two songs are more touching than biting. A disagreement inspires a sad parting. Trips abroad bring separation. There's no anger. There's no recrimination. The songs lament the situation, share feelings about it, and close. There's distance in the two relationships now, and the author leaves us to consider that sad situation. Sometimes in life, relationships end and it's just a matter of how you say goodbye—a principle that sets the scene for our capstone statement, "Restless Farewell."

The fact that Dylan returned to the studio on Halloween 1963 to record this freshly penned piece in the wake of rumors concerning the forthcoming *Newsweek* article suggests that this is a farewell statement. That attitude is reinforced by the liner note essays and the subsequent appearance during the Tom Paine award ceremony. The jig was up. The emperor had no clothes. All of which was probably fine with Dylan—he never wanted to wear *that* outfit anyway.

"Farewell" recalls the days with the narrator's friends, girlfriends, and enemies and how the time has come to move on. All those nights drinking with his friends, all those relationships that may have ended badly, and even his confrontations with his perceived enemies have reached their peaceful conclusion. He wishes nobody harm; he says goodbye until they meet once more. He discusses his songwriting and his need to express himself. Otherwise, he'd go "insane." Moreover, the songs were written for himself and his friends—not "special" audiences. But it has all gone wrong, as he relates in the final stanza:

> Oh a false clock tries to tick out my time
> To disgrace, distract, and bother me.
> And the dirt of gossip blows into my face,
> And the dust of rumors covers me.
> But if the arrow is straight
> And the point is slick,
> It can pierce through dust no matter how thick.
> So I'll make my stand
> And remain as I am
> And bid farewell and not give a damn.

There's not much mystery here. He tells his drinking buddies that the "corner sign" says "closing time." He tells his former lovers that he never meant to hurt anybody. He tells his foes that he fought his fights honorably. He tells us all that his songs aren't owned by anyone. And he closes by telling everybody why. But the guy is resilient, isn't he? His time is monitored by a false timepiece. He may be covered with the filth of gossip and rumors, but his aim remains true. Consequently, he's going to stick to his guns, remain true to himself, say goodbye, and not—for a moment—look back. Bob Dillon's rebellion is such an integral part of Bob Dylan's personality that he cannot stop himself from that last phrase. All the sincerity expressed to his friends, lovers, and foes shrinks into a biting kiss-off. The phrase foreshadows the oeuvre's next period in a compelling manner.

Still, "Restless" is only part of the farewell package. The personal observations featured in "11 Outline Epitaphs" reinforce the sentiments expressed in "Restless" to suggest that Dylan was most assuredly taking stock of his situation. The "Epitaphs" are quite a contrast to their "autobiographical" predecessor, "My Life In A Stolen Moment." The liner notes' use of the term "epitaphs" obviously suggests an ending or transition as well. The take on his Minnesota roots (epitaph #2), his commentary on organized politics and his preference for the emotive over the logical (#4), his rejection of hero worship (#6), his discussion of the folk process and authorship (#8), his tirade against journalists and their agendas (#9), and his identification with the many wordsmiths who have impressed him in one manner or another (#11) offer personal accounts on topics of concern to the artist, his audience, and his profession. Not all of these statements are negative. Dylan praises poetry (#5), his village friends (#10), and his creative challenge (again, #11) just as much as he rails against journalists, insincere activists, and idolatry. We should take a moment here to examine the specifics.

Epitaph 5 speaks to the narrator's love of poetry and its pleasures. He portrays a conversation with "Al's wife" as they speed through the "New Jersey night." Mrs. Al questions his happiness since he sings such depressing songs, but the narrator replies, "Lenny Bruce says there're no dirty words . . . just dirty minds an' I say there're no depressed words just depressed minds." The conversation continues with the narrator's insistence that "poetry makes me feel good" and how "it makes me feel happy." When asked about the songs he performs in concert, he replies that "they're nothin' but the unwindin' of my happiness." The epitaph is a simple exchange expressed through the writing style that characterizes Dylan's "proetry" at this point in time. Nevertheless, it takes a stand regarding his detachment from his songs. He may sing of depression, but that doesn't make him depressed. That he used Bruce as an example indicates that, well, this may be an *act*. He's fine, he declares. It's his *audience* that has all of the problems. I think that this is a compelling statement.

Epitaph 6 discusses Woody Guthrie and the Oklahoma bard's impact on the narrator. Guthrie was his "last idol" since he was the first person to teach him "face t' face" that "men are men"—an act that shattered "even himself as an idol." Through the simple eloquence of his example, Guthrie taught his disciple a valuable lesson; it just took a lot of mythmaking for the lesson to sink in, I presume. In any event, Dylan takes the time to praise this valuable lesson and the man who taught it. Bob Zimmerman's dedication to Woody Guthrie never, ever wanes.

These are the types of sentiments conveyed through the epitaphs. Sometimes they attack; at other times they praise. Some, such as number 8, offer responses to specific situations. Here is an extended excerpt from number 8's discussion of songwriting and the folk process:

> Yes, I am a thief of thoughts
> not, I pray, a stealer of souls
> I have built an' rebuilt
> upon what is waitin'
> for the sand on the beaches
> carves many castles
> on what has been opened
> before my time
> a word, a tune, a story, a line
> keys in the wind t' unlock my mind
> an' t' grant my closet thoughts backyard air
> it is not of me t' sit an' ponder
> wonderin' and wastin' time
> thinkin' of thoughts that haven't been thunk
> thinkin' of dreams that haven't been dreamt
> an' new ideas that haven't been wrote
> an' new words t' fit into rhyme
> (if it rhymes, it rhymes
> if it don't, it don't
> if it comes, it comes
> if it won't, it won't)

Through his now-familiar method of writing, Dylan speaks directly to his songwriting process. As we shall observe in the closing chapter, he has always been rather straightforward about how he "discovers" ideas that he doesn't claim as his, that is, he takes the "folk process" to heart and uses what he reads and hears and experiences as a means to unlock his "closet thoughts" (e.g., his "attitudes" toward those materials). It is, dear readers, as simple as that.

The epitaphs are a valuable part of the oeuvre. Though his means of expression occasionally cause distractions, the insights they offer shed light on his thinking. And think he does. In number 7, he describes an encounter with a German who related how Adolf Hitler is regarded by many Germans the way Robert E. Lee is treated by many Americans. Number 9 has a go at journalists and their questions about his clothes, eating habits, and lifestyle: "I never eat / I run naked when I can / my hobby's collectin' airplane glue." The next to last statement in number 11 connects the epitaphs to a familiar theme from writings gone by: "lonely? ah yes / but it is the flowers an' the mirrors / of flowers that now meet my / loneliness / an' mine shall be a strong loneliness / dissolvin' deep / t' the depths of my freedom / an' that, then, shall / remain my song." Once more, the revelations articulated through "Joan Baez in Concert, Part 2" come to the forefront.

The Times They Are A-Changin' is a calculated manifestation of the auteur's considerable talents. Unlike *Freewheelin'* and its raw demonstration of the writer's abilities, this project works from a two-pronged agenda. First, it satisfies his perceived market; second, it says goodbye to that constituency. Yet, what stands out is the poignancy of Dylan's observations. His acute understanding of his characters' lives on the Iron Range, in depressed farming communities, and in dysfunctional relationships; his understanding of the activists fighting for civil rights, against imperialism, and for their right to be heard; and his experiences with the celebrity's life directly inform his stories. Many of these accounts are quite sophisticated for a person of Zimmerman's age. Ultimately, the evidence suggests that the songwriter wanted to be heard, not investigated. He wanted to be appreciated, not worshipped. He wanted to express himself, not be a mascot for a movement. Zimmerman had successfully entered the world of professional music—that is for certain—and his mission of discovery was achieved. Now, his challenge involved that career's direction.

Another Side Of Bob Dylan

If ever an album were appropriately named "Another Side," this is it. With the folk-protest music movement shrinking in his rearview mirror, Bob Dylan turns from public commentary on public affairs to public commentary on personal affairs with his fourth album. The systematic editorials that dominate *Times* return to Dylan's narrative tool chest, where that storytelling strategy shall rest until George Jackson inspires its return. With that stylistic shift came a return to the playful humor and spiteful recrimination that made his topical songs so compelling. The king of protest merely shifts his subject matter, refocuses his aim, and deploys different narrative tools. Dylan explained his new approach to Nat Hentoff and *New Yorker*:

Those records I've already made, I'll stand behind them, but some of that was jumping into the scene to be heard and a lot of it was because I didn't see anybody else doing that kind of thing. Now a lot of people are doing finger-pointing songs. You know—pointing to all the things that are wrong. Me, I don't want to write *for* people anymore. You know—be a spokesman. Like I once wrote about Emmett Till in the first person, pretending I was him. From now on, I want to write from inside me, and to do that I'm going to have to get back to writing like I used to when I was ten—having everything come out naturally. The way I like to write is for it to come out the way I walk or talk.

Dylan conveyed that view to Hentoff just before that reporter joined producer Tom Wilson, Dylan, and several of the artist's friends for an all-night recording session (June 9, 1964). The results from that session became *Another Side*. Heylin's invaluable chronology indicates there were few outtakes from this concentrated enterprise that stressed an expressive, creative orientation. The songs flowed through Dylan in a natural, unforced manner—no editing, no overdubbing, pure expression. It must have been quite a night.

Another Side is, as the title suggests, a transitional statement. The album's eleven tracks (running over fifty minutes) feature three thematic orientations ranging from a trademark Dylan satire ("Motorpsycho Nightmare"), to seven songs about relationships ("All I Really Want To Do," "Black Crow Blues," "Spanish Harlem Incident," "To Ramona," "I Don't Believe You," "Ballad In Plain D," and "It Ain't Me, Babe"), to three songs that preview future writing trends ("Chimes Of Freedom," "I Shall Be Free No. 10," and "My Back Pages"). These last three tracks involve Dylan's emerging impressionism, in which the author moves from pure wordplay ("I Shall Be Free No. 10") to the more structured narrative impressionism technique ("My Back Pages" and "Chimes Of Freedom"). These two styles signal the wave of the songwriting future, as the former approach allows Dylan to play with words and sounds in a whimsical, free-form fashion while the latter uses refrains and musical punctuation to create the illusion of narrative structure. In both cases, we discover that one person's "metaphor" is another person's "game of Glissendorf."

Three stylistic attributes control this album: a shift away from the topical song subject matter, the steady increase in impressionism, and the demise of the humorous satire. The project features three three-song segments with two asides. There are three songs of relational ambition, three pieces of impressionism, three relational complaints/attacks, one relational editorial, and one wonderful satire. The change from societal concerns to relational matters demonstrates the accuracy of Dylan's remarks to Hentoff. Holding steady, however, is the intensity of these offerings. Whereas "It Ain't Me," "All I Really Want To Do," and "Black Crow" speak in general terms that lend themselves to analogy, songs such as "Ballad In Plain D" and "To Ramona" directly address personal situations. Like *Times'* societal complaints, these relational complaints are presented in plain, clear language. The author is not beating around his symbolic bush with these songs. Dylan writes that relationships need not be submissive ("All I Really"), that the circumstances around a relationship can be detrimental to its success ("To Ramona"), that it hurts when our partners ignore us ("I Don't Believe You"), and that Carla Rotolo was the problem with his relationship with Suze Rotolo ("Ballad In Plain D"). He may not have mentioned the sisters by name, but the song's contents are so pointed that they leave little doubt about their subject. That he publicly acknowledged the lyrics' personal qualities heightened this song's "finger-pointing" attributes in no uncertain terms.

The impressionism builds on the style established with "A Hard Rain's A-Gonna Fall." The use of brief lyrical refrains and repetitive musical structures frames the surreal images featured in "Chimes of Freedom" and "My Back Pages" in the manner of "Hard Rain." These songs *sound* like story ballads as they present characters doing different things, but nothing ever happens. There is no plot progression; instead, we consider characters in a thunderstorm contemplating life's injustices ("Chimes") and a narrator's cloudy reflections on his career ("My Back Pages"). The emphasis is on imaginative description—with the occasional moral prescription—as Dylan's wordplay advances down the path blazed by "Hard Rain."

The album's transitional qualities are also evident in our third stylistic trend, the demise of Dylan's trademark satires. "Motorpsycho Nightmare" is in the tradition of "Talking New York," "Talking Bear Mountain," and "Talkin' John Birch," with its portrayal of crazy characters doing weird things that somehow or another serve the story's moral. Dylan's adaptation of the "traveling salesman" story is skillful in its depiction of ignorant bigotry (once more, the Red Scare is prominently featured) and the silly conditions that foster that attitude. It is quite unfortunate that Dylan abandons this storytelling technique for an extended period after this recording. His sense of humor proved to be an effective storytelling tool.

"Motorpsycho" is a rhythmic little tune with nine verses. The story opens with our narrator standing outside of a farmhouse attempting to secure lodging for the night. Suddenly, a farmer answers his knock, points a gun at him, and demands to know if he's the traveling salesman about whom the farmer's been hearing. The traveling salesman declares, " 'No! No! No! / I'm a doctor and it's true / I'm a clean-cut kid / And I been to college, too.' " Predictably, the plot quickly thickens:

> Then in comes his daughter
> Whose name was Rita.
> She looked like she stepped out of
> La Dolce Vita.
> I immediately tried to cool it
> With her dad,
> And told him what a
> Nice, pretty farm he had.
> He said, "What do doctors
> Know about farms, pray tell?"
> I said, "I was born
> At the bottom of a wishing well."

That verse captures the song's rhythm as it effortlessly floats from scene to scene using puns and weird comments to paint a crazed version of the traveling salesman–farmer's daughter tale. Some lines work better than others. At times, we gain an insightful glimpse of the artist's "don't look back" writing/recording style. If a line works, Dylan may build on it; if it doesn't, he may use it anyway (it appears his rhyming scheme often dictates the decision).

The story continues with the farmer providing a place to sleep (a bed under the stove, no less) with two conditions: that the salesman refrain from touching his daughter and that he'll milk the cow in the morning. The salesman dutifully agrees. He goes to bed only to be awakened by Rita, standing over him, looking "just like Tony Perkins." She offers him a shower, and the salesman declares his need to leave (claiming he's seen all of this before—a clear reference to the movie *Psycho*). Yet, since he promised to milk the farmer's cow, he perceives the need to get thrown out in order to keep his word (!). So, he screams out, "I like Fidel Castro and his beard." The now-ubiquitous Red Rant rattles the farmer: He charges down the stairs, swings at the salesman, threatens to kill him, and runs the "unpatriotic doctor Commie rat" out the door. When the farmer reaches for his gun, the salesman does a somersault, lands in a flower bed, and escapes. The final stanza features the salesman reflecting on his experience, acknowledging that the farmer wants to turn him over to the FBI, and praising his right to free speech since it saved him from "the swamp." The song joins Dylan's other satires in its light sound, crazed images, and silly language. It also uses the ever-present Cold War reference to frame yet another morality play. "Free speech" facilitated his appeal to the farmer's ridiculous Cold War paranoia, and *that* saved his life. The salesman–farmer's daughter scenario, scenes from contemporary movies (*Psycho*), the Red Scare, and more all wrapped into one nutty story. Dylan is in his element here.

To complement this fun-loving romp through a standard joke, we turn to the other end of the songwriting spectrum and Dylan's emerging wordplay. As we've seen, the auteur's impressionism may use imagery that massages serious situations (e.g., "Hard Rain") or it may follow the "I Shall Be Free" format and toy with famous names, places, or historical events. The writer's proetry and songwriting now converge to produce a body of work that rejects message music and, in turn, unshackles Bob Dillon's rebellion. That new writing style is evident in "My Back Pages," "Chimes Of Freedom," and "I Shall Be Free #10." For the next few years, Hollis, Hattie, John Brown, and the other characters are relegated to bit parts in an idiosyncratic game of Glissendorf that not only liberated the auteur's pen, but also transformed songwriting forever.

"My Back Pages" may be the *professional* "Restless Farewell." That is, to the extent that "Farewell" speaks to *personal* situations in its own stinging way, "Back Pages" discusses Dylan's art in an impressionistic fashion. It uses what seems like a call-and-response pattern to communicate Dylan's rejection of the "old way" of working through his "new way" of expressing himself. The song—presented via six eight-line verses—is an introspective litany. Dylan wrestles with simplified advocacy, false prophecy, and inner turmoil in individual stanzas that close with the sarcastic response suggesting his artistic liberation. The song's opening is indicative of his new style:

> Crimson flames tied through my ears
> Rollin' high and mighty traps
> Pounced with fire on flaming roads
> Using ideas as my maps

"We'll meet on edges, soon," said I
Proud 'neath heated brow.
Ah, but I was so much older then,
I'm younger than that now.

From there, the song addresses four specific situations with varying degrees of clarity. First, Dylan recounts how he advocated simplified constructions of complicated societal situations that reduced his earlier work to that of a sloganeer. By reducing his subject matter to right and wrong, black and white slogans, he betrayed his own ideals. That romantic worldview was summarily used and abused. Second, he seems to decry the false prophecies that accompanied those simplified pronouncements. Bogus jealousies, antiquated politics, and dead advocates float through this cloudy stanza that is weak on its specifics, but strong in its sentiments. Third, he interjects his thoughts regarding the arbitrary qualities of language. He seems to suggest that words have personal attachments to their users (people are "married" to their words) and that those relationships must be acknowledged if true understanding is to take place. A cheap slogan is meaningless in the broader scope of things. To be sure, *this* is becoming a dominant theme. Dylan is questioning the power of words; yes, some people will rob you with a fountain pen. Finally, he reveals his inner frustrations over his artistic direction (he fears he opposes himself) and his understanding that his confusion may make him susceptible to betrayal. The final stanza sums his stance:

Yes, my guard stood hard when abstract threats
Too noble to neglect
Deceived me into thinking
I had something to protect
Good and bad, I define these terms
Quite clear, no doubt, somehow.
Ah, but I was so much older then,
I'm younger than that now.

Either Dylan is wrestling with his personal metaphysics or he's reporting the results of that experience. Much like the "Joan Baez in Concert, Part 2" essay, the writer fights off the knee-jerk philosophy that suggests that simplicity reveals truth. The idea that nothing exists unless you can touch it with your hands complements the notion that everything can be reduced to its black and white, yes-no essence. "Back Pages" takes issue with that stance and relates that reality is subjective. Those who reduce complex realities into simple slogans may have agendas that are less than noble. Thus, our narrator dismisses the old man's dogmatism for a younger man's subjectivity.

"My Back Pages" is a pivotal song. When you accept a philosophy that everything is subjective, you liberate your mind and open it to all sorts of perspectives. The "right" and "wrong" judgments that characterize most social movements become more than simplistic—they may be dangerous. When that "ship comes in," the liberated may resemble their former oppressors in more ways than one. The good guys simply trade places with the bad guys; nothing really changes. Consequently,

"Back Pages" reports the error of such thinking, Dylan's stance on that matter (which was always lingering in the background), and his acceptance of a more subjective worldview—a philosophy that he now puts to use in his art. The message music—with all of its trite platitudes—is about to become a thing of the past.

Further proof of this transition resides in the inclusive blessing that is "Chimes Of Freedom" (also presented through six eight-line verses). Here the auteur pauses to acknowledge those who struggle with their respective worlds. No remedies are proposed. No slogans are proffered. Instead, we have a group of people watching a serious storm (complete with wind, rain, hail, lightning, and thunder—only the locusts are missing!) and using those meteorological events as metaphors. The song opens, "Far between sundown's finish an' midnight's broken toll / We ducked inside the doorway, thunder crashing / As majestic bells of bolts struck shadows in the sounds / Seeming to be the chimes of freedom flashing." These majestic chimes flash for pacifist warriors, defenseless refugees, rebels, unfortunates, and victims of all stripes. The third stanza captures the song's rhythm of expression:

Through the mad mystic hammering of the wild ripping hail
The sky cracked its poems in naked wonder
That the clinging of the church bells blew far into the breeze
Leaving only bells of lightning and its thunder
Striking for the gentle, striking for the kind
Striking for the guardians and protectors of the mind
An' the unpawned painter behind beyond his rightful time
An' we gazed upon the chimes of freedom flashing.

Each verse follows a similar formula. Dylan offers a scenic observation as a preface to his blessing. Beautiful statements populate this inclusive prayer. The chimes toll for the disabled, for "the mistreated, mateless mother, the mistitled prostitute," and for hounded fugitives. But it doesn't stop there. The chimes toll for searchers, lovers, the falsely accused, and more: "For the countless confused, accused, misused, strung-out ones an' worse / An' for every hung-up person in the whole wide universe / An' we gazed upon the chimes of freedom flashing."

Few songs in popular music history reach out to disturbed folks in every location. That line captures "Chimes" in all of its majesty. The meteorological metaphors provide a symbolic starting point for a heartfelt acknowledgment of everybody who struggles in any way. Its inclusive rhetoric complements the subjectivity of "Back Pages" in that it refuses to draw lines of separation between any group or individual. The "chimes" toll for everybody; everybody's worldview has merit. Even hung-up elites like William Zanzinger are offered comfort through this inclusive blessing. That Dylan now stands on all sides of the picket line is evident in this song—the sloganeer is dead.

Or maybe the sloganeer isn't dead; he just lost his mind. What can be said about "I Shall Be Free No. 10"? The song's playful predecessor is tame when placed alongside this merry jaunt through Dylan's symbolic maze. The song's second stanza reflects its logic:

I was shadow-boxing earlier in the day
I figured I was ready for Cassius Clay
I said "Fee, fie, fo, fum, Cassius Clay, here I come
26, 27, 28, 29, I'm gonna make your face look just like mine
Five, four, three, two, one, Cassius Clay you'd better run
99, 100, 101, 102, your ma won't even recognize you
14, 15, 16, 17, 18, 19, gonna knock him clean right out of his spleen."

Proving that not all wordplay is *good* wordplay, each of the song's eleven stanzas involves a vignette much like the Cassius Clay example above. Our narrator wonders about the golden streets of heaven and what would happen if the Russians arrive there first (always, the Red Scare), acknowledges his liberal political philosophy and his refusal to allow his daughter to marry Barry Goldwater, recalls telling his monkey to do the "dog" and how it did the "cat" instead, describes his woman and her cooking habits, notes how his friends stab his photograph with a "bowie-knife" and vomit at the mention of his name ("I've got a million friends!" he declares), and more. The song closes in this manner:

Now you're probably wondering by now
Just what this song is all about
What's probably got you baffled more
Is what this thing here is for.
It's nothing
It's something I learned over in England.

With that, the wacky rejection of message music closes. Crazy vignettes that feature celebrity names or describe personal stances have replaced weird expressions of personal resolve. Notice the shift in language as well. There's no sign of the Okie, "My Life In A Stolen Moment," phonetic writing. Instead, clear language is used to portray outrageous events. However, the Dylan Edge remains. He pokes fun at Clay's rhyming raps. He laughs at his enemies who call themselves his friends. And he describes it all through a sneering smile; it is all about *nothing*.

I couldn't agree more. Nevertheless, there is news in this little piece of nothing. These three songs work in harmony to foreshadow Bob Dylan's songwriting future. The introspective moralizing of "Back Pages" joins the metaphoric acknowledgments of "Chimes" and the unrestrained chaos of "No. 10" to demonstrate that the auteur's protest music days are way, way behind him now. As a result, he's younger than he used to be—freed by his pen's liberation to praise, damn, or laugh at his subject matter in the manner of the moment. Our Glissendorf Master now plays by his own rules. Bob Dillon is pushing young Jack Fate into the background. From this point onward, Bob Dylan will point his fingers where he wishes in the manner of his choosing. He will sing for himself, using his talent in idiosyncratic explorations that may—or may not—ring true to outsiders. Bob Dylan, the voice of his generation, just told that generation to go to hell.

With that comes a new dedication to an old subject: loving relationships. Dylan has always written about love. He sang about Peggy-O, Barbara Allen, and ladies from the north country long before he tackled the Cold War or the military-industrial complex. But now he takes the venom of those finger-pointing protest songs and applies it to human relationships. The slight sarcasm of "Don't Think Twice" explodes into a frontal attack, and that narrative trend begins with the remaining songs on *Another Side*. The seven songs about loving relations feature three thematic trends. There are three songs of romantic ambition, three songs of complaint/attack, and one relational editorial. Once more, the insights of Dylan's comments to Hentoff are on display in these seven songs.

The three songs that open *Another Side* constitute a trilogy of romantic ambitions. The songs are neither positive nor negative. They're just hopeful. The things in life are uncertain ("Black Crow"), yet he believes in her power to save him ("Spanish Harlem"). He aspires to a relationship that is not characterized by dominance but by friendship ("All I Really"). The tone is established in the opening track, "All I Really Want To Do." The song states its case from the opening lines:

> I ain't lookin' to compete with you,
> Beat or cheat or mistreat you,
> Simplify you, classify you,
> Deny, defy or crucify you.
> All I really want to do
> Is, baby, be friends with you.

And that's that. The song continues with the same symbolic rhythm across its six six-line verses. He doesn't wish to scare her, disappoint her, interpret her, use her, limit her, or anything that could remotely be considered abusive. Instead,

> I don't want to fake you out,
> Take or shake or forsake you out,
> I ain't lookin' for you to feel like me,
> See like me or be like me.
> All I really want to do
> Is, baby, be friends with you.

Our narrator is searching for the classic soul mate. Someone to complement him, not mirror him. Someone occupied with her own ideas, not someone lost in his world. Someone who pursues individuality, not sycophancy. The song is direct, hopeful, and persistent.

The title "Black Crow Blues" indicates our next track's sonic orientation. Here our narrator pines for his "long-lost lover" and her interpretive abilities through a song that uses repetition to drive home its point throughout its five seven-line verses. The third stanza is representative of the song's style:

> If I got anything you need, babe,
> Let me tell you in front.
> If I got anything you need, babe,

Let me tell you in front.
You can come to me sometime,
Night time, day time,
Any time you want.

The narrator is uncertain of himself and in need of her special assistance. He's hopeful that she can make the much-needed difference in his life. Interestingly, the final verse introduces the black crow element by describing the birds as they gather across the highway in a meadow. That Dylan writes, "Though it's funny, honey, / I just don't feel much like a / Scarecrow today," suggests the nature of the relief he's pursuing. Is he sacrificing himself for others? Is he a fake warrior, fending off the enemy through appearances? Regardless, she is his perceived answer and he's hopeful of her return. The song is simple, direct, and firmly rooted in the blues tradition.

The "rescue me" theme is apparent in "Spanish Harlem" as well. This time, the narrator is hot for a gypsy girl with magical powers. That message is articulated though the now-standard structure of three eight-line verses. The opening verse establishes the story:

Gypsy gal, the hands of Harlem
Cannot hold you to its heat.
Your temperature's too hot for taming,
Your flaming feet burn up the street.
I am homeless, come and take me
Into reach of your rattling drums.
Let me know, babe, about my fortune
Down along my restless palms.

She's the answer. What she doesn't know, she can predict. He pleads for her intervention. He needs her help. She is the only way he can determine whether or not he's real. (There's that metaphysical angst again!) The song is without mystery.

These three songs initiate a thematic trend that reappears throughout the oeuvre. The "woman as savior" story line will recur with considerable frequency as Dylan praises one day what he damns or cries over the next. Perhaps this idealistic view of Woman fuels the relational anger when those ideals fail to materialize. Maybe he places his female characters on too high a pedestal. In any event, these three songs of relational hope indicate that Dylan's characters seek comradeship over domination, the wisdom to avoid superficial sacrifice, and the refuge of a wise partner. The narrators' submission is their most prominent attribute.

That submissive attitude is nowhere in sight in our songs of relational strife. The relational editorial, "To Ramona," sizes up his love interest's sad situation, points his accusing finger at those responsible for her plight, and leaves her to resolve her dilemma in whatever way she chooses. The song opens with pleas for Ramona to "come closer" to the narrator and follows with expressions of tenderness (e.g., he wants to kiss her "cracked country lips"). Although their attraction is "magnetic," the song quickly turns to her problems:

But it grieves my heart, love,
To see you tryin' to be part of
A world that just don't exist.
It's all just a dream, babe,
A vacuum, a scheme, babe,
That sucks you into feelin' like this.

Why does Ramona hold these unrealistic views on life? Because she's been brain-washed ("I can see that your head / Has been twisted and fed") by people who betray her: "From fixtures and forces and friends, / Your sorrow does stem, / That hype you and type you, / Making you feel / That you must be exactly like them." Although he'd love to keep talking, the narrator understands that his words blend into a "meaningless ring" and concludes,

For deep in my heart
I know there is no help I can bring.
Everything passes,
Everything changes,
Just do what you think you should do.
And someday maybe,
Who knows, baby,
I'll come and be cryin' to you.

With that, the five-verse editorial ends. The narrator diagnoses Ramona's situation, notes the futility of her outlook, blames her friends for feeding her distorted views, and leaves her to cope with her problem. He doesn't intervene on her behalf or suggest alternatives; rather, he's satisfied with identifying the problem and exiting. Much like "Back Pages," there are sinister forces in the world who advocate false prophecies that bring nothing but trouble. One gains the impression that the author is washing his hands of their activities—and encouraging Ramona to do the same.

Another Side's three songs of relational conflict deal with rejection. In one song, the narrator feels rejected ("I Don't Believe"); in another, specific people are rejected for specific reasons ("Plain D"); and in the other, the very notion of a supportive, nurturing relationship is rejected ("It Ain't Me"). Dylan's finger pointing takes aim at negligent lovers, the Rotolo sisters, and loving relationships via these sharp, cutting songs that—in some instances—come quite close to going too far. The weak sister here is the teen-angst tune, "I Don't Believe You (She Acts Like We Never Have Met)." Here, last night's hot lover turns cold. The narrator is perplexed by his date's lack of attention and spends considerable time complaining about it. The second of the song's five verses captures the situation:

It's all new t' me
Like some mystery,
It could even be like a myth.
Yet it's hard t' think on,
That she's the same one

That last night I was with.
From darkness, dreams're deserted,
Am I still dreamin' yet?
I wish she'd unlock
Her voice once an' talk,
'Stead of acting like we never have met.

He wonders if she's ill or if he's worn out his welcome. He desperately tries to comprehend why this is happening. In the end, he leaves; however, he has a new relational trick in his romantic arsenal: Ignore them and they'll want you. Our narrator has learned his lesson well.

From teenage histrionics, we turn to adult love wars—or at least the aftermath of a battle. "Ballad In Plain D" charts the demise of a failed romantic relationship in a manner reminiscent of "Master Of War" and Dylan's cutting-edge social commentary. The autobiography seems to be there—if you want it. But the bottom line involves the narrator's attack on his ex-lover's petty sister and her conniving ways. He admits to his role in the controversy, yet we are assured that the responsibility for the relationship's failure lies elsewhere. The song opens with descriptions of his innocent, gentle, departed lover. He claims he "stole her away" from her mother and sister and their failed lives. These people use guilt to manipulate our innocent victim. The narrator praises his former lover's sensitivity and creativity before he acknowledges how she was "easily undone" by the jealousies of those around her. The principal culprit is identified in the fourth verse:

For her parasite sister, I had no respect,
Bound by her boredom, her pride to protect.
Countless visions of the other she'd reflect
As a crutch for her scenes and her society.

Having said that, our narrator admits to telling lies in order to save the relationship; however, that was not the problem. The problem, it seems, was that the couple lived in a fantasy that *had* to end someday. When that day arrived, the fight between the narrator and the parasite sister was intense. Once the battle ended, he departed into the night, "leaving all of love's ashes behind" him. He finds himself unable to apologize, and hopeful that her new lover will appreciate his good fortune. The song ends with the narrator's understanding that he will never be free from the "chains" of her now-departed love.

"Plain D" is a clear, slow, prodding, thirteen-verse account of an interpersonal situation full of dreams, pettiness, hopes, and dysfunction. It is, in a word, a dirge. The narrator's beautiful "bronze" girlfriend is stolen away by pretentious family members whose evil ways both ruined his love and threatened his lover. Much like Ramona, this love interest is shackled by her surroundings and by people who hope to restrict her life so that it resembles theirs. So, ultimately, the narrator is a victim. He stepped into a situation that he could not overcome. He fought and lost. Nevertheless, he lost on his terms, and that is where it rests. He's free, but not free of the memories—or the thought of her love. This slow, heavy-handed dirge takes no prisoners. The Dylan Edge remains.

A dime store psychologist will tell you that people who get burned by various phenomena often cease to participate in the conditions that rendered those situations. Hence, submitted for your approval is the ultimate statement of relational defiance, "It Ain't Me, Babe." Looking for a nice, supportive, nurturing lover? Sorry. The song's opening lines set the scene nicely:

> Go 'way from my window,
> Leave at your own chosen speed.
> I'm not the one you want, babe,
> I'm not the one you need.
> You say you're lookin' for someone
> Never weak but always strong,
> To protect you an' defend you
> Whether you are right or wrong,
> Someone to open each and every door,
> But it ain't me, babe,
> No, no, no, it ain't me, babe,
> It ain't me you're lookin' for, babe.

That, my friends, pretty much sums up this three-verse song. It is a declaration of personal independence. When your girlfriends ignore you at parties and their families cause you more grief than joy, you develop *attitudes*. This is a song with an *attitude*. Take all of the traditional support systems that lovers expect from their partners and deny it all, this song reports. You want someone who'll promise their loyalty? You want someone who will sacrifice their life for yours? You hope for a lover who'll offer support, bring you flowers, or be responsive to your needs? Look elsewhere, then. Dylan's relational defiance is staggering. One immediately asks, "Well, what *will* you do?" While other Dylan songs will attack specific characters or situations, this entry casts a broad net and flat-out defies all the rules of relationships. What good is a relationship if your partner can't be supportive, dependable, kind, and loving? What good, indeed.

Bob Dylan's mission-oriented approach to art is on display in *Another Side*. Just as he positioned himself for his market with *Bob Dylan*, followed that opening statement with original songs that reinforced that orientation in *Freewheelin'*, and solidified his standing with the protest editorials of *Times*, Dylan now says goodbye to it all with *Another Side*. The author of *Another Side* is not only rejecting political groups and their trite messages, but he's also pushing everybody aside (as "It Ain't Me" reveals) and announcing his total independence. Two things stand out in this emancipative project: the album's transitional statement and its manner of production. Although Dylan shifts his gaze toward romantic relationships, he does it in a signature fashion. Images of abused, defenseless people populate these songs that suggest the enemy attacks from all sides. There is coherence to Dylan's argument that the slogans are only as good as the sloganeers, that the sloganeers may be as corrupt as their targets, and that the whole thing rests on the arbitrary nature of language. Hence, the transition portrayed here involves a shift from a group orientation to an individual one. Groups are doctrinaire and stifling. Whether the group supports the left or right, it constricts its membership in a manner that is not that different from the other side. Remember, when that ship comes in, the lynch mob will be ready to exact revenge, and in so doing, will simply change places with the oppressors. Consequently, *Another Side* tips its hat to the victims (via "Chimes"), declares the author's freedom (via "My Back Pages"), and argues for personal independence (via "It Ain't Me"). A signature satire and a series of relational commentaries float in and out of this otherwise focused enterprise.

Contributing to that focus is the record's manner of production. Dylan assembled his friends (and a reporter), grabbed his bottles of wine, and recorded these songs in one night. If he missed a line or changed a lyric, so be it. The "If it comes, it comes" school of music production was on display that June night. He may have deleted the original "Mr. Tambourine Man" (performed with Jack Elliot) from the final song list, but those edits were few on this production. The auteur brought his artistic agenda to the studio that evening and initiated the first installment of a two-part resolution to the opening phase of his career. This mission would be completed, appropriately enough, on Halloween. The times are about to permanently change.

Dylan's liner notes, "Some Other Kinds Of Songs," are an interesting addition to the *Another Side* package. Unlike our previous edition of notes ("11 Outlined Epitaphs") and its complementary relationship to "Restless Farewell," these poems stand independently—at least on the surface. Although they massage some of the issues currently before the auteur (e.g., word definitions and political philosophies), most of the eleven poems display no overt connection to the album's songs. More than anything, they take us one small step closer to *Tarantula* while simultaneously leaping away from any connection to the folk-protest movement. Dylan is about to respond to the folkies in the same manner as his character's lover in "I Don't Believe You." In a year, you'd think these people had never met.

Of the eleven entries, poem 5 is—by far—the most intriguing; still, let's take a moment to walk through this important work. The short, rhythmic bursts of words that are poem 1's account of "baby black" suggest an urban world of violence, lawbreaking, and pawnbroking. The narrator relates that baby black would pawn the world for "a dollar an' a quarter" and closes the segment by offering himself to her to pawn. Scenes of Paris in the spring float throughout poem 2's symbolic jaunt. Lines such as "the breeze yawns food" populate this chaotic account of Parisian life. Poem 3 is something to behold. It leaps from topic to topic with the occasional head-turning line or image. We move from a chess match, to a discussion of domestic drug use, to Nazis, to Barry Goldwater, to a kid's game of cowboys and Indians, to a ping-pong match with Henry Miller, to a scene with a college journalist, to another scene with another journalist, to a concluding statement about religious dogmatism. Sometimes the images are disturbing, such as this statement about domestic drug use: "outside of Chicago, private come down junkie nurse home heals countless common housewives strung out fully on drugstore dope, legally sold t' help clean the kitchen." During his encounter with a journalist, the narrator reports how she's attempting to manipulate him into saying things "she can understand." When asked about "humanity," he replies via the now-standard response of "i'm not sure what that word means." Finally, consider this observation about religion: "people pound their chests an' other people's chests an' interpret bibles t' suit their own means. respect is just a misinterpreted word an' if Jesus Christ himself came down through these streets, Christianity would start all over again." That the Dylan of the *Another Side* era is concerned with language, definitions, and the strategic manipulations of meanings is oh-so-clear. It is as if the "Masters Of War" have traded their military hardware for dictionaries and deploy the slogans of the day as their new weapons of choice. The great wordsmith is wrestling with the power of words. It is a sight to behold.

Poem 4 charts that mysterious card the "jack o' diamonds" as it examines the vicissitudes of playing that particular card through a rhythmic expression that resembles "baby black" in poem 1. Poem 5 represents the top shelf of this body of writings. It takes us from Joshua preparing for battle in Jericho, to a suicide attempt on the Brooklyn Bridge (the narrator wants the person to jump and is ashamed for it), to New Orleans and the crazy street scenes only available there, to New York, to a rich discussion of a "door enlargement" operation, to a scene on 14th Street, to Greece, to another discussion of language's arbitrary qualities, and to a series of personal prescriptions for living, then closes where it began with Joshua. It uses parenthetical comments to flash back to the jumper as it flows from scene to scene in its own rhythmic way. Poem 5 touches on subjects that appear in *Another Side*'s songs, albeit indirectly at times. The brief section on language offers further evidence that this was a topic of concern to the writer: "i talk t' people every day / involved in some scene / good an' evil are but words / invented by those / that are trapped in scenes." Suggesting the arguments advanced in "Ramona" and, to a lesser extent, "Plain D," this statement contends that realities are products of "scenes" that are controlled by certain people for specific reasons. Join a "scene" and prepare to be manipulated. The narrator states his case in these prescriptions for living:

> i can't believe that i have
> t' hate anybody
> an' when i do
> it will only be out of fear
> an' i'll know it
> i know no answers an' no truth
> for absolutely no soul alive
> i will listen t' no one
> Who tells me morals
> there are no morals
> an' i dream a lot

We've come a long way from "When The Ship Comes In" and "The Times They Are A-Changin'." There are no morals to change, no truths to evolve. The morals propagated on one ship are just as suspicious as the ones honored on another. It is all arbitrary; therefore, the narrator resolves himself to emotional, intellectual, and spiritual independence. Oh yes, "It ain't me, babe."

The poems continue with 6's brief discussion of "enzo" and the narrator's feelings for his competitor; 7's quick account of where "charlie" sleeps; 8's dark tale of a doomed hitchhiker, "liz taylor," Texas, and more; and 9's story of "little johnny"—

a nice kid that hammers nails through flies, traps young bumblebees, beats his brother, and forces his sister's hand into the garbage disposal. The kid couldn't get into the college of his choice, but he picked up a nice car anyway. Poem 11 returns to poem 1's "baby black" method of expression to rail on about weddings, vows, honeymoons, and religion. In the end, we're told, nothing matters, and "all is lost."

Poem 10's presentation of some sort of metaphysical-political debate is a reiteration of *Another Side*'s song themes. Echoing "Back Pages" (i.e., its metaphysical search) and "Chimes" (i.e., its prayer for *everybody*), the participants fight over the concept of politics ("an' i tell you there are no politics" is the narrator's frequent response), the hypocrisies that engulf life (his friend says he cares about people and steals cigarettes from vendors), and communications media, and the poem closes with a horrific description of an apartment building and its occupants. Several lines from the encounter offer compelling insights into the continuing search for metaphysical stability. For example: "you ask me questions / an I say that every question / if it's a truthful question / can be answered by asking it." *This* comes from the pen that told the world that the answer was blowing in the wind? Now, the *question* is adrift as well? That Bob Dylan has wrestled with the concept of propaganda—and how individuals use persuasive strategies to build enslaving realities for their constituents— is most evident in the *Another Side* package. Organizations trap Ramona through simplifications that not only obligate her to that organization, but also trivialize life's tragedies. Chimes toll, people preach profitable doctrines, religions subjugate by segregation, and the slogans that support the enterprise involve word games that are totally transparent. This is the message that runs through *Another Side*. When Bob Dylan recognized that the message business is a cheap application of a more entertaining (and, in his case, time-honored) phenomenon, he did more than exit that "scene"— he turned it on its head.

Another Side Of Bob Dylan is a powerful record. That Dylan was inspired to record this group of songs is evident in the method of their recording. I mean, one night! In order to muster the resources to record a series of songs of this emotional depth, the auteur had to be bursting at the seams with those feelings. Maybe it was the revenge afforded by "Plain D," the defiance available through "It Ain't Me," the whistle-blowing of "Back Pages" and "Ramona," or the opportunity to personally— or perhaps genuinely—identify with the plights of the oppressed through "Chimes." Whatever it was, *something* inspired this one-shot outpouring of emotion.

Or maybe it was the realization that this job—this *mission*—was complete. As I said at the outset, the folk-posturing period of Dylan's work is a diverse, intense, historic manifestation of the artist's considerable talent. His objective was realized in no uncertain terms; in fact, he may have overdone it. He positioned himself via *Bob Dylan*, he delivered with *Freewheelin'*, he reinforced that achievement with *Times*, and he sealed that deal with *Another Side*. The pivotal moment in all of this may have been *Times* and its calculated application of the skills showcased in *Freewheelin'*. As we've seen, to the extent that *Freewheelin'* is a raw manifestation of the writer's talents, *Times* is a packaged, targeted manifestation of those abilities. Subsequently, his audience expected these types of songs from him. Zimmerman closes the initial portion of a career predicated on defying expectation with the aesthetic correction that is *Another*

Side, as the writer declares his independence from *his* perceived oppressors, explains *his* situation, and closes this period of his career with his final slogan, "It Ain't Me, Babe."

To appreciate the growth that occurs throughout this opening period, you must consult all of the work. The proetry, the outtakes, and the live performances complement the albums in a manner that unveils the budding auteur. What is most intriguing is the fact that what blows in the wind changes. The enemy on that evil ship, as John Brown observed, looks just like the people on the good ship. The times change, but how? Zimmerman deploys Jack Fate's musical knowledge to devise songs that suit the needs of the moment, but the thinking that supports those songs evolves as we move through this era. What fuels this evolution? Why didn't Zimmerman's Dylan just acquiesce and churn out more of the protest stuff? After all, it was child's play for him.

The answer flows as quickly as the question is posed: Bob Dillon's rebellion.

When Bob Zimmerman packed his suitcase and headed east, his plan followed his instincts more than anything else. After all, the guy was twenty years old! Once he arrived in New York, the Jack Fate portion of his Bob Dylan character assumed the dominant position. He absorbed every influence. He assimilated all that he heard or read and rendered stylized versions of those materials. The tensions emerged at the outset. When "Talking New York" notes the club owner's preference for folk music over hillbilly music, well, the die was cast, wasn't it? Still, Fate's education forged onward. He mastered the folk-protest genre. He expanded the scope of his musical knowledge. And he somehow coped with Bob Dillon. You see, the Iron Range's rebellious biker-poet may have crept into a song here, an interview there, or a photo opportunity somewhere; however, he was submissive to Fate's musical education. It was the Jack Fate portion of Zimmerman's character that performed before the march on Washington, who wrote "Blowin' In The Wind," and who submitted to the protest movement with *Times*. But Dillon was always there. His rebellious sarcasm could be heard—sometimes darned clearly in that Dillon fuels much of the poetry from this era. Now, with the realization that the various protest organizations are probably as abusive as anybody else, Dillon has had enough. He restrained himself and allowed the Fate-fueled Dylan to become the darling of the protest genre. Now the characterological tide turns, Fate steps backstage (as Dillon did), and the Dillon-fueled Dylan assumes control.

Anyone for a game of Glissendorf?

What a ride. From "My Life In A Stolen Moment" to *Another Side*'s poem 5, from "Blowin' In The Wind" to "My Back Pages," from Woody and the Jack Fate–controlled Dylan to the new Dillon-controlled Dylan, we've witnessed an aesthetic evolution that is so unique, so historic, so fascinating that it is almost hard to believe. Zimmerman's Dylan doesn't work for money or fame; he works for himself. During the folk-posturing era of Zimmerman's career, Dylan discovers just who the Self is. He learns where he stands with his industry, his society, and himself. He knocks that Dust Bowl dirt off of his cap, tosses it away, dons Phil Spector's sunglasses, and has a go at *everybody*. But first, after what's happened over the past three years, it would be rude to exit and not say goodbye.

Jack Fate's Dylan says "So long" to his adoring audience on Halloween night 1964. The Dylan featured in that recording reminds me of a rebellious high school senior on the last day of school. He's giddy. He laughs at everybody and everything. While some classmates are crying over the end of an era, our rebellious one is anxious to get on with his life. His teachers taught him important lessons, but he's not talking about them. His friends played important roles in his development, but he's looking forward to new friends and new experiences (he is more than a little bit bored with those folks). The institution that educated him oppressed him more. So, the last day of school is a moment of liberation and, unlike graduation night, a time for *personal* celebration. Holy trick or treat! School's out forever.

Listening to *Bob Dylan: Live 1964* is such a joy. It is safe to say that no official recording of Bob Dylan sounds like this. Recorded at New York's Philharmonic Hall, the show runs through what is about to be an old repertoire. He even brings Joan Baez out for four songs toward the end. The show opens with "The Times They Are A-Changin'," as Dylan seems to offer lip service to a song that is already tired to him. His audience, however, is riveted. He marches through the list: "Spanish Harlem Incident"; "John Birch"; "Ramona"; "Davey Moore"; a new song, "Gates Of Eden" (which Dylan laughingly calls "A Sacrilegious Lullaby in D Minor"); "If You Gotta Go, Go Now"; another new song, "It's Alright, Ma (I'm Only Bleeding)" (Dylan calls the song, "It's All Right Ma, It's Life And Life Only"); "I Don't Believe You"; "Mr. Tambourine Man"; "Hard Rain"; "Talkin' World War III"; "Don't Think Twice"; and "Hattie Carroll." After Baez joins in for "Mama, You Been on My Mind," the traditional "Silver Dagger," "With God On Our Side," and "It Ain't Me," the show closes with a solo "All I Really Want To Do." It may have taken Columbia Records close to forty years to officially release this show, but it was worth the wait.

The reason this show is so important involves Dylan's between-song commentaries. He is playful beyond belief. He jokes about "John Birch" (noting that it is a "fictitious song"), forgets the opening lines to "I Don't Believe You" and finally asks the audience if anybody knows the first verse, and celebrates Halloween by declaring that he's wearing his "Bob Dylan mask." His laughter is contagious. His demeanor is a long, long way from the dour look on the cover of *Times*. His interplay with the audience is telltale. When he starts to explain a song, he stops and declares, "Who cares?" The liner notes report that when he introduced "Davey Moore," he announced: "This is a song about a boxer. It's got nothing to do with boxing, it's just a song about a boxer really. And, uh, it's not even having to do with a boxer really. It's got nothing to do with nothing. But I fit all these words together, that's all." Before his encore, his audience shouts requests. One request was "Mary Had A Little Lamb." Dylan pauses, asks if he recorded that, and inquires, "Is that a protest song?" When the mostly polite audience shouts something, he responds—again, with laughter or "Who cares?" He *is* giddy. It *is* his last day of school.

Sean Wilentz's liner notes for the 1964 show offer meaningful insights into this capstone event. Wilentz describes Dylan in this manner:

> He was the cynosure of hip, when hipness still wore pressed slacks and light brown suede boots (as I remember he did that night). Yet hipness

was transforming right on stage. Dylan had already moved on, well beyond the most knowing New Yorkers in the hall, and he was singing about
what he was finding. The concert was in part a summation of past work
and in part a summons to an explosion for which none of us, not even
he, was fully prepared.

That essay continues by highlighting the dynamic events of that chaotic period in
world history: the recent Kennedy assassination, the murder of three civil rights
workers in Mississippi, the passage of the Civil Rights Act, the emergence of Barry
Goldwater, the overthrow of Nikita Khrushchev, and the testing of an atomic
weapon by the Chinese. For Dylan, times were weird as well. After the *Newsweek* biography and the Tom Paine fiasco, Wilentz reports, the artist was mystified by the
poor response to *Another Side*. That Wilentz claims that album "offended" audiences
with its shift of emphasis from protest songs to personal matters foreshadows a future struggle. Publications such as *Sing Out!* decried the change, called Dylan a political sell-out, and warned him of the consequences of a shift in style. (As an aside,
Johnny Cash wrote *Sing Out!* and responded to its charges by defending Dylan—an
act that bonded the men forever.)

Wilentz does a mighty fine job of capturing the artist-audience struggle that
engulfed Dylan's career at this point. Those clever lines about wearing his "Bob Dylan
mask" and his declaration "I'm Masquerading!" are more than slightly symbolic.
Wilentz explains,

> The joke was serious. Bob Dylan, ne' Zimmerman, brilliantly cultivated
> his celebrity, but he was really an entertainer, a man behind a mask, a great
> entertainer, maybe, but basically just that—someone who threw words to-
> gether, astounding as they were. The burden of being something else—a
> guru, a political theorist, "the voice of a generation," as he facetiously put
> it in an interview a few years ago—was too much to ask of anyone. We
> in the audience were asking him to be all of that and more, but Dylan
> was slipping the yoke. All he really wanted to do was to be a friend, if
> possible, and an artist writing and singing his songs. He was telling us so,
> though we didn't want to believe it, and wouldn't let him leave it at that.
> We wanted more.

Wilentz continues with what happens next: the change of clothes, the change of
sounds (using a backing band on the next album), the English tour and movie (*Dont
Look Back*), the aesthetic war that opens with Newport 1965, and more. I don't know
of any artist that encountered the difficulties of audience expectations the way Dylan
did—and it all began with the *Another Side* project and the Halloween 1964 show.

The folk-posturing period of Bob Dylan's oeuvre is the most diverse, innovative, and enterprising period of his career. The traditional folk songs, the topical
songs, the emerging surrealism, the satirical songs, the liner notes, the magazine
commentaries, the public speeches, and—most significantly—the carefully contrived
image all convey the intense dedication that supported this period of time. The professional and personal motivation that inspired young Zimmerman to travel to New

York to hawk his wares intensified, diversified, and peaked during this period. The friendly folk singer who arrived in New York in 1961 had seriously changed by the spring of 1964. This description of Dylan in *Life* supports that conclusion: "[Dylan is] not exactly the image of the clean-cut boy you'd like your daughter to bring home to dinner. He is sloppy, disheveled, unshaven. He talks angrily and irreverently. But he is the most important writer of folk songs in the last 20 years." The young Woody Guthrie apprentice from 1961 did not talk "angrily and irreverently" (although he may have appeared "sloppy" and "disheveled"), and his Oklahoma persona displayed an innocent charm that inspired the New York folk community to assume an active role in his development. Robert Shelton's *New York Times* review fueled a celebrity skyrocket that quickly raised questions about his loyalty to the artistic movement that nurtured him. Zimmerman's Dylan character would now have to resolve the conflict between serving others and serving himself. As I've said before, the apprentice faced teachers wanting to collect fees for their services.

Once more, we turn to Shelton's book for crucial evidence regarding Dylan's situation. There, Dylan explained his response to the folk-posturing period in no uncertain terms. He admitted that he attached himself to the New York folk scene because of its growing audience. He realized that the move was temporary since that approach just wasn't his "thing." The problem was in the organizations that permeate New York City. He liked the people there, but not their organizations. Chief among those people was the man who motivated the trip to New York: Woody Guthrie. Dylan understood how Woody applied himself, and that impressed the budding artist. He told Shelton, "What drew me to him was that hearing his voice I could tell he was very lonesome, very alone, and very lost out in his time." Not only did Bob Dylan identify with Guthrie's image as the lonesome traveler, but he also intuitively understood how Guthrie used what was around him to pursue a personal agenda. That is, he understood Guthrie's *act* and he was hell-bent on applying that knowledge to his unfolding situation.

As Zimmerman mastered his trade through his adaptation of Guthrie's model, he developed stylistic tendencies—narrative signatures—that were unique to the emerging auteur, Bob Dylan. His command of the satirical topical song (in both its humorous and serious modes), the advent of his impressionism, and the intensity of his storytelling style energized a songwriting tradition soon to be abandoned. You see, this phase of Bob Zimmerman's career was *educational* in nature. He was actively feeding the Jack Fate portion of his emerging Dylan character while simultaneously restraining the rebellious Bob Dillon dimension. As the folk community crowds their beloved Dylan, Zimmerman's rebellion kicks in, Fate steps back, Dillon steps forward, and Dylan assumes a very different characterological stance. The "Who cares?" declaration from the Halloween show now attains the status of a code of honor. Scream all you want, Newport weirdos. Yell "Judas" till your vocal chords bleed, yuppy Brits. Set your wine down and boo till your ears ring, Forest Hill wankers. Bob Dylan is laughing at you, and the kicks began on Halloween 1964—the day the folk-posturing period of Bob Dylan's oeuvre ended. I love his laugh on the *Live 1964* recording. It is rich, sincere, and liberating. Now, dear readers, let's see what he does with his newfound freedom, shall we?

The Newport Mod Era

The giggling, playful, frisky performer who stood before an adoring audience at New York's Philharmonic Hall on Halloween night 1964 blossoms into something *nobody* anticipated during the Newport Mod portion of Bob Dylan's oeuvre. It was as if the heavily organized, tradition-addicted New York folk movement had gone to its sanctioned nursery, selected its preordained type of rose, planted it according to time-honored ritual, pruned it religiously (as dictated by a Library of Congress artifact), and awakened one morning to discover the sacred rosebud had turned into a rabbit who did more than surprise his benefactors—he ate all of the flowers in the garden and hopped off to find another nesting place. Never mind that the faithful folkies had been warned. They laughed heartily when their chosen one inquired if "Mary Had A Little Lamb" was a protest song that Halloween night. They totally missed the fact that their designated hero stood before them and mocked their sacred texts. Warnings were everywhere: on the first album ("Talking New York"), during the recording of the second album (and the electric-based outtakes), within the liner notes of his third and fourth albums, and in the thematic shifts on *Another Side*. No, they ignored it all, believing what they had ordained, they would realize. Their control was complete. Their traditions were inviolable.

No wonder those people went nuts in the summer of 1965.

"Radical" is the best descriptor for the changes we're about to observe. Although the seeds of Dylan's characterological evolution were planted on the Iron Range, they experienced a major growth spurt that incredible year that was 1965. The March release of *Bringing It All Back Home*, the spring tour of England and the filming of *Dont Look Back*, the July appearance at the Newport Folk Festival, and the August release of *Highway 61 Revisited* complemented Bob Dillon's dominance of the auteur's composite personality to render another creative synthesis. This time, our Glissendorf Master donned a new uniform, adopted a new philosophy, and created a new identity. In *American Song*, I introduced this phase of Dylan's oeuvre by describing how he incorporated the sights and sounds of the surging British youth movement—the "Mod" phenomenon—into his rapidly evolving act. Few youth movements have demonstrated the commitment to *image* that the Mods perfected in the mid-1960s. Their attention to detail was unsurpassed. They worked all week—often in dead-end jobs—for the money to buy the proper shoes, slacks, jackets, vehicles, records, and, of course, drugs (Mmmmmmoodds con-con-con-consumed lots of a-a-a-a-amphetamines). Pete Townshend's *Quadrophenia* chronicles how the

Mods' clothes were tailored to perfection, how their haircuts met rigid formulas, and how their musical affiliations reinforced their segregation from their rivals, the Rockers. They organized themselves into ranks: tickets (regular members), faces (leaders), and the group leader, the Ace Face. How weird it must have been to see perfectly dressed young people riding cheesy-looking motor scooters to resort locations just so they could gang fight their rivals (the leather-jacketed, greasy-haired Rockers actually rode *motorcycles*). The Mods and Rockers were *group* movements that used their respective uniforms and codes of conduct to promote group solidarity. Individualism in either group was a "ticket" for excommunication. Their intragroup rigor would have impressed the New York folk movement. They kept the troops in line.

Of course, once Bob Zimmerman saw all of this, he assimilated what he liked, dismissed what he did not, and transformed what he absorbed into a new "Bob Dylan." He merged Mod fashion and Mod attitude with Bob Dillon's rebellion and fashioned an *individual* free of affiliation. When he performed at the 1965 Newport Folk Festival Bob Dylan unveiled his new image, shocked his idolatrous following, and introduced what I call the "Newport Mod" period. Once more, I turn to English journalist Nik Cohn—a writer who thoroughly understands Mod culture—to articulate this characterological change:

> In place of the Minnesota boy scout, a whole new face emerged, watchful and withdrawn, cold and arrogant and often mean, full of conscious hipnesses. In particular, he became secret—he stonewalled and played games and pulled faces, let nobody intrude and, when he decided to put someone down, he'd stare at them without expression until they crawled, he'd be merciless. Definitely, this machine could kill. . . . At any rate, if his changes made him paranoid, they also improved his writing out of all recognition. No more schoolboy sermons and no more good intentions, his songs now were sharper, fiercer, stronger in every way. His melody lines got less hackneyed, his imagery less obvious, his jokes less cute. Instead, he was harsh and self-mocking and hurt, he laughed with his teeth, he packed real punch.

The charming apprentice of the folk-posturing era—Cohn's "Minnesota boy scout"—evolved into a combative celebrity unsure of his friends or enemies. The clothes, haircut, and eyewear may have changed, but Bob Zimmerman called upon the artistic independence of his Jacket Jamboree and St. Louis County Fair days to reinvigorate his act, reject his oppressors, and revive his art. For him, stonewalling games were old hat. He was more than prepared for the task at hand.

Now, my friends, this is not the same person who sang "Only A Pawn" at a Mississippi voter registration rally. This man was *not* present at the march on Washington. He did, however, attend the Tom Paine award ceremony. He was also responsible for all those liner notes. The "Bob Dylan" characterological composite now takes the Jack Fate–fueled experiences in Mississippi, Washington, and New York and sets them aside (at least publicly). For the next few years, the Bob Dillon dimension of the Dylan composite assumes control. The kid who warned people of huge, dangerous snakes slithering through Minnesota forests matures into a young man who warned people about themselves. Those who saw prophecy in his words would now have to refocus. Comments about weathermen and their observations may be more cartoon than social philosophy. Remarks about the president of the United States may be more mockery than polemic. Since so many people were (and, in many cases, still are) unwilling to accept anything other than "message music," our new Dylan devised a plan just for them, as he told *Playboy*'s Nat Hentoff: "Myself, what I'm going to do is rent Town Hall and put about 30 Western Union boys on the bill. I mean, then there'll *really* be some messages. People will be able to come and hear more messages than they've ever heard before in their life." The new Bob Dylan was up for his new mission.

The telegrams to be issued during that Town Hall show read like no others. Once again, we turn to Hentoff's 1966 *Playboy* interview for a slice of this new narrative pie. Hentoff asked a simple question—what inspired Dylan to play rock and roll—and this is the answer he received:

> Carelessness. I lost my one true love. I started drinking. The first thing I know, I'm in a card game. Then I'm in a crap game. I wake up in a pool hall. Then this big Mexican lady drags me off the table, takes me to Philadelphia. She leaves me alone in her house, and it burns down. I wind up in Phoenix. I get a job as a Chinaman. I start working in a dime store, and move in with a 13-year-old girl. Then this big Mexican lady from Philadelphia comes in and burns the house down. I go down to Dallas. I get a job as a "before" in a Charles Atlas "before and after" ad. I move in with a delivery boy who can cook fantastic chili and hot dogs. Then this 13-year-old girl from Phoenix comes and burns the house down. The delivery boy—he ain't so mild: He gives her the knife, and the next thing I know I'm in Omaha. It's so cold there, by this time I'm robbing my own bicycles and frying my own fish. I stumble onto some luck and get a job as a carburetor out at the hot-rod races every Thursday night. I move in with a high school teacher who also does a little plumbing on the side, who ain't much to look at, but who's built a special kind of refrigerator that can turn newspaper into lettuce. Everything's going good until that delivery boy shows up and tries to knife me. Needless to say, he burned the house down, and I hit the road. The first guy that picked me up asked me if I wanted to be a star. What could I say?
>
> **Playboy:** And that's how you became a rock-'n'-roll singer?
>
> **Dylan:** No, that's how I got tuberculosis.

Hey, hey, Woody Guthrie, the times sure have changed. During the Newport Mod era, a new narrative mission guides Bob Zimmerman's pen, and he uses the new Dylan as his weapon of choice. I apologize. But this "needle-in-the-haystack" imagery just will not leave me alone! Finding a "message" in this portion of the oeuvre is *not* like searching for that needle in that place. It is *more* like searching for a needle without any idea of what a needle looks like. The interpreters ask, "Is this one?" Then, enter self-proclaimed experts—some armed with computer programs and corresponding mental illnesses—who interpret Dylan's words like Pentecostal deacons translate a tent revival's "speaking in tongues." To noninitiates, the translations are more than problematic. The results of such practices evolved into "Dylanology."

Somewhere, over behind a tree, the kid who warned Echo Helstrom about those large snakes is laughing his head off. Glissendorf is a great game—if you enjoy that sort of thing. So, sit back and marvel at our Glissendorf Master's finest moment. From *Bringing It All Back Home*, to *Highway 61 Revisited*, to *Dont Look Back*, to *Blonde On Blonde*, to the ultimate game of Glissendorf that is *Tarantula*, Zimmerman achieves his mission of rejecting the messiah-seeking branch of Bob Dylan's constituency by generating lyrics unlike any before them. In so doing, our rebellious Bob Zimmerman did more than meet the needs of his creative moment. He changed songwriting forever.

Bringing It All Back Home

During the BBC's *The Bob Dylan Story*, John Lennon offers his recollections of sitting around with Dylan, drinking, and listening to his American colleague's new music. Lennon recalls Dylan's insistence that he focus on the lyrics, but the late Beatle reports he was too engrossed with the record's sonic qualities to bother with the words. That "sound" moved Lennon, and that is all that mattered to him. There was something distinctive about that sound. I bet they were listening to *Bringing It All Back Home* or *Highway 61 Revisited*. Just as Dylan claims to "find" the words and images that populate his songs, the Newport Mod era applies that inventive strategy to the sonic platforms that support his lyrics. Sounds from here and aural tricks from there work with words from everywhere to create songs that no Western Union messenger could imagine, much less deliver. Dylan described that sound to *Playboy*'s Ron Rosenbaum:

It's that thin, that wild mercury sound. It's metallic and bright gold, with whatever that conjures up. That's my particular sound. . . . It's the sound of the street with the sunrays, the sun shining down at a particular time, on a particular type of building. A particular type of people walking on a particular type of street. It's an outdoor sound that drifts even into open windows that you can hear. The sound of bells and distant railroad trains and arguments in apartments and the clinking of silverware and knives and forks and beating with leather straps. It's all—it's all there. Just lack of a jackhammer, you know. . . . Yeah, no jackhammer sounds, no airplane sounds. All pretty natural sounds. It's water, you know, water trickling down a brook . . . it's the sound and the words. Words don't interfere with it. They—they—punctuate it. You know, they give it purpose. [pause] And all the ideas for my songs, all the influences, all come out of that. All the influences, all the feelings, all the ideas come from that. I'm not doing it to see how good I can sound, or how perfect the melody can be, or how intricate the details can be woven or how perfectly written something can be. I don't care about those things.

What a wonderful statement. So this is what Lennon heard: natural sounds filtered through the colors in Bob Dylan's mind. Those sounds and the writer's words have a complementary relationship. Together, they unlock the artist's raw passions, and it is those raw feelings—those colorful emotions—that he endeavors to record. Forget perfection. Forget everything but those thin, wild sounds. This is the artistic philosophy that guides the Newport Mod.

Clinton Heylin's chronology relates that the first installment of this era—*Bringing It All Back Home*—was recorded in three sessions (on January 13, 14, and 15, 1965) and that several songs required but one take. Those sessions initiated a whirlwind year for the new Dylan. After recording *Bringing*, he toured the United States and England, filmed his first movie, recorded his follow-up to *Bringing*, started an aesthetic war, responded to that situation in song, issued his sixth album (*Highway 61*), faced the enemy in Forest Hills (New York) and beyond, and concluded the year by ending his run of New York–based recordings. Dylan's 1961 may rival his 1965 in terms of the sheer number of important career events; however, the media attention generated in 1965 joined Dylan's response to those activities to create as volatile a year as any artist has ever endured.

Produced by Tom Wilson, *Bringing It All Back Home* (released on March 22) was originally divided into two distinct sides—one containing acoustic songs and the other with an electric band. Dylan changed the sequence, and the "electric" songs were interspersed throughout the album. The record features eleven tracks (running over forty-seven minutes) that fall into two orientations: organized and disorganized wordplay. Under those two master categories, we have four subdivisions: narrative impressionism involving positive responses to romantic relationships ("She Belongs To Me" and "Love Minus Zero/No Limit"), narrative impressionism featuring sermonic prescriptions ("Gates Of Eden" and "It's Alright, Ma [I'm Only Bleeding]"), wordplay with a point ("Maggie's Farm" [rebellion], "It's All Over Now, Baby Blue" [relational], "Mr. Tambourine Man" [escape], and "Bob Dylan's 115th Dream" [history lesson]), and wordplay without a point ("Subterranean Homesick Blues," "Outlaw Blues," and "On The Road Again"). Interesting hybrids appear such as the evolution of the auteur's trademark satire ("115th Dream") that synthesizes Dylan's "tall tale with a moral" tradition with the impressionism that dominates the other songs. "Bob Dylan's 115th Dream" is this record's lone narrative—and a delightful one it is. The love songs refer to the narrator's romantic interests and their special characteristics, and leave us to contemplate those traits. Nothing ever happens, however. The same holds for the impressionistic sermons that feature rich descriptions without any story development, although the recurring tag lines (often containing the song's title) add coherence to the experience (in *Chronicles*, Dylan refers to these closing lines as a "ghost chorus"). Finally, Dylan's wordplay flirts with specific points or drifts into repetitive, idiosyncratic imagery. Through it all, the contrast between metaphor and folly may involve a distinction without a difference. Robert Shelton captures the results perfectly in a *New York Times* review: These songs are "musical Rorschach tests" with a potentially vast distance between artistic intention and audience interpretation. Dylan's imagination was having its way (he fired the Western Union boys), and he invited his audience to join in the fun, get out of the way, or prepare to fight.

The impressionistic love songs are warm, accessible, and respectful—they just do not tell stories. They are also our closest link to Dylan's songwriting past and, therefore, provide a bridge to the new style of writing. One song uses the repetitive lyric schemes one associates with pop music ("She Belongs"), while the other departs from that approach ("Love Minus") in the manner of the new style. Both songs worship their subjects. The opening verse of "She Belongs" captures the song's rhythm and its impressionistic tone:

> She's got everything she needs,
> She's an artist, she don't look back.
> She's got everything she needs,
> She's an artist, she don't look back.
> She can take the dark out of the nighttime
> And paint the daytime black.

All of the song's five verses follow the same six-line strategy. An observation is stated, then repeated, and the stanza closes with a surreal image. The narrator reports how anyone would be proud to steal for her, that she always maintains her balance, that she wears foreign jewelry, and that she deserves praise. Once he relates these points and repeats them, he turns to more cryptic conclusions. For example, after you gladly steal for her, you'll find yourself on your knees "peeking through her keyhole"; after describing her Egyptian jewelry, he observes that she is a "hypnotist collector" and "You are a walking antique"; finally, after saluting her on Sunday and on her birthday, we're told to give her a "trumpet" for Halloween and a "drum" for Christmas. As you can see, nothing ever happens in the song. It merely praises this woman, repeats that point, and drifts into idiosyncrasy. Yet, there is no doubt about the message: The narrator adores his woman and her magical powers.

"Love Minus Zero" follows part of this strategy while omitting the repetition. Here the impressionistic descriptions appear in couplets that are piled upon one another—all of them in praise of the song's subject. The song's four verses (with eight lines each) detail the wonders of this goddess who is faithful, simple, loyal, and gentle. She cannot be bought. She tempers her opinions. She is, in a word, idyllic. The song's last two verses demonstrate this song's rhythm of expression:

> The cloak and dagger dangles,
> Madams light the candles.
> In ceremonies of the horsemen,
> Even the pawn must hold a grudge.
> Statues made of match sticks,
> Crumble into one another,
> My love winks, she does not bother,
> She knows too much to argue or to judge.

The bridge at midnight trembles,
The country doctor rambles,
Bankers' nieces seek perfection,
Expecting all the gifts that wise men bring.
The wind howls like a hammer,
The night blows cold and rainy,
My love she's like some raven
At my window with a broken wing.

The song floats from image to image for no apparent reason. There's no sign of any story, just enigmatic praise for the adored one. Cloaks and knives sit alongside women lighting candles, and vengeful chess pieces coexist with frail, wooden statues that this wonderful woman embraces without prejudice. Bridges tremble at specific times. Winds sound like hammers. The weather is daunting. How interesting that this idyllic woman turns out to be fragile—even injured—as she arrives at her lover's home, perhaps in need of convalescence. At times, these images seem to wander off on their own (e.g., the activities of the country physician and bankers' relatives), but the principal point returns: This is one fine woman. While the impressionism floats in and out of these two love songs, their central thesis is driven home either through repetition or through the clear, compelling lines that close the various verses.

To the extent that Dylan's characters praise their women through blends of concrete observation and surreal imagery, they leap off the symbolic deep end as well. Turning to the auteur's wordplay, we open with its more extreme version and the unrestrained folly that is "Subterranean Homesick Blues" and its two weak sisters, "Outlaw Blues" and "On The Road Again." "Outlaw" and "On The Road" use lyrical repetition in the manner of "She Belongs" either to open a verse ("Outlaw") or to close one ("On The Road"). After or before, the word games flow; some create fascinating images, and others make you scratch your head in wonder. But the prize in this symbolic sandbox is the album's opening song, the lyrical masterpiece that is "Subterranean Homesick Blues." Here, the music grabs you in the manner John Lennon mentioned on the BBC broadcast. It seems to whirl around in some circus–honky-tonk–barrelhouse fashion that provides the perfect platform for the symbolic folly that accompanies those sounds. The opening verse says it all:

Johnny's in the basement
Mixing up the medicine
I'm on the pavement
Thinking about the government
The man in the trench coat
Badge out, laid off
Says he's got a bad cough
Wants to get it paid off
Look out kid
It's somethin' you did
God knows when

But you're doin' it again
You better duck down the alley way
Lookin' for a new friend
The man in the coon-skin cap
In the big pen
Wants eleven dollar bills
You only got ten

This is the "Subterranean" rhythm: Images flow for eight or nine lines across the song's four verses, each verse pauses for the "Look out kid" transition, and back we go to the symbolic jaunt. The second verse opens with Maggie's dirty face, references to a drug bust, and the infamous warning "You don't need a weather man / To know which way the wind blows." The short lyric bursts that are the various lines continue with the final two stanzas. For instance, the third verse opens,

Get sick, get well
Hang around a ink well
Ring bell, hard to tell
If anything is goin' to sell
Try hard, get barred
Get back, write Braille
Get jailed, jump bail
Join the army, if you fail
Look out kid . . .

Obviously, the song discusses the Magna Carta and its potential to guarantee basic liberties for extraterrestrials. (Actually, that interpretation has more credibility than I initially realized.) The song is an aural circus. The music merrily bops along with lines that operate with varying degrees of success floating in and out of proceedings. Symbolically, a line here or there may grab you, but when taken in its totality, the song *is* a musical Rorschach test; make of it what you will. Have fun! But watch what you say; being a Glissendorf victim can be embarrassing.

Our other examples of free-flowing wordplay are less imaginative than "Subterranean." "Outlaw Blues" deploys a basic blues beat and corresponding guitar work to drive home its vacuous points (which vary from verse to verse). Each of the five stanzas consists of six lines with two opening lines that are repeated and are followed with a two-line tag that may or may not have anything to do with the opening sentiment. The first verse talks about stumbling into a lagoon and closes with the time and temperature. The second verse states an unwillingness to hang a "picture frame" and declares that while the narrator looks like "Robert Ford," he feels like "Jesse James." The third verse longs to travel to Australia for a change of scenery. The final verse talks of a nameless, dark-skinned woman from Jackson that the narrator loves, it seems, despite the color of her skin. Of the five verses, the fourth captures the rhythm in an exemplarily fashion:

I got my dark sunglasses,
I got for good luck my black tooth.
I got my dark sunglasses,
I'm carryin' for good luck my black tooth.
Don't ask me nothin' about nothin',
I just might tell you the truth.

The simple street-blues pacing rushes these lines along at a steady pace. The song sounds like something you'd hear a Memphis street musician bang out in an alley off of Beale Street. Notice how Dylan spices the song with references to his trademark sunglasses, pauses for the line about his lucky tooth (classic blues), and closes with a warning that would make Abe Zimmerman proud (remember the rule: Don't ask a question if you're not prepared to hear the answer). It could also be that Mr. Message Man is rebelling once more.

"On The Road" uses the narrative impressionistic technique we first observed in "Hard Rain," in which (in this case) six lines preface a concluding two-line statement that is introduced by a blast of harmonica. Once more, the street blues beat rushes the verses along in a toe-tapping fashion. The first verse is indicative of the entire song:

Well, I woke up in the morning
There's frogs inside my socks
Your mamma, she's a-hidin'
Inside the icebox
Your daddy walks in wearin'
A Napoleon Bonaparte mask
[harmonica break]
Then you ask why I don't live here
Honey, do you have to ask?

The folly continues across the song's five verses as the narrator plays with a monkey and gets his face scratched, notices that Santa Claus is in the fireplace, sees a well-dressed milkman, complains about his meal (hey, it sounds great: rice, seaweed, and a "dirty hot dog"), discusses her weird family, and describes "fist fights" in the kitchen that involve opinionated postal workers and house servants. When we embrace all these weird happenings, it appears the narrator is explaining why he's leaving this crazed place where parents live in appliances and wear masks, service workers over-dress and overtalk, extended family members act strangely, and violence abounds. The last two lines sum the scene well: "Then you ask why I don't live here / Honey, how come you don't move?" Consequently, he's "on the road again"—no doubt, before someone comes and burns the house down.

These songs establish the tone for the writing style that dominates the Newport Mod era. Crazy activities may be used to convey some equally weird point ("On The Road"). Discontinuous images may be packed together in a fast-paced, rhythmically continuous manner ("Outlaw"). Or circling circus sounds may be deployed to paint a surreal image that fondles a variety of symbolic toys ("Subterranean"). The images rotate between genius, madness, and gibberish in unpredictable rhythms. If one line doesn't move you, be patient—the next one might (or it might not). No one had ever seen songs like this before.

Four of *Bringing It All Back Home*'s tracks use this songwriting strategy in a more focused manner. While they romp around the auteur's symbolic playpen in haphazard ways, they also display an anchor that holds everything in its own context. Whether the track discusses social rebellion, relational decline, or escape, or plays with historical events, that subject provides a focus that is absent on "Subterranean" and its cohorts. We begin with Dylan's statement of vocational rebellion, "Maggie's Farm." Here the "Subterranean" sonic circus supports five verses containing eight lines each that close with that one line tag of defiance. The opening verse establishes the song's point:

> I ain't gonna work on Maggie's farm no more.
> No, I ain't gonna work on Maggie's farm no more.
> Well, I wake in the morning,
> Fold my hands and pray for rain.
> I got a head full of ideas
> That are drivin' me insane.
> It's a shame the way she makes me scrub the floor.
> I ain't gonna work on Maggie's farm no more.

Our narrator has obviously had enough of Maggie's action. From there, he denounces Maggie's brother, father, and mother by describing how her brother gives him money and then takes it away for frivolous reasons, how her father is physically abusive, and how her mother extols virtues that she personally ignores. The place is a mess, and the narrator has had enough. The final verse is telltale:

> I ain't gonna work on Maggie's farm no more.
> No, I ain't gonna work on Maggie's farm no more.
> Well, I try my best
> To be just like I am,
> But everybody wants you
> To be just like them.
> They sing while you slave and I just get bored.
> I ain't gonna work on Maggie's farm no more.

This impressionism is tame in comparison to "Hard Rain" and its account of bleeding hammers, deceased poets, and despondent clowns; however, just as those scenes embellish the dire consequences of a world gone wrong, these images convey the dastardly qualities of hypocritical employers. Now, my friends, should we go out on a limb and conclude that Mr. Dylan is discussing the music business? Is he talking about those disillusioned folkies who would love to silence his individualism and have their bidding done? I'll let you decide.

That interpretation is also available with our next example, "It's All Over Now, Baby Blue." The ending of some form of relationship is chronicled in this four-verse track that uses four lines to establish scenes of varying clarity before closing with the title in the tag line. Consider the opening verse:

> You must leave now, take what you need, you think will last.
> But whatever you wish to keep, you better grab it fast.
> Yonder stands your orphan with his gun,
> Crying like a fire in the sun.
> Look out the saints are comin' through
> And it's all over now, Baby Blue.

Clearly, it is time to move on. Grab what you have and run, we're told quite directly before an image of an armed orphan with raging tears is featured. The second verse encourages the target to round up his or her experiences since the sky is giving way, while the third verse describes how the carpet is being pulled out from under a loving relationship. This need to break free is driven home in the final stanza:

> Leave your stepping stones behind, something calls for you.
> Forget the dead you've left, they will not follow you.
> The vagabond who's rapping at your door
> Is standing in the clothes that you once wore.
> Strike another match, go start anew
> And it's all over now, Baby Blue.

Through images of disgruntled orphans, wandering gamblers, weird painters, sick sailors, "reindeer armies" (??), and wayward lovers, the narrator drives home his straightforward point: It is time to go. Interpreting Dylan's work from this era in literal fashions is risky business; however, his references to "stepping stones," deceased followers, and encroaching wanderers wearing the subject's used clothes are pointed. To suggest that the author is dismissing his past, embracing his present, and anticipating his future (a cleansing fire?) seems reasonable. It is, simply, time to escape the past and start over.

From an enigmatic refusal to work for oppressive employers and a cryptic declaration of independence, we move to a magical escape from *everything*, "Mr. Tambourine Man." Supposedly inspired by a trip to New Orleans (excuse the pun), "Mr. Tambourine Man" massages a cosmic wanderlust that delivers everybody from everything. Wonderful, psychedelic imagery is anchored by—are you ready?—a *chorus* that asks Mr. Tambourine Man to play music for a wide-awake, uninhibited patron who's itching to follow him wherever he may lead. The song offers the chorus, follows with a verse, and moves back to the chorus in a systematic manner. The plea for escape is evident in the second stanza:

> Take me on a trip upon your magic swirlin' ship,
> My senses have been stripped, my hands can't feel to grip,
> My toes too numb to step, wait only for my boot heels

To be wanderin'.
I'm ready to go anywhere, I'm ready for to fade
Into my own parade, cast your dancing spell my way,
I promise to go under it.

Not only does our narrator wish to escape, but he also pledges his loyalty to his bene-factor. He'll go anywhere through a selfless dedication that ensures his prosperity. Dylan's writing is impeccable, as the final verse reveals:

Then take me disappearin' through the smoke rings of my mind,
Down the foggy ruins of time, far past the frozen leaves,
The haunted, frightened trees, out to the windy beach,
Far from the twisted reach of crazy sorrow.
Yes, to dance beneath the diamond sky with one hand waving free,
Silhouetted by the sea, circled by the circus sands,
With all memory and fate driven deep beneath the waves,
Let me forget about today until tomorrow.

What a fantasy! The narrator begs for escape, an exodus that would deliver him danc-ing beneath the magical heavens, surrounded by nature's beauty. "People" are beside the point now. What matters here is liberation. The narrator seeks to rid himself of his past, free his mind, and enjoy the results within an inclusive natural setting that buries the past and delays the present. Fascinating.

While "Mr. Tambourine Man" is an older song (remember, a version was recorded during the *Another Side* session but not used), the impressionistic trilogy that is "Maggie," "Baby Blue," and "Tambourine" works in harmony to produce yet an-other installment of the "Restless Farewell"–"My Back Pages" theme. Maybe these songs are more of an urge than a systematic statement; nevertheless, there is a theme here. The narrator is not going to work for oppressive people who treat him badly, limit the scope of his thinking, or restrict his imagination. It is, instead, time to leave the original path behind, forget the musically dead, throw away the old uniform, and follow his muse—the enigmatic Mr. Tambourine Man.

Perhaps Dylan places all of this in its proper context with our last piece of im-pressionism with a moral, "Bob Dylan's 115th Dream." Using the "I Shall Be Free" method of casting famous characters in weird scenes that parody historical events, this song explores the discovery of the New World and the strange, mean-spirited people who populate what became known as "America." With eleven stanzas con-taining either twelve or thirteen lines each, the song is a musical marathon. Our nar-rator—a sailor on board Captain Arab's whaling ship—gazes through his spyglass and spots land. The ship scurries over and docks, the narrator names his discovery, and the captain aspires to build a fort and purchase land with beads. Unfortunately, a police officer arrests the crew for carrying harpoons and the land-grabbing ceases for the moment. Once the narrator escapes, his adventure intensifies. He joins a picket line, dines at a French restaurant, tries to secure bail for his imprisoned comrades (unsuccessfully), gets mugged for his trouble (a French girl's partner steals his boots), seeks help for his friends from an unfriendly local citizen and a funeral parlor director (to no avail), and concludes that he'll just flip a coin to decide whether he should help his friends or return to the ship. The ship wins, and he returns, takes a parking citation off of the mast, and identifies himself as "Captain Kidd" to a passing "coast-guard boat." The story ends with our narrator leaving Arab behind in the arms of a "whale" who was married to a local police officer before stumbling onto three ships cruising toward the harbor. He asks the captain's name (as he inquires why he doesn't "drive a truck"), the man identifies himself as "Columbus," and our narrator wishes him "good luck."

What fun. The song's playfulness is established at the outset, when Dylan's first lines are interrupted by a laughing Tom Wilson. Both men enjoy a good belly laugh before Wilson restarts the recording. The auteur insisted that the glitch not be deleted. It sets the tone for the fantastic tale that follows. It is all one big laugh. As I noted during the discussion of *Another Side*, these satires are delightful examples of Dylan's imaginative writing. Just as the "Talkin'" songs and "Motorpsycho" take news events or traditional jokes and recast them in crazy ways, this song toys with history, fondles some moral (there's a lot of greedy people in this New Land), and leaves us to laugh at the results. This musical hybrid synthesizes Dylan's controlling impressionism, his narrative skills, and his sarcastic sense of humor into a rollicking story form that is about to go dormant.

The wave of Dylan's songwriting future is on display through the two examples of sermonic impressionism that are "Gates Of Eden" and "It's Alright, Ma (I'm Only Bleeding)." Proof of the transitional qualities of the *Live 1964* recording is evident in the fact that Dylan performed these two songs that Halloween evening. Here the vivid, surreal imagery of "Mr. Tambourine Man" marries the dark, foreboding symbolism of "Hard Rain" to create sermonic accounts of the world around us. Just as "With God On Our Side" exposes the cheap rhetoric that provides the moral justification for any conceivable act, "Eden" and "It's Alright" roam similar symbolic playgrounds, exposing hypocrisy, denouncing elitism, and advocating a social awakening. There are no jokes in these songs. The symbolism is *anything* but playful. These are two powerful works of art.

"Gates Of Eden" consists of nine seven-line verses, with the last line of each stanza featuring a reference to "Eden." Typically, the respective verses make some point about truth, life's futility, equality, or materialism and follow that observation with a response from "Eden." The first three verses are cloudy, as the song seems to suggest that truth is lost (except in Eden), the world is lifeless (with no help emerging from Eden), and life is futile. It is, indeed, easy to overreach with these opening verses. The sermon pivots, however, with the fourth verse:

With a time-rusted compass blade
Aladdin and his lamp
Sits with Utopian hermit monks
Side saddle on the Golden Calf
And on their promises of paradise
You will not hear a laugh
All except inside the Gates of Eden

These references to false indicators or divinations (e.g., an old compass, a genie, idealistic prophets, or magical creatures) and their fairytale explanations of the afterlife are laughable inside the Gates of Eden. Thus, our preacher opens his sermon with four stanzas that characterize the sorry state of the world, point to the silliness of worldly explanations, and refer us to the epicenter of Truth, "Eden."

The following five stanzas do a "compare and contrast" treatment of worldly attitudes and Eden's response. The fifth verse speaks of secular roles (owners, royalty) and declares, "There are no kings inside the Gates of Eden." The sixth verse describes a "motorcycle black madonna," her "silver-studded phantom cause," and a "gray flannel dwarf" who cries "to wicked birds of prey" who "pick up" his "bread crumb sins" before announcing there is no "sin" in Eden. The seventh verse denounces materialism and philosophy, and proclaims that there is equality of possessions and ideas in Eden. The eighth verse reveals that there are no judgments in Eden, and the song's final verse features a personal story. There the narrator describes his lover awakening in the morning and sharing her dreams. He responds,

> With no attempts to shovel the glimpse
> Into the ditch of what each one means
> At times I think there are no words
> But these to tell what's true
> And there are no truths outside the Gates of Eden.

"Gates Of Eden" reveals why the world has gone wrong and, in so doing, reinforces Dylan's commentary in his liner notes and elsewhere. Echoing *Another Side*'s "Some Other Kinds Of Songs," and poem 3's repudiation of unholy masters who manipulate words to their advantage and poem 5's pronouncement that language is dictated by scenic conditions, this song reinforces what is becoming a long-standing metaphysical position. The world is a series of "scenes" that attract, retain, and manipulate their participants through clever—and occasionally, time-honored—words and stories that may have a very loose relationship to anything tangible. In fact, these "kingdoms of Experience" (according to verse 7) may propagate these views as a means of maintaining the status quo, insuring their supremacy in their particular "scene" (at least in *their* eyes), and, in turn, promoting their longevity. Like "Masters Of War" or "Only A Pawn," there is evil in the worldly house, and the landlords propagate lies that keep their tenants in line. So, Reverend Dylan tells us where to go if we want equality, perfection, justice, and Truth: the Garden of Eden. The sermon preaches against certain earthbound evils, identifies the false prophecies that support those conditions, and argues for the principles that grant admission to paradise.

Dylan's impressionism demonstrates his ability to use different songwriting tools to build a case. He could have turned to a tight "Hattie Carroll"–type narrative to issue his point, or, as we shall see in the moral period, he could have deployed a hymnlike structure to present his argument. Instead, his impressionism carried the sermon in its own idiosyncratic way. What is most evident here is that these matters are on the writer's mind. He says these things in all sorts of ways. The liner notes are crystal clear. His stories leave no doubt. And his impressionism massages the same notions. Dylan is responding to his experience with social movements (political or religious). He understands the arbitrary qualities of language and its power to create realities for strategic reasons. What is overwhelmingly clear is that our auteur *does not trust* those who engage in these practices. The former sloganeer understands slogans and warns his audience of their manipulative powers. Do we hear the voice of experience? Truth, honesty, equality, justice, and more are not of *this* world. People use those terms to justify worldly—not heavenly—acts. *Individuals* must, therefore, stand up against *institutional* or *societal* structures, address their potentially evil practices, and advocate a better way. Dylan reinforces this point in his next sermon as well.

"It's Alright, Ma (I'm Only Bleeding)" is one powerhouse piece of impressionism. It features fifteen verses of six to seven lines each, which are divided into five segments separated by five three-line choruses. It builds and builds and builds until it reaches a most predictable resolution. Again, it is *not* a story in that there is no plot progression or character development; instead, the five segments establish points that are tied to that section's chorus. It is, in a way, sort of a mental "D-Day" in that it enjoins a battle for intellectual, emotional, and spiritual freedom. Let us march through this extraordinary song and examine Dylan's distinctive songwriting technique.

Segment 1 presents a personal challenge. The first verse establishes life's futility. The second relates how life requires work (using the marvelous statement "he not busy being born / Is busy dying"). The third verse reinforces the futility of the opening stanza by adding a touch of humility to the scenario. Dylan sums this situation with his first chorus:

> So don't fear if you hear
> A foreign sound to your ear
> It's alright, Ma, I'm only sighing.

This sigh over life's demanding nature gives way to a three-verse segment that identifies the evil that creates these difficult situations. Dylan denounces bigotry, commercialism, and wicked institutions in verses 4, 5, and 6, respectively. He condemns those who hate by claiming the only thing worth hating is hate. He contends that by selling anything and everything, nothing is held "sacred." He questions what preachers preach and what teachers teach, and announces the limitations of social institutions (culminating in his famous line about how "even" U.S. presidents must bare their weaknesses). Once more, the chorus brings it all together:

> An' though the rules of the road have been lodged
> It's only people's games that you got to dodge
> And it's alright, Ma, I can make it.

(There is more than a little irony in a statement where the Glissendorf Master warns of people's *games*, isn't there?) Having established the challenge and its enemy, segment 3 decries the media that enslave audiences through delusions of grandeur (verse 7), that entice people to lose themselves in these calculating lies (verse 8), and that require people to rise up against that situation through their individuality. The point is compelling: Through your individualism, you may fight off the media manipulations that cause people to lose their identities and abide by false standards. Once you lose sight of that identity, you're a target for evil. Again, the chorus sums the situation:

> Although the masters make the rules
> For the wise men and the fools
> I got nothing, Ma, to live up to.

The writer reiterates his case with the next segment. He describes the angry prisoners entrapped by their realities (verse 10), the false idols that abound (verse 11), and the false promises that enslave people and restrict them. Simply, the establishment creates false standards and demands that everyone conform to them—or else. People become angry at, and jealous of, those trying to break free. People in "scenes" condemn those who are not. People want others to suffer life as they do. Here the chorus reaches the simple conclusion that "it's alright, Ma, if I can't please him." If independence is going to anger people, inspire jealously, or prompt criticism, so be it.

The song's final segment returns to the lies and misplaced pride that result from this sorry situation and closes with a statement of rebellion. The sermon condemns the lies that support it all, having a go at the infamous root of all evil: "money doesn't talk, it swears." The preacher denounces the pride that protects that which is indefensible and grants a sense of false security. Finally, the resolution is at hand. Reverend Dylan has had enough. He dismisses the "false gods." He rejects "pettiness." He frees himself of these restrictions and mocks their conceit before he concludes,

> And if my thought-dreams could be seen
> They'd probably put my head in a guillotine
> But it's alright, Ma, it's life, and life only.

Wow.

At this point in Bob Zimmerman's career—after all of the liner notes, songs, interviews, and commentaries—one of two things has happened. Either Zimmerman used Jack Fate to give lip service to the social movements that played a central role in Dylan's emergence, or Zimmerman actually went there and rejected it. That is, when he wrote those protest songs, he meant them. Then, when he peeked behind the curtain and realized that one person's evil manipulation is another person's just cause, he realized that *everybody* is a sloganeer and that all of the slogans were potentially bogus. To be part of a "scene," you must follow that scene's prescriptions for living. If you don't, expect that scene's hierarchy to admonish you—perhaps in hurtful ways. Words are the crux of the problem. Apparently, Mr. Message Man realized how words are used by all sides to create and sustain the realities that rally their respective troops. When he became a pawn in *that* game, he not only quit, but also took up arms against his oppressors. "It's Alright, Ma" is that man's sermon on the mount—complete with fishes and loaves lyrics. After announcing our personal challenge (to overcome life's futility through humility and perseverance), identifying why that challenge exists (bigotry, materialism, and untrustworthy institutions), drawing the terms of the battle (rejecting media-inspired delusions that cause people to lose touch with themselves), and reiterating what must be resisted (jealousy, false idols, and false promises), our sermonic poet denounces the prideful lies that support it all and promises to fight the status quo. He may dismiss his battle as a natural consequence of contemporary living, but he's obviously up for the fight.

Bringing It All Back Home does exactly that. Mr. Message Man proclaims that it may very well be that all of these social movements—the essence of politics and religion—build their respective houses on sand and that the *real* answer is to "bring it all back home" and build that house on the rock of individuality. The guy who warned people that they may be pawns in someone else's game took that message to heart. The guy who described how people justify any imaginable act by asserting that the action was God's will came to recognize both edges of that particular sword. The guy who not-so-subtly threatened people by writing that if you resist the changing times, you'll lose everything realized that when that ship comes in, the enemy will be hard to detect (as per John Brown's lament). Once that guy watched how easily the righteous became self-righteous, he rebelled against it all. On the surface, these poetic word games dance to their own rhythms and open themselves to myriad interpretations. However, once you pull back, take a breath, and consider this record in its totality, a compelling statement is issued through *Bringing It All Back Home*. Individuality is the key. Don't work for oppressive employers. Don't believe institutional pronouncements just because institutions pronounced them. Do more than believe in Eden: Bring Eden to Earth by rejecting evil where you find it—even if you find it in supposedly holy places. Yes, at times Dylan toys with these ideas ("115th Dream"). Sure, at times he dreams of esoteric escape ("Mr. Tambourine Man"). But when taken as a whole, Dylan dismisses his perceived oppressors ("Baby Blue"), acknowledges his guiding principles ("Eden"), and wages war on those who'll never step one foot inside the Gates of Eden ("It's Alright, Ma"). That this character will undergo a religious conversion later in life is not surprising.

Bringing It All Back Home's liner notes provide the icing for this symbolic cake. These notes aren't as detailed as in the previous editions; nevertheless, they complement the album in the now-traditional manner. These notes read like an excerpt from the writer's crazed diary. The story opens with the narrator watching a parade, issues a "pause" for a seemingly confessional statement, and concludes by returning to the opening scene. The account begins with our narrator minding his own business, probing his feelings (he feels like a blend of Sleepy John Estes, Jayne Mansfield, Humphrey Bogart, "Mortimer Snerd," "Murph the Surf," and more), and watching the parade. An "erotic hitchhiker" wearing a "Japanese blanket" interrupts his pleasure by inquiring if he recognized our narrator from a Mexican hootenanny. The narrator assures him that that's impossible, since he is a member of the Supremes. In response, the hitchhiker tears off the blanket and reveals that he is a "middle-aged druggist" running for district attorney. He screams at the narrator, claiming that he is the cause of "all them riots" occurring in Vietnam. If elected, he promises those around him, he will ensure that our narrator is "electrocuted publicly on the next fourth of July." Since everyone around the narrator held "blowtorches," he decides to leave. He goes home and writes "WHAAAT" on his "favorite wall." When his recording engineer suddenly arrives via a jet plane, he informs our narrator that he is there to retrieve "you and your latest works of art."

At this point, a "pause" is issued. The writer offers views on his songwriting that claim he has "given up at making any attempt at perfection," since the White House is full of people who have never visited the "Apollo Theater" and neglected to invite Allen Ginsberg to participate in their inauguration. The plot thickens at this point. He declares he would rather "model harmonica holders" than "discuss aztec anthropology / english literature. or history of the united nations." He continues, "i accept chaos. i am not sure whether it accepts me. i know there're some people terrified of the bomb. . . . experience teaches that silence terrifies people the most." He declares that "all souls have some superior t' deal with" and how "in the face of this," terms such as "responsibility," "security," or "success" are meaningless. He announces that he wouldn't want to be Bach, Mozart, Tolstoy, Joe Hill, Gertrude Stein, or James Dean, since those people are dead. He talks about drawing a picture to explain what's going on even though he admits that he doesn't understand anything. He notes that death is inevitable and that "no death has ever stopped the world." His poems, he claims, are "written in a rhythm of unpoetic distortion / divided by pierced ears, false eyelashes / subtracted by people constantly torturing each other." He defines a song as "anything" that is able to "walk by itself." He recognizes that people call him a songwriter. He defines a poem as a "naked person." He acknowledges that "some people" call him a "poet." The "pause" ends, and our narrator asks the recording engineer to help him load the wall onto the plane.

These notes foreshadow the *Tarantula* writing style with the opening scene. Crazy characters with shifting identities doing weird things are the norm in Dylan's long-anticipated "novel." After writing the songs for *Bringing*, Dylan ceased writing songs and concentrated on the *Tarantula* project for an extended period. In fact, when the film *Dont Look Back* shows Dylan writing away on a typewriter in his hotel, he is reportedly writing *Tarantula*. Hence, these liner notes fall in line with that type of exposition. However, once the notes "pause" and Dylan writes about songwriting, poetry, and poets, we seem to venture back in time to the writing style evidenced in "11 Outlined Epitaphs" or "Some Other Kinds Of Songs." While he plays with definitions of songs and poems, he once more massages his views about creating "perfection" and answering to "superiors." Yes. The man who will one day pen the song "Gotta Serve Somebody" was examining that thesis fifteen years before he addressed the issue in song. These were fertile times. *Bringing It All Back Home* demonstrates the extent to which the auteur is wrestling with ideas, events, people, and places. The man who claimed that the answers were blowing in the wind and later argued that the questions were as well now seems to acknowledge that *everything* is blowing in that wind.

The extent to which Dylan was in touch with these metaphysical positions that are beginning to dominate his writing is uncertain. He was merely twenty-four years old. He could very well be articulating urges that, in hindsight, become coherent when assembled. But coherent they are. They guy who carried posters learned how to write them and now distrusts posters and the people who make them. He now stands alone. His principal concern, it seems to me, would be his next move. He's denounced his oppressors and freed his art. What next? The answer to his dilemma is as old as time itself. It was time to make a movie.

Artistic transitions occur in a variety of ways. A critical painting, a pivotal writing, any pioneering work of art may signal a shift in an artist's creative direction for contemporary audiences as well as capture that turning point for posterity. What may first appear to be radical idiosyncrasy ultimately opens the door to a new way of doing things, and as a result, changes how artists go about their particular tasks. *Dont Look Back* records one of those historic moments when one style of art yields to another. This film says goodbye to the solo acoustic Bob Dylan and hello to the Newport Mod. With *Bringing It All Back Home* fresh on the shelves and the single "Subterranean Homesick Blues" hot on the airwaves, *Dont Look Back* offers the new Dylan retiring the old one. Mr. Message Man delivers his farewell message, receives his adoring audiences' applause, embraces his new role, and concludes with his "vanishing American" act (in Bob Neuwirth's words). The filmmaking is as daring as its subject, and the results offer compelling evidence regarding Bob Zimmerman's career.

The film presents Bob Dylan's spring 1965 tour of England and portrays the controlled mayhem associated with the celebrity's travels across Her Majesty's United Kingdom. It records the media relations, the constant movement, the public relations, the preshow tensions, the management negotiations, the on-the-road tomfoolery, the postshow social life, the fans' reactions, and more as they unfold during Dylan's historic tour. *Dont Look Back* is not a "concert film." It is a "direct cinema" account of what it was like to be on the road with Bob at this point in his career. As direct cinema—in which every effort is made to record an event without interference—the movie offers raw views of its subject matter. Never does Dylan address the camera. Everyone goes about their business without regard for staging, since the film involves one camera shooting under natural lighting with minimal sound. In fact, director D. A. Pennebaker reports the project could not have happened just five years earlier, since recent technological developments enabled the direct cinema strategy. Consequently, we're afforded a useful glimpse of the celebrity-singer-songwriter in action. Not stage action, mind you, but in the offstage activities that often overwhelm—or at least distract—artists in potentially debilitating ways.

The film features no sense of time or place. It cuts from location to location and scene to scene in its own way, or, as Pennebaker states in his postproduction commentary, the movie is a marriage of "avant-garde filmmaking and avant-garde songwriting." Director/photographer/sound engineer/editor Pennebaker named his film after the famous line by baseball great Satchel Paige and registered his thoughts about his work during the audio commentary that accompanies the movie's release on DVD (a special feature that allows you to view the movie with Pennebaker and Dylan's road manager Bob Neuwirth's comments dubbed over the action). There, he describes the film:

> I didn't want it to be a concert film because the music was really absorbing…it was new music that people had never heard before. And I thought if I start out and make this a film of musical performances it's not gonna be about anything else. I want people to think that they're seeing behind the music. That the music isn't why they're there. The music is why he's there and that they're seeing somebody who's responsible for

the music. So, I thought to do that by shooting every night and then—
pretty much at the last minute . . . till the song began, I would wait and
then I would shoot something that seemed to me, right for the minute . . .
where we were in the tour. So, what I shot kinda came out of our experiences through that day or so leading up to that concert. I only wanted
bits of it.

Hence, we see shot after shot of Dylan walking onstage and starting a song before
the film cuts to another activity or we cut from some event to the middle of a song.
This movie is not about the music.

Although the film cuts from scene to scene in unpredictable ways, it focuses on
six specific contexts: hotel rooms, encounters with journalists, encounters with fans,
transportation scenes, green room (back stage) activities, and snippets of performances. The hotel scenes involve postshow parties; members of the entourage re-
laxing, joking around, and reading newspaper accounts of Dylan's activities (clipping
them and building a collage on the room's wall); or Dylan talking with fans, guests,
journalists, or friends. The camera is merely another occupant in a crowded room
where people sing, write, argue, work, joke, and play. Confrontations occur with hotel
management. Rowdy guests have to be reprimanded. Journalistic questions are repeated and receive rote answers. Parties abound. Fans worship. Dylan is at the heart
of it all.

Dylan's sessions with journalists seem to grow in intensity, as the film opens
with amiable exchanges during a welcoming hotel press conference, then moves to a
friendly interview with a BBC radio producer, a playful encounter with a college
newspaper music critic, and an aggressive scene with a *Time* magazine reporter. Two
things emerge from these scenes: You gain a feel for the conflicting agendas associated with these activities (i.e., the artist-versus-reporter dynamic), and Dylan drives
home his points about protest songs, folksinging, and his art's direction. He makes
it clear, Clear, CLEAR that he does not consider himself to be a protest singer, that
he is not an advocate for any political cause, that he is not a folksinger, and that everybody makes too much out of his words—often taking idiosyncratic expressions as
mass declarations. There is no doubt that the auteur *used* this opportunity to register
his views on these subjects.

The scenes featuring fan activities are—without exception—playful. Cute English girls whistle at his hotel room from the street and are invited up to meet their
idol (Dylan is quite gracious with these young ladies). Fans stand in the rain awaiting
a glimpse of the celebrity. Fans crowd Dylan's car as he departs a venue (these "escape scenes" recur throughout the film), and, in one instance, a female fan has to be
pulled from atop the vehicle. Fans are also shown entering venues, greeting Dylan at
the airport or on the road, and in conversation with Dylan backstage after shows.
Never is there any acrimony, disrespect, or anything negative presented in scenes involving fans; instead, we see loving fans embracing their respectful hero.

The transportation and green room scenes present the chaotic nature of these
tours. Shots of Dylan and his entourage traveling by car (often with Dylan reading
newspaper reports of his activities) or train create a sense of constant motion and
eternal activity. One shot of Dylan sitting alone on a train conveys the tiresome qual-

ities of this tour-on-the-run experience. The green room scenes communicate the preshow jitters, last-minute preparations, and constant distractions associated with the final moments before a performer goes onstage. Several of the film's most compelling moments occur in this setting, as Dylan is shown surrounded by his entourage (you get the feeling the guy is rarely alone), dealing with journalists, welcoming visitors and dignitaries, or just pacing back and forth smoking cigarette after cigarette, nervously plucking his guitar and adjusting his harmonica holder.

Performance scenes are—with one exception—short and sweet. Usually, Dylan is shown walking onstage starting a song, and the movie cuts to backstage activities, cuts to an "escape scene," or changes topics completely. A closing collage of songs from the Royal Albert Hall show offers the most depth with regard to Dylan's performances as the scene dissolves between several songs. Still, even though we are allowed but a snippet of a song, we witness the reverence Dylan's audiences extended and the general intensity that surrounded the experience. There are neither screaming teenagers shouting between songs nor any distractions whatsoever. My, how things will change in less than a year!

A consistent cast of characters fills these scenes. At the forefront are Dylan, Neuwirth, and manager Albert Grossman, with Joan Baez appearing often in the film's first half. Cameraman Howard Alk appears in the background of several scenes, with a host of cameo appearances (e.g., Alan Price, Donovan, Marianne Faithfull, John Mayall, Tom Wilson, and Allen Ginsberg) rounding out various segments. Occupying much of the film's ninety-six minutes are hotel staff members, unnamed journalists, fans, stage crew personnel, partygoers, and tour professionals. These people come and go as the scenes march along and, once more, convey the constant motion that characterizes a tour production of this magnitude.

An overview of the various scenes communicates the film's—and therefore the tour's—hectic pacing. The movie opens with a slight twist and the musical world's first "music video." Working to the tune "Subterranean Homesick Blues," the video features Dylan flipping through a large series of placards, with words, phrases, and ideas from the song appearing as they occur in the recording. Shot in a London alley, Dylan stands to the right with his cards while Allen Ginsberg and Neuwirth talk over to the far left. Dylan merely flips through the cards with a detached, perhaps occasionally disdainful, look on his face until the song ends; he holds a "What?" sign and tosses it down as he walks off, with Ginsberg and Neuwirth doing the same. Everyone goes in different directions. From there, we cut to our first green room shot of Dylan pacing before appearing onstage (he is searching for a missing walking cane). He walks out onto the stage, and the rollercoaster film begins with credits.

Scene 1 offers Team Dylan's arrival in London. The group parades through the airport with Neuwirth and Dylan singing "London Bridge" as fans and airport officials look and talk. Next, we enter a hotel press conference where Dylan playfully answers what appear to be the usual questions. When asked about the language in his songs, he kindly replies that people have their own definitions of those terms. A friendly female journalist inquires if Dylan reads the Bible; they talk. From here, a series of hotel scenes unfold: A photographer interacts with Baez, Dylan does more interviews, Dylan reads the paper and discovers that he smokes eighty cigarettes a day (to which he replies that he's happy he's not himself), former Animals pianist

Alan Price discusses the Donovan phenomenon, and the visual collage closes with party scenes. After a quick shot of Dylan and Neuwirth acting up at a reception (snapping their fingers in sarcastic rhythm to a lounge music act), we return to the hotel and a BBC radio interview (Dylan is very polite). When the reporter inquires how Dylan's career started, we're taken to the only piece of film not shot by the Pennebaker crew, Ed Emshwiller's footage of young Dylan singing "Only A Pawn In Their Game" at a Mississippi voter registration event. As the Mississippi gathering applauds the performance, the sound blends into an English audience welcoming Dylan onstage and the beginning of "The Times They Are A-Changin'." A stream of events follows: A reporter files his account of the show; another conversation about words and definitions takes place; an intense argument between Grossman and hotel management occurs (Grossman demonstrates why he is nicknamed "the Bear"); a car scene with Baez, Dylan, and a man reading a concert review follows; the scene with the whistling English girls unfolds; another performance snippet yields to another road trip scene that turns into another performance fragment that is followed by another conversation about writing and audiences that segues into another escape scene. The film pauses for a rather long hotel scene featuring Dylan pounding away on his typewriter as Baez sings and Faithfull observes (that scene ends with everyone singing Hank Williams songs). Tomfoolery occupies the following scenes as Dylan, Neuwirth, and Baez joke around, Baez sings during another road trip, and Neuwirth offers his fine imitation of Lyndon Johnson (!).

Here the movie pauses for a long scene featuring Grossman and music entrepreneur Tito Burns negotiating with the BBC and other venues over appearances and their corresponding fees. Suddenly, we're taken to a street scene and Dylan standing before a music instrument store window admiring the various electric guitars on display (hint, hint). After a brief shot of Dylan composing on piano with producer Tom Wilson listening and a shot of fans on the street awaiting Dylan's arrival, we witness a long green room conversation between Dylan and a college "science student" who also serves as his school paper's music critic. Dylan is sarcastically playful with the intense young Englishman, who fears his hosts are disrespectful and unappreciative. How interesting that we see this exchange just prior to Dylan receiving a local political official's wife and her invitation to visit her mansion on their next trip. Dylan is totally respectful of the woman and most gracious to her and her three sons (two of whom have the same name!). We return to the green room, to another performance fragment, to another transportation shot (this time, on a train), to a sound check, to yet another escape scene.

Suddenly, we're exposed to Bob Dylan's anger as he goes after his hotel room guests for throwing a glass out of a window onto a limousine parked below. He is furious. A fight nearly breaks out before the drunks and their angry host settle down and enjoy songs by Donovan and Dylan, respectively. More hotel, travel, and sound check shots appear before yet another interview occurs. This time, a *Time* magazine reporter is treated to a Dylan tirade on journalism (he is being used), his music's meaning, the power of language (words begin with upper and lower cases, you know), his musical style, and, after he calms down, a comparative musical argument (Dylan relates that he sings as well as Caruso). This is quite a scene. The reporter is clearly taken aback but remains calm. He cannot get a word in, as Dylan is on *fire* about these topics and how journalists misrepresent him. It is as if Dylan has simply had enough of this line of questioning and uses this encounter to vent.

The movie closes with a final green room scene, the collage of Royal Albert performances, one last escape scene, and closing comments from another backseat. Something is different this time, however. The tour is over. Grossman is obviously relaxed. Dylan reflects on his experience. And Team Dylan appears to unwind as the tour ends while Neuwirth's "vanishing American" act unfolds. When Grossman informs Dylan that the British press has labeled him an anarchist since he offers no solutions in his songs, the auteur sits back, lights a cigarette, and ponders this new label. He concludes, that the label is unattractive. With Neuwirth singing "It's All Over Now, Baby Blue" in the background, the film ends.

In his commentary on the film, road manager Bob Neuwirth describes the movie as an account of Dylan's "last acoustic tour" in which he says "goodbye to these arrangements of those songs." I agree, but with an additional point. This movie captures a moment. It documents a specific point in time in a major artist's career in which he dismisses one approach to his profession and embraces another. Along with the tour madness and its constant motion, the film relates Dylan's stance on his music's style (he is *not* a folksinger), his songs' meanings (those words have varying definitions—big and little letters, you know), his attitude toward his audience (telling one group that he doesn't care if people listen to him or not), and his views on the journalistic process (he is used by people he does not need). Though the film rotates between its six contexts in an uneven but steady manner, it reveals Dylan to be a clever, sarcastic young man with manners. The scenes with the English girls and the political official's wife and sons feature a kind, ingratiating celebrity respectful of his visitors. The hotel fiasco with the drunks throwing glasses from windows reveals a responsible character unwilling to endanger innocents; his actions appear instinctive and genuine. So, we have blends of personal characteristics, professional orientations, and tour madness. Pennebaker's strategy worked. Dylan posed for the cameras as he posed for everyone around him all the time. The single, unlit camera was just another audience member, and Dylan played to them all.

Pennebaker's commentary on the DVD release indicates the challenges he encountered in the film's editing and printing stages. Sitting here in a new millennium, it's difficult to fathom how unique this film was in its time. Concert films or celebrity-based nonsense movies (primarily, Elvis Presley films) were the norm, and this sort of offstage tour documentary was more than a little bit fresh. Upon his initial screening Dylan was hesitant, announcing that he would screen the film again and make a specific list of the changes he felt were necessary. When he attended the subsequent screening, Pennebaker tells us, he came armed with a large yellow pad on which to lodge his suggestions. After seeing the film a second time, he stood and displayed his observations. The pad was blank. The movie was approved and, therefore, complete.

Dont Look Back does so many things. It advances the direct cinema strategy in a positive way. It conveys the celebrity madness that accompanied mid-1960s concert tours. It demonstrates the artistic power of the lone performer onstage before large, responsive audiences. It communicates the impact of Bob Dylan's art, literally, around the world. It foreshadows the artist-journalist tensions that will intensify as the music press expands. What was once welcomed (media exposure) is now dreaded (media convolutions). It offers a sense of what Bob Dylan endured personally as he was rushed from place to place by a large entourage surrounded by fans, officials, media, and professional sycophants. I think more than anything it gives our evolving auteur a platform from which to announce his stances on his work. All of the talk about language and messages along with the antifolksinger comments and the electric guitar window-shopping scene communicate a clear, precise message that audiences will absorb in May 1967. Perhaps it was too little, too late.

Dylan returned from the UK and turned to his next album project. On June 15 and 16 he recorded his last track with producer Tom Wilson at Columbia's Studio A in New York. Wilson exited with a bang as Dylan, Mike Bloomfield (guitar), Paul Griffin (keyboards), Al Kooper (organ), Russ Savakus (bass), and Bobby Gregg (drums) recorded a song that many consider—and I'm watching my hyperbole here—to be the greatest rock song ever recorded, "Like A Rolling Stone." Rookie organ player Kooper claims the song was a one-take wonder in which Dylan asserted his ear's supremacy by turning up the organ lines (even though Kooper says he had never before played that instrument) and declaring the result to be a final product. The session charts tell another story (Clinton Heylin's records indicate there were around a dozen takes). Bob Johnston assumes the producer's chair with the July 29 sessions. Sessions on July 30, August 2, and August 4 rendered the recording the world knows as *Highway 61 Revisited*. But history takes a little turn before the July 29 sessions, and we must spend a moment with the madness that was the 1965 Newport Folk Festival.

The Legend of Newport is a strange one. The folk music fans from this era somehow missed what their hero was wearing, what he said, or anything other than their own hopes, desires, and perceived needs. I mean, *Bringing It Back Home* was released in *March*. The "Subterranean" single had been out for months. Dylan and his bandmates Bloomfield, Kooper, Barry Goldberg (piano), Jerome Arnold (bass), and Sam Lay (drums) assembled on Saturday and rehearsed all night at a Newport home (with people present). There was a sound check. The instruments were set up onstage (from an earlier performance by the Paul Butterfield Blues Band). How could anybody be surprised when Dylan took the stage that Sunday evening with an electric band? Did they bother with his new record? Did they listen to the radio?

The legend reports that Dylan was secretive about his plans. Of course he was! Remember how Bobby Zimmerman insisted that his band keep quiet their plans in order to surprise the audience? Dylan kept *everything* quiet. It was his nature, it seems. There was, however, compelling evidence of what was about to transpire. The sound check that Sunday may not have been typical, but Dylan was not onstage by himself with his guitar and harmonica holder. The Pete Seeger work clothes were nowhere in sight. He was dressed like the Newport Mod that he now was. From my examination of the biographers' reporting, there was *no evidence whatsoever to suggest that Dylan was going to perform a solo acoustic set*. NONE. Nevertheless, what unfolded was a scene for the ages.

When the Dylan Gang ran through "Maggie's Farm," "Rolling Stone," and "Phantom Engineer" (soon to evolve into "It Takes A Lot To Laugh, It Takes A Train To Cry"), legend has it that all hell broke loose. Again, reports vary. There are recordings available that yield inconclusive evidence. The soundboard recording indicates the band did a fine job, ragged at points but steady throughout the brief set (you can hear Dylan say, "Let's get outta here," after the final song). Nevertheless, can you imagine the shock of watching Pete Seeger attempting to sever the power cord with an axe? (That's one legend.) Newport 1965 must have been a weird experience. Can you imagine Albert Grossman wrestling with musicologist Alan Lomax in a fistfight over one of Grossman's acts? (That occurred earlier in the festival.) That was Newport. During the BBC's *The Bob Dylan Story*, stage manager Joe Boyd reports that Dylan's electric sound wasn't loud by contemporary standards, but it was ear-splitting by Newport 1965 standards. Some sources indicate that many in the audience were yelling to adjust the sound mix—not booing the performance. Other sources claim the audience *was* booing the performance and insisting that Dylan play folk music. As *Rolling Stone* reporter Joe Levy notes in *Biography*'s account of Dylan's career, an "aesthetic riot" broke out. At a *folk festival*, no less!

The Gang left the stage after the third number, and reportedly, Johnny Cash and Peter Yarrow convinced Dylan to return for a solo acoustic set. He did. After running through "It's All Over Now, Baby Blue" and "Mr. Tambourine Man," Dylan left the Newport stage, not to return for thirty-seven years (and when he returned in 2002, he performed wearing a fake beard and wig). I'm unsure how Dylan responded to all of this. In *Behind the Shades*, Clinton Heylin cites Jonathan Taplin's claim that Dylan was crying before he returned for the acoustic songs. The soundboard recording offers no evidence to support this; in fact, it offers proof to the contrary. For example, Dylan sounds relaxed as he asks for a harmonica before "Tambourine." He graciously accepts the audience's raucous applause at the close of his two-song encore. Still, Heylin quotes Maria Muldaur's recollection that Dylan was despondent afterward and responded to her invitation to dance with "I would, but my hands are on fire." Michael Bloomfield reports in Heylin's biography that Dylan "looked real shook up" after the show, but was his old self the following evening. In any event, the opening shots of that aesthetic war were fired that Sunday evening in July 1965. Things would get much worse before it all crashed in the summer of 1966.

I must say that I cannot imagine Dylan crying or in any way being upset about the events of July 25, 1965. If you can stand before a jeering and booing crowd when you are fifteen years old—as Bob Zimmerman did at the St. Louis County Fair—and walk confidently away from *that*, I doubt that a bunch of people that you do not even like are going to bother you when you are the ripe old age of twenty-four. Remember, in *Dont Look Back* Dylan is shown talking to an English band about how he does not care if his audience listens or not. Dylan's relationship with his audience has always been one of mutual coexistence—they may be dependent on him, but he is in no way reliant upon them. As we shall observe in the concluding chapter, the auteur writes and performs for an audience of one: himself. So, I conclude that the mischievous Glissendorf Master smelled the blood of a fine game brewing. But first, as Bruce Springsteen is fond of saying, the songwriter always gets the last shot.

Well, maybe not the *last* shot, but when Dylan returned to Studio A on July 29, he came armed with his response to the Newport craziness. His first recording session with new producer Johnston yielded three finished tracks; two would appear on the next album, and one was released as a single (issued that September). The single followed the path blazed by "Rolling Stone" as it quickly shot into the Top 10. Its opening lines left little doubt about this particular "message." "Positively 4th Street" starts with these words:

> You got a lotta nerve
> To say you are my friend
> When I was down
> You just stood there grinning

From there, Dylan uses twelve four-line verses to rant against those who claim they want to offer a "helping hand" but in reality just want to be on the winning side (verse 2), those who claim he disappointed them but fail to show injury (verse 3), and those who claim to have lost faith but in reality "had no faith to lose" (verse 4). Next Dylan communicates that he understands the game since he used to affiliate with that scene. He denounces their hypocrisy and acknowledges how they wish him harm. When he describes their disgruntled lives in verse 10, he proclaims that it is just not *his* problem. Dylan closes with two telltale verses:

> I wish that for just one time
> You could stand inside my shoes
> And just for that one moment
> I could be you
>
> Yes, I wish that for just one time
> You could stand inside my shoes
> You'd know what a drag it is
> To see you

That is "Positively 4th Street" and the auteur's response to the controversy surrounding his change in musical instruments. The writing is clear, direct, and without mystery. By using the Village address (Dylan lived on 4th Street), he focused his attack. By stating his understanding of that "crowd," he established both his previous affiliation and his departure. By recognizing their unhappiness with their lives, he declared his lack of interest and his complete disregard. And the concluding verses wrap up this "kiss-off" in a compelling, sneering fashion. Yes, I wish you could be me and realize the disappointment that accompanies seeing you. Our aesthetic war just escalated, don't you think?

While those attending the August 28 Forest Hills Music Festival were yet to hear the "Positively 4th Street" response to Newport, they were most certainly aware of the previous month's events. Dylan announced that there would be an electric set at the Forest Hills show, and the day before the event he told the *New York Times*, "It's all music: no more, no less . . . I know in my own mind what I'm doing. If anyone has imagination, he'll know what I'm doing. If they can't understand my songs they're missing something. If they can't understand green clocks, wet chairs, purple lamps or hostile statues, they're missing something, too." The battle lines were drawn. The guy who had the power yanked on him during a high school talent show was prepared to take on his so-called audience.

Dylan opened the Forest Hills show with acoustic numbers such as "She Belongs To Me," "To Ramona," "Gates Of Eden," and the debut of his powerful new song, "Desolation Row." After a thorough acoustic set and an intermission, Dylan returned with Kooper, Harvey Brooks (bass), Robbie Robertson (guitar), and Levon Helm (drums). War ensued. People called Dylan a "scum bag" (according to Robert Shelton's newspaper report), some threw fruit, and one audience member climbed onstage and knocked Al Kooper off of his stool. Dylan instructed the band to repeat the instrumental opening to the new "Ballad Of A Thin Man" for some five minutes, and that seemed to calm the crowd. When the show reached "Rolling Stone," Shelton maintains the audience sang along. What an evening.

Robertson and Helm were members of a Canadian band, the Hawks (so named for their role as singer Ronnie Hawkins's backing band). John Hammond Jr. used several members of the Hawks in a 1965 recording session, and, eventually, the band was signed to accompany Dylan on a world tour. Joining Robertson and Helm were Rick Danko (bass), Garth Hudson (organ), and Richard Manuel (piano). Arkansas native Levon Helm and his Canadian colleagues earned quite a reputation during their extended stay in Toronto supporting Hawkins's act. Once the band broke from Hawkins, moved to the east coast, and joined Dylan, the Hawks—later to be known as The Band—experienced a career change like no other in popular music history. The booing phenomenon died out on the east coast after Forest Hills, and a brief stay on the west coast saw nothing but appreciative audiences. Armed with the August 30 release of *Highway 61*, Dylan and his new backing band set off for a world tour that would make *Dont Look Back* seem tame by comparison. But first, we must examine the record named after one of the musical world's most famous roadways and the sonic adventure that Dylan, Bob Johnston, and the studio musicians assembled that crazed summer of 1965.

Highway 61 Revisited

Further proof that the Newport/Forest Hills experiences *inspired* Bob Dylan far more than they distracted, disturbed, or disillusioned him appears in the oeuvre's sixth album, *Highway 61 Revisited*. Released on August 30, 1965, and produced by Bob Johnston (with the exception of the opening track, Tom Wilson's "Like A Rolling Stone") the nine-track (running over fifty-one minutes) entry is a sonic masterpiece. Here the world's greatest wordsmith places his language in the backseat of this musical vehicle that is piloted by what the auteur called his "thin wild mercury sound." Foreshadowing 2001's *Love And Theft*, each track follows its own sonic strategy. The flamingo feel of "Desolation Row" complements the honky-tonk playfulness of "Tombstone Blues" and "From A Buick 6." The pondering circus hymn "Ballad Of A Thin Man" juxtaposes the rocking revelry of the title cut. It is all one big laugh. Dylan's harmonica never sounded better. His voice and harmonica provide lead sounds for the blues-based rhythms that are accented by churchy organs and barrelhouse pianos. The supporting musicians turn in outstanding performances. The roster differs between sources: Mike Bloomfield (guitar), Paul Griffin (keyboards), Al Kooper (keyboards), Russ Savakus (bass), Bobby Gregg (drums), Harvey Goldstein (bass; also listed as Harvey Brooks in Heylin's account), Sam Lay (drums; omitted from the liner notes listing), Frank Owens (piano), and Charlie McCoy (guitar). What a party.

This record is *designed* to make you crazy. The only way any of this makes any sense is if it is in some sort of code. However, each song features a sonic strategy that suggests meaning. Once you hear the opening piano of "Thin Man," you know there is something to this. As the guitar opens "Desolation Row," you can feel the story coming. But it is not there. Hey, what could be crazier than a messenger (the sound) without any message? These songs are, my friends, the quintessential examples of the "musical Rorschach test" strategy. The Dylan of *Dont Look Back* (with all of those comments about language and meaning) throws the dictionary out the window and destroys all the basic rules of language through songs that frolic about in their *musical*—not *symbolic*—sandboxes. Just listen: Someone is laughing in the background. Our Glissendorf Master is on top of his game.

The album is neatly divided into two parts: four pieces of narrative impressionism and five songs of unrestrained wordplay. The four impressionistic tracks explore two reliable topics, relationships ("Like A Rolling Stone," "It Takes A Lot To Laugh, It Takes A Train To Cry," and "From A Buick 6") and society ("Highway 61 Revisited"). From the portrayal of "Highway 61" as a harbinger of evil (home to murder, theft, and intrigue), to the celebration over the projected misfortunes of another person ("Rolling Stone"), to a character's cloudy warnings to his baby ("It Takes A Lot"), to a character's celebration of his girlfriend's heroic qualities ("Buick 6"), these songs establish loose storytelling contexts for a succession of images of varying clarity. The album's centerpiece is its five songs of wordplay: "Tombstone Blues," "Ballad Of A Thin Man," "Queen Jane Approximately," "Just Like Tom Thumb's Blues," and "Desolation Row." These songs range from enigmatic descriptions of people and places ("Tom Thumb's Blues") to organized chaos ("Desolation Row"). Any structure evident within these songs is musical, not narrative. Each track is its own universe.

We begin with the relational trilogy that is "Rolling Stone," "It Takes A Lot," and "Buick 6." This three-song set touches all of the bases as "Stone" projects the negative, "Buick" projects the positive, and "It Takes" offers mixed views on its subject. "Rolling Stone" contains four nine-line verses with a six-line chorus separating the respective stanzas. The sound is magical. The organ floats over a smooth rhythm section in a hymnlike manner. The piano dances in the background as Dylan's vocals bark out his case and his harmonica punctuates the experience. The song attacks a former insider who is now on the outs. Whether this is a former lover, friend, colleague, or gardener is *never* revealed. The target could be the folk movement, Joan Baez, or Lyndon Johnson. The evidence suggests that the song's target is a woman, since the first verse refers to the subject as "doll," the second verse makes reference to "Miss Lonely," and the fourth verse calls her "babe." But that could be misleading; Dylan often deploys slang or personal codes as camouflaging devices. Or maybe the song is simply words piled on top of one another via a loose framework. In all cases, the song needles its subject in a relentless fashion.

"Rolling Stone" opens with comments about the old days and the song target's attitudes toward the people in her social group. She was once on top of her game, carefree (as she tossed money to street people), and amused by the people around her. Apparently, she was warned that her luck may one day change. When it did, she found herself humbled by the experience and coping with her pride as she struggles for her "next meal" (this could be *anything*). Dylan drives home his point in the chorus:

> How does it feel
> How does it feel
> To be without a home
> Like a complete unknown
> Like a rolling stone?

(Subsequent choruses replace "To be without a home" with "To be on your own" and add the line "With no direction home" afterward.) Next, we're told that "Miss Lonely" attended the "finest school" but that education failed to prepare her for a life on the "street." Things she's never endured before are now confronting her, and the narrator loves it. He constantly attacks through metaphors that are difficult to unpack—if they are metaphors at all. He refers to a "mystery tramp" and some sort of "deal" that requires Miss Lonely to "compromise." He describes how unhappy circus performers entertained her in some way (very cloudy here) and her irresponsible response. He refers to her failed relationship with a thieving "diplomat" on a motorcycle with a cat on his shoulder. To be sure, these lines feature attacks, yet the nature of the verbal assault is evasive. Mystery tramps and diplomats with pets prompt compromises and disappointment in cryptic ways. The song is a lyrical game, and only the narrator's tone offers any hint as to what's unfolding. The final stanza demonstrates the song's style:

> Princess on the steeple and all the pretty people
> They're drinkin', thinkin' that they got it made
> Exchanging all kinds of precious gifts and things
> But you'd better lift your diamond ring, you'd better pawn it babe
> You used to be so amused
> At Napoleon in rags and the language that he used
> Go to him now, he calls you, you can't refuse
> When you got nothing, you got nothing to lose
> You're invisible now, you got no secrets to conceal.

Do with this what you will. The song's sonic qualities are its strength. The organ-piano interplay is stunning. Moreover, Dylan's voice is commanding, although his language is more than evasive. You *know* he's attacking someone or something, but his references to objects/people like Napoleon and an unnamed princess are private matters. His sermonic closing comments about her transparent independence are equally evasive. Considering this is the Archbishop of Anarchy, travel with caution.

"It Takes A Lot to Laugh, It Takes A Train to Cry" is a rolling blues tune that takes us to the Delta on a moonlit night. Another smooth rhythm section provides a platform for a countrified piano, Dylan's honky-tonk vocals, and his sterling harmonica. Little wonder that the record's liner notes refer to these tracks not as songs, but as "exercises in tonal breath control." The harmonica is the lead instrument here. Those sounds are complemented by Dylan's voice, not his *words* (more tonal breath control). The song features Dylan's most commonly used song structure: three eight-line verses. The first verse relates that the narrator rides an uneventful "mailtrain," that he was up the entire night leaning in his window, and his belief that if he dies "on top of the hill" and fails to "make it," he realizes that his "baby" will survive. The second verse features more train imagery as the narrator praises the sights (the moon shining through the forest, the sun setting over the ocean) and his beautiful woman who is "comin' after" him. With "All I Really Want To Do" echoing in the background, the third verse closes our beer joint blues in this fashion:

> Now the wintertime is coming,
> The windows are filled with frost.
> I went to tell everybody,
> But I could not get across.
> Well, I wanna be your lover, baby,
> I don't wanna be your boss.
> Don't say I never warned you
> When your train gets lost.

Our train metaphor is clearly the key to unlocking this track. He loves his baby, but something's amiss. He's qualifying the relationship for some reason before closing with his warning. From any other writer, one would shrug this off as a typical blues tune with vacuous references to trains, moons, and the seasons and enjoy the sounds of the Delta. But this is Dylan, so we think a bit harder, don't we?

We can stop thinking with "Buick 6" and that honky-tonk sound that characterizes so much of this album. "Buick" swings, that is for sure, but it says precious little. The song's four four-line verses seem to concentrate more on sonic rhythm than lyrical clarity. The first verse demonstrates my point:

> I got this graveyard woman, you know she keeps my kid
> But my soulful mamma, you know she keeps me hid
> She's a junkyard angel and she always gives me bread
> Well, if I go down dyin', you know she bound to put a blanket on my bed.

Each stanza closes with that last line, with the previous three lines describing some scene or characteristic that places the woman in a heroic light. The second verse offers a cryptic account of a "pipeline" breaking; the narrator stranded on a bridge, on a highway, and by the "water's edge"; and his rescue. The third verse praises the woman since her silence makes for a calm environment, her manner of walking is effortless, and she keeps her shotgun loaded. After a substantial harmonica break, Dylan closes in this manner:

> Well, you know I need a steam shovel mama to keep away the dead
> I need a dump truck mama to unload my head

She brings me everything and more, and just like I said
Well, if I go down dyin', you know she bound to put a blanket on my bed.

The bait has been placed on the hook. Watch yourself! If you want to characterize those old folkies as the "dead" or take the line about shedding his mental burdens as indicating something, go ahead. Whatever those metaphors refer to, this is one fine woman. She's armed. She's willing. She's capable. She also knows how to use a blanket. This is surely a song of relational praise clouded by god knows what. In any event, the band rocks!

Turning to our final piece of narrative impressionism and the cryptic moralizing of the title cut, we gain additional proof of the sonic majesty that dominates this recording. This song is an aural party. That crazy whistle makes you look for a silent film character waddling across your yard twirling a cane. The rhythm section drives and drives and drives as the keyboards cut loose at the close of the fifth line of the five seven-line stanzas. If there is a devil and it has a musical preference, this is it! The song dances with itself. "Highway 61 Revisited" is an amazing piece of music.

Complementing that sound are some of Dylan's finest lyrics. His imagery massages thoughts about murder, commercialism, family relations, and war. All I can say is that Highway 61 is an intriguing place. The first verse tosses around some famous names in a historical context:

Oh God said to Abraham, "Kill me a son"
Abe says, "Man, you must be puttin' me on"
God say, "No." Abe say, "What?"
God say, "You can do what you want Abe, but
The next time you see me comin' you better run"
Well Abe says, "Where do you want this killin' done?"
God says, "Out on Highway 61."

What fun. The language is clear; the story is direct. Next we have "Georgia Sam," who unfortunately has injured his nose and has no clothes. He seeks relief from "Howard," who uses his gun to point him in the direction of Highway 61. Having cleared that up, the third verse offers a conversation between "Mack the Finger" and "Louie the King." Poor Mack has invested poorly and finds himself with a bunch of colored shoestrings and a "thousand telephones that don't ring." Although I'd love one of those phones, Mack seeks advice as to where he might unload this unwanted merchandise. Louie ponders the situation and suggests that Highway 61 might be a viable option. Our fourth verse is a tad more complicated and requires that I offer it in its entirety:

Now the fifth daughter on the twelfth night
Told the first father that things weren't right
My complexion she said is much too white
He said come here and step into the light he says hmm you're right
Let me tell the second mother this has been done
But the second mother was with the seventh son
And they were both out on Highway 61.

Life can be so complicated. The fourth verse is certainly the photo negative of the first. One is crystal clear; the other is a game. This rollicking number closes where all good songs should: with a world war. It seems as though a homeless gambler seeks to relieve his boredom by starting a world war. He approaches a promoter who is without experience in such matters; nonetheless, he proposes a solution: Build a grandstand along Highway 61 and do it there. Highway 61 is one busy road! God wants a murder to take place there. Georgia Sam sees it as a place to convalesce. The road is an active marketplace populated by a variety of relatives. They even stage wars there. Yes, Highway 61 is a lively place. Thanks anyway; I think I'll take a different route.

Highway 61 Revisited's five songs of wordplay are something to behold. Each song displays its own distinctive sonic platform upon which the madness dances. Most of the time you have no idea what's going on in the song, but you're tapping your toe to the tune anyway ("Desolation Row" is the lone exception here; you just sit there with your mouth open). The man who wrote "Hattie Carroll" is not telling stories like that here. There's no Bear Mountain picnic, no spiteful love song, and no traveling salesman joke; there is not even a dream to interpret (or is there?). No sir, a master storyteller is going out of his way to obfuscate his lyrics. The results did more than change songwriting, as they killed Mr. Message Man stone dead.

We begin our review of *Highway 61*'s remaining tracks out west with "Tombstone Blues." Sounding much like "Buick 6" with its honky-tonk, manic blues, barroom sound, "Tombstone" features twelve four-line verses that are organized into pairs separated by six six-line choruses. Famous names (e.g., Paul Revere, Belle Starr, Jack the Ripper, John the Baptist, Galileo, Cecil B. DeMille, Ma Rainey, and Beethoven) join less famous people (e.g., Jezebel the nun, a crazy bride, a medicine man, a Commander-in-Chief, a king, Gypsy Davey, and more) and do things that may or may not make sense. The first verse establishes the song's rhythm:

> The sweet pretty things are in bed now of course
> The city fathers they're trying to endorse
> The reincarnation of Paul Revere's horse
> But the town has no need to be nervous

This is Dylan's wordplay at its finest. The imagery comes in droves as it shares the music's madcap qualities. Jezebel makes a "bald wig" for Jack the Ripper. A distressed bride seeks relief from a doctor. A medicine man offers weird advice. John the Baptist asks the Commander for a good place to throw up. Galileo throws a mathematics book at a laughing Delilah. Banks sell spiritual maps. And Dylan punctuates it all with this defining chorus:

> Mama's in the fact'ry
> She ain't got no shoes
> Daddy's in the alley
> He's lookin' for the fuse
> I'm in the streets
> With the tombstone blues

Just when I thought I understood "green clocks, wet chairs, purple lamps and hostile statues," Dylan throws this at me. Ever feel somebody's toying with you?

The pace calms considerably with the circus hymn that is "Ballad Of A Thin Man." Here the ringmaster preaches to his assembled congregation by speaking in tongues. Those who *know* nod approvingly. The piano provides a dramatic tension for the funeral sounds that are enlivened by that churchy organ that bends and weaves throughout the song. The song's eight eight-line verses are punctuated by seven three-line choruses (verses 4 and 5 don't have a chorus separating them). Things occur in the individual stanzas, and those events pause for the chorus: "Because something is happening here / But you don't know what it is / Do you, Mister Jones?"

Evidence that this is all one mighty fine game of Glissendorf appears in the second verse. Just as Bucklen and Zimmerman used to confuse their victims with their "I see it's raining–It isn't raining–what's the next first thing to cross you mind?" game, this verse romps in the same symbolic playground:

You raise up your head
And you ask, "Is this where it is?"
And somebody points to you and says
"It's his"
And you say, "What's mine?"
And somebody else says, "Where what is?"
And you say, "Oh my God
Am I here all alone?"

Classic Glissendorf. All I can say is that Mr. Jones is not alone. Verse 3 features a conversation with "the geek" (Dylan often states that the "geek"—a circus freak of some kind—is the inspiration for this song). Verse 4 offers a character that's friendly with lumberjacks, under attack for an active imagination, and expected to contribute to charity. Verse 5 presents a well-read individual who is admired by professors and lawyers. Verse 6 unveils a "sword swallower" who returns his throat to its rightful owner (what did I just say?). Verse 7 plays another round of Glissendorf in which a vertically and visually challenged individual shouts words that rhyme. Finally, verse 8 describes a man who walks like a camel, frowns, and places his eyes in his pockets and his "nose on the ground" as the narrator declares, "There ought to be a law / Against you comin' around / You should be made / To wear earphones." All I can say is I don't know or care who or what Mr. Jones is; I'm just terribly excited that I'm not him.

What makes "Thin Man" so special is its music. The slow, again churchy, piano-organ interplay works to a rhythm that betrays the wordplay. When "Tombstone" rushes along musically and lyrically, you sort of sit back and soak it all in, yet this song's hymnlike qualities create expectations that are totally violated. Imagine yourself in a religious ceremony listening to a solemn hymn that marches along at a reverent pace, but features lyrics that make no sense whatsoever. To suggest that all of this is metaphor is to step into a trap. At the moment of conception, a metaphor may have been in place, but once that neuron fired, it was gone. What magic.

"Queen Jane Approximately" uses coherent pop music sounds (smooth rhythm, timely piano flourishes, steady organ) and lyrical repetition to drive home the point that the narrator wishes Jane would visit. He appears to offer some sort of respite from all of the bad things in her life. The five five-line stanzas present three lines containing some observation about Jane before closing with the two-line invitation for her visit. Consider the opening verse:

When your mother sends back all your invitations
And your father to your sister he explains
That you're tired of yourself and all of your creations
Won't you come see me, Queen Jane?
Won't you come see me, Queen Jane?

The song continues with more negative scenes that are used to preface the invitation. Florists want their flowers back (they have lost their smell anyway), Jane's children "resent" her, clowns die in vain, "advisers" question Jane's "conclusions," and "bandits" that Jane has apparently absolved complain. The music swirls around as these lyrics unfold. Mr. Jones is not the only person in the dark on these matters: Just who or what "Queen Jane" is or represents is certainly fertile ground for the Dylanologists to plow. Have at it, folks!

"Just Like Tom Thumb's Blues" is the only sonically uneventful song on this album. The song conjures images of the old Dylan, strumming his guitar in support of his poetry. Although the piano-rhythm section interplay is unlike Dylan's earlier solo work, that *feel* is present and narrows one's focus to the song's lyrics over their orchestration. When you zoom in on these lyrics, bring your interpretative binoculars—you'll need them. The first verse reveals why:

When you're lost in the rain in Juarez
And it's Eastertime too
And your gravity fails
And negativity don't pull you through
Don't put on any airs
When you're down on Rue Morgue Avenue
They got some hungry women there
And they really make a mess outa you

The song's six verses march along in a similar fashion with a strong Dylan harmonica bridge separating the fifth and sixth stanzas. Verse 2 discusses "Saint Annie," the narrator's physical predicament, and a silent physician (are we talking drugs here?). Verse 3 introduces the "goddess of gloom" ("Sweet Melinda") and her strange powers. Verse 4 talks not about a person, but a place ("Housing Project Hill") where the police enjoy their independence. Verse 5 discusses what appear to be corrupt government officials and their impact on "Angel." The final verse features a personal statement from the narrator:

I started out on burgundy
But soon hit the harder stuff
Everybody said they'd stand behind me
When the game got rough
But the joke was on me
There was nobody even there to call my bluff
I'm going back to New York City
I do believe I've had enough

That verse has a sign posted: Beware of Poet. Whatever Tom's blues are about, I know of nothing "just like" them. There is a thread somewhere that holds this song together. The talk of negativity, undiagnosed illnesses, gloom, disillusionment, corruption, and betrayal is presented in a codelike fashion. Like "Queen Jane" there is a rhythm to the wordplay that suggests some form of logic. Whatever that logic might be, it is not readily available; consequently, experience counsels restraint.

One of the great things about our auteur is his ability to produce the one-of-a-kind song. Name a song that is like "Subterranean Homesick Blues." What tune sounds like "Rolling Stone"? Dylan's capacity for musical innovation is amazing. He pulls another musical rabbit out of his songwriting hat with "Desolation Row." The ten stanzas, with twelve lines per verse, consist of ten independently operating vignettes. While they all supposedly involve the location "Desolation Row," only one character appears in more than one vignette: the narrator. Introduced in the opening stanza and returning as the subject of the tenth verse, our narrator offers his or her take on the activities in and around Desolation Row. As with much of the Newport Mod's writing, the various characters—ranging from celebrities (e.g., Cinderella, Einstein, Ezra Pound, and T. S. Eliot) to individual locals (e.g., Ophelia, Dr. Filth, and Casanova) to an unnamed cast of thousands (e.g., sailors, a blind commissioner, the superhuman crew, and lovely mermaids)—are portrayed in wild and crazy ways, doing more than unlikely or absurd acts (e.g., smelling sewers while repeating the alphabet). The scenario unfolds via four characters profiles, five scenic descriptions, and the closing personal commentary from the narrator. The opening verse, a scenic vignette, offers a fine example of that particular style:

They're selling postcards of the hanging
They're painting the passports brown
The beauty parlor is filled with sailors
The circus is in town
Here comes the blind commissioner
They've got him in a trance
One hand is tied to the tight-rope walker
The other is in his pants
And the riot squad they're restless
They need somewhere to go
As Lady and I look out tonight
From Desolation Row

Well, what have we here? A "scene" where they sell photos of public executions, colorize public documents, glamorize military personnel, and where public officials fraternize with carnies. Notice the narrator's appearance in the penultimate line as he or she establishes his or her role in the unfolding scenario. The table is set for one weird Newport Mod meal.

Other scenic descriptions involve verse 3's account of a dark night in which most people hide inside, making love, while Cain, Abel, the hunchback of Notre Dame, and the Good Samaritan prepare for the evening's festivities; verse 7's portrayal of the Phantom of the Opera's and Casanova's activities as the neighborhood prepares for a feast (the Phantom yells at local "skinny girls" about Casanova's transgressions on Desolation Row); verse 8's report of the activities of the "superhuman crew" and local "insurance men" (they work in their own ways to insure that people do not escape to Desolation Row); and verse 9's chaotic description of conflicts on the *Titanic* (featuring a fight between Pound and Eliot as calypso singers laugh, fishermen clutch flowers, and everyone avoids thinking about Desolation Row). In each case, there is evidence of plot progression within the individual scenarios; however, the next verse drops that scene and moves on to the next.

Complementing these scenic descriptions are the character profiles that add another layer to this surreal situation. The second verse unveils Cinderella's conflict with Romeo and her penchant for cleanliness. The song's fourth verse offers this vignette:

> Now Ophelia, she's 'neath the window
> For her I feel so afraid
> On her twenty-second birthday
> She already is an old maid
> To her, death is quite romantic
> She wears an iron vest
> Her profession's her religion
> Her sin is her lifelessness
> And though her eyes are fixed upon
> Noah's great rainbow
> She spends her time peeking
> Into Desolation Row

Here we witness a profile of a young spinster and her dark life. Apparently, she is an outsider, looking in on the varied happenings of Desolation Row. With her romantic visions of death and her presumably protective attire, she worships her life away, transfixed by Noah's promise. Other character profiles involve verse 5's presentation of Einstein (who dresses like Robin Hood, hangs out with a jealous ecclesiastic, smells his way around town, and betrays his personal history) and verse 6's portrayal of Dr. Filth's weird world. Everyone is preparing for a night on Desolation Row, doing something strange on Desolation Row, winding down from a night on Desolation Row, peering in on the activities of Desolation Row, keeping people from going to Desolation Row, or practicing mental avoidance behaviors about that wild and crazy place.

The closing verse returns to the narrator's situation. He receives a letter, responds to its contents, questions his correspondent's sincerity, ridicules those people mentioned in the letter, and demands that no more letters be sent—unless they originate from "Desolation Row."

What song is like this? A blend of characters mixes and mingles through strange scenes that stand independently of one another. Nothing ever builds upon anything once a given vignette closes. Clearly, each vignette could easily be the *start* of its own song. A reference to "Desolation Row" is the only common thread amongst the mayhem. Where would an interpretation begin? With the circus' arrival? With Cinderella's cinematic poses and cleaning habits? With Cain and Abel's relationship with the Hunchback of Notre Dame? Where? Did Einstein somehow take from the rich and give to the poor? Or was Robin Hood really a brilliant scientist running a sociological study? By the way, what could possibly inspire someone to sniff drainpipes while saying the alphabet? A trademark harmonica bridge prefaces the final stanza that changes its presentational tone by shifting to a first person expression. Is Desolation Row some form of "Mr. Tambourine Man" escape for our narrator? Has he dismissed his correspondent's "scene" for the varied events of Desolation Row? Yes, there are more than a few faces and names exchanged in this song. What song is like this? It is most certainly not a narrative. It displays characteristics of narrative impressionism, although the references to Desolation Row are too fast and loose for that style. So, I place it in the wordplay category, and leave it at that. What a song.

Highway 61 Revisited is a one-of-a-kind recording. Both sonically and lyrically, it stands alone in the history of music. This record, more than any other in the Dylan Canon, demonstrates the auteur is unafraid of chaos; in fact, he embraces it. His impressionism is at its peak here. What began on *Bringing It All Back Home* culminates in the words and sounds of *Highway 61*. Both records deploy a raucous barrelhouse–honky-tonk–churchy-Delta blues aural strategy that Tom Wilson and Bob Johnston capture wonderfully. With that sonic platform in place, Dylan advances his Glissendorf skills in unprecedented ways. Yes, go ahead, interpret Einstein's relationship with Robin Hood, analyze the cryptic moralizing of "Highway 61," or read between "Tom Thumb's" lines. The Glissendorf Master issued his invitation into his world of word games and patiently awaits your participation. But, it may very well be that when all is said and done, John Lennon was right: The "sound" *is* magical.

There were but a few outtakes from the *Highway 61 Revisited* sessions. According to my sources, only the "Positively 4th Street" single, "Can You Please Crawl Out Your Window," and "Sitting On A Barbed-Wire Fence" were excluded from the album. Once more, the auteur penned liner notes for the album as well. Those notes—entitled "Highway 61 Revisited"—demonstrate the *Tarantula* writing style in a compelling fashion. Once you accept the flow of crazy-named characters, there is evidence of plot progression in this particular piece. The "story" traces the activities of "White Heap," the "hundred Inevitables," "Cream Judge," "the Clown," "Savage Rose," "Fixable," and "Autumn," and features cameos by "Tom Dooley," "the bartender," "Paul Sargent," "Madam John," "Rose," and "Lifelessness." They are all sort of out on the town, working their way—it *seems*—over to the "Insanity Factory" (operated by the "WIPE-OUT GANG"). Some of the characters are quite interesting. For example, we have Autumn, the poet. She's not, we're told, "extremely fat but rather progressively unhappy" as she writes her poetry and awaits the "slow train." We have Cream Judge, the author. Cream is currently writing a book "on the true meaning of a pear," which is a follow-up to last year's book on "famous dogs of the civil war." The bartender appears to be a nice fellow who "keeps a buffalo in his mind." At one point, the bar scene is disrupted by Paul Sargent of 4th Street, who arrests everyone "for being incredible" (no worries—no one was offended). I thought Clown went a bit too far when he gagged Autumn's mouth and prompted White Heap to challenge our poet regarding her relationship with spring. Apparently, Savage Rose and Fixable agreed (they kicked his brains and colored him pink "for being a phony philosopher"). Suddenly, a break in the action occurs, and we receive the statement about tonal breath control. That passage continues, "the subject matter—though meaningless as it is—has something to do with beautiful strangers . . . the beautiful strangers, Vivaldi's green jacket & the holy slow train." The liner notes close with a discussion of the word "eye," the author's inability to "say" that word any longer, and his conclusion that we're lucky since we "don't have to think about such things as eyes & rooftops & quazimodo." (Previously we were told that our roof was "demolished" and that quazimodo—along with john cohen and mozart—were right about, I think, the word eye.) What can you say?

Well, there you have it. What a ride!

The Newport Mod's mission of rejecting Mr. Message Man and his adoring constituency is nearing completion. Bob Zimmerman's exploration of the dark recesses of Bob Dylan's mind is coming to a close. Dillon's rebellion successfully pushed away those "New York organizations," dismissed the practice of sloganeering, and massaged his concerns over language by introducing his poetry to the practice of songwriting. His unique "proetry" also brought new life to liner notes. Jack Fate's musical education advanced as well. By bringing in a band to add color to his musical pictures, Fate synthesized his understanding of rock and roll, blues, country, and gospel into a stunning sonic portrait. Gospel music's traditional organ-piano counterpoint found a new home featuring a blues-based rhythm section, slashing rock-and-roll rhythm/lead guitar, and a country-style crooner. He may not sound like George Jones (or Caruso, for that matter), but he brought that emotional edge to both his voice and his harmonica—it was not about *perfection*, it was about feeling. The results issued a revolutionary sound combining a wailing voice/harmonica—the epitome of tonal breath control—projecting cryptic emotional statements through music that synthesized a host of sonic strategies. No wonder Fate's ear heard Kooper's organ in "Rolling Stone" and brought that sound forward despite Tom Wilson's protest. He recognized that sound and assimilated it into his design. By channeling Fate's knowledge through Dillon's rebellion, Zimmerman's Dylan stood everything on its head.

That fire burned very, very brightly. Writing *Tarantula*, the songs, the liner notes, and pieces for magazines such as "Alternatives To College," and constant *touring* would have to take a toll on the artist. After *Highway 61*, everything intensified. A new band, a new world tour (with all of its travel and media work), another movie project, the ever-present "novel," and changing recording studios for a new album made 1966 look even *tougher* than the incredible year that was 1965. It would be tougher, that is for sure, but it would not be better. Just look at 1965: *Bringing It All*

Songs for the next album, major per-
formances (e.g., the Hollywood Bowl shows), and unsuccessful recording sessions
rounded off a most productive 1965. Now, that fire begins to dim. The celebrity life,
the overheated word machine, the constant movement, and the flat-out fatigue set in
and bring a glorious era to a close. The marriage of words and music reached a creative peak in 1965, and Bob Dylan took it there.

Blonde On Blonde

Transitional projects tend to be confusing and, occasionally, suffer in their artistic impact. Bob Dylan's seventh album, the Nashville-produced *Blonde On Blonde*, is
such an album. The sonic innovations that powered *Highway 61 Revisited* disappear on
Blonde. The lyrical magic that fueled the Newport Mod period fades as well. Consequently, we have a fourteen-song album that splits straight down the middle, with
seven tunes from the clever songsmith who changed songwriting forever and seven
songs from a pop music version of the writer who preceded him on *Another Side*—
a songwriter who would eventually return and dominate the oeuvre. "Visions Of Johanna" and "Stuck Inside Of Mobile With The Memphis Blues Again" offer glimpses
of the brilliance that radiates from "Gates Of Eden" and "That's Alright, Ma," as
that historic genius evolves into a black hole that would forever feed upon itself. The
news here—aside from the Nashville influence that totally tamed the record's sonic
qualities—is that the topical master revisits his finger-pointing muse as he focuses on
that one topic that never ceases to inspire him: relational complaint.

To be sure, the sounds vary. From the raucous party of the opening track
("Rainy Day Women #12 & 35") through the variations of blues-oriented platforms
to the downright pop tunes that are "I Want You" and "4th Time Around" (only the
Beatles are missing here), this record marches along at its own Music City pace. Our
seven songs of relational complaint present another "greatest hits" package as they
touch all of the musical bases. We have three country tunes (remember, unless the
song is blues or a ballad, country songs follow Tin Pan Alley formats with choruses,
bridges, and middle eights—very un-Dylan), a New Orleans–style pop tune, a
Merseybeat–style pop song, a Sun Records–style pop song, and a pop variation of
the record's musical innovation, the Salvation Army Band song. Our impressionistic
songs also deploy diverse musical strategies with a decided emphasis on Tennessee
sounds (i.e., Nashville and Memphis styles) and Delta blues. The organ and guitar
work complement the steady Nashville rhythm section as they work through the various musical genres. In all cases, the harmonica remains dazzling, providing a sonic
signature that rarely fades.

Clinton Heylin's chronology reports the album's production process was a
marked departure from the spontaneous sessions that characterized Dylan's recording to that point and, therefore, represented "the writing on the wall for all subsequent terrors in the studio." Dylan, Bob Johnston, and the Hawks started the *Blonde*
project in Columbia's New York studios in October 1965 and carried on through the
end of January 1966. With little coming from those sessions, Dylan dismissed the
Hawks and traveled to Nashville with Johnston (a producer with considerable expe-

rience in Music City), Robbie Robertson (the Hawks' guitarist), and Dylan veteran Al Kooper to complete the recording. There Johnston brought in several seasoned musicians to work with an artist quite unlike anything the Nashville regulars had ever experienced. Veteran musicians such as Wayne Moss (guitar), Jerry Kennedy (guitar), Joe South (bass), Hargus Robbins (piano, listed as "Robinson" in Heylin's book), Kenneth Buttrey (drums), Henry Strzelecki (drums), Bill Aikins (not listed in Heylin), and informal leader (and *Highway 61* veteran) Charlie McCoy (guitar, harmonica) provided the backing sounds for the Newport Mod's unlikely appearance in Nashville. It was a unique experience for everybody. You see, Nashville musicians work in tightly supervised, professionally efficient sessions—a stark contrast to the Dylan Method, which relied on the improvisational skills of the accompanying musicians. On the BBC's *The Bob Dylan Story* the series host, Kris Kristofferson, recalls the sessions for the first double-album release in pop music history. How fascinating that the man who in a little over seven years would star in *Pat Garrett and Billy the Kid* was working at Columbia's Nashville studios as a *janitor*! When he recounts the experience, you can still hear the excitement in his deep, booming voice. During that BBC broadcast, Charlie McCoy explains how these sessions unfolded:

> It was a bit different. It had a totally different approach . . . up to that point it was almost a set rule that you would go into a studio at either 10, 2, 6, or 10 and record four songs. But he took his time . . . he wanted to make sure every lyric was exactly the way he wanted it. So we had a tendency to relax a bit more . . . wasn't quite as nervous . . . wasn't trying to beat the clock kind of situation.

Proof of McCoy's recollections exists in Heylin's chronology, in which he cites a 1965 conversation between Dylan and Allen Ginsberg where the songwriter described his writing-recording process. According to Ginsberg, Dylan would enter the studio, visit with the musicians, talk (Heylin describes it as "babble") into the microphone, listen to the replay, jot down what he liked, summon the musicians, and record the "new" material. Now, this is not the stuff of the patented Nashville Sound. In any event, the musicians played cards and ping-pong as Dylan "composed" his songs, stopped the game to record a new song, and resumed the game while Dylan prepared the next track. The spontaneous, "in-the-spirit" recording style that successfully captured the spontaneous, "in-the-spirit" messages was evolving in Nashville. Not until 2001's *Love And Theft* sessions would Dylan deploy this unique recording style to capture meaningful original material.

Blonde On Blonde reflects this transition in every way. Released on May 16, 1966, the fourteen-track double album (running over seventy-three minutes) offers two songs in the free-form, wordplay style (the aforementioned "Visions Of Johanna" and "Stuck Inside Of Mobile With The Memphis Blues Again"), five songs that employ the narrative impressionism technique ("Rainy Day Women #12 & 35," "Pledging My Time," "I Want You," "Leopard-Skin Pill-Box Hat," and "Sad Eyed Lady Of The Lowlands"), and seven *stories* about relationships ("One Of Us Must Know [Sooner Or Later]," "Just Like A Woman," "Most Likely You Go Your Way And I'll Go Mine," "Temporary Like Achilles," "Absolutely Sweet Marie," "4th Time

Around," and "Obviously Five Believers"). The relational songs establish a narrative trend that extends through the remainder of the lifework, while the wordplay and impressionism grind to a halt. The cavalier wordsmith's spontaneous utterances—like his spontaneous recording sessions—would now give way to more strategic, less inspirational art. It was as if the critics finally got what they always wanted—a thoughtful poet—and Dylan's art would never be the same again.

That the auteur's impressionistic inspiration had run its course is evident throughout the five pieces of narrative impressionism and the final two editions of wordplay. The absence of liner notes may signal that development as well. Indeed, my friends, the Newport Mod has left the building, never to return. So, let's celebrate! I think it is safe to say that the Nashville cats were yet to experience anything like the recording of "Rainy Day Women #12 & 35." Bob Johnston describes how "Rainy Day Women" emerged for the BBC:

> Dylan came to me and he sat down on the piano and he said, "I've got a song." And he started playing this thing. And I said, "Goddamn that sounds like a Salvation Army band." He said, "Well, see if you can get one." I think it was late at night and I called everywhere and I couldn't get one, so I talked with Charlie McCoy. And McCoy said "well I play trumpet and I know somebody who can play trombone."

McCoy recalls, "I said 'does he want it to be good?' And [Johnston] said no. I said when do you want him here. And he said midnight . . . so the guy showed up at ten till twelve . . . and went home at seventeen after . . . and it was done. Two takes." Wayne Moss recounts the details of that particular session for *The Bob Dylan Story*:

> [Dylan] wanted everybody to whoop and holler and act like they were having a party. So he said "what do you guys do to relax around here?" And Charlie McCoy says, "well we play golf and fish." He said, "naw, that's not what I mean." He said, "what can I do to make things loosen up a little bit so we can make this sound more like a party?" Charlie says, "oh I don't know, maybe everybody can drink a beer or something." . . . We got quite relaxed. To show you how foggy it is in my memory, Henry Strelecki and I have a difference of opinion as to who played bass on it. It was either he or I, I don't recall. Seems like to me I was playing foot pedals on the organ with my hands cause I couldn't stand up.

McCoy adds, "Bob was talking about how he wanted it to have a Salvation Army-type marching beat to it. And so someone . . . said why don't we just march around the room. And so, next thing you know . . . the bass drum was taken off the stand and Jerry Kerrigan strapped it around his chest and we physically marched around the room. But that had the feel that he wanted . . . no changes or nothing. That's the way it was supposed to be and that's the way it was."

Once the trombone player was on his way home and the track was completed, Dylan named his new song. Bob Johnston recalls the succession of titles the auteur considered: "I said what are you gonna call that . . . he said 'Rainy Day Women . . .

number 48 and 63.' No, 'number 18 and 24' . . . no 'number 12 and 35.' And it was just like [snaps his fingers] he knew when he hit 12 and 35 that was it. And that's what he called it." When asked about the significance of those particular numbers, Dylan told the BBC. "There was great significance to it *at the time.* . . . I know there must have been. It wouldn't have been titled that for no reason whatsoever. I don't know what that reason was. Everything had a reason back then. But then again, it could be a no reason. I'm not sure."

Turning to the song's specifics, "Rainy Day" features five six-line stanzas that are divided into two sections: four lines describing where people get stoned, and two tag lines stating the inevitable. The song, as the musicians' comments indicate, is an aural wonder. The piano swirls, a subtle harmonica floats throughout with a fine instrumental bridge between verses 3 and 4, and the crazy marching band sound effects (banging the drum, whooping and hollering) whip around to produce one rowdy song—so much so that the song is widely believed to be a "drug song," with Dylan's comments on oppression getting buried. The Salvation Army Band–inspired social statement opens in this manner:

> Well, they'll stone ya when you're trying to be so good,
> They'll stone ya just a-like they said they would.
> They'll stone ya when you're tryin' to go home.
> Then they'll stone ya when you're there all alone.
> But I would not feel so all alone,
> Everybody must get stoned.

That is the song's structure, plain and simple: four lines of stoning locations followed by the conclusion that that is just the way it is. Verse 2 reports that "they'll" oppress you while you're walking down the street, trying to hold your seat, walking across the floor, or going to the door. Verse 3 notes how "they'll" get you eating breakfast, during your able youth, and when you try to earn a living, and when all is said and done, these people will wish you well. A harmonica break segues into verse 4's comments about people oppressing you and then asserting closure, how they will come back for more, and go for you in your car; and, of course, there's no peace when you play your guitar, either. Yes, those stones come from every direction, all of the time—as the final verse drives home:

> Well, they'll stone you when you walk all alone.
> They'll stone you when you are walking home.
> They'll stone you and then say you are brave.
> They'll stone you when you are set down in your grave.
> But I would not feel so all alone,
> Everybody must get stoned.

This simple song of oppression betrays itself with the marching band, partying sound effects, so much so that I believe that this is the song that inspired Elvis Presley to seek a special U.S. marshall appointment from the president of the United States. He wanted to join the nation's drug enforcement efforts in order to

combat people who advocated policies like the ones he attributed to Dylan. Now,
that's irony.

Our other impressionistic songs concentrate on relational matters. "Pledging My Time" welcomes you to the Delta with its first note. This slow, prodding, blues tune features one compelling lesson in tonal breath control (especially during the bridge between verses 3 and 4), and Dylan's harmonica may very well reach its peak on this track. Complementing that harmonica work are some lightning-sharp guitar licks. I do not overstate the case when I suggest that this is a blues masterpiece. A long harmonica tag seals this Delta deal. Lyrically, the five six-line verses follow the 4:2 ratio of "Rainy Day" in that we have four lines of description before a two-line standard close. The first verse cites the narrator's daylong headache and his recovery as he states his commitment to his love interest. The second stanza demonstrates the song's method of expression:

> Well, the hobo jumped up,
> He came down natur'lly.
> After he stole my baby,
> Then he wanted to steal me.
> But I'm pledging my time to you,
> Hopin' you'll come through, too.

The song continues with verse 3's invitation to give the narrator a chance, then verse 4's comments about a stuffy room containing the two of them and the narrator's need to leave, and closes with this enigmatic verse:

> Well, they sent for the ambulance
> And one was sent.
> Somebody got lucky
> But it was an accident.
> Now I'm pledging my time to you,
> Hopin' you'll come through, too.

Here we observe a blues-oriented piece of impressionism. The song's complaint is indirect at best. The narrator talks around his concerns far more than he talks to them; nevertheless, the cloudy imagery featuring the hobo and the ambulance scene join cryptic remarks about giving the relationship a chance and the stuffy room scene to suggest that the narrator hopes to receive as much as he gives. There is no praise or celebration, just a hope for reciprocity. Dylan's voice and harmonica color this blues the appropriate hue.

Our relational theme advances with the pop sounds of "I Want You." This is one bouncy, happy, merry-go-lucky-sounding pop song that just bops along with some wonderful harmonica bits. The four verses of ten to eleven lines each feature seven or eight lines of surreal descriptions before turning to the four-line close stating the narrator's desires. Here we have a major songwriting innovation within the Dylan Canon: our first lyrical bridge. While Dylan has often deployed his harmonica or another instrument in the bridge role, he now steps straight into that Tin Pan

Alley tradition with a four-line bridge between the second and third verses. Welcome to Music City! The opening stanza sets the tone:

> The guilty undertaker sighs,
> The lonesome organ grinder cries,
> The silver saxophones say I should refuse you.
> The cracked bells and washed-out horns
> Blow into my face with scorn,
> But it's not that way,
> I wasn't born to lose you.
> I want you, I want you,
> I want you so bad,
> Honey, I want you.

Here we have a classic example of the narrative impressionism writing style. A contrite mortician, talking musical instruments, and more set the scene for the concluding appeal that occupies the final four lines. Verse 2 offers jumping politicians who have had too much to drink, crying mothers, sleeping saviors, and a reference to the narrator drinking from a "broken cup" (religion?). With that, we turn to the oeuvre's first bridge:

> Now all my fathers, they've gone down
> True love they've been without it.
> But all their daughters put me down
> 'Cause I don't think about it.

A bridge as clear as mud prefaces two closing verses that share that clarity. A conversation with the narrator's "chambermaid" occupies the third verse, with the final stanza offering an apology for any harm the narrator may have inflicted on his love interest's son. He was, after all, merely trying to protect her (I guess).

Though we've certainly seen this sort of writing before, rare has been the auteur's use of traditional pop song sonic and songwriting strategies to convey those words. The happy-go-lucky sounds and the "I want you" lines create impressions that the remaining lyrics dodge. The first four lines of each stanza are either Romper Room wordplay or a diabolical private code (or they could just as easily be words from the back of a cereal box written in the reverse order!). Our next impressionistic track, "Leopard-Skin Pill-Box Hat," follows more traditional methods.

"Leopard-Skin" is a slow, ripping Delta blues that represents the epitome of Dylan's beloved "thin wild mercury sound." The track sounds like the sort of song you might hear walking toward the Daisy Theater on Memphis' Beale Street. It makes you sweat to listen to its raw, pulsating Delta drive. Some of Dylan's finest guitar work appears in the instrumental bridge between verses 3 and 4. A strong guitar solo closes the song as well. The writing is in the blues tradition—except we have classic Dylan twists in their presentation. The five verses appear in four eight-line segments with an opening five-line stanza. In all cases, the final line provides the anchor for a series of scenes that go nowhere while flirting with a relational complaint.

The song opens with the narrator acknowledging his "baby's" new headwear and his curiosity regarding its impact on her head. Next, he does what anyone would do in this situation: He asks if he can jump on her new hat. He's clearly impressed with the hat, since he describes the fit as reminding him how a mattress balances atop a bottle. Before the dynamic guitar break, the third verse invites this well-adorned lady to accompany the narrator for a view of the sunrise in which he promises to wear his belt on his head while she wears her hat (what a loving photo that would make). The plot thickens with the final stanzas:

> Well, I asked the doctor if I could see you
> It's bad for your health, he said
> Yes, I disobeyed his orders
> I came to see you
> But I found him there instead
> You know, I don't mind him cheatin' on me
> But I sure wish he'd take that off his head
> Your brand new leopard-skin pill-box hat
>
> Well, I see you got a new boyfriend
> You know, I never seen him before
> Well, I saw him
> Makin' love to you
> You forgot to close the garage door
> You might think he loves you for your money
> But I know what he really loves you for
> It's your brand new leopard-skin pill-box hat.

Perhaps this isn't about the hat at all, but about the hypocritical doctor who lies to his patient for his own gratification (. . . right). Anyway, the final stanza lodges the relational complaint in its own, wonderful way.

Just look at the sonic strategies evidenced in these impressionistic songs! The Salvation Army sound, two pounding Delta blues tracks, and one merry pop tune set the scene for the impressionistic hymn that closes *Blonde*: "Sad-Eyed Lady Of The Lowlands." Wayne Moss recounts recording this eleven-minute track that occupied one whole side of the initial two-record set: "The first day . . . the first call . . . we were called at two. His plane was late. He showed up at six. And he said, 'Look, I gotta finish writing a song.' . . . we didn't start recording 'til four a.m. . . . and the song was 'Sad-Eyed Lady of the Lowlands' . . . a fourteen minute ballad . . . it was tough . . . we were lucky to hang with him. Everybody was very tired."

"Sad-Eyed" is a slow, slow, slow dirgelike piece that opens with a telling harmonica blast before settling into a pace that never changes. The song features five thirteen-line verses that share identical strategies: Each verse opens with a three-line statement of praise (of varying degrees), pauses for a question, follows with three more descriptive lines, pauses for another question, and closes with a five-line recurring statement. The song ends with a harmonica solo that runs the length of a stanza (that means it is *long*). The five-line closing statement holds the song together:

Sad-eyed lady of the lowlands,
Where the sad-eyed prophet says that no man comes,
My warehouse eyes, my Arabian drums,
Should I leave them by your gate,
Or, sad-eyed lady, should I wait?

We're a long way from sloganeering here. Otherwise, the song features lines and lines and lines of imagery, some of which extend to two lines. The opening verse captures the three-line-and-a-question approach:

With your mercury mouth in the missionary times,
And your eyes like smoke and your prayers like rhymes,
And your silver cross, and your voice like chimes,
Oh, who among them do they think could bury you?

The song goes on with layer after layer of description followed by questions such as above. Other questions ask who could "carry" her, who could "outguess" her, who could "impress" her, who wants to "kiss" her, who could "resist" her, who could "mistake" her, who could "persuade" her, who would "employ" her, and who would "destroy" her. What prefaces these questions, as the example above indicates, are lines of varying degrees of clarity or significance. Some examples include "And your street-car visions which you place on the grass"; "And your flesh like silk, and your face like glass"; "And your deck of cards missing the jack and ace"; "Into your eyes where the moonlight swims" (I thought he stopped using the word "eye"!); "With your childhood flames on your midnight rug"; and my favorite, "And your saintlike face and your ghostlike soul."

"Sad-Eyed" is an unprecedented song. From its length, to its placement on the *Blonde* album in that all-important capstone slot, to its lyrics, well, we don't see songs like this one very often. In a later song, Dylan will write that he wrote this song for his future wife, Sara. Whether or not that is accurate, it is most assuredly an impressionistic hymn of unadulterated adoration. This woman is wonderful, but under threat. Who would do that? the song asks. Moreover, the fourth and fifth stanzas make references to a former lover or spouse in negative terms (e.g., "And your magazine-husband who one day just had to go") that reinforce the biographical argument. One way or another, the song is a statement. But since it is a *Dylan* statement, we'll leave the speculation to the journalists and biographers.

The finest pieces of Newport Mod songwriting on *Blonde* are the record's two works of unrestrained wordplay. "Visions Of Johanna" and "Stuck Inside Of Mobile" are the last of their kind. Interestingly, both songs use variations of Memphis soul to carry the wordplay. Hints of that wonderful Booker T.–style organ provide a soulful jazz feel for the poetry that is "Johanna" and the "Green Onion"–style romp of "Stuck Inside." The guitar work also features flashes of Steve Cropper's Memphis magic, although Duck Dunn is nowhere to be heard within the Nashville rhythm section. Dylan's harmonica dances about as Dylan's harmonica does. The results—as they say on Broadway—work.

"Visions Of Johanna" consists of five verses: four with 9–10 lines, the fifth with *fourteen* lines. Only the recurring tag line about Johanna (and it varies) holds the thing together. The music provides a platform for the poetry, with a recurrent harmonica burst punctuating the respective stanzas. As with "Sad-Eyed," some images require 2–3 lines; others occupy single lines. There is no plot progression within the stanzas or throughout the song. "Grab a line and go" is the philosophy here. Yep, classic Dylan. The song opens with "Ain't it just like the night to play tricks when you're tryin' to be so quiet?" while the second verse offers, "The ghost of 'lectricity howls in the bones of her face." Verse 4 offers some imaginative sentiments: "Inside the museums, Infinity goes up on trial" and "But Mona Lisa musta had the highway blues / You can tell by the way she smiles" and "Oh, jewels and binoculars hang from the head of the mule." The lines come and go in their own enigmatic way. The final, extended verse is telltale:

> The peddler now speaks to the countess who's pretending to care for him
> Sayin', "Name me someone that's not a parasite and I'll go out and say a
>   prayer for him"
> But like Louise always says
> "Ya can't look at much, can ya man?"
> As she, herself, prepares for him
> And Madonna, she still has not showed
> We see this empty cage now corrode
> Where her cape of the stage once had flowed
> The fiddler, he now steps to the road
> He writes ev'rything's been returned which was owed
> On the back of the fish truck that loads
> While my conscience explodes
> The harmonicas play the skeleton keys and the rain
> And these visions of Johanna are now all that remain.

Echoing the liner notes from days gone by and foreshadowing *Tarantula*, these lyrics operate in a world of their own. Where do you find peddlers who have a countess look after them or such talented harmonicas? Originally entitled "Freeze Out," "Visions" was long in the making; consequently, you note the lively qualities of the Newport Mod's writing. To dust off the old axiom "They don't write songs like that anymore" demonstrates the utility of such silly slogans.

Proof of the unnatural qualities of the *Blonde* sessions for the Nashville musicians exists in the eleven and a half hours required to record "Stuck Inside Of Mobile With The Memphis Blues Again" on February 16 and 17. Here again, Memphis sounds appear through Nashville filters as the Booker T.–style organ leads a steady-charging Music City rhythm section that yields a musical hybrid I'll call "country soul." The sound is not quite country, not quite soul, not quite anything else either. Ho-hum. Another Newport Mod sonic innovation establishes a platform for the auteur's wordplay.

"Stuck Inside Of Mobile" is an impressive achievement. It contains nine eleven-line verses, each with a three-line recurring statement about Mobile and the Holy City of American Music (Memphis). The respective verses offer vignettes about specific characters in which that individual or location is identified and something unfolds from there. We hear about the ragman, Shakespeare, Mona, Grandpa, the senator, the preacher, the rainman, Ruthie, and the happenings on Grand Street. No choruses, no bridges, just a steady stream of vignettes, one after the other. Consider verses 2 and 3 of this now-perfected songwriting strategy:

> Well, Shakespeare, he's in the alley
> With his pointed shoes and his bells,
> Speaking to some French girl,
> Who says she knows me well.
> And I would send a message
> To find out if she's talked,
> But the post office has been stolen
> And the mailbox is locked.
> Oh, Mama, can this really be the end,
> To be stuck inside of Mobile
> With the Memphis blues again.
>
> Mona tried to tell me
> To stay away from the train line.
> She said that all the railroad men
> Just drink up your blood like wine.
> An' I said, "Oh, I didn't know that,
> But then again, there's only one I've met
> An' he just smoked my eyelids
> An' punched my cigarette."
> Oh, Mama, can this really be the end,
> To be stuck inside of Mobile
> With the Memphis blues again.

What can be said of this songwriting approach that we haven't already said? Notice the consistent strategy of introducing a famous or crazed name, having that character participate in some unlikely scenario, and winding up the whole thing with a recurrent image that may or may not have any possible connection to the weird scene that preceded it. Throughout, we witness touches of the old satires, dreams, and irreverence that populate the oeuvre. Whip them all together with some form of musical hybrid and you have another classic Bob Dylan song from the Newport Mod era. Simple, right? Don't try this at home, folks; this is a professional driver on a closed track.

But now it is almost over. Years later, *Tarantula* will demonstrate how this writing style works outside of songs, but we'll not see this type of songwriting again. Perhaps it was just too much—too much energy, too many demands, too little time for concentration, and, maybe just maybe, too many words. Still, it was a great ride, wasn't it? Now the musical portion of this incredible period crashes in a predictable place: Music City. I used to live in Memphis, and the folks there call Nashville "NashVegas" for a variety of reasons. We witness a few of them in the seven songs of relational complaint on *Blonde*. Weird things happen in these songs. Although the spiteful bite of the writer's relational commentary is festering and preparing for the Tidal Wave of romantic storytelling that would dominate the 1970s and beyond, these songs sift relational comments through a Nashville filter. Of these seven songs, five of them use Tin Pan Alley South–style bridges and one features a middle-eight (the first in the Dylan Canon). Somehow, someway, Dylan's muse encountered the soulless songwriting structures of that Nashville Sound and rendered a series of pop songs. We have Sun Records pop, New Orleans pop, English pop, Marching pop, and the place where we begin, country pop.

"One Of Us Must Know (Sooner Or Later)" is a country-style song with a churchy feel—thanks to the piano-organ interplay. Subtle guitars and rhythms provide an aural setting for a traditional pop songwriting strategy: three eight-line verses accompanied by three four-line choruses. The song is a simple "I'm sorry" tale that states its case in the opening four lines: "I didn't mean to treat you so bad / You shouldn't take it so personal / I didn't mean to make you so sad / You just happened to be there, that's all." From there, the narrator explains that he was unable to see or hear what she was showing or saying and admits that when she asked if he were leaving someplace with her or with another woman, he was confused by the situation. Let's examine the third verse/chorus for a sample of this formulaic songwriting approach:

> I couldn't see when it started snowin'
> Your voice was all that I heard
> I couldn't see where we were goin'
> But you said you knew an' I took your word
> And then you told me later, as I apologized
> That you were just kiddin' me, you weren't really from the farm
> An' I told you, as you clawed out my eyes
> That I never really meant to do you any harm
>
> But sooner or later, one of us must know
> You just did what you're supposed to do
> Sooner or later, one of us must know
> That I really did try to get close to you

This sort of no-fault relational song is unusual in the auteur's world. Nevertheless, the tale is straightforward: She did *her* job but he *failed*. He tried yet he just failed. Sorry. "One Of Us" is a simple pop song that follows a simple songwriting strategy that is simply unusual for this writer (despite the occasional biting or enigmatic line). Was the word machine running out of fuel?

Our next country-style composition reinforces that Nashville Trend as it uses a smooth harmonica introduction to establish a light musical backdrop for another standard pop song. In "Just Like A Woman," we witness our first Bob Dylan middle-eight. The song features three ten-line verses that contain six lines of commentary before a four-line tag that functions as an embedded chorus. Between verses 2 and 3, Dylan places his initial middle-eight. We have, therefore, a pop song articulated through that Nashville Sound. The track opens with our narrator sitting in the rain thinking about his "Baby" and her new look (new clothes, different hairdo). Next he refers to his friend ("Queen Mary") and how—when all is said and done—she is like everybody else, "With her fog, her amphetamine and her pearls." The middle-eight and final verse communicate the thrust of the song:

> It was raining from the first
> And I was dying there of thirst
> So I came in here
> And your long-time curse hurts
> But what's worse
> Is this pain in here
> I can't stay in here
> Ain't it clear that—
>
> I just can't fit
> Yes, I believe it's time for us to quit
> When we meet again
> Introduced as friends
> Please don't let on that you knew me when
> I was hungry and it was your world.
> Ah, you fake just like a woman, yes, you do
> You make love just like a woman, yes, you do
> Then you ache just like a woman
> But you break just like a little girl.

The final stanza lodges the relational complaint after the narrator expresses the pain he associates with the status quo. Consequently, it is time for a change—plain and simple. Though the track follows a standard songwriting formula, snippets of that Dylan Edge creep in on occasion. Just what does the songwriter mean by that last line? Do you break women like you do wild horses? Despite the tranquilizing Nashville influence, Bob Dillon's fire smolders.

Our final country-pop tune represents a blend of songwriting strategies presented through a fast-paced version of the Nashville Sound. "Absolutely Sweet Marie" synthesizes lines of relational complaint with impressionistic imagery that, at times, seems somewhat out of place. "Marie" contains five five-line verses with three different bridges. It opens with a complaint about what appear to be Marie's false promises. That sentiment continues in verse 2 when he describes how he "waited" for her when he was sick, hated, and stuck in traffic. Apparently, our narrator is in jail, taking stock. The lie theme advances in verse 3:

> Well, six white horses that you did promise
> Were fin'lly delivered down to the penitentiary
> But to live outside the law, you must be honest

I know you always say that you agree
But where are you tonight, sweet Marie?

That stanza is followed by the second bridge and its reference to a prescient boat captain and a plea for patience. The song closes with two cloudy verses about a stalking "Persian drunkard," the mail he received in jail, and his predicament with Marie. The song's final lines are representative:

And now I stand here lookin' at your yellow railroad
In the ruins of your balcony
Wond'ring where you are tonight, sweet Marie.

The complaint over Marie's absence drives the song in no uncertain terms; however, the enigmatic imagery of a colored railway, foreign drunks, and all-knowing riverboat captains paints an enigmatic picture of the events supporting the relational complaint. *Blonde*'s transitional qualities are on display, that is for certain.

This characteristic is also evident in the first of our parade of pop songs and the Merseybeat sounds of "4th Time Around." With sounds that remind you of the Beatles' "Norwegian Wood" swirling lightly in the background, this song portrays a series of exchanges between two lovers on the down side of a relationship (in fact, the final scene finds the narrator with another woman). The five nine-line verses feature no tag lines, bridges, or choruses as the story unfolds in its own obscure way. The first verse sets the tone:

When she said,
"Don't waste your words, they're just lies,"
I cried she was deaf.
And she worked on my face until breaking my eyes,
Then said, "What else you got left?"
It was then that I got up to leave
But she said, "Don't forget,
Everybody must give something back
For something they get."

Do you get the impression that we've just stepped into the middle of a scene? Obviously, there is conflict in the air, but the details are missing. A touch of impressionism is evident in the fourth line, signaling the song's transitional qualities once more.

From there, the narrator stands and hums, beats on drums, and gives away his gum (his generosity is evident in that it was his last stick). The plot thickens when she throws him out. But he forgot his shirt and returns for it. She answers the door and goes to fetch the shirt as he examines a photograph of her in a wheelchair. Upon her return, they argue. He makes her so mad that she falls to the floor, unconscious. Oddly, our narrator seizes the opportunity and rifles through her things. The story ends in this fashion:

And when I was through,
I filled up my shoe

And brought it to you.
And you, you took me in,
You loved me then,
You didn't waste time.
And I, I never took much,
I never asked for your crutch,
Now don't ask for mine.

The story sure takes a strange twist with that fifth verse when he takes one girl's possessions, stores them in his shoe, and delivers them to another woman. Right? Whatever is going on in the references to the wheelchair and crutches is anyone's guess (dependency, anyone?); in any event, the opening scene and the subsequent arguments indicate the relational difficulties that are at the heart of this slightly crazed pop song. The Newport Mod is hanging on for his life.

Our pop tour continues with the return of the Salvation Army Band and "Most Likely You Go Your Way (And I'll Go Mine)." Though nowhere nearly as demonstrative as "Rainy Day," the swirling organ, incisive harmonica, martial drumbeat, and subtle horns of this track provide a circuslike, Salvation Army sonic platform for the relational complaint that *completely* dominates this song. We pause occasionally for a weird image or two, but the proclamation regarding the relationship's termination controls this song. The track features three thirteen-line verses, each with a five-line embedded chorus. Between verses 2 and 3 is a five-line bridge. Thus, we have another pop song. The track opens in this manner:

You say you love me
And you're thinkin' of me,
But you know you could be wrong.
You say you told me
That you wanna hold me,
But you know you're not that strong.
I just can't do what I done before,
I just can't beg you any more.
I'm gonna let you pass
And I'll go last.
Then time will tell just who fell
And who's been left behind,
When you go your way and I go mine.

We're breaking up here, folks. The language is clear and the sentiment is conveyed without obfuscation. Notice that when the narrator raises his initial complaint, he does not call her a liar or question her sincerity; he merely notes that she *may* be in error. Whatever has happened must now cease, and time will reveal who was right; in the meantime, distance is the order of the day.

The second stanza advances the point. There, the narrator offers more reasons for his decision as he explains that all of her shaking, aching, and, in verse 3, lying have grown tiresome. It is time to stop. Suddenly, the bridge offers a cryptic warning:

> The judge, he holds a grudge,
> He's gonna call on you.
> But he's badly built
> And he walks on stilts,
> Watch out he don't fall on you.

Once more, the Newport Mod is wrestling with Nashville song structures: A traditional bridge provides a platform for a surreal expression—a threatening remark at that. The song concludes with a twist. The narrator reveals that he is aware that she has another lover. He departs after delivering a final blow: "You say my kisses are not like his, / But this time I'm not gonna tell you why that is." Instead, he is going to let her go. The end. Like "Restless Farewell," what good is a separation without a biting conclusion?

Our pop trip next enters the Crescent City and a New Orleans–style relational complaint, "Temporary Like Achilles." With Fats Domino–Nawlins-style piano complementing Dylan's vocals, this song contains four verses (three with seven lines, one with eight) that feature two-line tags. Two bridges are offered between verses 2 and 3 (vocal) and verses 3 and 4 (harmonica). Yes, we have yet another pop song about a relationship. The song's essence is conveyed in the first bridge:

> Like a poor fool in his prime,
> Yes, I know you can hear me walk,
> But is your heart made out of stone, or is it lime,
> Or is it just solid rock.

How many pop songs have used this imagery? That "heart of stone" has once more raised its cold self and threatens yet another relationship. Supporting that core is a litany of complaints such as "How come you don't send me no regards?" (verse 1), "How come you send someone out to have me barred?" (verse 2), "Just what do you think you have to guard?" (verse 3), and "How come you get someone like him to be your guard?" (verse 4). These complaints are set up in the preceding lines to create a fuzzy, but essentially direct, account of a dying relationship. The imagery may be idiosyncratic, but the point shines through.

Finally, the *Blonde On Blonde* pop tour ends upstream in the Bluff City and Memphis, Tennessee. With the sounds of Sun Studios providing the aural context, our final relational complaint is lodged by way of "Obviously Five Believers." Slashing guitars supported by rock-and-roll rhythms punctuated by Dylan's Delta blues harmonica conjure sounds from Union Avenue in this six-verse song that uses repetition to drive—and I mean *drive*—its point home. The seven-line verses repeat the first two lines of each stanza before a three-line closing that complains about the narrator's relational struggles. There are no vocal bridges, choruses, or recurring tag lines in this straightforward blues tune. The fact that the song repeats the first verse after the guitar bridge not only contributes to its repetitive qualities, but also separates this track from most Bob Dylan compositions. Although a rather common songwriting technique, Dylan seldom repeats an entire verse. The first verse says it all:

> Early in the mornin'
> Early in the mornin'
> I'm callin' you to
> I'm callin' you to
> Please come home
> Yes, I guess I could make it without you
> If I just didn't feel so all alone

This tune continues with the narrator explaining how he will not disappoint her as he urges her reciprocity (verse 2), how he is depressed over his situation (via the age-old "black dog" barking line of verse 3), and how her mother needs her (verse 4), then pauses for an odd description of his friends (the "believers" and "jugglers" of verse 5), and closes by repeating the first verse. Whatever his "friends" have to do with this account is a mystery to me; otherwise, the song follows a tried-and-true formula without deviation.

With that, we have *Blonde On Blonde*. The recording is a transitional statement that slowly bids farewell to the Newport Mod, fondles a variety of traditional musical structures, and shifts songwriting modes to accommodate those sonic platforms. The Newport Mod's brilliance is on display in "Johanna" and "Stuck Inside Of Mobile" as this newfound Tennessee sound is used to paint a surreal portrait and an enigmatic collage, respectively. They are, indeed, statements for the ages. The five songs of narrative impressionism indicate that the clever wordsmith who generated songs such as "Johanna" may be in need of a respite. As innovative as "Rainy Day Women" may be, the technique is clearly on the wane. In actuality, the musical diversity on *Blonde* offers our first glimpse of a soon-to-be standard Jack Fate tactic. When the muse is strained or lost, Fate turns to his musical repertoire, toys with those sounds, and searches for possibilities. We'll see this strategy surface again and again (from the *Basement Tapes* to *Love And Theft*). Although Dillon's rebellion fuels the creative urge, Fate's encyclopedic knowledge is the art's foundation. Subsequently, the songwriting complemented the songs' various sound designs. The principal finding here is in how Dylan adjusted his writing style to his environment. Our first lyrical bridges join the lifework's initial middle-eight and songs following Tin Pan Alley South prescriptions to create a songwriting moment that yields to Music City. This style of songwriting is unique to Dylan's Nashville pen.

While *Blonde* is without a doubt a product of its environment, a determination of just what kind of context generated our final topics is difficult to discern. The spring of 1966 world tour brings closure to a madcap era. The creative fire that somehow manages to assemble *Tarantula* burns out during a world tour that is the subject of the never-aired film, *Eat The Document*. That spring, the reverent audiences of *Dont Look Back* devolved into screaming beasts that confuse biblical characters with rock stars. The on-the-road-with-Bob scenes of *Dont* disintegrate into the in-hell-with-Dylan shots from *Eat The Document*. Perhaps in response or maybe in parallel, the auteur changes from the clever, confrontational hipster to a frail, detached icon. The booing gets so bad that Levon Helm quits the band and goes home. The road gets so long and tiresome that Jack Fate vanishes, leaving Bob Dillon's rebellion to carry the day. While Dillon's rebellion is a formidable entity, it is not sufficient in and or itself to sustain the auteur; hence, a motorcycle wreck eventually restores the proper balances that maintain Bob Dylan. To be sure, the eighteen months from January 1965 through July 1966 were a turbulent portion of Bob Zimmerman's career. We now turn to one of the products of that historic era and Bob Dylan's infamous book of words.

Tarantula and *Eat The Document*

Throughout this chapter, I have described many of Dylan's songs as "musical Rorschach tests"—make of them what you will. Enjoy. Now, we turn to this era's "literary Rorschach test" and *Tarantula*. Clinton Heylin describes *Tarantula* as a "series of in-jokes," while Howard Sounes refers to it as "a hundred and thirty-seven pages of liner notes." There is compelling evidence to support both claims. Here we consider the project's origins, walk through its contents, contemplate its value with the lifework, and invite you to check it out for yourself. There is only *one way* to appreciate *Tarantula*—you *must* go there yourself. Buckle up, my friends: *Tarantula* is something to behold.

Dylan's 1969 interview with *Rolling Stone* discusses the evolution of the *Tarantula* project in much detail. He told Jann Wenner that the project emerged because of reporters' inquiries about other forms of writing: "And I would say, 'Well, I don't write much of anything else.' And they would say . . . 'Do you write books?' And I'd say, 'Sure, I write books.'" After that, he claimed that all the major publishers started sending book contracts and he merely accepted the largest one and "then owed them a book." The interview continued: "But there was no book. We just took the biggest contract. Why? I don't know. . . . So I sat down and wrote them a book in the hotel rooms and different places, plus I got a lot of other papers laying around that other people had written, so I threw it all together in a week and sent it to them." Soon afterward, Dylan received his copy to proofread, rejected it (saying, "My gosh, did I write this? I'm not gonna have this out"), and relayed to the publisher that he had "corrections" to make. He wrote another "book" and sent it in only to repeat the process ("I just looked at the first paragraph—and knew I just couldn't let that stand"). After taking the manuscript on tour in an attempt to meet the publisher's deadline, the writer's frustrations grew: "But still, it wasn't any book; it was just to satisfy the publishers who wanted to print something that we had a contract for. Follow me? So eventually, I had my motorcycle accident and that just got me out of the whole thing." The publisher's notes to *Tarantula*'s original edition concur with Dylan's observations. After copies of galley proofs and advanced review copies filtered out through the press (and others), Macmillan and Dylan decided to publish the original set of writings, as the publisher states: "People change and their feelings change. But *Tarantula* hasn't been changed. Bob wants it published and so it is now time to publish it. This is Bob Dylan's first book. It is the way he wrote it when he was twenty-three—just this way—and now you know."

Tarantula contains forty-seven entries with crazy titles (e.g., "A Confederate Poke into King Arthur's Oakie") attributed to different authors (e.g., "Popeye Squirm"). Several entries kick about celebrity names in strange, unwieldy contexts; others introduce characters with wild street names that may (or may not) say something about those characterizations. Yet, once again, nothing ever seems to happen. Once the reader gains a feel for what is going on, everything changes. In these impressionistic antinarratives, characters appear and do things, suddenly disappear as the context instantly changes planets, and then reappear doing something totally unrelated to the previous act. These expressions involve a concerted effort to make plot progression or continuity impossible. Often, one finds oneself looking at words instead of reading or, as Matt Damsker writes for *Rolling Stone*, "Maybe it amounts to a lot more typing than writing, but *Tarantula* captures the teeming tenor of the bard at a moment when he seemed singularly capable of naming the unnameable [*sic*]."

But what do we expect? The author was unequivocal in his explanation of what he was, in fact, doing. Bob Dylan had nothing to say with *Tarantula*. It was writing for the sake of writing (or, more accurately, *publishing* for the sake of *publishing*). He received a contract and placed himself in the unfortunate position of having to deliver a manuscript with no purpose other than fulfilling his contractual obligation. That Macmillan accepted and published a work that its author disavowed says everything. The disbelief must have been intoxicating for Dylan, who was relentlessly churning out words that meant little to him and *everything* to *everybody* else. In the end, the project seems to have worn out the auteur. He toyed and toyed with the idea, placed it aside after the motorcycle accident, and finally acquiesced and allowed the original work to be published.

To take excerpts from *Tarantula* and present them as I do Dylan's song lyrics or his liner notes is to do nothing less than betray the work. There is just *no way* to extract a scene, examine its contents, and build an argument that is representative of the whole. To place the whole bloody book here is absurd (and illegal), so for the one time in this study, I *must* send you on *your* mission and urge you to check it out for yourself. In terms of this study's framework, however, I stand by Sounes's view that the book is "a hundred and thirty-seven pages of liner notes." Consequently, by returning to the various liner notes we've examined thus far, we may gain a feel for the type of writing in evidence within *Tarantula*. Good luck, and be careful—these kinds of trips to Desolation Row force you to dance with Mr. Tambourine Man, and *that's* potentially dangerous for your psyche.

Joining in that fondling of hazardous material is another project that hit the hold button after Dylan's Triumph motorcycle slid down that narrow Woodstock road. With D. A. Pennebaker and Howard Alk back on the cameras, Bob Neuwirth handling the sound (with Jones Cullinan), and music mixing by Phil Ramone, and with Dylan and Alk doing the editing, *Eat The Document* returns to the cinematic strategy of *Dont Look Back* and toys with that formula. With shots of press conferences, fans' goings and comings/rantings and ravings, hotel rooms, restaurants, green rooms, business dealings, and live performances, and image after image of constant motion (e.g., trains, buses, and cars) providing the raw materials, this film is almost too sketchy to be meaningful. Unlike *Dont*, the scenes are underdeveloped. There is no character in Bob Neuwirth's role (members of The Band appear here and there, but without the consistency of Neuwirth's role—everybody here plays Donovan's or Joan Baez's role). Pennebaker's coherent mission of capturing the activities occurring around the musical performances is absent. Though the film works hard to establish the controversy over Dylan's new band, it seems to concentrate more on the auteur's deteriorating situation than anything else. Still, the more concentrated performance scenes offer compelling insight into Dylan's new method of presenting his songs. That Bob Dylan is no longer that acoustic troubadour of old is made oh-so-clear by *Eat The Document*.

The movie's opening scene says it all. Here, Dylan and Richard Manuel are presented in a fine but empty restaurant (only a waiter stands off in the distance). Our first view of the auteur shows him bent over a table, consuming what would appear to be lines of cocaine (Manuel joins in the fun in a more obvious manner, using his fingernail to do the deed). Afterward, Dylan breaks into hysterical laughter—the kind of mad, uncontrollable laughter the characters of the movie *Reefer Madness* portray after smoking marijuana. The hysterics cease and Dylan moves to the piano for a bit of classical music. From there, we cut to image after image: train passengers, shots of the train, animals, countryside, back to the moving train, band members, strangers, and a jittery Dylan. With but a few exceptions, this is *Eat The Document*. The action is fast-paced, uneven, underdeveloped, and, more often than not, virtually incoherent.

The film moves to different scenes, from a sound check to the changing of the Buckingham Palace guards (Dylan looks *horrible*) featuring a menacing guard dog and an apocalyptic protestor; to a bus trip, shots of the street, a car cruising down a country road at a high speed, and a man recounting an accident on that road (I think); to a Dylan voice-over (apologizing for any mistake he has made); to scenes from a concert; to a series of shots featuring a blonde woman (appearing in and out of scenes for no apparent reason); to a press conference; to a scene with Dylan and Robbie Robertson writing songs in a hotel room (the movie cuts back to this scene from time to time and, in fact, ends there); and on and on. At one point, Dylan applies a fake mustache, different shots appear with different women (the blonde pops in and out of the mix), the Dylan-Robertson hotel scene returns, and shots of photographers awaiting Dylan and a series of fan reactions to Dylan's new method of performing are shown. *Nothing is ever developed.* We hop, skip, and jump our way through a maze of images that—unlike *Dont Look Back*—do not communicate anything. A scene with Johnny Cash joins brief appearances by Albert Grossman and John Lennon that are featured for no apparent reason—just like everything else. Yet, two segments achieve a measure of depth as the film captures the "going electric" controversy and offers its version of an Elvis Presley movie, respectively.

A long segment built around the performance of "Ballad Of A Thin Man" establishes the intensity of fans' reactions to Dylan's new band and performance style. I don't think it takes a rocket scientist to recognize how Dylan used "Thin Man" lyrics to frame the differing opinions and establish their lost qualities. Fans scream that the new show is rubbish, while others celebrate the show. A brief shot featuring a journalist offers a reporter–as–Mister Jones implication. There, Dylan is asked if he is ever not onstage, to which he merely shrugs his shoulders (the suggestion is clearly "no"). More fan rants follow as the song proceeds. Every side of the Story is told: Some fans are heated in their opinions (one man suggests that the auteur is languishing in the gutter), others are worshipful (one fan states that Dylan is superior to Elvis Presley), and one fan is utterly confused by the whole thing, as she just walks away. As the segment ends, Dylan yawns, adding his response to the mix as well. To suggest that this portion of *Eat The Document* is driven by an agenda is to offer the most obvious conclusion.

After a brief scene in which Dylan unsuccessfully pursues an elderly lady's opinion of "Tom Thumb's Blues," we move to the Elvis portion of *Eat The Document*. This protracted segment features Dylan and Richard Manuel (along with very brief shots of other band members) walking around a village, climbing through what appear to be ruins, and moving down a street. One shot shows Dylan standing by the road holding some flowers. As he walks around with his flowers, Dylan and Manuel come across a beautiful blonde sitting by the road with her apparent boyfriend. Seemingly speaking on Dylan's behalf (he stands behind Manuel, flowers in hand), Manuel bargains with the guy for his woman. He offers his jacket, adds a can opener and Chapstick, throws in his shirt, and inquires if she is a cigar smoker. Failing to close the deal and complaining about her business skills, Manuel raises the ante by tossing in his cigarettes. Manuel announces that that's all he has before asking the guy how much money is required. The guy is quick to respond, 2000 crowns. The segment closes with Manuel inquiring if he would accept Australian currency. Without question, this is—by far—the longest, most detailed scene in the movie. And so it goes.

For me, *the* telltale scene in *Eat The Document* involves the brief appearance by John Lennon. It opens with a shot through a car windshield that reveals a rainy ride through winding streets. A tight close-up of a sick, weary, about-to-vomit Bob Dylan follows. He is leaning forward, pale and gaunt. Suddenly we hear a supportive voice urging Dylan to pull himself together. The camera pulls back and Lennon appears, nonchalantly encouraging Dylan to rise to his occasion. The scene ends with the camera returning to the windshield shot.

Although *Eat The Document* effectively communicates the intensity of the fans' reactions to the new musical style that controlled Tour '66 and offers several extended examples of Dylan and the Hawks in action, the movie's significance lies elsewhere for me. From the opening scene to the segment with John Lennon, the film captures the State of Bob Dylan in unequivocal terms. The man is wasted. From his mad laughter after supposedly doing cocaine, to his death stare as he watches the changing of the palace guard, to his frenetic performances with the Hawks, to his tired exchanges with journalists, to the shots with Lennon, this film relates the necessity of a motorcycle accident—or its functional equivalent. The clever interactions between Dylan and reporters, the playful encounters with cute English girls, the polite reception of the politician's friendly wife, the focused intensity of his performances—all of those characteristics that make *Dont Look Back* a coherent representation of the 1965 British tour—are *totally* absent in *Eat The Document*. In their place is a series of disjointed scenes that flirt with *Dont*'s themes. Perhaps Dylan sums the situation best in one of the few scenes featuring Grossman. There, Grossman talks with Tito Burns (also featured in *Dont*) about some problem and Dylan responds that he is surprised by the difficulties he constantly endures.

That sums the Newport Mod era of Bob Dylan's career. What began with fun-loving music making that was designed to distance the auteur from the more dysfunctional elements of his audience slowly but surely evolved into a sad, sacrificial situation. He rejected all that hero worship through a good old-fashioned game of Glissendorf, and in so doing, changed songwriting forever. When he articulated those lyrics through a new musical style, all hell broke loose. Fortunately, Bob Zimmerman was prepared for that as well. Not only did the Iron Range's original biker-poet display the wherewithal to combat the Mr. Message Man branch of his constituency through his innovative word games, but he also knew how to stand before a rude audience and do his thing. This man was more than prepared for the task at hand. When his audience booed, fine. When his audience got lost in his words, wonderful. Bob Zimmerman's "Bob Dylan" was practically *trained* for his eventual profession.

But something happened. The difference in the Dylan of *Dont Look Back* and the Dylan of *Eat The Document* is staggering. The cocky, self-assured but polite poet of *Dont* disappeared into a wiry, jittery, distant performer whose wit and cutting humor devolved into blank expressions with nothing to say. For example, when you compare the journalistic encounters of *Dont* with the press scenes of *Eat*, the results are troublesome. Instead of sharp, attentive responses, we witness tired, empty platitudes—usually slurred and sloppy. When the reporter in *Eat* asked if Dylan ever ventured off stage, all he received was a shrug. In *Dont*, Dylan would have challenged the question, inquiring what was meant by "stage" or "performance" or some other detail. Yes, something happened. I could speculate on these personal matters, but I swore that off. Whatever it was, it caused that wonderful word machine that gave the world "Desolation Row" to run out of gas in Nashville during *Blonde On Blonde*. Whatever it was, it caused the sharp, witty personality of *Dont* to become anything but sharp or witty in *Eat*. Whatever it was, it caused the dynamic performer to evolve into a demonic actor. Whatever it was, it had to end. Or else, the Bob Dylan story would have closed here. The Newport Mod era of Bob Zimmerman's career required all of the talent, energy, and perseverance the man had to offer, and gave precious little back to him personally aside from the songs. Now it was time to purge. Now it was time for the Iron Range's original biker-poet to prove that he was more a poet than a biker.

The Americana Period

Few places are as beautiful as Paris in the spring. The French manicure their gardens in ways that complement their architecture to render magnificent vistas that reflect the grace and style of that nation's capitol city. What a wonderful place to celebrate your twenty-fifth birthday. How could you improve on *Paris* as the site of that once-in-a-lifetime occasion? Well, that may hold true for you and me, but that is not how it worked out for the voice of his generation on *his* twenty-fifth birthday. May 24, 1966, represented the first day of Bob Zimmerman's twenty-fifth year on this planet, and he celebrated through one of Bob Dylan's chaotic 1966 world tour's more cantankerous shows. With a huge American flag draped in the background, Dylan stood before a mixed audience. The biographers report that there were those who were offended by the flag, others who were pleased to see their musical hero on his birthday, and others who were there for the spectacle of a public confrontation. By all reports, Dylan was antagonistic. Robert Shelton claims that a fourteen-minute, mid-show tuning session inspired "jeers" from the audience that Dylan "silenced" by announcing, "I'm doing this for you. I couldn't care less. I wouldn't behave like that if I came to see you." During another tuning break he sneered, "Don't worry, I'm just as eager to finish and leave as you are."

Happy birthday, Bob.

The tour's final shows featured more of the same, including the infamous Royal Albert Hall concert and its historic confrontation between an audience member screaming "Judas" and an artist declaring that individual to be a "liar." This was not the London of *Dont Look Back*. That tour was nowhere in sight: no adoring English girls, no invitations to stay in mansions, no fun-loving escapes after shows. Tour '66 was hellish. Bob Dillon's mettle was thoroughly tested during this embattled world tour. The aesthetic riot that was rumored to have started in Newport and intensified in Forest Hills calmed during a fall 1965 west coast swing and, somehow or another, reignited in 1966. The Hawks' drummer, Levon Helm, had long since departed due to his inability to endure the hostility (he was replaced by Mickey Jones). Dillon's rebellion fueled Dylan's resistance, and, somehow or another, the troupe survived the grueling experience. To suggest that Bob Dylan returned to his native soil a road-worn celebrity is to use the kind of understatement that undermines my credibility as a human—the man was literally knocking on death's door. He was a ghostly figure, pale and gaunt. *All* reports confirm this situation—there are *no* exceptions. The *proof* is in *Eat The Document*.

What was in no way dying was the commercial juggernaut that operated under the name of "Bob Dylan." In May 1966, *Blonde On Blonde* was released. After the 1966 tour, the commercial hellhounds were on the auteur's trail. He owed ABC-TV the *Eat The Document* film. He owed Macmillan *Tarantula*. His contract with Columbia Records was expiring, and negotiations were underway with both Columbia and MGM (who reportedly offered a $1 million signing bonus). In addition, Albert Grossman had arranged a bearish tour of sixty-plus dates that was scheduled to begin that fall. At the heart of it all was a frail, weak, uninspired artist whose bohemian lifestyle, demanding schedule, and commercial obligations were more than overwhelming; they were potentially fatal. Love, however, was in his life, and Sara Dylan proved to be his personal savior. But something had to be done about all of these obligations. The creative fire of 1965 was not only extinguished by the hard rain of the 1966 tour; the man's life was threatened. He stood at that proverbial crossroads. Which way would he turn?

In *Bob Dylan, Bruce Springsteen & American Song*, I foolishly claimed that the motorcycle accident of July 29, 1966, "was a welcome reprieve" for Dylan. Though it relieved several of the commercial pressures of that moment, I now seriously doubt that it was "welcomed" by anyone. Or maybe it was. I simply don't know. Much mystery surrounds this point in time. Just what was the extent of his injuries? Cynical observers questioned if the accident happened at all. Supposedly, Dylan was riding his bike when his rear wheel locked and sent him reeling. Rumors of a broken neck, crushed vertebrae, disfigurement, death, and insanity followed. Grossman was exasperated. Macmillan was polite. ABC was silent. The record companies disappeared. "Bob Dylan" convalesced with his wife and growing family in the rural New York town of Woodstock, site of the motorcycle incident.

Whether or not Bob Zimmerman was riding that motorcycle with Bob Dylan is uncertain. Perhaps the Glissendorf Master orchestrated one of his greatest stunts. Or maybe not. Really, it does not matter. What matters is that Bob Dillon pushed Bob Dylan to the extent that something had to happen. The energy—whether naturally or unnaturally fueled—required to tour the world, generate a book, produce a film, and cope with a demanding industry and its constituency drained all of the rebellion, creativity, and health from the artist. Hence, the actual or metaphorical "accident" produced what is widely viewed as the lifework's pivotal turning point. Just as Dillon provided the rebellion necessary for Dylan to reject his folk audience and refocus his finger-pointing muse in unprecedented directions, Zimmerman would now rely on that other facet of his Dylan composite to save this new day, renew his damaged life, and reinvigorate his art. A new mission emerged after the 1966 tour—recovery—and to the rescue came none other than Jack Fate and his encyclopedic knowledge of music.

The biographers tell us that after that infamous wreck on the highway, Zimmerman refocused his life. He dismissed vices such as smoking cigarettes (which revived his voice), embraced fatherhood (four times), and in general quieted his life. All the while, he worked. He read. He painted. He toyed with *Eat The Document* (doing irreparable damage to some of the raw footage) and invited members of the Hawks to Woodstock to participate in some filmmaking ideas. Rick Danko and Richard Manuel ventured to Woodstock and eventually rented a secluded house in West

Saugerties with Garth Hudson. The split-level house was painted a shade of pink, so the boys named their new digs Big Pink. Soon, Robbie Robertson and his girlfriend obtained a place nearby, and, much later, Levon Helm found his way north as well. What started as informal music-making sessions in a room in Dylan's house (called the "Red Room") found a new home in the basement of Big Pink. The results were cathartic for all.

Here Zimmerman allowed the Jack Fate portion of the Dylan composite to flourish and, in so doing, initiated a creative strategy that would prove to be a magical elixir throughout his career. "The Basement Strategy" emerged during 1967; and whenever Dylan's art entered a state of uncertainty, Fate and the Basement Strategy would rescue the auteur. The Basement Strategy is a creative process by which Zimmerman turns to Fate's vast musical education as a means of relieving creative pressure by revisiting his artistic foundation, fondling its treasures, and rediscovering the inventive magic to be applied to the mission at hand. The lessons from Gatemouth Page's radio show and the records ordered through his mail-order system; the conversations with Jim Dandy and anybody that would talk about music; the experiences in Denver, Dinkytown, New Jersey, and New York; and all those hours with Library of Congress recordings and specialty record collections shaped Fate's immense knowledge. Consequently, Dylan used that musical library to reorient his creative impulse and refocus his artistic objectives. The strategy was perfected in 1967 and deployed at crucial moments over the next twenty-five years. It is, in every respect, a critical part of Zimmerman's career and, perhaps, the key to his longevity.

The results involved a wandering—at times, meandering—musical recovery. Along with the *Basement Tapes*, this phase contains six albums that I group into three segments: first, *John Wesley Harding* (released in December 1967) and *Nashville Skyline* (April 1969); second, *Self Portrait* (June 1970), *New Morning* (October 1970), and *Dylan* (November 1973); and third, *Planet Waves* (January 1974) and the "Tour '74" reunion. Here we observe Dylan struggling with his creative instincts—trying to rediscover the spontaneous reception of the inspirational signals that supplied his art. We move from the playful rejuvenation of the basement to the obligatory (and somewhat rebellious) acts that were *Harding* and *Skyline* to the confusion of the *Portrait-Morning-Dylan* episodes to the Big Show that was the Tour '74–*Planet Waves* explosion. Throughout, Dylan's mission of recovery is steadfastly pursued as he rebounds, rebels, reorients, and returns to his station as the musical world's leading act. As Jack Fate frolics in the basement with his buddies, returns to Nashville to record country music with Bob Johnston, rejects his adoring constituency through one of Bob Dillon's boldest acts, and revisits the stage with his 1966 cohorts, our auteur—Bob Dylan—leaves the 1960s behind and prepares himself for musical adventures that were, no doubt, unimaginable during this portion of his career. As a result, he refines the Basement Strategy, solidifies his artistic foundation, and enables his career's future. Our story begins underground, inside Big Pink.

The Basement Tapes

After the motorcycle incident, Dylan's activities slowed in a predictable fashion. He escaped the intrusions of celebrity via a six-week stay with a nearby physician, using a spare apartment in the doctor's home as his refuge. While he convalesced in and around the Woodstock area, his commercial engines churned onward in a steady, productive manner. His first "greatest hits" was issued in March 1967 (containing but one unreleased song, "Positively 4th Street"), and *Dont Look Back* appeared that May. Although *Tarantula*, *Eat The Document*, Grossman's protracted tour, and record contract negotiations were placed on hold, the Bob Dylan commercial machine continued to prosper. With a huge back catalog of outtakes and concerts in the Columbia vaults, Grossman and the Columbia team could conceivably hold out for quite a while. That reveals just how productive Bob Dylan had been over the previous five years.

Our story resumes in early 1967, when the Hawks—soon to be The Band— reassembled in the Woodstock area. The musical merriment that began in Dylan's Red Room soon moved over to Big Pink's basement, and a daily schedule emerged. Rick Danko told Howard Sounes that "Bob and Robbie . . . would come by every day, five to seven days a week for seven or eight months . . . [Bob] would show up like clockwork around noon." With Band members still adhering to their late-night on-the-road lifestyle, the new domesticated Dylan arrived "like clockwork" each day to brew high-test coffee as he typed away with song ideas (loudly, we are told) while the boys slowly awakened, and—once everyone was primed for the day—moved into the basement to play around with their musical ideas. The biographers describe the open windows, the dog on the floor, and the relaxed, free-flowing qualities of these musicology exercises in which the musicians played old and traditional songs, recorded them on minimal (but effective) equipment, and eventually used the exercise as the springboard to new material. Robbie Robertson described the process to *Basement Tape* expert Greil Marcus:

> We went in with a sense of humor. It was all a goof. We were playing with absolute freedom; we weren't doing anything we thought anybody else would ever hear, as long as we lived. But what started in that basement, what came out of it—and the Band came out of it, anthems, people holding hands and rocking back and forth all over the world singing "I Shall Be Released," the distance that all of this went—came out of this little conspiracy, of us amusing ourselves. Killing time.

What might appear to be killing time to one may actually be a product of a systematic plan, as Robertson indicated to biographer Clinton Heylin:

> With the covers Bob was educating us a little. The whole folkie thing was still very questionable to us—it wasn't the train we came in on. He'd be doing this Pete Seeger stuff and I'd be saying, "Oh God . . ." And then, it might be music you knew you didn't like, he'd come up with something like "[The Banks of the] Royal Canal," and you'd say, "This is so beautiful! The expression!" He wasn't so obvious about it. But he remembered too much, remembered too many songs too well. He'd come over to Big

Pink, or wherever we were, and pull out some old song—and he'd prepped for this. He'd practiced this, and then come out here, to show us.

On another occasion, Robertson told Marcus, "He would pull these songs out of nowhere. We didn't know if he wrote them or if he remembered them. When he sang them, you couldn't tell." From this, one gains images of Dylan massaging the Jack Fate portion of his composite personality by sitting in a candlelit room—after the kids are tucked away for the evening—sipping wine with Sara, practicing the songs he'd unveil to his sleepy-eyed colleagues the next day. There is always, my friends, a mission.

The songwriting that followed inspired all. It seeded The Band's career and fertilized Dylan's. Garth Hudson described the basement songwriting process in Heylin's biography: "We were doing seven, eight, ten, sometimes fifteen songs a day. Some were old ballads and traditional songs . . . but others Bob would make up as he went along. . . . We'd play the melody, he'd sing a few words he'd written, and then make up some more, or else just mouth sounds or even syllables as he went along. It's a pretty good way to write songs." Instead of hiring expensive Nashville session players to play cards or ping-pong while he prepared the next track to record (as per the *Blonde* sessions), Dylan adapted his method to Big Pink, deploying a similar strategy in a more relaxed fashion that invited more participation. As a result, coauthored gems such as "Tears Of Rage" (written with Manuel) and "This Wheel's On Fire" (written with Danko) emerged from Big Pink's basement.

To capture the fruits of their basement labors, Big Pink engineer Garth Hudson set up the home-cooked recording studio. Heylin's session chronology cites the specifics. He reports that about "a hundred" of the approximately 150 basement recordings exist from the sessions that unfolded from March–April 1967 through November (sources indicate The Band continued the practice after Dylan departed for Nashville in mid-October for the *John Wesley Harding* sessions into early 1968). Although critics describe the results as "home recordings," the equipment used represented one mighty fine home system. Heylin provides the details:

> [Hudson] was able to use some "leftovers" from the PA equipment used on the 1965–66 world tour. These included a couple of Altech PA tube (as opposed to transistor) "mixers" that allowed up to three microphone inputs per channel, and four or five studio quality Neumann microphones. The use of something as state of the art as Neumann mikes plus the two tube mixer units explains why the sound of the basements has that deliciously rich warmth (indeed what sounds suspiciously like reverb on Dylan's vocals is actually the result of this Neumann/Altech combination). Sadly the official CBS album conveys little of this richness.

Heylin is being uncharacteristically generous in that last comment. The Columbia version of the basement recordings is completely void of the wide stereo sound that one hears on unofficial versions. Having said that, the results of the Neumann-Altech arrangement were captured on a Uher reel-to-reel that was road-tested during the world tour as well. Dylan offered his views on the basement method to *Rolling Stone*'s

Jann Wenner in 1969: "You know, that's really the way to do a recording—in a peaceful, relaxed setting, in somebody's basement, with the windows open and a dog lying on the floor." Such was the bliss of Big Pink.

It would be misleading to suggest that the group entered the basement each day, fired up their system, and recorded whatever crossed their minds. This was not the case. They ran through songs before rolling tape. They deleted song fragments and false starts (most of them, anyway). Although it took a while for Hudson to gain his basement legs (several songs feature poor audio levels or distorted sounds), the process was more systematic than the legend suggests. Once more, evidence of a specific mission floats in and out of the varied accounts of basement happenings. Like a good college teacher, Professor Dylan created an educational environment that inspired *everyone*, including the instructor. (As a quick aside, Greil Marcus's incomparable discography charts the histories of all of the basement songs. It is an indispensable guide through this maze of recordings.)

Once the group started generating new material, Dylan's publisher realized the potential for other artists to record these new songs. Consequently, Dwarf Music dubbed fourteen songs from stereo to mono (via two "releases" of 10 and 4), pressed acetates of the demos, and sent them out to artists/publishers for consideration. Two important consequences flow from this decision. First, artists such as Peter, Paul and Mary ("Too Much Of Nothing"); Manfred Mann ("The Mighty Quinn"); the Byrds ("You Ain't Goin' Nowhere" and "Nothing Was Delivered"); Julie Driscoll and the Brian Auger Trinity ("This Wheel's On Fire"); and later, of course, The Band (selecting whatever they wanted for their *Music From Big Pink* album) recorded basement tunes and enjoyed varying degrees of prosperity with the results. Second, the "other" music industry was created. We'll save arguments regarding the pros and cons of the bootleg industry for another time; however, that channel for disseminating unofficial versions of songs, albums, and shows was literally born by way of the Basement Tapes. That *Rolling Stone* actually *reviewed* the bootlegged version of the Basement Tapes years before the official Columbia release is telltale. Subsequently, when Columbia finally got around to issuing a diluted version of the recordings (transforming the original stereo recordings into what Heylin terms "collapsed mono" and adding songs by The Band without Dylan), Dylan wryly observed that he thought everybody already had them. Such is the historical significance of this informal gathering of friendly musicians "killing time" in their basement.

Turning to the tapes themselves, we hear a wonderful example of musical collegiality as a group of road-weary veterans relax and play with musical ideas and, on occasion, just fool around. Incomplete songs such as "Baby, Won't You Be My Baby," "I'm Guilty Of Loving You," "Gimme Another Bourbon Street," and "Lock Your Door," and songs that would eventually appear on the official release such as "Open The Door, Homer," "Tears Of Rage #2," and "Nothing Was Delivered #1," demonstrate the work-in-progress qualities of the basement experience. At times, we hear awful recordings (e.g., "Going Down The Road" and "I Can't Come In With A Broken Heart") that indicate that engineer Hudson was gaining his basement bearings.

Essential to the Basement Strategy's success is the use of diverse cover songs to stimulate the sessions and unlock new ideas—or just to fool around. These cover songs emerge from every conceivable direction. Ranging from "Flight Of The Bum-ble Bee" (Rimsky-Korsakov) to "Cool Water" (Nolan) to "See You Later, Allen Ginsburg" (Guidry) to "People Get Ready" (Mayfield) to Johnny Cash tunes ("Big River," "Folsom Prison Blues," and "Belshazar") to John Lee Hooker songs ("I'm In The Mood" and "Tupelo") to classics such as "The Royal Canal" (Behan), "Four Strong Winds" (Tyson), "Wildwood Flower" (Carter) and "You Win Again" (Williams) to the silliness of "Coming Round The Mountain" (traditional), these songs extend from the ridiculous to the sublime to the more than ridiculous. At times, established songs such as "All American Boy" (Parsons/Lunsford) are transformed into new creations that Dylan's publishers actually copyrighted (as another aside, this particular revision captures the attentions of biographers due to what are considered to be biographical references to Albert Grossman). The use of traditional tunes such as "Going Down The Road," "Bonnie Ship The Diamond," "Po' Lazarus," and "Young But Daily Growing" demonstrate that Jack Fate's musical encyclopedia was wide open and flipping through its storied pages.

Yet, what is most revealing to me is the informal instruction and the tomfoolery that appear on many tracks. We hear Dylan coaching his team, calling out chord changes, or demonstrating harmonies. During "Big River #2," we hear Dylan asking if there's room on the tape for an ending. The auteur just breaks up laughing on "Get Your Rocks Off!" and "Lo And Behold #1" as well as several other tracks. His playful cursing colors "Next Time On The Highway." "Bring It On Home" is one big hoot as the boys search for a groove while laughing, talking, probing, and laughing some more. "The Spanish Song" is the basement version of "Rainy Day Women #12 & 35" as the boys yell, whistle, and fool around (after the second take, Dylan asks if "you wanna tape this one"—apparently unaware of the Big Pink engineer's activities). Finally, after recording a raucous "Hills Of Mexico," Dylan tells Hudson that he's just "wasting tape." These are the special moments that Columbia wasted when it elected to offer such sanitized versions of the basements. You can *hear* the convalescence while listening to these recordings. Under Jack Fate's direction, Bob Dylan is on the mend.

When we pull back and examine the 100 or so tracks and kick out the incomplete, unintelligible, or cover songs, three types of songs emerge: hymns, blues or 1950s rock-and-roll songs, and what I affectionately call "goof tunes." There are but a few exceptions. The folk-country masterpiece that is "I'm Not There (1956)" is one. What I deem to be "Band songs" (e.g., "Goin' To Acapulco" and the multiple tracks that appear on the official release) is another. Lastly, country songs such as "Next Time On The Highway" and "I'm A Fool For You" represent others. Otherwise, there is a steady emphasis on the hymnlike, 1950s-sounding, goofy songs. Let us turn to some examples that communicate just how the basements built a bridge between the *Blonde* and *Harding* projects while facilitating the auteur's mission of recovery.

We begin with the hymns. This designation has more to do with the songs' sonic qualities than anything else, since their lyrics display varying levels of clarity. Covers such as "People Get Ready" and "See That My Grave Is Kept Clean" are direct in their communicative style, whereas songs such as "I Shall Be Released" and "Tears Of Rage" sound like hymns while flirting with cloudy topics. I've selected three basement tunes that extend across a spectrum from classic narrative impressionism ("This Wheel's On Fire") to moderate clarity ("Too Much Of Nothing") to undeniable reverence ("Sign On The Cross"). Salvation, repentance, moral justice, and faith are recurrent songwriting themes throughout the oeuvre (as they will also appear in The Band's work), so the presence of these songs is no surprise. Here these inclinations assume a more enigmatic status due, no doubt, to the basement environment's exploratory nature. With the coauthored "Wheel's," the musicians create a solemn sonic platform for a series of observations that lack any sense of character development or story line; nevertheless, it preaches the value of a strong memory. The three stanzas are highly repetitive, with the opening seven lines loosely describing some scene before closing with a five-line sequence. The opening verse captures the strategy:

> If your mem'ry serves you well,
> We were goin' to meet again and wait,
> So I'm goin' to unpack all my things
> And sit before it gets too late.
> No man alive will come to you
> With another tale to tell,
> But you know that we shall meet again
> If your mem'ry serves you well.
> This wheel's on fire,
> Rolling down the road,
> Best notify my next of kin,
> This wheel shall explode!

Ever get the feeling that you just walked into the middle of a scene without any idea of what's happening? We've certainly felt that sensation before, haven't we? The next verse discusses how the narrator intended to "confiscate" the other person's "lace," tie it in a "sailor's knot," and hide it. He is uncertain if, in fact, it was that person's "lace" and we drift into the five-line closing. The final verse recalls how the narrator was called upon to get "them" to do the other person's "favors" but those plans "failed" and that was that. As you can see, this is a classic example of the narrative impressionism writing strategy in that the opening lines present some cryptic scene that is anchored by the recurring tag lines—the functional equivalent of a chorus. That "wheel" may surely be "on fire," but precious little insight is offered as to the nature of our wheel, the narrator, or his or her correspondent. Nevertheless, you find yourself wanting to respond with a hearty "amen" after each verse.

"Too Much Of Nothing" is evasive but not quite as cryptic. Here we have three eight-line verses that are followed by three four-line choruses in which the respective stanzas offer moral prescriptions regarding moderation, modesty, and patience (I think; they may also be about sewing, cooking, and gardening). Let's consider the second stanza and the chorus as our case in point:

> Too much of nothing
> Can make a man abuse a king.
> He can walk the streets and boast like most

But he wouldn't know a thing.
Now, it's all been done before,
It's all been written in the book,
But when there's too much of nothing,
Nobody should look.
Chorus: Say hello to Valerie
      Say hello to Vivian
      Send them all my salary
      On the waters of oblivion

Again, this is the verse I suggest involves some treatment of a modesty theme; yet, as you can see, it dances around that topic as much as anything. As the song proceeds through the respective lines, the music builds and builds in a haunting manner that contributes to the track's sermonic feel. Dylan sounds like Vincent Price in the pulpit as the stanza progresses toward the chorus. It is a creepy vocal, that is for sure. "Valerie" and "Vivian" rhyme nicely with "salary" and "oblivion," and therein may lie their significance. In any event, I suspect the author is massaging anxieties concerning the futility of some particular act or achievement. The last verse is insightful:

Too much of nothing
Can turn a man into a liar,
It can cause one man to sleep on nails
And another man to eat fire.
Ev'rybody's doin' somethin',
I heard it in a dream,
But when there's too much of nothing,
It just makes a fella mean.

Popular interpretations of this song typically focus on some type of celebrity angst by suggesting Dylan is frustrated by the perceived uselessness of his activities. From this perspective, the narrator's been involved in a whole lot of nothing, so he shares his disgust via a warning that reports that moderation, modesty, and patience may prove to be useful elixirs for those facing an overabundance of emptiness. Still, beware. Reading too much into these songs is risky business. In the basement of Big Pink, one person's metaphor is another person's folly.

"Sign On The Cross" follows a fundamentally different songwriting strategy. That this song is a hymn is beyond question. Not only does its slow, prodding musical structure follow that format, but the eleven-line testimonial placed between the fourth and fifth verses also fits firmly in that tradition. The verses vary. The song opens with two eight-line stanzas, is followed by two four-line verses and then the testimonial, and closes with a twelve-line stanza. Our narrator is a worried man. He appreciates his "fine" "gold mine," but all the while he knows it is misleading. He recalls his childhood ambitions and declares, "But I was lost on the moon / As I heard that front door slam," before he returns to his worries. The two four-line verses provide a bridge to the testimony as they ponder that "old sign," its significance, and his passing "friends." From there, we witness a spoken testimony that would make Hank Williams's "Luke the Drifter" character proud:

> Well, it seems to be the sign on the cross. Ev'ry day,
> ev'ry night, see the sign on the cross just layin' up
> on top of the hill. Yes, we thought it might have
> disappeared long ago, but I'm here to tell you, friends,
> that I'm afraid it's lyin' there still. Yes, just a
> little time is all you need, you might say, but I don't
> know 'bout that any more, because the bird is here and
> you might want to enter it, but, of course, the door might
> be closed. But I just would like to tell you one time,
> if I don't see you again, that the thing is, that the sign
> on the cross is the thing you might need the most.

Our sermon of perseverance continues with the closing stanza's message of encouragement. Reverend Dylan reports that "when your days are numbered" or "your nights are long," you may think that "you're weak" when in fact "you're strong." So, as your worries mount, relax, "sing" out, "And all your troubles will pass right on through." While "Wheel's" may tease you with its reverent sounds and "Too Much" may frighten you with its haunting, eerie vocals, "Sign On The Cross" is the real sermonic deal. The basement tent revival featured a blood-stained shade of pink when the tape rolled that day as the auteur and his cohorts fondled sentiments that never seem to be very far away from the songwriter's pen—a tendency that foreshadows the late 1970s in no uncertain terms.

To the extent that "Sign" previews the future, the 1950s-style tunes revisit the musical past. We consider two examples of this category: "Odds And Ends" and "Nothing Was Delivered." "Odds" is classic 1950s rock-and-roll song; it's vacuous beyond belief. The tune complains about a relationship and the narrator's partner's habit of "spillin' juice" all over him. Like so many of those 1950s songs, a central metaphor is the song's pivot—here, the "juice" reference. So have fun with this 1:46 ditty; that is, after all, what this genre is all about.

The three six-line stanzas pause for a spectacular guitar break between the second and third verses. This aural party is simple, coherent, and a solid example of a songwriting strategy that passed on almost the moment it arrived. Let's examine the opening verses for detail:

> I plan it all and I take my place
> You break your promise all over the place
> You promised to love me, but what do I see
> Just you comin' and spillin' juice over me
> Odds and ends, odds and ends
> Lost time is not found again
>
> Now, you take your file and you bend my head
> I never can remember anything that you said

You promised to love me, but what do I know
You're always spillin' juice on me like you got someplace to go
Odds and ends, odds and ends
Lost time is not found again

The moral about "lost time" is our most accessible line as the song plays with the "juice" imagery. Since there is no need to cry over spilt juice, we move on after appreciating this basement adaptation of an established genre.

"Nothing Was Delivered" is a Fats Domino–New Orleans–style sermon that could easily fit with the "hymns" I discussed previously. The track's sonic qualities move me to place it here, however. Classic 1950s piano work echoes upriver from the Big Easy and provides a musical context for lyrics that are as coherent as any basement offering. The three 8–9-line stanzas join three two-line choruses to create a balanced, steady sermon. The opening verse/chorus captures the song's prescriptive tone:

Nothing was delivered
And I tell this truth to you,
Not out of spite or anger
But simply because it's true.
Now, I hope you won't object to this,
Giving back all of what you owe,
The fewer words you have to waste on this,
The sooner you can go.
Chorus: Nothing is better, nothing is best,
        Take heed of this and get plenty of rest.

The moralizing continues with the second verse:

Nothing was delivered
But I can't say I sympathize
With what your fate is going to be,
Yes, for telling all those lies.
Now you must provide some answers
For what you sell has not been received,
And the sooner you come up with them,
The sooner you can leave.

The final stanza (which opens with an extra line, delivered in a deep, gospel-drenched voice, "Now you know") continues the sermon by reiterating the central point: You are going to have to resolve these matters before you are allowed to proceed. The song is straightforward as it announces that you must pay your debts, stop lying, and explain yourself. My friends, *somebody* is grinding an axe here.

If there is an axe flailing about in our "goof" songs, it is a foam rubber toy with chocolate fingerprints all over it. "Million Dollar Bash," "Yea! Heavy And A Bottle Of Bread," "Lo And Behold!" and "You Ain't Goin' Nowhere" are marvelous examples of what makes the basements so interesting. A master storyteller and enigmatic poet put down their respective songwriting tools in favor of a musical joyride to no particular destination. The boys find a simple instrumental groove and toy with words and images in these songs. The results were, no doubt, medicinal—perhaps in more ways than one.

"Million Dollar Bash" is about as goofy as it gets. The five eleven-line stanzas feature six lines of goofspeak before the five-line announcement of this inclusive gathering that is the "million dollar bash." Come one, come all to the mother of all parties. The song opens with a mentally challenged blonde and her weirdly named friend, follows with a grunt of inclusion, continues with a barn scene populated by the narrator's "counselor" and some storytelling friends, and closes with these two—highly representative—verses:

> Well, I'm hittin' it too hard
> My stones won't take
> I get up in the mornin'
> But it's too early to wake
> First it's hello, goodbye
> Then push and then crash
> But then we're all gonna make it
> At that million dollar bash
> Ooh, baby, ooh-ee
> Ooh, baby, ooh-ee
> It's that million dollar bash
>
> Well, I looked at my watch
> I looked at my wrist
> Punched myself in the face
> With my fist
> I took my potatoes
> Down to be mashed
> Then I made it over
> To that million dollar bash . . .

The song's light, bouncy rhythm complements the wordplay to create a classic basement number. It is all one big laugh full of strange scenes, crazy rhymes, and inclusive partying. Enjoy!

The basement folly continues with "Lo And Behold!" and its light—again, bouncy—tune that features up-front, tight vocals that suggest a country or pop tune with something to say, no matter how trite. Nothing could be further from the case. The world's most famous word machine is on shuffle and is generating phrases that share only a common language. The four eleven-line verses roam from San Antonio through Pittsburgh down to Tennessee and back to Pittsburgh for no apparent reason. The individual stanzas do not feature surreal imagery, clever associations, or narrative vignettes; rather, they are pure tomfoolery. The second and third verses offer insight as to this song's inner workings:

I bought my girl
A herd of moose,
One she could call her own.
Well, she came out the very next day
To see where they had flown.
I'm goin' down to Tennessee,
Get me a truck 'r somethin'.
Gonna save my money and rip it up!
Lo and behold! Lo and behold!
Lookin' for my lo and behold,
Get me outa here, my dear man!

Now, I come in on a ferris wheel
An' boys, I sure was slick.
I come in like a ton of bricks,
Laid a few tricks on 'em.
Goin' back to Pittsburgh,
Count up to thirty,
Round that horn and ride that herd,
Gonna thread up!
Lo and Behold! Lo and Behold! . . .

Of course, this is a direct invocation of the old "herd of flying moose" story with a slight twist for a pickup truck and a traveling carny. Lo and behold, indeed. This basement travelogue with its eight lines of gibberish followed by a three-line plea for escape is a fine example of the boys fooling around with a phrase or two and coloring it whatever shade comes to mind at that particular moment. There is no escaping the subterranean joy of this basement classic.

With "Yea! Heavy," the goofspeak explodes in its simplicity and repetition. The basement spills over with this playful ditty that goes beyond nowhere. The voice of his generation is in his lyrical diapers, hoping somehow to manage the damage caused by his natural urges. That the "bottle" is a major part of this song is to undermine the value of a good pun. The song's structure is indicative of its lyrical depth. The four six-line verses offer three lines of description followed by a single line that is repeated three times (two stanzas are identical and repeat the title, one urges somebody to get the "loot" quickly so they can go fishing, while the other aspires for a trip to California). The first and last verses open with these lines: "Well, the comic book and me, just us, we caught the bus / The poor little chauffeur, though, she was back in bed / On the very next day, with a nose full of pus." *That's* a great image to hang onto, as is the next verse: "It's a one-track town, just brown, and a breeze, too, / Pack up the meat, sweet, we're headin' out / For Wichita in a pile of fruit." Finally, verse 3 brings everything into perspective: "Now, pull that drummer out from behind that bottle. / Bring me my pipe, we're gonna shake it. / Slap that drummer with a pie that smells." Assuredly, "Yea! Heavy" is a master statement by a master spokesman. The basement must have been a bit foggy on that wonderful day.

Our final goofy tune involves a fine example of narrative impressionism—basement style. With "You Ain't Goin' Nowhere," we have classic Dylan scenic descriptions, character one-offs, and surreal images held together by a five-line tag/chorus about the arrival of the narrator's bride. The four eleven-line stanzas offer five lines of impressionism followed by the song title transition (the fourth verse substitutes an alternative line/segue) to the five-line embedded chorus. The first verse is telltale:

> Clouds so swift
> Rain won't lift
> Gate won't close
> Railings froze
> Get your mind off wintertime
> You ain't goin' nowhere
> Whoo-ee! Ride me high
> Tomorrow's the day
> My bride's gonna come
> Oh, oh, are we gonna fly
> Down in the easy chair!

The impressionism complements the song's catchy melody to create an enjoyable, light, and lively pop song. Let's examine the remaining verses' opening lines and enjoy this installment of basement impressionism. The second stanza opens, "I don't care / How many letters they sent / Morning came and morning went / Pick up your money / And pack up your tent / You ain't goin' nowhere." Simple rhymes support jumbled imagery with little to no relation to one another, as the final verse relates: "Genghis Khan / He could not keep / All his kings / Supplied with sleep / We'll climb that hill no matter how steep / When we get up to it." The smooth melody and catchy chorus provide a context for some traditional Dylan songwriting and one of Big Pink's stronger tracks. No wonder that this song did well for the Byrds—it works.

We close our exploration of the basements with a coauthored tune that became a staple for The Band's shows over the years that followed, "Tears Of Rage." The solemn sounds of yet another basement hymn support this cryptic account of relational angst. The three thirteen-line verses ramble through eight lines of cloudy complaint before the five-line closing lament concerning personal thievery and life's tentative qualities. After an evasive opening verse that appears to involve a rebellious "daughter," the song turns to more specific complaints:

> We pointed out the way to go
> And scratched your name in sand,
> Though you just thought it was nothing more
> Than a place for you to stand.
> Now, I want you to know that while we watched,
> You discover there was no one true.
> Most ev'rybody really thought
> It was a childish thing to do.

Tears of rage, tears of grief,
Must I always be the thief?
Come to me now, you know
We're so low
And life is brief.

It was all very painless
When you went out to receive
All that false instruction
Which we never could believe.
And now the heart is filled with gold
As if it was a purse.
But, oh, what kind of love is this
Which goes from bad to worse?
Tears of rage . . .

(Just kidding about that clarity, folks.)

Not only does the song's oh-so-slow delivery and churchy instrumentation create a context for a tale of complaint, but the lyrics hint at that interpretation from time to time as well. Like several of the basements, the track's music displays an incongruent relationship to the lyrics. The music suggests something as ponderous as "Sign On The Cross" or a sentimental romantic complaint as it establishes a context for receiving something like a prayer, plea, or promise. Instead, we absorb lines that are closer to "Lo And Behold!" than anything else.

One reason for this kind of writing—aside from the totally informal qualities of the entire exercise—is the method of production used. In Time-Life's *The History of Rock 'n' Roll* video, Levon Helm describes how Dylan and Richard Manuel wrote songs together: "Bob and Richard used to have a typewriter that sat on the coffee table there in the living room. And the two of them would go by, type little notes to each other, and one would read what the other one wrote and put a couple of lines under that. A lot of times, by the end of the day, we'd have a couple-three pages out of there." Such is the spirit of Big Pink. Professor Bob may deploy Jack Fate's repertoire of old songs to teach class by way of his carefully orchestrated notes, but he also made plenty of room for all sorts of improvisation. "All American Boy" may provide the starting point for a personal diatribe. A John Lee Hooker tune may offer the springboard to a musical rhythm that supports lyrical mayhem. Or a well-paced typewriter may serve as a harbinger for songs that rotate perspective with each line. In all cases, the musical laboratory that was Big Pink's basement operated under an open-door policy, and that philosophy served its purpose very, very well.

The basements are raw, impulsive creations. The boys may have run through a song's musical structure and developed a sonic strategy for the recording, but they gave one-off lip service to the writing. Hudson's right: There is as much mumbling and schoolboy rhyming as there are coherent stories or systematic lyrics in these recordings. Helm's recollections reinforce such a conclusion. Replacing the enigmatic ponderings of "Visions Of Johanna" is the type of vacuous pop platitudes that go dormant until *Under The Red Sky*. But it is the *process* that matters most here. The Basement Strategy was born under Big Pink, and *that* is as big a development as anything in Dylan's lifework. Zimmerman used Fate to initiate Dylan's systematic recovery during the spring, summer, and early fall of 1967. By fooling around with his musical playmates in the relaxed atmosphere of a secluded house with open windows, dogs laying about, an accessible typewriter, and the time to allow it all to happen, Dylan relaxed and released his talent in a way that unlocked the door to his recovery. What follows reveals the extent to which the Basement Strategy initiated what would eventually be a successful mission. Through the goofy songs, the hilarious covers, the uneven hymns, and the musical camaraderie, Bob Dylan turned the creative corner. Still, we have songs and songs and songs to go before we rest—some recoveries require time.

John Wesley Harding and *Nashville Skyline*

From the raucous freedom of Big Pink, we move to one of the musical world's most restrictive environments: Music City. They may want you to believe that they sit around with the windows open and the hunting dogs lounging as they pick and grin their way through songs in Nashville, but that is just not the truth of the matter. Those Nashville Cats are an uptight bunch with very specific, preconceived notions about what does and does not fit. The Nashville Sound is not inclusive. Hank Williams was kicked out. Elvis Presley was initially rejected. Willie Nelson and Waylon Jennings became "outlaws." This list goes on and on. But, somehow, Bob Dylan had his way with these musical warlords. They may have looked at Bob Dylan as some sort of freakish cash cow, but Bob Dillon could not have cared less what they thought. Williams, Presley, or the outlaws could only dream of the reservoir of rebellion available to the Iron Range's original biker-poet. It was, without doubt, the key to the Music City Victory that was *Blonde On Blonde*. So, with the fresh air of the New York mountains at his back, Bob Dylan brought Jack Fate and Bob Dillon back to Nashville, where the auteur would startle the locals by co-opting their methods of music production and confuse the musical world with the results. When we pull back and consider the success of the folk-posturing period (both in terms of art and publicity), the inventive intensity of the Newport Mod era (both in terms of art and publicity), and the creative recovery initiated by the Basement Strategy (both in terms of art and publicity), we observe the essence of a one-of-a-kind artistic force (both . . . well, you get it). Now, let's synthesize it all into a *country* album produced in *Nashville*.

How bold was *John Wesley Harding*? Do you have any idea what records populated the musical world in 1967? Let's see. In 1967, Brian Wilson of the Beach Boys was forced to abandon his follow-up to the highly successful—and *very* influential—1966 recording *Pet Sounds* (i.e., the *Smile* project) because it was driving him insane. That June, the Beatles issued *Sgt. Pepper's Lonely Hearts Club Band*. That November, Cream offered its second album, the land-breaking, richly impressionistic *Disraeli Gears*. That November, the Rolling Stones responded to the Beatles with *Their Satanic Majesties Request*. And gestating just over the horizon was the first record to be awarded "platinum" status by the music industry (selling over 4 million copies), Iron Butterfly's *In A Gadda Da Vida*. Complementing those provocative offerings was a new record by the most confrontational artist the musical world was yet to know, Bob

Dylan's *John Wesley Harding*. To that end, music critic Jon Landau reports that *Harding* is a "profoundly egotistical album" with an "essential lack of insecurity" that reveals Dylan to be "a truly independent artist who doesn't feel responsible to anyone else, whether they be fans or his contemporaries."

Two points stand out *immediately* regarding *John Wesley Harding*. This is an amazing act of artistic courage for *1967* (as per Landau's observations) and the concentrated application of portraiture as a storytelling strategy—portraits that are a long way from the basement's silly "Tiny Montgomery." Throughout these songs, the harmonica stands out as the project's most compelling sonic signature, opening tunes, punctuating verses, and closing songs in a consistent fashion. Otherwise, the musical structures on this album stick to simple, pared-down strategies that play a supporting role to the vocals and harmonica (there is, however, some outstanding bass guitar on these songs). Heylin's session chronology reports that producer Bob Johnston enlisted the support of Nashville regulars Charlie McCoy (bass), Kenneth Buttery (drums), and Pete Drake (pedal steel) for the three sessions required to record the album (Drake worked only during the third and final session). If Heylin is accurate, this is Nashville recording at its finest: quick, efficient, standardized. There are no unused songs from these sessions (and apparently only two outtakes!). From this, it is safe to say that Dylan totally abandoned his *Blonde On Blonde* production method and completely accepted Nashville's operating procedures. That—in and of itself—is newsworthy.

Turning to the writing, there is a specific tone to the portraits that dominate this album, and that tone is decidedly *biblical*. Characters are presented and developed in a fashion that culminates in moral conclusions. Like biblical parables, the scenes unfold simply, the conflict is quickly exposed, and the resolution yields a concrete point. Hence, *Harding* offers twelve songs in a rapid-fire thirty-eight minutes that follow six thematic orientations: two epic portraits ("John Wesley Harding" and "I Dreamed I Saw St. Augustine") and one not-so-epic portrait ("The Wicked Messenger"), three relational complaints (the fuzzy "As I Went Out One Morning" and the metaphorical "Dear Landlord" and "I Pity The Poor Immigrant"), an adaptation of Dylan's trademark satire ("The Ballad Of Frankie Lee And Judas Priest"), two individual complaints ("Drifter's Escape" and "I Am A Lonesome Hobo"), two love celebrations ("Down Along The Cove" and "I'll Be Your Baby Tonight"), and a piece of impressionism ("All Along The Watchtower"). The record's thematic diversity involves a blend of past and present. The modification of Dylan's satirical style via "The Ballad Of Frankie Lee" and its enigmatic parable about mistaken paradises recall the moralistic tales of earlier times (by the way, Clinton Heylin insists the song is not about "mistaken paradises" at all; rather, he focuses on the line "nothing is revealed" as the key to unlock this parable). The song synthesizes the folk-posturing period's narrative structures with the Newport Mod's idiosyncratic imagery (Tim Riley calls the song a "mock linear narrative") to introduce a songwriting hybrid. Dylan also revamps his impressionism with "Watchtower," dusts off his finger-pointing techniques via the complaints, and revisits the love song genre with the relational celebrations. We have, then, what could best be called a transitional piece. We begin with "The Ballad Of Frankie Lee And Judas Priest."

"Frankie Lee" is a smooth, relaxed tale of two friends and their domestic adventure. Like virtually all of *Harding*'s songs, the instrumental pattern—with its emphasis on the harmonica-vocal interplay supported by dynamic bass playing and light acoustic guitar-drums—provides an excellent platform for the unfolding story. The track's twelve verses range from four to nine lines each (most are eight lines), with only one break featuring the harmonica interludes that dominate this album. The song involves a simple tale with clever descriptive lines that lead to a rather cryptic ending. There are no choruses or bridges, or any type of refrain. The song is what it says it is: a ballad. Consequently, we witness a steady march through a slice-of-life story with a cloudy ending. The opening verses demonstrate Dylan's writing:

> Well, Frankie Lee and Judas Priest,
> They were the best of friends.
> So when Frankie Lee needed money one day,
> Judas quickly pulled out a roll of tens
> And placed them on a footstool
> Just above the plotted plain,
> Sayin', "Take your pick, Frankie Boy,
> My loss will be your gain."

> Well, Frankie Lee, he sat right down
> And put his fingers to his chin,
> But with the cold eyes of Judas on him,
> His head began to spin.
> "Would ya please not stare at me like that," he said,
> "It's just my foolish pride,
> But sometimes a man must be alone
> And this is no place to hide."

Notice the simplicity of the writing and its clever twists. The song immediately establishes the friendship and turns to little details that enliven the imagery—Judas' willing response to Frankie's need, and Frankie's subsequent embarrassment. The story continues with Judas granting Frankie's wish while warning him that his offer will not last forever. Judas departs for a location down the road that he calls "Eternity." When Frankie inquires what that means, Judas responds that his friend may know it by another name, "Paradise." They part. A stranger approaches Frankie and informs him that Judas is asking for him. It appears Judas is "stranded in a house" down the road, and Frankie quickly travels to his friend's side. Upon his arrival, Judas relates that his location is far more than a mere house; it is a "home." Frankie Lee contemplates the situation as he stares at this building with twenty-four windows, each featuring a woman's face. Suddenly, Frankie Lee storms upstairs and initiates "his midnight creep" that lasts for sixteen days. On the seventeenth day, he dies of "thirst" in his friend's arms. When they carry his body out, no one speaks except the guilty "neighbor boy," who utters Clinton Heylin's favorite line, "Nothing is revealed." (There's an understatement for you!) The songs closes with its self-proclaimed moral that one should not mistake "Paradise" for a neighboring house and a twenty-nine-second harmonica tag.

"The Ballad Of Frankie Lee And Judas Priest" extends Dylan's satirical storytelling formula as it uses the narrative detail we associate with the "Talkin'" songs or "Bob Dylan's 115th Dream" and add new twists. His emphasis on the two characters over their scenic conditions is a reversal of his established style. Here the emphasis is on portraiture. Moreover, the evasive qualities of the story's resolution add another modification. Unlike "Bear Mountain," "Motorpsycho Nightmare," or his other detailed narratives, this song omits crucial storytelling elements that leave aspects of the story's resolution in question. Is "Frankie Lee" as obvious as it seems? Did the guy wear himself out in a bordello? Did Judas know that Frankie's "paradise" would become his "eternity," and, if so, did he betray him? What was not "revealed"? The detailed plots of "Emmett Till," "Only A Pawn," or "John Birch" have made way for a more focused characterization, and this shift in narrative style paves the way for future songs such as "Lily, Rosemary And The Jack Of Hearts" and the kinds of portraits that populate later works. Make of this parable what you will, but notice the shift in style. This song represents a significant transition.

As we turn to the impressionistic tale "All Along The Watchtower," we note another stylistic evolution. Dylan told John Cohen and Happy Traum that the song has "the cycle of events working in a rather reverse order," which, in turn, opens it to a variety of interpretations: "anything we can imagine is really there." One reason for this open-ended approach is the song's brevity. It contains but three four-line verses. There are no recurring lines or bridges, just two characters who speak through cryptic morals before a brief scenic description closes the tune while opening the inverted story. With a lively harmonica and a most impressive bass guitar providing the aural context, Dylan introduces his characters in the opening verses:

"There must be some way out of here," said the joker to the thief,
"There's too much confusion, I can't get no relief.
Businessmen, they drink my wine, plowmen dig my earth,
None of them along the line know what any of it is worth."

"No reason to get excited," the thief, he kindly spoke,
"There are many here among us who feel that life is but a joke.
But you and I, we've been through that, and this is not our fate,
So let us not talk falsely now, the hour is getting late."

After establishing that people are inconsiderate and cynical, the song turns to its final lines and a quick description of the "watchtower" with its princes, women, and servants, while a distant wildcat growls as two approaching riders travel through gusty winds. If you take Dylan at his word, the two riders are the joker and the thief. Right? The song hints of their characters as they lament life's confusion, lack of sensitivity, and insincerity, but assuredly, "anything can happen" from there. This is not Dylan's trademark narrative impressionism or patented wordplay; to the contrary, the language is clear while the plot is jumbled. There are no weird juxtapositions, odd pairings, or celebrity convolutions here. It almost seems as if Dylan started the song and just stopped. In any event, Jimi Hendrix did very well with this song, and Dylan has played it in concert more than *any other song*. There are few songs in the Dylan Canon like "All Along The Watchtower."

We now turn to the meat of this record and Dylan's portraits. "Harding," "St. Augustine," "Poor Immigrant", and "Lonesome Hobo" spend considerable time developing their respective characters, and "Wicked Messenger" uses this songwriting strategy in a less concentrated fashion. Whether the narrative stresses the positive or negative qualities of its subject matter, Dylan describes the heroic, never foolish outlaw ("Harding"); the virtuous St. Augustine; the failed lives of a dishonest people ("Immigrant" and "Hobo"); and the perils of an unwanted "messenger" in a direct manner. The biblical imagery (Heylin cites Bert Cartwright's count of sixty-one biblical references throughout the album), the enigmatic metaphors, and the songs' brevity work with the writer's emerging portraiture to produce yet another hybrid of Dylan's storytelling signatures. Although he had certainly developed characters in the past, such characterizations typically appeared in service of the narrative. In these songs, the narrative flows from the characterization. Dylan songs often move too fast to embellish any single character (or scene, for that matter), so the energy spent developing these characters suggests an interesting shift in songwriting strategies. Let's go to the specifics for more detail.

The album's title cut and opening track establishes both the sonic and storytelling strategies that control this project. "John Wesley Harding" is an epic account of its subject's heroic qualities that appears in three 7–8-line verses. The opening harmonica and active bass, along with their supporting guitar and drums, pave the way for a song without repetition or variance of any kind. The opening stanza introduces our hero:

> John Wesley Harding
> Was a friend to the poor,
> He trav'led with a gun in ev'ry hand.
> All along this countryside,
> He opened a many a door,
> But he was never known
> To hurt an honest man.

Like Woody Guthrie's "Pretty Boy Floyd," our heroic outlaw uses his own brand of Robin Hood logic to have his way with the law while serving his populist social philosophy (it's perfectly fine to steal from the dishonest rich), proving that one bad turn deserves another. The implication here is that they deserve it. The second stanza describes an event in which the outlaw and his moll take a stand against somebody and straighten that "situation" out—whatever it was. The final verse seals the deal:

> All across the telegraph
> His name it did resound,
> But no charge held against him
> Could they prove.
> And there was no man around
> Who could track or chain him down,
> He was never known
> To make a foolish move.

The "us versus them" qualities of this tale are self-evident in this final stanza, in that "they" are unable to corral "our" heroic criminal. Never mind that the man has no respect for the law of the land; he never injures honest folk, he takes care of situations in helpful ways, and he refrains from foolishness (and thereby sustains his freedom). But you just *know* what's going to happen somewhere, someday. "They" always get these guys, don't they?

Another kind of character who always seems to get it in the end is the social warrior that confronts "them" by not hiding behind a gun, but by direct—unarmed—confrontation. With long blasts of harmonica painting the tragic backdrop for this portrait (featuring a :48 closing in a 3:53 track), Dylan offers his tale of martyrdom that is "I Dreamed I Saw St. Augustine." The three eight-line verses of this story use irony as a narrative pivot. The narrator's dream unfolds in three parts: First, St. Augustine is introduced and described, and his mission is established; second, he goes about his duty; and third, he pays the proverbial price as the narrator laments his participation in the martyr's persecution. The irony occurs in that through Augustine's denunciation of martyrdom, he becomes one. Dylan's storytelling is precise in its description of the hero with his "blanket underneath his arm" and his "coat of solid gold" as he searches for "souls" that have "already been sold." When he loudly lodges his "sad complaint" with the "gifted kings and queens" that "no martyr is among ye now," he closes by telling them to go "on your way accordingly" with the knowledge that they are "not alone." The dream ends with the hero's death, after which our narrator awakens "in anger" as he embraces his loneliness and terror: "I put my fingers against the glass / And bowed my head and cried." The epic character endures the tragedy of persecution, and Dylan's dreaming narrator wrestles with his role in his nightmare.

From gallant gunslingers and persecuted preachers, we move to the sad tale of the misguided messenger and "The Wicked Messenger." Here the band deploys its standard instrumental approach in a more lively manner as Dylan uses the three-verse (with seven lines each) strategy for yet another narrative vignette. This time, however, the lyrics drift toward impressionism and, in so doing, cloud the story in the manner of "Watchtower." Still, though cloudy, the tale unfolds in a linear fashion as the opening verse describes the messenger, the second stanza unveils the conflict, and the final verse provides the story's resolution (complete with moral). Consider the song's opening:

There was a wicked messenger
From Eli he did come,
With a mind that multiplied
The smallest matter.
When questioned who had sent for him,
He answered with his thumb,
For his tongue could not speak, but only flatter.

So, we have a character who exaggerates through flattery. The second stanza notes how he lives behind a public building (it houses the "assembly") and one day returned home with a statement that announced, "The soles of my feet, I swear they're burning." With that, the leaves fall from the trees, the oceans "part," and lots of people confront our metaphoric messenger (he should have followed Dylan's old Western Union boy style). The story ends with the messenger learning a lesson that "opened his heart" to the consensus opinion: "If ye cannot bring good news, then don't bring any." While the public impact of the messenger's impressionistic statement was obviously profound, the trite qualities of the song's resolution drive home the moral of story.

From clear portraits of heroism, martyrdom, and victimhood, we move to a series of relational complaints that deploy identical songwriting structures with varying degrees of clarity. Here we move from the enigmatic "As I Went Out One Morning" to the dogmatic "I Pity The Poor Immigrant" to the cryptic "Dear Landlord." "As I Went Out" features an odd portrayal of a threatening woman in chains and Tom Paine's successful intervention, while "Landlord" offers a cryptic characterization that drives a heartfelt complaint (*everyone* has a different interpretation of "Landlord") and "Immigrant" describes a wretched soul that inspired the narrator's contempt. There is, indeed, some interesting songwriting here. We begin with Paine, the woman in chains, and the song's opening verses:

> As I went out one morning
> To breathe the air around Tom Paine's,
> I spied the fairest damsel
> That ever did walk in chains.
> I offer'd her my hand,
> She took me by the arm.
> I knew that very instant,
> She meant to do me harm.
>
> "Depart from me this moment."
> I told her with my voice.
> Said she, "But I don't wish to,"
> Said I, "But you have no choice,"
> "I beg you, sir," she pleaded.
> From the corners of her mouth,
> "I will secretly accept you
> And together we'll fly south."

Suddenly Paine appears running toward the couple, yelling at the woman, ordering her to stop, and apologizing to the narrator for the trouble. The song ends. Now what have we here? A throwaway? An effort to massage the anxieties over a long-ago dinner date in Tom Paine's name ("liberty" enchained by oppressive celebrities)? The song is weird, but not impressionistic. The symbolic complaint is direct and relational. The narrator recognizes the threat the enslaved lady poses and instantly retreats. The symbolic structure is obvious, but the meaning is what they call "inside baseball" in politics—only the players understand the statement's significance.

The "inside baseball" continues with the auteur's switch to the piano and a track that sounds as if it came straight from the basement, "Dear Landlord." The song is an angst-ridden expression about a metaphorical landlord (no one would get this worked up over rent!) who appears to be a direct extension of basement gems such as "Too Much Of Nothing," "Nothing Was Delivered," and "I Shall Be Released." An evil is lurking in the shadows and, like Tom Paine's woman in chains, only the songwriter—here, represented by the narrator—knows what is transpiring. The song opens with the narrator stating his case:

> Dear landlord,
> Please don't put a price on my soul.
> My burden is heavy,
> My dreams are beyond control.
> When that steamboat whistle blows,
> I'm gonna give you all I got to give,
> And I do hope you receive it well,
> Dependin' on the way you feel that you live.

(I don't know about you, but when I'm behind on rent, my landlord doesn't give a damn about my soul, burdens, or dreams!) Now, this is rich. Who is this landlord? Grossman? Columbia Records? Dylan's audience? Richard Nixon? (Just kidding.) Again, following the emotional line of basement reasoning from the aforementioned songs, this falls directly in line with some sort of celebrity–music biz angst. The narrator's dreams are his burden and the essence of his soul, and his landlord uses the narrator's sincere efforts to maintain his lifestyle. The second of the song's three eight-line stanzas pleads for the landlord's understanding. Everybody suffers, the narrator reports, but we must not work in vain by pursuing materialism's false promise. The song closes,

> Dear landlord,
> Please don't dismiss my case.
> I'm not about to argue,
> I'm not about to move to no other place.
> Now, each of us has his own special gift
> And you know this was meant to be true,
> And if you don't underestimate me,
> I won't underestimate you.

There is more than a little bit of celebrity–music business–artistic angst working in this song. Again, the connection to the basement's "Too Much Of Nothing" and its colleagues is too direct to ignore. Like "One Morning," this is inside business, and all we can do is sit on the outside, contemplate the symbolic consistency in evidence, and enjoy the results.

Our final relational complaint falls in line with the others. "I Pity The Poor Immigrant" is one prodigious diatribe against *somebody* who happens to be from someplace else. Not only has this individual alienated the narrator, but he is also a dastardly soul whose evil ways are coming home to roost. The narrator paints a grim picture of a man "Who uses all his power to do evil" only to wind up abandoned; "who lies with ev'ry breath" and "passionately hates his life" while fearing death; who "eats" without satisfaction and "hears but does not see" while, according to our narrator, "he falls in love with wealth itself / And turns his back on me." Although most of the song expresses the narrator's "pity" for this fiend, that last line takes these descriptions from the abstract and anchors it in the narrator's direct experience with this monster. The third eight-line verse closes with more acrimony, as the narrator's pity is surely a prelude to the joy he will no doubt experience upon the immigrant's passing. To be sure, there is a darkness enveloping "One Morning," "Landlord," and "Immigrant," as somebody is grinding an axe about something. This thematic thread is just too obvious to ignore; moreover, its connection to the basements is also too direct to overlook. The songs' details are certainly different, but their themes wrestle with the same ideas—notions that carry over to the two songs of individual complaint as well.

"Drifter's Escape" and "I Am A Lonesome Hobo" address societal issues through the experiences of the songs' two central characters. In "Drifter's," an innocent wanderer is about to be victimized by a bloodthirsty jury before a divine intervention corrects that scenario. In "Hobo," the central character has fallen prey to personal weaknesses inspired—he says—by societal norms, and although he is resigned to his fate, he issues a warning for us all to heed. The world is full of evil landlords and heartless immigrants, and they occasionally form lynch mobs that scream for recreational justice and form social systems that lead to ruination. "Drifter's Escape" opens with the wanderer's plight and his complaint:

> "Oh help me in my weakness,"
> I heard the drifter say,
> As they carried him from the courtroom
> And were taking him away.
> "My trip hasn't been a pleasant one
> And my time it isn't long,
> And I still do not know
> What it was that I've done wrong."

As you can see, the story is direct and the complaint is coherent: A wanderer has been seized, accused of wrongdoing, and apparently convicted. The second of these three eight-line verses reports how the judge tosses his "robe" aside in tearful disgust over his bloodthirsty jury's decision while a "crowd" is "stirring" outside. The song concludes,

> "Oh, stop that cursed jury,"
> Cried the attendant and the nurse,
> "The trial was bad enough,
> But this is ten times worse."
> Just then a bolt of lightning
> Struck the courthouse out of shape,
> And while ev'rybody knelt to pray
> The drifter did escape.

Echoing "With God On Our Side," the song demonstrates the runaway qualities of a self-righteous jury willing to defy both the judge and the citizenry in order to exercise its divine right. However, the divine tables turned on the evil establishment and enabled the drifter's escape (an ending that disappointed me, since I was certain that John Wesley Harding was going to rescue our everyman wanderer). Using the narrative clarity of the folk-posturing period, Dylan tells his story through clear, understandable language presented through a coherent narrative structure. This trend holds true for our down-on-his-self-inflicted-luck hobo as well. "Lonesome Hobo" begins with a character sketch:

> I am a lonesome hobo
> Without family or friends,
> Where another man's life might begin,
> That's exactly where mine ends.
> I have tried my hand at bribery,
> Blackmail and deceit,
> And I've served time for ev'rything
> 'Cept beggin' on the street.

Having established the hobo's immigrant-like ways, the second of our three eight-line verses describes the hobo's fall from grace. He had it all: fine gold in his teeth, silk clothing—probably even a leopard-skin pillbox hat. But his distrust proved to be his undoing and his ultimate "doom." The song closes with this admonition:

> Kind ladies and kind gentlemen,
> Soon I will be gone,
> But let me just warn you all,
> Before I do pass on;
> Stay free from petty jealousies,
> Live by no man's code,
> And hold your judgment for yourself
> Lest you wind up on this road.

Once more, the Great Sloganeer of the folk-posturing era has plied his trade successfully. Probably like the dastardly immigrant, this character blames those around him for his failures—not his personal weaknesses. He lied and extorted because that is the way you play the game, he tells us. So refrain from the game and you will not have to grapple with your character. With lying and extorting comes insecurity that breeds jealousy, and from there spawns ruination. The game of life is refereed by the devil. This "The devil made me do it" escape clause is just what the immigrant, landlord, bloodthirsty jury, and persecuting dreamer need to lighten their respective loads. It is why "they" hunt down our good man, Harding. It is why the bearers of bad news are shunned. It is at the heart of the joker's and thief's concerns. And it is "With God On Our Side, Revisited."

Having established why the world *is* hell, we turn to the "Yea! Heavy, Music City" portion of *John Wesley Harding* and the album's two closing tunes of relational joy. These songs of loving celebration are, most assuredly, the stuff of traditional American pop and country songs. The snappy, piano-driven, basement-sounding, pop tune "Down Along The Cove" and the smooth country-and-western track "I'll Be Your Baby Tonight" convey their romantic celebrations in cute, direct, and loving styles. These pop songs are short, sweet, happy tunes that extol the virtues of romantic bliss. That they are celebrations is beyond all doubt. Perhaps when the preacher is in love, he or she can both celebrate that happy condition *and* take aim at the evil external threats that challenge us all.

Deploying the songwriting strategy that made Nashville Tin Pan Alley South, "Cove" and "Baby Tonight" are simple, repetitive songs with lively melodies. The dancing piano of "Cove" complements the pedal steel authenticity of "Baby Tonight" to provide traditional sonic platforms for the loving platitudes they espouse. In "Cove," the three six-line verses repeat the opening two lines as a preface for the two-line statement of adoration that closes the stanza. One needs but a single example to capture the joy:

> Down along the cove,
> I spied my true love comin' my way.
> Down along the cove,
> I spied my true love comin' my way.
> I say, "Lord, have mercy, mama,
> It sure is good to see you comin' today."

Proving that one loving turn deserves another, the second verse features *her* response after the repeated opening lines: "Lord, have mercy, honey, / I'm so glad you're my boy!" Supporting the notion that balance is always a desirable option in a Tin Pan Alley tune, the final verse portrays *our lovers* walking "hand in hand" as "ev'rybody watchin'" realizes the extent to which love is in the house. A forty-three-second harmonica blast offers a fine tag for 2:23 pop song. It is not hard to envision everybody dancing and singing to this bouncy Music City offering as they make their way out of a local bar and head down Nashville's famed Broadway Street.

Later that evening, when social schedules enter the realm of doubt, to the rescue comes our final pop entry and the reassurances of "I'll Be Your Baby Tonight." How fitting it is that our closing song involves three three-line verses with a patented Nashville *bridge* separating the second and third stanzas. Once more, a capstone statement is issued on a Bob Dylan album. The song opens with an order to "close" both your "eyes" and the "door" and relax with the realization that the narrator is available for the evening. More instructions follow as the narrator asks his love interest to shut off the lights, lower the shades, and forget all fears; tonight is the night. The song turns to the bridge and the telltale final verse:

> Well, that mockingbird's gonna sail away,
> We're gonna forget it.
> That big, fat moon is gonna shine like a spoon,
> But we're gonna let it,
> You won't regret it.

Kick your shoes off, do not fear,
Bring that bottle over here.
I'll be your baby tonight.

With that, *John Wesley Harding* comes to a close. After over thirty-three minutes of clear and not-so-clear moralizing, the record concludes with five minutes of loving bliss.

Further proof of *Harding*'s role in the oeuvre is available through the album's liner notes. There, the auteur presents a cloudy tale of three kings and their efforts to understand a new Bob Dylan record. The story begins with its characters: "There were three kings and a jolly three too. The first one had a broken nose, the second, a broken arm and the third was broke. 'Faith is the key!' said the first king. 'No, froth is the key!' said the second. 'You're both wrong,' said the third, 'the key is Frank!' " So, off they go to consult Frank. As they arrive late that evening, "Terry Shute" was "prying open a hairdresser" when Frank's wife, Vera, interrupts to announce the kings' arrival. She describes the kings to Terry in her own way. For some reason, the kings crawled into Frank's place, and he immediately demands that they get off of his freshly swept floor. When the second king inquires about Vera, Frank declares, "She's in the back of the house, flaming it up with an arrogant man, now come on, out with it, what's on our minds today?" No one responds.

Terry enters the room, derides the kings, and is promptly dismissed by Frank: "Get out of here, you ragged man! Come ye no more!" Terry departs. Frank presses on with his inquiry, and the first king finally responds, "Mr. Dylan has come out with a new record. This record of course features none but his own songs and we understand that you're the key." Frank concurs with their conclusion and asks, "How far would you like to go in?" The king responds, "Not too far but just far enough so's we can say that we've been there." Frank responds by sitting down and crossing his legs, leaping to his feet, ripping off his shirt, waving it around (dropping a light bulb and crushing it with his feet), punching out a plate glass window, sitting back down, and pulling a knife. This seems to satisfy the kings, who leave Frank, his wife, and Terry contemplating their visit while repairmen replace the window. The kings have, however, been cured: One king's nose healed, the other's arm was repaired, and the third was suddenly rich. They blow horns in celebration: " 'I've never been so happy in all my life!' sang the one with all the money." One may only presume that everyone lived happily ever after—or at least enjoyed themselves until the next Bob Dylan album appears.

The story is weird, but coherent. Unlike the previous editions of liner notes, Dylan presents a clear—albeit surreal—story without the moral undertones of the album's songwriting. It introduces and develops characters, there is plot progression, and the narrative conveys the value of knowledge (among other things) while poking fun at all of Dylan's interpreters. This is the *Harding* package: in turns playful and moralistic, but always a long, long way from *Highway 61*.

John Wesley Harding is a systematic album. There is a straightforward, methodical musical structure controlling the record. The harmonica lead-ins, between-verse punctuations, and tags join the active bass lines and passive guitar-drums to provide the aural context for all songs. The melody may vary slightly in its pacing, but the formula is all-controlling. There is a systematic songwriting strategy dominating this project as well. Nine of the album's twelve songs are structurally identical (give or take a line). Only the twelve verses of "Frankie Lee," the bridge in "Baby Tonight," and the brevity of "Watchtower" deviate from the basic structure of three eight-line stanzas that organizes these songs. Finally, there is a systematic storytelling style used that makes ten of the twelve songs more than accessible—they are predictable (only "Watchtower" and "As I Went Out One Morning" are exceptions). That Dylan co-opted a specific songwriting structure and strictly adhered to it is overwhelmingly clear. The question is "Why?"

Although I reserve direct commentary on Dylan's creative impulse and song-writing techniques until our concluding chapter, I need to pause here and draw from that material to explain what happened with the *Harding* project. During the second of his two 1978 *Rolling Stone* interviews with Jonathon Cott, Dylan described the evo-lution of his songwriting after *Blonde On Blonde*:

> Right through the time of *Blonde on Blonde* I was doing it unconsciously. Then one day I was half-stepping, and the lights went out. And since that point, I more or less had amnesia. Now, you can take that statement as literally or metaphysically as you need to, but that's what happened to me. It took me a long time to get to do consciously what I used to be able to do unconsciously. It happens to everybody. Think about the periods when people don't do anything, or they lose it and have to regain it, or lose it and gain something else. So it's taken me all this time, and the records I made along the way were like openers—trying to figure out whether it was this way or that way, just what *is* it, what's the simplest way I can tell the story and make this feeling real.

The Basement Strategy may have allowed the auteur an opportunity to exercise his musical muscles in the friendly confines of Big Pink and, in so doing, pursue his re-covery through Woodstock's sonic playground, but the writing in that wholesome basement paled in comparison to traditional Dylan standards. That period only "opened" part of the creative door. So, with the simple melodies of *Harding* provid-ing a starting point, Dylan focused on his writing during the *Harding* and, later, *Nashville Skyline* projects. He explained the process to Cott:

> *John Wesley Harding* was a fearful album—just dealing with fear . . . but dealing with the devil in a fearful way, almost. All I wanted to do was to get the words right. It was courageous to do it because I could have *not* done it, too. Anyway, on *Nashville Skyline* you had to read between the lines. I was trying to grasp something that would lead me on to where I thought I should be, and it didn't go nowhere—it just went down, down, down. I couldn't be anybody but myself, and at that point I didn't know it or want to know it.

What a fascinating statement! Notice Bob Zimmerman's frustrations over his inabil-ity to be "anybody" else and how that left him wrestling with his muse, using Jack

Fate's knowledge and Bob Dillon's resolve to fight through his "amnesia." There's truth here. When you read *Harding*'s lyrics in *Lyrics 1962–2001*, a strange thing happens with regard to a Bob Dylan song: *All the lyrics are accurate*. Never is a line reversed, omitted, or edited as the result of Dylan's live method of music production. No. Each line is carefully crafted and executed. The auteur was not wrestling with the devil; he was wrestling with his words about the devil. Hence, the strictly adhered to structures that control this record. He devised a formula. Fit his ideas within that structure. And stuck it out. The end result is that Zimmerman's talent pulled him through on this one, but the amnesia would soon overtake that as well. From the unbridled joy of the basement release to the systematic application of Bob Zimmerman's talent, our mission of recovery now backslides into the between-the-lines vacuity of *Nashville Skyline*.

Whereas *John Wesley Harding* departed from the poetic imperative that drove the Newport Mod to revolutionize songwriting, it still had the topical feel of Bob Dylan's pen. The portraits still had some edge—even if that edge lacked the bite we associate with the auteur's finest work. Well, dear friends, it's all gone here. *Nashville Skyline* is a pop record—regardless of whether it is country pop or what—that features formulaic songwriting and predictable sonic turns. This record is, in a word, *anti-Dylan*. There are five key signs that support this claim. First, the album—all of twenty-seven minutes in length—opens with a self-cover and an instrumental. Second, there is no harmonica (except for the instrumental), and guitars replace Dylan's signature instrument via standard interludes that punctuate the verses in predictable fashions. Third, the record's sonic strategy is lifeless (those great bass lines from *Harding* disappear); we're talking Total Music City here—more anti-Dylan. Fourth, Dylan's oh-so-sweet voice unveils the pop-singing specialist—more anti-Dylan. And fifth, the songwriting strategy is straight from Tin Pan Alley South: verse, verse, bridge, verse, verse, with guitar breaks between verses 3 and 4—totally formulaic, totally anti-Dylan. So, let's relax and read between the lines because there is nothing else there. After all, this is not George Jones; it is *Bob Dylan*. (By the way, Jones is great, but could you imagine him singing "Desolation Row"?)

Unlike *Harding*, this twenty-seven-minute, ten-song album focuses on a single topic: love. Those songs explore two predictable themes: celebration ("To Be Alone With You," "Peggy Day," "Lay Lady Lay," "Country Pie," and "Tonight I'll Be Staying Here With You") and complaint (the return of "Girl From The North Country" with Johnny Cash, "I Threw It All Away," "One More Night," and "Tell Me That It Isn't True"). This is a warm, friendly work that conveys heartfelt sentiments in brief, coherent snippets. Producer Bob Johnston and a Nashville cast of thousands (just kidding; there are close to a dozen musicians appearing on this record) complement Dylan's vocals to create what *Newsweek* calls "a relaxed get-together of expert musicians who seem to know each other's—and Dylan's—moves as if they were playing at the Grand Ole Opry." There it hangs, folks.

The playful metaphors in "Country Pie" and the cloudy love triangle in "Lay Lady Lay" (written for the movie *Midnight Cowboy*, but not used) are smooth complements to the direct portrayals of the character who had it all and now has nothing ("I Threw It All Away"), the character who pleads with his lover to denounce the rumors of infidelity ("Tell Me That It Isn't True"), the character who aspires for an evening of bliss ("Peggy Day"), and the determined lover forsaking all to be with his new woman ("Tonight I'll Be Staying"). These 2–3-minute pop songs follow standard Nashville recipes in a manner that, once again, demonstrates Dylan's capacity to co-opt a musical style. He explained the shift in style to *Newsweek*: "The songs reflect more of the inner me than the songs of the past. They're more to my base than, say, 'John Wesley Harding.' There I felt everyone expected me to be a poet so that's what I tried to be. But the smallest line in this new album means more to me than some of the songs on any of the previous albums I've made." He continued, "Those songs were all written in the New York atmosphere. I'd never have written any of them—or sung them the way I did—if I hadn't been sitting around listening to performers in New York cafes. . . . When I got to New York it was obvious that something was going on—folk music—and I did my best to learn and play it. I was just there at the right time with pen in hand. I suppose there was some ambition in what I did. But I tried to make the songs genuine." *Some ambition?* Again, the *mission* dictated the expression's form. The context plays a significant role in any Bob Dylan song's style, and the latest songs were recorded in "Nashville."

We begin with the love celebrations and "To Be Alone With You." This evenly balanced, piano-led, instrumentally uneventful little ditty (running 2:05) contains three eight-line verses that extol the virtues of spending time with the one you love. The opening verse says it all:

> To be alone with you
> Just you and me
> Now won't you tell me true
> Ain't that the way it oughta be?
> To hold each other tight
> The whole night through
> Ev'rything is always right
> When I'm alone with you.

The joy continues with lines that announce "That while life's pleasures be few / The only one I know / Is when I'm alone with you" and a bridge that declares that the "nighttime" is—guess what?—the "right time" to be with the one "you're always" busy "thinkin' of." The song closes with the narrator thanking the "Lord" for the "sweet reward" that life is with his baby. I'm still reading between the lines of this one, and I promise to get back to you if I find anything.

"Peggy Day" advances the nocturnal nature of true love theme with its four 3–4-line verses that pause for a five-line bridge and a pedal steel instrumental between verses 3 and 4 (replacing the harmonica's role in that standard slot). It does not take that long to drive this point home (the track runs 1:59), and "Day" cuts to the chase with its opening verse, in which the narrator reports that Peggy "stole" his heart and now he loves to "spend the night" with his new love. The second verse confirms that he enjoys his days with her as well. The bridge relates the narrator's state of mind:

> Well, you know that even before I learned her name,
> You know I loved her just the same.

An' I tell 'em all, wherever I may go,
Just so they'll know, that she's my little lady
And I love her so.

Ain't love grand! From there, our proud lover recalls how Peggy changed those "gray" skies to "blue" and announces, once again, that his nights are truly special.

The night moves theme continues with "Tonight I'll Be Staying Here With You" and its four five-line verses that repeat the opening verse to close the song (there is, once more, a four-line bridge in the middle of the song). A happy piano lead supported by *Skyline*'s standard instrumental arrangement paves the way for this tale of a dedicated lover's commitment to his newfound flame. The opening verse sets the scene:

Throw my ticket out the window,
Throw my suitcase out there, too,
Throw my troubles out the door,
I don't need them any more
'Cause tonight I'll be staying here with you.

The song continues with the narrator's announcement that he "should have left this town this morning" but was unable to remove himself from the "spell" cast by his new love. Seemingly, a one-night stand has blossomed into a full-fledged affair and the narrator is unable to pull himself away. So, as the train whistle blows and the "stationmaster" awaits, he offers his ticket to anyone (even a "poor boy on the street") because he's staying right where he is for another night of bliss.

Why would anyone be so committed so quickly? Probably, my friends, because this lady makes one fine "Country Pie." The metaphors run deep in this 1:35 account of culinary wonder in which the narrator declares his unrequited love for all kinds of pie. The lively piano-guitar interplay that leads this country rocker through its five four-line verses (with a four-line bridge and another guitar break—again, no harmonica) sets the tone for a song that reminds you of Big Pink's playfulness. The bridge says it all: "Raspberry, strawberry, lemon and lime / What do I care? / Blueberry, apple, cherry, pumpkin and plum / Call me for dinner, honey, I'll be there." Not only are his tastes inclusive, but he also promises not to be wasteful or to "throw" his pie "up in anybody's face." The guy just loves his pie, that's all. That commitment is evident in the closing verse when he declares, "Shake me up that old peach tree / Little Jack Horner's got nothin' on me." The word here is *anti-Dylan*.

From nocturnal wonders and sweet munchies, we turn to our final love celebration, the cloudy "Lay, Lady, Lay." Those Nashville Cats had airplay on their minds when they recorded this track. The pedal steel, organ, close vocals, and funky drumming on this song establish a precise aural setting for an uneven account of what appears to a love triangle. The song is quite repetitive across its four 4–5-line stanzas that unfold without bridges or choruses. The opening verse features the narrator's plea for this lady to relax, "lay across" his "big brass bed," and trust his ability to provide the "colors" that reside in her "mind." The plot thickens in the second verse:

Lay, lady, lay, lay across my big brass bed
Stay, lady, stay, stay with your man awhile
Until the break of day, let me see you make him smile
His clothes are dirty but his hands are clean
And you're the best thing that he's ever seen

Unless our narrator is enjoying an out-of-body experience, a third person has entered the fray. After another request for the lady to spend more time with her man, the narrator inquires, "Why wait any longer for the world to begin / You can have your cake and eat it too." This little piece of anti-Dylan communicates either the trite qualities of *Skyline*'s songwriting or its insatiable sweet tooth. In any event, the song closes with more requests, more night urges, and more repetition. The Music City pop engines are running full-bore here, and the auteur fully acquiesces to its hollow needs.

When the night moves grow stale and you overdose on pie (or cake), well, things change, don't they? Proving to be the well-balanced purveyor of love that it is, *Skyline* turns to the downside of loving relations with its remaining songs. After the Cash-Dylan cover of "Girl From The North Country" and that song's pining over the red-headed woman from the "borderline," *Skyline* presents a man who wasted his life, a guy in denial, and a fellow whose nights are less than pleasant. It is almost as if these songs represent the photo negative of the celebrations: One character "threw away" Peggy Day and regrets it, another realizes that the "stationmaster" might be right (it is time to leave), and yet another desperately misses his downtime with his woman—especially at night. All of these characters are on a diet. There is no country pie anywhere in sight.

"I Threw It All Away" is a well-constructed pop song. This sad, organ-drenched elegy unfolds in three five-line stanzas with a pivotal five-line bridge setting up the moral of the story. Our "Woe is me" tale opens with the narrator's acknowledgment of his ex-lover's commitment before he wasted it all through foolish cruelty. Next, he describes his fall. He had it all and did not realize it until it was gone. His remorse is complete and his lesson has been learned, as the bridge and final stanza relate:

Love is all there is, it makes the world go 'round,
Love and only love, it can't be denied.
No matter what you think about it
You just won't be able to do without it.
Take a tip from one who's tried.

So if you find someone that gives you all of her love,
Take it to your heart, don't let it stray,
For one thing that's certain,
You will surely be a-hurtin',
If you throw it all away.

The song is coherent, well-constructed, and evocative. There is no Peggy Day in this man's world. No. She is long gone, and the narrator transcends his pain by testifying before the world. He faces his sad state and shares his lot.

But at least he is not in denial, unlike the central character in "Tell Me That It Isn't True." The opening stanzas state this case in no uncertain terms:

> I have heard rumors all over town,
> They say that you're planning to put me down.
> All I would like you to do,
> Is tell me that it isn't true.
>
> They say that you've been seen with some other man,
> That he's tall, dark and handsome, and you're holding his hand.
> Darlin', I'm a-countin' on you,
> Tell me that it isn't true.

This country pie has grown stale, but this character still wants a slice. The brief two-line bridge expresses the injury the narrator endures before the song closes with two verses that repeat his dismay, his denial, and his plea for her loyalty. Unlike the character in "I Threw It All Away," this character gains sympathy through his apparent innocence and his longing for fidelity. But you know, don't you, that his perseverance will yield more emptiness.

This treatment of *Nashville Skyline* closes with one final night tale, appropriately titled "One More Night." The four 5–6-line verses with a pivotal two-line bridge communicate that the narrator's love is long gone, leaving him to cope with all of those moonlit nights of solitude. The song opens by describing the lonesome central character on a clear, starry night pining for his lost love. The second verse and bridge state his sad situation:

> Oh, it's shameful and it's sad,
> I lost the only pal I had,
> I just could not be what she wanted me to be.
> I will turn my head up high
> To that dark and rolling sky,
> For tonight no light will shine on me.
>
> I was so mistaken when I thought that she'd be true,
> I had no idea what a woman in love would do!

The plot thickens here a bit, doesn't it? He failed her expectations; therefore, he lost his pal—it appears to another man. The song closes with two repeated verses sandwiched around a guitar break. With the winds whipping about as his heart sinks further in his lonesome sorrow, another joyless night passes by.

Without question, *Nashville Skyline* is a balanced treatment of pop music's most extensively mined songwriting topic. Love is joyous. Love is hell. Infatuation is resplendent. Rejection—or treachery—is all-consuming. Wrap up these sentiments in 2–3-minute vignettes with steady—but uneventful—instrumental support, and you have, my friends, that patented Nashville Sound. Pure *anti-Dylan*. Push that vocal up-front so the listener cannot confuse the platitudes, provide those instrumental breaks on their regularly scheduled cues, hint of or wink at the emotions that support the expression, and you're on your way to a mighty fine Music City song. Now, if you've concentrated and read between those lines, be sure to send your conclusions to my editor. He is interested. Me? I'm off to celebrate the night with some good ol' country pie.

I'm not being a snob when I make fun of these pop songs. If I were writing about anyone other than Bob Dylan, I'd back off these insinuations. But I *am* writing about the voice of his generation, and I *am* wondering where all of this is heading. The *Skyline* sessions tell me exactly where that is, too. You see, most of the songs recorded during the four sessions that generated *Skyline* were covers of Johnny Cash tunes or selected Nashville standards. This is not the sort of activity that we would associate with the basement experience; rather, the biographers report that there was talk of a Cash-Dylan album, so the Cash songs and assorted covers were anything but throwaways or inspirational exercises. The auteur is searching for his bearings. His amnesia is genuine. He relies on Cash to play The Band's role in a more serious manner, and it does not work. So, now, we turn to the dark side of the Basement Strategy and that special moment when Jack Fate goes on vacation and Bob Dillon tells everyone to go to hell.

Self Portrait, *New Morning*, and *Dylan*

The Americana era of Bob Dylan's oeuvre was a dynamic, personally challenging period for the auteur. While the thrill of discovery massaged childhood dreams and the release of rebellion invoked lifelong personality traits, the transitions of recovery tested the Dylan composite's resilience. Jack Fate's musical education worked its muscles in Big Pink and Bob Dillon's rebellion fueled the *Harding* project (by accepting Nashville recording practices, he rebelled against everything), but all of the rough edges that characterize Dylan's art were smoothed and rounded during the *Skyline* venture. Using musicology exercises to relax and adhering to strict formulas to write had merely opened the door for Dylan's recovery. That mission was a long way from completion. Here we take a step back, a step forward, and a step sideways in this protracted process of creative rejuvenation. Had Bob Dylan not been so high on that artistic mountain, his fall would not have been so severe. But he was, and his climb back up that prodigious incline would take time and serious effort. What flowed so naturally for so long now had to find another way to surface. To begin, Jack Fate holds his nose, accepts the stench of commercial rebellion, and allows Bob Dillon to have his way—regardless of the cost. It is time to turn to Bob Dylan's self-portrait.

One of the prime movers of Dylan's career is his power of invention. The creation of the Bob Dylan character and its various spin-offs was more than clever; it was effective. His innovative finger-pointing songs transformed what songwriters thought they could say in a song. His unprecedented impressionism released the pens of every generation of songwriters to follow. Since Kris Kristofferson reports in *The Bob Dylan Story* that *Blonde On Blonde* was pop music's first double album, even his album formats revolutionized the industry. Now, in his own special way, Dylan offers another musical invention: karaoke. What Dylan and Bob Johnston were thinking when they expanded on the failed Dylan-Cash sessions is hard to say. The biographers claim the auteur was working on an album of Nashville standards. As we'll see, Dylan claims he was allowing Bob Dillon to do his thing. Whatever the reason, *Self Portrait* introduced the musical world to the possibilities of karaoke—whatever they may be.

Once more, Clinton Heylin's session chronology is invaluable to this understanding of just how the *Portrait* album came to pass. Sessions occurred over time, some in Nashville, others in New York; and overdubs were applied—yes, *overdubs*—in Nashville. Here, Dylan's method of record production shifted from its performance-based orientation to an ensemble method. Things would never be the same again. He applied his first vocal overdub during these sessions. After parts of some songs were recorded, the tapes were forwarded to Johnston in Nashville, where he recruited Dylan veterans Charlie McCoy and Ken Buttrey to add overdubs (to their disbelief). Several songs feature layers and layers of bass, drums, piano, fiddle, dobro, trombone, cello, keyboards, viola, violin, and saxophone, and according to Heylin, an arranger (Barry McDonald) worked the album's tenth session. Songs were also finished without Dylan's direct participation. Thus, we are a long, long way from the *Another Side Of Bob Dylan* sessions: "Yea! Heavy, Music City."

The results are . . . well, some are good, some are bad, and some fall somewhere in between. The twenty-four-track, seventy-four-minute double album was issued in June 1970. *Rolling Stone*'s review seems to reflect the consensus opinion with its lead: "What is this shit?" If you haven't heard *Portrait*, that comment may seem a bit harsh. If you have, you understand the sentiment. The album offers four songs from Dylan's performance at the Isle of Wight festival ("Like A Rolling Stone," "The Mighty Quinn," "Minstrel Boy," and "She Belongs To Me"), a host of surprising covers (e.g., "Let It Be Me," "Blue Moon," "The Boxer," and "Early Morning Rain"), traditional tunes (e.g., "Little Sadie"), and some "interesting" new songs (e.g., "All The Tired Horses" and "Wigwam"). Being the positive guy that I am, I'll open with the good news.

Despite what the popular press may suggest, there is good news on this record—if you look at it from a different point of view. Regardless of perspective, "Woogie Boogie" is a lot of fun. Despite the overdubs, the song is a classic example of the boogie-woogie musical style that inspires the most uptight individuals to take to their feet and move a bit. Correspondingly, the Isle of Wight track "She Belongs To Me" demonstrates the potential for a better recording to unveil a strong performance of a solid song. But what is truly interesting is the set of songs that have to be removed from their *Self Portrait* context, reorganized, and presented in a different light. You see, *Portrait* contains a show that I deem "the Bob Dylan Revue." These songs represent NashVegas at its finest—doors open at 2:00 A.M., folks. The layers upon layers of sound, the occasionally cheesy backing vocals by the Bobettes (who, from what I can ascertain, are Hilda Harris, Maeretha Stewart, and Albertine Robinson), and the auteur's crooning method of delivery yield one strong Las Vegas show dressed in a Nashville Nudie suit. The set opens with a swinging "Living The Blues," slows for the "Blue Moon" cover (Elvis is in the building), pauses for the obligatory bad number "Take A Message To Mary," rebounds with a strong "Take Me As I Am," continues with a compelling "Belle Isle," closes with a grand finale "Wigwam," and concludes the evening with the encore that is "Alberta #2." If the crowd is hot and the promoter gives an approving wink, the show may be expanded to include "Let It Be Me" and "It Hurts Me Too" (gotta get the crowd back to those poker machines in the lobby!). The show's ebb and flow are masterful as the voice of his generation opens with his own composition, "Living The Blues," as he strolls across the stage, crooning away while the backing vocals add the kind of musical depth you find only in NashVegas. The "Blue Moon" pause is pure genius, as is the "Take A Message" lull before the storm that is "Take Me" and "Belle Isle." But it's how you leave 'em in NashVegas, and the Bob Dylan Revue does not disappoint here either. "Wigwam" is a one-of-a-kind closer. With Big Horns blaring (and more to come!) and Dylan humming (that's right) along with the tune, the song cranks to an inspiring crescendo. I wonder what color of lamé Dylan wears as he sashays in front of the crowded tables, "la la la"ing his way through the number, accepting a soft rain of roses, panties, and tie-dyed boxer shorts. As the crowd nears exhaustion, the Revue returns for an encore that leaves them with "something" (even the harmonica has glitter on this song). What a night.

Somebody has a sense of humor.

Like all great art, *Self Portrait* embraces the yin and yang of life as well. To the extent that the Revue "works," there are those sad tracks that do not. When Dylan fights his way through "Early Morning Rain," you find yourself on the edge of your seat, anticipating The Band to appear and launch into the basement masterpiece "Hills Of Mexico." I mean, this has to be a joke, right? The laughs continue with what I call the Speechless Series—a group of songs that take you beyond words, for all of the wrong reasons. Here you wonder if Big Pink engineer Garth Hudson would have rolled tape or exercised better judgment. The Sadie Chronicles ("In Search Of Little Sadie" and "Little Sadie"—same song, different arrangement) would, no doubt, have been considered to be a waste of precious basement tape. "The Boxer" would have miraculously caused Big Pink's colors to devolve into a familiar shade of yellow, signifying its artistic value. Still, as the song proceeds, you get used to it—you know, sort of like you do when your eyes are dilated and you accept the disorientation. "Minstrel Boy" is a genuine basement outtake. The drunken vocals are pure Pink (at least I *hope* they're drunk!). But at the top of this list is the incredible version of "Rolling Stone" from Isle of Wight. I was wrong about this track in *American Song*. There I suggest that this song could be used as a motivational tape for karaoke performers. I'm younger than that now, and I realize that in karaoke you try to follow the tune in your own haphazard way. This is not like that at all. This is more like the kind of song four college freshmen would belt out while running away from the law during an underage drinking raid at a party—their minds are someplace else. (By the way, if caught, these guys would spend their time in jail singing *Portrait*'s "Mighty Quinn.") So, to the extent that the Bob Dylan Revue shines, these songs sink. The commercial art world is a challenging environment.

Finally, we turn to those songs that fall somewhere in between these extremes. The singing-talking voice used in "Days Of 49" fits within this category, as does another cover, "Copper Kettle." In the latter song, what starts out as "The Little Drummer Boy" quickly turns into "Bridge Over Troubled Water." The overproduction is staggering. Of genuine interest here is the musical style evidenced in "Gotta Travel On." Too hokey to be included in the Revue (oh my!), this song uses a production strategy that will come to dominate two future projects: *Dylan* and *Street-Legal*. The female backing vocals are almost overdone here; they drift closer to that destination in *Dylan*, and they achieve that status in *Street-Legal*. The gospel-style backing vocals introduced on *Portrait* represent the wave of the future in that Bob Dylan will, from time to time, rely heavily on this sonic strategy—at times, as per *Slow Train* and *Saved*, to marvelous ends; at others, as per *Street-Legal*, to less than positive results. And it all starts here, friends. The man with so many sonic innovations to his credit tries to sneak one past the musical world as he introduces a performance trend that should have resulted in his lynching. There *is* evidence of karaoke on *Self Portrait*. "Early Morning Rain" is the real thing. His use of different voices to fit different songs is also telltale. From the third track's "I Forgot More Than You'll Ever Know" to the fourth track's "Days Of 49" to the fifth track's "Early Morning Rain," Dylan deploys three distinct voices in service of the respective songs. Thank god the voice of his generation did not have a karaoke machine available.

What was Bob Dylan thinking as he allowed *Portrait* to be assembled? What were his objectives? He shared his motivations with *Rolling Stone*'s Kurt Loder and explained Bob Dillon's response to an audience that was increasingly debilitating:

> Well, fuck it, I wish these people would just *forget* about me. I wanna do something they *can't* possibly like, they *can't* relate to. They'll see it, and they'll listen, and they'll say, "Well, let's go on to the next person. He ain't sayin' it no more. He ain't givin' us what we want," you know? They'll go on to somebody else. But the whole idea backfired. Because the album went out there, and the people said, "*This* ain't what we want," and they got *more* resentful. And then I did this portrait for the cover. I mean, there was no *title* for that album. I knew somebody who had some paints and a square canvas, and I did the cover up in about five minutes. And I said, "Well, I'm gonna call this album *Self Portrait*". . . . And to me, it was a *joke*. [Loder asks why a double album.] Well, it wouldn't have held up as a single album—then it *really* would've been bad, you know. I mean, if you're gonna put a lot of crap on it, you might as well *load it up*!

These comments to Cameron Crowe are also instructive: "*Self Portrait* . . . was a bunch of tracks that we'd done all the time I'd gone to Nashville. We did that stuff to get a (studio) sound. To open up we'd do two or three songs, just to get things right and then we'd go on and do what we were going to do. And then there was a lot of other stuff that was just on the shelf. . . . So I just figured I'd put all this stuff together and put it out, my own bootleg record, so to speak. . . . Also, I wasn't going to be anybody's puppet and I figured this record would put an end to that."

This was Dylan's attitude at that time. With his manager allegedly abusing his publishing income, his critics overanalyzing every syllable of his work, his fans rummaging through his garbage and hassling his family, his connection with his creative instincts strained, bootleggers making fortunes off of his labors, and his contract with his record company under negotiation, Dylan decided to record cover versions of country, traditional, and pop songs, thereby resting the muse and, perhaps, reducing the publishing royalties. Producer Bob Johnston offers this strong response to *Portrait*'s critics in the BBC's *The Bob Dylan Story*:

> Critics are an eternal mediocrity living at the expense of genius either to belittle it or destroy it. A race of insects happily eating away at the foliage of art. [Wow. Thanks, Bob.] He came in and he said "What do you think about me doing other people's songs?" And I said, "Great man, whatdaya got?" And he got a bunch of bibles and books and poetry and all that shit, came in and sat down and he recorded as long as he wanted to and we had all of those songs. I thought a bunch of 'em were wonderful. Presley things and all of those others—"Leaving On A Jet Plane" . . . he loved the songs so he recorded 'em all. Wasn't any, like, hidden agenda.

This is not the Basement Strategy here. This is not a group of seasoned friends exploring music history. Dylan's and Johnston's comments are at odds with one another. Was Dylan telling his audience off? Was he making his own bootleg? Was he seriously exploring the songs searching for their possibilities? The extent to which problems on the business end affected the creative side of Dylan's work is uncertain. Assuredly, there were problems. In response, this thing was assembled in the crassest manner; however, if disassembled, it may be reassembled in a way that makes sense. Johnson's argument has merit. There *is* a NashVegas set here (though they are hardly "country standards"). There *is* a foreshadowing of *Street-Legal* here. And, to be sure, there *is* some filler here. Considering what Columbia Records had in its vaults, that filler *is* almost offensive.

If Dylan had amnesia, then whatever he did to trick out the lyrics for *Harding* enabled him to build another selection of songs for what would become *New Morning*. However, unlike *Harding*, *Morning*'s songs display a sonic diversity that is unique within the lifework. *Love And Theft* will fondle several genres, but not with the scope evidenced in *New Morning*. What is so strange is how Dylan made *Morning* while recording the cover songs that would find their way onto *Dylan*. As we will see in a moment, the *Dylan* project takes the Bob Dylan Revue, calms the overproduction, and moves us even closer to the *Street-Legal* format. How these two approaches to music making coexisted is anybody's guess. The gospel backing vocals appear to be the two projects' common denominator, so perhaps that was the bridge. The two albums deploy totally different sonic strategies, that is for certain. Heylin's session chronology reports that all sorts of projects may have been in the works. There was an awful lot of recording taking place, and several sources suggest that the covers that wound up on *Dylan* consumed more of the auteur's time than his new material—those songs appear to be afterthoughts. Take, for example, Heylin's account of the activities of June 3, 1970, when Team Dylan recorded "Jamaica Farewell" and "Long Black Veil" (which failed to make either cut); two takes of "Can't Help Falling In Love" and one of "Lily Of The West" (both songs are on *Dylan*, but different takes may have been used); and, at the end of the session, *New Morning*'s "One More Weekend." He recorded songs from his back catalog (e.g., "Blowin' In The Wind" and "Rainy Day Women"); new songs that wound up on his next greatest hits collection, released in November 1971 (e.g., "Watching The River Flow" and "When I Paint My Masterpiece"); and odd songs of different stripes (too many to mention here!). There are existing song lists that indicate that a blend of *Dylan* and *New Morning* was on the table—some kind of *Self Portrait, Vol. 2*. Maybe Dylan's Gemini personality was operating on two planes. Maybe he was as lost as he says he was and feeling his way out of his situation. Maybe he was as flat-out mad as he seems to be in the Loder interview. Whatever it was, it was a part of his recovery—a mission that regains momentum with *New Morning*.

That the Dylan commercial machine was aware of *Portrait*'s limitations is evident by the speed with which *New Morning* came to the rescue (they had the material, so why not use it?). Released October 21, 1970 (a little over three months after *Portrait*), this would be the last studio album of new material produced by Bob Johnston (Al Kooper, Leon Russell, and Dylan also sat in the producer's chair at one time or another). *Morning*'s twelve songs (running almost thirty-six minutes) focus on loving relationships with three exceptions: one song of personal celebration (the autobiographical "Day Of The Locusts") and two nonstories ("Three Angels" and "Father Of Night"). The nonstories differ from Dylan's wordplay or impressionism in that they offer clear, coherent lines that simply describe a scene ("Angels") and praise its subject ("Father"). The love songs, of course, focus on good and bad things (e.g., "Time Passes Slowly," the cloudy "Went To See The Gypsy," and "Sign On The Window"). The record is dominated by the six songs celebrating love: "If Not For You," "Winterlude," "If Dogs Run Free," "New Morning," "One More Weekend," and "The Man In Me." The joys of love are communicated through a variety of musical genres: a waltz ("Winterlude"), a scat jazz routine ("If Dogs"), classic pop songs ("If Not" and the title cut), rhythm and blues ("One More"), and country pop (the prayerful "The Man"). (The two nonstories feature a gospel quality that is interspersed throughout *Morning*—thanks to the backing vocals and churchy organ work.) The shift in musical approaches contributes to the album's pacing and reduces the narrative redundancy that occurs when songs say the same thing repeatedly.

We begin with songs of relational joy. The ecstasies of relational contentment are presented through a pop music lens with "If Not For You" and "New Morning." "If Not" offers our lone piece of harmonica as it otherwise sticks to tried-and-true pop music sound strategies. Presented in four 5–6-line stanzas with a six-line bridge, the song extols the wonders of relational codependence. "If not" for his lover, our narrator would unable to "find the door" or "see the floor," he would endure sleepless nights, his "winter would have no spring," he would be unable to "hear the robin sing," and his life would be turned on end. The bridge (which is repeated as the third verse) explains why:

> If not for you
> My sky would fall,
> Rain would gather too.
> Without your love I'd be nowhere at all,
> I'd be lost if not for you,
> And you know it's true.

The song is the epitome of the "I can't make it without you" love song as it goes about its business in its own light and lively way. That trend holds true for the second pop installment and the album's title cut. In "New Morning," Dylan deploys four verses (three with seven lines, the final verse with five) with a two-line bridge strategy to weave a systematic account of love's wonders. The strategy is simple: Each verse uses four lines for a scenic description, pauses for the "So happy just to see you smile" or "So happy just to be alive" segue, and closes with the two-line embedded chorus. The first verse demonstrates the technique:

> Can't you hear that rooster crowin'?
> Rabbit runnin' down across the road
> Underneath the bridge where the water flowed through
> So happy just to see you smile
> Underneath the sky of blue
> On this new morning, new morning
> On this new morning with you.

From there, the narrator ponders an automobile starting and moving down the road (verse 2), feels the sun shining as a groundhog frolics by a stream (verse 3), and simply enjoys his happy life (verse 4). Why? Because love is in his life, and for that he is very, very thankful. "If Not For You" and "New Morning" are classic pop compositions that feature direct language presented in a coherent way. They are without mystery.

To enliven this age-old tale, our auteur now turns to different ways of presenting it. Let's start with a waltz, shall we? "Winterlude" uses the *John Wesley Harding*–perfected structure of three eight-line verses to praise her once more. The opening stanza sets the pace:

> Winterlude, Winterlude, oh darlin',
> Winterlude by the road tonight.
> Tonight there will be no quarrelin',
> Ev'rything is gonna be all right.
> Oh, I see by the angel beside me
> That love has a reason to shine.
> You're the one I adore, come over here and give me more,
> Then Winterlude, this dude thinks you're fine.

The waltz tempo provides the perfect sonic backdrop for these slightly syrupy sentiments that continue as the narrator praises his "little apple," urges her to accompany him "down to the chapel," return and "cook up a meal" (!), and, afterward, enjoy the simple pleasures of a winter day. The final verse offers more of the same. What could be finer than love in the snow? Are Zimmerman's Minnesota roots on display?

Maybe a good dog run would be just as fine. Shifting sonic gears to a scat jazz format, this loving little number takes a while to get to where it is going. At first, the narrator is philosophical—"If dogs run free, then why not we?"—before he explains how his "ears hear a symphony / Of two mules, trains and rain" and conveys his optimism about the future. In the second verse, he reminds us that his "mind weaves a symphony / And tapestry of rhyme" as he concludes, "To each his own, it's all unknown." The third verse takes us home:

> If dogs run free, then what must be,
> Must be, and that is all.
> True love can make a blade of grass
> Stand up straight and tall.
> In harmony with the cosmic sea,
> True love needs no company,
> It can cure the soul, it can make it whole,
> If dogs run free.

As Dylan works through his treatise, the backing singer scats along, adding her emotional tones to the philosophical stances that lead to the inevitable conclusion that love is the end all be all. The song's philosophical bent is best communicated in its ending as a long fade lingers and trails off.

The demonstration of how to match romantic lyrics with musical genres continues with the Delta blues and country-pop tunes that are "One More Weekend" and "The Man In Me," respectively. With the sounds of Beale Street echoing in the background, the blues-based "Weekend" hammers home the fun of another holiday with the one you love. Using four four-line verses with a perfectly situated middle-eight to tell this very repetitive tale, the song uses that age-old blues vernacular to do the deed. For instance, we open with "Slippin' and slidin' like a weasel on the run, / I'm lookin' good to see you, yeah, and we can have some fun" before repeating the title for two lines and driving home the need for "one more weekend with you." (That weasel imagery clears it all up for me; how about you?) The metaphors do their thing in the following stanzas, as the narrator urges his love interest to "Come on down to my ship, honey, ride on deck" and announces that they will be "Comin' and goin' like a rabbit in the wood" before his concluding simile, "Like a needle in a haystack, I'm gonna find you yet, / You're the sweetest gone mama that this boy's ever gonna get." Get the drift?

We shift gears to country pop with "The Man In Me." With a classic structure of three four-line verses and a four-line bridge, "Man" works just like "Weekend." That is, two lines describe the man or his situation before the standard two-line tag. For example, the song opens with the narrator explaining that he will do "any task" without regard for "compensation" since, as the two tag lines relate, "Take a woman like you / To get through to the man in me." Storms may rage and he may sometimes hide from his oppressors, but she pulls him through. The bridge explains why:

> But, oh, what a wonderful feeling
> Just to know that you are near,
> Sets my heart a-reeling
> From my toes up to my ears.

Through these songs, our auteur mines the same songwriting vein, but with different tools. In each case, the lyrics are tailored to fit their soundstage. Pop songs use platitudes. Scat jazz jumps about. A waltz floats. Country pop is homely. And the blues are a bit randy. Just as he used the song's lyrical structure to shape his words in *John Wesley Harding*, Dylan uses these songs' sonic structures to do the same. He may have amnesia, but he is fighting it, searching for some key to unlock that once-unconscious lyrical magic. Maybe therein lies the problem: He's trying *too* hard.

The record's love complaints vary in their intensity. "Time Passes Slowly" and "Sign On The Window" leave little doubt about their points, whereas "Went To See The Gypsy" is more cryptic and evasive. All use the piano to establish their respective moods. A real "Woe is me" number, "Time" uses the standard four four-line verses with a four-line bridge format to state its case. In the first verse, the narrator describes how time passes slowly when you are amongst nature, lost in your dreams. Next, he reminisces about the days with his "sweetheart" and enjoying domestic life with her family. The bridge and final verse seal the deal:

> Ain't no reason to go in a wagon to town,
> Ain't no reason to go to the fair.
> Ain't no reason to go up, ain't no reason to go down,
> Ain't no reason to go anywhere.
>
> Time passes slowly up here in the daylight,
> We stare straight ahead and try so hard to stay right,
> Like the red rose of summer that blooms in the day,
> Time passes slowly and fades away.

From the sound of things, the narrator's situation is not about to improve anytime soon. That pessimism appears in "Sign On The Window" as well; however, this time, a turning point occurs and the song ends optimistically. The song, with three five-line verses with a three-line bridge, opens by offering a series of signs that appear on a window, a door, a street, and a porch. One says "Lonely," while another relates "No Company Allowed," another states "Y' Don't Own Me," and the fourth unveils our story: "Three's A Crowd." The second verse states our narrator's case:

> Her and her boyfriend went to California,
> Her and her boyfriend done changed their tune.
> My best friend said, "Now didn' I warn ya,
> Brighton girls are like the moon,
> Brighton girls are like the moon."

Interestingly, after the bridge reinforces the narrator's darkness, the tide turns. For some reason, he resolves to build a "cabin in Utah," get married, go fishing, and have a "bunch of kids who call me 'Pa'." He concludes, "That must be what it's all about," the next line repeats that view, and the story ends. Apparently, his optimism wins out.

We continue our exploration of *New Morning* with a slight relational complaint ("Gypsy") and a personal celebration ("Day Of The Locusts") that share identical songwriting strategies. Though their structures differ slightly, both march through their respective accounts from beginning to end. The autobiographical "Locusts" was written in response to Dylan's acceptance of an honorary doctorate from Princeton University and, therefore, recalls the events of that apparently hot and exasperating day. The song's four eight-line verses (the final stanza adds a line) use four lines to describe something from that day and the final four lines to praise those singing locusts who were celebrating the auteur's achievement ("Yeah, the locusts sang and they were singing just for me" closes each verse—the song features locust sound effects to drive home the point). First, the narrator captures the scene with its seats "stained" with "tears and perspiration," the busy birds, and the silent participants. He continues by describing a dark, smelly "chamber" in which the "judges" conferred, and how as he was leaving, he saw "light" enter the room. Next, he talks of the heat and a man standing next to him with an exploding head ("Well, I was prayin' the pieces wouldn't fall on me.") before concluding, "I put down my robe, picked up my diploma, / Took hold of my sweetheart and away we did drive, / Straight for the hills, the black hills of Dakota, / Sure was glad to get out of there alive." One gains an image of Dr. Dylan motoring away to a serenade of loving locusts.

"Went To See The Gypsy" follows a similar narrative logic in a more cryptic fashion. The song marches through the story, but the characters are not developed. Since the song pivots on the visit with the gypsy and we don't know who or what that is, well, things get pretty darned cloudy. In the first verse, the narrator meets the gypsy and they greet one another (a scene that seems like it came straight out of "Frankie Lee"). Suddenly, he ventures down to the lobby and meets a "pretty dancing girl" who shouts at him to go back upstairs to the gypsy, declaring, "Go on back to see the gypsy / He can move you from the rear, / Drive you from your fear, / Bring you through the mirror. / He did it in Las Vegas, / And he can do it here." The bridge pauses for a brief scene in which the narrator stares off at a "river of tears" with "music" in his "ears." Afterward, he returns to the gypsy's room only to find it vacated. Both the gypsy and the pretty dancing girl are gone. He decides to sit and watch the sun rise "From that little Minnesota town." Clearly, something is happening here and we do not know what it is, but it hints of a complaint of sorts. Something, somehow created that "river of tears," and either the gypsy or the girl were related in some manner. So, I suggest that this is some form of cryptic complaint along the lines of "I Pity The Poor Immigrant" or "Dear Landlord." We have, then, more "inside baseball."

Speaking of *John Wesley Harding* tunes, we witness an extension of the "All Along The Watchtower" songwriting strategy in "Three Angels" and "Father Of Night." These songs do not feature stories arranged in a reverse order; they are not stories at all. "Angels" is a twenty-line poem set to church music. The first four lines establish the context:

> Three angels up above the street,
> Each one playing a horn,
> Dressed in green robes with wings that stick out,
> They've been there since Christmas morn.

From there, we have line after line of street activity descriptions. The three angels look down on a wild guy from Montana, a brightly dressed lady, a rented trailer, a bus, dogs, pigeons, a man wearing a "badge," three guys "crawlin' on their way back to work," a bakery vehicle, and more. The track closes in this fashion:

> The angels play their horns all day,
> The whole earth in progression seems to pass by.
> But does anyone hear the music they play,
> Does anyone even try?

With that, our brief hymn (running 2:09) comes to a quiet close. The track describes the angels and moves on to the varied activities that unfold beneath them. People are too busy to look at Christmas displays, and this song charts what they do instead. This sound—the sound of *hymns*—is percolating in the auteur's musical mind. This is all leading to something, and "Father Of Night" supports that trend.

"Father" is three six-line verses of respectful praise. Its gospel sound is as undeniable as its faithful message. He is the "Father" of all things: day, night, black, white, mountains, time, dreams, the waterways, the grain, the wheat, cold and heat, air and trees, and time itself. The opening verse captures how this hymn of praise unfolds:

> Father of night, Father of day
> Father, who taketh the darkness away,
> Father, who teacheth the bird to fly,
> Builder of rainbows up in the sky,
> Father of loneliness and pain,
> Father of love and Father of rain.

The song continues with the list I cited above. The final line sums it all: "Father of whom we most solemnly praise." Much like *John Wesley Harding*'s closing and its two tracks of pop love songs, *New Morning* ends with two songs that address heavenly matters. Again, the capstone strategy recurs. Dylan followed *Harding* with an entire album of love songs. Would he repeat the practice with these hymns?

As we've seen, this is the most eclectic album in the oeuvre. The record uses pop, waltz, scat jazz, blues, gospel, and country sounds to—in more cases than not—articulate views on loving relations. Now, this may be viewed two ways. One is that it is a Good Thing since the writer deploys various sonic platforms to present his ideas. The other is that it is a Bad Thing since the work is directionless, void of any type of sonic anchor while wallowing in pop platitudes. There is, however, a *thematic anchor* holding this work in its designated place: Love is on the auteur's agenda. Nevertheless, like most of the writing of this era, the songwriting is formulaic. Bridges, middle-eights, and repeated lines and verses control most of these songs. That this is a transitional moment in the Dylan Canon is abundantly clear.

Contributing to that view is the gospel tone that permeates the record. While these songs may not be full-fledged gospel songs, the two nonstories surely embrace traditional gospel sentiments, and the churchy organ and backing vocals use gospel sounds in no uncertain terms. Perhaps this is because religion is moving its way into the songwriter's consciousness. Faith has always been a part of Dylan's writing, but perhaps it is moving closer to a position of dominance. Or, complementing that development but acting on their own imperative, the Bobettes influenced the tone of the songs. The Bob Dylan Revue certainly has a gospel feel to the vocals, but the productions were too over the top to fit within that genre. During the sessions that rendered *Morning*, however, that production strategy yielded to different sound—a sound that controls *Dylan*.

Released in November 1973, *Dylan* is widely viewed to be Columbia Records' "revenge" album. You see, for the one time in his protracted career, Dylan left Columbia after his contract expired in 1972. He signed a one-album-at-a-time deal with David Geffen and Asylum Records. While Geffen received but two albums before Dylan returned to his native label, the *Dylan* release was a shot over the old bow. There was, after all, album after album worth of outtakes, unreleased songs, and live shows in Columbia's vaults; therefore, releasing *Dylan* provided the writing on the commercial wall: Columbia is liable to do *anything* with Dylan's back catalog.

Where *Dylan* stands in the oeuvre is probably unfair. Since it has never been released in a compact disc format, it is largely considered to be a throwaway. That is too bad, since this record of covers is *nothing* like *Self Portrait* (although two of the album's nine songs are from those sessions). On *Dylan*, the artists are trying to record strong takes of their subject matter. There is no fooling around, as there is on *Portrait*. There are no layers of sound added for the sake of adding layers of sound. Until the final two tracks ("A Fool Such As I" and "Spanish Is The Loving Tongue"—the two songs from the *Portrait* project), the Bobettes restrain themselves and sing in the gospel—not NashVegas—tradition. Only on those two *Portrait* remnants does Dylan use his *Skyline* crooning voice. On the remaining seven tracks, we hear the Bob Dylan of days gone by.

The album opens with "Lily Of The West" (by Davies and Peterson) and continues with "Can't Help Falling In Love" (Weiss, Peretti, and Creatore), "Sarah Jane" (Dylan receives the credit here), "Mr. Bojangles" (Walker), "The Ballad Of Ira Hayes" (LaFarge), "Mary Ann" (traditional), "Big Yellow Taxi" (Mitchell), and closes with the two *Portrait* songs, "A Fool" (Abner) and "Loving Tongue" (traditional). (I'm working from the cassette, and the song order is different than on the vinyl version.) The covers jump all over the place. The Western saga "Lily" sounds like "Ghost Riders In The Sky" with seemingly misplaced backing vocals confusing its impact. The opening and closing harmonica solos on "Can't Help Falling" add a Dylan touch to a fine arrangement—the song is treated *seriously* in my view. "Sarah Jane" and "Mary Ann" sound like a Rolling Thunder Revue preview, while "Mr. Bojangles" is a honest-to-god cover. Dylan is true to the original and discovers his own groove until, that is, the backing vocals appear and kill the mood established to that point. "Ira Hayes" fits in with "Lily" in its approach and Dylan's talking segments add to the song's respectful treatment. "Big Yellow Taxi" is worth the price of admission. It's a hoot! With a cheesy-beyond-belief organ paving the way, the song instantly turns into comedy. It is just not believable. What is particularly funny is the shift in lyrics. Dylan changes but one set of lyrics, and it's that segment that contains the song's title. If you know the original, you understand that Joni Mitchell sings about two things in the song: paving paradise and losing her lover. "You just don't appreciate things until they're gone" is her hook. In the original, she moves from one topic to the other by describing how she heard a door slam and watched a cab—hence, the title—take her lover away. Well, Dylan cannot go *there* since there is a direct gender reference in the original, so he changes the line to describe a bulldozer (that is the same color as Mitchell's taxi) knocking over his home. Hence, the tune should be renamed "Big Yellow Bulldozer." What a scream.

Dylan, for some reason, closes with the over-the-top dimension of the Bob Dylan Revue. These songs fly out the basement window, past the sleeping dog, and straight for the Nevada desert. Unlike the other covers, they are—to my ears—flat-out disingenuous. They are the exception here, not the rule. "Bojangles" is sincere. "Can't Help Falling" is a signature treatment. "Lily" and "Ira" receive respect. And "Big Yellow Taxi" is straight from the basement—they had to edit out the laughter— it has *got* to be there somewhere.

So now we reach the end of a truly fascinating era. Dylan's mission of recovery takes those steps I mentioned earlier. He steps back with *Portrait*. He inches forward with *New Morning*. He steps to the side while easing forward just a hair with *Dylan*. The Basement Strategy reinvigorated his sonic instincts, but that is only part of Dylan's musical equation. *Harding* and *Skyline* provided opportunities for his pen that resulted in lyrical conformity—and conformity is *not* part of the auteur's musical equation. Then along comes this segment of work. *Portrait* was as rebellious as it gets; I mean, the Bob Dylan Revue? *New Morning* takes us back to *Harding* and *Skyline*, but with sonic twists. Not until the pop icon era will Dylan write in this fashion again. The "amnesia" is most evident in these three records. However, even with amnesia, there is some good work here. Bob Zimmerman has considerable talent, and the strength of some of these songs indicates the extent of those abilities. *Dylan*, on the other hand, truly foreshadows the future. We *will* revisit this sonic strategy very soon. Consequently, when we pull back and pause, we instantly observe the overwhelmingly transitional qualities of these efforts. Just as Dylan said about *Harding*, he could have just as easily *not done any of this*. Instead, he fought through the amnesia. How many artists would have settled for an album of outtakes, or the release of the shows that later found their way onto the music store shelves thirty years later (e.g., shows from the 1966 tour and 1964)? No, that is not what happened at all. You see, Bob Zimmerman does not just use Bob Dillon; he has to cope with him. Jack Fate provides the musical knowledge, but Bob Dillon provides the creative instinct. These instincts are pulling the artist through his self-diagnosed amnesia. Now, all of that hard work pays off. The amnesia is about to go away. It is time to return to where this mission began—with The Band.

Planet Waves and Tour '74

If you've ever been sick, been brokenhearted, or experienced any form of emotional, physical, or professional downturn, then you know just how grand that moment of recovery is. The best part of breaking up is making up, right? When I was a kid and I fell down or injured myself in some way, my dad used to tell me, "Just think how good it'll feel when it quits hurting." I used to think that he was a real jerk for saying that since I wanted sympathy, not some home-cooked Carolina platitude. But he was, as usual, right on. And if you've been under the weather for an extended period of time, and it's affected you in your most vulnerable way, you *really* enjoy that moment when you realize that you're back. It's over. You're on your feet again.

I hope Bob Dylan enjoyed that moment. He earned it.

Dylan's mission of recovery succeeds with the dual *Planet Waves*–Tour '74 project. Although the tour will dredge up bad memories and inspire yet another rebellious Bob Dillon response, the opportunity to record with The Band was apparently medicinal. Moreover, the voice of his generation had something to say when he entered the studio with the boys from Big Pink in November 1973. How do I know this? Because the old songwriting process returned, that's why. Dylan wrote the *Planet Waves* songs in a month. When the words flow that quickly for Dylan, the lyrical lights are alit, the creative fire is burning, and the mission is focused. *Waves* contains some extraordinary songs. There is no plugging phrases into predetermined structures. The Bobettes are on vacation. Nashville is over. Bob Dylan turns his corner. Let's take a moment to catch up with the various activities that led to this critical point in the auteur's rejuvenation.

In 1970, Dylan moved back to New York City and formally ended his relationship with Albert Grossman (although things would linger with the lawyers for a while). His move to the Big Apple stimulated his musical agenda. He recorded with George Harrison in early spring (with little to no yield). He worked on *Morning* and what would become *Dylan* during the spring and into the summer. *Self Portrait* was released that June while Dylan was hard at work in the studio. *Morning* appeared that October just before *Tarantula* was issued. It was a busy time. In March 1971, he recorded new songs that found their way onto his second greatest hits compilation, released that November (e.g., "Watching The River Flow"). He appeared in George Harrison's Concert for Bangladesh in August 1971 (his first performance since Isle of Wight in 1969). He returned to topical songwriting with the single "George Jackson" that fall (the song is about a San Quentin inmate's murder). He recorded with Allen Ginsberg. He recorded with Happy Traum. He played and recorded with Doug Sahm. It was a busy time.

Another major development occurred in November 1972. What better way to leave the past and concentrate on the future than to fulfill one of your childhood dreams. When Dylan played the wonderfully named character "Alias" in Sam Peckinpah's film *Pat Garrett and Billy the Kid*, the Iron Range's original biker-poet returned to his creative womb. So much of Dylan comes from those 1950s movies that Bob Zimmerman viewed over and over and over in Hibbing. Once he accepted the part, he loaded up his wife and kids and took off for those hills of Mexico. When he arrived in Durango to join former Columbia janitor–turned–prominent celebrity Kris Kristofferson and the rest of the cast, things turned weird fast. Peckinpah was out of control—drunk all day, we're told. Howard Sounes reports that the director urinated on the film screen during a daily screening and cites Kristofferson's response: "I remember Bob turning and looking at me with the most perfect reaction, you know: what the hell have we gotten ourselves into?" Peckinpah fought relentlessly with the film studio, MGM, and the conflict affected all involved. What could have been a great thing was not so great.

Part of Dylan's role in the project involved making his first movie soundtrack. The recording began in Mexico City and was completed in Burbank in early 1973.

He worked studiously writing songs and designing the film's score—often while watching footage and feeling his way through the scenes. Much of that work was in vain since MGM hacked away at Peckinpah's version and displaced several of Dylan's carefully arranged instrumentals. One untouched moment involved the song "Knockin' On Heaven's Door" and its beautiful placement in a sad scene. The song also charted well as a single. Dylan did a fine job with the movie's sound design, although he swore off the practice immediately afterward. Columbia released the soundtrack in July 1973 after some internal debate over its timing. When all was said and done, we can safely say the experience yielded mixed results for Bob Dylan. No doubt, he enjoyed the acting even though the soundtrack experience was disappointing. When considered in retrospect, these events offered meaningful lessons for an artist in transition. Heylin's session chronology offers this take on these events: "The experience of working with an arranger and a film producer, making music that was only part of a greater whole, and seeing that greater whole wrestled from its creator and overseer, Sam Peckinpah, only further convinced Dylan of the importance of retaining control of his own work. For his next recording, he would use the most tried and tested of bands, and would reserve production duties for himself and that old cohort, Robbie Robertson." After undergoing his own artistic-commercial struggles and observing the same with Peckinpah, Dylan assumed control over his affairs (e.g., forming his own publishing company), moved to California, and started anew.

Joining Big Pink as one of his career's pivotal moments, Dylan agreed to participate in the huge Tour '74 operation promoted by Bill Graham and David Geffen, left Columbia and signed with Geffen's label, and entered the studio with The Band to record the album that they would promote during the reunion tour. Dylan and The Band had unsuccessfully recorded together in the fall of 1965, and they certainly enjoyed themselves during their Woodstock days, but these Los Angeles sessions were different. The Band had developed its own musical style, established its own reputation, and enjoyed its own commercial success. Now, these 1966 road veterans would pull it all together and create music that synthesized their respective histories into a single statement. Dylan provided the songs. Remarkably, he wrote those songs the month before the November sessions—sessions that required a little over a week to complete. It was music making on the run. It was just like the old days.

Waves features eleven tracks (running just over forty-two minutes) that convey that which had never before been captured in the studio: the Dylan-Band sound that was perfected during the basement experience. This is not the sound heard during the 1966 tours, although you can hear bits of it amongst the noise that is the "She Belongs To Me" recording from Isle of Wight. The Band's musical style features a dynamic interplay between Robertson's guitar, Hudson's organ and accordion, and the Helm/Manual/Danko rhythm section. Their sound is a distinct version of American roots music—totally unique. Complementing these musical treks across Americana (every song feels like a carnival or a funeral) were Dylan's words and his vocal performances. No crooning here, as the old Dylan voice assumed control. His words concentrate on one topic with one exception: "Forever Young" (offered in two versions: one fast, one slow) is a prayer for his children's futures. Love controls the remaining nine tracks through songs that complain about ("Going, Going, Gone," "Hazel," and "Dirge") and celebrate that haphazard emotional state ("On A Night

In the summer of 1980, Dylan would release an album called *Saved*. But that
record should have been named *Saved, Revisited* because the original "saved" is in the
six songs of relational joy that appear on *Waves*. After celebrating love by the fireplace on a snowy night in "On A Night Like This," the five remaining love songs address how the glorious women featured in these stories saved their respective
narrators' lives. At times, these tributes appear as parts of other activities; at other
times, they are the focal point of the story. As our first example, we turn to "Tough
Mama." With a foot-stomping instrumental track leading the way, the song charts the
narrator's loving admiration for his wonderful and strong woman. The song—featuring four seven-line verses sandwiched around a nine-line stanza—opens with
praise for our tough lady, references to "sister" (currently on the road), "papa" (now
in jail), and admiring statements about her perseverance. Apparently, "tough mama"
has reasons for her toughness. The next verse discusses specific life events she has
endured (seemingly, old boyfriends) and how those days have passed for our "Sweet
Goddess." The narrator—her "perfect stranger"—promises a better future:

> Silver Angel
> With the badge of the lonesome road sewed in your sleeve,
> I'd be grateful if this golden ring you would receive.
> Today on the countryside it was a-hotter than a crotch,
> I stood alone upon the ridge and all I did was watch.
> Sweet Goddess
> It must be time to carve another notch.
>
> I'm crestfallen
> The world of illusion is at my door,
> I ain't a-haulin' any of my lambs to the marketplace anymore.
> The prison walls are crumblin', there is no end in sight,
> I've gained some recognition but I lost my appetite.
> Dark Beauty
> Meet me at the border late tonight.

The plot thickens here. After once again praising her strength, he asks her to marry
him and give love another try. Suddenly, he turns introspective. He is dispirited. He
perceives that things are falling apart. An illusionary world threatens him, and he is
fighting back. It sounds as though he has had "too much of nothing." His success
has cost him his drive. His solution? His "Dark Beauty." *She* is the way out of his
"prison" and its deteriorating situation. He believes in her power to save *him* just as
she has saved *herself*.

The woman-as-savior theme advances in "Something There Is About You." A
strong guitar opens this systematic account of the narrator's life and his new romantic
curiosity. The first verse observes how she reminds him of something from the
past—maybe the distant past. Next, he recalls his youth, his life in Duluth, and, once
more, how she puts him in touch with those "long-forgotten" sentiments in a mag-

ical way. Yet, this special lady does more than remind him of days gone by; she is the key to his uncertain future:

> Suddenly I found you and the spirit in me sings
> Don't have to look no further, you're the soul of many things.
> I could say that I'd be faithful, I could say it in one sweet, easy breath
> But to you that would be cruelty and to me it surely would be death.
>
> Something there is about you that moves with style and grace
> I was in a whirlwind, now I'm in some better place.
> My hand's on the saber and you've picked up the baton
> Somethin' there is about you that I can't quite put my finger on.

Clearly, the song pivots on the third of the four four-line verses. Her mystery is inspiring and he wants to commit to her, yet he is torn—apparently out of loyalty. He is just not going to lie to her, no matter how easy it is to do. The fourth verse reveals the state of the relationship. She saved him, and he is happier for it. Now he is prepared to address whatever conflict is before him with her by his side (sounds as if he is ready to wage war). Her mystery lingers, yet he believes in her. She is his answer.

"You Angel You" and "Never Say Goodbye" also involve the woman-as-savior theme; however, the songs are nowhere near as complex as "Mama" and "Something There Is." "You Angel" is a very repetitive, simple account of how that special woman did it again. With a pop song's structure providing the framework (four four-line verses with two identical five-line bridges), we hear statements of praise, commitment, adoration, and gratitude. The second bridge and final verse capture the story's essence:

> You know I can't sleep at night for trying
> Never did feel this way before,
> Never did get up and walk the floor.
> If this is love then gimmie more
> And more and more and more
>
> You angel you
> You got me under your wing.
> The way you walk and the way you talk
> It says everything.

As does this song! Our narrator has apparently never had to *work* in a relationship before, and he is loving the experience. The fact that he worries about her in the fine tradition of Ernest Tubb's "Walking The Floor Over You" just inspires him more. The harder he has to work, the more he has to worry, the deeper in love he falls. He surrenders to her loving ways and treasures his subservience.

"Never Say" opens with a splendid acoustic guitar that is joined by a sharp lead guitar, smooth bass, and that unique Band rhythm as it launches into its five four-line verses (the printed version features six stanzas). The first verse describes a snowy day by a frozen lake before the second verse explodes in emotion:

> You're beautiful beyond words
> You're beautiful to me
> You can make me cry
> Never say goodbye.

What else needs to be said? After a cloudy self-description in which the narrator declares his dreams to be "made of iron and steel" with a bouquet of roses that extends from the "heavens" to the "ground," he announces his need for her to "grab hold of my hand." He needs her. He loves her. The song is as simple as it is compelling.

Although "Mama" conveys respect, "Something" admires mystery, and "Angel" and "Goodbye" state undying devotion, *none* of these sentiments compares to the emotional power of "Wedding Song." Here Dylan performs unaccompanied on guitar and harmonica in a song that has got to be a personal message. Like other such instances (e.g., "Restless Farewell" from *The Times They Are A-Changin'*), Dylan appeared during the album's final mixing session and recorded this track—remarkably, the day after recording "Dirge." All of the details fit Dylan's life; therefore, like the folk-posturing period's revelation, a deeply personal tone permeates the expression. Its eight four-line verses march through line after line of praise, unadulterated commitment, and subservience. She not only saved him; she sustains him. The first verse establishes the song's depth of emotion:

> I love you more than ever, more than time and more than love,
> I love you more than money and more than the stars above,
> Love you more than madness, more than waves upon the sea,
> Love you more than life itself, you mean that much to me.

That she saved him is clear in the opening line of the next verse: "Ever since you walked right in, the circle's been complete." Now that she is there, he has rid himself of dark ("I've said goodbye to haunted rooms and faces in the street") and foolish things. Once she "breathed on" him, his tears dried and his life was renewed. She gave him children (and "saved" his "life") as she challenges him constantly (her love "cuts like a knife"); for that, he loves her more than life itself ("I'd sacrifice the world for you and watch my senses die"). The sixth verse is revealing:

> It's never been my duty to remake the world at large,
> Nor is it my intention to sound a battle charge,
> 'Cause I love you more than all of that with a love that doesn't bend,
> And if there is eternity I'd love you there again.

The auteur is nobody's spokesperson. He is nobody's leader. He seeks not followers, just his woman's enduring love. The valentine continues with more praise and pledges ("You're the other half of what I am, you're the missing piece"). Slight references to the "past" and what was "lost" hint at relational difficulties that have, in the end, strengthened the relationship. From top to bottom, "Wedding Song" is as powerful a love song as has ever been written. It is personal beyond belief. Dylan invites his audience into his heart. He publicly shares his innermost feelings. The song may have been written from a character's stance, but that seems quite unlikely. Actually, all of the evidence points elsewhere. When we pull back and think of what we've heard, the song's maturity is clearly its most powerful quality.

Feelings this strong often have another—equally powerful—side. The slavish devotion that characterizes these songs of loving adoration could—if threatened—turn dark. Elvis Costello made a career out of exploring this side of loving relationships. There is power in hatred as well as love. This side of love is first portrayed in "Going, Going, Gone." Here we have a solemn song about a man at the end of his relational rope. He has gone as far as he can, and now the relationship is over (we hope!). The four seven-line verses pause for a pivotal four-line bridge as they follow a consistent strategy as the song unfolds. Each verse spends four lines describing the relationship's demise before the three lines announcing his departure. The opening verse sets the pace: "I've just reached a place / Where the willow don't bend. / There's not much more to be said / It's the top of the end." After announcing that he is gone, the second verse reports that he is "closin' the book" on the relationship without regard for what follows. He is tired of "hangin' on threads" and playing fair, so he is cutting "loose" before he is too late. Interestingly, the bridge adds another element to the story:

> Grandma said, "Boy, go and follow your heart
> And you'll be fine at the end of the line.
> All that's gold isn't meant to shine.
> Don't you and your one true love ever part."

Grandma's wisdom may add tension to the situation, but it goes unheeded and the darkness returns with the final verse: "I been walkin' the road, / I been livin' on the edge, / Now, I've just got to go / Before I get to the ledge." He is going, going, gone. Not only is the song meaningful, but Dylan's singing also drives the desperation home further. The narrator loved as the love songs advocate, it failed, he pressed on with Grandma's advice in mind, and he just has to exit before it is too late. It appears that "too late" signifies serious closure. Consequently, the decision to leave is as lifesaving as it is unsatisfying. This is a simple yet powerful song.

It is, however, nothing like "Dirge." Sources like to refer to "Dirge" as "son of 'Positively 4th Street' " and, in so doing, suggest that the song flows from that wellspring. I totally disagree. "Positively 4th Street" is a nursery rhyme when placed alongside "Dirge." I know of no song like it. It is as damning a song as has ever been written. It is the photo negative of "Wedding Song"—and it was recorded the day before. Furthermore, it does not feature random potshots or the occasional wisecrack. No, it is a systematic statement that moves from point to point in a calculated manner. First, the narrator states his self-loathing for his predicament. Second, it conveys how he hates his lover's and his relational games. Third, he uses a metaphor to characterize his experience. Fourth, he describes his situation. Fifth, he attacks her one last time. And the sixth verse presents the resolution to this powerful statement. The song's opening cuts to the chase:

> I hate myself for lovin' you and the weakness that it showed
> You were just a painted face on a trip down Suicide Road.
> The stage was set, the lights went out all around the old hotel,
> I hate myself for lovin' you and I'm glad the curtain fell.

Our angry narrator *hates* their codependent relational games and his empty, sad feelings (verse 2). He regrets that he traded intense pain and suffering for a flash of pleasure (verse 3). He believes he has paid his dues for his isolation, and resolves to discover an answer to his plight (verse 4). He is so angry. In the fifth stanza, he denounces her value, derides her insincerity, and denies any chance for a reversal. The final verse fires another shot before his anger runs its course:

> So sing your praise of progress and of the Doom Machine,
> The naked truth is still taboo whenever it can be seen.
> Lady Luck, who shines on me, will tell you where I'm at,
> I hate myself for lovin' you, but I should get over that.

Here we witness clear, direct language arranged in understandable, coherent statements that build in a systematic fashion. The finger-pointing master uses his middle finger to communicate where he stands in this most abusive of all relationships. The self-loathing is revealing. He shares a measure of the responsibility. But clearly, she is the prime mover in this more than unhappy situation. The metaphor in the third stanza is compelling, as the narrator describes a character playing a game at his expense and abusing him until he submits. Hints of optimism appear when he reports he has paid his dues, but that quickly dissipates in favor of more invective. It is hopeless, isn't it? Apologies are worthless. The truth is forbidden. Now, he turns his optimism toward his recovery. What a song. From its introduction to its resolution, Bob Dylan paints a tale of devotion gone to relational hell. You must be very much in love to see it devolve into this. How could the same person write this and "Wedding Song" on the same album of recordings? I find it breathtaking. Although "Hazel" describes the narrator's love for his woman and his disappointment over her absence, it pales in its emotional impact when placed alongside "Going, Going, Gone" and "Dirge." Is it possible for a writer to fabricate this level of emotional intensity?

That level of emotional involvement carries over to our final song on *Planet Waves*. After all of this talk about love's positive and negative qualities, we turn to the results of love and a parent's adoration of his or her child. "Forever Young" is a prayer. Heylin reports that Dylan was embarrassed when an observer made fun of the song's sentiments and contemplated removing it from the album. Good sense prevailed. In fact, it prevailed to the point where the song appears twice—in a slow and fast tempo. In both instances, it is just not difficult to imagine a parent holding or staring down at their child and wishing this:

May God bless and keep you always,
May your wishes all come true,
May you always do for others
And let others do for you.
May you build a ladder to the stars
And climb on every rung,
May you stay forever young,
Forever young, forever young,
May you stay forever young.

May you grow up to be righteous,
May you grow up to be true,
May you always know the truth
And see the lights surrounding you.
May you always be courageous,
Stand upright and be strong,
May you stay forever young,
Forever young, forever young,
May you stay forever young.

The song continues with the last of its three nine-line verses as the narrator prays for busy hands, fast feet, moral strength, a happy heart, and self-fulfillment. The narrator wishes for all the blessings any parent would bestow upon their child: health, hope, happiness, strength, wisdom, success, and, most of all, joy. What a blessing. Though the songs for this album were prepared quickly, sources report that Dylan claims to have carried this one around with him for a while. That he was embarrassed suggests its heartfelt qualities. I doubt he was embarrassed over "Wedding Song" or "Dirge."

Like *John Wesley Harding* and *The Times They Are A-Changin'*, *Planet Waves* is a systematic work of art. The "saved series" is a clear, evocative group of songs that drive home a single point: Love is our savior. The belief that a righteous woman is the ultimate answer to our earthly woes supports these songs in no uncertain terms. The strength of that belief is best measured by the degree of negativity associated with love's failure. Nothing crashes as hard as a person's ideals. Nothing. If you truly believe in something, and it fails, the bitterness can be more than dysfunctional; it may lead you to that metaphorical—or not so metaphorical—ledge. *Waves* is not only systematic in its thematic orientation; the song's narrative structures share that trait as well. The songs set scenes, establish conflict, and provide resolutions in coherent fashions. A master storyteller is plying his trade here, and *that* is evidence of his recovery. The songs' narrative structures are complemented by their instrumental patterns. Virtually all of *Planet Waves* songs feature long instrumental tags. Songs end and harmonica, guitar, organ, or instrumental combinations follow for extended periods (sometimes occupying as much as a third of the track). No other Dylan record subscribes to this production formula to the extent of this project. Finally, one other trait emerges here: Dylan consistently fails to follow his lyric sheet. This particular habit is not as bad as it once was, but the auteur is back to his old game. Read 'em and weep. Unlike *Harding* or *Skyline* and his careful line-by-line devotion to his statement, the Dylan of *Waves* is free to follow his emotions without regard to the occasional blown line or verse. In its own special way, this signifies the man's return to business as usual.

Planet Waves is a special record. From that first note, you recognize this recording's unique qualities: That Sound. The magical interplay of the organ, harmonica, drums, guitar, and voice that made Bob Dylan and the Hawks the talk of 1966 is instantly on display in a new, more refined manner. That Robbie Robertson's guitar *is* that *thin wild mercury sound* is beyond doubt. And The Voice returns with The Harmonica. While Dylan's harmonica floats in and out of the last five albums, The Voice has—for the most part—been absent. That sweet voice of "Lay, Lady, Lay" is nowhere to be found, and the Dylan Edge that makes this performer's work *so* distinctive returns and dominates the proceedings.

From this, we have to conclude that chemistry must be everything. The songs appeared so quickly. The sessions unfolded just as fast. The results are startling. No song bites as hard as "Dirge." No song loves as much as "Wedding Song." No song prays as hard—and as sincerely—as "Forever Young." Whether the creative light just flicked back on or The Band inspired Dylan's muse or the guy just had something to say (or, more likely, a combination of everything)—whatever happened—the musical world had not witnessed this quality of writing for close to ten years. No word games and little mischief appear here. No. Just an explosion of talent occurred, an ability that laid dormant for close to a decade. Now, it was time to do something that had not happened in eight years: It was time to take these songs on the road.

"Tour '74" was the first of its kind. Dylan explained his motivation for the landbreaking event to *Newsweek*: "If there was something else out there to really give you a kick ... I would have thought differently about doing this. What I want to hear I can't hear so I have to make it myself." To explain what he wanted to hear, the auteur turned to his musical librarian, Jack Fate: "I just carry that other time around with me. The music of the late '50s and early '60s when music was at that root level—that for me is meaningful music. The singers and musicians I grew up with transcend nostalgia—Buddy Holly and Johnny Ace are just as valid to me today as then." Since those sounds never leave Dylan's head, he massaged them through an integral part of his career: performance. He told *Newsweek*, "It's as natural for me to do it as for a fish to swim." Having established his musical motivations for the tour, his ever-present musical allegiances, and his natural urge to perform, Dylan addressed the inevitable question regarding his role as an artist: "I am not looking to be that new messiah. That's not in the cards for me. That's all over, that's the past. I like the way Van Morrison sings it: 'You know I just can't help you now. It's not my job at all.' I go deep and far out to get my songs—that's what it is, there's no more than that." Hence, it was all about the songs, their pedigree, and his need to get that sound out to the public. Moreover, he perceived an opportunity to fill a void. In his *Rolling Stone* interview with Ben Fong-Torres, he explained his motivation through this short and sweet comment: "I saw daylight. I just took off."

In his conversation with Fong-Torres, Robbie Robertson followed a similar logic by returning to the 1966 tour to frame his rationale for the 1974 event: "We were going to do another one, and Bob had the motorcycle wreck. And for a long time it didn't seem like a good idea to us at all. All of a sudden it started to become clear. There was a space, an opening, a necessity, almost, that just pulled you into it. It was no clever maneuver on anybody's behalf to put the thing together, to expand our audience or get a few extra albums. Everybody just felt the same way at the same time." In order to maximize this shared need to return to performance, Dylan and The Band turned to David Geffen (chairman of Dylan's new record label, Elektra/Asylum) and Bill Graham.

Geffen placed the tour in context for *Newsweek*: "This event is the biggest thing of its kind in the history of show business." *Newsweek* reports that when the tour was announced via a series December 2, 1973, newspaper ads, "the post office was flooded with millions of envelopes." Since Dylan wanted people of all ages to have a chance to see the show (not just those stalwarts willing to camp out for days outside ticket windows), the promoters turned to a mail-order system. (*Rolling Stone* claims the mail-order system was also used to avoid "box-office riots.") Following that strategy, the tour booked large venues to accommodate the ticket demand. In the end, the six-week tour of thirty-nine shows in twenty cities had, according to *Newsweek*, a capacity of 658,000 seats available. There Geffen claims an estimated 2–3 million envelopes were returned. Demand was that great. With an unprecedented price of $9.50 per ticket, the tour projected a gross of over $5 million and a net profit of $2.5 million. Dylan told *Rolling Stone*, "Originally, I wanted to play small halls, but I was just talked out of that." Simply, he claimed, "I just let people know I was ready," and he willfully "put it in Bill Graham's hands."

The musical world had never seen such a ticket demand before. While complaints about the ticket prices echoed from post offices across the country, such views did not squelch ticket requests. When the *Newsweek* and *Rolling Stone* reporters inquired about the number of tickets sold and the size of the audiences attending the shows, Dylan responded in characteristic ways. First, he answered Maureen Orth's question regarding the ticket demand: "I'm not surprised by the response we've had for tickets to the tour, but I wouldn't be surprised if they only sold 1,000 tickets. I give out a hard dose—like penicillin. People don't have to worry if Dylan's conning them. If it works, it works. If they don't like it, they don't have to try the dose again." When Fong-Torres asked how he felt standing before such large crowds, Dylan responded, "No, 18,000 people yelling isn't that much of a thing. It's nothing new. See, I used to sit in the dark and dream about it, you know. It's all happened before." What revealing statements! After all the artist has endured—from the folk-posturing period to Newport to Tour '66 to the postaccident recovery—his attitudes display the same artistic orientation that served him during his high school talent contest: His vision controls him. He believes in that "hard dose" and its musical heritage. His loyalty is to *the songs*; consequently, the size of the audience is irrelevant—as is its behavior. Joining his commitment to his music is his belief in his vision. So, when he perceived a musical opportunity, he turned to his natural inclination to perform and his dedication to his musical heritage, solidified his attitude regarding his artistic role, and allowed Geffen and Graham to have their way. If they sold a million tickets, fine. If they sold a hundred tickets, fine. *That attitude* reveals the extent to which Bob Dylan's mission of recovery was completed. His loyalty to Jack Fate. His belief in his art. Bob Dillon's disdain for idolatry and business matters. All of this represents Bob

Dylan's artistic foundation—a professional orientation that overcame Albert Gross-man's abuses, the media's pressures, the audience's madness, and the world of celebrity's convolutions.

Maureen Orth describes what the auteur faced on opening night in Chicago: "The question was: what was Dylan's new message for the '70s? To get the answer, 19,000 fans, many busing, hitchhiking or driving hundreds of miles, braved a freezing Chicago evening to see and hear the minstrel who withdrew in 1966 at the height of his fame, told the world to get lost and, like Garbo, raised the status of celebrity to myth." According to Orth, those in attendance were not "teenyboppers" anticipating the kind of show perfected by acts like "Alice Cooper"; to the contrary, they were "eager, expectant people, mostly in their 20s, who sat patiently as the house lights went down and only an occasional whiff of marijuana rose." Once onstage, she claims, the audience greeted Dylan "not with the demoniac sounds of Mick Jagger's vicarious street-fighting men, but with the healthy gladness of friends greeting a long-absent friend." She sums her observations in this fashion: "After eight long years, the most important single personality in the American popular culture of his generation was back." That Fong-Torres observed tearful music critics fighting to regain their objectivity signals the emotional depth associated with the Tour '74 experience. All the talk of profiteering, publicity, and punditry ceased once the lights went down and that *sound* filled the air.

What these huge audiences saw was impressive. Fong-Torres reports the show opened with six Dylan songs followed by six songs by The Band. Three more Dylan tunes prefaced a fifteen-minute intermission. Dylan then returned for a solo acoustic set that lasted about five songs. Afterward, The Band performed three to four songs, Dylan rejoined the group for "a couple of" *Planet Waves* tracks, a finale of "Like A Rolling Stone" prefaced an encore of "Most Likely You Go Your Way (I'll Go Mine)." Later in the tour, "Most Likely" both opened and closed the evening, as Dylan explained, "It completes a circle in some way." A typical show involved around twenty-eight songs, many recast to meet the needs at hand, as Dylan told Fong-Torres: "You'll always stretch things out or cut it up, just to keep interested. If you can't stay interested that way, you'll have to lose track. But I'm me now, that's the way it comes out."

But I'm me now—fascinating.

Responses to Tour '74 vary with sources. The Band, it appears, was invigorated. Levon Helm describes opening night in his autobiography:

> We understood that people were excited by Bob's comeback from a long public absence, but we were astounded anyway when we walked onstage in the darkened hall in Chicago and saw the entire audience stand and hold up their flaring lighters in a roar of tribute to Bob. Imagine nineteen thousand candles in the dark, people calling and whooping. It was a moment, I'll tell you. I could see the normally taciturn Dylan was moved. He walked over to the drums and looked at me, about to say something, but instead he turned back to the microphone and launched into an old song of his called "Hero Blues," which caught everyone off guard, including us.

Robbie Robertson shared his response with Maureen Orth: "We were booed off of every stage in Europe. What happened tonight in Chicago is so reassuring for us. We don't have any fancy outfits or sparklers on our eyes, and we don't cut off any heads. I mean how many times can you set yourself on fire or rip off your shirts?" In a musical world populated by acts featuring incinerating theatrics, carnival stunts, and postmodern vaudeville, Bob Dylan and The Band simply played their music with passion and commitment. They recast their music to meet their perceived needs. They yielded to the commercial machines that drive such a far-reaching enterprise. They cooperated with the press. They harvested a fortune. The results pleased everyone, it seems, except the show's star.

In the interview with Cameron Crowe that accompanies the *Biograph* boxed set, Dylan spends considerable time explaining his response to Tour '74. While Robertson describes the tour as a "kind of a relief," Dylan assumes a different stance:

> I think I was just playing a role on that tour. I was playing Bob Dylan and The Band was playing The Band. It was all sort of mindless. The people that came out to see us came mostly to see what they missed the first time around. It was just more of a "legendary" kind of thing. They've heard about it, they'd bought the records, whatever, but what they saw didn't give any clue to what was. What got it to that level wasn't what they saw. What they saw you could compare to early Elvis and later Elvis, really. Because it wasn't quite the same, when we needed that acceptance it wasn't there. By this time it didn't matter. Time had proven them all wrong. We were cleaning up but it was an emotionless trip.
>
> Rock-and-roll had become a highly extravagant enterprise. T-shirts, concert booklets, lighting shows, costume changes, glitter and glamour . . . it was just a big show, a big circus except there weren't any elephants, nothing really exceptional just Sound and Lights, Sound and Lights, and more Sound and Lights. That's what it had become and that's what it still is. It is like those guys who watched the H bomb explode on Bikini Island and then turn to each other and say, "Beautiful, man, just incredibly beautiful." That's what this whole scene had become. The only thing people talked about was energy this, energy that. The highest compliments were things like, "Wow, lotta energy, man." It had become absurd. The bigger and louder something was, the more energy it was supposed to have. You know, like knock me out, drive me to the wall, kick my brains in, blow me up, whip me 'til it hurts, that's what people were accepting as heavy energy. Actually it was just big industry moving in on the music. Like the armaments manufacturers selling weapons to both sides in a war, inventing bigger and better things to take your head off while behind your back, there's a few people laughing and getting rich off your vanity. Have you ever seen a slaughter-house where they bring in a herd of cattle? They round them all up, put them all in one area, pacify 'em and slaughter them . . . big business, brings in lots of bucks, heavy energy. It always reminds me of that. The greatest praise we got on that tour was "incredible energy, man", it would make me want to puke. The scene had changed

somewhat when we stepped into that picture. We were expected to produce a show that lived up to everybody's expectations. And we did. It was utterly profound. What they saw wasn't really what they would have seen in '66 or '65. If they had seen that, that was much more demanding. That was a much more demanding show. People didn't know what it was at that point. When people don't know what something is, they don't understand it and they start to get, you know, weird and defensive. Nothing is predictable and you're always out on the edge. Anything can happen. I [always] had those songs though and so I always figured everything was alright.

What a long, winding, thorough assessment. Assuredly, Dylan's mission of recovery was achieved in more ways than one. Not only were his creative instincts renewed, but his commercial orientation achieved an equilibrium that enabled his career to continue. Joni Mitchell refers to this phenomenon as a balance between an artist's "creative child" and his or her "commercial shark." They are, indeed, two different things. Dylan's overriding commitment is obviously to his *songs*; however, now, after the 1965–1966 aesthetic riots, the Grossman debacle, the Columbia debate, and the Graham-Geffen–led spectacle, a new auteur emerged with a realization that it would take more than the songs for him to survive. From this point forward, Dylan's creative instincts would be balanced by his commercial cynicism—a well-earned, healthy commercial skepticism. As we will see, if an album is perceived to be "too good," Dylan will remove tracks accordingly. He will protect his songs by forming his own publishing company. He will play where and when he wants, rarely succumbing to the Tour '74 method of staging and promotion. The lessons from the folk-posturing, Newport Mod, and Americana periods have been learned and assimilated. His successful recovery leaves him with the independence necessary to sustain his career.

One of the roadblocks to that mission's success involved his public image. The voice of his generation did everything he could to dismiss the messiah-seeking branch of his constituency—often with mixed results. One place where the myth refused to die was in journalistic interviews. His talk with Maureen Orth reveals his new response to the question that will *never* go away:

> Idols are old hat. They aren't people, they're objects. But I'm no object. When we think of idols we think of those carved pieces of wood and stone people can relate to—that's what an idol is. They do the same thing to someone like Marlon Brando—they attach themselves to certain people because of a need. But I'm just doing exactly what a lot of other people would be doing if they could. I'm not standing at an altar, I'm working in the marketplace.

Though his creative missions will vary with their contexts, Bob Dylan reentered the musical world with a firm understanding of his role. From this point forward, he will confront the idolatry—whether it emanates from his audience or his industry. His commitment to Jack Fate's musical library will join Bob Dillon's relentless rebellion to do whatever Bob Dylan feels he needs to do to achieve his mission. And this, my friends, would not have been possible without the musicology exercises associated with Big Pink; the writing lessons involved with *John Wesley Harding, Nashville Skyline,* and *New Morning;* the commercial struggles that unfolded with *Self Portrait* and *Dylan;* and the reunion that was *Planet Waves* and Tour '74. This eight-year mission of recovery set the scene for all that follows. Without it, Bob Zimmerman's career may have crashed with that mythical motorcycle. But it did not, and Zimmerman's Dylan would deploy strategic combinations of Jack Fate and Bob Dillon to do his bidding in new, equally provocative missions that demonstrate his commercial savvy, his artistic commitments, and his considerable talent. Tour '74 was a capstone experience of one of the lifework's most demanding missions. What a ride!

The Crystallization Period

The Americana portion of Bob Dylan's oeuvre involved a long, systematic recovery from the white-hot intensity of the Newport Mod era. The seeds planted during the folk-posturing period matured and blossomed in a manner no one could have imagined way back in 1963. The songwriting innovations; the *Tarantula*, *Dont Look Back*, and *Eat The Document* projects; the unprecedented mayhem of the post-Newport chaos and 1965–1966 tours; and his conflicts with Columbia Records and Albert Grossman unfolded in strange—at times, surreal—fashions that crashed on a Triumph motorcycle running down a narrow country road. What might be an ending to some proved to be yet another creative opportunity for Bob Zimmerman. Instead of resting on his laurels, he recuperated in Big Pink's basement, resuscitated his pen in Nashville, rebelled via the Bob Dylan Revue, and reentered the musical mainstream on the road with The Band. Yet, Tour '74 unveiled a musical world gone wrong to Zimmerman. He may have recovered from the overscheduling, overindulging, and overthinking that characterized his career to that point during the Americana era, but that restoration opened his eyes to the corruption, abuse, and insincerity that plagued the commercial art industry. He may have negotiated his way through his songwriting to the point where he could write songs of the quality of "Forever Young," "Wedding Song," and "Dirge," but the spontaneous flame of music production that fired his lifework merely flickered during those magical Los Angeles sessions. In other words, there was still work to be done. Zimmerman now faced a reorientation that would address his creative-commercial situation on new terms. His career's future was at stake once more.

That process began on the business end. After the release of the Tour '74 concert album, *Before The Flood*, Dylan ended his brief residency with David Geffen's label and returned home to Columbia Records on August 1, 1974. Albert Grossman was in that metaphorical rearview mirror—although his lawyers littered the highway for quite a while. The auteur now produced himself. His publishing company obtained and maintained control over his work. Things had most certainly changed on the business side. New opportunities were at hand. On the creative end, the songwriting struggles associated with the *John Wesley Harding*, *Nashville Skyline*, *New Morning*, and, to a lesser degree, *Planet Waves* projects reached a critical turning point upon Dylan's temporary return to New York City. Friends of Sara Dylan introduced the Dylans to a seventy-three-year-old former boxer turned art teacher who helped the Iron Range's original biker-poet reorient his writing. Dylan discussed Norman Raeben's impact on his creativity with Jonathan Cott:

> He put my mind and my hand and my eye together in a way that allowed me to do consciously what I unconsciously felt. And I didn't know how to pull it off. I wasn't sure it could be done in songs because I'd never written a song like that. But when I started doing it, the first album I made was *Blood on the Tracks*. Everybody agrees that that was pretty different, and what's different about it is that there's a code in the lyrics and also there's no sense of time. There's no respect for it: you've got yesterday, today and tomorrow all in the same room, and there's very little that you can't imagine not happening . . . doing it unconsciously was doing it like a primitive, and it took everything out of me. Everything was gone, I was drained. I found out later that it was much wiser to do it consciously, and it could let things be much stronger, too. Actually, you might even live longer, but I'm not sure about that.

Raeben's definitions of philosophical abstractions such as love, truth, and beauty intrigued the man who not too long ago announced his distaste for "definitions." Subsequently, Dylan attended Raeben's classes, and a period of stylistic crystallization ensued in which the songwriter mastered his craft and, for the first time, officially invited others to participate in the process. The *Desire* project followed and featured Jacques Levy as Dylan's coauthor. Although Dylan related to Cott, "I don't remember who wrote what," during the collaborations, the fact that *anyone* participated in this previously intimate act was newsworthy. Things had most certainly changed on the creative side. New opportunities were at hand.

The crystallization period of Bob Dylan's oeuvre pursues a mission that will reappear later in the lifework. Now—as in the pop icon phase—Dylan's mission of reorientation guides his art. Through Raeben's instruction, the writer will bring to a conscious state what previously erupted on an unconscious level. Through his work with Levy, the artist will invite public participation into what had previously been the most private of matters (the Big Pink's songwriting is a noted exception; however, those songs were not intended for the general public). Through the Rolling Thunder Revue, Dylan will offer Tour '74's antithesis as his performances move from mail-order ticket solicitations and overflowing sports arenas to spontaneous appearances in old movie houses and smaller venues. Through the *Renaldo & Clara* film, the auteur will assimilate the lessons of *Dont Look Back*, *Eat The Document*, and *Pat Garrett and Billy The Kid* into his own cinematic style that massages the Bob Dylan Myth in its own idiosyncratic way. And through *Street-Legal* and *Live At Budokan*, Dylan will unleash the Bob Dylan Revue through an album of unrelenting negativity and a revisionist view of his back catalog, respectively. The search is on during this portion of the lifework. What starts with Raeben moves through Levy and into Rolling Thunder, percolates with *Renaldo & Clara*, and culminates with *Budokan* and *Street-Legal*. When the dust settles, we see that Raeben treated the symptoms, but not the disease. The slow train that Dylan mentions in the *Highway 61 Revisited* liner notes will carry the cure, yet at this point in Bob Zimmerman's career, that train is way down those holy rails; chugging along its long winding track to its inevitable destination, that train station the world called "Bob Dylan."

We now reach that point where Zimmerman transforms his art into a craft. Here the auteur reorients after his recovery from the "amnesia" that followed his motorcycle accident. Once his classes with Norman Raeben connect his eye, mind, and hand as a painter, he transfers that technique to his pen and gives the world *Blood On The Tracks* (released January 1975), *Desire* (released January 1976), and *Street-Legal* (released June 1978). The various songwriting strategies from the previous periods now crystallize into a creative repertoire that the artist consciously applies to the topics before him. For subject matter, the author—as always—turns to his *context* and, unfortunately, his deteriorating domestic situation and its aftermath. Clinton Heylin's biography quotes Dylan on Raeben's teachings, and life afterwards: "Needless to say it changed me. I went home after that and my wife never did understand me ever since that day. That's when our marriage started breaking up. She never knew what I was talking about, what I was thinking about, and I couldn't possibly explain it." Instead of explaining himself to Sara, he wrote *Blood On The Tracks*.

Blood On The Tracks

Our opening project, *Blood On The Tracks*, is a powerful entry in the Dylan Canon. When the auteur sits at the songwriting table with an agenda, well, the topical craftsman often yields startling results. To the extent that *Planet Waves* features That Sound, this record displays The Writing. While the sonic platforms upon which the writer places his words vary in their simplicity, the detail that flows from this writing is downright shocking. This is a masterpiece of topical songwriting—and that topic is *love*. The album contains *nothing* but relational complaints with but one exception, and *that* song involves relational duplicity. These romantic elegies differ somewhat in their storytelling strategies; however, there are no word games, there is minimal portraiture, there is no impressionism, and the trademark satire takes a fundamental turn. These songs articulate relational anxieties through coherent stories told in straightforward language. Such a strategy provides a level of detail that conveys specific accounts of love in trouble, love lost, love challenged, love suffered, and relational deceit. At times, the metaphors are almost too simple, revealing the extent to which the writer desired understanding over obfuscation. The practice of songwriting does not get much better than this.

As our opening remarks indicate, Norman Raeben played a central role in the inventive processes that generated *Blood On The Tracks*. Andy Gill and Kevin Odegard cite Dylan's comments to Pete Oppel regarding Raeben's impact on his work and, in broader terms, his life:

> He would tell me about myself when I was drawing something. I couldn't paint. I thought I could. I couldn't draw. I don't even remember 90 percent of the stuff he drove into me . . . and it wasn't art or painting. It was a course in something else. I had met magicians, but this guy is more powerful than any magician I've ever met. He looked into you and told you what you were. And he didn't play games about it.

That Dylan brought this confusion to his home life is evident in the previous remarks about his inability to communicate with his wife after working with Raeben. Since learning is nothing other than the resolution of confusion—and great teachers endeavor to instigate that confusion before resolving it—Raeben was obviously having an impact on his pupil. Gill and Odegard explain the manifestation of Raeben's magic within his student's songwriting:

> In particular, Raeben brought Dylan to a more fruitful understanding of time, enabling him to view narrative not in such strictly linear terms, but to telescope past, present, and future together to attain a more powerful, unified focus on the matter at hand. The immediate effect can be heard on *Blood on the Tracks*, most notably in a song like "Tangled Up in Blue," where temporality, location, and viewpoint shift back and forth from verse to verse, rather in the manner of montaged jump cuts in a movie, or in the fiction of Thomas Pynchon and Don DeLillo, allowing him to reveal underlying truths about the song's characters while letting them remain shadowy, secretive figures.

Gill and Odegard's book, *A Simple Twist Of Fate*, charts the evolution of the *Blood On The Tracks* project from beginning to end—often using the book as an opportunity to register the varied recollections of those who participated in the venture. To be sure, the book contains materials that are unavailable elsewhere; as a result, it yields valuable data for this study.

The biographers report that Dylan wrote the songs for *Blood* during the summer of 1974 at his new farm in Minnesota. He carried around a small red notebook in which he applied Raeben's teachings to the subject matter before him. Sadly, his deteriorating marriage appears to represent the bulk of that material. As you realize, dear reader, I don't go into these matters. The artist's relationship with his wife is a private affair, and I think interpreting songs based on biographical details is more than folly—it can be downright foolish. Remember, this is *the* Glissendorf Master. Writers occasionally look ridiculous when they boldly assert that this means this, that means that. I don't know why critics insist on engaging in these practices, but they do. Bob Dylan speaks to this matter in the liner notes to his career retrospective, *Biograph*, while discussing the song "You're A Big Girl Now":

> I read that this was supposed to be about my wife. I wish somebody would ask me first before they go ahead and print stuff like that. I mean it couldn't be about anybody else but my wife, right? Stupid and misleading jerks sometimes these interpreters are—I mean I'm always trying to stay one step ahead of myself and keep changing with the times right? Like that's my foolish mission. How many roles can I play? Fools, they limit you to their own unimaginative mentality. They never stop to think that somebody has been exposed to experiences that they haven't been . . . anyway it's not even the experience that counts, it's the attitude toward the experience.

I sincerely hope that this study avoids "stupid and misleading" conclusions, and I contend that by avoiding personal attributions, I may take a positive step in that direction. In that commentary, the auteur admits to having written a song from a personal stance *once* (I believe he is referring to "Ballad In Pain D") and how he has steadfastly avoided "confessional" writing ever since. There it hangs, my friends. So as we move though the writing on *Blood*, let's appreciate the "attitudes" evidenced within the work and leave the commentary about whether the song discusses new girlfriends, old girlfriends, prospective girlfriends, or women who just happen to look like the Queen of Diamonds to writers more experienced in these matters. After all, this is about the *art*, not the women in Bob Zimmerman's personal life. When *I* can sustain that level of personal scrutiny, I'll write finger-pointing books about others.

Blood On The Tracks features ten songs (running almost fifty-two minutes) and appears in two versions. The original New York recording presents the songs in a more instrumentally sparse but lyrically intense fashion. In order to temper the lyrics and lighten the record's heavy-handedness Dylan rerecorded half of the album in Minneapolis in a last-minute effort arranged by his brother. With the help of a group of Minnesota-based musicians, Dylan enlivened several songs (musically) and deflated others (lyrically) as his extemporaneous method of record production was replaced by a more deliberate, self-conscious process. The songwriting tide had turned.

The New York sessions were held in the auteur's musical home away from home, Columbia's Studio A on 54th Street, now sold and renamed A&R Recording (some sources refer to the studio as A&R Studios). When John Hammond recruited producer Phil Ramone to oversee the recording sessions, Ramone quickly obtained the services of guitarist Eric Weissberg (whose recent song "Dueling Banjos" from the 1973 film *Deliverance* was a worldwide hit) and his touring group, Deliverance (drummer Richard Crooks, guitarist Charlie Brown, bass player Tony Brown, and Tom McFaul on keyboards). Later, steel guitarist Buddy Cage and organist Paul Griffin joined the sessions (Clinton Heylin's session chronology reports that guitarist Barry Kornfeld also participated in the sessions, although Gill and Odegard contend that is a factual error). During the first session on September 16, 1974, Gill and Odegard claim the group recorded an amazing *thirty* tracks while Heylin cites a much smaller number (Heylin's records become very shaky at this point; some dates do not make any sense). Afterward, only bassist Tony Brown returned for the remaining New York sessions (supposedly on September 17, 19, and 24) with Griffin and Cage appearing as needed for overdubs (the records are inconsistent regarding dates and participants, but I'm sticking with Gill and Odegard). All of the New York participants were experienced session musicians; however, those experiences were challenged when the progenitor of that thin, wild mercury sound entered the recording studio.

When Dylan assembled the musicians in the center of the studio to begin the first session, he offered brief rundowns of the songs he wanted to record. There were no charts. He allowed no time for rehearsals. He insisted on rolling tape as soon as possible. Subsequently, the musicians grew increasingly frustrated. Charlie Brown offered his recollections to Gill and Odegard:

> It's not that he's wrong; it's just that it's a whole other way of thinking from what we were used to. He would run something down once, and

maybe halfway again, and that was it: Take it! Because he wanted the immediacy of the moment—he didn't care whether there were mistakes in there or not; that's just the way it happened. We, on the other hand, were used to getting it right. . . . And then we play with him, and he's like a bad boxer, he's throwing punches all over the place, and we're just trying to get out of the way! Eric and I would listen back and hear the mistakes and want to fix them, but we weren't allowed to.

Gill and Odegard note that Weissberg expressed concerns for his professional reputation, pleading for additional takes to correct obvious mistakes. When appeals to Ramone went unheard, they realized the nature of their situation, as Ramone revealed when he described his role in the proceedings: "My job was to make sure Bob was comfortable at the microphone . . . and just start recording." That Dylan refused to wear headphones and positioned himself where not all of the musicians could watch his hands exacerbated the situation. Several of the participants viewed these practices to be most unprofessional, while others accepted them as the nature of this artistic beast. When bassist Brown was asked to return for the remaining sessions, he prepared by listening to Charlie McCoy's bass work on *John Wesley Harding*. Sure enough, when you listen to various tracks from *Blood*, you hear shades of McCoy's wonderful work from *Harding*. Such was the nature of the New York sessions. Phil Ramone was convinced that Bob Dylan was pleased with the results.

Columbia wanted to release the new album as quickly as possible in order to ride the wave of success achieved earlier that year by *Planet Waves* and Tour '74. In fact, the label hoped to get out the new work in a few weeks or at least by December. While the pressing plant delayed the process due to the Christmas season overload, the auteur was busy rethinking his new project. Sources indicate that he questioned the sound supporting some of the songs; moreover, several of the songs' lyrics seemed to cry for revision. *All* of the biographers argue that the deeply personal qualities of songs such as "Idiot Wind" inspired the songwriter to temper those expressions and revise the songs. When he traveled to his Minnesota farm that December and played the acetate for his brother (who worked in radio-television advertising and managed local musical talent), David reportedly questioned the record's commercial value. Subsequently, David asked if he might call around, round up some local musicians, and have a go at revising several of the tracks. His brother agreed to his wishes.

David made calls to his high school classmate, drummer Bill Berg, as well as local guitarists Chris Weber and Kevin Odegard, bassist Bill Peterson, and keyboardist Greg Inhofer. He next secured a Minneapolis studio, Sound 80, and its engineer Paul Martinson. Everybody involved had experience working with one another on all sorts of projects ranging from advertising jingles, to jazz recordings, to pop songs and more. In particular, Berg and Peterson had a strong reputation as a jazz rhythm section. David obtained the necessary instruments, solicited additional talent as needed (e.g., Peter Ostroushko on mandolin), and set up a December 27 session to rerecord "Idiot Wind" and "You're A Big Girl Now." Dylan was so pleased with the results that the group returned on December 30 to rerecord "Tangled Up In Blue," "Lily, Rosemary And The Jack Of Hearts," and "If You See Her, Say Hello." Unlike the

New York sessions, Dylan took the time to teach the songs to Weber, who would then teach them to the remaining cast. Gill and Odegard report that as Martinson and the musicians prepared for the various takes, Dylan tailored the lyrics to meet his newfound needs. Clearly, this was not the Bob Dylan of the New York sessions. He instructed his band and allowed them to prepare themselves. He sought their input, listened to their ideas, and actually used those suggestions on "Tangled Up In Blue." Still, when Martinson began cleaning up the tracks and separating the sounds, the auteur stopped him and insisted on the original studio mixes. Since Martinson had done a fine job with the original recordings, they held up during the latter phases of the album's production. When all was said and done, Dylan was thrilled with the results. Bill Peterson recalled Dylan stopping him in the parking lot and thanking him for his work. He told Gill and Odegard,

> I'll never forget that. He must have been thinking, "Whoa, my brother pulled this one off!" He *really* dug it. David never gets any credit for putting all that together: He hired those jazz heads to be the rhythm section and put the pieces of that band together so it would work for Bob. It's brilliant in the way it went down. It could have easily been a disaster, too. Who knew? David did.

David is not alone on that measure. It is a pity the Minnesota musicians have never received any official credit for their work on *Blood On The Tracks*. Since the record was altered at the very last minute, the artwork was already printed. David assembled the musicians and assured them that subsequent printings would reflect their participation in the project, but that never happened. As a result, there are some hard feelings. Gill and Odegard report the variety of responses that range from outright animosity, to slight disappointment, to total indifference. In all cases, it is a shame the musical world has never officially acknowledged the Minnesota players' roles in the work since the five tracks they replaced had genuine impact on the record's tone and pacing. So, let's take a second here and offer a tip of the hat for a job well done.

There were a variety of responses from the New York musicians regarding the subsequent changes on *Blood*. Phil Ramone told Gill and Odegard that he was "quite shocked" by the revisions. Eric Weissberg regretted that his band was not extended the same opportunities the Minnesota players received regarding running through the various songs. Charlie Brown was downright angry. Richard Crooks was too busy to care. For Bob Dylan, *Blood* must have been a revelation. From incorporating Norman Raeben's teachings to modifying his traditional mode of recording, the auteur made fundamental adjustments in his methods of operation. Only time would reveal the extent to which these changes shifted the production of Bob Zimmerman's art in a permanent fashion.

We now turn to the ten songs that comprise *Blood On The Tracks*. The wonderful epic, "Lily, Rosemary And The Jack Of Hearts," extends Dylan's patented satire songwriting strategy. The nine romantic elegies vary in their intensity. From nostalgic memories and accounts of lessons learned ("Tangled Up In Blue") to heavy-hearted recollections of love lost ("Simple Twist Of Fate," "You're A Big Girl Now," "Meet Me In The Morning," "If You See Her, Say Hello," and "Shelter From The

Storm") to a straight on frontal attack ("Idiot Wind"), Dylan blends fact and fiction through unambiguous, succinct accounts of romantic failure. Several of these songs probe intense experiential attitudes: The persecuted man who is saved, then abandoned ("Shelter"), the utter desperation of a jilted lover ("You're A Big Girl"), and the flippant gamesmanship of "If You See Her" convey the heartfelt insights that often accompany direct experience. The "love hurts" thematic is so fully developed that one narrator anticipates the pain through "You're Gonna Make Me Lonesome When You Go" (along with the sense of warning emanating from "Shelter"). The abandonment theme may well be the record's dominant characteristic, with the narrators' responses shifting from tale to tale: the *confusion* in "Simple Twist," the *anger* in "Idiot," the *pain* in "You're A Big Girl," the *cavalier attitude* in "If You See Her," and the *suspicion* in "Shelter." The narrator from each song—as Tim Riley suggests—sounds "like the same person" and, therefore, intensifies the various accounts. This is, in every respect, romantic angst pushed to its outer limits.

I approach these songs based on the intensity of their portrayal of the album's controlling theme. "Lily" offers an account of relational duplicity that treats that theme in a more detached fashion—the deceit is the story's centerpiece, but the attention to scenic details dilutes its impact. "Tangled" and "Simple Twist" are more pointed in their enactments of relational angst; however, they too offer scenic details that tame their respective tales. "You're A Big Girl," "Idiot Wind," "You're Gonna Make Me," "Meet Me," and "If You See Her" are in the thick of it. The characters in these stories are up to their necks in relational strife, and the songs chart the results. "If You See Her" is cavalier at times, but that is clearly a defensive mechanism for the central character. The album reaches its peak in the keynote moment that is "Shelter." Here, the *Blood On The Tracks* message is laid out in clear and precise terms. Appropriately, the album concludes with the capstone statement that is "Buckets Of Rain." Our topical songwriting wizard is in his element, and the results are as systematic as "Only A Pawn," "Hattie Carroll," or "John Birch." We begin out west with a good old-fashioned bank robbery.

At nearly nine minutes in length, "Lily" is an epic account of people on the make. *Everybody* has a more than hidden agenda in this sixteen-verse (fifteen are performed) tale of diabolical relationships and interpersonal robbery. We have love triangles, con artists, possessive moguls, and a veritable cast of thousands as each stanza uses a fast-paced, five-line-per-verse method of expression to tell the tale. The song is *very* systematic. It marches through the various characters and their respective roles in the unfolding scenario. It features clever plot twists; some of which go unresolved and, therefore, invite speculation (is a sequel forthcoming?). In my view, the Minnesota revision of this song offers a more compelling sonic platform for the unfolding narrative in a fashion that keeps the action moving. "Love" is nowhere to be found in this story. Instead, the root of all evil is on display as the characters use one another in their individual pursuits of its false promises.

The story opens with a scenic description. We are evidently in a dying Western town that, for some reason, has endured curfews and is slowly dismantling. Our central character—the Jack of Hearts—is introduced as a mysterious man with a mysterious plan (the fact that somebody, somewhere is drilling through a wall offers a hint). In the second verse, Jack is presented. He walks in the room (a cabaret), buys drinks for all, and captures everyone's attention; afterward, "everyone commenced to do what they were doin' before he turned their heads." The third verse offers this fine scenic description: "Backstage the girls were playin' five-card stud by the stairs, / Lily had two queens, she was hopin' for a third to match her pair." Unfortunately, as the street action intensifies, she draws the "Jack of Hearts." The fourth verse introduces "Big Jim"—a man whose never-foolish ways insure his prosperity (of course, owning the town's "only diamond mine" adds a level of security). The fifth verse presents Rosemary, Big Jim's trophy girl. She arrives late and apologizes to her benefactor, but he is not paying attention; he is checking out Jack: " 'I know I've seen that face before,' Big Jim was thinkin' to himself, / 'Maybe down in Mexico or a picture up on somebody's shelf.' " The crowd grows restless, calling for the floor show to begin. The seventh verse presents Lily, a "fair-skinned" lady with a checkered past and a duplicitous present (she "wears Big Jim's ring"). The plot begins to thicken at this point. The corrupt "hangin' judge" is entertained as the drilling in the unnamed wall continues. Rosemary is getting loaded, holding a knife that yields her reflection, and reconsidering her relationship with Jim. Since she once tried to kill herself, she is hoping for a personal correction before she cashes in her chips. Lily converses with Jack and warns him to avoid a freshly painted wall (is this where they are drilling?). The stage manager becomes suspicious; he *knows* something is amiss. Lily grows apprehensive. Jim enters the room with Rosemary in tow (she is eyeing Jack all the while). "A cold revolver" clicks as "the boys" drill through the wall, clean out the bank vault, and escape to the river to await Jack (who has conned everybody). Suddenly, it is the following day. Jim has been murdered by Rosemary, who kindly stabbed him in the back. A sober "hangin' judge" does his thing (see ya, Rosemary). And Jack is nowhere to be found. The final verse relates that the cabaret is now closed for repairs, that Lily has changed her hair color, and that she is reflecting on her life— thinking about her distant dad, Rosemary, local jurisprudence, and of course (wanna guess?) Jack. The song closes with a fine forty-second harmonica tag.

What a story! Dylan's capacity to weave these "Bear Mountain," "115th Dream," or "Frankie Lee" satires has not diminished one bit. His attention to scenic detail complements his characterizations to yield a fine account of diabolical human relations with all sorts of personal payoffs. Norman Raeben's instruction has been carefully set aside here. This is a linear narrative in every respect. Certain details are either omitted or cleverly avoided in a way that adds a bit of mystery to the story. Did Jack get shot, or did he escape? Did Rosemary stab Jim because he shot Jack? Was Lily's father the president of the United States, or does he live on Desolation Row? (Just kidding.) What a story.

Although Raeben's teachings are not evident in "Lily," they most certainly appear in "Tangled Up In Blue" and "Simple Twist Of Fate." While the Minnesota revision of "Tangled" dismissed the pronoun games that twist the internal workings of the original song, there is evidence of Raeben's influence within the two songs. "Tangled" is presented via seven thirteen-line verses (the fifth verse features but twelve lines) that unfold in a nonlinear fashion. The story seems to hold together until the sixth verse, when everything suddenly changes. The opening stanza offers nostalgic recollections about an old love (he is laying in his bed, "Wond'rin' if she'd changed at all / If her hair was still red" and recalling the financial incongruities between their families), the second verse charts that relationship's history (she was married, then they ran away, traveled "out West," and "Split up on a dark sad night / Both agreeing it was best"), the third verse describes the narrator's history since the breakup (he has worked a variety of jobs, drifted down to New Orleans, but never quit thinking of his love: "But all the while I was alone / The past was close behind, / I seen a lot of women / But she never escaped my mind, and I just grew / Tangled up in blue"), the fourth stanza suggests some form of reunion (he visits a "topless bar" where she works, he begins to leave when he suddenly realizes she is standing behind him, she asks if she knows his name, he "mutters" a response, and he grows "uneasy" as she "bent down to tie the laces of my shoe"), the fifth verse describes their subsequent encounter (they visit and she reads a book of Italian poetry from "the thirteenth century" that sparks a responsive chord within the narrator), the sixth verse does its own thing (out of nowhere we go back in time to a basement apartment on "Montague Street," where "revolution" permeated the "air" and the narrator's roommate dealt "with slaves" at his own personal expense, an act that caused the narrator to withdraw, regroup, and commit himself to "keep on keepin' on like a bird that flew"), and the song closes with a statement of resolve:

> So now I'm goin' back again,
> I got to get to her somehow.
> All the people we used to know
> They're an illusion to me now.
> Some are mathematicians
> Some are carpenter's wives.
> Don't know how it all got started,
> I don't know what they're doin' with their lives.
> But me, I'm still on the road
> Headin' for another joint
> We always did feel the same,
> We just saw it from a different point of view,
> Tangled up in blue.

If you don't overthink everything, the song flows nicely. I mean, it's a song, not the Declaration of Independence. It is easy to rearrange the verse order and create a different story. Just take the first verse and place it in the sixth verse's spot, move the fourth verse to the opening slot, follow with the fifth, then to the third, then . . . oh, never mind. This is the kind of madness that quality art inspires. The auteur offers his response to the song in his *Biograph* liner notes:

> I was never really happy with it. I guess I was just trying to make it like a painting where you can see the different parts but then you also see the whole of it. With that particular song, that's what I was trying to do . . . with the concept of time, and the way the characters change from first person to the third person, and you're never quite sure if the third person is talking or the first person is talking. But as you look at the whole thing it really doesn't matter.

Again, the revised version of "Tangled" drops some of the pronoun folly that achieves the effect Dylan describes above; moreover, his major revisions of the song on *Real Live* and in various performances through the years demonstrates that this is one song that continues to be a "work in progress." In all cases, however, it remains a love complaint. The guy lost his girl, he is upset about it, and he is searching for her. Or maybe he was searching for her *before* he lost her and he is *about* to get upset about it. You decide.

"Simple Twist" is nowhere near as complicated, although my reading of it deviates from that of most critics, it seems. The song unfolds via six five-line verses and features two harmonica bridges (the bass work sounds *exactly* like Charlie McCoy's *John Wesley Harding* performance). The first person–third person characterological gymnastic is present here as well, yet a simple reading of the song unveils a simple twist of narrative. That is, the song offers a narrator telling a story about another guy's encounter with what appears to be a prostitute. The track opens with the couple sitting in the park, the man's romantic inspiration ("She looked at him and he felt a spark tingle to his bones"), their walk by the water ("They walked along by the old canal / A little confused, I remember well"), and their arrival at a hotel. Later, she leaves; he awakens the next morning and pretends not to care, but he cannot resist the urge to go down to the docks and seek a reunion—hoping for yet another "simple twist of fate." Suddenly, the sixth verse shifts to the *narrator's* relational situation and his sense of loss:

> People tell me it's a sin
> To know and feel too much within.
> I still believe she was my twin, but I lost the ring.
> She was born in spring, but I was born too late
> Blame it on a simple twist of fate.

The key to this interpretation is in the second stanza and the line about the couple's walk by the canal and their confusion. Clearly, the narrator is telling a story that he then shifts to his situation. The "simple twist of fate" that left the man pining for his hooker is evident in the narrator's life as well; therefore, he shares the other man's pain over the sense of loss. Now, Dylan could be shifting things around to obfuscate his story or to break down yet another aural painting, but my reading seems perfectly clear. Besides, I like my interpretation.

In both "Tangled" and "Simple Twist," we have relational complaints that are lodged from a distant point of view. "Tangled" leaps about as it lodges the complaint, while "Simple Twist" uses one story as a point of departure for another. They both talk around the issue as they fondle scenic conditions. Since the two songs open *Blood On The Tracks*, they seem to perform a scene-setting function for the next five songs, which are followed by the two-song resolution (I take "Lily" out of the mix at this point; "Lily" is its own island in this sea of relational remorse). Having established the album's theme, the record now dives into the relational abyss. We might as well take the songs in their order of appearance. Buckle up, dear readers; love *hurts*.

The pain begins with a sad song about a sad topic and "You're A Big Girl Now." The track features a light, virtually gentle, instrumental backdrop to set the scene for a tale of love lost. The five six-line stanzas unfold systematically—Norman Raeben has left the building. First, the song establishes the division: She is one place (on "dry land") while he is at another ("back in the rain"). The second stanza takes us to the crux of the matter:

> Bird on the horizon, sittin' on a fence,
> He's singin' his song for me at his own expense.
> And I'm just like that bird, oh, oh,
> Singin' just for you.
> I hope that you can hear,
> Hear me singin' through these tears.

Whatever inspired the breakup, the narrator swears he can repair it. He wants her desperately, but she has left him and, perhaps, she is with another person. He has learned the lessons that she understood all along, and he is left with that knowledge. His pain is evident in the closing verse:

> A change in the weather is known to be extreme
> But what's the sense of changing horses in midstream?
> I'm going out of my mind, oh, oh,
> With a pain that stops and starts
> Like a corkscrew to my heart
> Ever since we've been apart.

Dylan weaves a simple tale though transparent metaphors that establish his point. His character endures bad weather while his lost love enjoys a better place, he uses a jet to communicate how quickly life passes, the weather and changing horses lines are crystal clear, and, finally, the dreaded corkscrew drives his message home. Everywhere there is pain. This may be the "attitude" behind the "experience," but it is, indeed, one sad perspective. The written words "oh, oh" mean *absolutely nothing* when compared to Dylan's performance of those lines. This character is wailing away, sinking in the flood of his emotions.

Sometimes, when your emotions are stretched out in this fashion, it inspires anger—maybe, even, *intense* anger. Submitted, then, for your approval is "Idiot Wind." Many writers place this song alongside "Ballad In Plain D" and "Positively 4th Street" as one of the auteur's most biting songs. I couldn't agree more, although I think it pales in comparison to "Dirge." In any event, this rant unfolds in four segments that contain two five-line verses followed by a five-line chorus. The first segment establishes the narrator's personal situation and his frustrations with those around him (people place stories in the media and fall for rumors that distort their view of him). This inspires him to call his ex-lover an "idiot" and to note that everything she says rides on an "idiot wind." (By the way, Norman Raeben, we're told, was fond of calling his students "idiots." So, perhaps this is yet another influence.) The second segment explores the relational conflict and his intense anger over their predicament. He complains about his demanding life, the war they have waged on one another, and how she has hurt those close to him with her lies. He assures her that her day of reckoning is coming, claiming that with time, she will find herself wasted in a "ditch." The third segment describes their situation and how they grew apart. She did things for him, but they just were not enough; consequently, life is virtually upside down. The final segment just explodes in anger before succumbing to his true feelings. He cannot touch her things. She has no understanding of his feelings. This guy *hates* this woman. Then, suddenly, he calms down. It is as if he gets so worked up that he achieves some type of catharsis and ends up accepting a measure of responsibility for the breakup. The final verse/chorus establishes this point:

> I been double-crossed now for the very last time and now I'm finally free,
> I kissed goodbye the howling beast on the borderline which separated you
>   from me.
> You'll never know the hurt I suffered nor the pain I rise above,
> And I'll never know the same about you, your holiness or your kind of
>   love,
> And it makes me feel so sorry.

> Idiot wind, blowing through the buttons of our coats,
> Blowing through the letters that we wrote.
> Idiot wind, blowing through the dust upon our shelves,
> We're idiots, babe.
> It's a wonder we can even feed ourselves.

This song experienced significant changes when Dylan rerecorded it in Minnesota. The original is far more biting and, it seems, personal. Something as simple as the way he sings the word "idiot" changes the song's dramatic impact. In both versions, there is more than a little bit of "Like A Rolling Stone" here. This guy wants revenge! He wants this woman to crash and burn, and then crash and burn some more. What is interesting, once more, is the transition in the final segment. As you can see, he accepts his role in all of this at the very end. He has had his fit and now he is in some sort of postexplosion funk. I bet young Elvis Costello's heart stopped when he first heard this song since he made a *career* out of this sort of expression. This song is almost *too* powerful for its own good.

"You're Gonna Make Me Lonesome When You Go" is a fascinating follow-up to "Idiot Wind." It is as if this veteran of romantic wars has settled down from his love battles and accepted that this is the way loving relationships work: You fall deeply in love, she slashes your wrists, you have yourself a good bleed, and, with time, your injury heals and you move on to the next amorous laceration. With a bouncy harmonica, active bass (shades of McCoy once more), and lively acoustic guitar providing the sonic platform, this five-verse/two-bridge song articulates the *anticipation* of the end. The narrator is in love with a wonderful woman and, this song tells us, he is surely going to miss her after the bliss hits the fan. He sounds so carefree as he pronounces the inevitable. Verse 1 announces his experiences with love and the change he has witnessed with his new partner ("I've seen love go by my door / It's never been this close before"). The next stanza reports that he has "only known careless love" that frequently hits him where it hurts (down "below"); however, "This time around it's more correct / Right on target, so direct." In fact, things are so good she may be spoiling him. The first bridge explains why:

> Flowers on the hillside, bloomin' crazy,
> Crickets talkin' back and forth in rhyme,
> Blue river runnin' slow and lazy,
> I could stay with you forever
> And never realize the time.

Love is surely in the house. But the truth is just beyond that hillside, as always. He accepts his plight and understands the burden that he is destined to bear, as the next verse relates: "Situations have ended sad, / Relationships have all been bad. / Mine've been like Verlaine's and Rimbaud." I guess poets are just doomed to wrestle with all those attitudes. He reports that this time things sure are wonderful and when she leaves he will surely miss her; as a result, he may even search for her in Hawaii, California, and Ohio. In any event, when she is gone—and she *will* go—he will see her in nature and in his children's eyes.

This song is weird. It is a happy-go-lucky approach to the forthcoming pain of losing someone who is so wonderful that she makes time and nature stand and take notice. Yet that is just the way it is, so take the time to smell the roses, hold her close while you can, and take your medicine when that day arrives—and it *will* arrive. At first glance, you want to claim that this is cynical, but there is no cynicism present. It is acceptance. Love is like a root canal; just think how much better you will feel once the inevitable has passed.

While the pain is fresh, you might as well indulge it by way of a nice, simple blues tune. When we turn to "Meet Me In The Morning," we do just that. The six-stanza song (only five of the verses are performed) uses brief four-line segments that open with a line, repeat it, and close with a two-line statement that usually laments the deteriorating relationship. The song is brief and—when compared to the other songs that populate this record—pretty superficial. The track opens with a request for a meeting at "56th and Wabasha" streets, as the narrator comments how they could easily be in Kansas by the time the snow thaws (I only discuss that portion of the song in private). The second stanza captures the thrust of this particular song:

> They say the darkest hour is right before the dawn
> They say the darkest hour is right before the dawn
> But you wouldn't know it by me
> Every day's been darkness since you been gone.

That's "Meet Me" for you. The narrator continues by referencing a rooster crowing with "something on his mind" and how he shares that feeling since his woman treats him "so unkind." He claims he deserves better, but just as the sun sinks "like a ship," his heart has fallen and left him in his sorry state. The song is clear as can be: The narrator has the blues, and it is all because of her.

Our final track from this five-song segment takes us out of the fray and into the rationalizations that accompany time away from misery. In "If You See Her, Say

Hello," our narrator is conversing with an unnamed individual that he, for some reason, believes might meet his ex-lover. The song (presented in five four-line stanzas) is a sweet elegy in which the narrator continues to struggle with his feelings for a lost love. (Interestingly, this song is radically revised in the new *Lyrics 1962–2001* from the previous *Lyrics 1962–1985* and Dylan's website. This leaves me with an editorial decision. I've decided to stick with the original.) He continues to play games ("Say for me that I'm all right though things get kind of slow / She might think that I've forgotten her, don't tell her it isn't so") but his memories persist and, at times, still sting. The second verse recalls the night they split up, the chilling impact of that event, how their "separation" affected him, and his inability to rid himself of those thoughts ("She still lives inside of me, we've never been apart."). He asks this person to give her a kiss for him as he announces his respect for her decision to leave even though the "bitter taste" of that sad night "lingers." The fourth verse reports how her name pops up as he travels about and how he still struggles with his feelings ("Either I'm too sensitive or else I'm gettin' soft"). The final verse is telltale:

> Sundown, yellow moon, I replay the past
> I know every scene by heart, they all went by so fast
> If she's passin' back this way, I'm not that hard to find
> Tell her she can look me up if she's got the time.

The song, like "Idiot Wind," starts in one place and ends in another. From the gamesmanship of asking this person to avoid giving away his true feelings, the narrator eventually closes by making himself available for a visit. That he is dying for her is quite clear. He cannot rid himself of his thoughts. His confusion dominates him (he respects her for leaving, he hopes for her happiness, and he longs for her return). His misery causes him to question himself (is he just too sensitive?). "If You See Her" is a simple song with a complex message. The "it's *never* over" qualities of a deep-seated loving relationship can be maddening.

What an impressive series of songs! From the lamentations of "You're A Big Girl" to the vitriol of "Idiot Wind" to the self-fulfilling prophecies of "You're Gonna Make Me" to the simplicity of "Meet Me" to the confusion of "If You See Her," these songs touch all of the emotional bases associated with the game of love. All except one, that is: the joy that accompanies a successful relationship. You may develop defense mechanisms such as the acceptance portrayed in "You're Gonna Make Me" or the cavalier attitude in "If You See Her," but those are all short-term remedies. You may explode in anger and vent like a madman, but in the end, you realize that idiot wind blows from two directions. Yes, love *hurts*. Nowhere does it hurt *more* than on *Blood On The Tracks*.

What happened? What happened to make this natural situation that is a man's love for his woman so dire? Why is this so difficult? It is because idealistic people are just fine when their ideals deliver; however, when they fail to materialize, all hell breaks loose. Bob Dylan understands this "attitude." He has worked his way around all sides of this sorry situation, and now he closes this statement with his keynote address. After using Norman Raeben's teachings to introduce his theme, using the following five songs to probe deeply into the phenomenon, and pausing for an epic account of relational duplicity, the auteur is now primed to sum it all up via a two-song statement. Life is a hazardous adventure. Dangers of all sorts abound. People lie, cheat, steal, and stab you in the back with penknives. The best anyone can hope for is to find some form of shelter that protects you from life's varied storms. That is the only place where the promise of deliverance may unfold. When that, too, becomes a lie, well, you write albums like *Blood On The Tracks*. For a closer look at this sad situation, we turn to "Shelter From The Storm."

A simple acoustic guitar and a lively bass provide the aural context for this ten-verse portrayal of a relational life cycle. The writing is clear, accessible, and systematic. Each five-line stanza serves a particular function within the unfolding narrative; moreover, they all follow a specific structure in which a three-line statement about the narrator's circumstances, the woman's intervention, or their relationship prefaces a two-line invitation for refuge. The initial invitation demonstrates the songs narrative strategy:

'Twas in another lifetime, one of toil and blood
When blackness was a virtue and the road was full of mud
I came in from the wilderness, a creature void of form.
"Come in," she said,
"I'll give you shelter from the storm."

The narrator emerges from a dark, dirty, untamed life to receive her invitation for shelter. Subsequently, we have a statement of loyalty for the sanctuary she offers and the comfort she provides (verses 2 and 3) that is followed by a two-verse description of his dire circumstances and her successful intervention (4 and 5). A turning point appears in the sixth stanza ("Now there's a wall between us, somethin' there's been lost / I took too much for granted, got my signals crossed.") and the relationship dies (symbolized by references to "doom" and a "one-eyed undertaker" blowing a "futile horn"). At this point, we witness a series of reflections on life and its difficulties. Babies cry, senior citizens suffer through bad dental work and relational abandonment, and the narrator questions life's conditions. The song paints a sad, sad picture, and any shelter that may be offered appears to be a temporary respite.

The track offers an interesting twist with the final stanzas. The ninth verse mentions a village on a hill where the villagers gamble for the narrator's clothes. Do we have a Jesus complex here? He claims he "bargained for salvation" and received a "lethal dose" for his troubles; furthermore, he states he offered his "innocence" and received "scorn" in response. Here the song's written lyrics use the word "they" to signify those who abused the narrator; however, Dylan sings the line using "she." Usually, I accept the written version as the basis for my observations, but this change is compelling as it shifts the blame from unnamed villagers to the woman who offers shelter. She has, then, failed him. The final verse reflects on it all by describing beauty's evasive qualities, the narrator's desire to turn back time to the point where "God and her were born," and the final invitation for sanctuary.

"Shelter From The Storm" offers some intriguing imagery as it unfolds. The fifth verse's reference to the narrator's "crown of thorns" and the aforementioned comment about people gambling for his clothes are pretty pointed. When you consider the comment about the day God and the woman were born, the biblical qualities of these expressions add a curious dimension to the story. The narrator has been hounded, hunted, and hurt by life. These dire circumstances elevate the significance of the woman's intervention to the point that she assumes a godlike status. She is his personal messiah. Though *he* wears symbolic crowns and experiences ceaseless persecution, *she* plays the savior's role and offers the all-important invitation for salvation. Then she betrays him. She is graceful and well-adorned, and offers an idyllic escape from life's hell. Yet, in the end, it is all a lie. It is just not there. Still, the narrator perseveres in his belief that one day he will capture true beauty and experience heavenly bliss. One day, that invitation for sanctuary will be sincere. In other words, he still *believes*.

This song is most assuredly this record's centerpiece. The thorough description of the narrator's circumstance (and its Christlike qualities), her seemingly divine intervention and its false promises, and his subsequent response to it all capture the essence of *Blood On The Track*'s themes. "Idiot Wind" wrestles with these emotions and wages war on the perceived enemy only to capitulate and share the responsibility for the failure. "You're A Big Girl" suffers through the consequences of another false promise. "You're Gonna Make Me" winks at the game and, in so doing, attempts to transcend it. But "Shelter" embodies it all. Life is hard. Persecution is ubiquitous. The promised sanctuary is a mirage. The interesting thing about a mirage is that what you think you see *does* exist *somewhere*. That is why you think you see it—you want it so desperately it creates the hallucination. Love's idealistic qualities are on display here. The woman-as-messiah characterization drives a delusion that crashes as soon as it takes flight. Yet Dylan's characters persevere. Their belief in their ideals is unwavering despite all of the evidence to the contrary. This faith, as "Shelter" so clearly illustrates, may be misplaced and result in even more damage. That does not matter, though. The ideal is what is important, not the reality.

Blood closes with the capstone statement that is "Buckets Of Rain." The song contains five six-line verses that use soft—again, gentle—supporting music to sharpen the expression's clarity. Dylan keeps it simple here. The track opens by establishing the situation:

> Buckets of rain
> Buckets of tears
> Got all them buckets comin' out of my ears.
> Buckets of moonbeams in my hand,
> I got all the love, honey baby,
> You can stand.

Our narrator is full of emotion—magical feelings—that contribute to his undying devotion. The second verse explains how people come and go in life; nevertheless, if she needs him, he will be there for her. The next stanza tells us why. She is wonderful. He adores everything about her, and that brings nothing but sorrow. Still, his commitment is eternal, so he pledges to take her with him when he departs (I presume he means the Big Departure). He offers this resolution to his relational situation:

> Life is sad
> Life is a bust
> All ya can do is do what you must.
> You do what you must do and ya do it well,
> I'll do it for you, honey baby,
> Can't you tell?

Through stories of lost love and the search to regain it, to accounts of love's aftermath and their sad situations, to explosions of righteous indignation and their cathartic qualities, to portrayals of the defense mechanisms that help lovers lick their wounds, *Blood On The Tracks* charts a perilous mission. Promises of eternal shelter may prove to be lies. Those you trust the most may be the ones to inflict the most damage. Yet, in the end, love is the end all, be all of life. Through life's sadness, its disappointments, and its demands, the willingness to sacrifice whatever loves requires remains strong. There is just no other choice: You do what must be done, and you do it to the best of your ability.

Blood On The Tracks is most assuredly a statement from Bob Dylan. The fact that he revised his work in order to refine his message says so much about this project. This is not the Dylan of *Another Side*. Nor is this the artist who claims to disavow perfection in favor of spontaneous, raw expression. Here, Bob Dylan worked hard to communicate his "attitudes" about loving relations. His metaphors are as accessible as any he has ever written. Only the moral period will rival this record's clarity of expression. From the opening songs that establish the thematic context through the individual portrayals of specific relational situations to the capstone commentaries of the final songs, Dylan laid out his idealistic vision of love, its demanding nature, and its essential qualities. The women in these songs display every imaginable trait, but their most enduring characteristic is the salvation they offer. They represent nothing less than the Face of God—a God that is wrathful, evasive, merciless, redeeming, and, most of all, challenging. But that challenge must be accepted. There is no other choice. To step outside the game of love is to step outside of life itself. These are, indeed, some powerful "attitudes." Perhaps it is a good thing that there is only one *Blood On The Tracks*. Hopefully, facing the collapse of your most treasured ideals is a once-in-a-lifetime experience.

The extent to which *Blood* is autobiographical is a matter of speculation. It is a fact that Bob and Sara Dylan separated during this time frame. It is also a fact that they divorced years later. I'm confident in saying that those "experiences" informed the "attitudes" on display within this record. I'm also certain that other influences played a role in this project's development. In all cases, one compelling point stands out: The auteur *labored* over the articulation of this message. Whether he was struggling with his creative instincts, battling to make sense of Raeben's teachings as they applied to the generation of his art, or fine-tuning a personal expression in order to ensure its clarity, *Blood* received more of the auteur's attention than any work to date.

From that, we presume the man had a point he wanted to communicate—and what a point it was.

Desire

The combined successes of *Planet Waves*, Tour '74, and *Blood On The Tracks* demonstrated the creative power of a rejuvenated Bob Dylan. That eight-year period from *Blonde On Blonde* to *Planet Waves* was not the highly touted or widely reported artistic decline or creative decay of the voice of his generation; to the contrary, it represented an artistic transition that enabled his career to continue. It is, indeed, hard to imagine a forty-year career without these types of turning points—especially if the artist's work continues to evolve (a person *could* flatline their way through a fifty-year career in NashVegas, for example). After issuing his carefully plotted statement about love, the auteur's reorientation advanced by way of an unexpected child, *Desire*. Derek Barker offers Jacques Levy's recollections regarding his first encounter with Bob Dylan in the spring of 1974: "I was just walking out of the house right here on Bleecker Street and he was coming this way. I said 'hey, hi!' and he didn't know who I was, but he was familiar with my work with Roger [McGuinn]. We started talking and spent the evening together." They next met a little over a year later in the summer of 1975: "I bumped into him again on Bleecker Street, and again we came up here [Levy's loft]. He had no specific plans at the time to do anything, and he said something like, 'I really like the stuff you do with Roger. How about if you and I do something together?' Which was slightly strange, right? Because he knew I did lyrics and I knew he did lyrics. But I said, 'Sure, let's give it a shot.' " They wrote the song "Isis" immediately: "We were just having a great time laughing and coming up with one verse after another and we kept on going until five in the morning and we finished the song. And both of us thought it was great." From there, they wrote the song "Joey" (inspired by a dinner conversation with friends about mobster Joey Gallo's murder in April 1972). With that, a creative alliance was established with no particular outcome in mind. The two guys just wanted to write some songs in a basement somewhere—preferably in a building painted some shade of pink.

Jacques Levy is not your typical songwriter. He received his Ph.D. in psychology from Michigan State University; later practiced clinical psychology in Topeka, Kansas; and, while living in Topeka, worked as a director for a local community theater as a hobby. In 1965, he left the clinic and moved to New York City to pursue a career as a stage director. It worked! His credits include such Broadway productions as *Doonesbury, The Musical* and *Oh! Calcutta!* as well as a variety of off-Broadway projects. He has written songs with Roger McGuinn as well as for singers such as Joe Cocker, Carly Simon, and Jerry Lee Lewis. As Derek Barker points out, the collaboration with McGuinn set the table for his work with Dylan.

Levy described his work with Dylan to Barker: "Bob had a few very basic partly-worked tunes. . . . Some of them were just little phrases, some were a little more developed musically and some had a certain feeling to them." They first wrote "Isis" by working on the piano. With that success, they turned to the "Joey" idea along with "Romance In Durango," "Black Diamond Bay" (a song inspired by Joseph Conrad's book *Victory*), and eventually "Hurricane" (a song about boxer Rubin Carter's murder trial). During the process, Dylan's songwriting shifted once more, as Levy explains,

> [The songs] have strong narratives, and you really feel when you listen to them that you want to know what happens next. At least that's what I was trying for, and I hope it succeeds. Every once in a while Bob has tried to do that [he mentions "Lily" from *Blood*] but it's not easy for him to stick with a narrative. He's much stronger with a set of images, a series of images that are sometimes quite abstract, but little by little open up the idea that you're after. There may be many narratives in it for one or two verses, but the whole thing usually is not part of one long narrative. It is not his style, but it is a style that he likes. I guess it's a prose style, but it's also the style of movies and theatre.

Another significant shift occurred during the collaboration: Dylan was introduced to a rhyming dictionary for the first time. Levy used what he terms "old fashioned" songwriting techniques that feature "double syllable" rhymes and rhymes that extend "into the next line." Dylan loved the approach, according to Levy: "He got a big kick out of that stuff, he really enjoyed it, and when that would come up he would not only enjoy the fact of it but also singing it. He got a great kick out of bending those things around."

As Dylan observed at this chapter's outset, the writers worked so closely that neither one of them recalls who wrote what. Levy told Barker, "I have to say that we worked together very well . . . after a while you don't exactly know who came up with what, and that's the way it should be." The writing began in the city, but soon the men relocated to East Hampton for more concentrated sessions. When they had "eight or ten songs finished," Dylan called Columbia Records and announced that he was ready to record. Levy claims their intention was never to write an album of songs; however, when they reached that threshold, Dylan entered the studio. Interestingly, the Levy interview notes that Dylan-in-the-studio was quite unfamiliar with several of the songs and had to resort to lyric sheets: "Although we had worked on them together in the Hamptons and he pretty much had them down, when he got into the studio he still had to have notations of chords, and he had to look at the lyric sheet for most of the songs. Now, this was a very new experience for Bob." When backing singer Emmylou Harris joined in the recording, she too was unfamiliar with the material. There were no rehearsals. Levy recalls, "They would just start and Bob didn't tell her when to come in or when not to come in. It all comes out sounding very smooth, but there's a certain spontaneity to it that's very special." *This* was the effect Dylan attempted to achieve with the boys from Deliverance during the New York *Blood On The Tracks* sessions.

The studio work was rough initially. The biographers report that when Dylan entered the studio to record *Desire*, he had a huge band awaiting him. Clinton Heylin's session chronology cites one participant's recollection that as many as five guitarists were on hand (including Eric Clapton) along with a horn section, multiple backing vocalists, and all sorts of instrumentalists available for new producer Don DeVito. A major participant in the proceedings was violinist Scarlet Rivera. (The biographers tell a wonderful story about Dylan's recruitment of Rivera for this project, stopping her on the street and inviting her to a session simply because she was carrying her violin.) Without question, Rivera's work is *Desire*'s defining sonic signature. She takes Dylan's music to places it had never before ventured, adding musical textures that directly enhance the songs' narrative qualities. Eventually, DeVito turned to bass player Rob Stoner for advice regarding managing the huge band sound. Stoner encouraged the producer to dismiss the big act, hire a small band, and take it from there. DeVito did just that and the *Desire* cast settled into Harris on backing vocals, Stoner on bass, Rivera on violin, Howard Wyeth on drums, as well as Vincent Bell (bellzouki), Dom Cortese (accordion), Luther Rix (congas—listed only as "Luther" on the album liner notes), and Ronee Blakley and Steve Soles on backing vocals (Rix, Blakley, and Soles appear on but one song, "Hurricane"). In writing the story of the "Hurricane," Levy and Dylan messed up several crucial points that were viewed as potentially libelous by Columbia's lawyers ("who was doing what to whom"–type errors). A rewrite ensued, the factual errors were corrected or omitted (Barker says it took Levy five minutes), and the song was rerecorded. (Song character Patty Valentine sued anyway and lost eventually.)

Desire (released January 1976) contains nine tracks (running just over fifty-six minutes) with seven songs coauthored by the Dylan-Levy team (the two exceptions are "One More Cup Of Coffee" and "Sara"). *Desire* features two songs of societal complaint (the portraits, "Hurricane" and "Joey"), three sagas ("Isis," "Romance In Durango," and "Black Diamond Bay"), one scenic/love celebration ("Mozambique"), and three relational complaints ("One More Cup Of Coffee," "Oh, Sister," and "Sara"). Levy's influence supports an advance in the satire's evolution by way of the two portraits and the sagas (these songs advance the "Lily" style of storytelling); additionally, Dylan's songwriting travels abroad more than on any previous work through songs that feature faraway scenes, international intrigue, foreign languages, and—thanks in large part to Scarlet Rivera's violin—foreign sounds. Levy reported that his lyrical contributions enabled Dylan to focus on the music more than on previous projects, and the evidence reinforces the accuracy of that claim: *Desire* features some of the most sophisticated music to appear on a Bob Dylan project. The violin-harmonica interplay, Stoner's stellar bass work, Harris's marvelous singing, and the balance of sound DeVito achieves provide a strong sonic platform for Levy and Dylan's stories. We begin with the portraits.

The two portraits are actually photo negatives of one another. In one, a famous Black man is victimized by a racist judicial system hungry for action; in the other, a famous White man is victimized by a system outside the law—a culture with its own code of conduct. "Hurricane" says little about boxer Rubin Carter (one verse describes him) in favor of scenic embellishments that unveil the ludicrous qualities of the prosecution and the hideous consequences of the racism. "Joey" follows a different strategy as the story focuses on the central character's heroic traits. Both stories end negatively as Dylan is embarrassed by a judicial system that practices uncontrolled racism and angered by the law of the streets, hoping true justice will have its way in both cases (the auteur's ideals, it appears, transcend relational matters). Without the subtle humor and playfulness of "Lily," "Hurricane" and "Joey" use the same attention to detail to reintroduce the czar of the topical song and his anger, frustration, and indignation.

Dylan struggled with "Hurricane" in the studio. When Columbia demanded that the song be revised, he expanded the band and recorded track after track searching for the right take. Finally, he gave up and left DeVito to select the most suitable recording. DeVito responded, we're told, by assembling the song from the best portions of the respective takes. This ensemble method of record production is a long way from the *Another Side* sessions; nevertheless, the results offer a lively narrative presented through a fast-paced musical format. Rivera's violin works between verses to sustain the song's dramatic tension as the story builds and builds. Furthermore, the eleven nine-line verses contain three embedded choruses that add coherence to the detail that accompanies each line. The opening verse conveys this songwriting strategy:

> Pistol shots ring out in the barroom night
> Enter Patty Valentine from the upper hall.
> She sees the bartender in a pool of blood,
> Cries out, "My God, they killed them all!"
> Here comes the story of the Hurricane,
> The man the authorities came to blame
> For somethin' that he never done.
> Put in a prison cell, but one time he could-a been
> The champion of the world.

(The stanza's final five lines represent the embedded chorus that reappears in verses 5 and 11. In verse 5, it relates "This is" the story; and in verse 11, "That's" the story—the tactic adds considerable continuity to the rapid-fire narrative.) Notice how the song opens with action. Shots ring out and a character enters the scene. A *theater* writer is in evidence here.

The story unfolds systematically: The first two verses establish the crime and those on the scene; the third stanza presents Carter and his whereabouts that evening; the fourth verse relates the police's arrival and their activities (interviewing witnesses and discovering that one of the injured is still alive); the fifth stanza takes us to the hospital, where Carter is presented to the witness, who declares he is the wrong guy; the sixth verse jumps to four months later and the police's efforts to pressure so-called witness Arthur Dexter Bradley to name Carter as the assailant; the seventh stanza portrays more pressure as the police advance their racist assertions; the eighth stanza describes Carter-the-boxer; the ninth and tenth verses present the trial; and the song closes with the eleventh verse and its observations regarding a failed legal system and the concluding embedded chorus. The song is crystal clear. The emphasis on scenic detail produces a story that is long on plot progression, short on characterization. Only one character is actually developed, as "witnesses" Alfred Bello, Arthur Dexter Bradley, and Patty Valentine perform cameos and no police or court official is mentioned by name. The eighth verse presents the story's victim, Rubin Carter:

> Rubin could take a man out with just one punch
> But he never did like to talk about it all that much.

It's my work, he'd say, and I do it for pay
And when it's over I'd just as soon go on my way
Up to some paradise
Where the trout streams flow and the air is nice
And ride a horse along a trail.
But then they took him to the jailhouse
Where they try to turn a man into a mouse.

Consolidating the songwriting that produced "Hattie Carroll," "Only A Pawn," and "Oxford Town" with the narrative detail of "Frankie Lee," "115th Dream," and "Lily," "Hurricane" takes a point of view and hammers it home. Just like Maryland elites or Mississippi racists, the courts of Paterson, New Jersey, fail themselves, their constituents, and their country by their actions. The song's story is thorough and insightful, although its relationship with the truth is uncertain. Carter was released, eventually retried and reconvicted, and eventually rereleased. Though the truth is uncertain, Rubin Carter's story is a famous one, receiving treatments in song, film, and literature.

"Joey" shares this level of narrative detail. With a slow, steady musical platform creating space for the unfolding story, this twelve-stanza (with four lines per verse) epic is divided into five segments that use four-line choruses to punctuate the story. The song is a biography, plain and simple. It traces Joey Gallo's life from the cradle to the grave. He is, most assuredly, presented in a heroic light. He defends his brother, refuses to kill for the sake of killing, nobly does his time in prison, refrains from wearing a gun because he is around children, protects his family when "they" come to kill him, and dies honorably in the streets of Little Italy. The chorus drives home the song's point when it repeatedly inquires why did he have to die—what made "them" do it? The opening verse demonstrates the Dylan-Levy songwriting team's approach:

Born in Red Hook, Brooklyn, in the year of who knows when
Opened up his eyes to the tune of an accordion
Always on the outside of whatever side there was
When they asked him why it had to be that way, "Well," he answered, "just because."

The writing is colorful. When the police harassed him (referring to their target as "Mr. Smith") and eventually arrested him for conspiracy, the songwriters conclude that the police were not certain who he conspired "with" (there is one of those rhymes Levy mentioned earlier). When he faces the judge to be sentenced, the jurist inquires as to the time. Joey responds "five to ten," and the judge declares, "That's exactly what you get." While in prison, our hero reads Nietzsche and Wilhelm Reich, and does time "in the hole" for intervening during a "strike" (there are those rhymes again). He emerges from prison looking like "Jimmy Cagney" and returns to his life of crime. Eventually, "they" kill him and his relatives mourn. The writers conclude, "And someday if God's in heaven overlookin' His preserve / I know the men that shot him down will get what they deserve."

Although Levy claims that Dylan does not typically develop his narratives in this fashion, I have to point to several of the folk-posturing period's satires and protest songs as evidence to the contrary. Moreover, the narrative structures that hold together "Lily" on *Blood On The Tracks* and "Frankie Lee" on *John Wesley Harding* reflect this attention to detail. Levy's correct in that much of the Dylan Canon delves into idiosyncratic images, fragmented scenes, and uneven plots. The conclusion? The auteur's is a flexible pen. His work with Levy merely brings out that side of his songwriting. Levy's capacity to bring forward attributes that have laid dormant appears again in the three sagas, a point to which we now turn.

"Isis," "Durango," and "Black Diamond Bay" represent syntheses of the old Dylan, the more recent Dylan, and Jacques Levy's influence. With a lively instrumental track featuring wonderful interplay between Rivera's violin and Dylan's harmonica setting the aural scene, the thirteen four-line verses that present "Isis" take us back down one famous highway. The song is an account of a man, his strange relationship with his woman ("Isis"), and an *Indiana Jones*–like treasure hunt. Once more, the opening stanza describes the narrator's relationship with Isis and his sudden departure:

> I married Isis on the fifth day of May,
> But I could not hold on to her very long.
> So I cut off my hair and I rode straight way
> For the wild unknown country where I could not go wrong.

Say what? He married this woman, feared losing her (or did she leave him?), and exited for an adventure? With a starting point as clear as mud, the story begins. The narrator meets a stranger, the stranger invites him to join him on a trip, off they go, as he travels his mind wanders (thinking of a laundry list of treasures and, of course, Isis), they arrive at pyramids that are "embedded in ice," they start digging in search of a "body," the stranger dies for unknown reasons, the narrator keeps digging, he enters a tomb but there's no body or treasure, he places the stranger in the tomb and pays his last respects, and he seals the tomb and heads back to Isis. Upon his arrival, Isis inquires about his whereabouts, his new appearance, and if he plans to stay. The song ends with this statement:

> Isis, oh, Isis, you mystical child.
> What drives me to you is what drives me insane.
> I still can remember the way that you smiled
> On the fifth day of May in the drizzlin' rain.

This is a very superficial tale that stresses narrative progression over narrative development. Thing after thing happens with minimal detail. The narrator's relationship with Isis is central, but we know *nothing* about it—absolutely *nothing*. The song demonstrates the utility of character development in that, without it, the characters' actions have little meaning. The story races along, but why? It seems to take the clever omissions of "Lily" and elevate the tendency to the story's centerpiece. Herein lies our flash from the auteur's songwriting past. Much like "Highway 61 Revisited," we witness a series of actions without any understanding of who these people are or the motives for their activities. Why did God want a murder, how did Georgia Sam suffer his injuries, what in the world is Mack the Finger doing with all of those telephones, and what is up with that family? To be sure, songs are not novels or even short stories, so I'm not criticizing the writing. I am, however, noting the similarities in style. Aside from his considerable skills, Levy did not bring something new to the songwriting table as much as he dusted off that which was already there. And *that* is a positive step in the auteur's mission of reorientation.

"Romance In Durango" is another simple story. Here flamingo sounds provide the perfect stage for the activities that follow. The nine four-line verses are divided into four sections that are separated by four six-line choruses. The narrative is an unequivocal account of outlaws on the run from a murder charge. The characters are presented in the opening verse:

> Hot chili peppers in the blistering sun
> Dust on my face and my cape,
> Me and Magdalena on the run
> I think this time we shall escape.

The narrator sells his guitar for food and shelter. He dreams of the incident and "Ramon's" blood-drenched face. He questions his memory, seemingly unsure if he committed the crime. He dreams of "dancing the fandango" and tequila nights. He envisions their marriage. Suddenly, he thinks he hears "thunder" when he feels a "sharp pain." He hands his gun to his never-to-be-bride and encourages her aim. We are left to contemplate their circumstances. Alas, Magdalena is destined to dance the fandango in the Big House.

"Black Diamond" is a far more complicated story. This track *is* "Lily, Revisited," albeit with a significant stylistic twist. The long instrumental opening and closing that prefaced and concluded "Lily" are in evidence here as is the closing tag line for each verse (substituting "Black Diamond Bay" for the "Jack of Hearts"). The difference is that throughout the song's seven twelve-line verses, no character is ever developed. We learn of Lily's past, Big Jim's power, Rosemary's angst, and Jack's acting abilities as "Lily" progresses, but there is none of that here. Instead, a large cast of nameless characters—none of whom are ever developed in any meaningful way—go about their last-minute activities at a casino-hotel on an island about to be consumed by a volcano. Now, *that's* a story line. We have "the woman" (wearing a Panama hat), "the Greek," the "soldier," "the tiny man," the "desk clerk," and my favorite, "the loser." The song jumps from scene to scene, almost with each line. The woman floats around, apparently being courted by the soldier who presents her with a ring that she deems inadequate. The soldier and the tiny man negotiate the ring's price and, just before the end, contemplate their sexuality. The Greek wastes his time by hanging himself (a genuine waste of energy and rope when one is on an island about to sink into the ocean). The loser's busy losing until he wins big and then endures The Final Loss. The desk clerk busies himself coping with everyone else and monitoring the impending doom. The third verse demonstrates the song's busy qualities:

A soldier sits beneath the fan
Doin' business with a tiny man who sells him a ring.
Lightning strikes, the lights blow out.
The desk clerk wakes and begins to shout,
"Can you see anything?"
Then the Greek appears on the second floor
In his bare feet with a rope around his neck,
While a loser in the gambling room lights up a candle,
Says, "Open up another deck."
But the dealer says, "Attendez-vous, s'il vous plaît,"
As the rain beats down and the cranes fly away
From Black Diamond Bay.

(If nothing else, the Spanish lines in "Durango" and the French cited above demonstrate a new lyrical trend, the use of foreign tongues.)

The action keeps moving until the volcano finally erupts just as the loser breaks the bank, the Greek hangs from a light fixture, the tiny man and the soldier think "forbidden" thoughts, and the woman prays from the balcony. Suddenly, everything changes with the seventh and final verse:

I was sittin' home alone one night in L.A.,
Watchin' old Cronkite on the seven o'clock news.
It seems there was an earthquake that
Left nothin' but a Panama hat
And a pair of old Greek shoes.
Didn't seem like much was happenin',
So I turned it off and went to grab another beer.
Seems like every time you turn around
There's another hard-luck story that you're gonna hear
And there's really nothin' anyone can say
And I never did plan to go anyway
To Black Diamond Bay.

There is a shift in narrative contexts for you! Jacques Levy told Derek Barker that this song is about "apathy" and how people hear the worst news only to dismiss it and go for another beer. All I can say is that we certainly took the long way around to that point! "Black Diamond" is a fine story that uses trademark Dylan pacing and Levy's attention to scenic detail and dialogue, and merges them into a long-winded account of a ten-second evening news story. The story fails to develop its characters, but then again, that's television news, isn't it? Just like a news story, the song grabs the racy angle when and where it can, exploits it, and leaves us to contemplate a tale that is long on the sensational but short on the specifics. Levy cites this as his favorite Dylan-Levy song, and I can see why. It would make a grand theater production.

These complicated theatrical productions grind to a screeching halt with our tale of scenic-relational celebration, "Mozambique." I don't know if the writers had spent the day listening to Joni Mitchell travel tunes or not, but it sure sounds like it. Shades of "Carey" and "In France They Kiss On Main Street" float throughout this simple travelogue that deploys foreign sounds to convey the wonderful activities of this foreign paradise. The song's three six-line verses pause for a four-line bridge between the second and third stanzas as the song cruises along in its own state of relational-scenic bliss. The celebration opens with scenic descriptions of beautiful blue skies that quickly turn to the romance such an environment inspires. Couples dance "cheek to cheek." Time stops for romance. Everybody is friendly beyond belief. The bridge communicates the song's sentiments:

> Lying next to her by the ocean
> Reaching out and touching her hand,
> Whispering your secret emotion
> Magic in a magical land.

There it is, my friends: magical Mozambique. Unfortunately, all good things must come to an end sometime, and that holds true here as well. When the time comes to "say goodbye to sand and sea" along with all the wonderful "people living free," you turn your head for one "final peek" and move on, hopefully, to the next paradise. Assuredly, this is a simple pop song with a clear theme: Beautiful places inspire beautiful things, maybe even love.

Love is the central theme of the first installment of *Desire*'s relational trilogy, "Oh, Sister." The question here is "What kind of love are we discussing?" With solemn violin-harmonica contributing to the song's hymnlike feel, this work appears to discuss a brother-sister relationship that is obviously metaphorical. This message of devotion unfolds via three four-line verses and a four-line bridge, again between the second and third stanzas (a similar structure to that of "Mozambique"). The opening verse establishes the characters:

> Oh, Sister, when I come to lie in your arms
> You should not treat me like a stranger.
> Our Father would not like the way that you act
> And you must realize the danger.

Now, what have we here? The song continues with the narrator's belief that he deserves his sister's affection as they join together to "love and follow His direction." The bridge notes how they were raised together, "died," and "were reborn" before they were "mysteriously saved." The song ends with his plea for her continued commitment and his concern that he may soon be gone.

The song's worshipful qualities are self-apparent; however, the authors are more than vague in their presentation of the characters and their relationship—although the relational complaint is clearly lodged. Much like "Father Of Night" and "Three Angels" from *New Morning*, the track skirts around the religious references as much as anything. But it is most definitely there. Whoever these people are, they work together in *service*—a sentiment that will soon explode and dominate the auteur's work.

Our remaining entries from *Desire*'s love trilogy were written without Jacques Levy. "One More Cup Of Coffee" and "Sara" leave Levy's scenic embellishments behind in favor of some good old-fashioned character development, Bob Dylan style. Although the songs describe their respective settings, their emphasis is squarely focused on the mysterious gypsy girl of "One More Cup" and the magical woman and soon-to-be-ex-wife that is "Sara"—and from there, their respective relational complaints. Close your eyes when "One More Cup" cranks up and you can see the gypsies dancing. Rivera's violin and Dylan's gypsy malisma work in harmony to take us Over There to that magical place where the lovers dance wildly, the magic flows freely, and the wine flows—period. Dylan introduced this song in concert by recalling a visit with the "King of the Gypsies" and the varied activities that surrounded that trip. The track, it appears, conveys his attitude toward that particular experience. The song's three eight-line verses are punctuated by brief three-line choruses that repeat the song title and add *nothing* to the character descriptions featured in the respective verses. (Supposedly, the title came from Dylan's conversation with the king.) The opening stanza and chorus demonstrate this narrative approach:

> Your breath is sweet
> Your eyes are like two jewels in the sky.
> Your back is straight, your hair is smooth
> On the pillow where you lie.
> But I don't sense affection
> No gratitude or love
> Your loyalty is not to me
> But to the stars above.
>
> One more cup of coffee for the road,
> One more cup of coffee 'fore I go
> To the valley below.

Not only is this beautiful girl magical in her appearance, but she is also distant toward our narrator; hence, his complaint. Obviously, that intrigues him and piques his interest in this mysterious lady. The second stanza describes her father. He is a wandering bandit who leads his people, protects their way of life, and teaches his daughter self-defense (knives are the weapon of choice here). The final verse mentions her mother's and sister's clairvoyant qualities and how those skills contribute to her magically dark ways. Her skills come not from formal instruction; rather, she is a product of her culture—a worldview where pleasures abound, danger is ubiquitous, and coffee is served on demand. Nothing ever happens in "One More Cup," just layer after layer of character development.

That style of writing is evident in "Sara" as well; however, this final song places the central character in a concrete setting that clearly communicates the death of a relationship. The biographers report how Sara Dylan stood outside the studio and watched her husband record this song. *Everyone* argues for its deeply personal contents. Whether or not "Sara" is autobiographical, it certainly massages some powerful attitudes that suggest personal experience. The song is laid out systematically. The seven four-line verses describe a scene on the beach with the kids playing in the sand and enjoying a "Mozambique" moment. Occasionally, a verse may cut away to a foreign location and Sara's activities there (e.g., she shops in "Savanna-la-Mar") or mention another family outing (e.g., they appear to be camping at one point) or describe Sara and the narrator's initial meeting. But it is the beach scene that drives this tale. The choruses are another story. Throughout the six four-line choruses, the narrator embellishes "Sara's" attributes. In the first chorus, she's "So easy to look at, so hard to define." In the second, she's a "Radiant jewel, mystical wife." In the fourth chorus, she's a "beautiful lady, so dear to my heart." Additionally, the choruses communicate stances from the narrator regarding the relationship. The third chorus relates, "Lovin' you is the one thing I'll never regret"; the fifth pleads, "You must forgive me my unworthiness"; and the final chorus implores, "Don't ever leave me, don't ever go." These are some powerful *attitudes*.

Again, it is the beach scene that drives this story. After all the references to the family frolicking on the beach, the final verse presents an abandoned shoreline with only a fragment of some old ship present. No kids. No fun. Alas, no love. The narrator notes that she has always been there for him and now he needs to find her so that she may save him once more. The song extols the joys of family life all the while it praises the matriarch who makes such natural happiness possible. When she goes, it goes. Busy beaches become abandoned. Happy moments disappear. The song charts more than the breakup of a romantic ideal; it portrays the end of a family. I wonder what Sara Dylan thought as she watched the voice of his generation work his way through this song.

So many times in this study, I've referenced the "transitional" qualities of this or that. Yet, when you present a forty-plus year career, these moments occur with some frequency. Unless an artist plows away and never varies what he or she plants, some crop rotation is going to occur, and that requires a shift in modes of operation. *Desire* is yet another one of those occasions. Dylan planted narrative seeds this season, and Jacques Levy assisted with the harvest. To be sure, the auteur has worked this crop before, but new technologies, time, and changing circumstances have had an impact on his methods. *Desire*'s liner notes offer a concrete example of this synthesis of old and new Dylan. Here *Tarantula* meets the "Hurricane," and the results are instructive:

> Where do I begin . . . on the heels of Rimbaud moving like a dancing bullet thru the secret streets of a hot New Jersey night filled with venom and wonder. Meeting the Queen Angel in the reeds of Babylon and then to the fountain of sorrow to drift away in the hot mass of the deluge . . . to sing praise to the king of those dead streets, to grasp and let go in a heavenly way—streaming into the lost belly of civilization at a standstill. Romance is taking over. Tolstoy was right. These notes are being written in a bathtub in Maine under ideal conditions. . . .

The piece goes on to mention the characters and scenes from the album in odd ways. "Isis" joins the moon as they radiate above the writer. He plans to celebrate Rubin Carter's freedom in a California parking lot with historical significance. These lines suggest the liner notes of old, spiced with tidbits from the new songs. Dylan is taking his creative history and reorienting it to meet the needs of his artistic future. To sit back and observe something like this unfold is fascinating in that you know that it is happening beyond the artist's consciousness. His *talent* is leading this process. His creative *urges* inspire these activities. Bob Zimmerman gives way to the natural evolution of his artistic instincts, and that enables him to continue writing for Bob Dylan. Otherwise, Dylan would be riding his Triumph motorcycle searching for a slick spot in the road.

Here we have just considered the first coauthored entry in the Dylan oeuvre. Although the songwriting revisits the grand-narrative style featured in *Blood On The Tracks*' "Lily" (itself a reiteration of the trademark satires such as the "Talkin'" songs), these songs occasionally sacrifice emotional depth for scenic detail. Other times—such as in "One More Cup"—the emotional detail is all we get. With more complicated sonic strategies accompanying these detailed playlets, this record presents story after story—much like a book of short stories, stories that, for the first time, take place in foreign lands and use foreign tongues. Moreover, "Oh, Sister" revisits "Father Of Night" and "Three Angels" as it foreshadows the religious rhetoric that will soon dominate the work. "Black Diamond" is an extraordinary story that may move too fast to embellish any character or scene, yet its ending is a complete surprise. The "Joey" and "Hurricane" portraits present two victims of a legal system that does not always operate in *everyone*'s best interests. Bob Dylan's finger-pointing skills remain sharp. These narrative forms will now weave their way into the albums that follow. The artistic reorientation that started with Norman Raeben has now assimilated Jacques Levy's influence. With his songwriting on a new track, his attitude toward his industry on a new footing, and his business affairs—especially his publishing—on a more solid foundation, it was once more time to do what all great artists do in this situation: Take a road trip and make a movie.

The Rolling Thunder Review and *Renaldo & Clara*

So much has happened in Bob Dylan's public life. His early work got him labeled "the voice of his generation." He changed songwriting forever when he rejected the Mr. Message Man albatross and blazed a new artistic trail. He participated in groundbreaking movies. He fought with audiences around the world because he wanted to play an electric guitar. He wrote one wild and crazy "book of words." He crashed his motorcycle. He recovered by playing music in the basement of a pink house in the woods. He recorded country music when it was as out of vogue as it would ever get. He created the Bob Dylan Revue. He rejoined his old band, made a new record, and participated in the largest musical tour event to that point in history. He returned to topical writing and issued a treatise on love that deployed new songwriting techniques while refining old ones. He joined a professional writer to hone his craft even further. And now he goes mad. Not the bad mad, mind you, but pretty far out there. The Lollapalooza and the Lilith tours traversed the land with their own brands of musical theater in the early 1990s, but no tour from any era has *ever* captured the off-the-wall magic of the Rolling Thunder Review and its cinematic offspring, *Renaldo & Clara*. The word is that *everybody* who participated in the Rolling

Thunder Review either found religion or entered an infirmary afterward. We are about to discover why. The Rolling Thunder Review and *Renaldo & Clara* take our notion of artistic reorientation into the twilight zone.

Larry "Ratso" Sloman's book on the Rolling Thunder Revue ("RTR") is, in my view, the definitive account of the tour, the film, and the various participants' zany activities. He originally covered the tour for *Rolling Stone*, yet that quickly ended as his allegiance to the tour outweighed his commitment to the magazine and its reportorial agenda. Sloman's admiration for the RTR and its participants just gushes from each page; however, the Thunderers appear to reciprocate those feelings. As a result, Sloman offers insights that just do not appear in other sources—although Sam Shepard's book also yields valuable information. For instance, toward the end of Sloman's book he cites Bob Dylan's recollections regarding the origins of the RTR idea:

> I was just sitting in a field [in Corsica] overlooking some vineyards, the sky was pink, the sun was going down and the moon was sapphire, and I recall getting a ride into town with a man with a donkey cart and I was sitting on this donkey cart, bouncing around on the road there, and that's when it flashed on me that I was gonna go back to America and get serious and do what it is that I do, because by that time people didn't know what it was that I did. All kinds of people, most people don't know what I do, only the people that see our show know what it is that I do, the rest of the people just have to imagine it.

Notice how the comments complement Dylan's remarks from the *Biograph* essay featured previously. He certainly has a specific take on this matter. From all of this, we may conclude that Dylan's dissatisfaction with the Tour '74 experience solidified his view that "the people" were out of touch with his work. Although he told Sloman that the tour with The Band was in the "past" and that he was more concerned with his "present," the music industry's corporate orientation fueled his desire for a simpler, more accessible presentation of his music. I mean, just look at the scene he described to Sloman: riding a donkey-pulled cart across the Corsica landscape thinking of a kinder, gentler musical world in which "the people" gather around the musician and share in the magic of what he does. What an idealistic daydream. What an inspiration. Consequently, when he returned to America he was ready for the prescribed change, as he relayed to Gregg Kilday: "I was ready to do something different, something new, and this is what it turned out to be."

The biographers describe the post–*Blood On The Tracks* Bob Dylan, his return to New York City, his work with Jacques Levy, and his complicated personal situation. While writing with Levy and recording the new material with his new band, Dylan's urge for "something different" gained focus. As he enjoyed his social life with his old friends from the folk-posturing period, he devised a plan that would satisfy his creative state of mind, take his work to "the people," and explore a form of artistic expression that has always stimulated his imagination. Thus, the RTR tour and the *Renaldo & Clara* film were born. Bob Spitz reports that Dylan's motivations may have been more social that artistic. He claims the auteur desired "companionship" as much as anything else. Spitz explains,

> For many of those who survived the Sixties, it was a confusing and im-
> personal time. Reputations had faded, finances dwindled, and it became
> impossible for once-famous rock stars to nail down a paying gig. Bob
> Dylan wasn't affected professionally by the cruel generational shift, but
> he certainly ached for the good ol' days. And the camaraderie. His own
> family was falling apart. He was lonelier than hell. And so, as a result, he
> manufactured this big musical family to help fill the void.

That Dylan often referred to the RTR participants as a "family" reinforces Spitz's claim. Still, it is hard to say what the prime motivator was, but it is not hard to report that Dylan devised an unprecedented plan. He assembled his large musical family, hired the army of technicians necessary to stage the RTR shows and film the movie, retained the personnel necessary for the advance work (e.g., secure venues, obtain housing, organize transportation, and manage ticket sales), and charted a course through New England that stopped—virtually unannounced—at all sorts of venues (some small, some medium-sized, some large). Dylan's emphasis on smaller venues was a key ingredient of his new musical formula, as he explained to Sloman:

> Why small halls? Because the atmosphere in small halls is more conducive
> to what we do. We're gonna play big halls too, but there's no pattern for
> it. We got a big show so we're gonna have to, you know, we got expenses
> to meet. So we're gonna have to play some big halls; I think the biggest
> one is maybe twelve thousand.... The strongest handle that I have on
> this whole thing right now, is it's like a family thing, really. I was talking
> to David Blue the other night and we were saying about how you rode
> your fame to the fullest, then it was like you were recycling some of it....
> These are all the people that have meaning in my life, they're all involved
> in the show. I wouldn't do it otherwise.

As the idea unfolded, the Village "family" met to discuss the logistics. During one gathering at the Gramercy Hotel (celebrating Steve Soles's birthday), a bartender suggested that Dylan name his tour "Rolling Thunder." Sloman claims that Dylan stared at the bartender and replied, "I was just sitting outside my house one day, thinking about a name for this tour, when all of a sudden, I looked into the sky and I heard a *boom*!" Dylan reported that more "booms" followed, "rolling from west to east," so he decided to name his tour "Rolling Thunder." The bartender inquired if he understood what that phrase means to "the Indians," and Dylan answered no. According to our Remy-serving bartender, it means "speaking truth." A satisfied Bob Dylan returned to his beverage.

We begin with the RTR plan. Spitz, Sloman, and other sources cite Faris Bouhafa's recollections of his initial attempts to organize the tour and seek funding from Columbia Records. He contacted various promoters, venues, technical personnel, ticket outlets, bus lines, hotel/motel chains, and everything the tour would require. Bouhafa told Sloman that Dylan wanted some sort of off-Broadway-type production that could, in theory, run forever. In other words, the auteur wanted a self-contained tour. He wanted the RTR to have its own sound and lighting systems, supporting technical crew, and transportation so that all that would be necessary to acquire would be the stage itself. From this perspective, the RTR need only call ahead, secure a stage, bring in its own promotion staff (to distribute flyers, talk to radio stations, and set up ticket sales), and magically appear whenever and wherever it wanted. No Tour '74 mail-order ticket distribution here. No sir. The RTR would roll in, offer its thunder to the people, speak the truth, and move on to the next impulse. It was as simple—and magical—as that. Bouhafa put it all together, submitted his findings to Columbia (via either a two- or four-page memo; sources vary), and received a firm response from Dylan's record company; according to Spitz, it read, "Bullshit—this will never happen." Dylan's attempt to take his musical revue to the people during the nation's bicentennial celebration was considered to be a joke. Subsequently, the auteur took matters into his own hands.

First, he secured the "house band" by retaining the musicians who worked on *Desire* (Rob Stoner, Howie Wyeth, and Scarlett Rivera). He added Steve Soles, David Mansfield, Mick Ronson, Luther Rix, Roger McGuinn, T-Bone Burnette, Ronee Blakley (also an actress), David Blue, Jack Elliott, and a remarkable blast from Dylan's past, Joan Baez. After a ten-year separation, Bob Neuwirth returned to Team Dylan as well. Allen Ginsberg agreed to participate. Jacques Levy signed on to stage the show. Later, Joni Mitchell also joined the RTR. With a formidable list of musicians in tow, Dylan turned to an old friend from the early 1950s to manage the operation. Lou Kemp—a successful owner of several fish-processing operations in Minnesota—attended summer camp with young Bob Zimmerman, and they have remained friends ever since. He was entrusted with the RTR's supervision. For assistance, Kemp hired Barry Imhoff, formerly of Bill Graham's promotional business. Both men worked with Dylan during the Tour '74 operation. Therefore, they understood their business. The Kemp-Imhoff team secured the sound and lighting systems, built the promotional staff, conducted the necessary advance work, coordinated the tour's media relations (such as they were), and, perhaps most of all, insulated Dylan and the musicians from any outside distractions (hence, the very restrictive media plan). The RTR may have been a wild and crazy—and perhaps even impulsive—idea, but it was professionally managed.

This professional orientation appeared in the film side of the RTR operation as well. The plan was simple: Play the shows, pay the bills (everybody was salaried and received a daily road per diem), and channel any profits into the film. Team Dylan hired Mel Howard to oversee the filmmaking as well as experienced technicians such as David Meyers, Larry Johnson, and Dylan veteran Howard Alk. Sam Shepard was brought onboard as a screenwriter, although that role faded as quickly as Sloman's stint with *Rolling Stone*. With time, professional actors (e.g., Harry Dean Stanton and Helen Kallianiotes) were also invited to participate. As Dylan told Gregg Kilday much later, "We needed people who could stand in front of the camera and set an example for the rest of us." Four camera crews produced a reported 100 hours of film from the RTR shows that also contained the various scripted, spontaneous, and spontaneously scripted "scenes" that unfolded whenever and wherever the cinematic urge struck. What a crew! Ratso Sloman offers this colorful take on the RTR operation: "The Rolling Thunder Revue was a caravan of gypsies, hoboes, trapeze artists, lonesome guitar stranglers, and spiritual green berets who came into your town for your daughters and left with your minds. They took to the road in the fall of '75. . . . And they barnstormed for six weeks, shaking up the great Northeast, making a quick foray over the border into the land of snow. Then, with a bang at Madison Square Garden, playing to twenty thousand in a benefit for Rubin 'Hurricane' Carter, it was over." That was the first leg of the Rolling Thunder Revue.

The process was fascinating. Lou Kemp explained the ticket distribution plan as one that was, in fact, true to Dylan's Corsica dream of taking the music to the people. He told Sloman that ticket coordinator Jerry Seltzer entered a location where a venue was secured some five or six days before the scheduled show with printed tickets in hand (sometimes, Kemp or Imhoff did not even tell the venue who was performing). He would post handbills and visit local radio stations to announce the show (occasionally, he purchased a radio spot). From there, a word-of-mouth distribution plan took over and anybody could buy whatever they wanted. No mail order. No central processing. Just tickets on sale to the people for seven to nine dollars (reported ticket prices vary). On several occasions, the RTR did two shows in one night, thus doubling the ticket sales for that location. Without the glitter and glamour of the Tour '74 extravaganza, the RTR was a profitable enterprise. This was not a charity operation; to the contrary, the performers and technicians were paid, the audience paid for admission, and Kemp-Imhoff ran an efficient business that covered tour and film costs in a realistic manner.

The results involved one fantastic six-week period. Opening in Plymouth, Massachusetts (the Plymouth Rock–pilgrim imagery rang true in this bicentennial event), the RTR rolled across New England and through North Dartmouth, Lowell, Providence, Springfield, Burlington, Durham, Westbury, New Haven, over to Niagara Falls and Rochester, back to Worcester, Cambridge, Boston, Waltham, Hartford, up to Augusta and Bangor, across the border to Quebec City, Toronto, Montreal, down to Clinton State Prison (the New Jersey institution housing Carter) to New York for the Carter benefit, and over a month later to Houston, Texas, for a second Carter fundraiser. At one point in the tour, Chief Rolling Thunder (according to *Newsweek*, a "celebrated Cherokee medicine man") joined the troupe for a private ceremony by the ocean in which the participants blessed their gathering and celebrated their cause. Throughout the tour, the troupe scouted film locations, concocted scenes for the film, and filmed scenes wherever and whenever they could while the stagehands prepared for that night's show. After a day of filming or planning, the performers put on their show, the crew loaded their gear, and the postshow madness ensued. From the sources I've consulted, it appears that every location featured all of the hospitality that one associates with a professionally staged entertainment tour. Food and beverages were available at specific locations after shows. Security was maintained at all times. And the RTR participants frolicked in their traveling playpen.

Jacques Levy handled the show's staging. After his first full rehearsal, he immediately encountered a significant problem: The show was eight hours long! He quickly pared down the proceedings by eliminating Ginsberg's reading of "Howl" and cutting each act's set list until he reached a more manageable four-hour show. Shows typically opened with Neuwirth (who then served as the RTR master of ceremonies) followed by Burnett, Stoner, Soles, Ronson, Blakley, Elliott, and perhaps a song by McGuinn, then an unannounced Dylan appeared for several songs. After intermission, Dylan and Baez opened the show's second half, followed by a Baez set and various combinations of performers to close out the show. Typically, the stage filled for a unified closer via Woody Guthrie's "This Land Is Your Land." Levy explained his staging to Howard Sounes:

> I was able to make this stuff very theatrical in the sense that the audience was taken on a ride. For the beginning of the evening I would have the whole band come on and each of the guys would do a number. We'd go through a chunk of the program like that before we got to the next segment and during that time, in between songs, I would turn everything shadowy blueish. Some people would go off and others would come on and, at one point, I just had Bob come on without any introduction. At first the crowd didn't think it was him, because the big star usually comes on last. He had a hat on and he would be in the shadows, standing there with the band, and they would start up a song and, little by little, lights would come up and it would be him playing along on somebody else's song. The crowd would go crazy.

During the Halloween night show, Dylan appeared wearing a mask that Ginsberg deemed his "transparent life mask" (according to Sloman). Stagehands wore shirts with "Bob who?" inscribed across the front. Dylan's ever-present hat (draped with flowers) complemented his whiteface stage makeup to present the antistar (Dylan often told interviewers that the makeup idea came from Italian street actors). No big send-up introduced him to the crowd. No piercing spotlights separated him from his troupe. No. A subdued Bob Dylan appeared on stage only to erupt into some of the most dynamic, energetic performances of his entire career. Echoing the frenetic style that characterized his performances in *Eat The Document*, Dylan pranced across the stage, his blue eyes piercing through his stage makeup as he barked his way through his material. He debuted the new *Desire* material (Rivera's performances were stunning), he recast several older songs, and everything was performed via a manic intensity that was nothing less than electrifying. They may have brought him onstage in a low-key way, but once onstage, Bob Dylan exploded. Although Baez and the others offered memorable performances throughout the six weeks of the RTR, Dylan's acts were the tour's signature moments. The troupe established the show's tone, Levy dressed the proceedings systematically, and Dylan delivered performances that conveyed his satisfaction with this coordinated attempt to take his music to "the people."

There were, of course, those odd or uncomfortable moments in the tour. The show at Clinton State Prison had its rough edges (e.g., Joni Mitchell took the rude audience to task). The huge affair at Madison Square Garden provided its own problems. The music press cast its cynical views on the tour. The backstage melodramas unfolded night after night. But all in all, the plan succeeded. Dylan's wife, kids, and mother joined the tour. The camaraderie was joyful. The music was historic. It was all good. Later, in April 1976, Dylan reassembled much of the original crew and set off on a second leg, traveling throughout the South toward the West for two months. The second RTR leg opened in Lakeland, Florida, and traveled through St. Petersburg, Tampa, Clearwater, Orlando, Gainesville, Tallahassee, and Pensacola, up to Mobile and Hattiesburg, down to New Orleans and Baton Rouge, over to Houston, Corpus Christi, San Antonio, Austin, Gatesville, and Fort Worth, up to Oklahoma City and Wichita, and over to Fort Collins, Colorado, and Salt Lake City. The Fort Collins show was broadcast on NBC and released as an album. By all accounts, the RTR's second leg lacked the fire of its initial segment; nevertheless, Dylan's attempt to take what he does to the people was thorough. Still, that was only part of the Rolling Thunder Plan. As the troupe cruised across New England, into Canada, down to New Jersey, and up to New York City, the cameras rolled and rolled and rolled and rolled. The results came to be known as *Renaldo & Clara*.

During the discussion regarding the making of the *Desire* album and Jacques Levy's role in that process, I cited a comment from Levy about his coauthor's writing style. There, Levy noted that it is difficult for Bob Dylan to "stick with a narrative" when writing a song. Instead, Levy argued, Dylan prefers a "series of images" that are, at times, 'quite abstract." Levy maintained that these images work "little by little" to "open up the idea" that the auteur's pursuing, but instead of "one long narrative" carrying that "idea," Dylan elects to use "many narratives" to do his job (often lasting for a mere verse or two). Levy concluded that he brought a new approach to the Dylan process, one in the style of "prose," "movies," or "theatre." Levy has a compelling point. Though we understand that Dylan has used extended narratives to present his ideas on multiple occasions (most recently with "Lily" on *Blood On The Tracks*), the work with Levy embellished that approach. Now he ignores Levy's methods and deploys "many narratives" to tell the tale of *Renaldo & Clara*. In his 1978 *Playboy* interview, Dylan explained that his decision to use overlapping narratives was grounded in his experiences with the *Eat The Document* film. After spending hours and hours with the raw *Document* footage, Dylan learned a valuable lesson:

> Well, up until that time, they had been concerned with the linear story line. It was on one plane and in one dimension only. And the more I looked at the film, the more I realized that you could get more into film than just one train of thought. My mind works that way, anyway. We tend to work on different levels. So I was seeing a lot of those levels in the footage. But technically, I didn't know how to do what my mind was telling me could be done.

Through *Renaldo & Clara*, Bob Dylan brought his technical skills up to the level of his mental imagery.

The cinematic lessons of *Dont Look Back*, *Eat The Document*, and *Pat Garrett and Billy The Kid* are synthesized with Dylan's songwriting techniques in the three hours and fifty-two minutes of *Renaldo & Clara*. The direct cinema style appears in multiple scenes. Extended performance segments populate the film. A few—not many—but a few of the film's "many narratives" operate in linear fashions. And the storytelling style that rendered "Highway 61 Revisited" abounds. It is all here in *Renaldo & Clara*. This is not *Tarantula*. These narratives make sense in their own idiosyncratic ways. You might as well read *Tarantula* backwards. This is different. Characters do coherent things (weird, but coherent). There is plot progression from time to time. There are patterns—many of them quite interesting—that lend themselves to interpretation. Therefore, I may do here what I couldn't do with *Tarantula*; that is, I may interpret it. *Tarantula* is so chaotic that there is just not much you can say. There is a lot to say about *Renaldo & Clara*. While some scenes appear to be straight from a Keystone Cops flick, others are more representative of *Citizen Kane*. All of it is unique to Bob Dylan's oeuvre.

Renaldo & Clara was written, directed, and produced by Bob Dylan. He told Jonathan Cott that he made the movie "for a specific bunch of people and myself, and that's all." If so, this is quite the pet project. The film cost some $1.25 million to produce (according to the *Los Angeles Times*' Gregg Kilday and the *Washington Post*'s Joel Kotkin). Again, sources report Dylan accumulated over 100 hours of film (Kilday reports the movie was edited out of 40 hours of film) and set about the arduous task of molding his four-hour statement from those raw materials. The subsequent movie was distributed by David Zimmerman's Minnesota-based company, Circuit Films. The *Washington Post* also reports that "elaborate and potentially lucrative distribution and soundtrack deals from major companies" were rejected "in order to keep the project Dylan-dominated" (according to Dylan press aide Paul Wasserman). I guess Dylan learned a powerful lesson from his experiences with Sam Peckinpah and that director's problems with his sponsoring studio's editing procedures. The original four-hour version suffered immediate—and, on occasion, severely harsh—criticism, which inspired Dylan to turn over the film to his brother to cut it down to a more manageable two-hour version. That, too, was panned by the press. As a result, the filmmaker pulled his celluloid debut from the public view. It has never been released on video, and it is one of the many artifacts that the world of Dylanology treasures. To be sure, there is only one *Renaldo & Clara* (regardless of its length).

Dylan explained his motivations for the film to the *Washington Post*: "I don't know nothing about making movies. I don't consider myself a filmmaker in the fashionable sense of the word or in the scholastic sense of the word. I don't think of myself as a filmmaker. If DeVinci [*sic*] were alive or Van Gogh, or if Rembrandt were alive, they'd be making films too." Notice that Dylan didn't say "if James Joyce were alive" or "if Shakespeare were still with us," or, for that matter, "If Mozart, Beethoven, or Benny Goodman were alive, they'd be making films." No. He referenced *painters*. In *Renaldo & Clara*, Norman Raeben meets D. A. Pennebaker and Sam Peckinpah through the eyes of Bob Zimmerman of Hibbing, Minnesota, and the results are, in their own special way, predictable. Time and space are twisted, as per Raeben's instruction. Unobtrusive camera shots are frequently used, as per Pennebaker's methods. Scenes with an edge unfold in rebellious, melodramatic ways, as per Peckinpah's cinema. Bob Zimmerman assimilates instruction and information extraordinarily well—what he witnesses, he somehow makes his own—and this film is a product of that instinctive ability.

Mel Howard shared his thoughts about the film's style in an extended conversation with Ratso Sloman. There, he noted how documentary filmmakers like Dave Meyers were hired to make a film that turned out to be something other than a documentary. Howard explained how the film's characters would mug for the cameras and transform scenes in unpredictable ways. After all, most of the participants were not professional actors; therefore, they acted unconventionally. Although Dylan told

Kilday that he's "not too attuned to documentaries," he reported that the film could be construed in that fashion since "it was shot with 16mm hand-held cameras." In his *Rolling Stone* interview, Dylan describes the use of "hold shots" for dramatic effect and how the film could be divided into one third "improvised" scenes, one third "determined" scenes, and one third "blind luck." He also offers this explanation of the production process:

> What we did was to cut up reality and make it more real. . . . Everyone from the cameramen to the water boy, from the wardrobe people to the sound people was just as important as anyone else in the making of the film. There weren't any roles that well defined. The money was coming in the front door and going out the back door: the Rolling Thunder tour sponsored the movie. And I had faith and trust in the people who helped me do the film, and they had faith and trust in me.

Dylan described the results in a predictable fashion, telling *Playboy*, "The movie to me is more a painting than music. It *is* a painting. It's a painting coming alive off a wall. That's why we're making it. Painters can contain their artistic turmoil; in another age, moviemakers would most likely be painters." As you can see, Dylan is consistent in his accounts of his motivations, his orientation, and his objectives. He is not playing with the press in these *Renaldo & Clara* interviews. The man is on a mission.

To be sure, a lot of people hit the road with Bob and Sara Dylan and the Rolling Thunder Revue. Many of those people are present in *Renaldo & Clara*. The film features the Dylans, Joan Baez, Bob Neuwirth, Ronee Blakley, Allen Ginsberg, Jack Elliot, David Blue, Harry Dean Stanton, Steven Soles, Rob Stoner, Mick Ronson, Helen Kallianiotes, Sam Shepard, Ronnie Hawkins, and most of the musicians and singers from the tour. A few tour members—Joni Mitchell is one—requested not to be featured in the film (she lost). Jacques Levy is the film's stage director. Hurricane Carter appears for an extended segment. People from the street, the audience, or the road appear in droves. We have that veritable cast of thousands—and they appear in varying ways in just as many story lines.

The movie unfolds by way of four cinematic strategies: the running scene, the detailed segment, the one-off act, and musical performances. There is no master plot or overriding theme to this movie. To devise one is to impose order on intentional chaos. Certain running scenes punctuate the viewing experience, but they do not contribute any form of narrative structure or flow. The characters vary with each shot. You never know who is who. The movie opens with Dylan singing "When I Paint My Masterpiece" while wearing his transparent life mask (that is the kind of symbolism that permeates the film). He wears a clear but slightly distorted mask that does not communicate anything other than it is a mask. When Bob Dylan is Bob Dylan and when Bob Dylan is Renaldo is more than uncertain. Supposedly, Renaldo wears that colorful hat I mentioned earlier; however, that does not work either, since the one time Renaldo is identified *by name* he is without headwear. Dylan's explanation to Ron Rosenbaum about "Bob Dylan's" role in the film is utterly fascinating: "His voice is there, his songs are used, but Bob's not in the movie. It would be silly. Did you ever see a Picasso painting with Picasso in the picture? You only see his work." (There's a little "Bob-on-Bob" for you!) Hence, we conclude that when we see Bob

Zimmerman in this film, he is always Renaldo. When Sara Dylan is Clara, a hitch-hiker, a conspiring criminal, the "woman in white," or a hooker working in a brothel is as uncertain as Bob Neuwirth's ever-changing roles (the Masked Tortilla is classic Neuwirth—too bad he did not use his Lyndon Johnson imitation). David Blue is always David Blue. Ronnie Hawkins is always Bob Dylan (I think). Allen Ginsberg is always some variation of Allen Ginsberg. Characters are scene-dependent, and the scenes are dependent on the actors', the director's, and the moment's whims. To that end, Charles Champlin deems the film to be a "Gone With the Whim" home movie, proving that all critics are closet comedians.

The running scenes appear in two styles: one extended, the other less so. The controlling running scenes—and I use that phrase in the loosest possible sense—are the David Blue historical lessons; the love triangle between the woman in white, Renaldo, and Clara; the Jesus Series; the activities of a sporting house (in Renaldo's words); a diner scene with a consistent cast of unnamed characters; a cabaret featuring a variety of performances by different people (some identified, others not); and a bordello occupied by the women of the Rolling Thunder Revue and visited by their male colleagues. Those seven running scenes come and go whenever somebody decided for them to come and go. Other segments recur with less frequency, but they still attain the status of a running scene. There are a host of "movement" scenes that feature shots of trucks, trains, and campers rolling wherever they are going; there are three scenes from Columbia Records offices that discuss the marketing of Dylan's product or nothing in particular; two scenes feature Ronnie Hawkins as Bob Dylan (two other scenes involve Hawkins, but I don't know who he is at that particular moment); three scenes involve street preachers and their inflammatory oratory; Rob Stoner argues with a woman over his touring in two scenes; two moments offer Sara as a hitchhiker (I guess) who is offered a ride by a trucker; and two scenes present Renaldo in a restaurant receiving a lecture on relationships from some guy. You think that makes for a busy production? Hey, we're just getting warmed up!

David Blue's historical lessons are interesting. Five of his six segments feature him having his way with a pinball machine as he recounts his personal history, Bob Dylan's emergence in New York City, and the varied activities in Greenwich Village at that time. Obviously, this film delves into the Dylan Myth and the circumstances that surrounded that phenomenon; in so doing, it appears that Blue attempts to separate fact from fiction in these scenes. Blue recalls the writing of "Blowin' In The Wind" and that magical moment when it was written and performed right on the spot in a folk club. He describes the activities around Gerde's Folk City and the people who frequented that venue. He mentions the New York poets that only "Bob" knew. Each time, he addresses the camera (when he is not playing the machine) and achieves a level of credibility that other actors fail to realize. This is straightforward stuff. You find yourself questioning it because of the mayhem that surrounds this bit, but Blue's comments appear to be factually accurate. Blue's final appearance seems to sum his role as he walks away from the pinball machine, looks into the camera, and argues that we are witnessing a myth since Bob Dylan is a regular guy with a family. To consider Dylan to be anything else, Blue concludes, is silly. The viewer is left to contemplate their history lesson.

The running scenes involving the sporting house, the diner, and the cabaret are not as detailed. Once Renaldo and Jack Elliot announce that they are off to the unnamed sporting house (as Renaldo uses that phrase, we see him smile for the *only* time in this four-hour movie), we cut away to road shots of beautiful New England before entering through the sporting house kitchen. Elliot seems to know the lady proprietor (I believe this is the character everyone calls "Momma"), but everything becomes fragmented from there. The movie cuts to scenes featuring people talking at the bar, Momma sings and sells her wares, she dresses Baez in a wedding gown, Baez and Renaldo discuss their relationship and the "what if" they had married, Ronee Blakley describes the perfect man to Renaldo at the bar, and other moments occur in fuzzy ways (Momma reads palms, blesses Ginsberg, and other acts). The film cuts in and out of these scenes in a chaotic manner. Scenes just pop up and go. At times, I wonder if the sporting house and the bordello are one and the same, but I don't think they are. Baez appears to be two different people in these respective scenes, so I'm going to separate them. The diner and cabaret scenes are distinctive. In the former, people sit around a table and discuss seeing Bob Dylan, talk about the nature of truth, and hear the philosophical expositions of a guy who seems to be the owner (Dylan deems him to be the "Greek chorus" in interviews). In the latter, a master of ceremonies introduces acts such as Ginsberg who do their thing (in Ginsberg's case, he reads his poetry). Audience shots, dancing scenes, and a brief segment in which Ronnie Hawkins is barred from entry by a stubborn Mick Ronson comprise this particular running scene (by the way, Dylan designates Ronson to be the "Guardian of the Gates" in his commentary—hey, I knew that! Right . . .). The film ends in the cabaret and seems to signify an "It's all a show" concluding statement (watch yourself, Larry!).

The Jesus Series, the bordello, and the love triangle vary in their complexity. The Jesus Series addresses the Bob Dylan Myth in its own curious way. As the movie flows, visual cuts to a cemetery appear from time to time that feature shots of Christ on the cross and other religious statues. At one point, the camera focuses on the cross as dogs bark in the background. Hounding Christ on his cross, are we? The shots just pop in and pop out. (The jump cut is *Renaldo & Clara*'s preferred transition.) One such visual involves a long shot of Renaldo standing beneath Christ on the cross in a manner that more than communicates that these two characters share a common experience. In a more concrete expression, Renaldo and Ginsberg tour the cemetery, visit Jack Kerouac's grave site, and contemplate various famous graves and their experiences with them. The key to this running segment—if *anything* can be a key to *anything* in this film—involves that moment when Renaldo and Ginsberg exit the cemetery and encounter a group of kids. The men ask the children if they believe in God. They answer in unison, Yes! They ask the kids what God looks like; does he have eyes, a beard, and other facial features? Renaldo then inquires if he plays guitar? They answer in unison: No! Clearly, the film is sympathetic with the Jesus story. Dylan explained the symbolism to *Rolling Stone*: "Jesus is . . . well, I'm not using Jesus in the film so much as I'm using the *concept* of Jesus—the idea of Jesus as a man, not the virgin birth." That clears that up!

The bordello running scene rivals the love triangle in its frequency of appearance. Things get more than a little bit strange in these scenes: A violin-playing male angel appears (David Mansfield) and attracts his lady for the evening; Ginsberg bares his soul to his temporary concubines; people make out or dance in lustful ways; and our ladies of the evening sit about, manicure themselves, and discuss the vicissitudes of their way of life. At moments, the ladies lay about—seemingly piled upon one another—as they convey a sense of boredom with their circumstance. Though lustful love abounds, its transitory qualities are problematic for our ladies of the evening. Still, they render their services, listen to the babblings of their clients, and contemplate a better life.

The love triangle is *Renaldo & Clara*'s centerpiece. This running scene builds slowly. The woman in white (originally, Sara) is presented leaving a large home in a horse-drawn carriage, shots of and from the carriage appear via jump cuts, then she arrives at her destination carrying her rose (the women carry a lot of roses in this film), disembarks, enters a doorway, turns to walk up the stairs, and suddenly is replaced by Baez. It is a magical transformation. Sara's head is lowered as she exits the carriage, and when she raises her head, she is someone else. Eventually, the woman in white arrives outside an apartment or hotel door. We've seen the other side of that door for a few shots, but were unaware of it. Inside the room is none other than Renaldo and Clara, for the first time identified by name. Renaldo consumes his liquor straight from the bottle as he plays guitar for Clara, receives massages from Clara, makes out with Clara, and listens to Clara talk. Clara seems to be reeling in her man as snippets of conversation appear. Suddenly, the woman in white enters (always, red rose in hand). She simply stands there and gazes down on the scene before her. The film cuts to and from this scenario with considerable frequency; at times jumping to a shot of Baez standing there, or of Clara embracing Renaldo as Baez looks on with this blank expression on her face. Clara inquires as to the woman's identity and receives nothing but a worried look from her lover. Renaldo drinks and remains calm (you get the impression that he has been here before). Clara asks if the woman is in the correct room. No answer. A staredown ensues. After a trip to the cemetery with Renaldo and Ginsberg, Baez declares she can no longer share Renaldo. Renaldo addresses the two women. He promises to tell the truth (his eagerness betrays his sincerity). He asks what they would like to know about anything. He admits his feelings for both women. The movie cuts to a performance scene before returning to our relational drama. When we return, the ladies are beginning to bond as they laugh and have fun at Renaldo's expense. Baez gives Renaldo a note and tells him to travel to that address to meet her later. Clara just sits there. The woman in white departs. Renaldo and Clara resume their activities. We cut away. When we return, Clara announces her feelings for Baez (her newfound sister) as Renaldo turns to a mirror and applies the whiteface makeup that he wears as he performs during the Rolling Thunder Revue. Clara acknowledges her love for Renaldo and its temporary qualities. The scene cuts to a diner conversation about the nature of truthfulness before turning to a performance of "Tangled Up In Blue." Renaldo, Clara, and the woman in white disappear, probably awaiting the seventeen-hour sequel to *Renaldo & Clara*.

These running scenes are interspersed throughout the film in uneven ways. There is no balance or overt logic to their appearances. A shot of the woman in white's carriage may be placed between a performance scene or an one-off act in a fleeting manner—it is just a flash. David Blue's bit is the most direct. The diner and cabaret scenes are not difficult to follow, although they appear chaotically and their contents vary. The sporting house and bordello bits just appear without warning, and their respective scenes feature varying degrees of sophistication. The Jesus Series begs for interpretation just as the love triangle teases the interpretative process. Aside from Blue's nostalgia, none of these scenarios offers anything positive. The people in the bordello may get their jollies, but it is a vacuous experience. Everybody, it seems, has problems. People moan and groan all the time. The characters in the diner may enjoy a lively conversation, but nothing is ever resolved. The sporting house is a scene magnet, drawing us into a cracked mirror view of the characters involved. Like a busy bar on a Saturday night, there are dozens of dramas unfolding in their own ways. Regardless of their narrative complexity or coherence, the running scenes represent the heart of the *Renaldo & Clara* viewing experience.

The detailed segments portrayed in *Renaldo & Clara* are limited in number. An extended treatment of a party in an Indian community and the Rubin Carter segment are our two detailed episodes. Although we jump in and out of the Indian party scene, the "Hurricane" portion is presented in an uninterrupted manner. I'm not certain what the agenda was with the Indians. Actually, I'm not certain where the scene transpires. It appears to take place inside a church or some sort of community hall (we see shots of Indian kids running around outside in anticipation of the Rolling Thunder arrival), and the participants are most certainly Indians, so I make that conclusion. It is definitely a community of people. Our opening view of the festivities involves the fine meal the hosts have prepared for their guests. Apparently, the Rolling Thunder Revue arrives in shifts, as we see roadies and others eating and talking with their hosts while the musicians appear later. Renaldo's entrance is a grand one as the camera follows him as he makes his way through the crowd. Different things pop up and go away during this extended segment. The Masked Tortilla moves around, striking up aggressive conversations with people. A tribal leader gives a speech in which he traces the tribe's move from North Carolina, and discusses their storied past. The segment offers shot after shot of people milling around, dancing, arguing, or eating. When Renaldo arrives, we hear Dylan singing "People Get Ready" in the backing soundtrack as Renaldo greets his hosts. I presume, then, that *Renaldo & Clara* offers this detailed segment in order to demonstrate how the Revue reached out to all segments of society—not just those who could afford expensive tickets to a local sports arena. We have, then, a scene featuring "the people."

Our other detailed segment also reaches out to a minority group. The Rubin Carter segment is the film's longest single scene. Shot at the RTR appearance at Clinton State Prison, it opens with Roger McGuinn singing "Knockin' On Heaven's Door" before a predominantly Black audience. We see Ginsberg moving amongst the crowd and Joan Baez dancing with a Black guy before we cut to a Rubin Carter press conference. Of course, a Rolling Thunder version of "Hurricane" plays in the background, fading in and out. The segment displays an obvious agenda. It communicates, in no uncertain terms, Carter's and a sampling of Black people's opinions about his imprisonment. Carter sits calmly with his huge hands folded during the press conference. He answers each question—no matter how stupid it might be—in a strong, self-assured manner. He is as philosophical as humanly possible. He exudes confidence. From watching him, you would never think of him as a boxer—much less a murderer. He is far more like a professor addressing his class (the reporters even sit at his feet). The people on the street do not share this characteristic. We witness all sorts of Black people as the camera sets up camp on a busy (I presume) New Jersey street and solicits people's opinions of the Carter case. Several young kids do not have a clue, although they are pleased to be on television. One well-spoken Black lady seizes the opportunity to offer her version of the end times before someone informs her that that's not the question at hand (she gracefully dismisses herself at that point). One Black man offers his considered opinion that he's not disappointed with the Carter situation because he never had the expectation that justice would be served. When you don't hold that expectation, the man reasons, you can't suffer disappointment (he eats a hamburger as he talks in a most credible manner—unfortunately, this man makes a lot of sense). Several of the participants are rough in their expositions; nevertheless, they appear to know of which they speak: Rubin Carter was done in by the White System. Toward the end of this protracted segment, an older White man appears in his own grouchy way. When he finally understands what is going on, he refuses to offer his opinion for fear the crowd will have its way with him. He is a former cop.

These two detailed segments portray the Rolling Thunder Outreach Program. The Revue travels out to the hinterland and embraces the country's original citizenry. They graciously accept their hosts' hospitality (the Masked Tortilla is our lone exception; Neuwirth wants to argue with everybody) and provide a platform for their leaders to express themselves. It's all good. Then, the Revue goes to the city. There they embrace another minority group, this time in the name of the Hurricane. The man was a contender, but he was robbed. *Renaldo & Clara* takes time out of its busy schedule to relate how the former boxer and those around him feel about that situation. The moral of the story is crystal clear: You better watch White people. They will overthrow your culture, incarcerate your innocent, and build record companies to use and abuse your talent.

From our Rolling Thunder editorial page, we turn to the one-off acts that float interminably throughout this four-hour film. By my humble count, we have nine one-off scenes along with around six or seven sets of "nothing shots" that do even less than the one-offs. Herein lies the busyness of this very busy film. Our first one-off appears during the film's fourth scene, in which Renaldo is featured playing guitar with Helen Kallianiotes hanging lustfully over his shoulder while a mechanic moves about the room (a garage, I presume). The mechanic mutters something about a motorcycle, while the guitar player's and his woman's minds are obviously elsewhere. One compelling one-off features Ronnie Hawkins/Bob Dylan doing his best to persuade a local farm girl (Ruth Tyrangeil) to disobey her father's will and join the tour with him. Hawkins is relentless in this lengthy scene. He lays it on and on and on. At one point, she requests time to think, but Hawkins will have none of that. He is like a used car salesman running for president; providing time for thought will not serve his persuasive strategy. We have no idea what happens. (We see the girl later in the film, but she could have been playing Tarzan at that moment.)

Other one-offs involve a scene with Sara and a man (I think Sam Shepard) discussing the virtues of Jack Daniels and its important role in life. Another features the road crew systematically setting up that evening's show somewhere (the crew is *extremely* professional). Another portrays a conversation between Sara and Shepard in which they discuss their relationship, his relational needs, and her response to those conditions (Sara appears to be in her prostitute role, but I'm not certain). One one-off offers what appears to be the Revue's kickoff ceremonies. With a beautiful New England ocean scene as a backdrop, the troupe unifies in its mission and dutifully celebrates its cause (drinking, dancing, and chanting). Another one-off is a madcap portrayal of Harry Dean Stanton escaping jail with the assistance of Sara and Neuwirth. Sara walks through downtown streets carrying a huge rope, stops by a car containing Neuwirth and tosses the rope inside, Neuwirth walks down the street and throws the rope over the jailhouse wall, Stanton climbs over the wall, and they celebrate briefly before he scurries down the street in jail attire. We later see Stanton nervously riding in a train, but I'm not certain if he is the same character or not (he could have been Dick Tracy at that moment).

Stanton does appear in another one-off, however. In this particular tale, he is the owner of a horse that is traded for Joan Baez. I kid you not. Renaldo and Baez are stomping across a snow-covered field for some unknown reason. They walk up to a barn. The horse emerges, and the next thing we know Jack Elliot informs Stanton of the trade. Baez is delivered to him, and they promptly sit down and begin kissing passionately. Although Elliot is clearly disgusted by the trade and Renaldo just rides off, Stanton and Baez appear to be satisfied with the arrangement and continue to enjoy their moment. Joan Baez is traded for a horse. The symbolism is intoxicating.

What is not intoxicating is our final one-off and a domestic fight scene between "Ramon" (Steven Soles) and "Mrs. Dylan" (Ronee Blakley). This scene opens with Mrs. Dylan readying herself for that evening's show. As she applies her makeup she requests a drink, and Ramon dutifully responds. But something is bothering Ramon. He paces back and forth in an angry way. He complains about the time Mrs. Dylan requires to prepare for the gig, and lodges that complaint time and again (cursing the woman and her activities). She wants to know the *real* problem, but he is not talking. Finally, he explodes. He knows she is having an affair, and a fight breaks out. They throw each other around as Mrs. Dylan screams that this is the last time she will endure this treatment. The scene is quite violent. Once they calm down, she tells Ramon that he has driven her into the arms of another because of his inattentiveness (she claims they have not had sex for three years). He does not deny the claim. She persists. Then the scene cuts to a Blakley performance segment. Dylan is precise in his explanation of this particular scene in *Rolling Stone*. He recalls that this was a "half-improvised" scene in which Soles plays Mrs. Dylan's "dead lover" who "appears as a ghost in the bathroom, and they argue in front of the mirror." Oh my. There is *no way* to ascertain this from viewing the film; in fact, the scene extends beyond the mirror reflection and spills over into another room (not to mention that this ghost serves cocktails on demand). The "suspension of belief" quotient associated with *Renaldo & Clara* may reach its peak in this particular scene.

Well now, that's quite the sequence, isn't it? A guitar player and his girl with a mechanic, a jailbreak, the roadies at work, a conversation between lovers, a physical fight between Mrs. Dylan and a ghost, a defense for Jack Daniels' place in the world, a party, and a bit of Rolling Thunder–style commerce. What is the common thread? What holds this routine together? The answer arrives as quickly as the question is posed. All of the characters are carbon-based (oops, that fails too; one character was a ghost).

Taking us further into the Rolling Thunder twilight zone is the appropriately named "nothing" shot. Here some activity pops up for no apparent reason other than providing a segue to the next chaotic scene. The technique appears immediately. The moment our masked auteur completes his opening song, we're taken to a scene in which cast members (featuring McGuinn, Joni Mitchell, and others) discuss their per diem and the tour's business arrangements. We suddenly cut away, never to return. Nothing shots involve quick backstage scenes, road trip visuals (shots of landscapes, towns, and/or people), an encounter between Neuwirth and a train conductor, a shot of Baez lustfully caressing her hairdryer as she laments her loneliness, and several "Monkees shots" (a Monkees shot is a reference to the 1960s TV show that shares that name) in which Renaldo or some cast member is shown running down a street or up a flight of stairs or down an alley for no apparent reason. It's just there. Some segues are tied to the respective running scenes (the love triangle, in particular, unfolds in this manner), but most of them involve the one-offs and nothing shots. They add incoherent continuity to the unfolding chaos.

To the extent that *Renaldo & Clara*'s running scenes represent the heart of the movie, the performance scenes are its soul. Predictably, music is everywhere in this film. Kilday (and others) report that forty-seven different songs appear throughout the movie. During the one-offs or detailed segments, music plays in the background. At times, certain musical passages appear to be associated with a given scene, as Dylan deploys Wagner's leitmotif system of theatrical presentation to his strategic ends. (Yeah, right.) Some of the performance scenes resemble the *Dont Look Back* approach in which we're taken to the beginning or middle of some act. These scenes include the Masked Tortilla reading poetry, bits of Jack Elliot performances, the beginning of Joan Baez's "Diamonds And Rust," parts of Ginsberg singing or reading poetry, brief shots of Roger McGuinn singing, an enthusiastic performance of the opening to "Eight Miles High" featuring a dancing Joan Baez before cutting away, parts of a Renaldo-Baez duet, parts of a Renaldo-McGuinn duet, parts of the band doing Bob Dylan's song "Catfish," and so on. The film jumps in and out of these musical moments as it jumps in and out of everything else. Like Baez, this movie dances with itself.

The full-song performances do an outstanding job of capturing the Rolling Thunder Revue in action. Renaldo performs the opening song, "Masterpiece," as well as "Isis," "A Hard Rain's A-Gonna Fall," "It Ain't Me, Babe," "It Takes A Train To Laugh," "Romance In Durango," "One More Cup Of Coffee," "Sara," "Tangled Up In Blue," and "Just Like A Woman" throughout the film (most of these songs are presented in their entirety). These performance scenes portray the small, crowded stages that typified the Revue. We see the dazzling violin work that Scarlet Rivera brings to the new Dylan sound. Rob Stoner's superb bass supports a host of guitar players that cut in and out of performance scenes. But the star of this show is Renaldo. Wearing whiteface makeup and his Renaldo hat, he tears into these songs with a demonic intensity. He jumps about during "Isis" as if he is possessed by the song's power. His eyes are piercing during his performance of "Tangled Up In Blue" as the camera grabs a tight facial shot and holds it throughout the song. Once more, Renaldo's performances remind you of the *Eat The Document* concert scenes as he shivers and shakes in a frenetic fashion, aggressively tearing his way through his songs. He stretches out his lyrics through emotional wails. He is the prototypical "man possessed." There are no casual performances here. Everything is fever-pitched and melodramatic. The Rolling Thunder Revue may drift from city to city, but once the crew sets the stage and the performers appear, it *explodes*. These explosions are *Renaldo & Clara*'s reason for being—indeed, the movie's soul—and the other activities offer varying forms of supporting material. You'd like to say the supporting scenes offer a glimpse of the Revue's offstage activities as per *Dont Look Back*, but in all honesty, I don't think the jailbreak scene was real and I think Baez is worth more than *one* horse.

So, that is *Renaldo & Clara*. Hopefully, the Dylan team will rerelease the film so that the general public may enjoy its riches. The various running scenes, the two detailed segments, the diverse one-off acts and nothing shots, and the energetic performance segments work in their own chaotic way to capture the Rolling Thunder Revue and the meaning of life, respectively. That Dylan toys with much of the movie's symbolism is certain. It is equally clear that the movie strives to establish specific points via its Outreach Program with the Indians and the Hurricane ordeal. Why the film chooses to present the women of Rolling Thunder as whores is open for interpretation (Dylan told Cott that he thinks the women in the film are "beautiful," as they "look like they've stepped out of a painting"). Why all of the women carry roses (supposedly a sign of "fertility," according to the Cott interview) and then engage in the cheapest lifestyles is a mystery. Why the film offers a central character that would trade a woman for a horse is unclear. Why women are presented as commodities is equally curious. David Blue certainly plays a role, but what function does that role ultimately perform? The conscious motivations that support Bob Dylan's *Renaldo & Clara* are presented via the host of interviews he conducted in promoting the film.

Dylan's interpretations of his film are fantastic, but consistent. He explained to Kilday that the film used masks to "reveal the inner self" of the characters in order to convey this point: "Things that happen in the outerday world are just manifestations of the inner mind. And what I was trying to capture was what the inner mind was going through." Subsequently, despite all of the attributions to Bob Dylan's life, Dylan reported that the film "is actually very little about me" and, instead, represents a "dream" (and that dream is not Bob Dylan's). He elaborated on this point to Cott: "This film concerns itself with the dream. . . . This film concerns itself only with the depth of the dream—the dream as seen in the mirror." Hence, the film ends with Renaldo laying on the floor before cutting to the final cabaret scene featuring a gentleman singing "In The Morning." Why? As Dylan told Cott, "The film had to end with him because he represents the fact that Renaldo could be dreaming. And he might be singing for Renaldo—representing him, the darkness representing the light." OK. To sum, let's return to the layered narrative approach I mention at the outset. Dylan deploys layer after layer of dreams, fantasies, and snippets of "reality" in order to communicate depth; moreover, he uses his mirror metaphor to communicate how that depth is a reflection of the inner self. These remarks to Cott elaborate on this evasive point: "This film reveals that there's a whole lot to reveal beneath the surface of the soul, but it's unthinkable. . . . It reveals the depths that there are to reveal. And that's the most you can ask, because things are really very invisible. You can't reveal the invisible. And this film goes as far as we can to reveal that." Now *that's* a mouthful. Dylan's conscious explanations of his work are buried in his personal metaphysics and his intense search for a comprehensive explanation for the inner-world—outerworld duality. There is *conflict* going on here—*inner conflict*. Allow me to pursue this inner conflict by way of another line of argument. I think the film massages an unconscious motivation that is slowly, but surely, working its way from the auteur's inner mind into the outer world that is his oeuvre. A movement is afoot, and *Renaldo & Clara* communicates the essence of that perspective.

Recently, renowned poetry professor and noted Dylanologist Christopher Ricks issued his much-anticipated interpretation of Bob Dylan's lifework. It is a courageous project. Professor Ricks brings his unparalleled knowledge of poetry to his substantial understanding of Dylan's art and renders an argument that I think is mighty brave. He builds a framework and demonstrates how Dylan's writings fall within that interpretive structure. He presents the seven so-called deadly sins (envy, covetousness, greed, sloth, lust, anger, and pride), the four "virtues" (justice, prudence, temperance, and fortitude), and the three "heavenly graces" (faith, hope, and charity) and demonstrates how various songs fall within the respective categories. His is not an argument that implies creative intention; to the contrary, he is quite specific on that matter:

> I believe that an artist is someone more than usually blessed with a cooperative unconscious or subconscious, more than usually able to effect things with the help of instincts and intuitions of which he or she is not necessarily conscious. Like the great athlete, the great artist is at once highly trained and deeply instinctual. So if I am asked whether I believe that Dylan is *conscious* of all the subtle effects of wording and timing that I suggest, I am perfectly happy to say that he probably isn't. And if I am right, then in this he is not less the artist but more. There are such things as unconscious intentions (think of the unthinking Freudian slip). What matters is that Dylan is doing the imagining, not that he be fully deliberatedly [*sic*] conscious of the countless intimations that are his art.

From there, Professor Ricks does his thing. Using snippets of lyrics or portions of songs (at times, entire songs) to argue the manifestations of the sins, virtues, and heavenly graces within the lifework, he places those expressions alongside noted works of poetry and discusses their similarities or differences. The end result is a wonder to behold. Devising taxonomies of this nature can be risky business in that critics occasionally force what they see into their predetermined categories; nevertheless, Christopher Ricks offers one thorough reading of the Dylan Canon and, in doing so, produces a valuable entry for the science of Dylanology.

Whereas I shy away from that approach in my work, I think that framework offers an exciting tool for interpreting *Renaldo & Clara*. Using Ricks's taxonomy, we are afforded one interpretive glimpse of an artifact that does not lend itself to holistic analysis. Taking the film's purposely fragmented nature and treating it as a single statement is more than tricky, I think it is an interpretive black hole. But let's give it a shot. We open with the wonderful world of sin.

Renaldo & Clara is full of sin. The sins that are not directly enacted are systematically implied. Our first sin, envy, is the least direct in its appearance. The battle between Stoner and his woman portrays her envy over his relationship with his music. He begs her not to come between him and his music, but she persists. It is the bane of all artists: a relationship with a lover who interferes with The Work. Envy appears in the love triangle as well. As that running scene unfolds, it is interesting to note how the women overcome any sense of envy and bond. Baez's one-off scene with her symbolic hairdryer centers on her envy of those who have stable relationships and, in turn, avoid the type of loneliness that plagues her life. Finally, the David Blue history lessons suggest the envy young Bob Dylan endured as the Dylan Myth grew. Back in The Day, it appears those around Dylan were as jealous of his abilities as they were admiring of them. In *Renaldo & Clara*, envy does not control scenes as much as it supports them.

Covetousness appears in *Renaldo & Clara* in a fascinating way. It is not a stretch to argue that Bob Dylan's audience during the folk-posturing period coveted his talent. They longed to possess him, to control him, and to have him exercise their will. Much as Jesus endured the wrath of the Jewish leadership because of his special relationship with the Lord and his intimate knowledge of their worldly ways, "Bob Dylan" suffered at the hands of those who wanted to own him, treat him as a deity, and have *their* way with *his* talent. The result of all of this was artistic—or religious—persecution. I mean, c'mon, some fool called him Judas! That persecution fueled the Bob Dylan Myth, and this film toys with that phenomenon. Without question, the Jesus Series carries this conclusion to the forefront—especially when Renaldo stands beneath the cross with his convicted soul mate. Covetousness also appears in the love triangle for more than obvious reasons. Moreover, the brief but poignant scene with the New York street preachers displays the one deadly sin to receive its own biblical commandment. When the street preacher stands about the crowd in the aftermath of a fistfight he had just instigated, he declares that whatever is said to a man of God is said directly to God. The man's attempt to usurp the Lord's power is suggestive of his desire to possess it. Covetousness is directly portrayed in this film. I just wonder if the outer self covets the tranquility and public inaccessibility of its invisible inner counterpart.

Greed appears in multiple ways. The love triangle certainly features it via Renaldo's efforts to have both women in his life (regardless of what they supposedly represent). He loves them both in different ways, he reports; therefore, he requires them both. Sounds greedy to me. The mere presence of the scenes from Columbia Records suggests the stench of greed. But maybe that is just prejudice on my part. Still, the comments about airplay and its capacity to assist Dylan's efforts to bring justice to Hurricane Carter are suspicious. Who would benefit most from a single and extended airplay, the boxer or the record company? Greed also ties directly into covetousness when we consider the Jesus Series. Dylan's audience not only wanted to possess his talent, but they also abhorred the idea of sharing it. Hence, the additional persecution that accompanied Dylan's exodus from that scene. Greed—like envy—plays a supportive role in *Renaldo & Clara*.

With all of the energy conveyed through the Rolling Thunder Revue performances and all of the time spent presenting the troupe's constant movement, you would think laziness would be nowhere in sight. Wrong. Sloth creeps in and out of *Renaldo & Clara*. The bordello scenes feature shot after shot of the Rolling Thunder whores lounging, pampering themselves, engaging in idle talk, and assuming the roles stereotypically associated with "kept women." When Renaldo trades Joan Baez for a horse, he may have pursued personal commerce in an energetic manner, but it was a lazy response to his situation. Blue kills time playing pinball. Characters just hang out. Though sloth does not enjoy the prominence of other sins, it certainly floats in and out of scenes in its own lazy way.

Lust is the *Renaldo & Clara* sin of choice. It chases you from scene to scene. In a quintessential moment, when Baez (the woman in white) exits Renaldo and Clara's room, she moves past a couple who pass each other in the hallway. They *instantly* stop, smile at one another, embrace one another, and walk off to another room. These two apparent strangers enjoy an instant rendezvous. *That* is *Renaldo & Clara*. The movie's fourth scene featuring Dylan playing guitar with a woman hanging over him is very suggestive. Ronnie Hawkins's relentless hounding of the farm girl in his efforts to get her to forsake her father's will and join him in the paradise that is the tour just drips with lust—the cheap, insincere kind. Harry Dean Stanton may one day miss his horse, but you can't tell it by his response to Baez. And the bordello! Lust abounds in this film. These characters are searching for something, and they are finding their answers in the flesh of the outer world.

That anger is evident in *Renaldo & Clara* is crystal clear. We witness compelling examples of rage and violence in the street preacher scene. Not only do the participants yell at one another in angry ways, but one preacher hops off the top of the Volkswagen bus (he is preaching from atop the vehicle) and rushes into the crowd to manhandle a heckler. The Masked Tortilla's aggressive attack on a heckler during the poetry reading as well as his rude treatment of his hosts during the Indian sequence portray his angry attitude. Several of the Black men interviewed about Hurricane Carter's plight display their anger toward that situation and those who enable such conditions. A fight almost breaks out between Hawkins and Ronson as Ronson refuses to allow Hawkins to enter the cabaret. Hawkins tries to control his anger, but you just know what's about to happen. You sense he has been in this position before. But the scene between Ramon and Mrs. Dylan is the film's angriest moment. The violence is severe and, unfortunately, quite realistic. That scene is uncomfortable to watch. Its presence is suggestive of an agenda that, as Professor Ricks suggests, is festering beneath *Renaldo & Clara*'s surface. Sometimes, you expect anger and it doesn't appear. Clara is quite patient with both Renaldo and the woman in white. Renaldo, too, is calm as the love triangle becomes public. Hurricane Carter shows no sign of anger whatsoever; instead, he is serenely philosophical. Of the many emotions that float in and out of the film's chaotic sequences, anger is one of the most powerfully portrayed.

Finally, pride is featured directly and indirectly in *Renaldo & Clara*. The long scene at what appears to be an Indian reservation involves a speech by a tribal leader that is rich in pride concerning tribal history, culture, and attributes. The street preachers' pride facilitates their ready condemnations of those without their perceived Exclusive Knowledge; hence, their violent responses to their hecklers fail the test of humility that is central to their so-called creed. The Hurricane segment cuts back and forth to a serenely prideful Rubin Carter who communicates a "They can beat me up, but they can't beat me down" attitude (those are my words). Ronnie Hawkins plays a prideful Bob Dylan. "Momma" takes pride in her records, her apparent ability to foretell the future, and her sure grip that allows no coin to pass through her fingers. Yes, pride slips in and out of this film, but more importantly, humility is nowhere to be found. The diner owner offers his takes on the conversations of the moment with a conceited certainty. Mrs. Dylan does not accept a measure of responsibility for her infidelity; rather, she externalizes the cause of her indiscretions in a prideful counterattack (but then again, she *is* talking to a ghost!). Assuredly, pride rivals lust as the Rolling Thunder transgression of choice.

When we pull back and think about Professor Ricks's framework as it applies to *Renaldo & Clara*, the most interesting observation may involve what is *not* present in the film. While we have varying degrees of envy, covetousness, greed, sloth, lust, anger, and pride, there is absolutely no sign of the "virtues" that are justice, prudence, temperance, or fortitude. Moreover, the "heavenly graces"—faith, hope, and charity—are absent as well. The Indian and sporting house scenes portray "hospitality," but that is a long way from the virtues and heavenly graces. The *injustice* of the Indians' and Carter's situations is clearly on display. Everybody's *intemperance* is in plain view. While it might have involved an act of courage to remain on the Rolling Thunder Revue, to suggest that fortitude is anywhere in the film is a fantasy. The shows may have popped up out of the blue sky, but they charged for admission. The film's second scene featured the participants discussing their per diem, so nobody is working for free. There is no faith; in fact, it is mocked. There is no hope; in fact, it is parodied. And, dear reader, what could possibly be prudent about a four-hour film portraying fear and loathing in New England with the Rolling Thunder Revue? No, there is a darkness on the edge of this town—and that is the news that comes from applying Professor Ricks's ideas to *Renaldo & Clara*.

Why Bob Dylan did not name his first feature-length film *Sodom & Gomorrah* is open to debate. I mean, authors name characters or projects after geographical locations all the time. Perhaps that would be a bit *too* direct. Dylan goes past the Gates of Eden in *Renaldo & Clara* and straight into the Garden of Hell. The dark side controls this film. Lust is ubiquitous. Violence is just around the corner—ecclesiastics get into fights with those they endeavor to save only to emerge from the fracas to declare themselves *to be* God. Love is a game in which people labor to own one another. Lovers trade their partners for horses, which suggests they do, in fact, own each other. People are suspicious of one another. Human emotions—and everything else, for that matter—are trivialized. People are persecuted. Life is an act. Moreover, this film's soul—the performance segments—assume a demonic quality. The makeup, the performers' demeanor and feverish intensity, and their ultimate detachment suggest an exercise in devil worship presented through a vaudeville act.

In support of this interpretation is the absence of *anything* positive. Never do characters sit and laugh with one another. Nobody smiles when they perform. There is always a tension in the air. During the Monkees scenes in which Renaldo just runs away from something or somebody, you don't get the impression that this is a *good* thing. He looks flat-out fearful. No, this film is shrouded in darkness. The dingy-looking cabaret, the smoke-filled rooms of the sporting house, the emotional vacuity of the bordello, everywhere, there is darkness or, at least, an absence of light. The Rolling Thunder Revue may have aspired to elevate its spirituality as it gathered by the sea to pray for their adventure, but the treatment of that moment in *Renaldo & Clara* suggests anything but spiritual enlightenment. The Rolling Thunder Revue as presented in this film is the Devil's Tour. And that is not a good thing.

But the critics seem to miss this. Instead, reviewers demanded that the film be interpreted as an autobiographical statement. This, predictably, upset the filmmaker. His 1978 comments to Robert Hilburn capture his response:

> I can't say the critical reaction surprised me. Look, you get 10 people and seven of them aren't going to like it. That's the percentage I've been accustomed to with my music. Of the three who are left, one might love it, one might hate it, one might just blank out or something. But I was disappointed that the critics couldn't get beyond the superficial elements. They thought the movie was all about Bob Dylan, Joan Baez and Sara Dylan . . . and [it] wasn't. It had nothing to do with those people. But that's what kept coming back in review after review. It's like the old days. The times haven't changed. They're the same people who didn't like what I was singing about in the '60s.

He expanded that argument in his remarks to Greg Kilday: "The film could have been much better if people could have had a little more belief, been a little freer. There was a lot of conflict on this film. We had people who didn't understand what we were doing, but who were willing to go along with it." Bob Dylan's idealistic dreams yielded mixed results. On one hand, his Corsica dream was realized: He brought his music directly to the people. He circumvented the money-hungry mechanisms of the music industry by building his own operation. Although that approach did not forsake capitalism, it surely streamlined it. On the other hand, his cinematic exposé was compromised, as his audience was unwilling to participate in his metaphysical analysis. The film's idiosyncrasies were its downfall. Nevertheless, in both cases, this was one helluva plan. It cannot be criticized for its lack of ambition.

What a fascinating moment in Bob Zimmerman's career. He reaches back to Jack Fate's knowledge of music history and pulls out a vaudeville tour that satisfies Bob Dillon's need to rebel against the largesse of contemporary concert tours. He synthesizes his experiences in filmmaking and creates his own movie out of the vaudeville tour's footage and cinematic escapades. He modifies his back catalog and recreates old songs by way of his new sound. So many changes take place as he reorients himself in light of his new knowledge, attitudes, and circumstances. I don't know what Zimmerman thought about all of these developments, but I do know what Bob Dylan did after these creatively courageous activities. Up over the hill, moving its way through the valleys leading up to the depot, is the slow train. The characters in *Renaldo & Clara* are all lost and searching for the answers to their particular situations. Their invisible inner selves are in conflict with their flesh-controlled outer selves. The mirror yields a dark reflection. When Ron Rosenbaum asks what Renaldo needs from life, Dylan responds, "A good guitar and a dark street." When the *Playboy* interviewer inquires why the dark street, his subject answers, "Mostly because he needs a place to hide." When Rosenbaum pursues what Renaldo is hiding from, Dylan states, "From the demon within. But what we all know is that you can't hide on a dark street from the demon within. And there's our movie."

Yes, that is *Renaldo & Clara*. There is no comfort to be found in the lust, envy, greed, pride, anger, laziness, or covetousness portrayed in this film. No, that is the broad road of the outer world. What Rolling Thunder and *Renaldo & Clara* establish is the need for the narrow way and The Hard Choice that accompanies travel on the slim tracks that carry the slow train. But first, the lost confirm their situations as they adjust their eyes for the darkness that engulfs that street where life hangs out. The self-righteous will yield to the righteous; it is only a matter of time. That is the news from the Rolling Thunder Revue and *Renaldo & Clara*.

Street-Legal

During the Americana portion of his lifework, for one reason or another, Bob Dylan toyed with other songwriters' songs and invented the Bob Dylan Revue to record his versions of those compositions. While the Revue was somewhat over the top in its *Self Portrait* recordings, it settled into a more credible groove with *Dylan*. Though those songs were a long way from the traditional Dylan sound, they worked on their own plane. There was something to the Bob Dylan Revue—the full band sound, the interplay between Dylan and his backing singers, their rhythm of expression. The Revue had the worst thing in the world: potential. In fact, the Revue demonstrated its flexibility on *New Morning* as it compromised its NashVegas bombast for a more subtle, supporting role. Dylan and his backing singers discovered their own magic, and they display those skills for an extended period beginning with *Street-Legal*. What was once laughed off as a throwaway album or a revenge record created a sonic strategy that the auteur now deploys in service of a newfound agenda: The invisible world of the inner self is about to leap from the mirror and challenge the outer world's spiritual credibility.

Once the Rolling Thunder Revue disbanded and their Fort Collins show aired on NBC-TV that September (also released as the *Hard Rain* album) and Dylan appeared at The Band's farewell concert ("The Last Waltz") in November 1976, he worked on the *Renaldo & Clara* film throughout 1977. It was a busy time. His divorce from Sara Dylan involved a lengthy child custody fight that carried on for an extended period. He traveled to his Minnesota farm to write songs that summer. He also purchased his own rehearsal/recording facility in Santa Monica, California (the "Rundown Studios"). By December 1977, he had assembled most of the songs that he would record for his next album; however, according to the biographers, he concentrated on his new band and their 1978 world tour, and refrained from working on the new material. Instead, the band revised his old catalog for their upcoming tour. A lucrative deal with Tokyo's Budokan Hall resulted in a week's residency there and, from those shows, the live album *At Budokan*. From there, the Revue visited Australia and Europe, and, later that year, toured extensively across the United States. To suggest that the auteur used the Bob Dylan Revue concept to revise and extend his back catalog is one prodigious understatement. The sonic strategy that transformed "Mr. Bojangles" on *Dylan* had its way with "Mr. Tambourine Man" and "Blowin' In The Wind." Some songs are virtually unrecognizable in their Budokan and Tour '78 incarnations. Big instrumental openings, shifting tempos, new arrangements, and, in some instances, lyrical revisions took the Dylan oeuvre to new places in 1978 (say, for example, Las Vegas). But it was not a new sound. We have heard this approach before, and now we see it applied not to other songwriters' compositions or Dylan's back catalog, but to new material with a new perspective. That old inner self has grown weary.

The train that occupies the cover of the *Slow Train Coming* album is an old-fashioned steam engine—the type that emits a stream of smoke that is visible miles ahead of its arrival. Our first glimpse of that smoke appeared via *New Morning*'s gospel sounds and "Three Angels" and "Father Of Night." Our second view was accompanied by a faint train whistle as the slow train chugged through *Desire*'s "Oh, Sister." With Bob Dylan's new album, *Street-Legal*, that slow train has entered the city limits and, though it is not clearly visible from the train station, we hear its whistle loud and clear and smell the smoke bellowing from its engine. *Street-Legal* is a clear, straightforward, coherent statement: The world is in trouble.

That theme is established in the opening track, "Changing Of The Guards." There, we're told the world is wrong and the end times are coming unless a major change takes place. Those sentiments are certainly reinforced through the Bob Dylan Revue's call-and-response gospel sounds (a tactic that is often overdone on this record). The deal is sealed with "No Time To Think" and its incessant assessment of the situation. The evil enemy is identified and their works are exposed via this long, long diatribe. Finally, we witness the consequences of these dire conditions in "Señor." Here the world no longer makes any sense for the narrator. He is disillusioned. He is disoriented. He is flat-out lost. If we don't rebound, take the time to think through our predicament, change those guards, and revive what is almost totally lost, we'll find ourselves wallowing on the floor with the character from "Señor," doing what we can to dust ourselves off and regroup. These are powerful messages articulated through a robust musical strategy. Just as Dylan used the Minnesota musicians to unlock the colors that fueled the songs on *Blood On The Tracks*, the auteur deploys the Bob Dylan Revue to those ends in *Street-Legal*. The songs gain a certain strength from their aural contexts, and that rhythmic force inspires Dylan's vocal performance, supports the album's thematic continuity, and reinforces the record's sermon: The slow train *is* coming.

Recorded in the spring of 1978 and released that June, this Don DeVito production uses its gospel sound and Revelations rhetoric to say goodbye to Norman Raeben/Jacques Levy and hello to Jesus through nine songs that complain about society ("Changing Of The Guard," "No Time To Think," and "Señor [Tales Of Yankee Power]") and relationships ("New Pony," "Baby, Stop Crying," "Is Your Love In Vain?," "True Love Tends To Forget," "We Better Talk This Over," and "Where Are You Tonight? [Journey Through Dark Heat]"). While most of the relational songs use some sort of complaint to establish their contexts, confusion reigns afterward. Characters are torn, confused, and, on occasion, downright lost in these songs. There are no word games, no obscure references on this record; the metaphors communicate, not obfuscate. Moreover, the large band's full sound and the gospel vocals add an urgency to songs that, without question, stress the negative. With Ian Wallace (drums), Jerry Scheff (bass), Billy Cross (guitar), Alan Pasqua (keyboards), Bobbye Hall (percussion), Steve Douglas (saxophone), Steven Soles (guitar and vocals), David Mansfield (violin and mandolin), Steve Madaio (trumpet), and Carolyn Dennis, Jo Ann Harris, and Helena Springs on backing vocals, the *Street-Legal* sound takes the oeuvre from the dusty New England music halls of the Rolling Thunder Revue toward the cotton field–lined dirt roads that lead to a Black Baptist church near the Mississippi River. In order to be saved, you must recognize that you are lost. To that admission, we now turn.

The sermon opens with "Changing Of The Guards" and its big band, gospel-drenched presentation of what the world looks like after the Rolling Thunder Revue passes through town. The hyperactive backing singers complement the auteur's relentless vocal performance throughout this track's nine verses (there are no bridges or choruses here). Each verse contains five lines that slowly unfold due to the backing vocals' insistence on repeating every other word (or so it seems). The song is thorough. The first verse presents a field where the "good shepherd" grieves and people live divided lives; the second stanza takes us to the "marketplace" where thievery abounds; the third verse features a captain who mourns the loss of his lover under a "cold-blooded moon"; the fourth stanza presents a mysterious woman with a shaved head and a mysterious female messenger wearing a veil (they disappear as quickly as they appear); in the fifth verse, the narrator rises and cruises past ruins where flowers are distributed by "renegade priests" and "treacherous young witches"; the sixth stanza reports of a "palace of mirrors" where "dog soldiers" coexist with whispering angels; in the seventh verse, we're presented with a cryptic scene in which a woman awakens a man with long hair (the fuzzy scene seems to stress her subservience to this fellow); and the eighth and ninth verses bring all of this into a closer focus. The penultimate verse presents the narrator describing what appears to be a speech to a group of men in which an unidentified speaker reports that he no longer needs these people or their organizations, he has done his job (e.g., shining shoes, moving mountains, and marking cards), and he issues this warning that appears in the last half of the eighth verse and all of the ninth:

> But Eden is burning, either brace yourself for elimination
> Or else your hearts must have the courage for the changing of the guards.
>
> Peace will come
> With tranquility and splendor on the wheels of fire
> But will bring us no reward when her false idols fall
> And cruel death surrenders with its pale ghost retreating
> Between the King and the Queen of Swords.

Using imagery reminiscent of "Chimes Of Freedom," this song paints a bleak picture of worldly affairs that literally *demands* the changing of the metaphorical guards. Eden is on fire. Peace on earth will arrive only after the cleansing fire. The false gods must also go; moreover, their lies will be exposed. The message is clear: Change your hearts or accept the consequences.

The imagery is surreal at times, but the account builds and builds to the conclusion that you just know is coming. An idiot wind has swept across the land, and it is time for a correction—or else. But just in case you missed Dylan's point, he revisits his stance with the prodigious reiteration that is "No Time To Think." This song is relentless. It truly is. With the band and backing vocalists revved up to a fever pitch, the *eighteen* four-line verses of this track are divided into nine segments punctuated by the title (that appears in the last line as per "Lily" and "Black Diamond Bay"—again, Dylan's "ghost chorus") and a brief horn break. The song marches along in the fashion reminiscent of "A Hard Rain's A-Gonna Fall." It is ceaseless. "No Time" presents a litany of negative images that point to life's disintegrating qualities and the pressures that leave you without time for spiritual reflection. In so doing, it follows a very specific formula. Each segment opens with a verse that describes a dire situation; the segment continues with a second verse that begins with a line that lists four attributes associated with that situation, moves to two more negative lines, and the segment closes with the conclusion that is the song's title. The respective segments unfold quite slowly. Once more, like "Hard Rain," the song overwhelms you with its incessant imagery.

The first segment appears to describe a lonely search for trust, presenting "Loneliness, tenderness, high society, notoriety" as the key attributes in that pivotal first line of the second stanza. The second segment stresses betrayal, using "Memory, ecstasy, tyranny, hypocrisy" to drive home its point. The third segment seems to massage notions of injustice, using "China doll, alcohol, duality, mortality" as its symbolic anchor (such as it is). The fourth segment seems to discuss idolatry, using "Paradise, sacrifice, mortality, reality." The fifth toys with acquiescence to the system, using more direct attributes such as "Equality, liberty, humility, simplicity" to hammer home the complaint. The sixth segment plays with life's futility, using "Mercury, gravity, nobility, humility" as its symbolic centerpiece. The seventh segment describes our subservience to a foolish system, using "Socialism, hypnotism, patriotism, materialism" to state the case. The eighth segment references the coming of the end times, using "Loyalty, unity, epitome, rigidity." And the song closes by summarizing the sorry state of it all. You can be shot, killed, or whatever, but when it is all said and done, you had better prepare yourself to receive His word. No, there is no time for thinking now and it will not change at the end. You'll either be ready or you'll suffer the consequences. There will be no time for goodbyes, preparations, or suffering. When That Time arrives, you'd better be ready.

Much like "Changing Of The Guards," a good bit of "No Time" is difficult to unpack. Some of the expressions are cryptic, and others are disjointed. The pivotal four-word statement that opens the second stanza in each segment appears to be the key to unlocking this sermonic warning. Everything in life rushes past so fast that it prohibits thinking; so, this song warns you'd better do it now and not wait until it's too late. In a world of loneliness, betrayal, false promises, idolatry, injustice, corruption, and oppression, there is only one escape, and this song preaches a warning that if left unheeded will result in eternal ruination. The topical songwriting craftsman is certainly turning to face The Big Topic, and the results are predictably thorough.

To close this sermonic trilogy, we turn to the consequences of ignoring this protracted warning and "Señor (Tales Of Yankee Power)." With a smooth, south-of-the-border aural backdrop (featuring wonderful horn work) establishing the song's context, the Bob Dylan Revue paints a sad picture in this tale of love lost, societal unrest, and their consequences. The song unfolds via seven four-line verses that pause for two instrumental breaks (one with horns, the other with guitar). The story opens with a compelling romantic complaint, turns to the narrator's subsequent confusion and apparent nostalgia, shifts to another planet, and returns to the aforementioned intrapersonal confusion. Throughout, the narrator appears to be in a conversation with an unnamed man (referred to as "señor"). In the first stanza the narrator questions his direction, his destination, and his experiences on that particular path (asking señor if he has been there before). The second and third stanzas explore a failed relationship. Our narrator talks with señor, wonders where his love is hiding, anxiously anticipates her return, and wallows in the past, recounting a powerful moment of relational bonding. The narrator not only is off balance regarding the relationship, but also seems to be confused about everything. He suddenly shifts the conversation from his romantic nostalgia to a surreal scene that conveys even more disorientation. The fifth and sixth stanzas capture the situation:

> Well, the last thing I remember before I stripped and kneeled
> Was that trainload of fools bogged down in a magnetic field.
> A gypsy with a broken flag and a flashing ring
> Said, "Son, this ain't a dream no more, it's the real thing."

> Señor, señor, you know their hearts is as hard as leather.
> Well, give me a minute, let me get it together.
> I just gotta pick myself up off the floor.
> I'm ready when you are, señor.

Say what? Yes, let's allow the gentleman a moment to regroup. From an account of love lost and anxious anticipation over the future, "Señor" turns to a surreal description of an unpleasant scene. For some reason, the narrator has these oppressive images that suggest some sort of reckoning with hard-hearted people. Whatever happened to this man, it was powerful. What a scene! Who are the fools on the train? Where are they trapped? Who is this gypsy? Who are "they," and why are they so hateful? Whatever happened, our narrator's disorientation is complete. The song closes with his final admission of confusion and yet another request for clarity. The two men are waiting for something. Perhaps something that will rectify the narrator's situation and clear his head. Something thorough—like a cleansing fire.

The character in "Señor" is lost. His love broke his heart. His world is oppressive. He is directionless and in need of reorientation. Throughout it all, he remains polite, requesting patience and understanding from his unnamed comrade. The deteriorating situation that demands a changing of the guards and denies us the time to think straight has victimized the narrator in "Señor." Eden is afire. Betrayal is ubiquitous. Even the gypsies are sanctimonious. The result? People are lost. Without time to think or regroup, the rising tide of evil is about to drown everybody unless they awaken, shift their ways, and gain their bearings. But this confusion does not stop here. It permeates the most treasured of all human conditions—it threatens love.

When we turn to *Street-Legal*'s six songs of relational complaint, we immediately notice the confusion conveyed by the respective characters. "Baby, Stop Crying" is a cryptic account of relational forgiveness; however, the remaining five songs wrestle with questions of relational security, commitment, and perseverance. In many respects, it is as if these relational problems or insecurities are the symptoms of a greater, all-encompassing disease. If we don't change that guard, pull back, and think, our relationships are going to end up like the narrator's in "Señor" and provide the springboard to ruination. Let's turn to the specifics.

"Baby, Stop Crying" is a cloudy song. With its big instrumental send-up and smooth, flowing organ paving the way, the song is a soulful pop tune. The track contains four four-line verses that are separated by four five-line identical choruses that drive home the song's point: "Baby, pleeaaassseee stop crying." Thus, we have a specific songwriting structure that is deployed on behalf of an unspecific relational sentiment. While the chorus concentrates on the narrator's request for his baby to get a hold of herself, the opening verse establishes the context for her behavior:

> You been down to the bottom with a bad man, babe,
> But you're back where you belong.
> Go get me my pistol, babe,
> Honey, I can't tell right from wrong.

The stench of infidelity is certainly in the air. She has stepped out and come home, and now he is thinking about stepping up to defend their honor. In the second stanza, the narrator offers to meet his baby "down" at the "river," where he will gladly "pay" her "fare" (offering the path to relational redemption?). The song continues with his offer of friendship, understanding, and acceptance. If she needs a friend for conversation, he is available. If she needs understanding for the pain she has endured in life, he is available for that as well. The Bob Dylan Revue is cooking on this number, but the symbolic stew that flows from that effort is bland and uneventful. Alas, "Baby" is one of the few genuine pop songs in the Dylan oeuvre. It is highly repetitive, thoroughly structured, and totally vacuous.

Those pop sensibilities take a blues turn with "New Pony." This song uses repeated lines, hyperactive backing vocals, a wicked saxophone, and a cutting guitar to issue a relational complaint through a transparent metaphor. As in most of these songs, the complaint is fleeting and yields to a relational confusion spawned from the narrator's desire to continue the relationship. So, we have a series of "You're bad but I love you anyway" stories that convey varying degrees of romantic uncertainty. In "Pony," we have a playful metaphor that is articulated through heavy repetition and driving instrumental support—classic blues. The backing vocals repeat "how much longer" over and over as the verses roll by. The first of the song's six four-line verses (only five of which are performed) recounts the unfortunate demise of the narrator's pony, Lucifer. She broke her leg, and he had to shoot her. Next, we totally shift topics to "Miss X" and her perplexing, unpredictable ways. Next, we shift back to horse business and the narrator's new pony, her various skills, and compelling appearance.

Suddenly, we change subjects once more as the narrator turns to his baby and issues a warning and an invitation:

> They say you're usin' voodoo, your feet walk by themselves (how much
>   longer)
> They say you're usin' voodoo, I seen your feet walk by themselves (how
>   much longer)
> Oh, baby, that god you been prayin' to
> Is gonna give ya back what you're wishin' on someone else.
>
> Come over here pony, I, I wanna climb up one time on you (how much
>   longer)
> Come over here pony, I, I wanna climb up one time on you (how much
>   longer)
> Well, you're so bad and nasty
> But I love you, yes I do

This simple blues tune captures the essence of the relational songs that populate *Street-Legal*. Typically, the narrator expresses some difficulty with his love interest (via varying degrees of negativity) only to set them aside and leap back into the romantic fray. The fact that this narrator shot his pony with the provocative name, warned his lover to abandon her idolatry, and then shook it all off for a ride on his controversial pony demonstrates his confused, but apparently complete, dedication to his love. But, then, blues tunes do this. Blues songs often take an idiosyncratic metaphor, play with it, and pound it home through heavy repetition. In so doing, they are often pretty doggone randy. "New Pony" is most certainly a blues tune. I wonder what kind of hat that pony wears. Perhaps a "Leopard-Skin Pill-Box Hat" would fit her nicely.

The remaining relational complaints are more concrete—and less playful—in their storytelling. "Is Your Love In Vain?" uses a long instrumental wind-up (you can feel a desert breeze blowing in from Vegas) to tell the story of what happens to lovers who have been promised shelter from life's varied storms and then kicked out. There are times when a person's insecurity is warranted, and that appears to be the case here. The three six-line verses (with a four-line bridge) follow specific strategies that take this composition firmly into the realm of a pop song. The stanzas repeat the title in the closing line, and, in a very unusual move, Dylan interrupts the closing instrumental to repeat the hokey four lines that close the final verse, asking his love interest if her domestic skills—cooking, sewing, gardening, as well as her knowledge of his condition and his perceived pain—are strong enough for the long haul, or is their romance a waste of time? "Is Your Love" unfolds systematically. In the opening verse, the narrator questions his love interest's motives. Is this love, kindness, or guilt? The second verse and bridge reveal why our narrator is so insecure:

> Are you so fast that you cannot see that I must have solitude?
> When I am in the darkness, why do you intrude?
> Do you know my world, do you know my kind

Or must I explain?
Will you let me be myself
Or is your love in vain?

Well I've been to the mountain and I've been in the wind,
I've been in and out of happiness.
I have dined with kings, I've been offered wings
And I've never been too impressed.

The relational complaint is straightforward. Is she up for this job? He is just not sure. His experiences have left him empty, jaded, and suspicious. His requirements are special. He is not like other people. Can she cope with this, or is this a waste? The final stanza presents what seems to happen in all of these songs: He acquiesces. Suddenly, after the above bridge, he gives in and announces that he will give love a try once more. It is odd that after all of the commentary regarding his special needs, he turns to her domestic skills for support. Yes, he asks once more if she is up for this job, but inquiring as to her cooking, sewing, and gardening skills seems disjointed when placed alongside all of these remarks about his special requirements. I guess those personal demands are lessened when one has a full belly, darned socks, and a house full of plants. Still, our narrator is suspicious: "Once bitten, twice shy" is the expression, I believe.

The pop sounds of the Bob Dylan Revue churn on with "True Love Tends To Forget." "True Love" also advances the relational insecurity theme in a direct fashion. This pop song unfolds via four four-line verses that pause for two appearances of a four-line bridge. In this tale, the narrator questions love's memory and, ultimately, its perseverance. He expresses romantic uncertainty in the first verse (he gazes into her eyes and questions what he sees) and drives his point home in the second stanza when he proclaims that each day with his love is like a game of "Russian roulette." Now *that's* relational insecurity! Nonetheless, he pleads with her to embrace him and provide her special form of love. Our narrator seems to be a bit confused. The repeated bridge captures his predicament and state of mind:

I was lyin' down in the reeds without any oxygen
I saw you in the wilderness among the men.
Saw you drift into infinity and come back again
All you got to do is wait and I'll tell you when.

Well, what have we here? Did he deprive himself of oxygen and induce a hallucination? Whatever is happening in this dreamy statement, it suggests insecurity. In the third verse, the narrator admits he is captivated by his lover even though she makes life difficult. When all is said and done, the song closes with the narrator pleading with his love to stand by his side and rescue his life. The "love hurts" thematic just flat-out dominates *Street-Legal*.

When love becomes an unbearable strain, wise participants stop drinking, sit down, and discuss their situation by hurling insults at one another. Right? Well, that appears to be the scenario in "We Better Talk This Over." The seven four-line verses of this song (with four different two-line bridges) move along at a brisk pace. Throughout, the song is one strong relational complaint. Line after line of defiant indignation emerges as we progress through the song. He has done everything he possibly can, but the situation continues to deteriorate. He resolves to stop this foolishness and allow time to heal their wounds. Why? She is "two-faced" and "double-dealing." He dared to take a chance on love and got burned, badly it seems. The fourth verse articulates the narrator's relational dilemma:

> Oh, child, why you wanna hurt me?
> I'm exiled, you can't convert me.
> I'm lost in the haze of your delicate ways
> With both eyes glazed.

Yes, this man is *lost*. He thinks she is as well (the second bridge announces that there must be a home for her somewhere in the "universe"). Suddenly, his attitude changes. He announces his departure, but he hopes they will meet again in a few days and share a laugh. He predicts what will really happen in the sixth verse:

> But I don't think it's liable to happen
> Like the sound of one hand clappin'.
> The vows that we kept are now broken and swept
> 'Neath the bed where we slept.

This guy is laughing at this situation. Maybe we have evidence of drunken confusion here. I don't know. Yet, after ripping on her for her evil ways, announcing the end, and then hoping for a good laugh in a couple days, he grows pensive. He encourages her not to be nostalgic about the relationship, but instead just appreciate the time they had together. The song closes with the narrator's wish for a magical resolution that would end this relationship once and for all. They have broken their vows, and it is time to move on to whatever awaits them. What an interesting song.

The love-is-a-tug-of-war scenario reaches its lyrical and musical peak with "Where Are You Tonight? (Journey Through Dark Heat)." The Bob Dylan Revue is smokin' in the *Street-Legal* finale. The song is presented in three segments, each with a 6–8-line verse and its own five-line bridge. The rhythm is consistent. Each stanza slowly works its way through a series of observations that the bridge seems to respond to in a direct or indirect manner. In all cases, this is a "life is a living hell" testimony that contains a series of powerful observations about a relationship and its serious downturn. The narrator offers several hard commentaries on life, but it all turns to her, the hell she has caused, and, remarkably, his longing for more (communicated by invoking the song's title in each segment's final line). The first segment complains about his absent lover and their wayward relationship. The second segment explores where the relationship went wrong and their frustrations. He is oh-so-torn by this relationship. As she undresses, he pledges not to look and then instantly suggests that he might anyway. Let's examine the third segment and enjoy the living hell of the narrator's life:

I fought with my twin, that enemy within, 'til both of us fell by the way.

Horseplay and disease is killing me by degrees while the law looks the
other way.

Your partners in crime hit me up for nickels and dimes, the guy you were
lovin' couldn't stay clean.

It felt outa place, my foot in his face, but he should-a stayed where his
money was green.

I bit the root of forbidden fruit with the juice running down my leg.

Then I dealt with your boss, who'd never known about loss and who always was too proud to beg.

There's a white diamond gloom on the dark side of this room and a path-
way that leads up to the stars.

If you don't believe there's a price for this sweet paradise, remind me to
show you the scars.

There's a new day at dawn and I've finally arrived.

If I'm there in the morning, baby, you'll know I've survived.

I can't believe it, I can't believe I'm alive.

But without you it just doesn't seem right.

Oh, where are you tonight?

(Do pause and appreciate those Jacques Levy–type internal rhyming schemes. They
are something to behold.) Now, dear reader, read these lines once more. I looked up
the word "diatribe" in my dictionary and, sure enough, it features a copy of these
lyrics as an example. What state of mind do you think our narrator is currently enjoying? He has fought with himself, and both sides lost. He is slowly disintegrating,
and nobody cares. His lover's friends stole from him, and his lover's lover got the
proverbial swift kick in the face (I love those lines!). He has tasted what is forbidden,
and that metaphor is dripping all over him. But the last two lines of this stanza—oh
my! Read them once more. There is a bright path extending to the heavens, a path
that transcends the pain that yielded the injuries the narrator's endured. This man is
speaking of redemption. When we get to the bridge, we revisit his predicament. Survival, it appears, is day-to-day. Each morning, it seems, is a miracle. Yet those miracles are meaningless without her. This man is lost. He is also in love.

With *Street-Legal* the inner self has emerged, gazed into the mirror, and recognized the need for change. As it is, the inner self is unable to negotiate with the outer
self and its world. Unlike "Frankie Lee," where nothing was revealed, the truth is revealed in *Street-Legal* and it's not pretty. The layers of the self that Dylan endeavored
to expose in *Renaldo & Clara* are peeled back here, the raw nerves that comprise our
earthly bodies are exposed, and the results are presented for our consideration. The
"attitudes" exemplified by Dylan's characters have taken a serious turn—not a *sudden*
turn, but a *serious* turn. This transition is presented on two planes (and after *Renaldo
& Clara*, that is quite a relief). First, the record establishes the sorry state of the
world. "Changing Of The Guards" exposes the conditions that warrant a change,
that is, it reveals the *need* for a change. "No Time To Think" explains *why* this need

exists. There is more than a little bit of biblical imagery in "No Time." Furthermore, its laundry list of human attributes drives home time and again the compelling rationale for a pause, a regrouping, and a reorientation. Finally, "Señor" demonstrates the *consequences* of a failure to act. If we don't think, and change, well, prepare to pick yourself up by your own lapel, excuse yourself for your all-controlling confusion, and find a soft place to crash again. As "Señor" conveys, what starts on a societal level will creep into the house of love and drive a wedge of confusion between lovers.

That manifestation of the end times rhetoric controls the second plane of *Street-Legal*'s manifesto for change. While "New Pony" and "Baby, Stop Crying" sort of toy with relational strife (although naming your pony "Lucifer" is telltale, don't you think?), the remaining songs embellish the condition. "Is Your Love" wallows in insecurity. "True Love" operates from a fearful position. I mean, a love that resembles a game of Russian roulette is a frightening proposition: You never know when that bullet is going to fly from that chamber. "We Better Talk" communicates the narrator's confusion in no uncertain terms. He rotates from yelling at her, to wanting to laugh with her, to trying to wish it all away. Finally, "Where Are You" is yet another Bob Dylan capstone statement. In the tradition of "Restless Farewell" and "Buckets Of Rain," "Where Are You" lays out the *Street-Legal* case for all to see. The song's intensity is staggering. While the two opening segments focus on the relational hell that is consuming the narrator, the final segment is wide-ranging and, therefore, demonstrates the all-encompassing qualities of the narrator's situation. He is at war with himself, his lover, and his world. The respite she offers is, no doubt, temporary. Yes, here we return to the false promises of "Shelter From The Storm." You approach the shelter she offers, she opens the door to welcome you in, then you enter and stare at the back door, knowing that one day soon it, too, will open and call for you. *Street-Legal* exposes the vicious cycles of life that are fondled dismissively in *Renaldo & Clara*. The woman in white has been soiled. Her false promises are exposed. You may wonder where she is tonight, but you just *know* where you'll be in the morning. *Street-Legal* is a powerful statement.

It is but one powerful statement among many from this era. Notice how so many things converged during this portion of the oeuvre. That a crystallization of diverse stylistic techniques occurred within this timeframe is beyond question. First, Norman Raeben helped Dylan bring to a conscious level that which had always operated on a subconscious level. While at first it appeared that Raeben taught Dylan new songwriting methods, in actuality, he merely reacquainted the songwriter with skills he already possessed. Dylan simply reoriented his approach. Next, Jacques Levy helped Dylan place his songwriting ideas in a linear narrative mode. While at first it appeared that Levy introduced the auteur to a new mode of operation, in actuality, he merely dusted off songwriting techniques from days gone by. When he wanted, Bob Dylan could always generate a nice, thorough, linear story. Dylan simply reoriented his approach. Next, we witnessed one ambitious—totally rebellious—project. The Rolling Thunder Revue and *Renaldo & Clara* project took everything that had passed before it, selected what was needed, and reoriented that knowledge for the outlandish task at hand. The RTR was a vaudeville hootenanny. It took the Greenwich Village players from The Day, loaded them on buses, and moved them across New England on a joyful romp. They played with silly makeup and used electricity during the show, but it was all a flash from that grand hootenanny past crystallized into a rebellious response to their perceived musical world. The family enjoyed a hectic, loving working vacation. The *Renaldo & Clara* portion of that project also deployed all that passed before it in service of the *scene de jour*. The movie represents the culmination of *Dont Look Back*, *Eat The Document*, and *Pat Garrett* twisted into a new mode. Norman Raeben was most certainly a factor in *Renaldo & Clara's* narrative design. While at first it appeared the movie introduced a new method of expression, it merely reoriented Dylan's songwriting technique to a new medium. Layers of occasionally incongruent imagery piled upon themselves in ways that fed Dylan's idiosyncratic metaphysics (i.e., a visual "Hard Rain's A-Gonna Fall"). An agenda is percolating inside the Archbishop of Anarchy. Finally, with *Street-Legal* the topical songwriting master returned to his narrative element through songs that blended the systematic structural techniques of *John Wesley Harding* with the surreal imagery of *Highway 61 Revisited* and the storytelling strategies of *The Times They Are A-Changin'*. What at first appeared as a Las Vegas adaptation of the Bob Dylan Revue was merely a sonic reorientation that set the musical table for what is about to follow. Everywhere, reorientation. Everywhere, systematic evolution of style. Everywhere, artistic maturation.

Something else was *everywhere*, too. Negativity was flat-out ubiquitous in this portion of Bob Dylan's oeuvre. From the angry heartbreak of *Blood On The Tracks* to the detached cynicism of *Desire* to the fear and loathing in New England of the RTR to the dark musings of *Renaldo & Clara* to the Revelations rhetoric of *Street-Legal*, a darkness is creeping up on the edge of Bob Dylan's work. Something is going on, and the auteur intuitively knows what it is at this point. It is as if that thunder that Dylan heard while he was thinking about a name for the RTR blossomed into a full-fledged storm. Perhaps a raging tornado popped out of that storm and ripped its way across the land and through people's homes. This huge, dangerous tornado just tore its way through the countryside, ruining towns, challenging relationships, and destroying lives. You know what they say about tornados: When you're hunkered down in your dark cellar listening to the havoc being wreaked above, a tornado sounds just like a *train*.

The Moral Period

During the wave of *Renaldo & Clara* interviews that Bob Dylan granted to promote his new film, he occasionally allowed the questioning to wander off in different directions. He was surprisingly open to all sorts of queries. He also seemed sincere in his replies. He talked about his youth in Minnesota, his varied musical influences, his professional history (e.g., the New York days), possible future film projects, and more. Due to *Renaldo & Clara*'s "Jesus Series" (i.e., those scenes featuring religious statuary, a dog barking at Christ on the cross, and the Renaldo and Ginsberg cemetery visit) and all of the filmmaker's metaphysical explanations regarding the film's symbolism, inquiries into his faith were frequent. In the extremely long *Playboy* interview, he responded to Ron Rosenbaum's question—"Do you think Christ is an answer?"—in this manner:

> What is it that attracts people to Christ? The fact that it was such a tragedy, is what. Who does Christ become when he lives inside a certain person? Many people say that Christ lives inside them: Well, what does that mean? I've talked to many people whom Christ lives inside; I haven't met one who would want to trade places with Christ. Not one of his people put himself on the line when it came down to the final hour. What would Christ be in this day and age if he came back? What would he be? What would he be to fulfill his function and purpose? He would have to be a leader, I suppose.

Rosenbaum continued by asking if Dylan's Jewish heritage influenced his formative years in any significant way; Dylan answered, "No . . . I've never felt Jewish. I don't really consider myself Jewish or non-Jewish. . . . I'm not a patriot to any creed. I believe in all of them and none of them. A devout Christian or Moslem can be just as effective as a devout Jew." Rosenbaum followed by asking his subject about his "sense of God." Dylan replied,

> I feel a heartfelt God. I don't particularly think that God wants me thinking about Him all the time. I think that would be a tremendous burden on Him, you know. He's got enough people asking Him for favors. He's got enough people asking Him to pull strings. I'll pull my own strings, you know. I remember seeing a *Time* magazine on an airplane a few years back

and it had a big cover headline, "IS GOD DEAD?" I mean, that was—would you think that was a responsible thing to do? What does God think of that? I mean, if you were God, how would you like to see that written about yourself? You know, I think the country's gone downhill since that day.

After you read those words, place your ear on the ground and fall silent: You can hear the slow train coming down the tracks, can't you? What a powerful series of comments. Bob Dylan seems to maintain quite a bit of empathy for this character the world knows as Jesus Christ. A man who was betrayed by his so-called following understands those who endured similar experiences. A man who is constantly hounded by the messiah-seeking branch of his audience understands the demands True Believers place on their perceived benefactors. And a man who has been lambasted by the press certainly feels for another media victim. Yes, there is quite a bit of identification in these remarks—an identification that crystallized in the Renaldo-on-the-cross-with-Jesus shot in *Renaldo & Clara*. Placing that symbolic association aside, what truly stands out is that Bob Dylan was obviously *thinking* about these matters. Jesus—the personification of Christian doctrine—was on the Archbishop of Anarchy's mind.

Further proof of this phenomenon exists in his *Rolling Stone* interview promoting *Renaldo & Clara*. There, Jonathan Cott also probed the film's religious symbolism, and the conversation branches off in a now-familiar direction. Remember, this is the interview in which Dylan claimed that his movie does not involve Jesus; rather, it massages the *concept* of Jesus. In that segment of the interview, Dylan described why people are attracted to the crucifixion and its bloody portrayals (e.g., spikes through Jesus' hands and the like). He maintained, "People are attracted to blood. I'm personally not consumed by the desire to drink the blood." That may very well be; nevertheless, he was certainly *thinking* about the *concept*. As the conversation rolled on and the two men discussed Sufi philosophy and other metaphysical conceptualizations, Dylan suddenly announced, "You know, I'll tell you: lately I've been catching myself. I've been in some scenes, and I say, 'Holy shit, I'm not here alone.' I've never had that experience before the past few months. I've felt this strange, eerie feeling that I wasn't all alone, and I'd better know it." The slow train was pulling into that station the world knows as "Bob Dylan."

Religion has always been a part of Bob Dylan's rhetoric, and the current version of those spiritual musings gestated during the *Renaldo & Clara* production process and throughout his Tour '78 travels. No doubt, those wonderful backing singers in the Bob Dylan Revue *had* to take his mind toward the church with their soulful inflections and committed vocals (created by gospel singers, no less). The story goes that that mysterious presence Dylan mentioned to *Rolling Stone* revealed itself after a fan tossed a cross on the stage during a show, Dylan pocketed it and later, in his hotel room, he accepted Christ into his life. To my knowledge, Dylan does not talk about that private moment in any substantive way. But Paul Williams does. So, I consulted his essay, "Dylan—What Happened?" for more details (reprinted in 1996's *Watching The River Flow*). I turn to Williams because of his love for Bob Dylan, and the fact that Dylan directly confirmed Williams's observations (according to Williams, Dylan bought 100 copies of the "instant book" and distributed it to people). Moreover, after attending seven consecutive nights of Dylan's gospel show's November 1979 debut and returning home to chronicle his observations about his beloved subject, I find myself comfortable with his conclusions. When push comes to shove, history has to trust *somebody*. Williams argues his case in this manner:

> What happened? Well, in the very simplest terms, the divorce happened. Simple terms are misleading, however, Bob and Sara Dylan were divorced in 1977, following a separation in 1974 (*Blood on the Tracks*) and a reconciliation in 1975 (*Desire*). . . . And ultimately, I think, the failure of the marriage (augmented by the frustrations of single life), led Dylan the Gemini to a painful and inescapable confrontation with the irreconcilable differences within himself. Dylan has always believed, not unreasonably, in the power of Woman. When he finally lost faith in the ability of women to save him (and he seems to have explored the matter very thoroughly, in and out of marriage, in the years 1974 through '78), his need for an alternative grew very great indeed, and he found what people in our culture most often find in the same circumstances: the uncritical hospitality of Jesus Christ. What the man needed to save himself from, I surmise, was guilt, unendurable restlessness, alcohol, self-hatred.

Now, this is provocative stuff. Williams acknowledges the troublesome nature of such conclusions and prefaces them by admitting that he is relying on "the public record; I don't have no inside line" as he concentrates on the text—the oeuvre—to trace not just an artistic evolution, but also a personal revelation. Since we have consistently observed how Dylan's context affects his art, Williams's argument gains support. After all, it was Bob Dylan, not Paul Williams, who made these most private matters public. Finally, in all honesty, I have *no idea* if Bob Zimmerman of Hibbing, Minnesota, accepted Christ as his savior. None whatsoever. There is, however, compelling evidence that Bob Dylan did. Since this study is about the *auteur*—and not a biography of Bob Zimmerman—we accept the auteur's public stance and turn to his new artistic mission: serving his Lord.

Interestingly, as Dylan professed his newfound beliefs in song, he endeavored to perfect that message—no more bottles of wine or overnight recording sessions. In the spirit of the Minnesota *Blood On The Tracks* recordings, attention to detail must be served on this project as well. The artist wanted a particular sound for a specific message; consequently, he reached for the musical world's top shelf and Jerry Wexler. Richard Buskin describes Wexler as "the man who coined the term *rhythm and blues* to replace the title of 'race records' on the black music charts" and—through his work with Professor Longhair, Big Joe Turner, Ray Charles, Ruth Brown, LaVern Baker, the Drifters, Aretha Franklin, Wilson Pickett, and Solomon Burke—brought "black music to the masses." His work in Muscle Shoals, Alabama, not only transformed the tiny studio into a "major recording center," but also created a sound unique within the world of popular music. There is no way to overestimate the impact of Jerry Wexler's work. He shared his recollections of his Dylan experiences with Buskin:

When Bob Dylan came to me and asked me to do that first gospel album . . . I had no idea what I was in for. All I knew was that the genius had done me the honor of saying that he wanted me to produce an album with him. However, it soon transpired that he wanted the structure and the sonority that he had heard in Ray Charles, Aretha Franklin, and Wilson Pickett records, as opposed to Woody Guthrie rambling and scrambling down the road with his guitar on his back and making eleven-and-a-half-bar mistakes. He wanted that structure. That was in 1977. Many years before, around 1972, Bob came by a session that I was doing, and we took a break and went back to my office, we lit up a cheroot, and he said to me, "Man, I've done the word thing, now I want to do the music thing." I wasn't sure what he meant, it was just idle chatter to me, but sure enough, when he came to me many years later I understood what he meant. When you listen to *Slow Train* it surely sounds different to anything else that he ever did. I'm not saying that it's better, but if Dylan hadn't gone through that Woody Guthrie/Rambling Jack Elliott phase, making mistakes on chords and going into odd meters and so on, he wouldn't have been Bob Dylan. He had to do that, but now he was saying, "I want a taste of Otis Redding."

The "music thing" did not replace the "word thing" entirely. Dylan was motivated by his God to say the Right Things and by his muse to present them properly. The two albums from the Jerry Wexler/Barry Beckett/Bob Dylan creative team—the "Alabama Chronicles" that are 1979's *Slow Train Coming* and 1980's *Saved*—are best considered together; they are, as their name suggests, cut from the same sonic cloth. That Paul Williams reports how the initial San Francisco shows featured songs from both albums indicates the extent to which the Alabama Chronicles are an integrated work. They also provide the musical foundation for the Bob Dylan Crusade. The records tell a two-part story that performs specific functions during live performances, yet they also stand separately as albums. The cause is served via the Alabama Chronicles' two segments: Part 1, "Beware: The slow train's coming" and Part 2, "Thank you Lord!"

This chapter examines the Alabama Chronicles along with the 1981 recording *Shot Of Love*. I also pause to consider the tours associated with these projects and the internal workings of what I call the Bob Dylan Crusade. The Crusade's gospel shows were quite the departure from the man-with-a-guitar programs from the folk-posturing period, or the screaming bombasts of the Newport Mod era, or the state-of-the-industry spectacles of Tour '74, or the vaudeville hootenannies of the Rolling Thunder Revue, or the glittery sounds of the Bob Dylan Revue and Tour '78. No, the gospel shows were nothing like those performances. The gospel-era shows complemented the moral period's albums as they work in unison in pursuit of this phase's mission of faithful service. During this portion of the auteur's oeuvre, we witness the first of two service-oriented missions that appear within the lifework. As a result, this period is quite systematic. The songs serve the cause. The shows give life to the songs and place them in a specific context that also serves the cause. And the songs-in-context provide the springboard to the Bob Dylan Crusade's overt adaptation of the Christian faith's guiding ambition: conversion. During the moral period, Bob Dylan accepts both Christ and His mission as the artist uses his art to serve his Lord by articulating The Word, orchestrating his public performances in service of The Word, and using those shows as an avenue for converting people to Christianity. Throughout this study, we've observed Dylan as he diligently fought for his various missions. He applied his skills well in his efforts to be discovered during the folk-posturing era. He allowed Bob Dillon to prosper within his rebellious mission to dismiss Mr. Message Man during the Newport Mod period. He deployed Jack Fate to productive ends in his mission of recovery during the Americana era. Lastly, he used his cumulative knowledge—refined through his exposure to Norman Raeben, Jacques Levy, and the RTR/*Renaldo & Clara* experiences—to reorient his creative bearings and continue his career. Now, we witness unconditional service. Personal agendas are seemingly set aside. Commercial agendas are set aside. Devotion assumes control over the art. The czar of topical songwriting now takes his trade to The Word. Service is the new creed. The results are startling.

The Alabama Chronicles

The biographers and Clinton Heylin's session chronology indicate that the *Slow Train* and *Saved* projects are products of different creative orientations. *Slow Train*'s inclusion of Dire Straits guitarist Mark Knopfler and drummer Pick Withers helped Jerry Wexler cope with Dylan's traditional recording method in a fashion that assisted the producer's efforts to layer the sound in the famous Muscle Shoals style. As the producer and the auteur negotiated a working process, the sessions came together in most respects. This was not the case for *Saved*—recorded a mere nine months later after a three-month tour. The good news is that the tour featured the new songs, so the band returned to Alabama with fully formed arrangements. The bad news is that band members were exhausted and their fatigue was evident. Although the disparity in sound and the quality of the performances may vary, the Alabama Chronicles' narratives capture Dylan's muse in an excited state. The Word was flowing through the auteur, and it was delivered with passion.

We start with Part 1's warnings of the slow train's impending arrival. *Slow Train* (released August 1979) contains nine tracks (running 46:44) that address four subjects: songs of warning ("Gotta Serve Somebody," "Precious Angel," "Slow Train," "Gonna Change My Way Of Thinking," "When You Gonna Wake Up?" and "When He Returns"), a song of commitment ("I Believe In You"), a moral prescription ("Do Right To Me Baby [Do Unto Others]"), and a celebration of God's works: the Sunday school tale, "Man Gave Names To All The Animals." The album's thematic leaves little to the imagination: Worldly concerns are not going to protect you (or serve you) in the end; it is time to "change the guard." The songs are not heavy-handed in their prescriptions, just insistent in their warnings. The musicians—Barry Beckett (keyboards), Pick Withers (drums), Tim Drummond (bass), Mark Knopfler (guitar), the Muscle Shoals Horns, and the backing vocalists, Carolyn Dennis, Helena Springs, and Regina Havis—communicate these themes through songs that bring gospel's traditional call-and-response format into the realm of blues, soul, rock, and pop songs. This portion of the Alabama Chronicles is nothing less than a sonic masterpiece.

Next, we turn to Part 2 and the "Thank you Lord!" segment of the Alabama Chronicles. You know, I think it is fascinating that underneath Bob Zimmerman's senior portrait in his high school annual rests a statement regarding his life's goal: "to join the band of Little Richard." Richard may not have been *physically* present during the recording of *Saved* in Muscle Shoals, but his *spirit* was most assuredly in Alabama. The rich, traditional gospel sounds of the Southern Black church joined a talented wordsmith from Minnesota to scream "Praise the Lord" for forty-three minutes in 1980's *Saved* (released in June). The sound may not have been perfect. The band may have been tired. Dylan and Wexler may have had difficulty communicating. But The Spirit was there, and it requires little to transcend the production difficulties and share in the experience.

Saved closes with yet another warning of the end times' impending arrival ("Are You Ready?"), and it is that cautionary tag that pulls the record from the heavenly clouds of divine celebration. From the opening cover of Hayes and Rhodes's "A Satisfied Mind" to the seven songs of sanctification that follow, the "Praise the Lord" thematic demonstrates the spiritual—not *religious*—fervor that inspired the Alabama Chronicles. Biographers and critics condemn this work for its damnation dogma, and their claims are simply unfounded. This record *celebrates* the joy of salvation and urges the audience to join in the blissful fun through the all-important *invitation* that accompanies the celebration (by rule, I might add). "Saved" (coauthored with bass player Tim Drummond) is a gospel tour de force, "Covenant Woman" is a special thank you for the lady who paved the narrator's path to the Lord, "What Can I Do For You" communicates a "thanks for The Answer" statement and a desire for reciprocity, "Solid Rock" and "Pressing On" are declarations of dedication, "In The Garden" is a hymn of loving recognition (and a history lesson as well), and "Saving Grace" is a paean of thanks for the narrator's salvation (the critical testimony portion of the conversion process). All of the celebrations constitute one big invitation—the call that comes with "Are You Ready?" The participants—Tim Drummond (bass), Jim Keltner (drums), Fred Tackett (guitar), Spooner Oldham (keyboards), Terry Young (keyboards/vocals), and the backing vocalists, Clydie King, Regina Havis, Mona Lisa Young—may have been tired from the tour, but their spirit seems strong. These two albums are wonderfully complementary in their functional pursuit of Divine Service. Let us slide comfortably into our respective pews and contemplate the specifics. The Alabama Chronicles are something to behold.

Part 1's theme—"Beware: The slow train's coming"—centers on *Slow Train*'s six songs of warning. That message kicks off in a grand style by way of the swampy, ominous sounds of "Gotta Serve Somebody." Under Wexler's guidance, the musicians created a suspenseful sonic environment for Dylan's sacred adaptation of Cole Porter's list-song strategy. Moreover, the backing vocals are nothing like the ones we heard during the Bob Dylan Revue as Dennis, Springs, and Havis offer subtle support, caressing Dylan's sermons with a gentle, worshipful vocal style. The song unfolds via seven four-line verses that are separated by a standard four-line chorus (there are no bridges or extended instrumental breaks here). The results declare this warning: No matter who you are or what you do, you are going to have to accept service into your life. The opening segment captures the sentiment and the song's rhythm of expression:

You may be an ambassador to England or France,
You may like to gamble, you might like to dance,
You may be the heavyweight champion of the world,
You may be a socialite with a long string of pearls

But you're gonna have to serve somebody, yes indeed
You're gonna have to serve somebody,
Well, it may be the devil or it may be the Lord
But you're gonna have to serve somebody.

You may be a rock star, an entrepreneur, a physician or leader, a policeman, a media executive, wealthy or afflicted, hiding, living in luxury, an arms dealer (those ever-present masters of war), a financier, a minister, a corrupt politician, or a barber, but no matter your role or position, you must serve. It does not matter what you wear, drink, eat, or what you call the narrator; you must serve. The song is without mystery. It also demonstrates that magical Muscle Shoals touch. This is gospel music at its swampy, Southern finest.

When you accept service into your life, you should pause to thank your spiritual benefactors, and Dylan does that with his second song of warning, "Precious Angel." With a rock sound featuring a strong gospel organ and fine Muscle Shoals horn work paving the way, the six four-line verses of this song pursue another two-dimensional strategy: Warn and give thanks. In so doing, the song is broken into three segments that are punctuated by a standard five-line chorus (there is an excellent instrumental break between the second and third segments). Thus, we have a warning with a twist. The song praises the glorious woman who saved the narrator while it simultaneously articulates the battle that they face together. After praising his angel for pulling him through, the narrator establishes the terms of engagement in this powerful second verse:

Now there's spiritual warfare and flesh and blood breaking down.
Ya either got faith or ya got unbelief and there ain't no neutral ground.
The enemy is subtle, how be it we are so deceived
When the truth's in our hearts and we still don't believe?

These are the terms of the conflict. Step one way or the other—into the light or into the darkness—for like service itself, the choice is unavoidable. The opposition may, in fact, be crafty, but this characterization surely is not. The song pounds its message home. The track continues with a warning for the narrator's friends, presents a dream in which his beloved woman praised everybody (e.g., Buddha and Mohammed) *but* Christ, and turns to a statement of praise and warning in the sixth verse:

You're the queen of my flesh, girl, you're my woman, you're my delight,
You're the lamp of my soul, girl, and you touch up the night.
But there's violence in the eyes, girl, so let us not be enticed
On the way out of Egypt, through Ethiopia, to the judgment hall of
    Christ.

There is nothing like two loving soul mates on a determined mission, is there? What writing. What praise. His lady is his queen. She shines a spiritual light on his inner self and assists his pilgrimage down the narrow road toward Christ. In the chorus, the narrator drives it home time and again. He would be lost without his soul mate. She brought him The Word, and now they must serve together. Oh, by the way, "Precious Angel" makes one other point as well: You better join Christ or prepare to burn in hell.

Slow Train's warning thematic reaches its apex with the track that could easily serve as the theme song for *Renaldo & Clara*: "Slow Train." With a wicked guitar initiating the song's trainlike rhythm, and timely, complementary backing vocals supporting Dylan's passionate singing, this track generates a blues-based sense of urgency. The slow train churns to the beat of the blues as it grinds its way down its holy tracks. The song is our second direct warning of the inevitable Second Coming. Like service, there is no avoiding the Final Judgment. The song's seven five-line verses march along without a bridge or chorus, pause for a strong guitar break, and use that traditional repeated last line to solidify its point. The song literally comes at you like a train. The Bob Dylan Crusade is in its element here. Each verse paints a picture of sin, threat, or worldly foolishness. The third stanza demonstrates the strategy:

> All that foreign oil controlling American soil,
> Look around you, it's just bound to make you embarrassed.
> Sheiks walkin' around like kings, wearing fancy jewels and nose rings,
> Deciding America's future from Amsterdam and to Paris
> And there's a slow, slow train comin' up around the bend.

Yes, the slow train even plows through the politics of petroleum. (Remember, this is 1979—a year when the energy crisis had settled into a way of life for Americans; therefore, this is a persuasive pitch.) After a swipe at worldly egos and vanity, the narrator comes down hard once more in the fifth verse:

> Big-time negotiators, false healers and woman haters,
> Masters of the bluff and masters of the proposition
> But the enemy I see wears a cloak of decency,
> All non-believers and men stealers talkin' in the name of religion
> And there's a slow, slow train comin' up around the bend.

Indeed, the slow train is coming. The world is more than chaotic—it is foolish. Society wastes money by storing food when it would be cheaper—and more humane—to give it away. Egos feed on themselves and exploit others in the process. Interestingly, the narrator closes this diatribe with what appears to be a personal reference. He fears for his family, their manipulation by the evil system, and his inability to intervene on their behalf. After all of the talk about international politics, domestic policies, blasphemous religious leaders, and out-of-control egomaniacs, the message comes home to the narrator's family as well. The slow train is certainly inclusive. There are no boundaries. This warning is for *everybody*.

Consequently, the remedy is simple: Receive The Word and change the guard. Using the sonic strategy that powered the "Slow Train," "Gonna Change My Way Of Thinking" deploys that ominous, threatening, blues-based big sound to issue yet another warning (the backing vocalists take a break on this one, though). Not only does the song use a blues-based sonic framework, but the lyrical structure follows that genre as well. The eight six-line verses all subscribe to a basic format in which two lines are offered, repeated, and followed with a two-line statement of warning—a warning that is frequently based on some dark observation. The first verse reveals the song's style:

> Gonna change my way of thinking,
> Make myself a different set of rules.
> Gonna change my way of thinking,
> Make myself a different set of rules.
> Gonna put my good foot forward,
> And stop being influenced by fools.

From this statement of personal transformation, the song articulates just what these lost fools propagate. It is not pretty. I mean, when sons marry their mothers and men create "whores" out of their daughters, well, the slow train needs to put another log in the engine and speed that sucker up. Our preaching narrator is up for his task. He derides the oppression, physical injury, temptations, and threats that face us all. He, once more, praises his spiritual partner just before he issues a no-holds-barred warning in the seventh stanza:

> Jesus said, "Be ready,
> For you know not the hour in which I come."
> Jesus said, "Be ready,
> For you know not the hour in which I come."
> He said, "He who is not for Me is against Me,"
> Just so you know where He's coming from.

(Dylan sings these lines differently on the recording.) Yes, you must reorient those priorities. Those earthly pains will vanish one magical day. You've got to accept The Word, change that guard, and ready yourself for the end times—or else. This is divisive rhetoric. Some of these threats border on coercion.

Slow Train is so systematic. In its next song of warning, the album poses the question that flows naturally from a command to change your mode of thinking. "When You Gonna Wake Up?" uses that swampy sound from "Gotta Serve," adds a layer of wonderful Muscle Shoals horn work, and marches its way through nine two-line statements that are punctuated by a standard two-line chorus that uses the song's title as a call to action. The song works in that revelatory realm between "No Time To Think" and *Oh Mercy*'s "Everything Is Broken" in that this is one song of righteous indignation. The track resembles a call-and-response sermon in which the preacher barks out some evil situation and the congregation replies with a plea for a spiritual awakening. We're told that God doesn't lie, that worldly philosophies are bogus, that injustice is ubiquitous, that people are out of control, and that earthly treasures are impermanent. At times, these statements are startling; for example, the fifth verse declares, "Adulterers in churches and pornography in the schools, / You got gangsters in power and lawbreakers making rules." Perhaps the slow train should convert to nuclear power in order to hasten its advance. How much worse could it possibly get? When the church is the home of infidelity, when society's youth are hounded by perverts, and when the lawless control the law, well, what else is there? The time is at hand, and one of the first to receive His wrath will be those who manipulated His Word to their worldly ends, as the seventh stanza relates: "Do you ever wonder just what God requires? / You think He's just an errand boy to satisfy your wandering desires." This song warns through confrontation. These are not passive statements of spiritual humility; to the contrary, they are frontal attacks. Literally, they are sermonic wake-up calls. "Wake up and rise to the occasion or suffer eternal damnation" is this sermon's essence. God's Word is the light; however, when extinguished, a consuming fire rages in its aftermath. There is more than a little bit of threat in these songs.

Slow Train's final warning is a powerful one, and it manifests in a signature style. Bob Dylan's use of the compelling capstone statement has appeared time after time as we've progressed through the oeuvre. He uses the tactic again with "When He Returns." Accompanied only by Barry Beckett's splendid piano, Dylan sings a powerful hymn of warning in the album's closing song. This is a traditional hymn performed in a time-honored manner. It is stunning. The song also serves a vital role for *Slow Train Coming*. It is the invitation. The Bob Dylan Crusade offers many important lessons, testimonies, celebratory statements, and warnings, yet none of those expressions is as central to the process of conversion as the invitation. Functionally, the song closes the ceremony that is *Slow Train Coming*. Thus, Dylan issues the invitation for service (the traditional "call"), restates the warnings that dominate this record, celebrates the Lord's immense power, and opens the door for his congregation's salvation. The opening stanza sets the pace:

> The iron hand it ain't no match for the iron rod,
> The strongest wall will crumble and fall to a mighty God.
> For all those who have eyes and all those who have ears
> It is only He who can reduce me to tears.
> Don't you cry and don't you die and don't you burn
> For like a thief in the night, He'll replace wrong with right
> When He returns.

This verse does it all, doesn't it? It announces respect for the Lord's immense power. It offers testimony as to His impact on the preaching narrator. It urges your surrender to His Will. It reveals The Answer.

The second verse presents the narrow way and compares it to the prejudicial lies of the unwashed and their broad way. The sermon asks, "How long can you remain intoxicated on fear, pride, and instability? What will it take for you to accept worldly limitations, set them aside, and travel with the Lord?" (my words). The final verse issues The Call:

Surrender your crown on this blood-stained ground, take off your mask,
He sees your deeds, He knows your needs even before you ask.
How long can you falsify and deny what is real?
How long can you hate yourself for the weakness you conceal?
Of every earthly plan that be known to man, He is unconcerned,
He's got plans of His own to set up His throne
When He returns.

Just as Billy Graham used "Just As I Am" for decades of invitations during his cru-
sades, Bob Dylan deploys "When He Returns" in the same slot on this first edition
of the Alabama Chronicles. All the warnings, all the revelatory rhetoric, and all of
the threats cast in this record were not attempts to divide or cast damnation. No.
They were used to establish the context for this song. The invitation to service is the
end all, be all of this extended ceremony. Stripped down to the lone voice accompanied by a sanctified piano, the service reaches its capstone moment—and a magical moment it is.

I must say that I find it utterly fascinating that Bob Dylan's call for spiritual surrender urges you to remove your *mask*. Maybe this is just a rhyme. Maybe this is one
of the most revealing moments on this record—or perhaps his career. You decide.
But after all of the *Renaldo & Clara* talk about masks, inner selves, and intrapersonal
deception, I think the remark is substantive.

What drives this conviction? What supports the commitment to serve? *Slow
Train Coming* answers this question in no uncertain terms with its hymn of eternal
faith, "I Believe In You." With its slow, simple instrumental platform and smooth
guitar break and closing, these four seven-line verses repeat the title in that telltale
last line and use two six-line bridges to weave a sermon of faith. The song is, assuredly, a straightforward statement of commitment. The narrator's belief sustains
him. No matter if people think he is lying and push him away (verse 1), if people reject him over his devotion (verse 2), or if he wanders, endures criticism, or faces
threats (verses 3 and 4)—our narrator *believes*. The bridges explain why. The first
bridge states,

I believe in you even through the tears and the laughter,
I believe in you even though we be apart.
I believe in you even on the morning after.
Oh, when the dawn is nearing
Oh, when the night is disappearing
Oh, this feeling is still here in my heart.

Regardless of the emotions, their separation, or the time of day, he believes. This
declaration of devotion continues in the second bridge:

I believe in you when winter turn to summer,
I believe in you when white turn to black,
I believe in you even though I be outnumbered.
Oh, though the earth may shake me

Oh, though my friends forsake me
Oh, even that couldn't make me go back.

Belief is the essence of faith, and this song declares that *belief*—and therefore *faith*—is in this narrator's heart. His conviction is unshakeable. His determination is unwavering. His aim is true. *This* is what stands behind and supports the warnings that dominate this album. Without the necessary faith to see the faithful through their challenging days, the pressures to follow the broad way—the way of sin—would prove to be so formidable that anyone could stray off the narrow road to Him. This is powerful stuff. What is also interesting is how this song could easily be interpreted as a love song. Perhaps that is the trick behind this track in that it communicates the *love* of the *faith* that sustains *belief*.

But the washed must develop practices that keep their faith resolute. Skills must be honed that allow the saved to remain strong, to avoid backsliding into the halls of sin, and, just as importantly, to set the example for those around them. *Slow Train* delivers on this measure as well by way of the prescriptive message of "Do Right To Me Baby (Do Unto Others)." The song uses the funky, soulful instrumental style of "Gotta Serve" to articulate a song that follows "Gotta Serve" in its lyrical approach as well. That is, it deploys the list songwriting strategy through its five four-line verses that are separated by five four-line choruses that declare that the Golden Rule is the way to righteousness. The result is a laundry list of things to avoid followed by a chorus that reiterates the simple morals of the Golden Rule. The opening section establishes the approach:

> Don't wanna judge nobody, don't wanna be judged,
> Don't wanna touch nobody, don't wanna be touched.
> Don't wanna hurt nobody, don't wanna be hurt,
> Don't wanna treat nobody like they was dirt.
>
> But if you do right to me, baby,
> I'll do right to you, too.
> Ya got to do unto others
> Like you'd have them, like you'd have them, do unto you.

Our Sunday school lesson continues in this steady, consistent manner. The narrator does not want to shoot, buy, bury, marry (somebody that is already married, that is), burn, learn from, cheat, defeat, wink at, confuse, amuse, betray, play with, miss, or misplace his faith in anybody; moreover, he does not want these things to happen to him, either. The song's simplicity underscores its moral. This is the quintessential "Follow the Golden Rule" Sunday school lesson. The path to righteousness is paved with equality. This is the song's moral prescription for living: Treat those around you as you hope to be treated, and the light of the Lord will shine upon you. Hey, it's that simple. Have faith, be fair, and prosper in the Holy Spirit. The song gains a breath of fresh air by eliminating the threat that controls most of these songs. Do not treat people kindly to avoid burning in hell; do it because it makes everybody happier in the ways of the Lord. Sounds like Abe and Beatty's rule to me.

Our treatment of *Slow Train* closes with our second Sunday school lesson, "Man Gave Names To All The Animals." The song's theme is reinforced by its light reggae-fueled sonic platform that uses the soft instrumental and backing vocal styles as though the band were addressing a group of children. After the fire-and-brimstone rhetoric that carries the warnings on this record, the delicacy of "Man Gave Names" certainly stands out. So, from the church nursery comes a tale of wonderment regarding the Lord's marvelous creations. With a recurring four-line chorus establishing our context, this Sunday school lesson recounts the naming of God's animal kingdom through six four-line verses (the final verse contains but three lines). The opening segment presents the song's strategy:

> Man gave names to all the animals
> In the beginning, in the beginning.
> Man gave names to all the animals
> In the beginning, long time ago.
>
> He saw an animal that liked to growl,
> Big furry paws and he liked to howl,
> Great big furry back and furry hair.
> "Ah, think I'll call it a bear."

(The practice of placing the chorus in the song's opening previews the songwriting style that controls *Saved*.) The song is cute, concise, and convincing. It bounces along with descriptions of cows, bulls, pigs, and sheep, and in a clever move, the final stanza describes one last creation but stops short of providing its name. After describing its silky exterior, its sliding means of locomotion, and its home near a lake, the song stops short. It never labels the creature a snake. Yes, man gave names to all of the Lord's animals, but this song refrains from naming the lone reptile—a creature that obtained mythical status in the Garden of Eden.

What a systematic statement this record is. *Slow Train Coming* touches all of the metaphorical bases as it warns of the impending doom to the unwashed face, thanks those responsible for bringing people to the Lord, stresses the key ingredient that enables salvation, and offers a simple rule of thumb for sustaining His Way. After all is said and done, *Slow Train* pauses to marvel at His Works through a memorable nursery story that reinforces the heavenly magic that surrounds us all. The Muscle Shoals sound carries these messages effortlessly. From the swampy sounds that add suspense, to the blues-based platforms that suggest urgency, to the lighthearted instrumentals that support a nursery rhyme, to the sparse, time-honored presentation of the invitation to service, Jerry Wexler and Barry Beckett's production carried off the "sound thing" in an exemplary manner. Not only do Dylan's lyrics articulate his stance in a clear, resolute fashion, but the musicians' interplay and the backing vocalists' subtle style carry those words in a graceful, respectful way. To be sure, the Revelations rhetoric is threatening at times, but that is what it takes to do this particular job. This ride is not for tourists.

When you pull back and consider *Slow Train Coming*'s songs in their totality, it seems as though the record offers a series of rules that pave the way to salvation, sustain those who have accepted Christ, and invite the lost to join His flock. These rules are simple, yet essential. Rule 1 stipulates that service is required ("Gotta Serve"). Rule 2 maintains that gratitude be extended to those who help us along the narrow way ("Precious Angel"). Rule 3 declares that faith is essential ("I Believe In You"). Rule 4 warns that the end is imminent ("Slow Train"). Rule 5 urges an acceptance of The Light or else facing the consequences ("Gonna Change"). Rule 6 is a classic: Follow the Golden Rule ("Do Right"). Rule 7 aggressively demands a spiritual awakening and a response to the call to service ("When You Gonna Wake Up?"). Rule 8 requests that we marvel at His mighty works ("Man Gave Names"). Finally, rule 9 invokes the strongest law of all—that everyone everywhere be extended the invitation to serve in His name. Yes, this is a systematic record. It stands on its own. But the Bob Dylan Crusade used these songs to perform specific functions within its services; therefore, they represent but one portion of the Alabama Chronicle's two-part statement. After understanding all that we face on the narrow path to righteousness, we should pause to celebrate. That takes us to Part 2: "Praise the Lord!"

The celebratory portion of the Alabama Chronicles opens with a cover of Hayes and Rhodes's "Satisfied Mind." It is a brief tune (1:57) that serves an important function in this album. As everybody moans and groans (seemingly, they are warming up for the show) and the preacher sounds as though he is parading in front of his congregation, this song poses a central observation: You may have all the money in the world, but it is meaningless without a "satisfied mind." Now, a truly satisfied mind is not for sale or loan. No. It comes with Him. By accepting Christ as your savior, satisfaction is but one of many joys to follow. It is the path to eternal life. It is, indeed, something to celebrate. And that's *exactly* what we are about to do.

Coauthored with Tim Drummond, "Saved" (the track that follows "Satisfied Mind") plays an identical role to *Slow Train*'s "Gotta Serve Somebody." That is, it sets the pace for the entire album. Just as "Gotta Serve" uses that swampy, ominous sound to paint its portrait of required service, "Saved" uses the jubilant sounds of the Southern Black fundamentalist church as a sonic platform for the unadulterated celebration that emanates from this song. Yes, the joy of eternal salvation is on display and even Leonid Brezhnev (the most dour face I can recall) would find himself tapping his Communist toe to this tune. The song unfolds via three eight-line stanzas that are separated by a standard thirteen-line chorus (several lines consist of but one word, the song title). Thus, the track offers a celebratory testimony (in the respective verses) that is followed by a choral statement of eternal gratitude. The first stanza provides the initial testimony:

> I was blinded by the devil,
> Born already ruined,
> Stone-cold dead
> As I stepped out of the womb.
> By His grace I have been touched,
> By His word I have been healed,
> By His hand I've been delivered,
> By His spirit I've been sealed.

Born into original sin, the narrator has been freed of his natural burdens, he embraced his supernatural benefactor, and he celebrates his deliverance. After a chorus of thanks, the second verse declares how the Lord's light shines strength, endurance, security, and freedom upon our reborn narrator. After another round of joyous thanks, our narrating preacher offers his final testimony:

Nobody to rescue me,
Nobody would dare,
I was going down for the last time,
But by His mercy I've been spared.
Not by works,
But by faith in Him who called,
For so long I've been hindered,
For so long I've been stalled.

Notice the message here: Faith is the key. It is that faith that this song celebrates—not good works or purity, but faith. Faith is the Answer. Faith inspires this call to celebration. *Saved*'s opening message is crystal clear: A satisfied mind comes only from faith, and once satisfied, a celebration is in order. Rest assured, this portion of the Alabama Chronicles concentrates on that joyous task.

Once more, following the *Slow Train* prescription and demonstrating the Chronicle's systematic methods, after using the album's opening segment to establish the record's thematic orientation, we pause to give thanks to that special woman who made it all happen. In "Covenant Woman," the celebration focuses on the earthly prime mover who led the narrator to Him. It is not just that he loves this woman; he is *grateful* for what she has done for him. Through her graceful faith, she brought him into the fold. For that, he offers his heartfelt gratitude to our "Precious Angel" / "Covenant Woman." The song unfolds in three segments (each with a four-line verse followed by a standard nine-line chorus). The second segment demonstrates the song's rhythm of expression as well as the basis for the narrator's undying gratitude:

I've been broken, shattered like an empty cup.
I'm just waiting on the Lord to rebuild and fill me up
And I know He will do it 'cause He's faithful and He's true,
He must have loved me so much to send me someone as fine as you.

And I just got to tell you
I do intend
To stay closer than any friend.
I just got to thank you
Once again
For making your prayers known
Unto heaven for me
And to you, always, so grateful
I will forever be.

Pretty straightforward, isn't it? The time-honored "broken cup" metaphor is deployed in its traditional manner. The cup is repaired and filled with His love, and it is all because of the graceful faith of the narrator's loving partner. Our narrator even received a worldly reward for his heavenly commitment: He has her. After a sanctified organ break, the song closes with a personal statement of relational intimacy. He cherishes her, he trusts her, and he is prepared to do the Lord's work in the devil's world with her by his side. Thus, we have an inclusive celebration: love of woman, love of God, love of the fight against the devil. A celebration is most assuredly in order.

With "What Can I Do For You?" our celebratory parade pauses for reciprocity. After praising his covenant woman, our narrating minister says thank you some more—this time with a nod toward returning that which he has so happily received. The four-line chorus controls this song that uses three five-line verses to state its case. Each chorus changes the point of its praise and follows with a standard implementation of the song's title. The opening segment conveys this approach:

> You have given everything to me.
> What can I do for You?
> You have given me eyes to see.
> What can I do for You?
>
> Pulled me out of bondage and You made me renewed inside,
> Filled up a hunger that had always been denied,
> Opened up a door no man can shut and You opened it up so wide
> What can I do for You?

The use of a capital letter for "You" indicates that the narrator is talking to Him. His covenant woman may have brought the narrator to the heavenly door, but He opened it, and for that, our reborn one wants to express his gratitude and reciprocate in some manner. To be sure, this hymn says more than "Thank you." It says, "Now it's your turn—how can *I* help *You*?" How do you repay God? Service? Commitment? What? Bob Dylan replies with his only harmonica solo in the Alabama Chronicles (there is also a faint harmonica in the background of the closing of "Are You Ready?")—an act that seems to suggest a "use your talent in service" response to the question. That is probably a stretch, but it is such a signature moment.

At this point, *Saved* moves from a general celebration of faith and thanks toward a celebration of commitment via the two-song segment, "Solid Rock" and "Pressing On." In both songs, the narrator is an active Servant. He is either hanging on to the rock of salvation or pressing forward in His name. Both tracks use the "What Can I Do" songwriting strategy in which the chorus paves the way for the celebratory testimony that follows. In fact, most Bob Dylan Crusade services close with the chore that awaits the congregation: to press onward with the Word of God (using "Pressing On" in that capacity). The two-part statement begins with the rocking entry, "Solid Rock."

Like the album's title track, this song burns with the pure heat of faith. It contains a simple, clear message that lends itself to communal expression. It literally demands that you stand, proclaim your faith, celebrate that commitment, and go forward to do The Work. The chorus opens the song by proclaiming perseverance in service (the four-line chorus opens and closes the song with two four-line verses and another chorus placed between them). A mythical place known for its extreme temperatures will freeze over before this narrator will relinquish his grasp on the rock of salvation. Why does he cling so tightly to his faith? Because the world poses challenges, as the first stanza relates:

> For me He was chastised, for me He was hated,
> For me He was rejected by a world that He created.
> Nations are angry, cursed are some,
> People are expecting a false peace to come.

Again, notice the reciprocity—the duty—associated with the commitment to serve. After all He endured for the narrator, the duty to deal with frustrated people who are lost in worldly expectations is compelling. Following another round of committed praise, our celebration pauses once more to assess the battle that rages:

> It's the ways of the flesh to war against the spirit
> Twenty-four hours a day you can feel it and you can hear it
> Using all the devices under the sun.
> And He never give up 'til the battle's lost or won.

With everybody using everything to thwart His work, it requires genuine commitment to sustain the fight. This song celebrates that perseverance via a pledge to hang on, fight the fight, and exercise His will against the ways of the lost. Interestingly, according to that last line, the outcome is in doubt. What would happen if the devil won? What would happen if *that* ship came into port? I can only imagine that that answer, too, is blowing in some far-off wind.

A good church service—like any other public presentation—benefits from the ebb and flow of a strategically paced program. So, from the rocking sounds of "Solid Rock," we move to the quiet, pensive song of determined belief that is "Pressing On." Building in a slow, thoughtful manner, this song mirrors the lyrical structure of its predecessor, using the three four-line choruses to organize the song with two four-line verses interspersed between them. After opening the hymn by announcing the commitment to press onward in His name, the first verse explains why:

> Many try to stop me, shake me up in my mind,
> Say, "Prove to me that He is Lord, show me a sign."
> What kind of sign they need when it all come from within,
> When what's lost has been found, what's to come has already been?

After explaining the inner self's faithful battle with the outer world (sound familiar?), pausing for another statement of determined commitment via the chorus, the second verse offers what could be called a spiritual pep rally:

> Shake the dust off of your feet, don't look back.
> Nothing now can hold you down, nothing that you lack.

Temptation's not an easy thing, Adam given the devil reign
Because he sinned I got no choice, it run in my vein.

Even with the disadvantages posed by the original sin, the preaching narrator rallies the troops, encourages their commitment, warns of the impending difficulty, and pledges his loyalty. This song acknowledges the fight for lost souls and celebrates the determination required to save them. What is sad about this song is how sin is presented as a natural part of the human condition. Yet, that is the way most Christian doctrine works. We're not born good; to the contrary, we're born evil. Fighting against one's nature is an all-consuming act, and this song offers support for that formidable challenge. Conversion is not an option—it is a requirement.

At this point, the celebratory sounds of *Saved* take time out for a history lesson. In so doing, the auteur revisits a songwriting strategy from days gone by with a slight twist. Using repeated lines to open and close each verse as in "A Hard Rain's A-Gonna Fall," "In The Garden" expands the repetition of the opening/closing lines and contracts the middle lines as it recounts pivotal events in the life of Christ. The song's five six-line stanzas raise questions about Him (via two opening lines), then the song pauses for a two-line comment on that question and closes with the two opening lines. The questions are fundamental to His story. Did "they" realize who He was when "they" arrested Him in that infamous garden? Did "they" hear Him when He spoke? Did "they" see the miracles He performed? Did "they" speak against Him? Do "they" believe in His ascension? Once the question is posed, a two-line comment responds. For example, when the question of His identity is raised, the song responds, "Did they know He was the Son of God, did they know that He was Lord? / Did they hear when He told Peter, 'Peter, put up your sword'?" When asked if His miracles were seen, the preaching narrator responds, "When He said, 'Pick up your bed and walk, why must you criticize? / Same thing My Father do, I can do likewise.' " When asked if His ascension is understood, the song replies, "He said, 'All power is given to Me in heaven and on earth.' / Did they know right then and there what that power was worth?" The song certainly celebrates The Word, but this time a historical context is used to support the story. Did "they" understand what was happening? Did "they" even have a clue? To celebrate what *is*, you must know what *was*, and this song marries those two perspectives. His power is awesome, widely underappreciated, and frequently challenged; nevertheless, these are the challenges that the saved face. So celebrate Him, the challenge, and go forward with The Word.

Having established what it takes to enjoy a satisfied mind, thanking those responsible for that sanctified state, celebrating the commitment required by the battle with evil, and placing it all in its historical context, the second portion of the Alabama Chronicles concludes with its final testimony and warning. Testimony is a key ingredient in the conversion recipe. Through identification with the plights of the lost, the found build a bridge to salvation. The threat that is so central to Christian rhetoric seems to dissipate somewhat in testimony. Testimony, it seems, is a kindler, gentler mode of invitation. Humility is often the key. To argue that you've "been there," suffered the consequences, endured the pain of confusion, and resolved that misery through accepting Christ takes the saved off of their pedestal, diminishes their judgmental tone, and invites identification though humility. After that bridge is built, the celebration reinforces the wisdom of conviction. It is, dear readers, a tried and tested formula—a prescription that is filled by way of "Saving Grace."

"Saving Grace" uses a slow, solemn instrumental strategy that features outstanding guitar-organ interplay to underscore the emotional qualities of the testimony. The tune is drenched in humility. "Saving Grace" contains five four-line stanzas that unfold systematically. First, the narrator announces his humility by offering an apology (he is alive, he says, only because of Him, and he apparently perceives the need to apologize for any transgressions). Next, he declares his salvation (the second verse). He follows that with a statement of belief (third verse) that leads to a characterization of the struggle (fourth verse). The song closes with a declaration of commitment. This is a systematic process. For specifics, consider the narrator's celebration of belief in the third stanza:

> Well, the death of life, then come the resurrection,
> Wherever I am welcome is where I'll be.
> I put all my confidence in Him, my sole protection
> Is the saving grace that's over me.

A stunning guitar-organ break prefaces the narrator's portrayal of the evil that produces the struggle for righteousness (again, verse 4) before the testimony closes with its proclamation of perseverance:

> The wicked know no peace and you just can't fake it,
> There's only one road and it leads to Calvary.
> It gets discouraging at times, but I know I'll make it
> By the saving grace that's over me.

Through testimony, the congregation identifies with the cause and humbly accepts the challenge of the narrow road to eternal bliss. Will you be discouraged at times? You bet. Will the world tease you with false promises? You bet. Will you make it to heaven if you accept the Lord's saving grace? You bet. But just in case this point evaded you for some reason or another, let's close the service with one more round of good old-fashioned threats.

The Alabama Chronicles conclude with a reiteration of *Slow Train*'s warning thematic and the call to action that is "Are You Ready?" This closing track is a classic, blues-based gospel song with well-timed call-and-response backing vocals and dramatic guitar-organ fills. The song offers a strong, compelling sonic platform from which to preach the threat of eternal damnation. The track offers yet another example of the chorus-driven songwriting strategy that controls this album; this time, Dylan brings that method to his capstone song tradition. After all of the celebrations, this capstone statement warns of the end times' impending arrival. With Dylan and his backing vocalists inquiring about *everybody's* readiness (barking over and over the song title or turning the question on themselves—asking "Am I ready?"), we have five four-line stanzas that generate an urgent need for preparedness. First, our worthiness is questioned. Will Jesus accept us or turn away on that fateful day? This is not the stuff of inclusion. The warning lacks any subtlety whatsoever. Humility is nowhere in sight. Will he "know" you or not? Since your salvation depends on you knowing Him, this song suggests you'd better get with the program—or else.

After the chorus raises the readiness question once more, the second verse probes the narrator's personal commitment, and in doing so, invites you to do the same:

> Am I ready to lay down my life for the brethren
> And to take up my cross?
> Have I surrendered to the will of God
> Or am I still acting like the boss?

There is no mystery there: Salvation involves submission. Have you submitted? If you have, you may be ready; if you have not, the third verse suggests that you might want to pick up the pace a hair. The third stanza returns to the "No Time To Think" scenario and urges you to decide your fate. What will it be? Heaven or hell. The warning marches on with the fourth verse as it implores you to rid yourself of worldly distractions. If something for some reason is restricting your commitment, you had better do the right thing and dismiss that evil. Why? The fifth verse nails down the situation in no uncertain terms:

> Are you ready for the judgment?
> Are you ready for that terrible swift sword?
> Are you ready for Armageddon?
> Are you ready for the day of the Lord?
>
> Are you ready, I hope you're ready.

Me, too.

With the imagery of the end times and divine retribution fresh in our minds, the Alabama Chronicles come to a close. This has been one systematic march through fundamentalist Christian doctrine. No traditional stone has been left unturned. We've been warned. We've been told to give thanks. We've been encouraged to celebrate. We've been taught why. And we've been threatened repeatedly. When considered in their totality, the Alabama Chronicles are thorough. When taken separately, they also work within their own dimensions. To the extent that *Slow Train* issues a series of rules, *Saved* walks through a series of phases that reinforce *Slow Train*'s prescriptions for holy living. The first phase celebrates the satisfaction that accompanies salvation ("Satisfied Mind" and "Saved"). Worldly pleasures will offer little comfort on that fateful day. The second phase calls for thanks to those who helped us find the Lord and requests reciprocity wherever possible ("Covenant Woman" and "What Can I Do For You?"). The third phase offers straightforward statements of commitment ("Solid Rock" and "Pressing On"). Your salvation is no moment's task. It takes work. The fourth phase pauses for a history lesson that communicates His great power while questioning "their" knowledge of His abilities ("In The Garden"). The final phase concludes the proceedings in a time-honored manner by offering a final testimony ("Saving Grace") followed by one last heavenly shot across the worldly bow and "Are Your Ready?" Yes, *Saved*'s five phases thoroughly reinforce the rules propagated by *Slow Train*. To be sure, they are integrated works.

Throughout these rules and phases, the Alabama Chronicles have demonstrated a strict dedication to its Muscle Shoals interpretation of traditional gospel music. The smooth sonic platforms of *Slow Train* are a contrast to the rougher, perhaps more conventional sounds of *Saved*. That is certain. While the biographers and critics attack *Saved* for its production qualities, those raw, tinny, excited sounds that characterize "Saved" and "Solid Rock" are authentic representations of a gospel show's dynamic nature—especially a Southern Black gospel show. Therefore, it stands to reason that the songs recorded before the Bob Dylan Crusade hit the road would lack the cumulative edge of songs recorded after an extended tour. Moreover, the songs on *Saved* are chorus-driven. This internal repetition has its own strategic purpose: It allows for audience participation. The chorus makes its point, and the verses support it. A fundamentalist gathering may lower its collective head and sing along to the written verses of "Gotta Serve Somebody"; however, that audience will lower their hymnals and scream out that they are "Saved" at the top of their collective voices. "Pressing On" invites the congregation's support in ways that "I Believe In You" cannot. "Are Your Ready?" facilitates audience participation in a way that the majestic "When He Returns" just cannot. But when the Alabama Chronicles are used *together*, we have the essential ingredients of the Bob Dylan Crusade. As a result, I think the Chronicles rival the *Bringing It All Back Home–Highway 61 Revisited* and *Time Out Of Mind–Love And Theft* one-two punches. The former changed songwriting forever, while the latter demonstrated Jack Fate's resilience; consequently, they represent compelling two-album statements that performed crucial roles in the auteur's oeuvre. The Alabama Chronicles also serve in that capacity. Therein lies their unique magic.

To claim that the topical songwriting wizard effectively dusted off his subject-driven pen and produced two exemplary contributions to the gospel tradition through the Alabama Chronicles is a sustainable argument. The sanctified marriage of the "word thing" and the "music thing" was orchestrated by Wexler and Beckett in a manner that provided the raw materials for the Bob Dylan Crusade. The results are thorough, effectively grounded in fundamentalist doctrine, and loyal to gospel musical traditions. Now, Bob Dylan and his holy colleagues face the daunting challenge of taking the Lord's music out into the devil's world. They must face the darkness by shining His musical light wherever necessary. This will take courage—the kind of courage required to perform before Englishmen who call you "Judas" or New Yorkers who throw fruit or Parisians who scream insults or locals attending their county fair who are unfamiliar with the magical style of Little Richard's piano bashing. Bob Dylan has faced this sort of thing before, and now he must face it again as he stands in the shadow of the cross. It promises to be quite the experience. Are you ready?

Shot Of Love

We've surely experienced multiple transitional moments as Bob Dylan's lifework progresses, but this particular point in time may be one of the most—if not *the* most—compelling. While we're certainly bringing closure to the oeuvre's moral period, an odd thing occurs here. It is almost as if the Alabama Chronicles never happened. *Shot Of Love* is a direct, systematic reiteration of *Street-Legal*. Virtually all of this record screams out a cry of worldly complaint. Echoing "Changing Of The Guards" and "No Time To Think," the songs from *Shot* point to worldly wrongs, evil acts or characteristics, and secular skullduggery time after time. Even the uneven treatment of Lenny Bruce's career hints of societal victimage as it celebrates the comedian's life. Everywhere there is darkness in *Shot Of Love*. A song may praise a lover, but that adoration is accompanied by ominous descriptions of worldly woes. A song may offer a metaphysical resolution to the auteur's spiritual quest, yet it too is surrounded by secular transgressions and wrongheaded ways. My friends, *Shot Of Love* is *Street-Legal II*. It transcends the Alabama Chronicles by leapfrogging backwards to the preconversion anxieties that warranted the acceptance of Christ in the first place. What happened to the Muscle Shoals movement? What happened to that systematic statement of warning, acceptance, celebration, and challenge? It has flat-out disappeared. It is as if it never happened.

Clinton Heylin's chronology suggests the *Shot Of Love* production process extended across thirteen sessions that occurred over a ten-month period (from September 1980 to May 1981). Several people occupied the producer's chair during that timeframe. The album credits Chuck Plotkin and Dylan as the album's producers (with a credit given to Bumps Blackwell for the title track's production). Heylin reports that Arthur Rosato and Jimmy Iovine also produced sessions during the record's production. The cast of musicians is reminiscent of the original *Desire* sessions. There are lots of people involved, so much so that the album's liner notes list the musicians for each song as opposed to the traditional single listing. Jim Keltner (drums), Fred Tackett (guitar), and Tim Drummond (bass) participated in virtually all of the sessions. The Bob Dylan Crusade's backing vocalists—Clydie King, Regina McCrary, Carolyn Dennis, and Madelyn Quebec—were present for the bulk of the sessions as well. Steve Riply, Ron Wood, and Danny Kortchmar make appearances on guitar; Smitty Smith, Carl Pickhardt, and Benchmont Tench appear on keyboards; Duck Dunn plays some bass; Steve Douglas plays saxophone; and Ringo Starr beats on the tom-toms. The session outtake "The Groom's Still Waiting At the Altar" was added to the mix when the original album was released as a compact disc. Other outtakes have appeared over time as well: "Caribbean Wind" (on *Biograph*) and "You Changed My Life," "Need A Woman," and "Angelina" are featured on *The Bootleg Series* initial set. A large cast supervised by multiple producers generated a wealth of songs during the *Shot Of Love* creative period. The results are a long, long way from Muscle Shoals.

While Dylan's music would forever be infused with spiritual messages and, occasionally, gospel sounds, the Alabama Chronicle's rhetoric faded during the closing legs of the Bob Dylan Crusade. The auteur explained the thematic shift to Robert Hilburn: "I've made my statement and I don't think I could make it any better than in some of those songs. Once I've said what I need to say in a song, that's it. I don't want to repeat myself." Consequently, the oeuvre's moral period comes to a close with *Shot Of Love* (issued August 1981)—a record that certainly does not repeat the Muscle Shoals message. Still, *Shot Of Love* provides the resolution to the spiritual quest that fueled the Crusade. This is most assuredly a major transitional piece.

Shot Of Love contains ten songs (running 44:58) that address five themes: worldly complaint ("Shot Of Love," "Trouble," "The Groom's Still Waiting At The Altar," "Dead Man, Dead Man," and "Property Of Jesus"), relational complaint ("Heart Of Mine" and "Watered-Down Love"), a relational celebration ("In The Summertime"), a portrait ("Lenny Bruce"), and a spiritual resolution ("Every Grain Of Sand"). The record presents these topics via a variety of musical genres: gospel, blues, Delta blues, pop, rock, and reggae. Not since *New Morning* have we witnessed this level of sonic diversity. *Transition* is stamped everywhere on this project. The multiple producers, the variety of players, the diversity of themes, and the sampler of musical styles suggest an artist contemplating alternatives and searching for direction. Therefore, we have moments that recall what inspired the trip to Alabama, moments that conjure the spirit of the Alabama Chronicles, and signs of things to come on this record. We begin where *Street-Legal* left off and the worldly complaints that control this album.

Old Bob Dylan acts never die; they just go dormant until they are needed again. So, ladies and gentlemen, welcome back to the Bob Dylan Revue and *Shot Of Love*'s title cut—our first song of worldly complaint. With a big powerful sound featuring the Bobettes' backing vocals, this track's six four-line verses come at you with a vengeance (the song uses the one-line repeated refrain—the song title—in the chorus). Complementing this sonic blast from the past is the intense statement of negativity that controls these lyrics. Line after line of interpersonal complaint, hellish imagery, or nightmarish fantasy appears as the song progresses. For every negative raised, a shot of love is requested. In the first verse, the overwhelmed narrator declares he needs not drugs for his disease, turpentine to stagger him, drugs to assist his repentance, or liquor to fuel his ambitions—no, he needs a shot of love. The second stanza pounds home the tirade:

> Doctor, can you hear me? I need some Medicaid.
> I seen the kingdoms of the world and it's makin' me feel afraid.
> What I got ain't painful, it's just bound to kill me dead
> Like the men that followed Jesus when they put a price upon His head.

To the rescue, the narrator proposes a shot of love. Love is the cure, according to our frightful narrator. The song turns to relational matters at this point as the narrator decries the rumors that surround a hurtful relationship in decline (verse 3) before the rant takes a major turn toward hell on earth:

> Why would I want to take your life?
> You've only murdered my father, raped his wife,
> Tattooed my babies with a poison pen,
> Mocked my God, humiliated my friends.

Whatever action our conflicted narrator is contemplating appears to be justified. Whoever kills a man, rapes his wife, and tortures children deserves a one-way ticket to Dante's deepest inferno. The negativity continues in the final verses as statements of rejection, fear, threat, anxiety, and dismay appear. Sounds to me like that shot of love had better be a double! This is a *Street-Legal*-sized dose of intense negativity. It is also a conflicted statement. The narrator may want a shot of love, but he also wants some revenge. Reminding us of "When The Ship Comes In" from the folk-posturing period, when that day of equality arrives, vengeance will be the conqueror's. The Love here may emanate from the House of Jesus, yet it is filtered through worldly emotions. I do not sense any willingness to turn the other cheek in "Shot Of Love."

The "humility takes a vacation" sentiments continue with another inclusive statement of negativity and "Trouble." The Revue travels to Memphis on this track, and much of the band takes a break as "Trouble" grinds to the sounds of Delta blues. If ever a song's words matched its music, this is it. You feel as though you are walking down Beale Street when you suddenly hear this screeching out of some nearby alley. In other words, this is simple, state-of-the-art Delta blues. "Trouble" is *everywhere* in this highly repetitious track featuring five three-line stanzas that are supported by a recurring three-line chorus (which merely repeats the song's title). Yes, indeed, just in case you forgot where trouble resides, this song offers advice as to where to look. The first stanza relates that trouble resides in urban and rural areas (no geographical discrimination here!); moreover, it declares that those lucky charms you've been hoarding aren't enough to fight it off. Next, we're told trouble is in the air and the water, and—like those essential natural elements—it exists all over the planet. Trouble has achieved ubiquity, as the third verse indicates:

> Drought and starvation, packaging of the soul,
> Persecution, execution, governments out of control.
> You can see the writing on the wall inviting trouble.

This is pure *Street-Legal*, isn't it? After a reminder that it has always been this way and an interesting observation about how people often feel that someone is in an empty room with them (verse 4's reiteration of Dylan's comment to *Rolling Stone* about sensing a presence when he is alone), the final stanza offers no sign of relief:

> Nightclubs of the broken-hearted, stadiums of the damned,
> Legislature, perverted nature, doors that are rudely slammed.
> Look into infinity, all you see is trouble.

From this perspective, we'd better get used to the idea of trouble. Since it is everywhere—and it will sustain that status for eternity—there is nothing else we can do, according to this song. The swift sword of the Alabama Chronicles is nowhere in sight here. Seemingly, the Final Judgment itself will be nothing but trouble. To change the guards is a waste of energy. So, go down to south Memphis, grab some barbeque, and accept the inevitable with a side of coleslaw. That's just the way it is.

What's going on here? What happened to our revelatory rhetoric and its ultimate solution? Why all this unresolved negativity? I *may* be stretching it here, but I believe the answer can be found in our third statement of worldly complaint, "The Groom's Still Waiting At The Altar." Sonically, the song reveals that the Bob Dylan Revue is off break and fired up for a big, loud, honky-tonk blues tune. This song has a Big Sound, and it reinforces the Big Negative advanced in its lyrics. The track's five four-line verses are separated by five four-line choruses that vary slightly (the written-performed variance appears here as well). It also joins the "Changing Of The Guards"–"No Time To Think" two-songs-on-the-same-theme strategy in that I think this song is a companion to "Property Of Jesus." "The Groom's Still Waiting" presents dreadful scenes and follows with the chorus in a simple but relentless manner. The opening stanza presents scenes of the narrator face-down on the ground praying, mentions a massacre and a boxer dying, and glimpses at general deterioration. The second stanza seems to take these observations into the personal realm:

> Try to be pure at heart, they arrest you for robbery,
> Mistake your shyness for aloofness, your shyness for snobbery,
> Got the message this morning, the one that was sent to me
> About the madness of becomin' what one was never meant to be.

Good intentions take you to jail, personal characteristics are misinterpreted, and mental instability are the fruits to be harvested from this particular tree. The fun advances with a portrayal of a dying relationship (verse 3), lifeless people (verse 4), and, finally, the fifth stanza explodes:

> Cities on fire, phones out of order,
> They're killing nuns and soldiers, there's fighting on the border.
> What can I say about Claudette? Ain't seen her since January,
> She could be respectably married or running a whorehouse in Buenos
>   Aires.

(Claudette is in the relationship mentioned in verse 3, and, to be sure, Jacques Levy cringed at that last rhyme.) Just what is going on here? What does all of this negativity have to do with the song's title? Who is getting married or being stood up by his bride? Well, here goes. The "church" is Christ's bride, right? Has the church failed, brought havoc into the world, and left Him standing at the altar, waiting? Has religion failed Him? Has organized faith lost sight of its mission? Something is most assuredly not working in this portrayal. I sense disappointment—perhaps even anger—over the failure of the Alabama Chronicles to deliver on their promised ideals.

That anger permeates our next song of worldly complaint and "Dead Man, Dead Man." With a bouncy reggae beat supported by a big band with howling backing vocals paving the way, this four-verse statement (with five lines per stanza) uses a standard four-line chorus to reiterate the *Street-Legal* rhetoric that dominates this album. This song is a rant. Each verse just tears into a topic and lays waste. First, our angry narrator conveys his sadness over a nameless individual's propensity to propagate false doctrines. The chorus follows by chanting the song title, asking when the dead one plans on returning, and describing his dazed condition (cloudy mind, dusty eyes). The second stanza sharpens the attack:

> Satan got you by the heel, there's a bird's nest in your hair.
> Do you have any faith at all? Do you have any love to share?
> The way that you hold your head, cursin' God with every move,

Ooh, I can't stand it, I can't stand it,
What are you tryin' to prove?

This dead guy is taking quite a beating here. Next, our narrator goes after what appears to be a smug, heartless politician (verse 3) before the final diatribe that's verse 4:

What are you tryin' to overpower me with, the doctrine or the gun?
My back is already to the wall, where can I run?
The tuxedo that you're wearin', the flower in your lapel,
Ooh, I can't stand it, I can't stand it,
You wanna take me down to hell.

Whatever our dead one represents, he wreaks havoc upon the world. He preaches false doctrines. He is faithless and without love. He is smug and pretentious. And he uses worldly tools to cast his victims into hell. This is unadulterated *Street-Legal*. All of the conditions that warranted the Alabama Chronicles have persisted in their aftermath. It is as if the Bob Dylan Crusade failed and the Reverend Dylan is angry about that result.

That anger borders on unpleasantness with our final song of worldly complaint and "The Groom's Still Waiting" companion piece that is "Property Of Jesus." A driving rock sound with light backing vocals provides the sonic platform for this counterattack of five four-line verses (the track also features a recurring four-line chorus). Here the author of "Positively 4th Street" and "Ballad In Plain D" plies his trade in response to his secular critics. Yes, in its own way the song celebrates the oppressed subject's relationship with Christ; however, there is a bit more brewing here than that. The song portrays an individual who belongs to Him but is loathed, mocked, and envied by everybody else. So, my friends, the track has a go *at them*. The you-got-a-lot-of-nerve-you-parasite response is thorough. In the opening verse, the narrator observes how people make fun of the saved one because he inspires thought, practices temperance, and deflects cheap shots with apparent grace. In the second verse, the narrator notes how people wish the saved one ill because he has transcended their worldly ways (e.g., hoping the poor guy will fall down in the street). The track's third segment yields a fine example of this song's rhythm:

When the whip that's keeping you in line doesn't make him jump,
Say he's hard-of-hearin', say that he's a chump.
Say he's out of step with reality as you try to test his nerve
Because he doesn't pay no tribute to the king that you serve.

He's the property of Jesus
Resent him to the bone
You got something better
You've got a heart of stone

The narrator offers a thorough defense for the saved one. The song clearly communicates that the saved one is what his oppressors are not, so go ahead—you heathen—resent him and pile some more dirt on your life. Since the song's not presented in the first person, a bit of its edge is removed. Nevertheless, worldly retribution is in the air here, and it is unbecoming.

When five of an album's ten songs stress a single subject, you've got to conclude that something's happening within the project. Dylan did not lie: Trouble is everywhere, or at least it is everywhere in these songs. A shot of love is the only response the narrator can muster in the face of all the negativity depicted in the title track. "Dead Man" articulates the disgust the narrator holds toward that entity that ruins the world for everybody. The praise-Jesus-with-a-twist-of-counterattack message of "Property" reinforces the dastardly qualities of those who have oppressed the Enlightened through their doctrine of darkness and corresponding jealousies. Finally, while the groom awaits his bride, the world churns in its own hell, moving deeper and deeper in the abyss of sin. The songs are the second edition of *Street-Legal's* Book of Revelations. *Street-Legal's* version of that account is not like the more famous edition in that the Second Coming is nowhere in sight. That swift sword has evidently dulled. The unwashed in these songs are decried, but they are left to their chores. The ruination continues. The cleansing fire is nowhere in sight. The Alabama Chronicles *never* happened. Could this be?

Although I think this *Street-Legal II* storytelling certainly leads us to that conclusion, one song suggests otherwise. "In The Summertime" is our final reiteration of the "Precious Angel"–"Covenant Woman" statement of thanks. This simple instrumental track with its signature harmonica solos uses the tried-and-true strategy of three eight-line stanzas (with a recurring two-line chorus stressing the song's title) to say thanks, thanks, thanks to that special woman who saved the narrator. He cherishes memories of the summertime when they were together (the recurring chorus), and the song traces moments in their relationship. The first verse offers a cloudy account of a meeting by the ocean and their feelings for one another. The plot thickens as the second stanza turns to their loving battles for Him:

> I got the heart and you got the blood,
> We cut through iron and we cut through mud.
> Then came the warnin' that was before the flood
> That set everybody free.
> Fools they made a mock of sin,
> Our loyalty they tried to win
> But you were closer to me than my next of kin
> When they didn't want to know or see.

After more seasonal nostalgia, the narrator offers one final blast of eternal thanks in the concluding verse:

> Strangers, they meddled in our affairs,
> Poverty and shame was theirs.
> But all that sufferin' was not to be compared
> With the glory that is to be.
> And I'm still carrying the gift you gave,

> It's a part of me now, it's been cherished and saved,
> It'll be with me unto the grave
> And then unto eternity.

Obviously, this is yet another thank you for the wonderful "Precious Angel"/ "Covenant Woman" who brought our worldly narrator to the ways of the Lord. That this song would fit nicely within the Alabama Chronicles is beyond all doubt. Its placement in *Shot Of Love* is intriguing, though. This acknowledgment of the narrator's acceptance of Christ and his corresponding gratitude to the one who exposed him to The Light seems to suggest that the narrator did, in fact, enter service. So what is with all of this negativity? Negativity as a preface to the call for service invokes the warning narrative strategy that we witnessed on *Slow Train*. However, to raise the negative and not resolve it is to return to the *Street-Legal*/preconversion storytelling style in which songs just wallow in the horror. Subsequently, I must conclude that the Crusade failed—at least for the preacher. He served, he fought, and nothing changed. Remember, when Dylan penned these songs the Crusade was in full bore. After the initial legs of the Crusade and their emphasis on the Alabama Chronicles, Dylan's back catalog began creeping into the service (more on this in a moment). Could it be that as those songs entered the show, a dwindling of the spiritual fervor accompanied that shift of emphasis? Yes, this is a transitional project. The evidence—the five songs of worldly complaint and the final song of loving, faithful gratitude—indicates that Reverend Dylan responded to The Call and, for some reason or another, it unraveled. Did the ideal succumb to the reality? Did the dream die in the face of the oppressive reality of worldly affairs?

Whether or not that scenario accounts for this change of tone, the ideal-reality conflict is the central organizing principle of *Shot Of Love*'s two songs of relational complaint. The ideal versus reality—pure love versus impure love—contrasts represent the heart of "Watered-Down Love." Here we witness a full-fledged pop song with a big instrumental sound and passive backing vocals supporting the track's four four-line verses that are separated by a standard three-line chorus. The song extols the mighty virtues of love and contrasts that with the diluted version preferred by what appears to be a current lover. We're told that love is pure, it's not manipulative, and it won't extort your heart (verse 1), but she doesn't want that, no, she wants a substandard love (chorus). The plot thickens with the second segment:

> Love that's pure, it don't make no claims,
> Intercedes for you 'stead of casting you blame,
> Will not deceive you or lead you to transgression,
> Won't write it up and make you sign a false confession.

> You don't want a love that's pure
> You wanna drown love
> You want a watered-down love

The song is without mystery: the "ideal" love versus the compromised "reality" of its diluted counterpart. The narrator continues by declaring that pure love will not divert you, corrupt you, or inspire jealousy or suspicion. Pure love is a fine thing, but she is after something else—something malicious, something dishonorable. The song leaves us to consider that sad situation and contrast that reality with the story's notion of an ideal love. The narrator's disappointment is evident in his anger. So, perhaps this song is not about a woman at all. Maybe it is about something else, something more sinister. Perhaps this song is about faith and how a pure faith is diluted by impure religion. I don't know. It seems to be a stretch. Yet, when placed alongside "The Groom's Still Waiting," it resonates. I guess it's best to let you decide.

Love's precarious qualities inspire caution, and that theme is massaged via our second song of relational complaint, "Heart Of Mine." With an interesting blues-ragtime-pop sound supporting the song's four six-line verses (as written, the track has five stanzas; however, the recording collapses two verses into one), this number offers the always-informative internal dialog. Our narrator is torn between his feelings and his experiences, and the song charts that intrapersonal battle. Each verse follows an identical strategy in which the stanza opens with a two-line warning to his heart before turning to a four-line statement of relational deception or personal resolve. The first verse captures the conversational pattern:

> Heart of mine be still,
> You can play with fire but you'll get the bill.
> Don't let her know
> Don't let her know that you love her.
> Don't be a fool, don't be blind
> Heart of mine.

With his veteran mind and his risk-taking heart struggling for power, the narrator continues by telling his heart to go home, quit fooling around, and hide his need for her. The guy just does not trust himself—much less anybody else. The final verse demonstrates the predicament and his resolve:

> Heart of mine so malicious and so full of guile,
> Give you an inch and you'll take a mile.
> Don't let yourself fall
> Don't let yourself stumble.
> If you can't do the time, don't do the crime
> Heart of mine.

I guess once you've left a gallon or two of blood on those metaphorical tracks you learn not to trust your instincts, right? Clearly, this man knows himself. He chastises his heart as a parent would a child: Provide a trickle of opportunity, and prepare for a flood of activity. But that penultimate line captures the crux of this situation best. If you're not prepared for failure, don't enter the contest. Unfortunately, with an attitude like this, the narrator is doomed to suffer at the hands of this self-fulfilling prophecy. This character has listened to "Dirge" so often that he is blind to relational alternatives—like success. Once again the moral is lodged: Once bitten, twice shy.

Having said all of this, *Shot Of Love* offers two more songs that provide additional evidence of this record's transitional qualities. The portrait, "Lenny Bruce," is a shot from nowhere. The track features a hymnlike sound with soft piano and light backing vocals. Its four five-line verses are prayerful. The songwriting strategy represents shades of "Joey," but in a lifeless way. The passionate singing that recounted Gallo's history yields to a passionless voice, almost void of emotion. It is as if the singer has the entire obituary section to record, so Bruce is but one of the 300 people to die that day and receive an aural salute. The first verse announces the outlaw Lenny is gone. Yet, even with his aspirations unfulfilled, his spirit lingers. The second stanza shares the depth of the narrator's emotion:

> Maybe he had some problems, maybe some things that he couldn't work
> out
> But he sure was funny and he sure told the truth and he knew what he
> was talkin' about.
> Never robbed any churches nor cut off any babies' heads,
> He just took the folks in high places and he shined a light in their beds.
> He's on some other shore, he didn't wanna live anymore.

This isn't the most moving eulogy I've heard lately. Still, Lenny was an innocent man even though he made cab rides seem interminable (verse 3). Our superficial hymn of tribute ends in this fashion:

> They said he was sick 'cause he didn't play by the rules
> He just showed the wise men of his day to be nothing more than fools.
> They stamped him and they labeled him like they do with pants and shirts,
> He fought a war on a battlefield where every victory hurts.
> Lenny Bruce was bad, he was the brother that you never had.

What a weird song. Never underestimate the impact of a cab ride, I suppose. While there is more than a small amount of societal criticism in this song, the biography is vacuous and the performance is lifeless. The rhyme scheme is pedestrian as well—especially for the voice of his generation. All of this foreshadows the next portion of the oeuvre in a very direct fashion. The pop icon era of Dylan's lifework is chock full of these types of compositions. Hence, the song offers further proof of *Shot Of Love*'s transitional qualities.

Our final track also demonstrates this record's passage into Dylan's next songwriting period; however, this time, we use the time-honored capstone statement to bring closure to the metaphysical search that supported this era's mission of service. As a result, this song not only closes out an album, but also ends a mission. With "Every Grain Of Sand," Bob Dylan resolves his metaphysical quest. He comes to peace with his conceptualization of "God." The answer is not religion; that is just more "trouble." The answer is in the majesty of His wonderful works, and this song celebrates that pantheistic resolution. Using a reverent, solemn instrumental style that is complemented by the backing vocalists' subtle support, the song's six four-line verses are divided into three segments that are punctuated by the ever-present song-title-in-the-last-line method. My friends, the harmonica-backing vocalist interplay that occurs between the fourth and fifth stanzas is as fine an aural moment as any in the Dylan Canon. "Every Grain Of Sand" is a majestic song, and it rivals any composition from any period in the oeuvre. The opening segment establishes the song's controlling argument:

> In the time of my confession, in the hour of my deepest need
> When the pool of tears beneath my feet flood every newborn seed
> There's a dyin' voice within me reaching out somewhere,
> Toiling in the danger and in the morals of despair.
>
> Don't have the inclination to look back on any mistake,
> Like Cain, I now behold this chain of events that I must break.
> In the fury of the moment I can see the Master's hand
> In every leaf that trembles, in every grain of sand.

The second and third segments work in harmony to reinforce this initial statement. The narrator sees God's work in simple things like individual human characteristics and articles of nature. He feels a direct connection to those who have traveled before him. He feels the Lord's presence in empty rooms (there is that *Rolling Stone* comment again!). He now understands the "reality" of our existence and is prepared not only to cope with it, but also to worship at nature's altar. This song represents a magical moment.

Yes, the auteur seals the deal and closes this period's mission of service with as fine a metaphysical statement as anyone will find anywhere in popular music. With "Every Grain Of Sand," Dylan proclaims his pantheism, accepts his spiritual reality, and dismisses the ideals that populate the Alabama Chronicles. Religious prescriptions and organizational dogma foster as much "trouble" as any other worldly—or "watered-down"—enterprise; for salvation, one need merely accept the majesty of God's labors as they manifest in the most mundane items: grains of sand, leaves on trees, strands of hair. Unlike those who have judged Dylan in "Property Of Jesus," Dylan forsakes worldly judgment in favor of spiritual acceptance. God is everywhere. Praise Him. Marvel at the wonders He provides. The auteur explained his pantheism to Neil Hickey and *TV Guide* years *before* his conversion to Christ:

> I can see God in a daisy. I can see God at night in the wind and rain. I see creation just about everywhere. The highest form of song is prayer. King David's, Solomon's, the wailing of a coyote, the rumble of the earth. It must be wonderful to be God. There's so much going on out there that you can't get to it all. It would take longer than forever. You're talking to somebody who doesn't comprehend the values most people operate under. Greed and lust I can understand, but I can't understand the values of definition and confinement. Definition destroys. Besides, there's nothing definite in this world.

The Bob Dylan who has always disavowed definitions is evident in this statement. He may have subscribed to Norman Raeben's prescriptions for a time, but those conclusions were short-lived. The guy who reported to *Playboy* in 1978 that he envisioned a "heartfelt God" offered similar sentiments to *TV Guide* on September 11, 1976. These comments magically work with "Every Grain Of Sand" to suggest that the Alabama Chronicles were a flash in the metaphysical pan. What he said in 1976 is repeated in 1981. So what happened?

I contend that those old devils "definitions and confinement" happened, that's what. Constricting definitions have always been Bob Dillon's archenemy. For the Iron Range's original biker-poet, subscribe to somebody else's rules and prepare to suffer a fate worse than any form of death—prepare to endure mediocrity. So, whenever Bob Dylan drifted toward an acceptance of someone else's agenda, Bob Dillon did his thing. His rebellion is a *driving* force in the auteur. Consequently, when Christianity's promise became Christianity's confinement, Dillon moved Dylan to reconsider Christianity's definitions. The glorious proclamations of the Alabama Chronicles received additional scrutiny. When the Christian movement squeezed Dylan in the fashion of the folk movement, he refused to be a pawn in that game either. Exactly when this occurred is uncertain to me; however, there is evidence of a turning point when we examine the specifics of the Bob Dylan Crusade. In November 1980, His Light began to flicker.

Shot Of Love is such a compelling moment. It is, most assuredly, *Street-Legal II*. It is, most assuredly, a transition into the pop icon era. It is, most assuredly, a counterattack against those who derided Dylan's conversion. It is, most assuredly, an ending. And what a grand ending it was. Rivaling "Restless Farewell," "Sara," or a number of other capstone statements, "Every Grain Of Sand" takes us right back to the 1976 *TV Guide* statement. We go full circle. For the first time in his protracted career, the Bob Dylan of the moral period became an *advocate* for a cause. He publicly carried his message of salvation to the world. He stood before disbelievers and stated the Lord's case just as he stood before Tour '66's hecklers and ignored or derided them. Then he left it. As the Bob Dylan Crusade progressed, something happened. Something that transported the auteur back to the *Street-Legal* frame of mind. For more detail into those events, let's take a closer look at the Crusade and the various legs of its three-year campaign. I suspect the answers to our questions may be found there.

The Bob Dylan Crusade

The Alabama Chronicles provided the raw materials for one mighty fine gospel show—a performance that adhered to a specific format based on time-honored rituals. Before examining the service itself and its enactment of *Slow Train*'s "Beware: The slow train's coming" theme and *Saved*'s "Praise the Lord!" statements, we would be wise to pause and place this *totally* new performance style in a context. Bob Dylan has certainly changed over the years. These shows are an awful long way from a Bill Graham–sponsored celebrity tour or a madcap vaudeville caravan. Actually, I don't think Bob Dylan ever thought he would perform in this manner. He says he dreamt about it so much as a kid that nothing is ever a fresh experience for him. I'd wager he didn't fantasize about this scenario. I'd bet *the farm* on that. Consider, for instance, the infamous (and reportedly contrived) 1966 interview with *Playboy*'s Nat Hentoff that features several insightful, humorous, and facetious moments. The interview captures the Newport Mod in all his glory. None of those comments contains the irony of Dylan's response to a question regarding his status as an opinion leader for America's youth—the proverbial "voice of his generation" question. When Hentoff reported that "thousands of young people look up to you as a kind of folk hero" and asked Dylan if he feels "some sense of responsibility toward them," the Archbishop of Anarchy replied:

> I don't feel I have any responsibility, no. Whoever it is that listens to my songs owes *me* nothing. How could I possibly have any responsibility to any kind of thousands? What could possibly make me think that I owe anybody anything who just happens to be there? I've never written any song that begins with the words "I've gathered you here tonight . . ." I'm not about to tell anybody to be a good boy or a good girl and they'll go to heaven. I really don't know what the people who are on the receiving end of these songs think of me, anyway. It's horrible. I'll bet Tony Bennett doesn't have to go through this kind of thing. I wonder what Billy the Kid would have answered to such a question?

(I agree, by the way; I bet nobody ever asked Billy that question. I'm prepared to extend another wager.)

Gosh, it sounds trite to say that change is our only constant in this mission-oriented march through forty years of art, but it *is* accurate. That principle also appears within the six phases of the Bob Dylan Crusade that initially focused on the *Slow Train* and *Saved* statements, later expanded to include Dylan's back catalog, and eventually featured the *Shot Of Love* album. The 1979, 1980, and 1981 tours varied in their internal workings in a way that charts Dylan's progress through this particular mission. It is as if the various legs of the tour evolved from a strict fundamentalist ceremony into a more relaxed contemporary service and, later, a secular show. Throughout the fundamentalist portion of the Crusade, Bob Dylan assumed a role of *advocacy* in the performances. Never before has the auteur placed himself in this position. He posed before the folkies. He mocked the Mr. Message Man faithful. He detached himself from *everything* during the Americana recuperation. He danced with *everybody* in the crystallization period. This time, he was the preacher, his band conjured the spirit, and his backing vocalists were his choir. Together, they engaged their audiences in an attempt to move them—to *convert* them—to a specific point of view. The Call may have been subtle at times, but it was ever-present. Dylan, therefore, was a public advocate. As the crusade unfolded, and the advocate's spiritual quest endured the oppression of organized religion, we observe that the Reverend Dylan, too, had Bob Dillon on his side. As the *Shot Of Love* sampler indicated, the spiritual questions that fueled the Crusade's initial legs achieved a resolution that transcended the organizational constrictions associated with religions. Hence, public service yielded to private service and an era reached its conclusion. Still, we *must* explore the Bob Dylan Crusade's specifics in order to fully appreciate the comprehensive qualities of this portion of the oeuvre. This was quite a show.

The Bob Dylan Crusade kicked off in a grand way with a *Saturday Night Live* appearance on October 20, 1979. The gospel band featured Fred Tackett (guitar), Spooner Oldham (keyboards), Tim Drummond (bass), Terry Young (keyboards), Jim Keltner (drums), and Regina Havis, Helena Springs, and Mona Lisa Young as backing vocalists. That Saturday night they ran through "Gotta Serve Somebody," "I Believe In You," and "When You Gonna Wake Up?" and initiated a three-year, six-phase international tour that would see little change in the band (Willie Smith replaced Terry Young and Spooner Oldham in late 1980, Steve Ripley [guitar] joined in 1981, and Al Kooper joined the Crusade's final leg) and steady comings and goings among the backing vocalists (at one point or another, Carolyn Dennis, Regina Peebles, Clydie King, Mary Elizabeth Bridges, Gwen Evans, and Madelyn Quebec rotated through the ranks). The steady cast developed a standard show that allowed everyone to grow in their respective roles. They evolved into a formidable musical unit. They were committed to their job.

The six phases of the Crusade opened with a fourteen-night residency in San Francisco's Warfield Theater on November 1, 1979. The opening phase—by far the most fundamentalist in orientation—extended into December as the Crusade set up a four-night stand in Santa Monica as well as two-night visits to Tempe, San Diego, Albuquerque, and Tucson. The second leg convened in January 1980 and also stressed multiple-night shows in Portland (Oregon), Seattle, Spokane, Denver, Omaha, Kansas City, Memphis, Birmingham, Knoxville, and Charleston (West Virginia). The use of concentrated visits ended in the Crusade's third phase (that April and May) after a famed four-night stay in Toronto, four more nights in Montreal, and two- or three-night stays in Albany, Buffalo, Worchester, Syracuse, Hartford, Portland (Maine), Providence, Pittsburgh, Akron, and single-night trips to Columbus and Dayton, Ohio. The Crusade reassembled for its fourth leg in November by once again appearing at San Francisco's Warfield for a multiple-night stand (featuring twelve shows this time). Afterward, the show extended into another December with two-night trips to Seattle and Portland (Oregon), and one-night stands in Tucson, San Diego, and Salem, Oregon. The Bob Dylan Crusade next toured the following summer with a brief June schedule featuring shows in Elgin, Illinois; Clarkston, Michigan; and Columbia, Maryland. After that warmup, the Crusade traveled abroad that June and July with shows in France, England, Sweden, Norway, Denmark, Germany, Austria, and Switzerland, closing in Avignon, France. The Crusade concluded with a thorough October and November schedule that extended across America from Milwaukee to Boston to College Park to Toronto and Montreal to Cincinnati to Ann Arbor to New Orleans to Nashville to Florida and many, many locations in between. By all standards, it was an extensive tour. Each phase unfolded in a concentrated fashion, moving from location to location in a rapid manner. The Bob Dylan Crusade was a working crew—and they labored diligently in His name.

The extent of the Crusade's concentration on that service varied as the respective phases passed. In its opening phase, the fact that the troupe came to town for extended stays demonstrated a focused conversion strategy. The Crusade's capacity to draw the unwashed, provide a successful intervention/conversion, and reinforce that experience was deeply enhanced by multiple-night residencies. As time passed and the fever dissipated, the strategy relaxed and conventional touring scheduling resumed control. Furthermore, the initial legs of the Crusade followed a more tightly controlled script. There was little variance in the set list, and the service moved through its rituals in an established pattern. Just as the concentrated residency ended as time passed, so too did this aspect. Finally, the early phases of the Crusade offered more testimony than latter periods. The time allocated to extended statements of faith dwindled, literally, with each phase. As we are about to discover, early in his mission of service the Reverend Dylan worked his audience. He enthusiastically endorsed his divine product. An examination of the show's internal workings demonstrates how they evolved throughout the Crusade's various phases.

Before delving into the Crusade's performances, I must pause and thank the world of Dylanology for its contributions to our understanding of this crucial portion of Bob Dylan's oeuvre. Websites around the world have accumulated the set lists, critical commentaries, participant interviews, and, in many cases, audience recordings of these shows and archived them for posterity. When you check out that information, it is more often than not darned accurate. The "Still on the Road" site maintained by Sweden's Olof Bjorner is a wonder to behold. Not only does the site offer the set lists for shows, but it also lists the musicians, charts the number of shows in a given tour (breaking down a tour into its various legs), as well as gives a transcription of *anything* that Dylan said during the performance. Now, that last bit of information is usually pretty trivial (e.g., his jokes and band introductions); however, during the Bob Dylan Crusade, these statements involved the preacher's testimonies, invitations, and sermons. Hence, they are invaluable. The accuracy of these transcriptions may be confirmed by comparing them to audience recordings of those performances. So much would be lost without the fine work of these Dylanologists. My thanks go out to the World of Bob.

The records indicate that the Bob Dylan Crusade featured a three-part show until its final phases. The opening segment involved the backing vocalists (for a 6–7-song set), the second portion offered 8–10 songs from Dylan and the band, then the evening paused for a backing vocalist solo and continued with the third segment's seven or eight songs with the full band. A two-song encore typically closed the service. During the 1979 phase of the Crusade, the set list solidified into a standard show. The midshow solo rotated between the various backing vocalists, but the remaining portions were awfully consistent. The program opened with a Regina Havis monologue about an elderly lady's travels to visit her fatally ill son. Havis told a touching story in a masterful way. The old lady was destitute, yet determined to make her way to her son. While traveling on a train, she steadfastly avoided the conductor for she had no ticket. He finally caught her, stopped the train, and ordered her off. The elderly lady took to her knees and prayed (Havis's voice is magical as she sings the lady's prayer). The conductor was so moved that he pleaded with her to come back on board, since her ticket has been purchased by the Lord. A dynamite gospel set ensued. The rich, emotive gospel singing transported the audience directly into a Southern Black church. The Crusade was aflame with The Word.

Dylan and the full band appeared via the opening number, "Gotta Serve Somebody." This first set typically included "I Believe In You," "When You Gonna Wake Up?" "When He Returns," "Man Gave Names," "Precious Angel," "Slow Train," and "Covenant Woman" (during the 1979 phase, there was virtually no variation here).

After the backing vocalist solo, the second set carried on with "Gonna Change My Way Of Thinking," "Do Right To Me," "Solid Rock," "What Can I Do For You?" "Saved," and "In The Garden." Again, virtually no exceptions to this set list occurred in 1979 and early 1980. The encore of "Blessed Be The Name" and "Pressing On" closed the service. This was a standard show that was organized to serve specific functions at strategic times within the service.

The first leg of the 1980 tour followed a similar pattern. While "Saving Grace" was added to the second set, the rest of the show followed the 1979 formula. The backing vocalist solo shifted songs and performers throughout the tour, but everything else held consistent. The second 1980 leg witnessed a slight shift in programming as "Ain't Gonna Go To Hell For Anybody" and "Cover Down, Break Through" entered the opening set and various songs were moved around to accommodate their entry (e.g., one night "Covenant Woman" would be deleted or another night something else would be shifted around). The backing vocalists' midshow segment was expanded to two songs, and "Are You Ready?" replaced "Blessed Be The Name" in the encore. As the second 1980 tour progressed, more changes followed. The structure remained the same, just different songs were introduced into the mix.

The first major shift in the Crusade's set list appeared during the twelve-night residency that opened the third leg of the 1980 tour in November. Here old Dylan songs (e.g., "Like A Rolling Stone," "Girl From The North Country," "Señor," and even "Blowin' In The Wind") were added to the show. Dick Holler's "Abraham, Martin And John" also appeared on the new set list. The backing vocalists split their solos into two breaks during this period. As the tour proceeded, more old Dylan songs found their way into the show (e.g., "It's All Over Now, Baby Blue," "Simple Twist Of Fate," "Just Like A Woman," and "Love Minus Zero/No Limit"). During the November 12 San Francisco show, a new song—"Caribbean Wind"—was performed, if I'm not mistaken, for the only time in Dylan's career. By the end of the San Francisco residency, the set list had grown to twenty-five songs as more and more Dylan standards made their way into the show. All the while the song list grew, the testimonies faded. The backing vocalists' set and the gospel arrangements kept the Crusade on sonic message, but that format was becoming increasingly diversified. The power of the Alabama Chronicles was systematically "watered-down."

By the time the Bob Dylan Crusade entered the 1981 portion of its three-year tour, the *Shot Of Love* songs made their way into the show. "Dead Man, Dead Man," "Watered-Down Love," and even "Lenny Bruce" could be heard on any given night. More Dylan standards were added as well (e.g., "Ballad Of A Thin Man," "Forever Young," "Maggie's Farm," and "Masters Of War"). The testimonials were by now a thing of the past. As the Crusade ventured "over there" for the European portion of the 1981 tour, the show maintained its gospel feel, but the gospel fervor was gone. Rare was any mention of His name. In fact, during an Earls Court London show, Dylan introduced "In The Garden" by mentioning a visit with George Harrison that occurred in Harrison's garden, so the song was offered in *his* honor. That trend continued during the Crusade's final leg and the extensive fall 1981 tour. Here the backing vocalists slots disappeared. Dylan joked with his audience (often encouraging them to grab another box of popcorn before playing "Mr. Tambourine Man"), stated that he hoped he played something the audience came to hear, or commented on gospel songs such as "Solid Rock" in offhand ways. Yes, the spiritual fire was gone as the Crusade made its way across America. What began as a fundamentalist service had mutated into a gospel-tinged rock show. In 1980 the Crusade shifted to, shall we say, a contemporary service; yet, even that was gone in the 1981 shows. One telltale moment occurred in Bethlehem, Pennsylvania. After the Dylan standard "I Want You," retired Reverend Dylan asked, "Bethlehem? Is this Bethlehem? . . . Somebody famous was born here, right? Who was it?" There is no way Bob Dylan would have said this in November 1979. No way. The thrill was gone.

What made the early legs of the Bob Dylan Crusade so unique was the testimony Dylan offered in advocacy of his Lord. Never before had the voice of his generation stood before an audience with a personal point of view guiding his performance. Oh sure, he had feigned stances all over the world, yet this time, he invested himself through, once more, time-honored practices. He did not shirk from his responsibility to Deliver the Word. At specific points in the show, he stepped forward and proclaimed his purpose. Robert Hilburn's review of the Los Angeles shows cites this Dylan testimonial: "Christ will return to set up His kingdom in Jerusalem. . . . There really is a slow train coming you know . . . and it is picking up speed. . . . Some people call Satan the real God of this world. All you have to do is look around to see that's true. But I wonder how many of you know that Satan has been defeated by the cross. . . . [After many cheered, he replied] Well, it doesn't look like we're alone tonight." Paul Williams reports that Dylan introduced songs with Christian slogans and sayings (e.g., "I'd like to say we're presenting the show tonight under the authority of Jesus Christ") and that as the tour advanced, he had more to say. According to Williams, Dylan issued "a rap about Satan before 'Saved,' a rap about 'a God that can raise the dead' before 'When You Gonna Wake Up,' a rap about Peter and Jesus in the garden of Gethsemane before 'In the Garden,' and an extended rap about Moses while introducing 'Ordinary People' (sung by Mona Lisa Young)."

The wonderful world of Dylanology provides an excellent example of Dylan's testimony from a May 11, 1980, show in Providence, Rhode Island. After a powerful version of "Ain't Gonna Go To Hell For Anybody," Dylan stepped forward and announced,

> All right, thank you. I "Ain't Gonna Go To Hell For Anybody." I know it's not fashionable. It's not fashionable to be thinking about Heaven and Hell. I know that. But God's always in fashion. So we're gonna be talking about Jesus tonight. And I warn you right know, that if you've got any demons inside of you at all they're not gonna like that name, Jesus. They're gonna rebel against that. I know a lot of you think of yourselves as rebels. But let me tell you something, you ain't no rebel at all unless you rebel against the devil.

That is a standard introduction of purpose. For centuries, fundamentalist preachers have opened their respective ceremonies with this type of introduction. The lines are drawn. The initial statement of advocacy has been delivered. Now, it's show time. After several songs, the Message intensified during Dylan's talk before playing "Slow Train":

Thank you. Well, I'd like to say right now we're not gonna give an altar call tonight. There's a pit here in front of the stage. But I am gonna try to implant the words of God in you. I know, you cast out seeds; you cast out on the wayside. Some seeds they go on to the rock. Other seeds they go into the thorns, then there are some seeds go on the fertile ground. I know some of you are gonna hear this. You're gonna hear Jesus died for your sins and to destroy the works of the devil and you're gonna rejoice when you hear that. A lot of you don't know . . . an oath, you figure it's a political system or something. You don't know that the devil's behind politics. You don't know you are the tree that God believes in. Anyway, some of you are gonna hear that word, it's like throwing it out to the wayside. You hear it, but you're gonna leave this room, it's gonna disappear immediately. Others of you are gonna hear it, it's gonna be like putting [it] on a rock, you're also gonna rejoice. But you're gonna go out there and it's not gonna take any deep root. It's gonna be snatched away by the enemy. I don't mean that old enemy that Waylon Jennings talks about, and Willie Nelson, and Jackson Browne, and Henry Kissinger, any of those people. I mean the real enemy, that one that wants your soul. All right, some of you, you're so choked by the riches of this world, the cares of this world, that those riches and those cares are gonna choke this word. I know all about that. But others, I know, are gonna plant the word in fertile ground. For these are the last days, these dark times. It's the midnight hour. I know some of you are on the verge of committing suicide. Some of you, you think you got it all together; it don't matter. Jesus came for all nations. Every knee shall bow, every tongue will confess.

Take away the celebrity references, and preachers of all stripes have used this analogy for centuries. The horticulture metaphor is, in fact, biblical. Dylan's working from a standard playbook. His advocacy follows traditional practices. He is, in every way, focused in his service to the Lord. By the way, later in that particular show, Dylan declared, "Well, we're hanging on to a solid rock. I don't know what you're hanging on to, but we're hanging on to a solid rock." That line will change radically in a short period of time.

An essential element in the conversion rhetoric involves the use of contrasts. The us versus them discourse promotes both a sense of unity for believers and an invitation for nonbelievers to join the cause. It also reinforces the conflict that supports the holy war against evil. Dylan deployed this persuasive strategy during a December 20, 1980, show in Toronto. There he drew distinctions between the narrow way of the Lord and the broad road to darkness and sin:

Man asked me on the street today, he said, "Well, if you believe all those things," he said, "I just can't seem to love my enemy." That's a tough thing to do, you know? That's an impossible thing to do actually. Cause the natural mind, you know, can't comprehend that. So if you're in the natural mind you just can't comprehend loving your enemy. That seems like a foolish thing to do, and it is. However, the supernatural mind can comprehend that. So when Jesus says, "love thy neighbor as thyself," he wasn't exactly saying "roll over and play dead."

Later in that testimony, preacher Dylan sharpened his persuasive strategy by zeroing in on the anti-Christ as the enemy to be defeated:

> Now we've had a lot of previews of what the anti-Christ could be like. We had that Jim Jones, he's like a preview. We had Adolf Hitler, a preview. Anyway, the anti-Christ is gonna be a little bit different than that. He's gonna bring peace to the world for a certain length of time. But he will eventually be defeated too. Supernaturally defeated. And God will intervene. But you're still gonna have to be aware of these things. You need something strong to hang on to. I don't know what you got to hang on to, but I got something called a solid rock to hang on to that was manifested in the flesh, and justified in the spirit, and seen by angels, preached on in the world.

Dylan's natural versus supernatural dichotomy provided the contrast essential to his persuasive strategy. By adding the anti-Christ to the mix, he sharpened that distinction in no uncertain terms. Reverend Dylan steadfastly followed traditional prescriptions.

During the Toronto testimony, preacher Dylan told a long story about a show in Tempe, Arizona, in November 1979. The Tempe show featured one of the more hostile audiences of the Bob Dylan Crusade's three-year adventure. That audience was so confrontational that the show closed without its usual encore. After the *second* song of the full-band set, Dylan attacked the Arizona audience:

> Well. What a rude bunch tonight, huh? You all know how to be real rude. You know about the spirit of the anti-Christ? Does anybody here know about that? Well, it's clear the anti-Christ is loose right now, let me give you an example. You know, I got a place out, ah, somebody stopped by my house and gave me this, uh, tape cassette. Some of these kind of people, you know, there's many false deceivers running around these days. There's only one gospel. The Bible says anybody who preaches anything other than that one gospel, let him be accursed. [Audience: "Rock-n-roll!"] Anyway, you know, this fellow stopped by my house one time and wanted to, so called, "turn me on" to a . . . well I'm not gonna mention his name, he's a certain guru. I don't want to mention his name right now, but ah, he, he has a place out there, near LA. [Audience: "Malibu!"] And ah, he stopped by and he gave me this taped cassette to show me. . . .
>
> [Audience: "Rock-n-roll!"] You wanna rock-n-roll you can go down and rock-n-roll. You can go see Kiss and you rock-n-roll your way down to the pit.

Dylan fought on with his story. He worked his way through shouts of "rock-n-roll" and "praise the Lord with puke" before the various factions in the audience wound up screaming at one another. Dylan fought onward. He described this "guru" and his materialistic ways of the flesh (this guy even declared himself to be God and encouraged his followers to do the same). Boos rained down as they had years before, and this time Dylan maintained his composure, advocated his cause, and worked his way through the heckling. Struggling all the way, Dylan concluded his Tempe sermon:

> I want to tell you this because there's many of these people walking around. They might not come right out and say they're God, but they're just waiting for the opportunity to. And there is only one God. And let me hear you say who that God is? [Audience: shouting] Their God, he makes promises that he doesn't keep. There's only two kinds of people like the preacher says–only two kinds of people. Color don't separate them, neither does their clothes. . . . [Audience: "Rock-n-roll!"] You still want to rock-n-roll? I'll tell you what the two kinds of people are. Don't matter how much money you got, there's only two kinds of people: There are saved people and there's lost people. [Audience: applause] Yeah. Now remember that I told you that. You may never see me again. I may not be coming though here again, you may not see me, sometime down the line you'll remember you heard it here. That Jesus is Lord. And every knee shall bow to him.

Dylan may have stammered his way through his message, but he completed the job in the face of all of the heckling and distractions. He issued the invitation by drawing the line in His sand: There are two types of people on this planet—"When You Gonna Wake Up?" The Bible's Great Commission was served through testimony. As this example demonstrates, Brother Dylan was remarkably thorough in his testimonies and sermons. He drew contrasts between the lost and the saved, he described the villainous anti-Christ (often through historical references), he decried false prophets (e.g., this "guru"), he used widely known biblical stories to establish his points, and he thoroughly denounced the dark ways of the world. He was a staunch advocate for Christ's cause. He served.

On occasion, Dylan's past came into play and he used it to his rhetorical advantage. Once more, the Tempe show offers an example of this tactic. In the long testimonial spot reserved before "Solid Rock," the preacher embraced his past with pride:

> How many people here are aware that we're living in the end of times right now? How many people are aware of that? Anybody wanna know that? Anybody interested in knowing that we're living in the end times? How many people do know that? Just yell out or do something. How many people don't know that? Well, we are, we're living in the end times. [Audience: "The times they are a-changin'."] That's right. I told you that. I told you "the times they are a-changin' " twenty years ago. And I don't believe I've ever lied to you. I don't think I said anything that's been a lie. I never told you to vote for nobody. Never told you to follow nobody.

From there, a long sermon ensued. Dylan recounted the tale of Christ's intervention on behalf of a prostitute threatened by a public stoning; urging those without sin to cast the legendary first stone. He traced the three ways the Lord punishes a nation that falls off the path of righteousness (through the "economy," through the "ecology," and by war). Finally, he marched through the "Battle of Armageddon" by describing the participants and their imminent clash. He encouraged the college students in attendance to consult their professors and confirm his facts. Bob Dylan was a confident preacher. He was secure in his advocacy. Before the concluding song, "In The Garden," Dylan offered his parting message: "Remember what I said, if you ever hear it some other time, that there is a way. There's a truth and a life and a way. You may not get it now. It may not be the next week or so. It may not be the next year or so. But remember the next time it happens." With that, the Great Commission was served.

Dylan's testimonies occasionally took current events and used them to demonstrate his point. During the San Francisco show on November 15, 1979, he used that tactic: "Well, you read in the newspapers everyday how bad the world is getting. The situation in Iran. The students are rebelling, you know, even over here they're rebelling. They won't let the Iranian students into the whorehouses in the valley anymore. Anyway, but that don't bother us because we know this world will be destroyed. Christ will set his kingdom up for a thousand years, we know that it's true. So it's a slow train coming, but it's picking up speed." What an interesting example; I mean, "whorehouses" in Iran? On other occasions, he played off of his audience's comments as he delivered his remarks. Here is a case in point from a November 19, 1979, show in Santa Monica: "Satan is called the God of this world. Is there anybody here who knows that? [Audience: cheering] That's right, he is called the God of this world and the Prince of the Power of the Air. [Audience: "He sucks!"] That's right, he does. [Audience: laughter] But anyhow, we know he's been defeated at the cross." As the 1979 tour continued, these commentaries expanded. Stories about John the Baptist, Peter raising his sword in Jesus' defense when the Romans arrested Him, the Garden of Eden, and more occurred during standard slots in the program. The Crusade was systematic in its 1979–early 1980 phases. My favorite testimony occurred during a November 27 show in San Diego. There, for the only time I'm aware of, Dylan talked about that fateful day when he picked up that cross that was tossed on stage:

> Last time I was here in San Diego, I was here about a year ago . . . wasn't it a year ago? I don't know but . . . I was coming from someplace and I was feeling real sick when I got through here. And on the day of the show, I don't think it was in here . . . I think it was in another place . . . [Audience: "Talk about Jesus!"] anyway, after, it was just about a year ago I think, after it was just, just about, towards the end of the show somebody out of the crowd—they knew I wasn't feeling too well, I think they could sense that—and they threw a silver cross on the stage. Now, usually I don't pick things up that are thrown on the front of the stage. Once in a while I do, but sometimes, most times I don't. But, uh, I looked down at this cross and I said, "I got to pick that up." I picked up that cross and I put it into my pocket. It was a silver cross, I think maybe about so high—and

I put it, brought it backstage and I brought it with me to the next town which was off in Arizona, Phoenix. Anyway, ah, when I got back there I was feeling even worse that I had felt when I was in San Diego, and I said, "Well, I really need something tonight," and, I didn't know what it was, I was using all kinds of things, and I said, "I need something tonight that I never really had before." And I looked in my pocket and I had this cross that someone threw before when I was in San Diego. So if that person is here tonight I want to thank him for that cross.

In the traditional manner of recalling that moment of conversion, Bob Dylan re-counted his personal experience with salvation. His stammering and halting delivery added to his statement's authenticity. He humbly testified before his audience, and in so doing, offered thanks to his unknown benefactor. He was sick, turned his back on the old remedies, and accepted a new medicine: the Word of God. His remarks from a December 5 show in Albuquerque demonstrated the strength of his conviction as he once more anchored it in his famous past: "I told you 'The Times They Are A-Changing' and they did! I said the answer was 'Blowin' In The Wind' and it was! And I'm saying to you now, Jesus is coming back, and he is! There is no other way to sal-vation."

When the Crusade returned to San Francisco in November 1980, the testimo-nials ended. On November 12, Dylan replaced stories about Jesus with tales of Lead-belly and Muddy Waters. On the 15, he recounted hearing the blues in Chicago when he was young. On the 16, he told a joke about meeting a transvestite before the show. Jesus had left the building. By 1981, the show continued to emphasize a gospel sound, but the Christian rhetoric was completely gone. During the latter portions of the summer 1981 European leg, the opening gospel set disappeared. A horrible moment occurred during the Crusade's final European show in Avignon when a patron fell into the electric cables and delayed the show. The program eventually resumed, but it was a symbolic moment. By the time the final leg of the Crusade opened in Mil-waukee on October 16, Dylan's approach had reversed itself. After performing "Solid Rock," he remarked, "Hanging on to a solid rock. I'd better be hanging on to some-thing." The gospel songs remained in the show as it cruised across America, but the 25–30-song set now emphasized Dylan's back catalog as much as anything. When the Crusade ended in Lakeland, Florida, on November 21, 1981, there was no mention of Jesus outside of the songs. Perhaps in His place, Dylan debuted "Every Grain Of Sand"—placed neatly between "Ballad Of A Thin Man" and "All Along The Watch-tower."

The Bob Dylan Crusade was yet another fascinating era in a career known for its extremes. Just as Dylan confronted his hecklers with a wall of sound in 1966, re-jected the commercialism of the times with the Rolling Thunder Revue in 1975, and radically revised his back catalog through the Bob Dylan Revue in 1978, he—for the first time in his career—assumed an advocate's stance with the Bob Dylan Crusade. But just as the madness of 1966 crashed on a motorcycle, the RTR lost its steam, and the Revue closed, the Crusade also lost momentum and slowly ground to a halt. As we've seen, the Crusade wound down gradually. The first thing to go was the ad-vocacy. The preacher who told his hecklers to go see a Kiss show if they wanted to rock 'n' roll lost that fire within a year's time. When the back catalog entered the set, the Lord exited the show. The Alabama Chronicles continued to flavor the concert, but the main course changed. A brief, but powerful, era came to a close.

For years afterward, critics, biographers, and the curious probed Dylan's conversion for insight into its rationale and relevance. Speculation ran far and wide. Most subscribed to Paul Williams's theory; others posited alternative accounts. Writing for *New York Magazine* (and reprinted in Thomson and Gutman's anthology), Ron Rosenbaum of *Playboy* fame offered four theories about Dylan's conversion: (1) "Cherchez la femme" (the combination of Dylan meeting his "precious angel" and exiting his marriage inspired the change), (2) "Dylan is trying to erase once and for all his Jewish identity," (3) "he hasn't really changed at all" (the "he's faking" argument), and (4) "the trouble is not the Christianity but the Californian in the conversion." That last point is intriguing and represents Rosenbaum's take on the matter. He contends that the hedonistic California lifestyle was the "culprit" by claiming, "One could argue that any sensitive human being who lived in Malibu and Marina Del Ray for more than a year would be driven to seek a transcendent saviour from those modern Babylons." Rosenbaum concluded on a personal note, "As for me, Bob, I don't necessarily want you to leave Christ and come back to your roots. But I do think you ought to leave California and come back to New York."

After the fundamentalist portion of the Bob Dylan Crusade had passed, the auteur sat down with the *Los Angeles Times'* Robert Hilburn before the November 1980 leg of the Crusade opened in San Francisco and submitted to his first interview questions about his conversion (reprinted in Carl Benson's 1998 anthology). There, he offered an explanation that is a long way from any of Rosenbaum's conclusions:

> The funny thing is a lot of people think that Jesus comes into a person's life only when they are either down and out or are miserable or just old and withering away. That's not the way it was for me. I was doing fine. I had come a long way in just the year we were on the road [in 1978]. I was relatively content, but a very close friend of mine mentioned a couple of things to me and one of them was Jesus. Well, the whole idea of Jesus was foreign to me. I said to myself, "I can't deal with that. Maybe later." But later it occurred to me that I trusted this person and I had nothing to do for the next couple of days so I called the person back and said I was willing to listen about Jesus.

Later, Dylan talked with "two young pastors" and asked all sorts of basic questions. The auteur concluded, "Jesus is real and I wanted that. . . . I knew He wasn't going to come into my life and make it miserable, so one thing led to another . . . until I had this feeling, this vision and feeling." Afterward, he attended a Bible school for an extended period and he accepted Christ.

Hilburn inquired about the 1979 shows and their emphasis on the Alabama Chronicles to the exclusion of all else. Since Dylan had announced that the November 1980 phase of the Crusade would include songs from his back catalog, Hilburn was interested in the change. Dylan replied, "I truly had a born-again experience. If you want to call it that. It's an over-used term, but it's something that people can relate to. It happened in 1978. I always knew there was a God or a creator of the universe and a creator of the mountains and the sea and all that kind of thing, but I wasn't conscious of Jesus and what that had to do with the supreme creator." So the 1979–1980 shows were a response to his newfound convictions. Besides, Dylan claimed that he just was not in touch with his old songs anymore. He was captivated by his faith. When Hilburn asked if Dylan had any "second thoughts" about that advocacy, he declared, "No. By that time, I was into it. When I believe in something, I don't care what anybody else thinks."

Interestingly, Dylan told Hilburn that he originally wrote the Alabama Chronicles for Carolyn Dennis to record. He planned to produce her, but changed his mind. Now, he changed his mind once more. He reacquainted himself with his old songs and it felt good. Everything was reconnected, as he told Hilburn: "It's like I said, this show evolved out of that last tour. It's like the [older] songs aren't . . . how can I put it? Those songs weren't anti-God at all. I wasn't sure about that for a while." Later, he added, "I love those songs, they're still part of me." Therefore, the Crusade changed. Dylan reported that the Lord was in his "system" and that he was secure with that condition. So secure, in fact, that he no longer perceived the need to testify during his shows: "I don't feel compelled to do it. I was doing a bit of that last year on the stage. I was saying stuff I figured people needed to know. I thought I was giving people an idea of what was behind the songs. I don't think it's necessary anymore." Here is where Dylan offered the remarks that I mentioned at the opening of the *Shot Of Love* section. When Hilburn asked about the new songs (that eventually appeared on *Shot*) and their shift in tone, Dylan responded that he has "made his statement" to the best of his ability and now it is time to move on and avoid repeating himself.

What a revealing interview! During the session, Hilburn asked if Dylan were searching for a religious answer when Christ came into his life. He inquired about a trip to Israel and its significance. Dylan responded through a now-familiar argument. He claimed that if he *was* searching for anything during that or any other trip, it was the "root reality of the way things are, to pull the mask off." Ah yes, the mask! Bob Dylan's quest to discover what's behind *the mask* is a consuming passion, isn't it? He wore his Bob Dylan mask on Halloween night 1964. *Renaldo & Clara* was one big maskfest. And now, he used his mask metaphor here. Did another mask appear during his conversion to Christ? Perhaps. When Hilburn probed Dylan's response to political organizations that use The Word to their own ends, he offered this insightful answer: "I think people have to be careful about all that. . . . It's real dangerous. You can find anything you want in the Bible. You can twist it around any way you want and a lot of people do that. . . . The basic thing, I feel, is to get in touch with Christ yourself. He will lead you. Any preacher who is a real preacher will tell you that: 'Don't follow me, follow Christ.' "

I think Bob Dylan sincerely accepted Christ, assimilated that doctrine within his pantheistic worldview (notice the comments to Hilburn about the creator of mountains, seas, and so on—a direct reiteration of themes from "Last Thoughts On Woody Guthrie" and "Joan Baez in Concert, Part 2"), wrote songs of praise for that position, advocated that stance throughout the early legs of the Bob Dylan Crusade, and, as time passed and he peeked behind the mask of organized religion, concluded his religious affiliations while not forsaking his spiritual worldview. As a result, the need to testify waned. He reaffirmed his commitment to his old work and synthesized it into a revised Crusade. His aim remained true; it was merely refocused. Another interview with Robert Hilburn—this time in 1983—seems to confirm that observation. There, the *Los Angeles Times* reporter asked about the born-again period in retrospect:

> I don't think it (the issue) is relevant right now. First of all, "born again" is a hype term. It's a media term that throws people into a corner and leaves them there. Whether people realize it or not all the political and religious labels are irrelevant. That ("born again" period) was all part of my experience. It had to happen. When I get involved in something, I get totally involved. I don't just play around on the fringes. . . . I don't particularly regret telling people how to get their souls saved . . . I don't particularly regret any of that. . . . But maybe the time for me to say that has just come and gone. Now it's time for me to do something else. . . . It's like sometimes those things appear very quickly and disappear. Jesus himself only preached for three years.

And Renaldo was in but one movie. As time passed, Dylan's responses to the moral period echoed these comments. He had certainly achieved his mission and moved on to his next chore. But as these 1997 comments to *Newsweek*'s David Gates indicate, he left that era with something special: "Here's the thing with me and the religious thing. This is the flat-out truth: I find the religiosity and philosophy in the music. I don't find it anywhere else. Songs like 'Let Me Rest on a Peaceful Mountain' or 'I Saw the Light'—that's my religion. I don't adhere to rabbis, preachers, evangelists, all of that. I've learned more from the songs than I've learned from any of this kind of entity. The songs are my lexicon. I believe the songs."

The moral period of Bob Dylan's oeuvre once again demonstrates the auteur's capacity to *orchestrate* an artistic expression in service of a specific mission. This time, however, there was a major distinction in this creative quest: He became a public *advocate* for his cause. Therefore, this was not a "phase" that the artist passed through; rather, it was a mission that he publicly accepted. He submitted to his mission of service, fulfilled it, and left before he became that dreaded pawn in yet another organizational game. He looked behind religion's mask, and guess what he saw? Still, like the folk-posturing era, he mastered a genre and its "definitions." Like the folk-posturing era, he left that scene rather than allow it to "confine" or dominate him. What I wonder is, like the folk-posturing era, was the auteur posing?

I don't think he was.

The Pop Icon Period

If, by chance, you study artists for a living, well, you don't have this discussion too often. Artists just don't create in fifty-year life cycles. One way or another, artists—like everybody else—seem to wind down over time. This is especially true, it appears, with *commercial* artists. The industry negotiations and accompanying multilevel frustrations, celebrity-based pressures, media demands and intrusions, audience expectations, and more tax the muse and take their toll on an artist as he or she moves through the years. Sources of inspiration also evolve, devolve, disappear, and disappoint over time. So, artistic careers have a tendency to taper off as the years pass. A seemingly natural ebb and flow characterizes the twenty-first-century commercial art world in which artists come and go with seamless regularity. There are few exceptions—*especially* in this celebrity-intensive, media-driven environment. Consequently, the burning question is "When those pivotal transitional moments occur, does a given artist passively retreat or does he or she respond in some way?" Rare is the individual who is able to reinvigorate him or herself time and again. It just does not happen that way, and it probably never did. How many changes can a creative person endure and still produce quality—hopefully, innovative—work?

This chapter explores that phenomenon as it manifests in Bob Dylan's oeuvre once more. As we witnessed during the Americana and crystallization periods, Bob Zimmerman perseveres because of his rebellious resilience. His history demonstrates that his ability to reorient his creative powers facilitated the transitions that enabled his career to not only continue, but also advance. That skill is complemented by Zimmerman's mission-oriented method of operation. Through his mission-oriented approach, he sizes up the situation before him, organizes his resources, revises as needed, and applies "Bob Dylan" in service of that specific objective. Now, unlike the crystallization period's systematic reorientation, this process unfolds in a more haphazard fashion during the 1980s and early 1990s. This time frame—the pop icon period—most assuredly pursues reorientation; however, Zimmerman feels his way through this mission more than he orchestrates it. The results involve the oeuvre's most uneven segment. Everything enters the mix here: Little Richard–style rock 'n' roll, folk songs, message music, impressionism, 1980s rock, pop tunes, roots music, *disco*, show tunes, gospel songs, the Bob Dylan Revue—*everything* appears here except *Tarantula*-style liner notes and sermonic public testimonials. The pop icon era involves an artist in search of his creative bearings. It features a struggle unlike any we've witnessed to date. That the auteur almost gave up his fight for creative survival indicates the extent to which his mettle was tested. Bob Zimmerman's eventual victory was hard-earned. There are no basements in pastel-colored houses, no ex-boxers-turned-art-teachers, no Broadway stage directors, and no fundamentalist preachers in this story. This is about a man struggling with his creative life's direction. It is, once more, quite a story.

Chapter 9 considers Zimmerman's inventive methods and his approach to music production in an in-depth fashion; yet, I must open this chapter by noting that his search for a creative comfort zone is the prime mover in this period of his career. The artist's struggles with producers joined his difficulties with contemporary recording practices to upset his creative equilibrium, thereby rendering a wayward auteur in the 1980s and early 1990s. We saw this coming. Although Tom Wilson, Bob Johnston, and Don DeVito developed practices that served Zimmerman's agenda well, the spontaneous flow of musical inspiration that Dylan sought in the studio was increasingly difficult to manufacture. The "Let's capture lightning in a bottle" recording process just failed to materialize on a regular basis. Those days were over. The difficulties with the *Blood On The Tracks* sessions are a prime example. They may have captured that elusive lightning during the *Desire* sessions, but that mode of operation was rapidly becoming a thing of the distant past. It was nowhere in sight in Alabama. It was totally absent during *Shot Of Love*'s recording, in which five producers (including Dylan) plied their trade over a nine-month period. Furthermore, as the *Shot Of Love* songs languished over time, they lost their focus. When the writer attempted to reinvigorate them, he too had lost the original inspiration and the songs lacked that famed Dylan Edge—that thin, wild mercurial spark of spontaneity. Once the voice of his generation accepted the practice of punching in new lyrics and sounds during a record's final production stages, the creative tide turned.

When Dylan exited the moral period, he apparently had a lot on his mind, and the *Infidels* album conveys those sentiments with compelling clarity. With Mark Knopfler in the producer's chair, Dylan recorded some of his lifework's best tunes. When Knopfler returned to England to resume his recording career and the record entered postproduction, Dylan proceeded to tamper with everything. He deleted two of the record's strongest songs, rearranged the track order, and seriously diluted the final product. With that, the writing appeared on that pop icon period wall. The man known for recording a track and not looking back now recorded a song and stared it down. With *Empire Burlesque*, the plot thickened to the point where famed disco remix master Arthur Baker entered the fray and took the Bob Dylan Revue to the dance floors of his mind. Dave Stewart and Tom Petty also joined Dylan in the producer's role, and the studio mayhem advanced through the recording of *Knocked Out Loaded* and *Down In The Groove*. Layers and layers of sound, increasingly disjointed songwriting, and the return of *Self Portrait/Dylan*–style cover songs dominate these recordings. This is not to suggest that the Bob Dylan Revue was bad or in any way inferior; to the contrary, it handled the reggae version of "Precious Memories" with the same deft skills it used in performing "Mr. Bojangles." But it was *different*. That Dylan Edge was nowhere to be found. When the Irish band U2's front man, Bono, recommended producer Daniel Lanois to record *Oh Mercy* in New Orleans, Dylan's confusion seemed to dissipate. But it didn't really. Things had changed forever, and Dylan's time in Louisiana was but a temporary respite (of sorts). So when Dylan

recorded *Under The Red Sky* under the direction of Don Was and David Weiss, he
ended a protracted era in his own way. *Red Sky* features an all-star band rocking to
1950s-style rock 'n' roll—a genre that prides itself on its vacuity. The songs from this
album bounce along at their own merry pace and say absolutely nothing—"Wiggle
Wiggle," indeed. It was a return to the womb for the Iron Range's original biker-poet.
From Knopfler to Baker to Lanois to Was, the search for creative comfort advanced
without resolution. As a result, Bob Zimmerman secretly modified (read: *retired*) "Bob
Dylan."

Complementing this revolving-door studio mayhem was the craziness outside
of the various recording facilities from this era. Bob Dylan was all over the place in
the 1980s. He made music videos, appeared at multiple charity events (an appearance
at one event actually created another), toured with name acts, acted in a movie, and
accepted awards for his historic labors. He may have been adrift in his creative seas,
but he moved around like a determined steamer on a systematic course. Let's run
down some of the highlights from the pop icon period. We begin in February 1982
when Dylan recorded Allen Ginsberg at his Rundown Studios in California. That, in
and of itself, had to be a life-altering event. The next month he was inducted into
the Songwriters Hall of Fame in New York. In the spring of 1983 he recorded the
Infidels album, changed everything around that summer, and released the revision that
November. He appeared at the Grammy awards in February 1984; performed on
David Letterman's television program that March; toured Europe that May, June, and
July with Mick Taylor (guitar), Greg Sutton (bass), Ian McLagen (keyboards), and
Colin Allen (drums); and released a live album featuring selected performances of
that tour in December (the *Real Live* album). For Dylan, 1985 was the year of the
charity performance as he participated in the "We Are The World" recording/video
that January; appeared at the "Live Aid" concert in Philadelphia that July; after mentioning at Live Aid that the American farmers could use a little help as well, he performed with Tom Petty and the Heartbreakers as his backup band at the inaugural
Farm Aid concert that September; and between the Aids Live and Farm, he participated in Steve Van Zant's Sun City event during the summer. That year he also released *Empire Burlesque* (in June) and his impressive career retrospective, *Biograph*,
appeared in November. Dylan kicked off 1986 by appearing in the "Tribute to Martin Luther King, Jr." at the Kennedy Center for the Performing Arts in Washington,
D.C. That February and March, he (and assorted backing singers from the Bob Dylan
Revue—our beloved "Bobettes") toured New Zealand, Australia, and Japan with
Tom Petty and the Heartbreakers (an HBO television special, *Hard to Handle*, was
filmed in Australia). *Knocked Out Loaded* was released that June. In June, July, and August, Dylan, the Bobettes, and the Tom Petty band took their "True Confessions"
tour across the United States and into Canada. A portion of that tour featured a twin
billing with the Grateful Dead. That fall Dylan participated in the film *Hearts Of Fire*,
acting and recording songs for the movie's soundtrack. The film was never released
in American movie theaters, but was issued in video form in 1990. By the way, Dylan
played an aging rock star in the film. In July 1987 Dylan toured with the Grateful
Dead, and that September the Temple in Flames tour with Tom Petty and the Heartbreakers cruised across Europe. The auteur kicked off 1988 with his induction in the
Rock & Roll Hall of Fame (inducted by Bruce Springsteen). That April and May he

recorded with Petty, Jeff Lynne, Roy Orbison, and George Harrison under the name of the Traveling Wilburys and released an album that October. That album was an unexpected multiplatinum success. In May, *Down In The Groove* was issued. It did not go platinum. From June into October, Dylan toured the United States with his new band featuring G. E. Smith (guitar), Kenny Aaronson (bass), and Christopher Parker (drums). He concluded 1988 with an appearance at Neil Young's annual Bridge School Benefit. In March 1989 Dylan traveled to New Orleans and recorded *Oh Mercy* with Daniel Lanois (issued that September). From May into September, Dylan toured Europe and the United States with Smith, Parker, and new bassist Tony Garnier. That ensemble traversed the United States that October and November as well. The pop icon era moved toward closure with the January–March recording of *Under The Red Sky* (released in September); a January and February tour of the United States, Brazil, and Europe with Smith, Garnier, and Parker; an April 1990 recording session with the Wilburys (this time, without Orbison, who passed away shortly after the initial project's completion); and another extensive tour from May through November. During that last tour, the band began changing as Smith departed, other guitarists entered the ensemble, and the steady change of personnel that characterizes Dylan's hectic touring schedule began. Only Tony Garnier has remained in the band over the years.

Bob Dylan was a very busy artist in the pop icon period. Yet rare was that special flash of fire that characterizes his art. A "Foot Of Pride" appeared here, a "Most Of The Time" there, a "Dirty Love" somewhere, but the thin, wild mercury thing was absent with few exceptions. And nobody knew this more than the artist. We now *know* what we previously *suspected* because of his autobiography. *Chronicles* and the interviews that accompanied its release detail this pivotal moment in precise terms. My friends, the pop icon period was a trying time for Bob Zimmerman of Hibbing, Minnesota. Things fell apart, came together, fell apart again, and came together again as the auteur finally reoriented his craft, realigned his talent, and revised his career. Typically, I'd present this story as the music unfolds during this period; however, I'm going to tell this story first, then we'll examine the albums that demonstrate this evolutionary process by which Dylan saved his career. As I said before: This is quite a story.

Dylan cites the year as 1987. His hand was badly injured in an accident and he wondered if he would ever play guitar again. This was more than a little bit ironic. Two major revelations had converged to transform Dylan's thinking about his vocal technique and musical approach to his songs. He had discovered the key to unlock his future. He was excited about his new possibilities. Now, his hand was in a cast up to his elbow, and everything seemed more uncertain than it had before his revelations. Everything, it seemed, was up in that air once more.

Except for one thing, that is. One thing was crystal clear to Bob Dylan: The old way could not continue. In *Chronicles*, Dylan reports that he was "whitewashed and wasted out professionally" by 1987. The ten years leading to this point left him an "empty burned-out wreck" with "too much static" in his brain. He explains, "Wherever I am, I'm a '60s troubadour, a folk-rock relic, a wordsmith from bygone days, a fictitious head of state from a place nobody knows. I'm in the bottomless pit of cultural oblivion." Bob Dylan believed himself to be a pop icon. He reckoned he'd "shot" himself in his "foot" too often for things to continue. He argued that it is "nice to be known as a legend" and have people come to see you perform; however, for most of those people, one visit sufficed. Dylan reasoned that he "hadn't gone away yet," although he was "lingering out on the pavement." The auteur realized that there was a "missing person inside" of himself and that he "needed to find him." He could no longer kid himself and exploit "whatever talent I had beyond the breaking point." A reorientation was in order.

This was a multifaceted problem. First, Dylan was unhappy with his performances of his songs. In the recording studio, he felt that the songs "had only been sketched out but never brought from the shadows." As a result, he believed that he had left many of his songs "on the floor like shot rabbits" in both his recordings and live performances. His frustrations with his live performances were particularly acute. He steadfastly believed that his live performances failed to "capture the inner spirit" of his songs. He also feared that this left his audience feeling as though it had traveled through "deserted orchards and dead grass" (how rare for Dylan to express concern for his audience). One gains the impression that Dylan was traveling with those people as well. Dylan concluded that "too many distractions" had transformed his "musical path into a jungle of vines." It was time to change or quit.

For some time, quitting seemed to be the more viable option. During his prolonged tour with Tom Petty and the Heartbreakers, he realized that he had "no connection" to any form of "inspiration." He explained his stance in his first broadcast interview in nineteen years, when he told National Public Radio, "I did some tours with the Tom Petty band and then I did a short tour with the Grateful Dead and . . . as you could probably expect, really didn't feel like my heart was in it anymore." When asked if his songs were "alien" to him, he responded, "That's true. If you talk to any of the people who were around me at that time, I couldn't quite reach the meaning of the whole pantheon . . . of the songs of which I'd written. I thought maybe they didn't really hold up conceptually or something like that or maybe the music scene had passed me by." In *Chronicles*, Dylan maintains that his songs became "strangers" for him and he was just unable to "touch their raw nerves" or "penetrate their surfaces." Remarkably, the Archbishop of Anarchy said his songs were like "carrying a package of heavy rotting meat." Well, that's no fun. Consequently, he resigned himself to the view that it was no longer his "moment in history." He concluded that one more "big payday" with the Petty gang would seal his deal. Dylan summarizes his situation in this fashion: "The problem was that after relying so long on instinct and intuition, both these ladies had turned into vultures and were sucking me dry. Even spontaneity had become a blind goat." The man has a way with words, doesn't he?

I don't know about you, but when I'm lugging around a load of disintegrating, nasty flesh and vultures are hovering around me with vicious sucking noises—and when my principal means of operation becomes a disabled farm animal—I do what I can to muster the resources to change my situation. It's not that I'm this pragmatic genius or anything. What would you do?

And that is how Bob Dylan viewed it as well. Just as he accepted the decision to pack it in, two significant events transformed this unfortunate situation. Years before, guitarist Lonnie Johnson taught Dylan a style of guitar playing based on an odd-numerical, rather than the traditional even-numerical, system. Dylan tells us in *Chronicles* that Johnson acted as if this was some sort of secret code—a method only to be shared with the right people. People who dared to be different. After all, shifting numerical systems changed the entire melodic process. It could be a radical move. Still, Dylan never deployed the strategy until he realized that he could use it to phrase his vocals differently. He could, as he reports in his autobiography, "ignore musical custom" by changing melodies to odd-numbered-based arrangements, use that to support the tune as opposed to his traditional emphasis on lyrics, and subsequently use the framework to "unconsciously drag endless skeletons from the closet." That is, he recast his old musical repertoire in a new melodic light. His songs were reborn, and he felt as though he could play them forever. That rotted meat dissolved into caviar.

The second significant event transpired after Dylan agreed to conduct a brief tour with the Grateful Dead. The Dead wanted to play songs that Dylan could no longer fathom, as he told NPR: "They [the Grateful Dead] always have seemed to have known my stuff in a lot of ways deeper than me. They found great meaning in those songs. They could play them pretty accurately, but I couldn't do that." *Chronicles* also discusses this situation. There Dylan recalls that during a rehearsal, he told the band that he left something in his hotel room and he left with no intention of returning. He was not up for that task any longer. It is perfectly clear that Bob Zimmerman was finished with all of those Bob Dylan songs. While strolling down the street in a light rain, he concluded that he had simply made a mistake when he agreed to tour again and, according to his autobiography, he needed to "go someplace for the mentally ill and think about it." He kept walking in the rain until he came across a small bar with a jazz combo performing inside. He felt compelled to enter the bar, walked up to the edge of the stage, ordered a beverage, and listened. The singer inspired him, as he related to NPR: "A lot happened for me when I went in there and heard them. And I felt like I could do something again or I had a fix on something that I hadn't had for many, many years . . . it was the singer who got to me there. I mean, those things happen sometimes, mostly when they do happen, they happen to a person when they're much younger."

Dylan describes this moment in no uncertain terms in his autobiography: "Suddenly and without warning, it was like the guy had an open window to my soul." Our unnamed jazz singer reacquainted Dylan with techniques that were so "elemental," but he had forgotten how to do them. He returned to the Grateful Dead's rehearsal facility and tried his luck. It was not easy. Dylan claims it was like boring a hole into a wall: "All I did was taste the dust." Yet, it worked. The experience was "revelatory." He was on the road to recovery. He had discovered a way to reorient his singing and revisit his old songs.

But this reorientation was not yet completed. When he returned to touring with Tom Petty, he now allowed the band to do what it had always wanted to do and play a wide variety of songs from Dylan's back catalog. Dylan confirmed his rejuvenation. He rediscovered his voice. Nevertheless, while the vocal technique was reoriented, his spirit was a long way from being renewed. Touring had flat-out lost its flair. Dylan admits in *Chronicles* that his appearances were an "act" and those "rituals" bored him. Thus, retirement remained on the table. He was comfortable with the idea. It was his future.

Then everything turned upside down during a show in Locarno, Switzerland. When he attempted to sing during an outdoor show that night, nothing was there. He tried everything and he just couldn't trick the vocals out. He claims he stood clueless before 30,000 people. Suddenly, he "conjured up" a new vocal recipe and "cast" his "own spell to drive out the devil." It worked. He was shocked. Not only did it all return, but he also claims it reappeared in a multidimensional form. Dylan contends that the "energy was coming from a hundred different angles, completely unpredictable ones." He writes that after thirty years of performance, he discovered a completely new orientation. He was, he says, in a totally new "place." Retirement plans were abandoned.

Subsequently, he devised a three-year plan through which he would reorient his approach, revise his audience (it had grown more than stale for the auteur), and revitalize his performances. He met with Elliot Roberts (who had arranged the Petty and Dead tours) and discussed his new plan. Roberts urged patience, and Dylan accepted his advice. The man felt as though he had invented a "new genre" that would be uniquely his. He would play at an unprecedented rate (he mentions as many as 200 shows a year), allow "word of mouth" to carry the news of his revival (those Rolling Thunder dreams die hard, don't they?), attract a new audience (ditto), and carry on forever (ditto). (This is why I term this process "reorientation." The artist does not invent a new solution as much as he dusts off an old tool or technique for a new job.) As he declares in *Chronicles*, "All the cylinders were working and the vehicle was for hire." Our mission-oriented auteur was in his element: He had a plan.

And then he mangled his hand.

It was all within his grasp. He would use Johnson's guitar techniques to support his forgotten vocal methods, revive his interest in his old songs, revise his audience over time, and carry on. But the hand injury placed it all in doubt. He considered a career change. He asked a friend for some ideas, and his friend delivered. He suggested businesses of all kinds: furniture factories, sugarcane operations, fish farms, and, in an insightful move, a North Carolina factory that made "wooden legs." Dylan was considering all sorts of possibilities, yet the *one thing* he did not think about at all was *writing songs*. He rediscovered an old vocal approach and revisited a musical pattern that would support that strategy, and in turn, enliven his songs; however, writing *new songs* never crossed his mind. So much thought went into every detail of his reorientation—new voice, new sound, new audience, new old songs—but not a moment's thought about new songs. That is amazing. After all, the *writing* was what made his career—not his voice, guitar playing, stage presence, or touring schedule.

One night while his family slept, Dylan sat at his kitchen table and the last piece fell into place. He wrote some twenty verses of a song that he named "Political World." He maintains that he might not have written the twenty or so songs that "arrived" so suddenly had he not been injured. But he was, and they came. Next was "What Good Am I?" It was followed by "Dignity," then "Disease Of Conceit" arrived. The muse was in Bob Dylan's house by the ocean, and he dutifully responded to her urges. He may be in a woodshop on his property, and a song would say hello. He may be gazing out at the Pacific, and a song would arrive with the breeze. He wrote the songs—many with no melody or idea of one—and placed them securely in a drawer. There they lived together, and the auteur claims he felt "their presence."

Finally, his hand recovered. His doctor encouraged him to play guitar to facilitate its rehabilitation. And he quit writing.

On another night, guests visited for dinner. One guest, U2's Bono, sat up with Dylan after everyone else retired for the evening. The Irishman inquired if the voice of his generation had any new songs, and that drawer opened. Even without any hints of any melodies, Bono liked what he saw, we're told. He encouraged his host to record the new songs, but Dylan was weary of that and suggested that the best plan might be to burn them. Dylan just didn't enjoy the recording studio—never had, really. Bono called Daniel Lanois since Lanois had worked with U2 with some success. Lanois and Dylan talked over the telephone. They agreed to meet the next time Dylan visited New Orleans. They eventually met. They plotted and negotiated. They made *Oh Mercy*.

But *Oh Mercy* is only a sidebar to the real story here. The *real* news involves Dylan's reorientation strategy and its plans for a new vocal style supported by a new instrumental pattern that was designed to both revitalize the artist and attract a new audience. *These* revelations will take Bob Dylan to the Never Ending Series of Tours (NEST) and his career's final period. (As an aside, Dylanologists refer to Dylan's tours as the Never Ending Tour; however, the auteur balks at that label by saying it is inaccurate. His tours end and another begins. So, let's accommodate the artist with a simple word. Seems fair, doesn't it?) These revelations supported a much-needed shift in the Bob Dylan composite personality. Dylan was right. It would require some three years to fully realize the change. Over that timeframe he would continue to tour, reeducate or revise his audience, pause to record *Under The Red Sky*, secure the services of Tony Garnier, and systematically reintroduce "Bob Dylan" in a way that brought the Jack Fate dimension of the "Dylan" composite to the forefront. New vocal technique, new instrumental pattern, new old songs, new life, and a not-new-at-all, seasoned, accomplished controlling factor: Jack Fate.

Again, dear reader, what a story! Still, to fully appreciate what happens when Fate assumes control and the NEST takes off, we must pause and closely examine the four phases of the pop icon period that brought about this evolution. As you realize, I don't use the word "phase" to characterize the various portions of Dylan's oeuvre. Instead, I see each era in terms of its mission: discovery, rebellion, recovery, reorientation, service, and another reorientation. I contend that each mission is independent. Assuredly, they influence one another. Yet, in each case, the auteur systematically plans his strategy, organizes his resources, and *orchestrates* his artistic statement. That does not happen here. The pop icon period unfolds in *phases*—developmental phases. His ability to orchestrate his art dissipates and he virtually loses control. As that control slips further and further away, he contemplates retirement. The missions motivate Bob Zimmerman. When Zimmerman writes for Dylan, he has an agenda. Without that mission, Zimmerman's Dylan is lost. The pop icon period, then, charts an at times haphazard journey. One thing leads to another in uncharacteristic ways. As our story just indicated, it was a delicate journey. If the voice does not discover its old ways, or Johnson's secret teachings go unheeded, or the hand injury does not inspire his pen, or the hand injury does not heal properly, well, everything could be lost and Bob Zimmerman could be found somewhere in North Carolina running a factory that makes wooden legs for retired pirates.

The pop icon period's four phases are the *Street-Legal III* phase (featuring 1983's *Infidels*), the return of the Bob Dylan Revue phase (involving 1985's *Empire Burlesque*, 1986's *Knocked Out Loaded*, and 1988's *Down In The Groove*), the "swampspeak" phase (featuring 1989's *Oh Mercy*), and the concluding Retirement Party phase (featuring 1990's *Under The Red Sky*). Here we see different producers with different musicians working with different styles of music to different ends. Whatever motivated *Infidels* floats away and is replaced by whatever inspired the Bob Dylan Revue. The process recycles with visits to the Bayou and *American Bandstand*, respectively. Bob Zimmerman fights through this era. His discouragement is evident in Lanois's swampy sermons. The fact that we circle the cars, turn on the headlights, and get out and dance to "Handy Dandy" on the radios signifies that, for some reason, a party was in order. Here we discover why. Sometimes retirement is not the answer: All that is needed is an enlivening career change. We begin with the end of the world.

The *Street-Legal III* Phase

I guess it's hard to let a good thing go. After the *Street-Legal* declaration of decadence and its companion piece, *Shot Of Love*, the man the British press of 1965 deemed an "anarchist" has another go at the evils of the world with *Infidels*. Here—as much as with any Bob Dylan album from any timeframe—the project's title fits its thematic orientation like that famed glove. With *Infidels*, Bob Dylan sheds any sign of the personal agenda associated with *Shot Of Love*'s counterattacks or statements of eternal faith and concentrates on his role as his generation's op-ed editorial writer. Released in November 1983, *Infidels* contains eight songs (running over forty-two minutes) that report one overriding fact: The devil is among us. This editorial works systematically. First, we're told that the devil is, in fact, a "Jokerman" who is capable of assuming a host of strategic identities—even that of a "Man Of Peace." Once he assumes his station, the devil propagates acts of violence ("License To Kill"), fosters oppression ("Neighborhood Bully"), and generates greed ("Union Sundown"). Unfortunately, the devil may actually reside in us all. You never know exactly where Satan lives at any given time. Hence, you better stop and search yourself ("I And I"). Still, even with the devil on the prowl, weaving his dark magic to the ruination of us all, love is present. However, like the love songs "Precious Angel" and "Covenant Woman," these love interests join in the battle against the darkness ("Sweetheart Like You" and "Don't Fall Apart On Me Tonight") as the songs' narrators praise their women and acknowledge their perilous tasks. Yes, our brothers and sisters of the English press thought Bob Dylan was an anarchist when he sang songs that described negative situations without any solutions offered. If he was, his anarchy was in its infancy. It's grown up now. There are no solutions anywhere on this record. None whatsoever. Why? Why doesn't Bob Dylan return to the Alabama Chronicles and offer a ray of His Light in the face of all of this darkness? Where is the heartfelt proclamation of "Every Grain Of Sand"? I just don't know the answers to those questions. But I suspect our editorial writer thinks that the world is hopelessly lost. At least that is what is reported in *Infidels*. Our prospects don't look too good.

The biographers offer mixed responses to *Infidels*. To the extent that they praise Dylan's choice of musicians (Sly Dunbar on drums, Robbie Shakespeare on bass,

Mick Taylor on guitar, Mark Knopfler on guitar, Alan Clark on keyboards, and Clydie King on backing vocals), they lament the decision to omit strong tracks such as "Blind Willie McTell," "Foot Of Pride," and more. Clinton Heylin's session chronology dubs the work Dylan's "great lost album" in that the inclusion of these two songs would have elevated the record's stature within the lifework. As released, the project most certainly prefaced the period of artistic ambivalence to come.

Much of this uncertainty was a product of the auteur's shift from spontaneous recording to more structured sessions. Dylan admitted to the *Los Angeles Times* that he had certainly changed recording styles: "I decided (this time) to take my time like other people do. The extra little bit of time helped. That's going to be my pattern from now on. I'm not going to release a record until I feel it is worked out properly." In his attempt to bring those songs out from those shadows and into the light, he turned to his *Slow Train* colleague, Mark Knopfler, as his producer. Dylan was pleased with this arrangement, as he told the *Chicago Tribune*: "This was the easiest record I ever made because of Mark. He understood the songs so well. . . . Actually, we are soul mates. . . . He helped me make this record in a thousand ways, not only musically, which in itself would have been enough." Interestingly, once the soul mates completed their work (in May) and Knopfler departed, Dylan changed everything (in June–July). It is at this point, the biographers report, that Dylan fell in love with the vocal overdub. He actually admitted to Paul Zollo that his songwriting on *Infidels* was overdone: "Lots of songs on that album got away from me. . . . They hung around too long. They were better before they were tampered with. Of course, it was me tampering with them." By "tampering" with the album's lyrics, vocals, and song order, Dylan communicated the uncertainty of his artistic situation. Heylin's biography offers supporting evidence when he claims that "Angelina" (omitted from the final edition of *Shot Of Love*) was composed via a rhyming dictionary and that "Foot Of Pride" required an "unprecedented forty-three attempts" to complete. As I note in *American Song*, Dylan's soul mate may have been a brother in the recording studio, but the auteur desperately needed a parent, and this absence of direction would control the pop icon period.

We begin with the man in charge of all of these dastardly scenarios and that infamous "Jokerman." With a world music, meandering sonic platform adding dramatic tension as the song progresses through its six six-line stanzas and accompanying three-line choruses, Dylan synthesizes his impressionistic and portrait songwriting strategies on this song. In this instance, we move away from gangsters and dark comedians and toward the "prince of the air" (according to the moral period's sermons), the devil himself. Yes, there is a joker in the deck of life, and this song profiles him. What a joker he is! The first verse offers meaningful insights into the dark one when it describes his birth: He was born during a hurricane, clutching snakes in each hand. That is certainly a fine image. For Satan, freedom is closer than truth. This gives him reason for optimism. A vacuous chorus follows that depicts our Jokerman dancing to the nightingale's song while birds soar in the moonlight. Sounds harmless, right? Not really. The second stanza presents his evasive ways (he even sheds his skin—does he live by a lake?), while the third verse associates the Jokerman with the halls of sin and the fires of hell. More dark descriptions follow in the fourth verse before the negativity crystallizes in the closing stanzas. Consider, for example, the ominous scenes from the fifth verse:

> Well, the rifleman's stalking the sick and the lame,
> Preacherman seeks the same, who'll get there first is uncertain.
> Nightsticks and water cannons, tear gas, padlocks,
> Molotov cocktails and rocks behind every curtain,
> False-hearted judges dying in the webs that they spin,
> Only a matter of time 'til night comes steppin' in.

If gunmen and preachers compete over the afflicted, violence abounds through a variety of means, justice is corrupt, and, by all signs, the end times are near, the Jokerman is surely on an upswing. This is a dreadful scenario. It does not get any better in the final stanza:

> It's a shadowy world, skies are slippery gray,
> A woman just gave birth to a prince today and dressed him in scarlet.
> He'll put the priest in his pocket, put the blade to the heat,
> Take the motherless children off the street
> And place them at the feet of a harlot.
> Oh, Jokerman, you know what he wants,
> Oh, Jokerman, you don't show any response.

From the beginning, we're thrust right into yet another *Street-Legal* treatise. Just look at the scene presented above. Nothing is sacred, corruption is ubiquitous, and the Jokerman stands quietly by, absorbing the fruits of his ultimate victory. Once more, Dylan intimates that we need to stop and think, realize that the Jokerman is hard at work laboring toward the inevitable, and take heed. However, at no time are we told to change the guards. No hope is offered. No remedy is proposed. Just layers and layers of evil are exposed. You just know that the Jokerman has a plan to blow up those railroad tracks and disrupt the slow train's progress. That will buy him more time to pay off priests, harvest orphans, and weave his evil web.

Yes, the Jokerman is a clever adversary. He is so resourceful that he wears disguises to mask his true intentions or actions. I wonder what role he played in *Renaldo & Clara* (my money's on "Bob Dylan"). As the rocking sounds and powerful backbeat of the eight five-line verses of "Man Of Peace" reveal, he may even appear as a proponent of eternal love. That Jokerman is really something. He systematically destroys the world by isolating the righteous and providing humans with a license for self-annihilation, then tops it off with that old shape-shifting routine. The guy could be *anywhere*. One great place to hide is in the hero's garb. The first two verses establish the context for this ultimate deception:

> Look out your window, baby, there's a scene you'd like to catch,
> The band is playing "Dixie," a man got his hand outstretched.
> Could be the Fuhrer

Could be the local priest.
You know sometimes Satan comes as a man of peace.

He got a sweet gift of gab, he got a harmonious tongue,
He knows every song of love that ever has been sung.
Good intentions can be evil,
Both hands can be full of grease.
You know that sometimes Satan comes as a man of peace.

After this, our narrators in "Sweetheart" and "Don't Fall Apart" had better take another look at their dream girls—they, too, could be the Jokerman. The Jokerman disguises himself as a peace warrior; just as the Good Book warns. He is elusive (verse 3), he exploits our weaknesses (verse 4), he is intriguing (verse 5), he is deceptive (verse 6), and he is preparing for the end times (verses 7 and 8). This is one dire situation. No hope is offered. No remedy is proposed. The song establishes doubt and pounds on it for a while. Assuredly, this song communicates trust issues. I'm keeping a closer eye on my neighbors these days.

OK, so you want to be pragmatic. You want to question if this Jokerman is as formidable a threat as these two songs say he is. How do we know these things? Our anarchist provides the answers to those queries through the Hell Trilogy that is "License To Kill," "Neighborhood Bully," and "Union Sundown." We open with that special gift for self-destruction and "License." A simple instrumental platform provides room for this sermon to breathe as it moves through its four stanzas, four choruses, and six-line bridge. The song is totally systematic. It communicates that the Jokerman has issued a license for self-destruction, and he is enjoying the results. The track follows a simple pattern in which a verse describes some form of self-inflicted injury followed by the chorus' description of a woman sitting in dismay hoping someone, somehow will intervene and stop this madness. *That* is unlikely. The first verse captures this installment of the *Street-Legal* story line:

Man thinks 'cause he rules the earth he can do with it as he please
And if things don't change soon, he will.
Oh, man has invented his doom,
First step was touching the moon.

From there, we jump to the lady hoping for a reversal. But her chances do not look good either. The second stanza reports of a dark life cycle in which humans are traded about as preowned automobiles and treated as a commodity. The third verse explains why man is in such a sorrowful predicament:

Now, he's hell-bent for destruction, he's afraid and confused,
And his brain has been mismanaged with great skill.
All he believes are his eyes
And his eyes, they just tell him lies.

The Jokerman is thorough. He has manipulated our brains and convoluted our thinking, and this distorts what we observe in ways that lead to our ruination. Smart plan, don't you think? The song continues with more descriptions of humankind's descent. People are greedy, and the Jokerman exploits that trait to wonderful ends: self-destruction as a way of life. The doom and gloom are as much a part of our existence as nitrogen and oxygen. There is *no sign* of Muscle Shoals here. No hope is offered. No remedy is proposed. I guess you have to learn to live with the Jokerman. He is not going anywhere. The world is his playpen.

He is sophisticated as well. He has mastered the art of the divide-and-conquer rhetorical ploy in a fashion that allows humankind to channel its self-destructive urges against groups of people. I mean, he has respect for people. The Jokerman just does not expect us to sit at home and kill ourselves over nothing, so he provides reasons for murdering one another. Besides, death with a purpose is far more inspiring than death for death's sake. In response to his understanding of this strategic undertaking, the auteur serves up a case in point with "Neighborhood Bully." A drum-driven, guitar-slashing rock format sets the sonic scene for the eleven five-line verses that use that famous last-line reiteration to anchor the song's stance. In this instance, Dylan presents a straightforward, insistent, eleven-verse complaint on behalf of Israel. Israel is the "neighborhood bully," and it's occupying one tough, mean-spirited geographical location. Actually, our bully is more victim than oppressor. The song relates that the so-called bully is outnumbered, hated, criticized, hunted, abandoned, isolated, unappreciated, abused, and misunderstood. Who are these people, and what is their deal? The third verse responds to that inquiry:

> The neighborhood bully been driven out of every land,
> He's wandered the earth an exiled man.
> Seen his family scattered, his people hounded and torn,
> He's always on trial for just being born.
> He's the neighborhood bully.

Our bully has certainly hoed a tough row. How ironic that a faith that disavows the notion of original sin endures the assertion of instant guilt just because of its existence. But that irony is just the springboard for more descriptions of misunderstandings and mistreatment, all of which lead to the moral of the story, which is presented in the song's eighth stanza:

> Every empire that's enslaved him is gone,
> Egypt and Rome, even the great Babylon.
> He's made a garden of paradise in the desert sand,
> In bed with nobody, under no one's command.
> He's the neighborhood bully.

This bully is a formidable adversary, that is for sure. So, as those around our bully continue to soil his sacred texts, lie to him in treaties, ignore his resourcefulness, and mock his achievements, they had better realize that that license to kill may, in fact, meet with some serious opposition. That sword cuts two ways, and Dylan's eighth verse is clearly a not-so-veiled threat (shades of "The Time They Are A-Changin' "). Besides, as the final verse reports, this neighborhood bully is just biding his time, awaiting the True Justice that will arrive on board the slow train.

Oh yes, that Jokerman is oh-so-clever. He has granted everyone a license to kill, pretended to be a peacemonger by characterizing the innocent as the guilty, and mobilized his legions for the ultimate prank: to rid the holy from the Holy Land. But the Jokerman maintains a domestic agenda as well. It is not enough to have nations wage war against nations. No, he undermines internally, too. Remember what preacher Bob said during the Bob Dylan Crusade? He said the Lord deals with the unholy in three ways: the economy, the ecology, and war. Well, if Christ—the ultimate man of peace—deploys such tactics, it stands to reason that the Jokerman also has these tools available. Thus, from waging war on the innocent and promoting an environment of self-destruction, we turn to economic issues and "Union Sundown." Here Woody Guthrie rolls over in his grave as his apprentice attacks one of his most treasured ideals: labor unions. In this song, the rocking big sounds of the previous tracks are complemented by Clydie King's backing vocals and a disco-like backbeat to pound home a balanced statement of economic self-destruction. The five eight-line verses and accompanying four-line choruses unfold systematically, once more. This argument is methodical: The Jokerman has ravaged the countryside so thoroughly that he has even infiltrated Guthrie's precious unions. Using a fine blend of the "Gotta Serve Somebody" list format and *Street-Legal*'s end times rhetoric, this song articulates the Jokerman's control over the economy. How did he manage that, you ask? He manipulated human greed to his strategic advantage. The opening verses present a laundry list of everyday goods—shoes, linens, clothes, jewelry, and furniture—that are no longer made by Americans, but by underpaid Third World laborers. The third verse explains why: American labor has priced itself out of the market. Throughout the song, the chorus explains that as well. Simply, a good idea was destroyed by greed. Consider the fourth verse's explanation, in which the music pauses and the bass guitar heightens the vocal's dramatic effect:

> Well, the job that you used to have,
> They gave it to somebody down in El Salvador.
> The unions are big business, friend,
> And they're goin' out like a dinosaur.
> They used to grow food in Kansas
> Now they want to grow it on the moon and eat it raw.
> I can see the day coming when even your home garden
> Is gonna be against the law.

Sorry Woody. After the chorus revisits the greed theme, the controlling *Street-Legal* rhetoric articulates the story's moral in the final stanza:

> Democracy don't rule the world,
> You'd better get that in your head.
> This world is ruled by violence
> But I guess that's better left unsaid.

From Broadway to the Milky Way,
That's a lot of territory indeed
And a man's gonna do what he has to do
When he's got a hungry mouth to feed.

And if he cannot feed his family, well, you know what happens. "Hollis Brown" told that story. I'm sure the Jokerman will provide just enough cash for those shotgun shells. When push comes to shove, that license to kill is inclusive—everybody, everywhere is fair game. The Jokerman has his bets covered.

I'm looking back over my notes and Dylan's lyrics, searching for something to hang onto here. Is there any remedy proposed? No. Is there any hope anywhere? No. Is there even an invitation to change those guards? No. Is a cleansing slow train moving over the horizon? No. The Jokerman has blown the tracks, has built a moat around his playpen, and enjoys the fruits of his own little recreational alternative: watching the world feed upon itself. When people feel as though they have a right—perhaps even a duty—to kill one another; when nations oppress one another and offer little to no opportunities for reconciliation or negotiation; and when economic systems self-destruct because of their unabashed greed, you have all of the makings of the end times. Hey! I need a sermon here. Can anybody give me The Word? Some hope? A chance? Somebody, somewhere may offer a message of hope, but you won't find them on Bob Dylan's *Infidels*. This is, most assuredly, *Street-Legal III*. But this version—like *Street-Legal II* (that is, *Shot Of Love*)—does not set the table for an intervention. You can't see the smoke bellowing from the slow train as it works its way down those long and winding tracks. Nope. This is the way it is. You better wonder at that grain of sand and marvel at that beautiful sunset because someone is liable to sneak up behind you wearing your best friend's clothes, stick a penknife in your back, lift your wallet, and tell the police you bullied him or her into a self-defensive act. A hard, cleansing rain would be a welcome sight in this dreadful portrait of human relations. I can only presume that some infidel shot Bob Dylan's dog out of spite the morning he wrote these songs. This is angry stuff.

And it does not stop with outside threats. You could just as easily be at war with yourself. Your left brain could be bullying your right brain. You could be stealing from yourself. Have you checked lately? Dylan does on "I And I." A creepy, swampy Dire Straits sound provides a passive, supportive backdrop for the five four-line verses and accompanying four-line choruses of this introspective analysis. A simple scene featuring a woman quietly sleeping in the narrator's bed provides a springboard for a cryptic individual complaint about the ways of the world and the narrator's internal struggles. After a couple of verses describing our sleeping beauty, the third stanza ponders Old Testament reasoning, and the fourth verse pauses to mention two men awaiting a train (is it *that* train?) and thoughts of the end times. The song's final segment captures its sentiments:

Noontime, and I'm still pushin' myself along the road, the darkest part,
Into the narrow lanes, I can't stumble or stay put.
Someone else is speakin' with my mouth, but I'm listening only to my
    heart.

I've made shoes for everyone, even you, while I still go barefoot.
I and I
In creation where one's nature neither honors nor forgives.
I and I
One says to the other, no man sees my face and lives.

Our narrator is not a happy camper, and he obviously feels used and torn. Yet, this song flirts with these sentiments as much as anything. It teases these internal tensions. I sense that, once again, the Jokerman is toying with the narrator and, from there, us. Beware!

With all of this turmoil engulfing us, how nice of *Infidels* to pause and celebrate that soft, beautiful rose that is growing in that pile of manure that is the world as we know it. With simple instrumental support, "Sweetheart Like You" deploys that time-honored last-line-as-narrative-anchor strategy as its five seven-line verses unfold (along with two four-line bridges). Using the "What's a nice girl like you doing in a place like this?" story line to praise this unnamed lady, this song builds directly on the dark imagery of "Jokerman" and the Hell Trilogy. Thanks to the Jokerman, the world is one big dump. However, "she" stands out, and this inspires the narrator's curiosity. The song sort of floats along, describing odd scenes, complimenting this fine lady, and encouraging her to find a more suitable environment where her virtues will be appreciated. The plot thickens with the fourth verse:

> You know, news of you has come down the line
> Even before ya came in the door.
> They say in your father's house, there's many mansions
> Each one of them got a fireproof floor.
> Snap out of it, baby, people are jealous of you,
> They smile to your face, but behind your back they hiss.
> What's a sweetheart like you doin' in a dump like this?

This song is getting interesting. The second bridge follows with what seem to be visions of hell: To be in the narrator's shoes, you must propagate evil and suffer for it. Suddenly, the scene shifts in the final verse and the *Street-Legal* rhetoric assumes complete control:

> They say that patriotism is the last refuge
> To which a scoundrel clings.
> Steal a little and they throw you in jail,
> Steal a lot and they make you king.
> There's only one step down from here, baby,
> It's called the land of permanent bliss,
> What's a sweetheart like you doin' in a dump like this?

Upon initial review, this is yet another salute to our "precious angel–covenant woman–in the summertime" spiritual benefactor in that this mysterious woman is a potential ray of light in a very dark world. The celebration is implied more than in the other songs, yet it is there. Then again, there is the fourth verse's reference to her father's home. Could this be more "The Groom's Still Waiting" metaphors? Does "she" represent "the church"? The lone shaft of light in a dark, Jokerman-controlled world? I don't know. But I do recognize this story line. *Street-Legal*'s themes are dominating this record.

This line of storytelling continues in that treasured capstone statement slot as Dylan closes his version of *Infidels* with "Don't Fall Apart On Me Tonight." The song follows a bouncy, country-tinged harmonica open with soft sounds that move to a big backbeat. The track unfolds by way of four eight-line stanzas with accompanying six-line, standard choruses and a good old-fashioned middle-eight between the third and fourth segments. Much like "Sweetheart" and its predecessors, this song issues a relational plea (that implies praise) that gains strength due to the sorry state of the world. The first segment pleads for her perseverance since the world is falling apart. He begs her to stay. He desperately needs her. The ways of the world are too much to handle by himself. The second and third segments follow the same line of reasoning except individual complaints replace worldly observations while the closing stanza argues that the relationship will improve if she stays. Throughout, the narrator pleads and pleads. Let's examine the second segment for insight into this song's approach:

> Come over here from over there, girl,
> Sit down here. You can have my chair.
> I can't see us goin' anywhere, girl.
> The only place open is a thousand miles away and I can't take you there.
> I wish I'd have been a doctor,
> Maybe I'd have saved some life that had been lost,
> Maybe I'd have done some good in the world
> 'Stead of burning every bridge I crossed.
>
> Don't fall apart on me tonight,
> I just don't think that I could handle it.
> Don't fall apart on me tonight,
> Yesterday's just a memory,
> Tomorrow is never what it's supposed to be
> And I need you, oh, yeah.

Yes, the *Street-Legal* declaration of decadence is the controlling factor in *Infidels*. No remedies are proposed. No answers are offered. But "she" helps him endure, and *that* is our capstone statement. In a hopeless world full of personal regrets and ceaseless unwanted obligations, the last avenue of survival is that precious angel who provides shelter from life's varied storms. The Jokerman has control. He is pounding on the door. And this narrator does not want to run and hide. He wants to stay at home with his woman and weather the experience. Besides, you can't hide anyway. The Jokerman could actually appear from within—or, even worse, you could look into your lover's eyes and see him laughing at you. This is depressing. I need a hug.

When Mark Knopfler left his soul mate in New York to resume his career with his own band, he evidently had no idea what Dylan would do with their work. They had recorded a number of songs that failed to make their final list. Covers such as "The Green, Green Grass Of Home," Willie Nelson's "Angel Flying Too Close To The Ground," and Knopfler's own "Sultans Of Swing" were supposedly in the can, as were outtakes like "Tell Me," "Someone's Got A Hold Of My Heart" (an early version of a track that appears on *Empire Burlesque*), "Lord Protect My Child," "Death Is Not The End," and others. While "Death Is Not" wound up on *Down In The Groove* and "Tell Me," "Someone's Got," and "Lord Protect" were featured on the original *Bootleg Series* installment, the real mystery involved two stellar songs, "Blind Willie McTell" and "Foot Of Pride" (versions of both are also included in the first *Bootleg* release). Why Dylan cut these songs from the original list, added "Union Sundown," and reduced the song list from the original nine to eight tracks is anybody's guess. The biographers report that he tampered with the songs he'd recorded with Knopfler in order to reduce their predictability. Dylan is often quoted as saying that he wanted to avoid the predictable patterns he heard on records like those by the Eagles, so he had his way with these songs in order to disrupt any unwanted rhythms. The principal emphasis on the overdubs involved the vocals, but as we see, he went farther than that.

"McTell" follows the narrative strategy we've observed in Dylan's recent love songs; that is, he uses his profile of "McTell" as a springboard to worldly complaint. He extols McTell and decries the ways of the world. The five eight-line stanzas follow a set format in which the opening six lines paint a picture of some scene before the verse closes with the two-line comment praising McTell's abilities. This is, my friends, a tried-and-true songwriting formula within the oeuvre. The opening verse demonstrates this style:

> Seen the arrow on the doorpost
> Saying, "This land is condemned
> All the way from New Orleans
> To Jerusalem."
> I traveled through East Texas
> Where many martyrs fell
> And I know no one can sing the blues
> Like Blind Willie McTell

Do you see how this works? Dylan reports on the sorry state of the world, praises the unnamed heroes of eastern Texas, and salutes McTell's singing ability. The second, third, and fourth verses concentrate on McTell by recalling him playing under the starlit night (verse 2), portraying scenes of the slavery that inspired the blues (verse 3), and describing a romantic encounter by a river with a chain gang bellowing in the distance (verse 4). Suddenly, we're thrust into the present and the narrator's thoughts of that moment as the song closes:

> Well, God is in His heaven
> And we all want what's his

But power and greed and corruptible seed
Seem to be all that there is
I'm gazing out the window
Of the St. James Hotel
And I know no one can sing the blues
Like Blind Willie McTell

McTell sings like the "Covenant Woman" loves—both occur in the face of a decaying world. To the extent that she can pull her lover through the hell of life on earth, McTell's singing provides a soundtrack for the slow train's arrival. His vast experiences offer a context for an all-knowing account of the world's never-ending misery. Sit back, relax, and let Blind Willie chart the ways of abusive power mongers, cheesy greedy exploiters, and their corrupted, contaminated offspring. Willie knows because Willie's been there, and that fuels his singing. Nobody can sing those blues like him because nobody would want that skill—the price is just too high.

I don't know if the biographers are accurate in their claims that the original *Infidels* was so much superior to the released version. But I will say this: Although I think "Don't Fall Apart" is a fine capstone statement that argues from a traditional position within the oeuvre, I get a chill when I consider the possibility of "Foot Of Pride" filling that position. Had "Foot Of Pride" occupied that special spot, it would have not only closed *Infidels*, it would have also concluded one of the more protracted statements of the Dylan Canon. *Street-Legal*'s declaration of decadence has carried on for quite a while. Though it paused for The Answer that was conveyed by way of the Alabama Chronicles, it quickly returned via portions of *Shot Of Love* before rising to dominance in *Infidels*. Actually, *Street-Legal*'s rhetoric has carried on longer than any other systematic statement in the lifework. The heaven and hell of love is always present in the auteur's work, that's for certain. That aside, no other theme achieves the depth and determination of the declaration of decadence. And "Foot Of Pride" is one compelling capstone statement for a five-album exploration of the ways of the devil, its manifestations on earth, and their consequences.

As Christopher Ricks will tell you, pride is a sin. In "Foot Of Pride," it rises to a position of dominance. The six eight-line verses with their corresponding three-line choruses offer a series of vignettes that are tied together by their darkness. A steady beat, driving guitar, and punctuating harmonica (appearing briefly after each chorus) provide a powerful backdrop for a song strong enough to challenge the Jokerman to a duel. The opening verse portrays a funeral scene full of unsavory sentiments (lions rip off flesh, women appear as men, preachers talk of betrayal, and aspirations crash) before the chorus declares that you pass the point of no return when you interject your pride. The second verse tells a cryptic story through vivid imagery. The narrator addresses an unnamed person with a sick-sounding, vengeful brother; rants about the ways of the world; and derides her for her thinking. The third verse is equally enigmatic. There we hear of a retired man's evil business practices and how they are complemented by his woman's wicked ways. When we get to the fourth and fifth stanzas, Brother Bob has worked himself into a frenzy, as you can see:

Well they'll choose a man for you to meet tonight
You'll play the fool and learn how to walk through doors
How to enter into the gates of paradise
No, how to carry a burden too heavy to be yours
Yeah, from the stage they'll be tryin' to get water outa rocks
A whore will pass the hat, collect a hundred grand and say thanks
They like to take all this money from sin, build big universities to study
    in
Sing "Amazing Grace" all the way to the Swiss banks

Well, there ain't no goin' back when your foot of pride come down
Ain't no goin' back

They got some beautiful people out there, man
They can be a terror to your mind and show you how to hold your tongue
They got mystery written all over their forehead
They kill babies in the crib and say only the good die young
They don't believe in mercy
Judgment on them is something that you'll never see
They can exalt you up or bring you down main route
Turn you into anything that they want you to be

See what I mean? This is the capstone statement for the oeuvre's declaration of decadence. False prophets secure real profits by offering a fake path to heaven. They will cajole you into subservience through false miracles, use the wicked to take your cash, and build tributes to themselves that further their prideful deceit. "They" are a bad bunch, they are. "They" appear physically attractive and mysterious as they dominate your mind and, therefore, control your life. No, there is no mercy here. When people kill babies under false pretenses and lead their followers down the broad path of sin, there is no hope in sight. "They" *are* the Jokerman. That is for sure. When the song closes with yet another cryptic vignette, it just hammers that final nail into this unsavory coffin.

    Infidels is a *protest* record. It is not, however, some cheesy topical album that panders to some specific cause or organization. Coming out of his spiritual exploration, the auteur now knows exactly who the enemy is, and he attacks that devil with all he's got. That the most damning song of all—"Foot Of Pride"—was deleted demonstrates Dylan's willingness to pull back the reins on himself (much like the *Blood On The Tracks* revisions). Pity. The song captures the *Street-Legal* declaration of decadence so very, very well. Nevertheless, the young topical writer has evolved through his spiritual maturation into a piercing protest writer without any fear. Bob Dillon watched it all unfold and inspired Bob Dylan to issue a response worthy of the Iron Range's original biker-poet. Just as Bob Dylan told the Mr. Message Man constituency to go to hell, he now attacks the agents of hell on earth. This is not a pretty sight. The Jokerman owns The Church. The devil is in His House. Join hands with your lover, abandon your prideful ways, cooperate with your neighbors, dismiss violence and greed, and buy yourself a sturdy wraparound bulletproof vest. Grab a helmet if you can find one. When that man of peace sends his whores out to collect their fees, you had better follow the Lord's advice to Abraham. I strongly recommend *running*.

Well, that's that. Thank goodness, I don't think I can stay in this place much longer. The *Street-Legal* declaration of decadence is a lot to swallow. It keeps you up at night. When he changed the guards and discovered it did not work, he took the time to find out why. This is some powerful songwriting. I agree with Christopher Ricks when he claims that much of this operates beyond the artist's consciousness. As we'll observe in chapter 9, Dylan claims that he is a medium in his songwriting. He picks up signals from somewhere, interprets them, and presents them in his own unique style. Now, he switches frequencies. The *Street-Legal* era is functionally over. Dylan will issue a rant from time to time, but the concentrated emphasis on the sad state of the world comes to a close with the *Infidels* project. Again, this was heavy stuff for me. So much negativity brings a guy down. I think I'll take a vacation and recoup. Yes, that's a good idea. Where should I go? I know! I'm off to Las Vegas to see one of my *favorite* acts: the Bob Dylan Revue.

The Bob Dylan Revue Phase

Well, we've ranted and raved for five albums, haven't we? After the volcano erupted on "Black Diamond Bay," the mayhem spread all over the world. The *Street-Legal* declarations warranted the Alabama Chronicles and the Bob Dylan Crusade, they ran their course, and the auteur closed that book with *Shot Of Love*. Then he fired one last warning shot across the horizon through *Infidels*—this time, without any sign of any hope. All we can do is grit our teeth and bear the pains of *this* life. Having achieved closure on that dire subject, the oeuvre now turns to a sustained treatment of loving relations articulated through the dramatic calls and responses of the Bob Dylan Revue. Here we have cover songs in the style of *Dylan*, love songs that follow sonic formulas introduced on *Street-Legal*, a grand narrative that recalls those *Desire* days with Jacques Levy, a protest song that sounds like a party, and a variety of coauthored songs that praise ugly lovers, announce trips to foreign lands, and declare relational subservience. In *Empire Burlesque*, *Knocked Out Loaded*, and *Down In The Groove* we take all of these themes, shake them up, and pour them out through a musical style that deploys a huge cast of famous musicians, Bob Dylan's unique voice, and the wonderful support of the backing vocalists, the delightful Bobettes. While the biographers and critics often ridicule this segment of the lifework, I find it a welcome reprieve from the fire and brimstone of the end times storytelling. Still, this phase of the pop icon period does indicate the extent to which the auteur was adrift in his search for creative equilibrium. The principal difference in this phase involves the absence of that famed Dylan Edge. That Edge may have been a bit too prickly in *Infidels*, so we may experience a bit of a backlash during the Revue-based albums. Nevertheless, these albums sound great, their performances are sharp, and their songs suit the purpose at hand—a reorientation is underway, and these projects are the result of that extended process.

Empire Burlesque (released in June 1985) contains ten tracks (running 46:55), involves Tom Petty and the Heartbreakers (and a host of other musicians, including guitarists Mick Taylor, Ted Perlman, Ron Wood, Al Kooper, Stu Kimball, Syd

McGuiness, and Ira Ingber; drummers Sly Dunbar, Don Heffington, Jim Keltner, Anton Fig, and Bashiri Johnson; bass players Robbie Shakespeare, Bob Glaub, and John Paris; keyboard and synthesizer work by Richard Scher, Alan Clark, Vince Melamed; and horns by Chops, David Watson, and Urban Bright Horns) and the Bobettes (Carol Dennis, Queen Esther Marrow, Peggi Blu, Madelyn Quebec, and Debra Byrd), and was produced by Arthur Baker, Dylan, Petty, and Dave Stewart (depending upon the track in question). Heylin's chronology reports that it required nine sessions to complete the thematically diverse project that features six relational complaints ("Tight Connection To My Heart (Has Anybody Seen My Love)," "Seeing The Real You At Last," "I'll Remember You," "Never Gonna Be The Same Again," "When the Night Comes Falling From The Sky," and "Something's Burning, Baby"), a relational celebration ("Emotionally Yours"), two societal complaints ("Clean Cut Kid" and the cryptic "Dark Eyes"), and an *Infidels*-fueled warning ("Trust Yourself"). The record is an interesting blend of production innovation and superficial lyrics (remember, this is the album that Paul Williams claims is full of movie dialogue). While "Clean Cut" and "Trust Yourself" have something to say, most of these tunes are vacuous, contemporary pop songs. Besides, there is nothing wrong with a good, old-fashioned pop song—especially after all those songs about the devil and the end of the world!

We start with this album's dominant theme and the relational complaints. *Empire Burlesque* kicks off with the Revue in high gear and the revision of the *Infidels* outtake "Someone's Got A Hold Of My Heart" and "Tight Connection." With layers of sounds and the Bobettes' precise backing vocals plowing the way, the track appears in three segments (each contains a twelve-line verse, a four-line stanza, and a five-line repeated chorus). This pop standard complains about a disintegrating relationship that the narrator probably doesn't want anyway. You get the feeling that Paul Williams's observations about the lyrics manifest here, as clever lines seem to emerge from thin air. As a result, there is not much continuity in this song's story. The opening segment conveys this style as well as any:

> Well, I had to move fast
> And I couldn't with you around my neck.
> I said I'd send for you and I did
> What did you expect?
> My hands are sweating
> And we haven't even started yet.
> I'll go along with the charade
> Until I can think my way out.
> I know it was all a big joke
> Whatever it was about.
> Someday maybe
> I'll remember to forget.
>
> I'm gonna get my coat,
> I feel the breath of a storm.

There's something I've got to do tonight,
You go inside and stay warm.

Has anybody seen my love,
Has anybody seen my love,
Has anybody seen my love,
I don't know,
Has anybody seem my love?

As you can see, the hint of complaint exists, but it sort of hovers over the song. The narrator thinks the relationship was a game or a joke that he looks forward to forgetting. It is also a fairly cloudy story. The four-line verse raises a scene that is never developed in any way. That is how this song works—in fragments. The track continues with the couple attempting to talk things over before everything drifts off into a dreamlike recollection about a visit with "Madame Butterfly." The song concludes with more fragmented images of blues singers singing about the Holy City of American Music (Memphis) in the summertime, guys in blue wigs, and a faint final complaint. Both in its sound and content, this is one vacuous pop song. But, hey, that's OK. At least there is no sign of the slow train or the devil!

The vacuity dissipates with the second song, "Seeing The Real You." Here the narrator has a real go at his soon-to-be-ex-lover. The song is relentless across its ten four-line verses that are divided into five segments with that ever-present last line punctuating the respective segments. Moreover, the Revue rocks on this song with layers of horns, guitar, and backing vocals coloring the story. Yes, this is a big-time pop platform for a tune that conveys that the relational tide has turned, the narrator's finally seen the truth, and he is angrily coping with the results. The first segment features the narrator's hope for a relational recovery, and his subsequent realization that that is just not going to happen. It's over. Now let's complain about it. The second segments reviews the chances he took for the relationship and, once more, celebrates the truth's arrival on that deteriorating scene. The song's third segment indicates why he is so relieved by this relational revelation:

I'm hungry and I'm irritable
And I'm tired of this bag of tricks.
At one time there was nothing wrong with me
That you could not fix.

Well, I sailed through the storm
Strapped to the mast,
But the time has come
And I'm seeing the real you at last.

That is a vivid description! For the narrator, his relationship was like being tied to a sailing mast and cruising through a heavy storm. I guess that's love for you; struggling through wind, rain, and hail while you're shifting to and fro, unable to move freely, trapped. Still, he had high hopes and he would have accepted a normal amount of difficulty, but that did not happen. This was just too much. He admits his problems, suggests she has got some as well, and urges her to do whatever she needs to do—quickly. He is ready to move on, plain and simple.

Not all relationships end in such acrimony, and "I'll Remember You" and "Never Gonna Be The Same Again" communicate remorse rather than righteous indignation. In "I'll Remember," the Revue does a genuine love song with the light vocal accompaniment (featuring Quebec) complementing the soft, piano-driven music as the number moves through its three 10–11-line verses (with a four-line bridge). This is a classic pop song (I mean *classic* classic—as in Cole Porter or Johnny Mercer). Clear, straightforward language chronicles the narrator's nostalgia for a lost love. Of all the lovers he has ever known, when he is all alone pondering his life, he will think of her (verse 1). He reiterates that feeling in the second stanza and the bridge:

> I'll remember you
> At the end of the trail,
> I had so much left to do,
> I had so little time to fail.
> There's some people that
> You don't forget,
> Even though you've only seen'm
> One time or two.
> When the roses fade
> And I'm in the shade,
> I'll remember you.
>
> Didn't I, didn't I try to love you?
> Didn't I, didn't I try to care?
> Didn't I sleep, didn't I weep beside you
> With the rain blowing in your hair?

(Once more, Jacques Levy would love those internal rhymes.) Yes—as the final stanza repeats yet again—she is the one who got away. In his sunset years, he will still be pining for this wonderful lady who knew him well. But he failed her, and now all he has are his memories of his now-departed friend. Lyrically, sonically, and emotionally, this song communicates that deep sense of loss that accompanies losing a lover who was also your friend. That is a special combination, and this narrator surely misses it.

As does the narrator in the second installment of this theme, "Never Gonna Be The Same Again." With *two* synthesizers participating in the layers and layers of sound (complete with the Bobettes weaving their magic), this three-verse pop song (with a four-line bridge) also uses that telltale last line to drive home the song's title and message. The Revue is at its pop finest here. "Never Gonna" is a simple, sad song of remorse presented in a sonically dense fashion. The narrator states his case, and the Bobettes echo those sentiments as only they can. The opening verse celebrates her wonders and quickly crashes over her departure. The second stanza and bridge provide the sad details:

Sorry if I hurt you, baby,
Sorry if I did.
Sorry if I touched the place
Where your secrets are hid.
But you meant more than everything,
And I could not pretend,
I ain't never gonna be the same again.

You give me something to think about, baby,
Every time I see ya.
Don't worry, baby, I don't mind leaving,
I'd just like it to be my idea.

Classic Bob Dylan, isn't it? Amongst all of the remorse and regret, the narrator coyly comments that he does not mind the breakup—he just resents being the victim. We may only presume that if *he* were the one doing the deed, he would be just fine. But he didn't, and he's not. The song closes with the narrator's continuing lament. She did it all for him, and now she is gone. He cannot change what is already done, so he has to accept the fact that she changed his life, she has departed, and he will have forever to consider the consequences.

In our final installments of the relational complaint thematic, the Revue tries on a couple of interesting musical hats for these portrayals of romantic angst. With "Something's Burning," the Revue deploys a martial beat as military-style drums lead a simple sonic strategy that facilitates a steady march through this track's nine four-line verses. At times cryptic, at times pedestrian, this song tells another account of love on the wane. It opens by communicating the narrator's uncertainty regarding the relationship. Does she still love him? Why does she seem to be pulling away? He is confused. The third and fourth stanzas relate his uncertainty and corresponding suspicions:

I know everything about this place, or so it seems
Am I no longer a part of your plans or your dreams?
Well, it is so obvious that something has changed
What's happening, baby, to make you act so strange?

Something is burning, baby, here's what I say
Even the bloodhounds of London couldn't find you today
I see the shadow of a man, baby, makin' you blue
Who is he, baby, and what's he to you?

The song marches on from there. The narrator just does not know what she is thinking, but he smells the smoke of love aflame, and he is growing increasingly suspicious. He senses the relationship's deterioration in the night and in the wind. Everywhere, he feels the relational decline unfolding around him. When the song ends, he seems willing to give the relationship another try, but whatever is on fire needs to be handled. The martial beat adds an interesting dimension to this time-conscious story. It is almost as if the sound represents a clock ticking as the time winds down on the relationship.

From the distinctive sonority of "Something's Burning," we turn to another highly recognizable beat for our final song of relational complaint, "When The Night Comes Falling From The Sky." I guess it just *had* to happen. The Bob Dylan Revue goes disco for the ten verses of a song that unfolds in five two-verse segments punctuated by the title-in-the-last-line strategy. Arthur Baker does his thing here. The song is a straightforward relational complaint that dances to the sounds of That Day. Synthesizers abound in this highly layered production. It is really sort of amazing: Bob Dylan goes disco. In the story, the narrator seems to enjoy his lover's pain as this "that'll be the day" story unfolds. The narrator in this song is through with this woman, and it will be a cold day in the Jokerman's native home before he even *thinks* about rekindling this relationship. In the opening scene, she is burning his letters in the fireplace, but it does not matter to our narrator. She toys with her fate, and it will catch up to her one day (segment 2). The narrator complains about those around him as well as her cheating ways in the third segment. You can sense it coming; He goes for the jugular in the fourth segment:

> In your teardrops, I can see my own reflection,
> It was on the northern border of Texas where I crossed the line.
> I don't want to be a fool starving for affection,
> I don't want to drown in someone else's wine.
>
> For all eternity I think I will remember
> That icy wind that's howling in your eye.
> You will seek me and you'll find me
> In the wasteland of your mind
> When the night comes falling from the sky.

They're biting, but what great lines: seeing your image in another person's tears, imagining drowning in another's pleasures, existing in the barren expanses of someone's mind. After yet another swipe at his new ex-lover, the song closes with the narrator's declaration of independence. What a song. In many ways, it is as if "Like A Rolling Stone" went disco. I guess it is nice to know that mean-spirited relational complaints know no musical boundaries. Bob Dylan's disco song—amazing.

What a tour of the relational world gone wrong. These songs take us everywhere—everywhere *except* for a ride on the slow train or a trip to the Jokerman's lair, that is. Couples drift through surreal, fragmented dreams ("Tight Connection"), remove one another's masks ("Seeing The Real"), take joy in the other's sorry state and ultimate demise ("When The Night"), cope with relational quandaries and their corresponding suspicions ("Something's Burning"), and wallow in nostalgic pain ("I'll Remember" and "Never Gonna"). And they do all this from different musical points of view. Las Vegas show tunes, disco beats, torch standards, martial sounds, and rock songs carry these tales of relational decline. Throughout, the Revue performs with impeccable taste. The Bobettes add the right touches at the right times, demonstrating that they have come a long way since *Street-Legal*'s overuse of their considerable skills. Though this sonic sampler drifts in its own space, it packs its own punch in its own powerful way. You have to admit: This is the other side of the musical world from *Infidels*.

But we do touch that thematic base with our two songs of societal complaint, "Clean–Cut Kid" and "Dark Eyes," and Dylan's forceful warning, "Trust Yourself." We open with *Empire Burlesque*'s capstone song, "Dark Eyes." There is nothing on this record like "Dark Eyes," and that inspires some curiosity. It features Dylan, unaccompanied, with his harmonica and guitar. The song's four four-line verses unfold with brief harmonica interludes between verses, but without choruses or bridges. A lone voice conveys cryptic images of life with one recurring trait: everywhere he sees "Dark Eyes." First, the narrator describes the world in which he lives with its extreme conditions, metaphoric jewelry, and cloudy recollections (a fuzzy scene involving men talking, drinking, and walking under the late-night moon by the river). The second stanza is even more cryptic: A chicken crows, a soldier prays, a mother searches for her lost son, and the narrator stares at that ever-present set of eyes while images of the end times seem to float around him. Let's examine the final verses and explore what the auteur is saying in this fascinating capstone statement:

> They tell me to be discreet for all intended purposes,
> They tell me revenge is sweet and from where they stand, I'm sure it is.
> But I feel nothing for their game where beauty goes unrecognized,
> All I feel is heat and flame and all I see are dark eyes.

> Oh, the French girl, she's in paradise and a drunken man is at the wheel,
> Hunger pays a heavy price to the falling gods of speed and steel.
> Oh, time is short and the days are sweet and passion rules the arrow that
> flies,
> A million faces at my feet but all I see are dark eyes.

This is the old Bob Dylan. With lines reminiscent of "A Hard Rain's Gonna Fall" or "Chimes Of Freedom," the Iron Range's original biker-poet roams through those historic back pages here. Following a rich tradition of innovative songwriting, each line could be the starting point for another song. The first two lines of the final stanza tie together, but the other lines seem to operate on their own plane. Through it all, the aroma of societal complaint fills the air. "They" tell the narrator things, and he does not seem to care for them. The reference to a life full of fire sounds pretty bleak. Whatever is going on with the French girl and her intoxicated driver is unclear, yet it does not seem too good to me. With all of these straightforward pop songs populating this project, this capstone commentary is a bit abrupt. The stark presentation and the cryptic writing are genuine blasts from the auteur's past. Perhaps therein lies its significance, in that the song demonstrates that that aspect of Dylan's pen is alive and well. That Dylan Edge is in evidence here, although the expression seems out of place on the album that contains the auteur's first disco track. Alas, such is the nature of the pop icon period. (In *Chronicles*, Dylan reports that Arthur Baker requested an acoustic song to close this album, and he wrote this in response to a young lady he passed in a hotel corridor and submitted it to Baker.)

Further proof that the patented Dylan Edge is alive, well, and heading for a vacation exists in the powerful "Clean–Cut Kid." Existing on the other end of the sonic spectrum from "Dark Eyes," this song deploys the Big Sound in this chorus-driven message. Throughout the track, a three-line chorus surrounds a series of serious two-line statements that seem to be trivialized by the musical bombast. Layers of horns, slashing guitars, bouncy piano, and the Bobettes' insistent doo-wop backing vocals work to bury the song's biting sentiments. After listening to this track, you find yourself wondering what the Revue could do with "Hollis Brown." I mean, this story is every bit as sad. It charts how "they" (clearly, the American government/military) took an all-American boy, toyed with his mind, converted him into a killing machine, used him, and then just flat-out dumped him back into the world. So, he reenters society, does off-the-wall things, and eventually kills himself, leaving everyone in dismay. There are some great lines here. Consider the opening verse and chorus:

> Everybody wants to know why he couldn't adjust
> Adjust to what, a dream that bust?
>
> He was a clean-cut kid
> But they made a killer out of him,
> That's what they did

There it hangs, friends. After "they" transformed this churchgoing Boy Scout into a killer and abandoned him once they had their way with him, the song describes his new condition:

> He bought the American dream but it put him in debt
> The only game he could play was Russian roulette

When our clean-cut one was not playing with firearms, he entertained himself by stealing a Rolls Royce and driving it into a Hollywood swimming pool. Eventually, this clean-cut guy makes his break:

> He was wearing boxing gloves, took a dive one day
> Off the Golden Gate Bridge into China Bay

The story ends with everyone wondering what happened. He could have had a great life. He prepared himself for a virtuous existence with unlimited potential. Yet, he was literally abducted by his government, transformed into something that could not be undone, and left to his own devices once his service was completed. Instead of working a steady job, he wound up wandering around. Instead of singing in the church choir, he wound up killing himself.

"Clean–Cut Kid" is a heavy story. What contemporary war does to its soldiers is not just hideous; it is also fundamentally irresponsible for a government to place people in such a situation and then abandon them. Having said that, I must also report that this song is strange. In a way, it is as if the Revue is mocking this sad story. The way the tune bounces along and its doo-wop musical format seem to trivialize the song's sentiments. There is a "Ho-hum, here's another tragedy" feel to this number, and, I must say, it's disturbing. The song parties while the story cries. Its cynicism betrays its observations. But maybe that's just me. I seldom feel like dancing after a war veteran kills him or herself.

Nevertheless, when you think about that clean-cut, all-American kid and how he was victimized by a ruthless government and its masters of war, you learn a quick lesson. In fact, Dylan articulates that stance in "Clean–Cut Kid" when he reports, "Well, everybody's asking why he couldn't adjust / All he ever wanted was somebody to trust." Yes, this is the crux of this matter. The kid entered an honorable profession, he trusted his superiors, and they betrayed that trust. As a result, the boy had serious trust issues—feelings that could only be resolved by his own ultimate solution. The Bob Dylan Revue discusses this matter fully via *Empire Burlesque*'s song of warning, "Trust Yourself." Here the Revue travels to Memphis as it uses that famed Bluff City sound (i.e., heavy backbeat, soulful keyboards, and light gospel-fueled backing vocals) throughout this song's three seven-line verses and four-line bridge. Indeed, this is a funky piece of Memphis-style soul with a direct message that is conveyed through the song's title. Don't trust the narrator—or anybody else, for that matter—to demonstrate beauty, truth, and love (verses 1–3, respectively); rely on yourself. If you don't, this song declares, you may as well prepare yourself to visit a bridge near you. This song's bridge and closing stanza fully represent this simple but wise message:

> Well, you're on your own, you always were,
> In a land of wolves and thieves.
> Don't put your hope in ungodly man
> Or be a slave to what somebody else believes.
>
> Trust yourself
> And you won't be disappointed when vain people let you down.
> Trust yourself
> And look not for answers where no answers can be found.
> Don't trust me to show you love
> When my love may be only lust.
> If you want somebody you can trust, trust yourself.

After all of those *Street-Legal* declarations, we arrive at this straightforward conclusion. After the clean-cut one jumped to his death and provided a concrete example of this song's point, we arrive at this conclusion. After all of the relational turmoil and false shelters from threatening relational storms, we arrive at this conclusion. Don't trust the external world; trust the internal one. Don't trust that reflection in that mirror; trust what no one can see: your soul. Unlike "Clean–Cut," this song's sonic support truly reinforces its simple but systematic statement. The messiah-seeking branch of Dylan's constituency just received its wake-up call. How appropriate that this message would be buried amongst a wall of pop songs. *This* is that Dylan Edge. "Clean–Cut" may dance around its point in an evasive or careless way, but this song drives home a compelling observation in a consistent, forceful manner.

Having published this final editorial, that Dylan Edge now vacations until its return down in the Louisiana swamps. As always, when it does appear, it appears forcefully.

Our last *Empire Burlesque* song is the album's lone account of relational bliss, "Emotionally Yours." Through all of the romantic and societal complaint that ultimately leads to the "Trust Yourself" conclusion, we have but one song of celebration. The electronic toy box is reopened here as the Revue uses synthesizer-based horns and layers of sound to present this dreamy 1980s-style pop song. In this three-verse song (with a four-line bridge), the narrator concentrates on a single task: unadulterated praise for his wonderful woman. No matter where he is or what he is doing, he belongs to her. His love is complete. His dedication is genuine. The bridge and closing verse convey the sentiment well:

> It's like my whole life never happened,
> When I see you, it's as if I never had a thought.
> I know this dream, it might be crazy,
> But it's the only one I've got.
>
> Come baby, shake me, come baby, take me, I would be satisfied.
> Come baby, hold me, come baby, help me, my arms are open wide.
> I could be unraveling wherever I'm traveling, even to foreign shores.
> But I will always be emotionally yours.

Pop songs are not supposed to say that much, and this track is true to form. It simply, and sufficiently, communicates its message and concludes. The synth horns are a signature moment on this record. A drum machine is awaiting just around the musical corner, don't you think?

Empire Burlesque is, most assuredly, a pop record. "Clean–Cut" may identify what the government does to the young people that they transform into killers, but its pop veneer camouflages the attack. "Dark Eyes" may revisit songwriting strategies from days gone by, but that visit is a quick one. "Trust Yourself" may provide a resolution to situations posed throughout the oeuvre, but it, too, uses a slick sonic strategy to support that point. Those songs aside, the rest of this project concentrates on a series of pop songs about loving relationships. Throughout, smooth, professional sonic textures serve as backdrops for these 1980s-style pop tunes. Arthur Baker left no musical stone unturned in his treatment of "When The Night." The Bobettes bring their stylish, gospel-tinged vocals to the proceedings in a colorful and entertaining way. Finally, as *Burlesque* massages its love theme from all sorts of angles—the attack of "Seeing The Real You," the remorse of "I'll Remember" and "Never Gonna Be," the dedication of "Emotionally Yours," the uncertainty of "Something's Burning," and the cavalier attitude of "Tight Connection"—it also deploys different sounds to support those accounts. The writing may be uneven at times. The sounds may be distracting from time to time. However, the record not only works in its own way, but also clearly demonstrates the emotional breadth of the auteur's pen. While dancing about with relational matters, he pauses to issue "Clean–Cut" and "Trust Yourself." Yes, we're transitioning from *Infidels* into new realms, musical domains that were previewed in—of all places—*Self Portrait* and *Dylan*. The Bob Dylan Revue is just getting warmed up.

The Revue cranks out two albums with similar sonic features during the second half of the 1980s. Both projects rely heavily on cover songs and the layered method of production we've just witnessed on *Burlesque*. Both projects offer no sign of that Dylan Edge. Produced by Dylan (there are no producer credits on either *Knocked Out Loaded* or *Down In The Groove*), these records offer another sonic sampler (*Loaded*) and a fun-filled trip to 1950s-style rock 'n' roll (*Groove*) as the original material focuses on relational matters once more. For the biographers and the critics, these were perplexing projects. Articles and reviews that questioned the auteur's creative direction were in the mainstream. In fact, Clinton Heylin's session chronology concludes that *Groove* joined the lackluster *Loaded* to confirm "in many an ex-fan's mind that the man had nothing left to say." Let's examine the specifics and evaluate Heylin's argument.

Knocked Out Loaded (released in August 1986) contains a blend of covers and coauthored and original material. The new songs concentrate exclusively on the relational complaint theme. As is the pop icon period's norm, the album features a host of musicians, including T-Bone Burnett, Jack Sherman, Ron Wood, Mike Campbell, Ira Ingber, Tom Petty, and Dave Stewart (guitars); James Jamerson, Vito San Filippo, John Paris, Howie Epstein, Carl Sealove, and John McKenzie (bass); Al Kooper, Bentmont Tench, Vince Melamed, and Patrick Seymour (keyboards); Raymond Lee Pounds, Anton Fig, Don Heffington, Stan Lynch, and Clem Burke (drums); Steve Douglas and Steve Madaio (horns); backing vocalists Carolyn Dennis, Madelyn Quebec, Muffy Hendrix, Elisecia Wright, Peggi Blu, Queen Esther Marrow, and Annette May Thomas; and, on one track ("They Killed Him"), the Children's Choir (there are other assorted musicians appearing on different tracks as well). Obviously, there is no standard sonic strategy controlling this album with such a diverse cast of musicians present. The record contains eight tracks (running over thirty-five minutes) with five originals (three coauthored: "Brownsville Girl" with Sam Shepard, "Got My Mind Made Up" with Tom Petty, and "Under Your Spell" with Carole Bayer Sager, as well as Dylan's "Driftin' Too Far From Shore" and "Maybe Someday"), one traditional ("Precious Memories"), and two covers (Parker's "You Wanna Ramble" and Kristofferson's "They Killed Him"). The blend of music directly contributes to the album's pacing. Actually, *Loaded*'s sounds are quite restless. The album features (in order) a 1950s rocker, a hymn, a disco track, reggae, a pop tune, a theatrical ballad (with a gospel chorus), a Tom Petty–style 1980s rocker, and a touch of blue-eyed soul. As you can see, this album rivals *New Morning*'s sonic diversity.

The covers feature something old, something recent, and something traditional with a twist. The Delta blues guitars and the Bobettes' wonderful backing vocals take us straight into the 1950s with "You Wanna Ramble." The song previews the sounds of *Groove* and, later, *Under The Red Sky* as it hops along to the 1950s Sun Records musical formula. We change planets with the following track and "They Killed Him." Here we move from Sun Studios down to the Reverend Al Green's Memphis church as the sanctified Bobettes are joined by the Children's Choir to tell the tale of fallen spiritual leaders Mahatma Gandhi, Martin Luther King Jr., and Jesus Christ. To the extent that "Ramble" is true to its musical formula, so is "They Killed Him." It does, however, seem out of place. The revised "Precious Memories" does not suffer that trait. The Revue takes a trip to the Islands with this reggae version of a timeless hymn. The treatment is respectful and demonstrates how that joyful Jamaican rhythm enlivens virtually anything it embraces. What a diverse series of covers! One senses the presence of that famed Basement Strategy as Dylan uses a host of sounds to unpack these three cover songs. To some, he is lost and feeling his way through his own musical maze. To others, he is rollicking in his musical playpen with his friends. To me, Dylan is having it both ways. Jack Fate is on the scene, and Bob Dylan is responding to his presence.

The relational complaints offer a fine thematic sampler as they explore a lover who is straying ("Driftin' Too Far"), hold out doubtful hope for the future ("Maybe Someday"), wax nostalgic for a lost love ("Brownsville"), bid adios ("Got My Mind"), and pine for an absent lover ("Under Your Spell"). That the songs deploy different sounds as they tell their respective stories contributes to *Loaded*'s pacing, since we focus on one subject by way of different spins on that topic. We open on the dance floor.

The Revue weaves its magic in a rock/pop/disco format as it tells the tale of a relationship on the wane through the eight four-line verses and repetitive choruses of "Driftin' Too Far From Shore." With Bob Dylan on the synthesizer (that's right!), this track repeats over and over that the narrator's love interest is drifting away—even though I gain the impression that she is being pushed as much as anything. Our narrator is doggone aggressive, as the third and fourth stanzas relate:

> I ain't gonna get lost in this current,
> I don't like playing cat and mouse.
> No gentleman likes making love to a servant.
> Especially when he's in his father's house.

> I never could guess your weight, baby,
> Never needed to call you my whore.
> I always thought you were straight, baby,
> But you're driftin' too far from shore.

That is the way this complaint works: aggressively. In the opening section, the narrator offers the usual suspicions of infidelity and the typical complaints regarding money. There he claims he reached out for her but she is, of course, drifting away. The above verses demonstrate how the scene heats up, and that tone carries throughout the rest of the tune. At times, he is curious. At others, he is damning. In all cases, it is over. Once you rip the telephones out of the wall and characterize the situation as a war, well, it is time to move on—and that is exactly what this narrator declares.

The relational world continues to turn via the five eight-line verses of "Maybe Someday." Here the Revue relies on the classic sounds of 1980s rock to convey another complaint, this time with a touch of nostalgia added to the mix. The song opens with an attack as the narrator maintains that maybe after she has lost everything and hit rock bottom, she will realize what she had. Oh yes, someday she will be sorry, as the second stanza relates:

Maybe someday you'll have nowhere to turn,
You'll look back and wonder 'bout the bridges you have burned.
You'll look back sometime when the lights grow dim
And you'll see you look much better with me than you do with him.
Through hostile cities and unfriendly towns,
Thirty pieces of silver, no money down.
Maybe someday, you will understand
That something for nothing is everybody's plan.

Anybody sense a hint of betrayal in the air? For a famous amount of money, another relationship bites the dust. That Dylan Edge may be on vacation, but the occasional postcard reminds us of its power. The track continues with more of the same. Maybe his attitude was a problem. Maybe he should have fought harder for the relationship. Nevertheless, she will be sorry—of that, this narrator is certain. The final stanza demonstrates the strength of the narrator's convictions on this matter:

Maybe someday there'll be nothing to tell.
I'm just as happy as you, baby, I just can't say it so well.
Never slumbered or slept or waited for lightning to strike.
There's no excuse for you to say that we don't think alike.
You said you were going to 'Frisco, stay a couple of months.
I always liked San Francisco, I was there for a party once.
Maybe someday you'll see that it's true
There was no greater love than what I had for you.

The narrator is convinced that she will never do better than she did with him, and that inspires his flippant attitude toward her departure. His belief that she will regret her decision is so thorough that you get the impression that he is trying to convince himself that this is the case. Having said that, notice the difference in the two verses I've selected. One bites, while the other moans. Such is the nature of the pop icon period's songwriting.

Well, let's see, the Revue has hit the dance floor and visited the rock sounds of the times, so what's next? How else might Dylan expresses the anxieties of love? I know. How about a Broadway production? And that is exactly what we get with the first of our coauthored pieces, the eleven minutes of "Brownsville Girl." This epic account of relational nostalgia takes us back to the Jacques Levy era with its detailed, systematic narratives. I suppose we may conclude that when Bob Dylan works with stage writers like Levy and Sam Shepard, we get this type of story. Through *seventeen* four-line verses and irregularly placed standard four-line choruses, the Bobettes, the horns, and more send this track to a unique place in the oeuvre. This is, indeed, a one-of-a-kind song in the Dylan Canon. We open with the narrator's recollections of an inspirational Gregory Peck movie (verses 1 and 2). Suddenly, the story shifts to the heart of the song and the narrator's nostalgia over a lost love. In the third verse, he expresses his feelings for his lost love:

Well, I keep seeing this stuff and it just comes a-rolling in
And you know it blows right through me like a ball and chain.

You know I can't believe we've lived so long and are still so far apart.
The memory of you keeps callin' after me like a rollin' train.

He thinks back to their last meeting (verse 4) and their trip to San Antonio, where she left him (verse 5). Again, suddenly, we leap to another time and another trip with another woman (verse 6), we pause for a chorus break, then the traveling couple arrives at an old friend's home in Amarillo, where times are hard (verses 7, 8, and 9). "Ruby" informs the road couple that their friend—one "Henry Porter"—is away, and she welcomes them to the "land of the living dead." They visit. Our attention-deficit-controlled narrator once more returns to the Peck film (verse 10) before the chaotic chorus just pops up once more (it merely repeats the song's title and describes her curly hair and beautiful teeth).

The plot thickens at this point. In the eleventh verse, we learn that our narrator is a wanted man and that his ex-lover testified (and lied) on his behalf (verse 12). He ponders his lot and longs for his Brownsville baby (verse 13). Predictably, this takes him back to Gregory Peck—this time, he is waiting to see a new movie starring his hero (verse 14). This man has been deeply affected by Peck's work. Personally, I don't think it's very healthy, but then again, what do I know? After another chorus and a fine saxophone break, our narrator thinks about his old girlfriend some more, remembering that Henry Porter was not Henry Porter at all and thinking about New Orleans (verse 15). In the sixteenth stanza, he nostalgically remembers the wisdom of her ways:

> Strange how people who suffer together have stronger connections than people who are most content.
> I don't have any regrets, they can talk about me plenty when I'm gone.
> You always said people don't do what they believe in, they just do what's most convenient, then they repent.
> And I always said, "Hang on to me, baby, and let's hope that the roof stays on."

Would you like to guess what happens next? Good job. Yes, the song concludes with another reference to our gun-carrying hero, Gregory Peck, and one last blast from the chorus. The story ends exactly where it began.

What a weird song. It floats here and there, cuts away to the Gregory Peck references, and anchors itself in relational nostalgia. What happened on the road trip with the new girlfriend? It is a mystery. Who are Henry Porter and Ruth? It is a mystery. Whatever happened to the Brownsville Madonna? It is a mystery. Something tells me that Porter was really the Jack of Hearts and that Ruth was a character from "Highway 61 Revisited." But maybe that's just a silly guess and, after all, I'm a professional, so I shouldn't wallow in conjecture. In any event, I know for a *fact* that the Brownsville Girl was Joan Baez. (Just kidding.) Sometimes a storyteller just tells a story for the sake of telling a story, and this is a case in point.

Knocked Out Loaded concludes with two more coauthored pieces that also address relational matters. In "Got My Mind Made Up," Bob Dylan is joined by Tom Petty (the coauthor) and the Heartbreakers for a song that sounds *exactly* like a Tom

Petty and the Heartbreakers song with a guest appearance by the Bobettes. In life, some people insist on standing by their convictions, and that is the story in the Petty-fueled 1980s pop-rock song. Throughout this track, the Bobettes display their impeccable timing and the narrator demonstrates the strength of his convictions as the song rolls onward. The opening verses essentially tell this tale:

Don't ever try to change me,
I been in this thing too long.
There's nothin' you can say or do
To make me think I'm wrong.

Well, I'm goin' off to Libya,
There's a guy I gotta see.
He's been living there three years now,
In an oil refinery.
I've got my mind made up.
Oh, I've got my mind made up.

For the life of me, I swear that this is the first song I've *ever* seen in which a central character is abandoning his or her lover for a trip to Libya. But then again, maybe I should get out more. He may be off to Libya, but he departs in a responsible manner. The narrator urges his baby to call her mother to reassure her that everything will work out well; he repeats his commitment to her, reassures her as well, mentions some mysterious person who will seemingly protect her, and repeats his convictions over and over. He is gone. Sorry! If she cannot handle it, well, that is her problem. From movies starring Gregory Peck to trips to Libya, what could possibly be next?

To the extent that the narrator in "Brownsville" was dedicated to Peck and the narrator in "I've Got My Mind" was committed to his travel plans, the central character in "Under Your Spell" is hooked on her. Coauthored with Carole Bayer Sager, this soft, slightly soulful pop song unfolds via seven three-line verses and a four-line bridge. It is a straightforward account of a man who is under a woman's thumb and his efforts to cope with her absence. He is hurting (verse 1). He recalls that fateful night when he was "knocked out and loaded" and she rescued him (verse 2's shades of "Shelter From The Storm"). She sounds perfect. She knows him well and comforts him, and he longs for her wonderful ways. He is away for some reason—seemingly in trouble—but he promises to return. Really, he has to go back, and the fourth verse and bridge explain why:

Well it's four in the morning by the sound of the birds,
I'm starin' at your picture, I'm hearin' your words.
Baby, they ring in my head like a bell.

Everywhere you go it's enough to break hearts
Someone always gets hurt, a fire always starts.
You were too hot to handle, you were breaking every vow.
I trusted you baby, you can trust me now.

Her difficulty was apparently inspirational. Whatever she did remains a mystery; nevertheless, there is no doubt about his conviction. The fifth verse seems to suggest he made his way back to her, but he has to leave again. He asks her to pray for him on his journey, and we're left to contemplate the sadness. Throughout this story, the Bobettes set the emotional tone in their own marvelous way. Love can be so sad—so close and yet so far.

So what is wrong with a thirty-six-minute pop record that deploys a specific approach to different musical genres? Dylan and the Bobettes (the approach) tackle a host of sounds (reggae, show tunes, Tom Petty sounds, and so on) through a variety of new and old songs. The project sounds great. The songs have integrity. The method is consistent. So what is the problem?

This is Bob Dylan.

For anybody other than the voice of his generation, this would be just fine. However, things get more than a little weird on this record. For instance, "Brownsville" is *way* over the top. This isn't "Hurricane," "Durango," or "Black Diamond Bay." "Brownsville" has no soul. Despite the Bobettes' earnest efforts, this track offers eleven lifeless minutes of verbiage. We have the occasional strong line, but that is not enough to salvage this wayward Broadway production. Then we drift into the world of anti-Dylan. The remaining coauthored pieces make you stop and scratch your head. The Tom Petty–sounding Libya story is one odd combination. The Sager installment has its cute, funky rhyme schemes, but they chug along in a hapless manner. As such, the songs transcend vacuity and we gain insight into Dylan's comments from *Chronicles* (cited in this chapter's introduction). The auteur does appear to lack inspiration, that is for sure. Nevertheless, this patient is still breathing. Lines from "Driftin' Too Far" and "Maybe Someday" demonstrate that Dylan has not totally succumbed to whatever is ailing him. This is, indeed, a strange time. There is a sense of malaise present, and it is going to get worse before it passes.

This musical trend advances with 1988's *Down In The Groove* (also produced by Dylan)—a ten-track (running 32 minutes) piece with six covers, two coauthored numbers (with Robert Hunter, the portrait "Silvio" and the relational celebration "Ugliest Girl In The World"), and two originals: the celebratory "Death Is Not The End" and "Had A Dream About You, Baby." Although the inclusion of classics such as "Shenandoah" and "Rank Strangers To Me" (along with other covers such as Wilbert Harrison's "Let's Stick Together"; Bullock and Whiting's "When Did You Leave Heaven"; Alexander, Montgomery, and Stafford's "Sally Sue Brown"; and Blair and Robertson's "Ninety Miles An Hour [Down A Dead End Street]") suggests the invocation of the Basement Strategy in the recording studio, the originals appear uninspired. One exception, "Death Is Not," sounds as though it were a *Saved* outtake (it is, in fact, an *Infidels* outtake) and demonstrates the moral period's lasting impact on the auteur's pen—an attribute that controls this album as much as any other. That is, the slow, respectful, gospel sound of "Death" joins the covers (e.g., "When Did You," "Shenandoah," and "Rank Strangers") to provide a striking contrast to the rocking frolics of the album's other tracks. Thematically, the relational celebrations and portrait are, in a phrase, too sketchy to be meaningful. Still, their presence stands in contrast to the previous albums' concentrated use of the relational complaint theme.

Hunter's influence is evident in the humor that makes "Ugliest Girl" and "Silvio" fun songs with their "you may bark at the moon, but you're mine" and "I'm The Man" story lines (although "Silvio" has its thoughtful moments). Perhaps Heylin's chronology captures *Groove*'s uneven qualities best: "The studio techniques [Dylan] had previously abhorred that 'touched-up' recordings, overdubbed new instruments, and allowed new vocal tracks or 'punch ins,' were for the first time in full evidence." So much so that, once more, Dylan recast the record after test pressings appeared. Songs that appeared on the *Hearts Of Fire* soundtrack and other cover songs were added or deleted, and the song list continually changed until, somehow or another, Dylan reached closure. There is, however, a decided emphasis on 1950s-era sounds—an act that, once more, foreshadowed future events.

Once again, each song on this album has its own musical cast. The project features Danny Kortchmar, Steve Jones, Mark Knopfler, and Eric Clapton (guitars); Randy Jackson, Paul Simonon, Robbie Shakespeare, Ron Wood, Kip Winger, Nathan East, and Larry Klein (bass); Steve Jordan, Stephen Shelton, Myron Grambacher, Sly Dunbar, Henry Spinetti, and Mike Baird (drums); Kevin Savigar, Alan Clarke, Beau Hill, Mitchell Froom, Stephen Shelton, and Bobette Madelyn Quebec (keyboards); a group called Full Force, Bobby King, Willie Green, Jerry Garcia, Bob Weir, and Brent Mydland on backing vocals; and the Bobettes: Quebec, Clydie King, Carolyn Dennis, Peggi Blu, and Alexandra Brown. We have quite a mix here, and that sonic strategy contributes to the record's uneven qualities in a most direct manner.

The six cover songs provide the bookends for *Groove*. The album opens with a rocking "Let's Stick"; moves into the dramatic, somber "When Did You Leave" (making this the second consecutive album to open with a rocker and follow with a hymn-like track); and continues with another rocker, "Sally Sue." The 1950s rock 'n' roll attitude is evident in the first and third tracks, that is for sure. The album closes with another triple-cover sequence by way of "Ninety Miles," "Shenandoah," and "Rank Strangers." These songs are much slower than the opening tunes and, therefore, wind the album down in a more theatrical, less raucous, manner. The gospel-tinged sounds of adulterers on the run in "Ninety Miles" set up the harmonica-drenched, respectful treatment of the traditional "Shenandoah" (the big backing vocals make this track quite the production), which leads to our first capstone cover since *Bob Dylan*, "Rank Strangers To Me" (once more, treated very respectfully). Whether we have evidence of the Basement Strategy or the *Self Portrait* approach in action here is open for debate. By and large, the biographers and critics conclude that the latter is the guiding philosophy of this day. To me, Dylan's *Chronicles* commentary suggests that we are actually somewhere in the middle of those two extremes.

The four original compositions on *Groove* share an interesting twist: They are all celebrations of one sort or another. "Death Is Not The End" uses its four six-line verses (with a four-line bridge) and slow, solemn instrumental style to return to the Alabama Chronicles by issuing a message of hope. No matter what you encounter in this life, the afterlife holds promise for the sanctified—and *that* is a cause for respectful celebration. The opening verse relates that when you're lonely and your ideals seem forgotten, the afterlife will relieve your misery. Next, we're reminded that when you are at life's turning points and it all seems hopeless, something better is awaiting you. The third verse and bridge are telltale:

When the storm clouds gather 'round you, and heavy rains descend
Just remember that death is not the end
And there's no one there to comfort you, with a helpin' hand to lend
Just remember that death is not the end
Not the end, not the end
Just remember that death is not the end

Oh, the tree of life is growing
Where the spirit never dies
And the bright light of salvation shines
In dark and empty skies

No matter how rough things may become, that shining light of redemption casts a heavenly glow onto the darkness. The message is clear: Be patient—your reward is awaiting you. The hymn closes with scenes of the end times—the world is ablaze and evil abounds—but there are no worries for the washed, because death is not the end. I find it utterly fascinating that this is an *Infidels* outtake. To be sure, this song would have stood out amongst the darkness that enveloped that record. From this, we may conclude that Dylan did have an answer to all of that declaration of decadence rhetoric and decided not to invoke it.

The slashing guitars and big backbeat of "Had A Dream About You, Baby" take us rocking into our first relational celebration. The song unfolds through a series of five two-line verses that are punctuated with a series of standard three-line choruses and a repeated seven-line bridge. As a result, the track is driven by a chorus that basically repeats the song title over and over. The song is nothing but a tribute to that woman who inspires the narrator's dreams—in this case, *good* dreams. She is so wonderful that she makes the narrator jumpy, nervous, and downright overheated. The bridge and the fourth verse sum this situation nicely:

The joint is jumpin'
It's really somethin'
The beat is pumpin'
My heart is thumpin'
Spent my money on you honey
My limbs are shakin'
My heart is breakin'

You kiss me, baby, in the coffee shop
You make me nervous, you gotta stop.

(We shall revisit this 1950s-style songwriting more thoroughly in the near future.) I think that all I can say at this point is that someone should douse this guy with a bucket of cold water—quick! Seriously, the bridge says it all, doesn't it? We are clearly in the songwriting style of Dylan's youth—Little Richard is in the house.

To close our discussion of *Groove*, we turn to the two songs coauthored with Grateful Dead songwriter Robert Hunter, "Ugliest Girl In The World" and "Silvio."

With "Ugliest," the 1950s parade continues in this five-verse, four-chorus pop song in which the Bobettes carry the day. Perfectly timed backing vocals take this song on a hilarious joyride to days gone by—we are in Leiber and Stoller country. Here, we celebrate a woman who is adored by her lover even though she fails to meet the minimal standards of physical attractiveness (i.e., she is *ugly*). Oh, but the narrator is in love. He cherishes her crooked nose and worn-out clothes (verse 1); therefore, he is madly in love (verse 2), as the Leiber and Stoller–type line indicates: "When she says babababababy I l-l-love you / There ain't nothing I the world that I wouldn't do." Anybody care for a little "Jailhouse Rock"? The third and fourth verses join the chorus to capture these 1950s sentiments in all of their glory:

> The woman that I love she got two flat feet
> Her knees knock together walking down the street
> She cracks her knuckles and she snores in bed
> She ain't much to look at but like I said
>
> You know I love her
> Yeah I love her
> I'm in love with the Ugliest Girl in the World
>
> I don't mean to say that she got nothin' goin'
> She got a weird sense of humor that's all her own
> When I get low she sets me on my feet
> Got a five inch smile but her breath is sweet

Yes, dear readers, beauty is in the eye of the beholder—regardless of his state of mind.

That joy permeates the sounds of "Silvio" as well. Here Dylan and Hunter offer a pop portrait that operates from an autobiographical stance. No, it is not about Bob Dylan. The narrator talks about himself and his situation at length across the six four-line verses of this chorus-driven song. That chorus simply states the song title, notes that money cannot bring the dead to life, and cites the narrator's urge to discover what only the dead understand. The opening verse sets the scene well:

> Stake my future on a hell of a past
> Looks like tomorrow is coming on fast
> Ain't complaining 'bout what I got
> Seen better times, but who has not?

Is our narrator sick and about to meet his Maker in the afterlife? After this opening proclamation, he describes himself. He is a determined guy—in control of the weather and people's health—and he is persuasive, but also *wise*, as the fifth verse relates:

> I can tell you fancy, I can tell you plain
> You give something up for everything you gain

Since every pleasure's got an edge of pain
Pay for your ticket and don't complain

With such wisdom in mind, he fantasizes of a day when he may travel into the "valley," sing his song loudly, and cast his fate in its echo. Again, I think our narrator is on his way Out. We should wish him luck with his journey since he approaches his demise with such a joyful attitude.

That joyful attitude is this album's centerpiece. The cover songs are not as celebratory as the original compositions, but this record bops along in its 1950s milieu in a happy-go-lucky manner. Although "Silvio" has several thoughtful lines, most of these songs just cruise along in that traditional rock 'n' roll style. They are danceable, laughable, and often forgettable. Now, you can be *mean* and say that the auteur has nothing to say, or you can be *kind* and say that he is exploring the song structures of his youth. With the benefit of history, we know that this writer isn't "done" yet, but without that benefit, you'd wonder. In any event, this is a great-sounding record: clear, balanced, and with little nuances that suggest authorship. Nevertheless—at thirty-two minutes—this would have been a song in 1966, so the standards get a little skewed when we talk about the voice of his generation.

However, lest we forget, this is the Bob Dylan Revue. This is not Mr. Message Man with his guitar or the Newport Mod screaming over the Hawks or even the Rolling Thunder Revue; rather, it is Bob and the Bobettes doing their thing. Please keep in mind that until we get to the NEST, this represents the lifework's longest running act. Beginning with *Self Portrait* and *Dylan*, pausing for minor roles in *New Morning*, and then exploding on the scene via *Street-Legal*, this act has done its rounds. When the Revue entered the moral period, it donned its choir robes and respectfully performed the Alabama Chronicles via the Bob Dylan Crusade. They did their service and did it well. After the *Infidels* interlude, the Revue returned for a three-album set that mixed and matched the sounds of yesteryear with assorted twists (e.g., the 1950s-style songs of *Groove*). Indeed, the Revue is a pivotal aspect of the auteur's oeuvre. He has used it to fool around, to complement songs, to warn of the end times, to preach, and to perform in variety shows that demonstrated the artist's latest musical whims. The Bob Dylan Revue now rides off into that famed sunset, glowing from a job well-done. At times, Bob and the Bobettes overreached; at other times, they fell just short of the mark; and at still other moments, they were downright perfect. I don't know about you, but I'm going to miss them. Though I've never cared for Las Vegas, I adore the Bob Dylan Revue. Could I hear "Mr. Bojangles" once last time?

The Swampspeak Phase

I'm so happy that Dylan discusses the "making of *Oh Mercy*" in his autobiography. It is such a revelatory, and informative, story. Remember? It is 1987 and Dylan is flat-out lost. He can no longer manage to do what he has been doing. His singing, his writing, his enthusiasm, and his guitar playing are leaving him feeling flat, totally uninspired. Something—somehow—must change, or he is quitting the music business. He is searching for the right musical combination to reinvigorate his muse, reorient his techniques (vocally and instrumentally), and rejuvenate his performances. He just has to find another way. He discovers it! And then he injures his hand—perhaps irreparably. Now, he is staring into the darkness, contemplating the end of his historic career. Yes, he is thinking about buying a North Carolina factory that makes wooden legs. *That* would certainly be a change. While sitting at his kitchen table and soaking in the sights, inspiration strikes and the songs suddenly flow. Many appear with no sign of melody, but Dylan writes away, placing his work in a drawer where it may rest until the right moment arrives. The drawer quickly fills, Bono visits, the drawer is opened, the Irishman admires what he sees, and he recommends Daniel Lanois as a possible solution. The hand heals. Dylan places a new plan in action, slowly. Eventually, he travels to New Orleans, he meets with Lanois, and *Oh Mercy* is born.

The musical world heralded the results as a triumphant return and a hopeful sign for the future. *Oh Mercy* is most certainly a strong record, yet it was merely a flash in the musical pan. Dylan took his drawer full of songs to the swamps of Louisiana, then negotiated with Lanois over their arrangement, and together they captured that magic for posterity. It was, however, a one-of-a-kind project, not the start of some sort of trend. Having satisfied that particular impulse, Bob Zimmerman will follow *Oh Mercy* with a major adjustment to his "Bob Dylan" character. His first—and only—edition of swampspeak did not feature his new vocal technique or instrumental style, or involve his three-year plan to revise his act and attract a new audience. Those activities are unfolding *around* the Lanois project, and they continue to develop until the end of the pop icon period. Consequently, *Oh Mercy* could be accurately construed as Dylan's swan song. A remarkable era is about to yield to a new day.

Oh Mercy contains ten songs (running thirty-nine minutes) that address three topics with varying degrees of clarity. There are six relational complaints ("Where Teardrops Fall," "Man In The Long Black Coat," "Most Of The Time," "What Good Am I," "What Was It You Wanted," and "Shooting Star"), two societal complaints ("Political World" and "Everything Is Broken"), and two warnings ("Ring Them Bells" and "Disease Of Conceit"). Recorded in New Orleans in just three sessions (according to Heylin), the album demonstrates Lanois's control over his subject matter as well as the utility of leadership in the producer's chair for our occasionally wayward auteur. Nevertheless, the omission of several strong songs (e.g., "Born In Time," "God Knows," "Dignity," and "Series Of Dreams") indicates that the artist's faith in his producer's decision making was not complete. Another change involved Dylan's reliance on a steady cast of musicians instead of the ten-musicians-per-track method of the previous pop icon era recordings. The *Oh Mercy* musical cast featured Lanois on lap steel, dobro, guitar, and omnichord; Paul Synegal, Mason Ruffner, and Brian Stoltz on guitar; Larry Jolivet and Tony Hall on bass; Willie Green and Alton Rubin on drums, as well as Cyril Neville and Daryl Johnson on percussion; and Malcolm Burn on keyboards, John Hart on saxophone, David Rubin on scrub board, and Rockin' Dopsie on accordion. Together, these men emptied Dylan's drawer, soaked the songs in swamp water, and created sonic platforms that are more than distinct—they're haunting. That thin, wild mercury sound was replaced by the thick, ominous sounds of the Louisiana swamps. The results are startling. We begin with the archbishop's finger-pointing specialty and the statements of anarchy that are the societal complaints.

A steady, rolling beat that offers little variance supports the *eleven* four-line verses of the opening track, "Political World." Remember, this was the first song in the drawer, and it indicates the extent to which our anarchist has awakened from his brief rest. The song is a steady roll of negativity. The opening line of each verse repeats the song title, and a three-line statement follows—no choruses or bridges here. The opening stanza sets the pace and demonstrates the strategy:

> We live in a political world,
> Love don't have any place.
> We're living in times where men commit crimes
> And crime don't have a face

Sounds bleak. From there, the tune reports of a chilly world where marriages exist and angels perform under cloudy—perhaps threatening—skies. The third verse captures the essence of this situation:

> We live in a political world,
> Wisdom is thrown into jail,
> It rots in a cell, is misguided as hell
> Leaving no one to pick up a trail.

OK, so far we've established that love has disappeared, crime is disguised (and therefore unrecognizable), and wisdom has been forcefully abandoned. It gets worse from here. This wail of negativity screams out that mercy is threatened (verse 4), courage has been abdicated (verse 5), life is corrupt (verse 6), people are isolated (verse 7), self-incrimination abounds (verse 8), life is simplistic (verse 9), the world is violent (verse 10), and doubt is all-controlling (verse 11). This is most assuredly another dose of that *Street-Legal* worldview.

Are any solutions offered? No. Any possibilities suggested? No. Any hope anywhere? No. This sermon from the swamp is not very optimistic, is it? It raises all of these negative scenarios and just throws them at us. Everywhere, things are either corrupt, evil, or in some state of decay. What are we to do? Perhaps more importantly, what happened to bring all of this mayhem into the world? How could this be? The anarchist responds with "Everything Is Broken."

Is it me, or is that the theme song from *Peter Gunn* that opens "Everything Is Broken"? Wonderful bass lines and balanced sounds pave the way for our second swamp sermon and the four seven-line verses and two two-line bridges of "Broken." Why is our "Political World" so corrupt? Because *everything* is in tatters, that's why. The opening verse both sets the tone and demonstrates this song's rhythm of expression:

> Broken lines, broken strings,
> Broken threads, broken springs,
> Broken idols, broken heads,
> People sleeping in broken beds.

Ain't no use jiving
Ain't no use joking
Everything is broken.

Yes, we'd better break out that golden dustpan because this is a mess and somebody's going to have to clean it up—or else. The world is full of broken houseware, broken language, disappointed lovers, broken legal systems, and broken people; in fact, as the bridge reminds us, just when you think the coast is clear—bam! There went something else. The last verse hammers it all back home:

Broken hands on broken ploughs,
Broken treaties, broken vows,
Broken pipes, broken tools,
People bending broken rules.
Hound dog howling, bull frog croaking,
Everything is broken.

Well, this is a mess. People make treaties and take vows just to break them. The rules are made to be broken, as per that age-old saying. Hey, we can't fix this because our tools are shattered as well. Solutions? No. Possibilities? No. Hope? No. Litter? You bet. The swamp is full of trash; I mean, you have to take all of this broken stuff somewhere, right?

After hearing how the political world is corrupt and the world is broken, it is time to ring those church bells, seek salvation, and prepare for what will most assuredly be a better day. With all of this, the end times will be a welcomed reprieve. *Oh Mercy* discusses this option in the first of its two songs of warning, "Ring Them Bells." This swampy hymn with its solemn piano-organ interplay unfolds via four eight-line verses and a seven-line bridge. The first bell tolls in the opening verse:

Ring them bells, ye heathen
From the city that dreams,
Ring them bells from the sanctuaries
'Cross the valleys and streams,
For they're deep and they're wide
And the world's on its side
And time is running backwards
And so is the bride.

Is this yet another reference to Christ's bride, the church, and her unsteady state? The song requests that the bell be rung by none other than St. Peter so that everyone will know just what time it is (verse 2); moreover, it issues a plea to ring those bells loudly in God's name so that His power is affirmed and all of the lost sheep may hear the call home (verse 3). The song crystallizes in this "Chimes Of Freedom" bridge:

Ring them bells for the blind and the deaf,
Ring them bells for all of us who are left,

Ring them bells for the chosen few
Who will judge the many when the game is through.
Ring them bells, for the time that flies,
For the child that cries
When innocence dies.

Yes, in a world of corruption and self-inflicted damage, the time has arrived to ring those bells that usher in the Big Solution and the slow train's arrival. The slow train is working its way through the swamps on its way to a bell tower near you. When the bells ring and the judgments begin, you'll be glad your heart is in the right place. These swampy sermons carry an old message through a new channel.

Our second song of warning deals more with a personality trait than with the end of the world. "Disease Of Conceit" features a simple, piano-based musical platform from which Dylan's haunting voice proclaims the evils of self-love. Throughout its four ten-line verses (with a four-line bridge), the warning is clear and concise, as the opening verses indicate:

There's a whole lot of people suffering tonight
From the disease of conceit.
Whole lot of people struggling tonight
From the disease of conceit.
Comes right down the highway,
Straight down the line,
Rips into your senses
Through your body and your mind.
Nothing about it that's sweet,
The disease of conceit.

There's a whole lot of hearts breaking tonight
From the disease of conceit,
Whole lot of hearts shaking tonight
From the disease of conceit.
Steps into your room,
Eats your soul,
Over your senses
You have no control.
Ain't nothing too discreet
About of disease of conceit.

Conceit kills. Conceit constrains. Conceit causes trouble. And conceit blinds. The doctors are clueless. The prognosis is bleak. Better lose your delusions or prepare for the worst, this sermon proclaims. There is no mystery to this warning. As you can see, it uses brief, almost choppy lines to pound home its insistent warning: Abandon your ego trip and seek His mercy. Is there any clue as to how to go about this? No. Any remedies proposed? No. Any hope? Well, maybe. These sermons from the swamp do not offer many direct solutions; however, their warnings are overwhelmingly clear and suggestive of an Answer from days gone by.

These four songs of societal complaint and warning work systematically. Whether they emerged from the drawer with that plan in place or Dylan's thinking just happened to flow in one current, the idea that the political system has been broken by conceited people for whom those sacred bells will soon toll is made abundantly clear. This is, indeed, one coherent swamp-fueled sermon. The auteur lays out a laundry list of political ills and broken institutions in the same fashion that he announced that service is required of everybody in "Gotta Serve Somebody." In so doing, we set the worldly table in a fashion similar to "Changing Of The Guards." When the bells ring out, and the slow train approaches, this sermon declares that you'd better shed your vanity, humbly repent, and prepare for His arrival. Not only do these songs work in harmony, but Lanois and his musicians also provide sonic backdrops that heighten the message's emotional impact. The result? One compelling series of songs that are shaped by that famed Dylan Edge. This may have been a temporary stopover, but our auteur is in his element in *Oh Mercy*. At times, it is as if Brother Bob of the Bob Dylan Crusade has come out of retirement for one last shot at saving our souls. This is powerful stuff, don't you think?

Oh Mercy's six songs of relational complaint share the musical features of our sermon from the swamp except they display a greater range of symbolism. That is, some of these songs are crystal clear while others are more suggestive, cryptic, or flat-out evasive. There, too, we find evidence of that Dylan Edge as the songwriter conveys his thoughts on love in insightful, and at times cutting or damning, ways. Our first song from the swamp of love, where the quicksand abounds and the threats are unceasing, is "Most Of The Time." This track displays a dreamy ambiance that arrests you, attacks your senses, and gives you pause. Assuredly, this four-verse statement emerges from the "If You See Her, Say Hello" school of relational gamesmanship as it, too, portrays a lover in denial. This creepy—again, dreamy—song offers a narrator attempting to cope with a lost love. He stays so focused and on his chosen path that he fails to notice her absence—most of the time (verse 1). He feels he made the right decision, he is prepared to stick to his position, and she never crosses his mind—most of the time (verse 2). But doubt lingers, and the third verse and the middle-eight communicate those swampy sentiments:

> Most of the time
> My head is on straight,
> Most of the time
> I'm strong enough not to hate.
> I don't build up illusion 'til it makes me sick,
> I ain't afraid of confusion no matter how thick
> I can smile in the face of mankind.
> Don't even remember what her lips felt like on mine
> Most of the time.
>
> Most of the time
> She ain't even in my mind,

> I wouldn't know her if I saw her
> She's that far behind.
> Most of the time
> I can't even be sure
> If she was ever with me
> Or if I was with her.

What writing. This man is conducting a personal pep rally in an effort to fight off his internal anxieties. He faces his confusion, he says, but his comments about kissing his lover suggest that those old feelings are fresher than he would like to admit. He claims he would not recognize her if he saw her, but we know better, don't we? His suggestion that she is just a distant memory fails to connect and drifts aimlessly into the swampy night. Those sentiments advance in the closing stanza. There he takes comfort in his feelings, he gains strength from his convictions, and he refuses to pretend otherwise—most of the time.

As the narrator of "Most Of The Time" demonstrates, after a relationship concludes, the memories are what plague us most. The pain heals, and time passes, but those memories occasionally drift back nostalgically to those blissful days of relational content. Dylan touches this emotional vein once more in *Oh Mercy*'s capstone statement, "Shooting Star." More simple, but serene, swamp sounds support the three 7–9-line verses and seven-line bridge of this statement of relational nostalgia that features an interesting twist as it closes. The opening verses tell this tale in no uncertain terms:

> Seen a shooting star tonight
> And I thought of you.
> You were trying to break into another world
> A world I never knew.
> I always kind of wondered
> If you ever made it through.
> Seen a shooting star tonight
> And I thought of you.
>
> Seen a shooting star tonight
> And I thought of me.
> If I was still the same
> If I ever became what you wanted me to be
> Did I miss the mark or
> Over-step the line
> That only you could see?
> Seen a shooting star tonight
> And I thought of me.

You can't be more direct than that. He thinks of her and wonders if she's well. He thinks of himself and his potential failures. Clearly, doubt remains and he copes with its aftereffects. The twist occurs in the third stanza when the song invokes images of the end times. The last prayers, sermons, and songs are occurring. The world is coming to a close, and it is too late to say what should have been said years ago. Our narrator, it seems, is left with that realization. A shooting star rips over the swamp and the gators moan, "Never more."

Our remaining songs of relational complaint are not as straightforward as the first installments. Cloudy scenes, cryptic characters, and ambiguous story lines control the remaining *Oh Mercy* tracks. In "Where Teardrops Fall," smoky and seductive swamp sounds create a mysterious ambiance for a murky relational commentary. Here our narrator longs for a lost love who is off in some faraway place where the tears are pouring down. The first of the song's four four-line verses establishes that she is gone, but we know not where. The second stanza reports that wherever she is, it is a long way away. The first of our two six-line bridges sheds some light on this muddy story:

> We banged the drum slowly
> And played the fife lowly
> You know the song in my heart
> In the turning of twilight
> In the shadows of moonlight
> You can show me a new place to start.

Whatever is going on in this story, we know that the narrator cares passionately for his departed lover. The next stanza supports that observation as he admits his dire condition (with his torn clothing and empty cup) and reveals that he spends his nights thinking of her. Something separated this couple, and the narrator's reconciliatory tone is evident in the second bridge:

> By the rivers of blindness
> In love and with kindness
> We could hold up a toast if we meet
> To the cuttin' of fences
> To sharpen the senses
> That linger in the fireball heat.

Clearly, he is willing to mend whatever has been broken in the relationship. Further proof exists in the final stanza's "roses are red, violets are blue"–based indication that he just might muster the resources to go see her in the land of the falling tears— wherever that is. Like so many songs in the oeuvre, this track features the lonesome man wallowing in his relational remorse. Lanois's production exacerbates this song's emotional stance through its simple but suggestive soundscape. The concluding saxophone solo adds just the right touch as it leaves us in the bayou with thoughts of missing love.

The ambiguity continues with "What Was It You Wanted?" With a simple guitar, bass, and harmonica interplay providing the backdrop, this five-verse, two-bridge track is chock full of good old-fashioned swampspeak. *Everything* is a mystery here. The first verse just raises the question "What do 'you' want?" The second verse builds on that opening by reporting that "you" have the narrator's attention; now, what do "you" want? The third verse finds the narrator (and me) wondering if he has missed something or somebody. Still, it does reveal that a relationship of some sort exists between the narrator and whoever he is addressing (she kissed him, and he is suspicious). The first bridge offers an example of this song's mysterious story:

> Whatever you wanted
> Slipped out of my mind,
> Would you remind me again
> If you'd be so kind.
> Has the record been breaking,
> Did the needle just skip,
> Is there somebody waitin',
> Was there a slip of the lip?

More swampspeak flows from there. Now, he questions her identity. This guy is just full of unresolved questions. He wonders if this is important. The tide turns in the second bridge as the questions continue to mount:

> Whatever you wanted
> What could it be
> Did somebody tell you
> That you could get it from me,
> Is it something that comes natural
> Is it easy to say,
> Why do you want it,
> Who are you anyway?

The swampy game of twenty questions continues in the concluding verse. Just what is happening? Who does she want, he asks. Finally, he poses the pivotal question: "Are you talking to me?"

What a curious song! It establishes two characters having what appears to be some sort of conversation, but it just floats from there. The music truly elevates the mystery. It drifts along with the endless series of inquiries that just go nowhere. That the narrator ends up asking if, in fact, she is talking to him is revealing. The song just goes round and round. You gain a sense that there is a rich story in the background and that it supports of all these mysterious comments and questions, yet we have no sign of it. You feel as though the song left you standing on the street on a foggy New Orleans night, peering into the shadows, wondering who is there—and why.

The questions continue—albeit in a more concrete manner—in our next track, "What Good Am I?" Throughout the four four-line verses (with a four-line bridge) of this simple, almost quiet song, the narrator copes with feelings of self-worth. I guess some people suffer from conceit, while others question their relevance. *Oh Mercy*, then, covers both extremes. In this somber, introspective song, the narrator questions his worth in the face of various life events. First, he wonders about his value if he acts like everybody else and turns away from her sorrow (verse 1). Next, he questions his failure to respond to their situation and his avoidance of what seems to be the painful truth (verse 2). Let's examine the third verse and bridge for more detail:

> What good am I while you softly weep
> And I hear in my head what you say in your sleep,
> And I freeze in the moment like the rest who don't try,
> What good am I?
>
> What good am I then to others and me
> If I've had every chance and yet still fail to see
> If my hands are tied must I not wonder within
> Who tied them and why and where must I have been?

This character is also full of questions; however, he anchors most of them in his concern over his self-worth in light of his relational failures. The song concludes with more of the same. He says silly things, he laughs at sadness, and he passively ignores his lover's pain. Perhaps our narrator has compelling reasons to question his value. He stands idly by and allows the relational darkness to grow darker still. He obviously feels worthless, and maybe he should.

The swamp comes alive via cricket sound effects and dreamy harmonica riffs in our final *Oh Mercy* track, "Man In The Long Black Coat." Here, too, mystery abounds in this cryptic account of a woman leaving her life behind to join a gentleman with symbolic outerwear. Like most of these songs, we learn very little about the characters in this story, but the sermonic images flow in rich segments across the track's four seven-line verses (with a five-line bridge). The song opens with scenic descriptions (e.g., references to the crickets, high water, open windows, and bent-over trees—sounds genuinely swampy to me) as we learn that "she" departed with this stranger and did not tell anyone. Who "she" is, and who he is, is yet another bayou mystery. The second stanza reports that this guy in the black coat was seen at the local dance hall and that "she" asked this Bible-quoting stranger to dance. What happened afterward is a mystery. Suddenly we hear from a minister who appears out of the blue in the third verse and bridge. His wisdom is rich, but his insight into the story is minimal:

> Preacher was a talkin' there's a sermon he gave,
> He said every man's conscience is vile and depraved,
> You cannot depend on it to be your guide
> When it's you who must keep it satisfied.
> It ain't easy to swallow, it sticks in the throat,
> She gave her heart to the man
> In the long black coat.
>
> There are no mistakes in life some people say
> It is true sometimes you can see it that way.
> But people don't live or die, people just float.

She went with the man
In the long black coat.

OK. What does *this* have to do with anything? Is depravity in the air? Did somebody make a mistake? Where did she go, and who is this guy? I guess we'll never know. The song concludes with more scenic descriptions (e.g., smoky water, uprooted trees, and a crescent moon—again, we are definitely in the swamp); a reference to somebody, somewhere pounding on a "dead horse"; and a final comment about her silent departure with this shadowy guy. The song hints at complaint because of its consistent comments about her sudden, quiet departure. Was she kidnapped? Did he kill her? Was he a Communist? It is all a mystery. There it hangs—or, more accurately, floats.

I tell you, Daniel Lanois gave a very specific form of life to a series of songs that came from both ends of that drawer. The rich, thick sonic textures used to present these songs is from the other end of the musical universe from that thin, wild mercury sound of yesteryear. The echo Lanois applied to Dylan's voice rendered a chilling, ominous quality to his vocals. The hushed, pensive instrumental platforms that support the songs of relational complaint contribute directly to their mysterious qualities. On the other hand, when Dylan describes the broken political world in which we live, those sounds disappear, the echo dissipates, and the attack leaps forward. So, we witness two distinct production strategies on *Oh Mercy*. This principle holds true for the songwriting as well. Yes, there are two ends to the drawer that housed these songs. On one end is the clear, specific writing of "Political World," "Everything Is Broken," "Disease Of Conceit," "Shooting Star," and "Most Of The Time." Dylan states his case in a straightforward manner that pounds home his societal and relational complaints. On the other end of that drawer is the cryptic, evasive writing of the relational complaints: "Teardrops" fall someplace for somebody; somebody, someplace wants something from somebody; and a shadowy character in a long coat takes off with a nameless woman from a unidentified location. Of course, in the middle of that drawer we find songs such as "What Good" and "Ring Them Bells." To be sure, Lanois and Dylan cover the clarity spectrum as they roam from the totally enigmatic to the severely concrete. In all cases, the sound complements the song. *Oh Mercy* is quite an achievement.

The outtakes followed a similar pattern. For example, the swampy sounds and cryptic commentary of "Series Of Dreams" are quite different from the clear instrumental pattern and straightforward sermon in "Dignity." In the former, a narrator recalls his perplexing dreams; in the latter, the narrator conducts an endless search for honor. Both are strong songs. Consider the bridge and third verse from "Dreams," in which the narrator considers the tenuous qualities of life (bridge) before recalling a recent series of sleeping visions:

Dreams where the umbrella is folded
Into the path you are hurled
And the cards are no good that you're holding
Unless they're from another world

In one, numbers were burning
In another, I witnessed a crime
In one, I was running, and in another
All I seemed to be doing was climb
Wasn't looking for any special assistance
Not going to any great extremes
I'd already gone the distance
Just thinking of a series of dreams

Dreams work that way, don't they? Your anxieties creep into odd scenes that portray weird or demanding situations. Images of constant running or climbing, feelings of futility, surreal or abstract visuals, and more populate our dreams. What does it all mean? It is another bayou mystery. Where is it all heading? It is another swampy curiosity. Like "What Was It You Wanted?" and "Man In The Long Black Coat," Lanois places "Dreams" in just the right aural context. The song *sounds* like a dream—a creepy, swampy, slithering dream.

Then we travel to the other end of the drawer for "Dignity." The music marches along in its uninterrupted rhythmic pattern as Dylan recounts a series of vignettes about his continuing search for honor in what appears to be a dishonorable world. The scenes roll by as the music rolls onward. The opening verses capture this "Gotta Serve Somebody"–"Everything Is Broken" list-oriented method of songwriting:

Fat man lookin' in a blade of steel
Thin man lookin' at his last meal
Hollow man lookin' in a cottonfield
For dignity

Wise man lookin' in a blade of grass
Young man lookin' in the shadows that pass
Poor man lookin' through painted glass
For dignity

Everybody everywhere is looking for dignity. I don't get the sense that they find it, however. The narrator searches everywhere, asks the police for help, take perilous trips (e.g., where vultures hang out and fires rage), and examines the great works of art, but he never stops even though he finds no sign of dignity. In the final stanza he questions what this is going to require, yet his resolve seems unshakeable. He is not going to give up until he finds dignity.

When we consult *Chronicles*, we discover that these list-based songs were among the first to enter the drawer. Perhaps the auteur experienced some triggering inspiration and rode that moment through these fragmented expressions that bounce along to that particular theme. The more cryptic songs came along as well; consequently, we have evidence of a seasoned songwriter tapping into his repertoire of writing strategies and reintroducing himself to them. You have to wonder what would have happened to these songs had not Bono recommended Daniel Lanois. Would they have ever seen the light of day? Since Dylan admits that many of these songs had no melodic framework at all, we must conclude that Lanois influenced the songs' eventual sound in compelling ways. One thing is certain: These songs have a distinctive tone. That makes the swampspeak segment of the pop icon period a unique, and intriguing, entry in the Dylan Canon. Throughout the oeuvre, there is only one *Oh Mercy.*

The Retirement Party Phase

The man the world knows as "Bob Dylan" has enjoyed one hell of a run. As I've mentioned before, Bob Zimmerman claims that as a child he dreamt of many of the professional experiences he eventually encountered in his career. I just don't think that he anticipated all that would unfold when he left the Iron Range, synthesized his rebellious personality and encyclopedic knowledge of music into the composite personality that is his "Bob Dylan" character, and traveled the world in pursuit of his destiny. He may have known what that destiny was, but I doubt he envisioned the various missions that arose as he followed his chosen path. I do not believe that he foresaw the Rolling Thunder Revue, or the Bob Dylan Crusade (I'll accept wagers on that one!), or the Bob Dylan Revue, or the transition he is about to undertake. Sure, he dreamt of the fame, the fortune, his confrontations with various establishments, and that sort of thing. He may even have fantasized about making an old-fashioned, 1950s-style, rock 'n' roll record that featured an all-star musical cast. But I suspect that the radical ebb and flow of his career surprised him as much as anybody. How could you anticipate the kinds of changes we've witnessed here? It would require one supernaturally charged Cajun mystic to have foreseen all of this, don't you think?

Our auteur is about to make a major—and final—characterological change to his Bob Dylan composite personality. As we discussed in this chapter's introduction, Zimmerman miraculously discovered a new vocal technique that he married to Lonnie Johnson's secretive system of guitar playing. With that, a revitalizing reorientation ensued in which Zimmerman would reinvigorate his stage act, revise his audience, and remodel Bob Dylan. He calculated that it would require some three years to complete this final transition. He paused to visit New Orleans and empty his drawer full of songs, but now that that has passed, he returned to his plan. The "Bob Dylan" we've known for all of these years is about to retire. Zimmerman now transforms his character in a fashion that complements his new plan; that is, Bob Dillon abdicates his leadership role to Jack Fate. The anarchist retires. His rebellion tapers off—although it *never* dies. The new Dylan is a roving bluesman with a new vocal technique, a new instrumental style, and a new approach to those old Bob Dylan songs. As time passes, Zimmerman will write for Fate as he did for Mr. Message Man, the Newport Mod, country Bob, Brother Bob, and the legendary Bob. A new musical dawn is breaking and it took a long, long night to get there. After such a strenuous journey, a retirement party is in order. And that is *exactly* what transpires with *Under The Red Sky.*

With David [Was] Weiss, Don Was, and Jack Frost (Dylan) as producers and an all-star cast of musicians present (e.g., Stevie Ray and Jimmie Vaughn, Elton John,

Al Kooper, Slash, George Harrison, David Crosby, and Bruce Hornsby as well as Kenny Aronoff [drums], Randy Jackson [bass], David Lindley [guitar], Paulinho Da Costa [percussion], and Waddy Wachtel [guitar]), one might anticipate a rousing response to the creative momentum established by *Mercy*. This was not the case. It was rousing, but it was not a response. Released in September 1990, *Under The Red Sky*'s ten songs (running over thirty-five minutes) contain a compelling innovation within its four thematic orientations. We have a romantic complaint ("Born In Time"), a celebration ("God Knows"), two societal complaints ("T.V. Talkin' Song" and "Unbelievable"), and six installments of the innovative nonsense song: "Wiggle Wiggle," "Under The Red Sky," "10,000 Men," "2 × 2," "Handy Dandy," and "Cat's In The Well." The nonsense songs are presented in a fun, energetic manner. They are, my friends, classic 1950s-era rock 'n' roll parties. Their pop song lyrics do not feature word games with playful/creative imagery, surreal scenes, or poetic impressions on a specific topic; here, Dylan's word machine has a party. It appears that *everybody* misunderstood it.

We begin our retirement party on the more coherent end of the *Red Sky* spectrum and the societal complaints. After *Red Sky*'s opening tracks get you dancing ("Wiggle") and thinking about little boys and girls on the Iron Range ("Under The Red Sky"), the album's third song brings that rocking sound to a more meaningful context. Here we place a bit more symbolic meat on the 1950s-style rock 'n' roll bones. The narrator in "Unbelievable" is incredulous, and it manifests in a variety of ways across the song's four verses. The first verse describes the directionless qualities of the modern world and expresses dismay that we've carried on for as long as we have—it's unbelievable. The second stanza relates the narrator's disbelief over how easily wealth may be accumulated in this materialistic land—it's unbelievable. The bridge reinforces those observations (describing the world's dignified poseurs and their money-grabbing empty ways) before the third verse and second bridge go off the deep end:

> It's unbelievable like a lead balloon,
> It's so impossible to even learn the tune.
> Kill that beast and feed that swine,
> Scale that wall and smoke that vine,
> Feed that horse and saddle up the drum.
> It's unbelievable, the day would finally come.
>
> Once there was a man who had no eyes,
> Every lady in the land told him lies,
> He stood beneath the silver skies
> And his heart began to bleed.
> Every brain is civilized,
> Every nerve is analyzed,
> Everything is criticized when you are in need.

We're a long way from "Jailhouse Rock" here. The song may *sound* like a rocking Little Richard tune, but it reads like Bob Dylan. Everything he sees renders disbelief. He bops along in dismay. The song subscribes to that long-standing Pete Townshend prescription that encourages us all to face our problems and dance all over them.

While not as danceable as "Unbelievable," our second societal complaint bounces to a smooth, swinging, pop-rock beat in which quick pacing supports a fast-moving story. "T.V. Talkin' Song" takes us back to the folk-posturing period's "Talkin'" series with a splash of "Black Diamond Bay" tossed in for good measure. That the story unfolds via eight four-line verses without a bridge and chorus reveals its narrative strategy. This is a fun story in which the narrator recounts his experiences in London's Hyde Park and its famous Speaker's Corner. There the narrator witnessed a man proclaiming the evils of television. The opening verse takes us to Speaker's Corner, the next stanza introduces the unnamed speaker's topic, the following verse describes the narrator moving closer to the speaker to gain a better view (two guys were in a fistfight and he couldn't see), and the fourth and fifth stanzas present the speaker's argument. Let's check it out:

> "The news of the day is on all the time,
> All the latest gossip, all the latest rhyme,
> Your mind is your temple, keep it beautiful and free,
> Don't let an egg get laid in it by something you can't see."

> "Pray for peace!" he said, you could feel it in the crowd.
> My thoughts began to wander. His voice was ringing loud,
> "It will destroy your family, your happy home is gone
> No one can protect you from it once you turn it on."

The speaker's rant continues in the sixth verse as he recommends the Elvis solution to his Speaker's Corner audience (i.e., pick up a gun and shoot the thing) and pounds his message still further in the seventh stanza. The song closes with a riot breaking out, a television crew arriving to capture the action, and the narrator returning to his hotel (or wherever he is staying) to watch all of the action on television.

Shades of "Bear Mountain" and "John Birch" blend with that "Black Diamond" closing twist to generate a fun story about a popular concern: the impact of television. Any doubts about the topical songwriter's ability to take a situation and capture it in song must be dismissed by this simple little story. "T.V. Talkin'" has little plot twists that enliven the story (e.g., two guys get in a fight and the narrator moves away, the Elvis reference, and the song's ending), uses humorous dialogue to keep the tale moving, and, in its own way, issues a moral of the story. Obviously, the auteur can write these songs when and if he wants to do it. Although I don't talk about those songs here, the two songs Dylan wrote for the Traveling Wilburys reinforce this point. When he sat with his new kinfolk to write songs for their new project, Dylan—according to George Harrison in the BBC's *The Bob Dylan Story*—instantly wanted to write a "Prince" song and ripped out "Dirty World" as a parody. Similarly, when he penned "Tweeter And The Monkey Man" for that project, he directly aped Bruce Springsteen's songwriting style with all sorts of references to New Jersey, characters with street names, and shady urban criminal activity. Indeed, Bob Zimmerman could still write these songs when he wanted, whether he was writing as a Dylan, a Wilbury, a Larry Smith, or, very soon, a Jack Fate.

Also demonstrating that those old skills are alive and well is the auteur's 1950s-style presentation of the Alabama Chronicles by way of the celebratory "God Knows." This track features an instrumental pattern that builds and builds as the celebration unfolds via another of those "Political World"–type list songs. The song is also *very* repetitious (the song title is sung over and over and over). Thus, the 1950s sound and songwriting style are co-opted in service of an old theme: praising Him. God knows a lot, and this song shares some of His insights. We begin with the realization that God knows the narrator's love interest is not pretty (shades of "Ugliest Girl") but his dedication to her is complete. Weightier matters quickly follow. God realizes life is tough, and He is prepared to cleanse His world (verse 2). God understands life is frail, tenuous, and frightful, and, as the fourth and fifth verses indicate, He understands our hearts and warns us of our materialism:

> God knows that when you see it,
> God knows you've got to weep,
> God knows the secrets of your heart,
> He'll tell them to you when you're asleep.
>
> God knows there's a river,
> God knows how to make it flow,
> God knows you ain't gonna be taking
> Nothing with you when you go.

This is pretty straightforward stuff. The list continues from there. God knows there is hope, and He understands we can make it to salvation. Yes, God knows a lot, and the voice of his generation reminds us of that fact through a musical style that blends nicely within the *Red Sky* format.

Our *Red Sky* thematic sampler continues to touch all of the traditional Bob Dylan storytelling bases with, you guessed it, a relational complaint that is presented in a smooth, pop-song style that features a graceful piano and complementary backing vocals (by David Crosby). "Born In Time" is a pretty song. The four-verse track (with two eight-line bridges) is a simple romantic complaint that is driven by the two bridges. The verses toy with images of the nighttime and relational nostalgia (verse 1), her thinking of him on a hot day in town (verse 2), a drive down a curvy road and thoughts of relational justice (verse 3), and a closing verse of resignation. The bridges lodge the relational complaint, as the initial installment reveals:

> Not one more night, not one more kiss,
> Not this time baby, no more of this,
> Takes too much skill, takes too much will,
> It's revealing.
> You came, you saw, just like the law
> You married young, just like your ma,

You tried and tried, you made me slide
You left me reelin' with this feelin.'

(That last one is for you, Jacques.) This is a straightforward relational complaint that is spiced with nostalgia. He loves her, but the time to part is at hand. The second bridge demonstrates the narrator's conflicting feelings:

You pressed me once, you pressed me twice,
You hang the flame, you'll pay the price,
Oh babe, that fire
Is still smokin'.
You were snow, you were rain
You were striped, you were plain,
Oh babe, truer words
Have not been spoken or broken.

So, our narrator is struggling with the end. He believes that she will pay for her relational transgressions, acknowledges his feelings remain intense, and displays confidence in his conclusions. Classic Dylan presented in a pop format that fits *Red Sky* just fine.

Herein lies the most concrete support for my contention that this is a retirement party. When an individual retires, people rise, acknowledge that person, and recount tales from days gone by, right? A story from this era, a joke from that time, and maybe a personal anecdote from somewhere provide the material for this final tip of the hat to the departing one. In this case, the auteur is returning to songwriting staples from days gone by, recasting them in the sonic style of the moment, and, in my view, saying, "So long." We have a "talkin' "-era satire—let's have some fun and point that finger. We've witnessed an excerpt from the Alabama Chronicles period—His knowledge is complete and, by the way, did you hear a train whistle? We've had a moment with that tried-and-true songwriting staple that is the romantic complaint with a nostalgic twist—I just love the way you hurt me. And we experienced the wrath of righteous indignation over the state of the world—it's unbelievable. They are all here at the retirement party, dancing in the milieu of the moment featuring the sounds of Bob Zimmerman's youth. Not that they are presented through Little Richard's screaming rhythms, but they invoke the beats, singing styles, and writing techniques of that era. Was this conscious? I don't know. Let's not forget what Professor Ricks had to say on that matter. Me? I'm sticking to my interpretative guns: This is a retirement party.

Often, retirement parties get a little carried away. The drinks flow, the hugs abound, and the dance floor action intensifies as the night continues. What a great moment. Everybody cuts loose in their own special way. In this case, the music explodes as that fabled word machine shuts down and gives us the postspeech portion of the retirement party and the nonsense songs. Everybody jumps and shakes to "Wiggle Wiggle." The alcohol-inspired tears flow from the vacuity of "Under A Red Sky" (it is like being emotionally caught up in an episode of *Lassie*). People sing along to "10,000 Men," although they do not know why. "Cat's In The Well" and "2 × 2" keep the dance floor occupied. Finally, someone falls while swinging from the chandelier during "Handy Dandy." When the cops arrive, the party grinds to a halt. Unfortunately, nobody remembers just what happened—or they are not telling.

Let's take just a moment to look over these nonsense songs—after all, they are unique within the oeuvre. In the opening song, we quickly make the transition from swampspeak to wigglespeak. The conversion is easy. You just turn off your mind and turn on your feet. The fourth verse offers a glimpse of this track's symbolic depth:

> Wiggle, wiggle, wiggle like satin and silk,
> Wiggle, wiggle, wiggle like a pail of milk,
> Wiggle, wiggle, wiggle, rattle and shake,
> Wiggle like a big fat snake.

Would you believe me if I told you that Bob Dylan wrote this? I didn't think so.

When we move to the second track and the title cut, the pace slows a bit, and the mood grows nostalgic. While you'd like to say that this is a sweet little ditty about growing up in Minnesota, in actuality, this is a sweet little ditty about absolutely *nothing*. The magical combination of the song's first bridge and third verse exposes the wonders of this songwriting strategy:

> Someday little girl, everything for you is gonna be new
> Someday little girl, you'll have a diamond as big as your shoe
>
> Let the wind blow low, let the wind blow high.
> One day the little boy and the little girl were both baked in a pie.
> Let the wind blow low, let the wind blow high.
> One day the little boy and the little girl were both baked in a pie.

Moving, isn't it? If I told you that Bob Dylan wrote this song, would you believe me? Don't get angry, now!

We turn to the blues for the nine three-line verses of "10,000 Men." Everybody knows how important pacing is to a party, so we pause for a little Delta break here. This is a straight-up, old-fashioned blues tune about large numbers of people. We have 10,000 men, 10,000 women, and a nice person who serves tea. Ten thousand men stand on a hill for no apparent reason (verse 1). We have 10,000 men moving in ways that your mother would sanction (verse 3). We also have 10,000 well-groomed men searching for precious minerals (verse 4). Oh yeah, we shouldn't forget the 10,000 women saying goodnight to the narrator (verse 6). Then, of course, there's the 10,000 women cleaning his room (verse 8). Well, get it? When you pull back and think about this, verse 5 deviates from this pattern in a richly symbolic fashion:

> Hey! Who could your lover be?
> Hey! Who could your lover be?
> Let me eat off his head so you can really see!

I don't think it required 10,000 people to write this song. If I told you Bob Dylan—oh, never mind.

Our numerological theme carries on with the controversial "2 × 2." A simple, steady rock beat supports the varying three verses of this reiteration of "Man Gave Names To All The Animals" as the song offers its nursery rhyme account of rhyming numbers. There is a hint of complaint that is elevated in the bridges; otherwise, the rhymes bounce along. Submitted for your dining and dancing pleasure, here is the opening verse and bridge:

> One by one, they followed the sun,
> One by one, until there were none.
> Two by two, to their lovers they flew,
> Two by two, into the foggy dew.
> Three by three, they danced on the sea,
> Four by four, they danced on the shore,
> Five by five, they tried to survive,
> Six by six, they were playing with tricks.
>
> How many paths did they try and fail?
> How many of their brothers and sisters lingered in jail?
> How much poison did they inhale?
> How many black cats crossed their trail?

What can you say? (I guess you could say that you haven't seen this kind of numerological folly since "I Shall Be Free No. 10.") As I mentioned earlier, there is the hint of complaint in these lines that throw out negative images and move along to the next rhyme. The song closes with references to Noah's Ark, people turning keys, and following the sun. The rhymes just flow—for no discernable reason. But hey, this is a party, right?

And the Bob Dylan Retirement Party concludes in a grand style. The penultimate "Handy Dandy" does a marvelous job of setting up that capstone commentary that is "Cat's In The Well." The full sound of the bouncy "Handy" keeps the party moving toward its sad ending. This tune is about somebody named Handy Dandy. He is controversial, well-traveled, and tough, and plays with an all-female orchestra (verses 1 and 2). Yes, he is rich and has plenty of time on his hands (verse 3). The final stanzas round off this insightful profile:

> Handy Dandy, sitting with a girl named Nancy in a garden feelin' kind of
>   lazy
> He says, "Ya want a gun? I'll give you one." She says, "Boy, you talking
>   crazy."
> Handy Dandy, just like sugar and candy
> Handy Dandy, pour him another brandy
>
> Handy Dandy, he got a basket of flowers and a bag full of sorrow
> He finishes his drink, he gets up from the table he says,

"Okay, boys, I'll see you tomorrow."
Handy Dandy, Handy Dandy, just like sugar and candy
Handy Dandy, just like sugar and candy.

OK, close your eyes, let your imagination flow, and you can see everybody swinging and swaying to this happy-go-lucky tune about a guy drinking brandy and offering guns to ladies. I tell you, that Bob Zimmerman sure knows how to throw a party.

To cap off *Under The Red Sky*, we return to the swamp and the swinging sounds of zydeco music. With a wonderful Cajun beat supporting this five-verse, two-bridge, blues-based song, we get the whole party up and dancing to a tale of a cat on the move. The cat's in the well, and a wolf is peering down at its potential dinner. While the wolf gapes, a woman sleeps, houses bounce, barns are occupied, and leaves fall. Serious stuff, right? The bridges take our Cajun ditty to another plane:

The cat's in the well and grief is showing its face
The world's being slaughtered and it's such a bloody disgrace.

Ahhh yes, the old threatened cat metaphor at work here. The wolf stares down—no doubt, drooling—while the cat grows pensive and worried about the state of the world. How unusual: a selfless cat. The second bridge lightens the load a bit:

The cat's in the well, and pappa is reading the news.
His hair is falling out and all of his daughters need shoes.

The choice between a hairpiece and shoes for the kids must be a challenging one. The track just skips along noting that the barn is full, the drinks are made, and the dogs are prepared for combat. The song—and the Bob Dylan retirement party—conclude in an appropriate fashion: "Goodnight, my love, may the Lord have mercy on us all." With that, the evening comes to a close. Assuredly, a good time was had by all. I don't know about you, but I had a blast.

Under The Red Sky does its job well. But I don't think the critics caught on to my argument. For instance, *Musician* reports the "lyrics often strike a somewhat bizarre but genuinely haunting balance between children's tales and biblical fables"; *Rolling Stone* suggests the record is "at best workmanlike; at worst, perfunctory" and calls *Red Sky* "a kind of Dylan-Lite"; and the *New York Post* describes the lyrics as "not bad—they're ominous, pessimistic and determinedly enigmatic—but it's doubtful that today's high school students are going to use them to make the old case for Bob Dylan as great American poet." Wow. No, the writers of that time had no idea what was to follow; hence, in all fairness, they were at a decided disadvantage. For them, this was evidence of a backslide past *Oh Mercy* to the albums of covers and coauthored pieces that preceded the trip to the swamps. For them, *Under The Red Sky* was a bad sign. For us, the record plays a very different role within the oeuvre. It is an ending—that is for sure—but it is also a transition to a new beginning. Jack Fate is preparing to come onstage for a long, long stay.

There is no other segment of Bob Dylan's oeuvre like the pop icon period. Throughout its four phases, we witnessed an auteur in search of himself. His anger raged in *Infidels*. After the moral period and its *Shot Of Love* resolution, the writer paused to offer one more edition of his *Street-Legal* declaration of decadence and take a final shot at the Jokerman responsible for this hell on earth. Yet, he cannot leave his work alone. Dylan toyed and toyed with the project until he deleted the work's pivotal statement ("Foot Of Pride") and subsequently diluted the final product. The writing, as the biographers report, was on the wall at that point in that this kind of production folly would plague the rest of this songwriting period. As *Red Sky* producer Don Was told biographer Clinton Heylin, "I started to develop this unified field theory, that if something was too beautiful, if it looked like it was trying to please, then it was against his purposes. . . . It's not necessarily out of a lack of generosity of spirit. . . . It says more about . . . his inability to yield to audience-pleasing." Bob Dillon's rebellion is ever-present, isn't it?

The search continued as the auteur called upon the Bob Dylan Revue for a three-album set. There, relational matters by and large replaced the *Street-Legal* rhetoric as Dylan sang songs of love mixed in with covers and coauthored pieces that performed a host of functions—some of which remain a secret to this day. As *Chronicles* reports, Dylan lost his bearings during this period, and his reorientation required time. Time he had, and time he gave. Eventually, it all came together, but he injured his hand. Because of that injury, he had more time to offer. Just when he was about to enter the wooden leg business, the muse returned, the songs flowed, he received solid advice from Bono, and the swampspeak phase ensued. Dylan emptied his drawer full of songs, received the musical world's praise, and continued with his new plan. At this point, his reorientation dropped its wandering ways and grew more and more systematic. I think this is remarkable. This is so very, very rare. Few artists have a career that extends this long and still have the resources necessary to muster yet another comeback—not an Elvis 1968-type comeback, but an artistic renewal. Dear reader, name *one artist* who has successfully achieved this goal. Finally, with the plan in place, the method of operation under control, and the willpower to see his ambitions through, Bob Zimmerman made his final adjustments to his "Bob Dylan" composite character. Just as Bob Dillon rose to the occasion during the Newport Mod era, Jack Fate now assumes control of the final leg of the auteur's fifty-year (to date) career. With all of that in place, Zimmerman paused to celebrate his youth on the Iron Range. The sounds of The Day supported samples of songwriting from that era as well as the songwriting styles of that timeframe (i.e., a blend of songwriting styles). The curtain dropped with the auteur wishing God's mercy on us all. A new day dawned, and Jack Fate is now on the case. What a story. Still, we're not finished. In fact, the story gets better. To the final period of Bob Dylan's lifework, we now turn.

The Jack Fate Era

That Bob Dylan is sincerely grateful for those crucial revisions of his vocal and instrumental techniques is evident in his slavish commitment to performance during the Jack Fate era. The Never Ending Series of Tours (NEST) is flat-out incredible. *No major artist performs in this manner—not one.* This is *not* a resident performer in Nashville, Berlin, Branson, Tokyo, Reno, or Las Vegas. Bob Zimmerman takes his Jack Fate–fueled Bob Dylan character on tour for an average of 100 shows a year. *One hundred shows!* A single year of the "Bob Dylan Show" is something to behold in and of itself. Now, shall we take that year and multiply it times, say, *seventeen* (and counting)? Bob Zimmerman's dedication to performance is controlling, and he actively deploys his Bob Dylan character in service of that reborn mission. Our seasoned bluesman, Jack Fate, synthesizes his encyclopedic knowledge of American Song with his intimate understanding of the Dylan Canon and his undying devotion to "the road" to render a new "Bob Dylan"—a character that embodies Bob Dillon's rebellious resolve, Fate's musical education, and Bob Zimmerman's lifelong professional drive. This is impressive stuff. I think it's safe to report that it is also unprecedented: Never before has an individual career achieved this level of depth, determination, and devotion.

As *Chronicles* and the pop icon period reveal, the musical evolution that facilitated the Jack Fate era was a slow process. Certainly, young Bob Dylan never anticipated that he would remain on the road for so long. In fact, in October 1965 he told Allen Stone, "I don't really plan to do it [perform] for the rest of my life or anything." From *Chronicles*, we learn that our auteur may not have understood his deepseated commitment to performance until it was physically threatened. When he faced the possibility of operating a factory that manufactured wooden legs or some other vocational alternative, he apparently realized just how important performance was to his life and his perceived moment in history. Why was performance suddenly so important? What inspired this change in attitude that supported the new plan involving a shift in vocal style, a reorientation of his instrumental approach, and a gradual revision of his audience? What prompted Zimmerman to accent the Jack Fate dimension of his Dylan composite persona? I think I know. I reported this finding in *Bob Dylan, Bruce Springsteen & American Song*. Bob Zimmerman loves "American song." He adores that music. It is his life. He treasures his contributions to American song's development as well. From all of those nights listening to the radio in Hibbing; to all those days sitting around listening to and playing music in Denver, Dinkytown, the Village, and the Folklore Center, with Woody Guthrie's friends, and more; to the hours in the basement with The Band; to the weeks on the Rolling Thunder highway; to his wayward days in the 1980s practicing with different bands, Bob Zimmerman has listened to, interpreted, dissected, and devoured the sonic blessings of this musical movement that is American song. Consequently, the answer to our question is simple: Bob Zimmerman loves the *songs*. Now, he deploys his Dylan composite in service for the second time. To the extent that he once served his Lord, he now serves those songs. Read *Chronicles*. Whether he is talking about Leadbelly, Hank Williams, an inspirational song entitled "Pirate Jenny," or his own "Desolation Row," it is overwhelmingly evident that the author *adores* these songs. In the Jack Fate era, he commits his life to their performance. This mission of service is, once again, all-consuming.

And why not? Zimmerman's life is punctuated by these songs. Johnny Ray is *still* his hero. Woody Guthrie *still* provides inspiration. Hank Williams is *still* his songwriting teacher. Harold Arlen is *still* a favorite. Remember what he said to David Gates when asked about the moral period and his religion? Dylan was unequivocal: "Here's the thing with me and the religious thing. This is the flat-out truth: I find the religiosity and philosophy in the music. I don't find it anywhere else. Songs like 'Let Me Rest on a Peaceful Mountain' or 'I Saw the Light'—that's my religion. I don't adhere to rabbis, preachers, evangelists, all of that. I've learned more from the songs than I've learned from any of this kind of entity. The songs are my lexicon. I believe the songs." In a 2004 interview with Robert Hilburn, Dylan elaborated on this point by explaining how music dominates his consciousness and, in turn, inspires his pen:

> Well, you have to understand that I'm not a melodist. My songs are either based on old Protestant hymns or Carter family songs or variations of the blues form. What happens is, I'll take a song I know and simply start playing it in my head. That's the way I meditate. A lot of people will look at a crack on the wall and meditate, or count sheep or angels or money or something, and it's a proven fact that it'll help them relax. I don't meditate on any of that stuff. I meditate on a song. I'll be playing Bob Nolan's "Tumbling Tumbleweeds," for instance, in my head constantly—while I'm driving a car or talking to a person or sitting around or whatever. People will think they are talking to me and I'm talking back, but I'm not. I'm listening to the song in my head. At a certain point, some of the words will change and I'll start writing a song.

There, Dylan reported that "Blowin' In The Wind" is "probably" a variation on a Carter Family tune, that "The Times They Are A-Changin' " is "probably" from a "Scottish folk song," and that—remarkably—"Subterranean Homesick Blues" is a spin-off of Chuck Berry's "Too Much Monkey Business" merged with some "scat songs" from the 1940s. Throughout the Hilburn interview, Dylan strummed his guitar (an occasionally annoying habit that can be heard in many recorded interviews and is featured in *Dont Look Back*'s scene involving the science student–journalist "interview"). Eventually, Hilburn recognized the tune. It was Irving Berlin's "Blue Skies." Hilburn inquired if Dylan were composing a new song, as per the method he just explained. The voice of his generation smiled and replied, "No . . . I'm just showing you what I do."

We'll discuss Zimmerman's approach to writing in more detail in the next chapter; however, notice how the old songs represent his creative foundation. They provide the springboard to new songs. They offer a means of meditative relaxation. They are the language of his life. In the Jack Fate era, they—and the Dylan oeuvre— become his creative currency. The period opens with the Basement Strategy and two albums of traditional folk and blues songs: 1992's *Good As I Been To You* and 1993's *World Gone Wrong*. There we witness Zimmerman doing what he does to sustain his art: He reorients his creative focus in service of a new mission. As we discussed in the previous chapter, once he decided to shift the vocal, instrumental, and audience-based dimensions of his work, he envisioned a three-year transitional period. After 1993's *World Gone Wrong*, that transition was virtually completed. His appearance on MTV's *Unplugged* series (recorded in November 1994) publicly reinforced that new orientation with its revisions of old songs such as "Tombstone Blues" and "Rainy Day Women #12 & 35." The NEST marched on from there, using the stylistic variations that accompanied shifts in his musical cast to enliven and reformulate the songs over time. We must also remember that Dylan has consistently stated that he started writing songs because he needed something to sing. He has said this time and again. This rule manifested in the Jack Fate era as well when Zimmerman penned a series of songs for Fate by way of 1997's *Time Out Of Mind* and 2001's *Love And Theft*. These two records feature a substantial thematic shift as—once again—Zimmerman wrote specifically for his character. Consequently, these songs take us from Bob Dylan's famed anarchy to Jack Fate's seasoned sermonic reflections. The new songs are a marked departure from Dylan's previous work, that's for certain. They, most assuredly, give Fate something to sing. To demonstrate that his creative reorientation was complete, Zimmerman did what he often does when he finds himself in this situation: He made a movie. In 2003's *Masked And Anonymous*, Jack Fate appears in all his raging glory. He wears the cowboy hat and Western suits that he unveiled in his recent editions of the NEST. He speaks in the calm, assured style of the veteran rounder that he is. And he embraces a world gone oh-so-wrong. To be sure, a creative equilibrium is established and sustained during this period of the oeuvre. The NEST prompts the creative instinct, and the songwriting, moviemaking, and autobiography follow that inspiration. Correspondingly, the public tide turned as the auteur won multiple Grammy awards for *Time Out Of Mind* and an Oscar for "Things Have Changed" (in 2001 for a song featured in the film *The Wonder Boys*), demonstrated his topical songwriting skills via the epic " 'Cross The Green Mountain" (composed for the 2003 Civil War film, *Gods & Generals*), and publicly laughed at the Dylan myth in *Masked*. Finally, during another David Gates interview—this time, regarding his autobiography—he revealed that other albums are in the works. Yes, Bob Zimmerman serves American song during the Jack Fate era, and that service renders a creative renaissance that contributes to an unprecedented extension of an already historic career.

The centerpiece of this revitalization is Zimmerman's surprising emphasis on performance. When we pause and consider the lifework, only the folk-posturing period reflects this commitment to performance. In his youth, Zimmerman's Dylan character embraced performance as his road to victory, using folk clubs, festivals, protest events, and whatever was available to hawk his wares. Subsequent eras, however, displayed the opposite trait. The Newport Mod's rebellion rendered an antagonistic orientation in which the emerging auteur faced hostile audiences with loud, confrontational responses. The young man stood his ground in the face of oppressive audiences—in fact, he counterattacked. The Americana period's mission of recovery found Dylan stumbling toward performance, struggling to regain his show legs and performance bearings. When he regained those bearings in the crystallization era, he leaped overboard by way of the melodramatic shows of the Rolling Thunder Revue. There, no performance stone was left unturned as Renaldo's appearance, screaming vocals, and stage demeanor took shows way over the top. That trend advanced into Tour '78's presentation of the Bob Dylan Revue. The Revue revised the Dylan back catalog in surprising, and at times challenging, ways. Unfortunately, Dylan's detachment was often the Revue's most prominent characteristic. The Bob Dylan Crusade strategically transformed elements of the Revue as it pursued the lifework's first mission of service. Finally, the pop icon era featured a wandering auteur in search of his creative foundation. That exploration yielded powerful results: It generated Jack Fate's emergence into a position of prominence. Thus, the folk-posturing period and the Jack Fate era serve as bookends for a career that has displayed varying approaches to performance. An energized performer (e.g., the 1964 Halloween show) rotated with a lethargic act (e.g., portions of Tour '66's acoustic set), a madcap performance (e.g., any Rolling Thunder show), a weird act (e.g., the 1978 Budokan show), a sermonic presentation (e.g., the early Crusade shows), and a wayward act (e.g., the tours with Tom Petty), culminating in Jack Fate's precise shows (e.g., the post-1994 NEST shows). This is quite a journey. Zimmerman's characters, it seems, have stood on all sides of the performance issue. Therefore, I maintain that the NEST's commitment to excellence is grounded in these diverse experiences. Zimmerman understands the differences in these various styles, and he uses that knowledge to Jack Fate's advantage.

As we conclude this study, please notice that Bobby Zimmerman of Hibbing, Minnesota, created more than a series of characters to support his artistic ambitions when he molded the Bob Dylan composite persona. He did much more than that. He built a musical highway that allows his genius to travel where it must. Never forget: Talent does what it can, but genius does what it must. For Zimmerman, this journey was never about the Dylan characters. No. He told Hilburn in that 2004 interview, "To me, the performer is here and gone. The songs are the star of the show, not me." He also makes that statement in *Chronicles*. Never have truer words been spoken. So, sit back and enjoy another characterological shift as Zimmerman turns to Jack Fate to bring his songs out of the "shadows," merge them with other jewels from American song's musical crown, and present the results for the world to embellish. Much like that famed capstone statement that the auteur used time and again to end an album, his songs play that role as the lifework turns its final corner. Now, Zimmerman separates himself from his peers and offers concrete evidence for the claim that

Jack Fate, the Basement Strategy, and the Never Ending Series of Tours

Everybody should have some variation of the Basement Strategy available for their particular needs. We all need some means of regrouping, reorienting, and re-bounding from the various challenges in life. Maybe a particular book, movie, loca-tion, or person takes you to a special place and assists your efforts to meet the demands of any given day or period. Bob Zimmerman surely perfected his Basement Strategy. *Chronicles* spends quite a bit of space delineating how his friends' libraries (both musical and literary), New York's Folklore Center and public library, and his various cohorts fed the budding auteur's brain—and ambitions—in multiple ways. Clearly, the man systematically educated himself. As a result, he knew *exactly* what to do after his motorcycle accident. Remember what Robbie Robertson said? Dylan prepped for those sessions in Big Pink's basement. He knew those songs a little *too* well. He was on a private mission that he took seriously. There were also elements of the Basement Strategy in the Rolling Thunder Revue, the Bob Dylan Revue, the Bob Dylan Crusade, and all of those rehearsals with different bands in the 1980s. Many times in the 1980s, musical colleagues reported that the unofficial music mak-ing (e.g., rehearsals and studio warmups) was far superior to the official proceedings (live or recorded). To that end, Clinton Heylin quotes Tom Petty's ambition to "take the rehearsals on the stage," and Mikal Gilmore describes rehearsals with Christmas songs, gospel tunes, and stunning revisions of old Dylan tracks ("inventive versions of wondrous songs come and go and are never heard again"). Dylan relished play-ing old songs in a spontaneous musical environment and only reluctantly recorded (or rehearsed) the material that warranted the rehearsal. This reliance on the Base-ment Strategy—and the creative rejuvenation it fosters—would ultimately pull the artist through this final musical reorientation.

The biographers report that this process began in Chicago in mid-June 1992. Dylan and an unnamed group of musicians assembled at Acme Recording Studios and recorded a series of traditional songs that never saw the light of day. Clinton Heylin's session chronology claims that songs such as "Casey Jones," "Duncan and Brady," and "Polly Vaughn" were taped there, and Michael Gray cites a report that Dylan recorded twenty-six songs during those sessions. Dylan subsequently shifted the Basement Strategy from a group experience to a solo endeavor when he recorded *Good As I Been To You* and *World Gone Wrong* in his personal studio at his Malibu, Cal-ifornia, home. Just imagine Dylan with his guitar and harmonica all alone in his garage with those timeworn songs. It must have been a medicinal moment.

Or was it? Heylin's biography maintains these two albums are nothing but con-tractual filler as he derides the vocal and instrumental performance (contending Dylan did not tune his guitar or change its strings during the exercise), cites a London *Times* critic's denunciation of the results, and demeans the projects' mastering. He goes as far as to suggest that Dylan deleted songs from the final version's order to maximize the publishing revenue associated with the venture. Heylin's response is harsh. Michael Gray—a Dylanologist who never shies away from critical attacks—offers a totally different perspective:

> "Good As I Been To You" and "World Gone Wrong" turn a radio tele-scope upon the past, retrieving that which seems light years away in the era of Microsoft, McDonald's and MTV. These albums are anthologies of individualism but they also champion the dignity of labour, the silenced and oppressed. They celebrate oral history, working-class history, history that struggled across oceans. As "Bob Dylan" [the debut album] did, they also reject 'purity.' There are songs here of dodgy provenance—songs as likely to have been sanitised by nineteenth-century Irish clergymen as come down orally intact; songs that might be North American or Irish; songs with composers' names attached to them through accidents of publishing history; songs that may not be half the age they hint at. Above all, these collections embrace material that has belonged jointly to black America and white, as well as songs that have arisen in one camp or the other.

If you subscribe to Gray's perspective, the raw qualities of the recordings may very well be in service of their respective histories—an act not of laziness, but of au-thentication. Gray contends that "Dylan's concern here is not a looking-back at him-self and his own past but a shepherding us out into an older and wider world." In other words, a public sharing of the Basement process. On the other hand, after Gray's incredible analysis of the two projects' material (the man offers a detailed his-tory of the various songs, explaining how each bar or vowel is derivative of some af-flicted Southern bluesman's or drunken Highlander's work—this is the state of the art of Applied Dylanology), he concludes, "Among other things, these two albums are an investigation on Dylan's part as to how far he can remain true to, as it were, this folksong part of himself." Gray's writing seems contradictory, but his point is compelling. I think Dylan pursued both objectives. He shed light on the past, him-self, and their intersection. In so doing, he may have satisfied both a contract and a creative urge. Of that, I'm more than uncertain. But I *am* certain of this: Instead of allowing this edition of the Basement Strategy to be distributed through unofficial sources, he channeled them through Columbia Records. Bob Dylan learned *that* les-son very, very well.

We now turn to the albums themselves and examine the thematic qualities of their respective songs. We begin with 1992's *Good As I Been To You* and its thirteen songs about relationships, personal woes, and worldly disaster. The relational stories range from "Arthur McBride" and its long, winding account about two cousins (the story's relational dimension) out for a Christmas morning walk and their chance en-counter with two soldiers and a little drummer boy (the soldiers attempt to recruit the cousins, the cousins reject the offer and insult the soldiers, a fight ensues, and the cousins defeat the soldiers before continuing their walk) to "Sittin' On Top Of The World" and its happy-go-lucky tale of a gentlemen who lost his lover and relishes the results; to "Canadee-I-O" and its complicated story about a sailor who smuggles his girl on board his ship bound for "Canadee-I-O," only to have her discovered by his mates who want to toss her overboard and the captain's successful intervention (he is so successful that she marries him and lives happily ever after). The remaining relational tunes focus on some form of romantic angst. For example, in "Frankie & Albert" the man, Albert, cheats on Frankie and winds up on the wrong end of a .44 caliber bullet. Everybody suffers in this time-honored tale when Frankie is convicted of second degree murder and, presumably, hangs for her troubles. "Blackjack Davey" portrays a gambler (Davey) who convinces a sixteen-year-old wife to run away from home with him, leaving her husband and baby behind. Her husband tracks them down. You just *know* he is going to kill them both, but he does not. He accepts his wife's decision and apparently leaves her to her new life. "Little Maggie" features a blue-eyed, gun-carrying lady who is the apple of the narrator's eye. Alas, she loves another man and our narrator abdicates his romantic efforts for another destination. More relational angst appears by way of "Step It Up And Go" (the narrator has one bad woman, and he needs to "step up" and get out of there), "Tomorrow Night" (the narrator just *knows* that tomorrow his love will be in vain), and the self-evident expectations of "You're Gonna Quit Me," in which the narrator is at a loss regarding his woman's obvious desire to leave him (he laments, why would you go, "as good as I been to you"). Yes, relational misery abounds in these old stories of cheating partners, runaway lovers, and romantic decline.

But the agony doesn't end there, no sir. *Good*'s three tales of individual angst probe the frustrations of being exiled to Australia ("Jim Jones"), the vicissitudes of daily living ("Hard Times"), and the drudgery of working for oppressive employers with jewels in their names ("Diamond Joe"). "Jim" had a choice, and he apparently picked the wrong one. He could have stayed in England and died for his crimes, but he opted for life in a penal colony instead. Oh well, at least he has his revenge fantasies to occupy his mind. Unlike Jim, the narrator in "Hard Times" has no choice but to wallow in his misery and wish for better days. With all of those hard times hanging around his door, you'd think the guy would just move away and leave them there. Finally, in "Diamond Joe" the narrator could go work for someone else, but no, he would rather complain about Joe and endure the anxieties of working for that cheap scoundrel. Individual pain abounds in these old stories of criminal exile, economic hardship, and hardhearted, diamond-studded employers. "Woe is me" is the slogan of the day.

The angst hits the fan in our capstone story of worldly disaster, "Froggie Went A Courtin'." This extremely repetitive story conjures memories of "Man Gave Names To All The Animals" in its fairy tale account of a frog's efforts to marry the mouse of his dreams. Froggie states his ambitions, and she asks her uncle—a rat—for his blessings. He grants Froggie's wish, and they have a wedding dinner in a hollow tree. They plan the meal and receive visits from a moth, a june bug, a bumblebee, a flea, a cow, a tick, a snake, and a cat. Unfortunately, the cat violates decorum and eats the bride and her uncle. Cats! To complement that indiscretion, Froggie is consumed by a passing duck (I didn't know ducks ate frogs, did you?). The story ends with the announcement that if you want any more of this story, well, you'll have to sing it yourself. To be sure, the world has gone wrong.

Good As I Been To You features an artist in his songwriting sandbox vigorously playing with tunes of significance to him—and perhaps him alone. Critics offered varied opinions regarding the result. There were a few writers who seemed to embrace the argument advanced here, so I present their findings out of good taste. For example, the *New York Times'* Karen Schoemer remarks, "Like some 1930's field recording, the album is more a document than art, more an attempt to preserve a moment than make a statement. . . . By re-examining his roots and reaffirming his past, Dylan has actually given a strange gift to the younger audience: the chance to experience, firsthand, some of the abrasive beauty and unapologetic dignity that must have jarred listeners 30 years ago. He's reintroducing himself, all over again." Peter Puterbaugh opines, "The album is a personal move, with Dylan endeavoring to reclaim his roots and recover his soul. Yet the signals it sends to the scene around him bear an indelible message: It's time to go back to beginnings if we hope to get back on course, not only in music but in other spheres of American life as well." *Rolling Stone*'s David Wild concurs, "This fascinating exploration of musical roots is more than a diversion for musicologists. *Good As I Been to You* shows that sometimes one can look back and find something that's both timeless and relevant." Similarly, David Hinckley maintains that the record "offers another detail for the vast canvass from which Dylan's own music came," and Larry Katz concludes, "Dylan's performances of this folk material are often remarkable. His voice is crabbed, but assured. For the most part, the lyrics are clear, not mumbled. But what's most noteable [*sic*] is his guitar playing, which borders on masterful." Talk of contractual filler, out-of-tune guitars, and lazy guitar mechanics are nowhere in sight in these commentaries; instead, critics seem to grasp the significance of this particular exercise. A reorientation is underway, and not all of the musical world turned a blind eye to its development.

That process continued with our second Basement Strategy entry: 1993's *World Gone Wrong*. Things turn a bit darker in this ten-track work that features four songs from the "love kills" tradition ("World Gone Wrong," "Love Henry," "Ragged & Dirty," and "Delia"), a three-song set I deem the Death Diaries ("Stack-A-Lee," "Two Soldiers," and "Lone Pilgrim"), two songs that shift the "love complaint" theme to a "lust complaint" orientation ("Blood In My Eyes" and "Broke Down Engine"), and, lo and behold, the 1990s Basement Strategy's first positive tune, the love victory of "Jack-A-Roe." Throughout most of the recording, Dylan's voice, guitar, and harmonica subscribe to a blues format more than the folk style of *Good As I Been*. The songs have a bit more edge. The specifics yield additional insights.

The "love kills" songs are diverse in their thematic enactments. We have the threat of murder, two actual killings, and a sullen acceptance of death's eventuality. The threat appears in the title cut and its straightforward yarn about a failing relationship that is precipitated by worldly demise. The world has turned strange, robbed the narrator of his home, and mandated that he either leave or kill his disloyal woman. He pauses to warn others of this sad scenario before grabbing his suitcase and hat and leaving forever. The story traces the problems associated with an externally controlled lover—or he is using those trends to his advantage. You decide. The act-right-or-I'll-leave theme reappears in "Ragged & Dirty" as well. Here a young, jilted lover requests one last night with his older, cheating companion. If she refuses, he asks if he may just sit outside her door, promising to depart before her other man returns. Nothing works for this poor soul, and he pleads for sympathy. That fails as well, so he decides to leave town. He has been mistreated, and he is prepared to die and end his frustrations. Yes, dear reader, love hurts.

In fact, love kills. You just can't explore American song without a few good old-fashioned "killin' songs." From the "you better watch what you say" portion of the songbook, we have "Love Henry" and its account of a big mouth opened one too many times. When Henry's love of the moment requests a night of bliss, he not only turns her down, but also tells her why. Bad move. He admits he loves another woman more, and pays the price for that indiscretion. She kills him, dumps him in the well to rot (do people drink from these things?), and invites her parrot to visit her. This parrot is no fool. It refuses on the basis that anybody who would kill her lover is unlikely to treat anything else any better. Smart bird. Dumb Henry. No, excuse me: Dead Henry. Death enters the house once more by way of "Delia" and another sad tale of poor taste. Obviously, Delia did not listen to her parents when they warned her to choose her friends wisely. Delia is a gambling girl who loved to hang out with the rounders. Our narrator is not of that crowd, and he loves Delia so much. One day a rounder named Curtis uses that dreaded .44 caliber bullet to do another dastardly deed. Delia is dead. Curtis pleads his case to the judge and loses. He gets ninety-nine years to contemplate his crime. Meanwhile, the narrator sings of his friend's passing and her poor decisions. Yes, my friends, love kills.

The Death Diaries reinforce this thematic trend by way of a story about a vicious brute who kills a guy over a hat ("Stack-A-Lee"), a tale of two ill-fated soldiers ("Two Soldiers"), and an account of a peaceful dead man's words from beyond ("Lone Pilgrim"). "Stack-A-Lee" is a mean-spirited bully. If you want evidence of a world gone wrong, submitted for your approval is this tale of a family man killed for his headwear. Apparently, Billy Lyons and Stack fought over a Stetson hat. I presume Lyons won that battle but lost the war when Stack shot him—appropriately enough—in the head. Stack goes to jail, no one will make his bail, and we're left hoping that he'll wind up in . . . no I'm not going to make that rhyme. To the extent that "Stack-A-Lee" trivializes death, "Two Soldiers" immortalizes it. "Soldiers" is a sad story. Two men talk before entering battle, and one asks the other to write his mother should he perish. With that understanding, they charge the enemy and both men die. No letter is sent. Unlike John Brown's mom, this mother is left in the lurch, wondering. That is not the case in our final episode of the Death Diaries, "Lone Pilgrim." An instrumental pattern that sounds remarkably like the guitar work in "Dark Eyes" provides the backdrop for a simple story about a narrator who walks up to a grave and hears a whisper from beyond. The voice conveys neither sorrow nor remorse, but peace and contentment. Apparently, he answered the call for service and paid the ultimate price; nevertheless, he is peaceful and at home with his master. Subsequently, he calls out from the grave to the narrator and urges him to tell everyone that everything is fine.

After all of this death and despair, we need a little comic relief, don't you think? I mean, we need a break! *World Gone Wrong* provides that little interlude via "Jack-A-Roe." This is a fast-paced, intense song that features a wealthy woman and her war-torn lover. She is the daughter of a successful London merchant and is in love with a sailor named Jackie. He goes off to war, then she disguises herself as a sailor and follows him. Eventually she finds him dying on a battlefield. She carries him off, secures a doctor, saves his life, and marries him. The story ends with the narrator telling the woman of his dreams that love worked for these people, so why won't it work for them? What a happy, heroic story. A rich girl sacrifices everything for her gallant lover. She wins the day and is richly rewarded. Yes, our lone ray of sunshine in a world gone truly wrong.

Our remaining songs, the "lust complaints," appear back-to-back. No one dies or is threatened by death in these songs that describe out-of-control libidos. From the "impatience is no virtue" chapter of the love manual, we have "Blood In My Eyes" and its tale of a lover who makes a simple but sincere demand: Make love to me or return my cash. He saw her, fell for her (hence the blood in his eyes), dressed up and spent his money on her, and wants her horribly. She responds to his plea for lovemaking with a simple request: Be patient. Well, the blood has left this guy's eyes for a more demanding location and his response indicates the results. His argument is without mystery: "Your body or my money" (my words). I'm not certain what happened, but I think he got his money back. You never know. Uncertainty drives our second edition of the "lust complaints," "Broke Down Engine." Here, an automobile metaphor is used to complain about an absent lover. This highly repetitive yarn invokes the oeuvre's second reference to "the Georgia Crawl" (also featured in *Slow Train*'s "Gonna Change My Way Of Thinking") as the narrator prays and prays and prays for his lover's return and an end to his misery. Only she—and her no doubt magical ways—can stop his crying. Yes, my friends, lust hurts.

The auteur's stroll down memory lane concluded with the Basement Strategy's second installment, *World Gone Wrong*. To cap off this exercise, Dylan contributed to the science that bears his name by including liner notes that feature musical histories and personal responses to *World*'s songs. The essay takes us back in time to those liner notes of yesteryear with its humorous observations and cryptic references. Thoughts of days gone by and their implications for the future occupied the minds of critics as well. For instance, *Spin*'s Steve Anderson writes, "Achy but not anxious, soothing but not soporific, Dylan's vocals float across the melodies, his blurred timbre gently chafing notes instead of shredding them. . . . The result is no 'unplugged' rite of passion, where some middle-aged rocker turns reflective and avuncular in his dusking career. . . . Dylan's singing is wily and nuanced enough to avoid a benign roots homage." Bill Flanagan observes in *Musician*, "Dylan demonstrates that he can say more in someone else's song than most artists can say in their own. . . . The weight of nobility and loss are as appropriate to this older Dylan's singing as anger and hunger were to the snarl of his youth." The *San Francisco Examiner*'s Craig Marine reports, "These are tales of war, love gone mad, corruption, defilement, murder, redemption and longing. Dylan's attachment to this type of social documentation is evident in the intensity and effort he brings to his interpretations." Lastly, *Acoustic Guitar*'s Derk Richardson places the two albums in context: "*World Gone Wrong* both illuminates *Good as I Been to You* as a necessary first step and lifts the curtain on a performer willing to express the kind of complex, ambivalent self-reflection that his best work used to enkindle in his audience." Although there were reviews that decried Dylan's singing and denounced the work as contractual filler, most critics emphasized

Dylan's commitment to American song and the album's potential to spark a creative renewal.

Perhaps a future edition of *Chronicles* will reveal the extent to which *Good As I Been* and *World Gone Wrong* represent contractual filler, a systematic application of the Basement Strategy, some combination of the two, or something else entirely. From the evidence I've examined, I'm quite comfortable with my argument that these records were our last formal implementation of a traditional practice. The artist who publicly states that American song and its ancestors are his art's lifeblood and his personal inspiration turned to those materials to conclude a reorientation that was years in the making. I admire Zimmerman for his patience. Instead of rushing his Dylan character in one direction or another, he bided his time, thought through his plans, and provided time for their maturation. He may have experienced a performance epiphany in Switzerland. He may have suddenly understood what Lonnie Johnson explained to him years ago. He may have discovered a method of singing that would support his longevity. But he allowed it all an opportunity to gestate. Once his hand recovered and he returned to touring, he patiently bided his time there as well. While I believe that his plan required more than the three years he allotted for his reorientation, it appears everything came together in the mid-1990s. Yes, love is a powerful thing. Whether those feelings extend toward another person, a cause, a country, or an art form, it is a most influential factor in an individual's daily life. In this case, Bob Zimmerman's love for American song—and his contributions to its development—provided the foundation for yet another artistic renewal. Yes, as the performers come and go, the songs remain. Bob Zimmerman is not quite ready to ride off into that musical sunset. Not yet, anyway. First, he has one more characterological card up his sleeve. His new character will keep his old name. That character will continue to play the songs associated with that name. But a new ratio emerges at this point, as Jack Fate assumes the helm and takes Bob Dylan's oeuvre on the road for an unprecedented run. We now turn to this phenomenon that is the Never Ending Series of Tours. I think you'll agree that there's nothing quite like it.

Paul Williams's three-volume set on Bob Dylan as a performing artist certainly conveys his belief that performance is the key to unlocking the auteur's art. Although I think there are times when Williams focuses a bit too tightly on individual acts or specific moments, I find his aim to be generally true. The rising tide of Bob Dylan's art certainly lifts all Dylanological ships—whether those vessels contain Michael Gray's emphasis on musicological detail, Christopher Rick's concentration on poetry, Clinton Heylin's diehard commitment to personal biography, or my focus on Zimmerman's creative missions and his stylistic responses to those challenges. Bob Zimmerman's lifework is capable of supporting all of these inquiries and, no doubt, more. Williams's position is certainly reinforced by Dylan's comments about his songwriting and its origins. That he claims his writing began in response to his performance needs certainly elevates this dimension of the lifework. Yet, as I mentioned at the outset, his attitude toward performance is, at the very least, fluid. We've traveled across a variety of extremes over the years, and we've rarely settled into any sort of compromise when it comes to performance. Perhaps Dylan's 1997 comments to Jon Pareles explains why:

A lot of people don't like the road . . . but it's as natural to me as breathing. I do it because I'm driven to do it, and I either hate it or love it. I'm mortified to be on the stage, but then again, it's the only place where I'm happy. It's the only place you can be who you want to be. You can't be who you want to be in daily life. I don't care who you are, you're going to be disappointed in daily life. But the cure-all for all that is to get on the stage, and that's why performers do it. But in saying that, I don't want to put on the mask of celebrity. I'd rather just do my work and see it as a trade.

What a statement! He loves touring. He hates touring. He can be whomever he wants to be onstage. There are no interviews when he is onstage. Nobody wants his autograph when he is onstage. The lawyers and Dylanologists leave him alone when he is onstage. In the sometimes threatening storms that comprise Bob Zimmerman's life, the stage is his one, true shelter. Yes, the stage is the "cure-all" for the Archbishop of Anarchy as he pursues his trade—and rejects his celebrity—through the Never Ending Series of Tours.

I noted earlier that the biographers refer to these tours as the Never Ending Tour. Dylan emphatically rejects that title, and he offers evidence to support his contention. In *World Gone Wrong*'s liner notes, he tackles the issue straight on. There he identifies a series of tours by their names; for example, there was the fall 1991 "The Money Never Runs Out Tour," the 1992 "Southern Sympathizer Tour," the European 1992 "Why Do You Look At Me So Strangely Tour," the Australian/U.S. West coast 1992 "The One Sad Cry Of Pity Tour," the Mexico/South American "Principles Of Action Tour," the 1992 "Outburst Of Consciousness Tour," the 1993 "Dont Let Your Deal Go Down Tour," and, according to Dylan, "others too many to mention." In his interview with Derek Barker, former guitar technician and NEST band member Cesar Diaz recalled other tour names such as 1988's "It's a Hard Tour," the "Where Is The Oil Tour," and "It's A Parody Of Himself Tour." Obviously, much of this tour-naming stuff is private folly and subject to the labeling trends of that particular moment. With all of this in mind, why not respect the auteur's wishes and simply modify the Never Ending Tour title to the Never Ending *Series* of Tours? Besides, it works.

All source agree that the NEST opened on June 7, 1988, in Concord, California. That show featured the first NEST band with G. E. Smith (guitar), Kenny Aaronson (bass), and Christopher Parker (drums). This ensemble toured for approximately seventy-eight shows (ending in June 8, 1989). Since that time, there have been eighteen other NEST bands, and we would be wise to take a moment to run down the list. Although a few of the ensembles were short-lived, other groups carried on over hundreds of shows and, in so doing, placed their own unique stamps on the NEST as well as on Dylan's songs' continued development. That is, the G. E. Smith–based "Masters Of War" is quite distinct from the Charlie Sexton–Larry Campbell version. Furthermore, the show's format varied in relation to the various bands' approaches to the music. We have an urban sound, a Tennessee period, a Texas orientation, and an eclectic sound. One thing is absolutely certain: This is a dynamic operation. Change is constant. Variety is most assuredly the spice of the NEST's life.

Tony Garnier replaced Kenny Aaronson on bass for a June 3, 1989, show and returned *forever* on June 10 of that year. I think it is quite clear that Tony Garnier is the backbone of the Never Ending Series of Tours' bands. Only Bob Dylan has appeared in more shows. It is a joy to watch Garnier work. His eyes burn through Dylan. He obviously knows his every inclination, and instructs the band based on that knowledge. As the guitarists and drummers come and go, Tony Garnier remains. See one show, my friends, and you'll understand my point. When Garnier smiles, the band is officially smiling as well. When Garnier steps forward and faces the drummer, the song ends. He reads Dylan, and the band reads him. He is the last member of the group to be introduced, and *that* is symbolic for this musical troupe. Tony Garnier is the heart of the NEST bands.

That second NEST band—featuring Smith, Garnier, and Parker—worked some 163 shows before disbanding on October 19, 1990. The third NEST group played a mere twenty-two shows (from October 21 to November 18, 1990) and featured John Staehely and Cesar Diaz in G. E. Smith's slot. Staehely gave way to John Jackson and Ian Wallace replaced Parker on drums on January 28, 1991, for twenty-one shows (until March 2, 1991) during the brief fourth NEST group. When Diaz departed that April 19, the fifth NEST band was born (playing approximately eighty shows until November 20, 1991). Pedal steel and slide guitarist Bucky Baxter joined Jackson (guitar), Garnier (bass), and Wallace (drums) for twenty-two shows (from March 18 to April 24, 1992) for the short stint that was the sixth band. Another short-lived variation occurred on April 27 of that year, when Charlie Quintana was added on percussion, rendering the seventh NEST ensemble (running for some forty-four shows until September 5). The dust hardly settled on the seventh band when the eighth NEST group appeared on September 6, 1992, for around twenty-six shows (Winston Watson replaced Quintana at that time). As you can see, there was a lot of activity in the band during this period. I conclude, then, that Dylan was searching for that magical combination that was performing in his head.

He must have found it in early 1993. The longest-running NEST band took the stage on February 5, 1993. The ninth group—featuring Baxter, Jackson, Garnier, and Watson—played some 358 shows until disbanding on August 4, 1996. *This* is the band that I maintain supported the new Bob Dylan—read, Jack Fate—and discovered a performance equilibrium that carries on to this very day. After all of the adjustments that occurred during the late 1980s and early 1990s, the NEST settled into a remarkable groove for the three and a half years of the ninth band's tenure. A brief modification occurred on October 17, 1996, when David Kemper replaced Watson and ushered in the tenth NEST band (they played but thirty-nine shows together). Another long-running act unfolded with the eleventh band, in which Larry Campbell replaced Jackson on guitar for a 242-show stint that extended from March 31, 1997, until May 2, 1999. The NEST shows took a decided turn in the spring of 1999. On June 5, 1999, Charlie Sexton joined the band in Bucky Baxter's slot and initiated the twelfth band's 288-show run (carrying on until November 24, 2001). The Sexton (guitar), Campbell (assorted guitars), Garnier (bass), and Kemper (drums) troupe supported Dylan in the recording of *Love And Theft* as well. George Recile replaced Kemper on drums for a brief run beginning January 31, 2002, until April 21 (the thirteenth NEST band); he yielded to Jim Keltner for sixteen shows (the fourteenth band's April

23 to May 12 stint), and returned until the thirteenth band's conclusion on November 22, 2002. When the Never Ending Series of Tours restarted in Australia for a short eleven-show tour in February 2003, it featured the fifteenth group of this protracted series (Bill Burnette replaced Sexton). Freddie Koella took over for Burnette on April 18, 2003, and that group—the sixteenth NEST band—worked some ninety-four shows that paused for the addition of drummer Richie Hayward for a twenty-six-show period (the seventeenth NEST band ran from February 28 to April 4, 2004). Hayward departed, and Koella, Campbell, Garnier, and Recile completed the sixteenth band's business on April 24, 2004. The eighteenth NEST band opened for business on June 4, 2004, with Stu Kimball in Koella's slot. Kimball (guitar), Campbell (a host of stringed instruments from acoustic and electric guitars to pedal steel, violin, and more—the man is incredible), Garnier (bass), and Recile (drums) completed their fall 2004 tour of college campuses with a closed performance before the students of Harvard University in November. The nineteenth NEST band appeared in the spring of 2005 featuring Denny Freeman, Donnie Herron, and Elana Fremerman as replacements for Larry Campbell. The NEST marches on with a new, bigger, more diverse sound. My friends, as you can plainly see, this is some serious business. The Bob Dylan Show is a busy operation that rarely pauses for extensive breaks. True to the blues tradition, they play and they play an awful lot. Consequently, they are one tight musical ensemble that virtually never experiences an "off night" in the typical use of that phrase.

As the various bands appeared over the years, certain distinctive musical styles or tendencies emerged that singled out a particular ensemble and its unique approach to the music or show structure. One revealing aspect of a given NEST band is its treatment of the acoustic-electric song balance. Until the April 1999 European tour opened, the NEST followed a structural pattern that I refer to as the "donut" strategy in which the, say, sixth or seventh song through the ninth or tenth number featured an acoustic format. During this era, the show opened with a rocking series of electric guitar–based songs, paused for the 3–5 acoustic numbers, and returned to the electric format to conclude the evening. Occasionally, an acoustic song or two appeared toward the night's end as well (encores and the like). Exceptions to this rule were few and far between. That approach changed in the spring of 1999. That April, the European shows opened with a traditional tune performed in an acoustic style (e.g., "Roving Gambler" or "You're Gonna Quit Me" from *Good As I Been*, or "Oh Baby It Ain't No Lie") or the Grateful Dead's "Friend Of The Devil," which was followed by 6–8 additional acoustic songs before cranking up the electric guitars— and that was done subtly. This trend advanced with Charlie Sexton's arrival in the summer of 1999. Traditional songs such as "Hallelujah, I'm Ready To Go," "Cocaine Blues," "Somebody Touched Me," "I Am The Man, Thomas," "Duncan And Brady," "Humming Bird," "Wait For The Light To Shine," and "A Voice From On High" joined "Roving Gambler" or "Oh Baby" in the leadoff spot. Acoustic treatments of Dylan songs followed and extended through the sixth, seventh, or eighth number. The practice ended during the fall of 2002 tour of the United States. From that point onward, the NEST shows opened with a variety of Dylan tunes performed in different fashions. Much like the traditional songs that opened the Sexton era, certain compositions rotated in the opening slot (e.g., "Drifter's Escape," "Rainy Day Women" and "To Be Alone With You"). From there, the show rotated from acoustic-based to electric-based songs in a manner that added an ebb and flow to the evening. Thus, we note how the NEST has always kept an eye on the show's pacing. These bands do not just march out and run through a set play list; to the contrary, systematic strategies are deployed that serve the particular characteristics of that specific Never Ending ensemble. Bob Dylan's shows are *orchestrated*.

Another structural shift involved the auteur's gradual transition from the guitar to the electric piano. To my knowledge, there is no official explanation for this change. Talk of arthritis or other physical limitations abounds. Who knows? But by the early summer of 2003, Dylan performed exclusively on piano (and, of course, harmonica). Again, there are very few exceptions to this new rule. How interesting that the man who wrote in his high school yearbook that he wished to join Little Richard's band would end up on the piano! He also plays it while standing—further shades of Richard. Thus, we come full circle since Zimmerman's early bands featured him on the piano as well. One major consequence of this shift is its impact on Dylan's singing. Since his move to the keyboards (usually positioned on the left side of the stage, facing the band as opposed to the audience), he seems to concentrate more on his enunciation. He bends and stretches his words in a more profound manner. He mumbles much less. Since his keyboard playing occurs in flourishes, he seems to concentrate more on his vocal inflections and, in general, his verbal theatrics. When watching Dylan perform in this manner, there are times when I bend over laughing. He will stretch, Stretch, STRETCH out a sound, cut it off with a weird facial expression, and carry on in genuinely funny ways. This is quite the departure from the imperturbable method of singing that characterized early NEST performances. Early in the series, the voice was there, but the thrill seemed to be gone. I mean, there is detachment, then there is *detachment*. That is, assuredly, no longer the case. The band maintains a stoic presence on stage; however, when you watch closely, they turn their backs to the audience and smile at one another or offer other gestures that communicate their musical collegiality.

There have been other stylistic variations as well. The early NEST bands—especially those featuring G. E. Smith—offered stripped-down, fast-paced versions of songs. One early tour was deemed "The Fastbreak Tour" (January–February 1990), and never was a show more appropriately named. Smith, Garnier, and Parker raced through songs. Even the acoustic numbers appeared to have a stopwatch attached to them. This is not to suggest that these performances were in any way inferior, but they were distinct. When Smith's edgy electric guitar stormed through a song, Dylan's vocals followed suit. He never lagged behind or offered any indication that this was anything other than the sonic strategy of the day. No NEST band ever played with this emphasis on *speed*. These bands took songs such as the revised, electric "Masters Of War" to new places. All of this contributed to the early bands' urban feel: These were city boys whipping through a series of smart songs.

When Memphis guitarist John Jackson joined the band in early 1991, this tempo began to change. I guess it's a Memphis thing, as they say in the Bluff City. By the time Bucky Baxter entered the group in the spring of 1992, a new strategy assumed control. As the NEST bands evolved through their sixth, seventh, and eighth incarnations, this change in tempo progressed. That process was completed during the ninth band's extensive 358-show run. Baxter's pedal steel and slide guitar work directly complemented Jackson's stunning Memphis-fueled style to provide a rich musical platform for Dylan's improving—and slower—vocals. For years, the voice of his generation had been criticized for mumbling, jumbling, and fumbling through his lyrics. While a more generous critic might acknowledge the difficulties in *remembering* all those song lyrics—few of which follow moon-and-June rhyming structures—the most frequent commentaries were void of such considerations. Maybe the early NEST bands just played too quickly. I don't know. But I do know that the Baxter-Jackson bands facilitated improvements in Dylan's vocal performances. They also supplied a rhythmic context for his new method of guitar playing and its emphasis on counterpoint. During this era, you can hear Dylan's guitar slicing and dicing its way through songs—often appearing in an otherworldly way, seemingly doing its own thing in opposition to the rhythm of that moment. That Dylan enjoys that particular effect is evident in Freddy Koella's guitar work in the sixteenth and seventeenth bands. When I first heard Koella, I noticed that I had heard that approach somewhere before. And I had! It was Dylan's guitar during this era and in the Sexton-Campbell stage. Although both the Smith-based and Baxter-Jackson–based ensembles steadfastly subscribed to the donut playlist strategy, they featured substantial differences in their instrumental approaches in terms of the shows' pace, sound (the pedal steel provides a very different aural context from Smith's jagged guitar licks), and, from there, Dylan's vocal work. There is a decidedly Tennessee feel to the Baxter-Jackson bands. It is as if Jackson's Memphis influences merge with Baxter's Nashville methods to render an aural style that sharpens the songs' presentation. If nothing else, the length of this band's run indicates that Dylan was pleased with this approach.

Larry Campbell is as good a guitar player as any in the musical world. He brought a virtuosity to the NEST that enabled his bands to go to magical places. The other NEST guitarists were certainly strong players, but Campbell stands by himself in the pantheon. When he joined Baxter, Garnier, and Kemper in March 1997, his performances were subtle. He would step forward with a blistering solo, then retreat to the shadows. Once Charlie Sexton joined the band in 1999, yet another NEST page was turned. Sexton is an extraordinary guitar player, and he has his own albums to support that claim. When he joined Campbell, the results were most impressive. For many Dylanologists, the shows of the 1999–2000 era represent the NEST at its finest. The show moved from the G. E. Smith–based rapid-fire blues explosion through the Tennessee-flavored era of Baxter and Jackson and into a Texas-style swing period that stressed more refined, instrumentally complicated versions of Dylan's—and other's—songs. Sexton and Campbell were in their element, playing off of one another in majestic ways that complemented Dylan's vocals in every way. When they opened shows with a traditional song, they conveyed a respect that set the evening's tone. Garnier along with Kemper, Keltner, or Recile provided a rhythmic platform that supported Sexton's and Campbell's virtuosity, which, in turn, seemed to inspire Dylan's vocals. This band's chemistry paved the way to a performance level that I believe would inspire Miles Davis to smile. I guess it was that Texas groove. Remember, this was the band that accompanied Dylan in recording *Love And Theft* (with Kemper on the drums) and appeared with Jack Fate in *Masked And Anony-*

mous (with Recile replacing Kemper) as the band known as the "Simple Twist of Fate" (a label that, in and of itself, offers much insight into that film).

The unpredictable, occasionally strange guitar work of Freddie Koella was a marked departure from the smooth, swinging instrumentals of the Sexton-Campbell era and signified the tour's evolution into a more eclectic period. While Campbell, Garnier, and Recile maintained their established approaches to the respective songs, Dylan's move to the piano and Koella's distinctive solos added yet another twist to the NEST sound. I must confess that this is my favorite NEST band. I've had few joys that compare to watching Larry Campbell laugh out loud at Freddie Koella's guitar work. Koella initiated guitar riffs that left serious doubts as to what was going on in the song. You'd find yourself wondering, "How's he going to get out of this?" Koella opened solos on the low end of the scale, wandered around that range plucking random notes, and somehow or another pulled himself from that slightly organized chaos. On occasion, his approach just flat-out failed, leaving Campbell or Dylan to come to his rescue. On other occasions, he achieved what appeared to be the impossible, reaching for odd combinations and solutions that left an amazed Larry Campbell laughing in Koella's wake. These tendencies, too, would leave Miles Davis—or any other improvisational jazz musician—with a knowing smile. Koella's imagination knew no boundaries, and he most certainly pushed it every night. Koella's guitar and Dylan's phrasing led to more than a few laughs during this phase of the NEST.

The 2004 band—featuring Stu Kimball in Koella's role—represented a return to the virtuosity that characterized the Sexton-Campbell era, but without that Texas swing. The solos are powerful, slightly more predictable, and ultimately quite refined. Koella's "Let's search for something and hope we find it" style is definitely a thing of the past. Like Campbell and Sexton, Campbell and Kimball traded thoughtful licks in precise fashions that systematically supported Dylan's singing. Campbell was the key to this band's success. His ability to play the mandolin, pedal steel, cittern, slide guitar, violin, and more provides the pivotal ingredient that took an old or new song to a different place. For example, when he shifted to pedal steel for the opening of the time-honored closing number, "All Along The Watchtower," he completely transformed the song. The NEST has closed many, many shows with this song, but *never* has it sounded as it did with Campbell on pedal steel. These are the little things the NEST bands do that enliven songs, change a show's pacing, and provide the variety of experience that brings fans back to shows time and again. I imagine it alleviates any sense of boredom for the band as well. Bob Zimmerman devised one smart plan when his hand was bandaged and he feared for his future. The NEST is as novel, and as smart, a musical endeavor as you will find anywhere, in any genre.

Dylan's bandmates rarely talk about their experiences with their respective bands. When they do, it is often instructive. In one instance, Cesar Diaz described Dylan's guitar work in a *Guitar Player* article that he and Derek Barker discussed in a subsequent interview. Their discussion offered compelling insight into Dylan's playing and the band's musical strategy. According to Barker's piece, Diaz told *Guitar Player*,

Well, he's not the most incredible guitarist, but only because he doesn't want to be. I call him the mother of invention—he is the most inventive guy I've ever met. He can play one of his songs many different ways in five minutes. He is just brilliant at what he does, which is reinventing everything that he's already done. It's his antidote to boredom. He's trying to come up with a whole different approach to playing the guitar. It's kind of like you're playing the guitar, but you act like you're playing the cello.

When Barker suggests that Dylan plays guitar like a "wind instrument," Diaz countered, "or a piano." Notice how these comments echo what Dylan reported in *Chronicles*. Remember? He described the endless possibilities of the Lonnie Johnson system. Clearly, Diaz's remarks demonstrate Dylan's implementation of that principle. That unpredictability extended to other facets of the band's performance, as Diaz explained:

> The band would sometimes get criticised for not being tight but it was usually a case of Bob going his way and the band going their way. I would always wait for Bob to make his move and then I would make my move. Some of the other guys would try to make their move before Bob and Bob would just go the other way out of spite! He would just fuck with them to prove a point, so they would realise that you can never really know what he's going to do. So, in reality the band was fairly tight. Bob was the one that would throw the whole thing into chaos.

So now we understand why Tony Garnier just *stares* at his singer! Comments about Dylan's unpredictable—or mischievous—stage behaviors appear to be the common denominator in the available interviews with band members. Winston Watson reports in Clinton Heylin's biography that you just have to keep your eyes on Dylan and his "body english." He is that unpredictable. It is not hard to imagine how such stage intensity contributed to the performance's energy. Dylan-onstage did what Dylan-in-the-studio aspired to do, that is, use spontaneity to spark creativity. If everyone is on edge, wondering what the next move might be, there is a chance that a special spark may fly or an unexpected move might magically appear.

Contributing to this spontaneous mix is the auteur's mood. Bucky Baxter discussed Dylan's onstage mood swings and its impact on the experience in Heylin's biography. Baxter contends that what is great one moment may not be so great the next. When Baxter's friends inquire what it is like to work with Dylan, the pedal steel player offers mixed views: It's not "much fun," but it is "incredibly interesting." Sounds like music making without a net, doesn't it? With an orientation that pursues spontaneity, then punishes band members if they follow the wrong impulse; with a strategy that requires constant attention to the singer in order to follow his whims, then rewards or punishes the musicians with those nonverbal responses; and with an approach that keeps bandmates so much on the edge that it drains the fun out of the experience while simultaneously challenging them, well, we have a dynamic—and potentially confusing—interpersonal situation here. *Everyone*, it appears, is on edge. Michael Gray offers this response to Dylan's spontaneous performance strategy:

His chameleon ability as a performer is as noticeable as his bravery, and if there are concerts as poor as Hammersmith 1991 there are those as marvellous as Hammersmith 1990. You'd get neither from a performer less reliant on the spontaneity of the moment. Nor would you get to see songs reflected in so many different lights; you get this from Dylan because he is still open to being caught in such a wide sweep of moods. Sometimes he's not engaged; usually you can sense his getting into, and drifting away from, his material, often in mid-song, let alone mid-concert. The results can be extreme.

No doubt, Tony Garnier provides relief within this demanding experience since his prolonged stay signifies a form of stability. Yet, please note that all of these comments fall in line with the Dylan Method we have observed throughout the lifework. "Never rehearse the life out of the songs" is a major rule. "Never allow yourself to fall into predictable patterns" is an honored creed. "Never succumb to the expected" is a guiding commandment. Therein lies the NEST's magic; therein lies the NEST's trap. Energy is not cheap. The members of the Never Ending Series of Tours bands understand that lesson very, very well.

Writers of different orientations have offered a host of opinions regarding the NEST and its particular characteristics. Usually, arguments focus on Dylan's motivations, his abilities, or his audience's demographics and level of involvement. The world of Dylanology is far-reaching, and its yield is extensive. Alex Ross offers an example of the follow-the-tour-and-talk-to-fans method of data collection. He describes his findings in this manner:

> What are these shows like? How are they different from the classic-rock nostalgia acts that clutter summer stages? I've been to ten Dylan concerts in the past year, including a six-day, six-show stretch that took three thousand miles off the life of a rental car. The crowds were more diverse than I'd expected: young urban record-collector types, grizzled weirdos, well-dressed ex-hippies, and enthusiastic kids in Grateful Dead T-shirts. . . . I asked some of the younger fans how they had become interested in Dylan, since he is not exactly omnipresent on MTV. Most had discovered him, they said, while browsing through their parents' old LPs. One kid, who had been listening to a 45-rpm single of "Hurricane," thought that he should come and check out the man behind it. The younger fans didn't seem to be bothered by the fact that Dylan was three times their age. A literate teenager asked me, "Do you have to be from Elizabethan England to appreciate Shakespeare?"

As Ross's observations reflect, so much of the audience's curiosity has to do with the man, Bob Dylan. The living legend phenomenon that Dylan discusses in *Chronicles* is most certainly a factor in this equation. Still, as Dylan states in *Chronicles*, that legend has to deliver something unavailable elsewhere if those audiences are going to return and spread the word about the show. (Dylan clearly supports word-of-mouth publicity. He plans for it in *Chronicles*, and it was the principal strategy in the Rolling Thunder Revue.) Consequently, he orchestrates the NEST bands' personnel, the show's contents, and the production's staging with that principle in mind.

To achieve that end, Dylan assembles strong bands and, from there, sets the performance standards through his own efforts. Rolling Thunder participant Sam Shepard described his former colleague's performance style to Howard Sounes: "He's an extraordinary writer but he's also one of the most amazing live performers I've ever seen. When you see his *nature* on stage, his true rhythmic soul, it just blows you away. He's like a little Banty rooster with his tail up." Alex Ross ventures this view after his road experiences with the NEST: "But to hear Dylan live is to realize that he *is* a musician—of an eccentric and mesmerizing kind. It's hard to pin down what he does: he is a composer and a performer at once, and his shows cause his songs to mutate, so that no definitive or ideal version exists. Dylan's legacy will be the sum of thousands of performances, over many decades."

The key to our eccentric, mesmerizing Banty rooster's longevity involves his ability to harness his moods, preserve his voice, and orchestrate his band's performances on a consistently high standard. That is a big order. NEST expert Andrew Muir offers his take on this delicate process:

> Dylan had to develop a way of performing that allowed him to put on around one hundred shows a year without ruining his voice and . . . his lungs. One way to do this was to pace himself; to hold back from giving his all on every song, every night. He didn't stop trying, but he came to rely on an increasingly polished band to help him put on a good show even when he was not entirely on top of his own game. Rather than the more extreme variance of the earlier N.E.T. years, when Dylan's performance seemed to be a mirror of his mood of the moment, we have now had years of consistently "fine" shows.

Muir's analysis falls in line with the observations cited thus far. As Dylan learned to harness his moods, concentrate his energies on the bigger picture, cultivate his voice to the needs of the moment, and allow his band to form its own personality (i.e., its Tennessee, Texas, or eclectic style), he slowly but surely developed the orientation necessary to fulfill his ambitious touring schedules.

Yet, the mission is one of service—and this service involves not his voice, demeanor, band dynamics, or audience. No, this service involves the songs. He had to do as Ross observed and allow the songs to "mutate" and unfold into versions that suited their continued development. To achieve those ends, Dylan had to play a variety of songs, not focus on a select playlist. He had to open the door to all sorts of ideas. Michael Gray offers insights into how the auteur pursued this goal:

> Some statistics: on the North American section of the 'True Confessions' tour in the summer of 1986, Dylan performed 'only' fifty-eight different songs in the course of forty-seven concerts (a total of 999 song performances); on the early 1990 dates, up to and including the Hammersmith Odeon, in a mere fourteen concerts he sang eighty different songs (within

a total of 246 song-performances)....What other performer could or
would do that?

383

The Jack Fate Era

In pursuing this strategy of opening the back catalog and allowing the songs to flow
forth in a variety of ways, Dylan has incurred some harsh criticism for living in the
past (remarkably, Gray is often one of those critics). On the other hand, as Ross's
comments indicated, this delights other observers. The key, obviously, is to strike the
right balance.

Alan Davis discusses Dylan's efforts to do just that and, as a result, responds
to Michael Gray's claim that, according to Davis's account of Gray's writing, "Dylan's
preoccupation with his old songs" is a sign of "creative bankruptcy." Davis could
not disagree more. In response to Gray's contention that "today's Bob Dylan voice"
should sing "today's Bob Dylan songs," Davis offers this view:

> What I want to suggest is that actually Dylan is doing exactly that. Dylan
> himself has given us some strong clues about his present view of his own
> art. With remarkable clarity, he's explained that his *old* songs are very much
> alive, for him; that his recordings should be regarded not as definitive per-
> formances, but as "*blueprints*," and that those blueprints mark the begin-
> nings of the lives of the songs, not the end. In other words, it would be
> entirely wrong to regard '*It's All Over Now, Baby Blue*' as a museum item
> filed away in some pigeon-hole of Dylan's past, to be taken out and dusted
> off when required for performances so that he and we can wallow in nos-
> talgia. No, it's still one of *today's* Bob Dylan songs, to be explored and in-
> vested with new meaning in performance. Whether or not we approve,
> and whether or not we're willing to accept it, it's primarily *this*, not the
> recording of new songs, which is currently the essential nature of Dylan's
> new work.

Davis expressed these views years in advance of *Chronicles* and its corresponding interviews in which the auteur states this view in no uncertain terms (Davis's piece was
first published in 2001). In his *Newsweek* interview promoting *Chronicles*, Dylan told
David Gates that his career is going in a positive direction, stating, "I'm sort of doing
what I want to do? I mean not *sort of* what I want to do, I *am* doing what I want to
do. Or what I believe I was put here to do." Part of that mission involves his re-
working of older material and rerecording them "with proper structures." He told
Gates, "A lot of these songs can have, like, a dozen different structures to them. I
can't hope to do all that. But I can provide a few things for future generations." Such
a statement must provide great pleasure for Alan Davis, who closed his 2001 piece
in this manner:

> An artist is known to be great through his *best* work. And Dylan's best
> work, today, lies in his magnificent reinterpretations of his *old* songs; in
> finding within and through those songs important new meanings, depths,
> perceptions and ways of musical expression, using the insight and self-
> knowledge gained through a lifetime of experience. It's a road that car-

ries risks, but then the highway always was for gamblers—Bob Dylan said that.

(Davis closes with a T. S. Eliot quote in a cute reference to a famous 1965 performance in which Dylan substituted Eliot's name during the closing of "Talkin' World War III.")

Yes, Bob Zimmerman devised quite a plan while his hand was healing in the late 1980s. If ever there was evidence that Zimmerman *orchestrates* his art, this would join the Rolling Thunder Revue, the Bob Dylan Revue, and the Bob Dylan Crusade as concrete demonstrations of that argument. He reoriented his voice and guitar, assembled and tested a host of musicians, devised specific plans of attack for his shows, and submitted his back catalog to the various influences of his ongoing experiment. And he did it all *his way*. I think Andrew Muir's quote from Gregory Peck (of "Brownsville Girl" fame) captures this phenomenon oh-so-clearly: "He is surprises and disguises; he is a searcher with his songs. In him we hear the echo of old American voices: Whitman and Mark Twain, blues singers, fiddlers and balladeers. Bob Dylan's voice reaches just as high and will linger just as long." I couldn't agree more, except I would add one major point: He does it all in service of the songs. Whether he wrote it or not, Dylan is a slave to the songs that flow through that voice accompanied by those bands performing night after night. The Never Ending Series of Tours represents the epitome of artistic commitment. It stands alone in the musical world.

Before closing our discussion of the NEST and its role in the lifework, I'd like to pause and share some personal observations about this unprecedented musical phenomenon. Like Alex Ross, I prepared for this portion of this study by attending a series of 2004 NEST shows that just happened to unfold in distinct ways. I'd love to say that I planned to see shows that displayed different traits and formats, but I didn't because I couldn't. While I'd hoped to see multiple shows in 2004, you never know what's coming before it's announced; so, I was more lucky than good (and you can't have enough of that!). Of the eleven 2004 shows I attended, one involved the sixteenth NEST band (Campbell, Garnier, Koella, and Recile), five featured the seventeenth ensemble (add Richie Hayward to the mix), and five involved the eighteenth band (with Stu Kimball replacing Koella). The shows followed three different, shall we say, formats. Two shows were from a four-night Chicago residency in which Dylan opened at Chicago's Aragon Ballroom, moved to the Riviera Theatre, and closed with performances at the Vic and Park West theaters (I was unable to secure tickets for the last two shows because one seats maybe 1,000 and the other less than 800). Each venue was smaller in size, as per his plans. A *Billboard* review concluded that as the venue shrank, Dylan improved. The second set of shows involved a three-night stay at the same venue: Detroit's State Theatre. There Dylan and his troupe were able to set up camp for an extended stay, and I was interested in how this might impact the shows. The third format involved three different types of shows. One performance occurred at Columbia, South Carolina's historic Township Auditorium and represented the end of the tour featuring the Chicago and Detroit shows (that tour concluded at the next stop and three Atlanta events). I next saw the NEST as part of a minor league baseball stadium tour that involved Willie Nelson. This was quite the departure from the previous shows in that it occurred outdoors with a major opening act that had a decided influence on the audiences' composition (I will never forget Nelson's fans openly weeping as he walked onto the stage—it was a moving thing to witness, and it happened *every* night!). These two acts were extraordinarily different, as I noted in the preface. Contributing to my experience was the fact that I saw three Dylan-Nelson shows in three truly different locations: Lexington, Kentucky; South Bend, Indiana; and Madison, Wisconsin (the tears flowed everywhere). I concluded my little ethnographic adventure with Dylan's fall 2004 college tour and shows at Purdue University (in West Lafayette, Indiana) and The Ohio State University (in Columbus, Ohio).

Regardless of the location or venue, the shows featured minimal staging. They used relatively fixed lighting strategies (no spotlights and minimal effects) and were essentially conservative productions. Shows opened with the band standing before the tour's logo (a drawing of an eye with lavish eyelashes that features a crown sitting atop the eye) placed on a black backdrop. Around midshow in several performances, that backdrop was lifted in favor of a standard stage curtain with fixed lighting that created a ballroom design for the stage. Stage activity was minimal. Larry Campbell might stride toward center stage during an extended guitar solo (seemingly attempting to draw responses from Koella or Kimball, but rarely gaining one); otherwise, the bandmates stayed in their respective locations: Dylan to the left of the stage playing a keyboard that faced the band, not the audience; Koella or Kimball to his immediate left; Recile (along with Hayward when the dual drum kits were used) in the center; Garnier immediately to the drum kits' left; and Campbell standing on the right side of the stage, where his pedal steel and *bank* of guitars were located. Dylan occasionally walked over to Garnier between songs or moved around his piano in preparation for the next number (e.g., selecting harmonicas); otherwise, it was a quiet stage. A microphone was positioned in the center of the stage and it was used but one time: during the band introductions (the only time Dylan addressed the audience).

Each evening opened with a recording of Aaron Copeland's "Fanfare For The Common Man" prefacing a long recorded introduction in which Dylan was characterized as the "poet laureate of rock and roll" before a brief rundown of his professional history (he merged folk and rock, he got lost in drugs, he found Jesus, he rebounded from a downward spiral to create some of his best work in the late 1990s—that sort of thing). The band walked onstage as the recording played. Afterward, the show ran through around fourteen songs, then the band accepted the audience's applause, left the stage, and returned for a three-song, standard encore. Dylan introduced his band either before the final song of the opening set (which was *always* "Summer Days") or during the encore. Rarely did this format vary. It did in Detroit, and I wonder if it was a function of performing in the same venue for three straight nights. The second night, the band returned and performed Bob Seger's "Get Out Of Denver" in a second encore (the previous day was "Bob Seger Day" in the state of Michigan, since Seger had just been selected for the Rock & Roll Hall of Fame); and on the final night, Jack White of the White Stripes appeared with the band for a second encore. Interestingly, Dylan and White performed a White Stripes song ("Ball And Biscuit") as opposed to a Dylan composition. Needless to say, the Detroit crowd went wild over the Seger song and White's appearance.

A few details stand out, and allow me to share them with you. First, the band's demeanor was decidedly professional. They all wore suits, often with formal head-wear (although Campbell never donned a hat), and acted in a most reserved manner. Dylan appeared as—you guessed it—Jack Fate. He wore either a white or black cowboy hat, a dark colored Western-style suit (with minimal decoration; I don't think you'd call these Nudie suits), and a scarf or Western-style tie. The band never removed their coats regardless of the heat. At times, you could see the sweat *pouring* off of Dylan's face. He would be drenched in perspiration before the night's end, but that coat and hat remained in place. In every venue, at all times, this professional demeanor never subsided. (As a quick aside, I saw the band perform in a bar in Little Rock, Arkansas, in 2003. It was hot as blazes in there since, for some reason, the venue cut off the air conditioning during the show. The band actually took their coats off, but Dylan fought on. I mean, I worried for the man's health! He had to lose five pounds that night, and, to be honest, he doesn't have five pounds to lose. It was an amazing sight. The man works extremely hard.)

This is not to suggest that the guys did not have a good time. Although they constantly stared at Dylan (Garnier looks *through* the guy), the occasional laugh or nod to one another occurred. During the Nelson shows, Willie and his son appeared for a song with the NEST band. In Lexington, the group did Dylan's "I Shall Be Released." Nelson's relationship with the lyrics was one of mutual existence, not mastery. Dylan was bent over laughing as he tutored his colleague through the number (one word at a time). Humor appeared in a standard slot in the shows, however. After the band introductions, Dylan invariably told a stupid joke. It was so weird. For him to say nothing all night long and then spew out a corny joke was so odd, and refreshing. In Columbia, Dylan introduced Freddy Koella by saying that he came from a "broken home"—his kids "broke everything in the house." During the college tour, after introducing Recile (seemingly his favorite target), Dylan announced that George was from Louisiana. Back home, George has all sorts of snakes around, so when it rains, he places them on his windshield and calls them "windshield vipers." Apparently, Dylan has a fondness for this type of humor. Actually, there is a scene in *Masked And Anonymous* when Luke Wilson's character interrupts a tense moment with one of these silly jokes. I guess we may conclude that not everything in the Archbishop of Anarchy's world is written on tablets of stone.

I think the most telling moment in not only the 2004 shows, but also in every show I've witnessed since the mid-1990s, is the manner in which the band accepted the audience's applause. I closed *Bob Dylan, Bruce Springsteen, & American Song* with a reference to this practice by comparing it to how Springsteen closed his shows (e.g., spotlights on band members, appearing one at a time, and stretching out the adulation). In the NEST, the band stood expressionless, instruments and arms dangled by their side or folded behind their backs, and received their applause. Dylan weaved side to side, acting in a shy, nervous manner. After a few seconds, they politely marched offstage. Once they completed the encore, they repeated the practice. There may be an occasional smile, but it is rare (and it was *always* Campbell smiling). It is almost as if there is a band fine or something if you get busted for smiling. They were all *so serious*. Why? Why would they strike such a pose? I think I know why. The NEST shows are about the songs, not the performers. Just as Dylan said at this chapter's outset, the songs are the stars of the show—not the performers. Consequently, nothing transpires that would detract attention from the songs. No flashy lighting, no stage theatrics, no chatty banter with the audience, and no aspect of the performance detracts from the songs. The band dresses up, I think, out of respect for the performance. The only departure from this strict behavioral code involves Dylan's jokes. There is no way you could take *them* seriously.

The Never Ending Series of Tours features the most professional shows I've ever witnessed. The fans may hoot and holler, scream out for their favorite songs, and act like fifty-five-year-old freaks, but onstage, it's all business. Silent Bob Dylan concentrates on his singing and playing. The band concentrates on Silent Bob. The lighting and staging concentrate on the music. And all of this concentration renders a strange phenomenon: Rare, if ever, is the bad night. Dylan may do as Gray suggested and lose interest in a particular song, but he quickly snaps back with the next tune. The band members seem to challenge one another in idiosyncratic ways, and that keeps them quite focused. Tommy Morrongiello and the stage and sound crew are flawless in their stage design and coordination—regardless of the venue. Yes, Bob Zimmerman devised quite a plan. Make sure you see it if you have the chance; there is nothing like it anywhere. As NEST expert Andrew Muir responds when asked why Dylan stays out on the road,

> Finally,—to turn the question around—why shouldn't Dylan be touring? What is so surprising about him practising his particular trade? Out of which we get the munificent bounty that is the N.E.T.; we get the greatest artist of his time going out year after year recreating his magic in front of our very eyes and ears. Far from the ceaseless re-working of his old songs being a sign of loss of artistic creativity, it is the very centre and expression of his art. The refusal to take the easy option and just sing the songs the same way time after time is borne out of his inherent understanding that the core of his art is the never ending challenge of the new performance.

I couldn't agree more with these observations. I think the art actively bears witness to the accuracy of these conclusions. However, this story is not yet complete. Zimmerman may use the NEST to recast his Dylan catalog in innovative and inspiring ways, but his history indicates that he will write something new in support of his new stage character. When he placed young Bob Dylan before his adoring following, Zimmerman gave him something to say. When Renaldo hit the back roads of New England, Zimmerman (and Levy) gave him something to say. When Bob Dylan praised his Lord, he had something to say. Now, Jack Fate has transformed the NEST into a crack musical unit capable of reinterpreting his musical knowledge in scores of ways, and Bob Zimmerman gave him something to say—and, for added measure, a movie to boot. So, we now turn to the new Bob Dylan—read, Jack Fate—and the end of anarchy. This Bob Dylan has traveled the world, seen its sights, smelled its smells, and listened to its occupants as they go about their daily lives, and wouldn't you know it, he has something to say.

Jack's Scripts: *Time Out Of Mind* and *Love And Theft*

We turn to the Dylan Method's standard mode of operation in this section and the script that Jack Fate carries on the road to complement his revisions of Bob Dylan's lifework. Not only did Bob Zimmerman offer Jack a series of jokes that would make Rodney Dangerfield cringe, but he also wrote a few dozen songs that any seasoned rounder would be proud to perform. Had Woody lived to perform into his seventies, he would have sung songs like these. So would Hank. These songs are looks *back* on life, reflections that center on that lifelong struggle with love and its accouterments. Insightful responses to human events that would have prompted anger or scorn thirty years ago are now treated with calm resolve. Pain is part of love; don't take it personally. Jealousy is a twisted form of flattery; rise above it. War is an act of nature; accept it. These are the types of sermonic reflections that float in and out of 1997's *Time Out Of Mind* and 2001's *Love And Theft*. In the former production, Dylan turned to Daniel Lanois once more; in the latter installment, he relied on his road-tested crew to bring that Texas Sound into the studio and help him do the deed. In both instances, Dylan finds a comfort zone in the recording studio; as a result, the songs respond to the players, the technical staff, and the singer in a telltale fashion. From all of this, one thing is certain: Bob Dylan (read: Jack Fate) had something to say.

Jack's script begins with *Time Out Of Mind*. Here Daniel Lanois proves an important point: You can take the producer out of the swamp, but you can't take the swamp out of the producer. The swamp crew traveled to Miami, Florida, for these sessions, added several new players to the roster, and produced an eleven-song (running seventy-three minutes) exploration of loving relationships that won multiple Grammy awards. This was one prodigious comeback. Lanois (who plays a variety of guitars) and coproducer Jack Frost (read, Bob Dylan) supervised a blend of Dylan's road band (David Kemper and Winston Watson [drums], Bucky Baxter [guitars], and Tony Garnier [bass]), several seasoned musicians of considerable ability (Jim Dickenson and Auggie Meyers [keyboards], Duke Robillard [guitars], and Jim Keltner [drums]), as well as assorted performers such as Robert Britt (guitars), Cindy Cashdollar (guitar), along with Brian Blade (drums) and Tony Mangurian (percussion). Together, these musicians find a sonic groove and ride it—a rhythmic mode of expression that creeps straight out of those Louisiana swamps and into that Miami recording studio. Some of these tunes are downright creepy. The organ-guitar interplay, subtle bass and drum work, and timely guitar flourishes complement Dylan's haunting vocals to render songs that make you pause to look over your shoulder at life and its occasionally harsh circumstances. *Nothing* on this record is low-key. *Everything* is thought-provoking, often disconcerting, and frequently eerie. Yes, Jack has his own script, and its opening installment is one heavy treatise on loving relationships and the conditions they foster.

To suggest the record's nine romantic elegies present mature feelings about love lost and love's obsessive qualities without word games or cavalier commentary is to transcend understatement and enter the realm of presidential speech writing. They don't play Glissendorf in the swamps, my friends. The songs are piercingly direct. The deep-seated irony of "Love Sick"; the bouncy devotion of "Dirt Road Blues";

the emotional slavery of "Standing In The Doorway"; the anguish of "Million Miles," "Cold Irons Bound," and "Not Dark Yet," the rationalizations of " 'Til I Fell In Love With You"; and the haunting resignation of "Tryin' To Get To Heaven" communicate an unflinching honesty regarding loving relationships and their precarious situations. Dylan reports that a rational romantic angst is a lifelong condition, not the unique province of youthful inexperience or immature folly. In fact, the more you know, the more you may be injured by that knowledge. *Time* also features the loving pledge "Make You Feel My Love" (even though by that point in the album, you know she's going to stab him in the back with a penknife someday). Finally, in that famed capstone position, we have one fascinating personal testimony—the sixteen-minute saga, "Highlands"—in which a seasoned rounder wistfully looks back on life and massages his new ambition: to rest in a comfortable place. *Time Out Of Mind* is one impressive comeback, but I'm surprised everybody didn't kill themselves after making the recording. Jack's script is pretty dark.

We open with the nine relational complaints. I think the best way to present these songs is to just march right through them in their order of appearance. I thought of several ways to organize the songs based on certain characteristics, but they just divert our attention from the heart of the matter. Yet, one organizing scheme that yields promise is to separate the songs on the basis of what happens to the narrator in the end. As you'll see, most of these people are going to kill themselves, and how they'd do it is instructive. For instance, we could build a continuum with self-decapitation on one end (that's a tricky maneuver, you know), gunshot wounds and poisonings somewhere in the middle, and self-starvation on the other extreme. I applied this model, but with disappointing results. You see, from my reading of these songs, *everyone* winds up in the self-starvation category. There is no better way for these characters to end their lives. Sitting in the dark—probably in some New Orleans alley—slowly but surely disintegrating into nothingness, all the while thinking, thinking, thinking, about that woman or circumstance that precipitated their perceived ruination. That's how they'd all end. Cutting your head off or shooting yourself is too quick. Poisons just make you go to sleep after a few convulsions. Yes, self-starvation is the trick—slow, agonizing, swamp-induced, *and self-inflicted* misery. You think I'm fooling around, don't you? Let's go to the songs and you'll see what I mean.

The opening track, "Love Sick," instantly takes us up to our necks in swampy relational muck. Throughout the five verses and three choruses of this slow, slow, slow song, we delve deeper and deeper into some serious relational angst. Our narrator is walking the streets on what feels like a cold, rainy, desolate New Orleans night. The track's sonic strategy enables you to feel the fog, smell the musty mist, and literally walk in the narrator's shoes with him. He's ill all right. Dreadfully so, as the opening segment reveals:

> I'm walking through streets that are dead
> Walking, walking with you in my head
> My feet are so tired, my brain is so wired
> And the clouds are weeping

Did I hear someone tell a lie?
Did I hear someone's distant cry?
I spoke like a child; you destroyed me with a smile
While I was sleeping

I'm sick of love but I'm in the thick of it
This kind of love I'm so sick of it

This doesn't sound too good, does it? He walks onward, seeing lovers in a field and amorous shadows in the windows. He is utterly despondent. The silence pounds and inspires urges of escape. Could she ever be loyal and faithful? He's uncertain—downright doubtful. Suddenly, the final chorus reveals his intentions to slam that door shut: He is sick of these feelings, regrets knowing her, and resolves to forget her. *Then*, just as quickly (or as quickly as anything happens in this song), he stops dead in his tracks and admits the truth: He would gladly do whatever it takes to be with her once more.

Oh my. After all of these dark ruminations, heartfelt anxieties, and disturbing conclusions, this guy would *instantly* pack them all in just to gaze into her eyes once more. Yes, he is "love sick." The moral is pretty darned clear here: No matter your age or standing in life, love hurts. "Love Sick" is the Fort Sumter of this album's relational war. The first shot has been fired. Just like that particular conflict, a lot of what is about to happen is totally unnecessary. Why can't reasonable people sit down and work through their differences? Why, indeed.

From the ragtime portion of the swamp songbook comes our second track, "Dirt Road Blues." Here we have a merry, happy-go-lucky, sonic platform supporting a highly repetitive five-verse song. Each stanza offers a line, it is repeated, and the verse closes with a relational wail. Our narrator is going to walk down that dusty, dirty country road until something gives. The struggle is all-consuming here as well. In the first verse, the narrator announces he is going to keep walking until he catches a ride; moreover, he declares that if he cannot find his love, he is going to disappear—one presumes forever. The track's essence is conveyed in the second and third verses:

I been pacing around the room hoping maybe she'd come back
Pacing 'round the room hoping maybe she'd come back
Well, I been praying for salvation laying 'round in a one room country
    shack

Gon' walk down that dirt road until my eyes begin to bleed
Gon' walk down that dirt road until my eyes begin to bleed
'Til there's nothing left to see, 'til the chains have been shattered and I've
    been freed

You just *know* that that is never going to happen. He will never be free. This man is a slave! The track concludes as the journey continues. He gazes off into the colorful distance, marches through inclement weather, and searches for love's happy side. He might as well go back to that shack and resume praying, because that is not going to happen on this record—maybe the sequel. In any event, the fifth verse varies in its written and performed versions. As written, he is going to seclude himself; as performed, he is going to carry on until she returns. I vote for seclusion. How about you?

We move from characters that are confused and relentless down into the relational abyss with "Standing In The Doorway." The track's smooth, swampy, quietly supportive instrumentals provide the perfect backdrop for the five ten-line verses of this incredibly depressing song. Like "Love Sick," this song paints an unmistakable portrait. This narrator is in utter despair, torn by his relational dilemma. The opening verse sets the table for this indigestible relational meal:

> I'm walking through the summer nights
> Jukebox playing low
> Yesterday everything was going too fast
> Today, it's moving too slow
> I got no place left to turn
> I got nothing left to burn
> Don't know if I saw you, if I would kiss you or kill you
> It probably wouldn't matter to you anyhow
> You left me standing in the doorway, crying
> I got nothing to go back to now

Read it again. What can you say? Times are dark for this narrator, that is for certain. The merriment continues with the second stanza's depressing account of a sick narrator attempting to shut out laughter that inspires sadness, to close his eyes to blood-stained visions, and to dismiss the feelings that haunt him. This is grim stuff. The relational dilemma sharpens in the third verse:

> Maybe they'll get me and maybe they won't
> But not tonight and it won't be here
> There are things I could say but I don't
> I know the mercy of God must be near
> I've been riding the midnight train
> Got ice water in my veins
> I would be crazy if I took you back
> It would go up against every rule
> You left me standing in the doorway, crying
> Suffering like a fool

I don't think those rules mean much anymore, and I don't believe his claim to strength. He may persuade himself, but he's not going to convince me. The fourth verse communicates his helplessness and defeatist views. He tries a stranger's love, but it only worsens his lot. Nothing works. The song closes with the narrator offering a flash of perseverance, believing that, ultimately, he will not end up all alone. Still, this oh-so-sad song ends with images of the narrator's shadow in a doorway that leads nowhere. There is an extremely good chance that he will end up alone, so he will have to learn to cope—or face dire consequences. These are powerful images, aren't they? I need a break.

Jack's script does not feature breaks today; however, he does manage a smile in our fourth relational bomb, "Million Miles." With wonderful organ fills and piercing guitar licks knifing their way through this dreamy Delta blues, the eight four-line verses of this song lighten our relational load just a bit, moving us from the heavy angst of the previous numbers to the moderate angst portrayed here. This narrator hurts, that is for certain, yet he seems to smile from time to time, as the opening verse indicates,

> You took a part of me that I really miss
> I keep asking myself how long it can go on like this
> You told yourself a lie; that's all right mama, I told myself one too
> I'm trying to get closer but I'm still a million miles from you

She hurt him, he is questioning his resilience, and yet he remains compassionate. "Hey relax, we all lied," he seems to say. That scene sets the pace for this story. The second stanza explains how she abandoned him (she took everything!). The third verse relates his disbelief. The fourth verse states his need for her in his life. Consequently, the fifth stanza announces his frustrations, then one more faint smile emerges with the sixth verse:

> The last thing you said before you hit the street
> "Gonna find me a janitor to sweep me off my feet"
> I said, "That's all right mama. . . . you . . . you do what you gotta do"
> Well, I'm tryin' to get closer; I'm still a million miles from you

That's our Jack Fate for you! Nothing like a little levity to spice up the dreary conversation. You just get the impression that this narrator has been here before. He has seen everything here more than once. Therefore, he is resilient. The song ends with a playful plea for her return and his belief that he can make it despite everything. Yes, Jack has been down a million of these one-mile stretches of highway—a million miles the hard way—and his experience is evident. You'd think he'd try a different route after a while, wouldn't you?

How nice of Dylan to dust off his harmonica for the next entry, "Tryin' To Get To Heaven." A subtle, pensive swamp sound accompanies the five eight-line verses of this song (with that ever-present "ghost chorus" that uses the song title to frame stanzas). Here we have a rounder so damaged by love that the rounds are no longer made, and he sits—wallowing in his introspection—awaiting the end. The opening verse sets this sad scene well:

> The air is getting hotter
> There's a rumbling in the skies
> I've been wading through the high muddy water
> With the heat rising in my eyes
> Every day your memory grows dimmer
> It doesn't haunt me like it did before

I've been walking through the middle of nowhere
Trying to get to heaven before they close the door

Perhaps if this character lives long enough, those memories will fade completely, but that is a real long shot. His walks have taken him to Missouri, where he thought of her (verse 2). He travels to the train station where folks await their passage, and—for some reason or another—he reaches the sad conclusion that there's always room to lose more than you've already lost (verse 3). He goes to the river and down to New Orleans (of course!), where people offer vacuous comforts (verse 4). Finally, he stops moving and reflects on his life in the final stanza:

> Gonna sleep down in the parlor
> And relive my dreams
> I'll close my eyes and I wonder
> If everything is as hollow as it seems
> Some trains don't pull no gamblers
> No midnight ramblers, like they did before
> I been to Sugar Town, I shook the sugar down
> Now I'm trying to get to heaven before they close the door

Our rounder has made his rounds and, apparently, come up empty. What he *really* wants is her. She is nowhere in sight, though. The sadness is stifling and inspires thoughts of bigger pictures—notions about life itself. Is it all as bad as it seems? It would appear so.

For those of you who enjoy the practice of externalizing your troubles, here's one for you: " 'Til I Fell In Love With You." The slashing swamp guitars and pianos paint this blues a darker hue across the five six-line verses of this track (that ghost chorus remains ever-present). There is anger in the air here, and that clanging guitar signifies its presence—it literally burns through the swampy fog that this music creates. Complementing that sonic strategy is yet another appearance of our "Love Sick" thematic and this tale of a narrator frustrated by love's refusal to come home. The opening verses tell this tale in its entirety:

> Well my nerves are exploding and my body's tense
> I feel like the whole world got me pinned up against the fence
> I've been hit too hard; I've seen too much
> Nothing can heal me now, but your touch
> I don't know what I'm gonna do
> I was all right 'til I fell in love with you
>
> Well my house is on fire; burning to the sky
> I thought it would rain but the clouds passed by
> Now I feel like I'm coming to the end of my way
> But I know God is my shield and he won't lead me astray
> Still I don't know what I'm gonna do
> I was all right 'til I fell in love with you

Everything is a reiteration from here. Our narrator feels oppressed, his home has burned down, and he is counting on the Lord to invigorate his coping skills. This, my friends, is a bad scene. He hopes she will remember him and his accomplishments when he departs (verse 3). He feels as though he is physically dismantling over her absence (verse 4). Finally, he grows weary of the fight, accepts the futility of the struggle, and resolves to take his problems down South, where they will, no doubt, continue to fester. The narrator can run, but he cannot hide. Love's capacity to injure knows no boundaries, and you'd think this guy would realize this by now. But, evidently, he does not, so the running will continue—for now.

Dreamy, pensive swamp sounds provide the backdrop for the four six-line verses (with that ghost chorus) of the seventh track, "Not Dark Yet." Well, it may not be dark, but this narrator is standing in pitch blackness holding a fading flashlight. Or perhaps he is on the other side of darkness, looking back in some depressed funk. Whatever "attitude" sparked this song should be banned by some higher authority. The opening verse sets this woeful scene: It is near dusk, it is swampy and hot, and he is thinking of his various ills—it is, assuredly, an unproductive way to close the day. But hang on, this is bound to get worse, as the second stanza reveals:

> Well my sense of humanity has gone down the drain
> Behind every beautiful thing there's been some kind of pain
> She wrote me a letter and she wrote it so kind
> She put down in writing what was in her mind
> I just don't see why I should even care
> It's not dark yet, but it's getting there

It is, indeed, hard to follow up on that. Besides, he is right: He would be better off not caring. The third verse traces his travels, preaching of worldly lies and heavy personal burdens. This is grim stuff, revisited. The fourth verse drops a curtain that should be burned:

> I was born here and I'll die here against my will
> I know it looks like I'm moving, but I'm standing still
> Every nerve in my body is so vacant and numb
> I can't even remember what it was I came here to get away from
> Don't even hear a murmur of a prayer
> It's not dark yet, but it's getting there.

Oh my. This man is clearly having a painful out-of-body experience. When you can't hear a whisper of hope, it's time to reassess your options. I guess being a seasoned rounder may not be all that it's cracked up to be. The twilight of life sounds dangerously like purgatory to me. The imagery in these songs is absolutely dreadful. I need to take a break and listen to the B-52s or something.

Well, I'm back, and dancing didn't help one bit. There was a shadow standing in the corner crying, so I thought I'd better get back to work. The swamp rocks on the ninth track, "Cold Irons Bound." The song unfolds in five segments that contain

an opening four-line verse followed by a three-or four-line verse that contains the
ghost chorus tag. This story offers an interesting blend of the narrator's remorse over
a failed relationship and his sermonic reflections on life. Regardless of the topic, it
is all dark. The opening segment unveils his plight: He lost his love interest, but his
love just will not quit. From there, he turns introspective, as the second segment's
opening stanza reveals:

> The walls of pride are high and wide
> Can't see over to the other side
> It's such a sad thing to see beauty decay
> It's sadder still, to feel your heart torn away

That sums everything nicely! He continues his reminiscing with memories of friends
who were not friends at all, how she was his life and now both are lies, and how life's
ebb and flow tend toward extremes; and, finally, he focuses on his resolution in the
fifth segment's opening verse:

> Well the fat's in the fire and the water's in the tank
> The whiskey's in the jar and the money's in the bank
> I tried to love and protect you because I cared
> I'm gonna remember forever the joy that we shared

The song concludes with our narrator on his knees in front of his bewildered ex-
lover. So close, yet so far away—maybe as far as twenty miles, in fact. These cold
irons of relational slavery are more than inhibiting; they may be life threatening.
Maybe this character should consider turning and heading in the other direction.

I'm so overwhelmed by these songs that I *can't wait* to move to something positive, and that desire sets the scene of our last song of relational complaint: "Can't Wait."
The song takes us into the realm of swamp funk with its slashing guitar and organ and
their cutting, sharp counterpoints. There's tension in the air, that's for sure. They say
that misery loves company, and this track (with four six-line verses and a two-line
bridge) has eight pals to keep it company. I don't think that this character is impatient
or pushy; I think he's been *hammered* by love and he simply needs a resolution to his relational dilemma. The opening verse establishes that he is up late, moving amongst
people, trying to sort through his thoughts. The second stanza reports why:

> I'm your man; I'm trying to recover the sweet love that we knew
> You understand that my heart can't go on beating without you
> Well, your loveliness has wounded me, I'm reeling from the blow
> I wish I knew what it was keeps me loving you so
> I'm breathing hard, standing at the gate
> But I don't know how much longer I can wait

That says a lot. Not only can he not recover from this relationship, but he also cannot continue without it. When Dylan sings about his breathing, you can sense that
emotional state. My hands are sweating (OK, I'm lying). My goodness, there is ten-

sion in the air. It continues with the third verse and his failed search for a ray of hope; still, if it happened, he would not know what to do. He is lost in comprehensive relational confusion. The bridge and closing verse sum this sad character's sad lot in life:

> I'm doomed to love you, I've been rolling through stormy weather
> I'm thinking of you and all the places we could roam together

> It's mighty funny; the end of time has just begun
> Oh, honey, after all these years you're still the one
> While I'm strolling through the lonely graveyard of my mind
> I left my life with you somewhere back there along the line
> I thought somehow that I would be spared this fate
> But I don't know how much longer I can wait.

What imagery. The end of time is upon us, but his thoughts remain with her. I think that's a telltale line. I think that if this character doesn't resolve this situation soon, he'll surely cease waiting—and that's a bad thing. This war is about to end, and the resolution looks bleak for our troubled narrator.

What a series of songs. I can't think of anything to compare with them. Maybe the Alabama Chronicles, but nothing else. What other series of songs probes so deeply into its subject matter? The Alabama Chronicles certainly delve into their warning and celebration messages with an unbridled conviction, but even those wonderful songs fail to fathom the emotional conditions of their situations to the extent Jack's relational script achieves. The *Street-Legal* stories lodge their complaints in no uncertain terms, but they, too, fail to expose the emotional depths associated with these stories. Sure, "Hollis Brown" goes there, but that is one song. Yes, *Blood On The Tracks* visits that neighborhood through its anger, yet it flails away, either caught in the emotions of the moment or reporting cryptic observations. This is what I meant with my remarks about the narrators' ultimate destinations. All of these men are at their wits' end. None of them seems to have the slightest ray of hope. It all starts at the top. The all-consuming confusion of "Love Sick" truly sets the pace for this record's relational songs. All that talk about people and their lying ways, the difficulties of loneliness, and the insecurities of life with a faithless person suddenly disappears with the admission that he would give *anything* to rejoin her. He would happily endure all of these insecurities for her presence. I hope these guys made it to therapy before it was too late. Something tells me they didn't. What do you think?

Where do these types of emotions come from, and what sustains their intensity? To respond to that inquiry, we turn to our swampy hymn of loving adoration, "Make You Feel My Love." Both sonically and lyrically, this track is a hymn in that rich Southern tradition. It features four four-line verses, two four-line bridges, and our beloved ghost chorus. Throughout, we witness a pledge of eternal adoration, plain and simple. The four verses promise the narrator's loyalty. When the weather is harsh and the world is oppressive, he will be there for her (verse 1). When the day closes and she is enduring life's difficult moments, he will be there for her (verse 2). He would go through hell in a gasoline suit for her (the paraphrased third verse). Finally, he promises to do anything and go anywhere for her (verse 4). Why is he so persuasive? What motivates this level of commitment? The first bridge suggests the answer:

> I know you haven't made your mind up yet
> But I would never do you wrong
> I've known it from the moment that we met
> No doubt in my mind where you belong

Oh, so that's it: She is in doubt. Thus, to assist her in her relational decision making, he sells himself and his undying commitment. Yes, whatever it takes, he will provide. Besides, Jack has made the rounds. He knows how the deal goes down. Consequently, she would be wise to travel with an experienced partner, as the second bridge states:

> The storms are raging on the rollin' sea
> And on the highway of regret
> The winds of change are blowing wild and free
> You ain't seen nothing like me yet

Threat abounds, so she had better wise up and latch on to a capable partner. That is the argument here. Let's all wish this guy luck so he doesn't end up in cold irons on a lovesick dirt road a million miles from that sad and lonely doorway to heaven—or something darker.

We close *Time Out Of Mind* with our famed capstone song, in this instance "Highlands." This is one of the oeuvre's finest capstone commentaries—and that says a lot since we've seen some powerful examples of this strategy. Here, we enter the realm of swamp rap by way of this *twenty-verse* treatise (each stanza consists of five lines with no choruses or bridges). The music features a soft, light sound for the pensive storytelling it supports. The song is a wistful, introspective look back at life, the narrator's situation, and a belligerent Boston waitress. It unfolds in three parts: dreamy, longing nostalgia (verses 1–7); a reality hit (verses 8–14); and a closing, introspective nostalgia (verses 15–20). This is quite a ride.

The opening section offers beautiful descriptions of that wonderful place that the narrator hopes to visit when he gains the strength for the trip. Is he ill? Near death? We don't know. He just longs for those "Highlands" and contrasts them with the hell that is his life. The second stanza communicates his boredom with life: different day, same deal. It is not that he wants anything from anybody, but he is taking stock of his situation and his declining years (verse 3). The fourth verse takes us back to that wonderful place where the trees dangle their buckeyes in rhythm with the wind. He longs to hear them. Suddenly, he is playing a Neil Young record, getting hassled for the volume, and contemplating his circumstances (verse 5). This guy is just fed up with it all and prepared to pawn whatever he has left (verse 6). All of this despair takes him to his thoughts of the highlands and its beautiful waters, inspiring sunrises, and majestic clouds. He closes the opening segment by reporting that the highlands are the only destination that remains for him. I wish he'd send me a postcard when—and if—he makes it.

We shift planets with the middle section and the narrator's encounter with a Boston waitress. I call this section a "reality hit" because it portrays how difficult people can be for no apparent reason; as a result, it inspires thoughts of those sacred highlands and its hopeful alternative. Our narrator enters an empty Boston restaurant without a clue as to what he wants (verse 8). The waitress approaches, and the song charts their first conversation in two ways: as written, the narrator asks for boiled eggs; as performed, he asks her to tell him what he wants. Now this is a big difference in that when she tells him that he wants the boiled eggs, he agrees, and *then* she reports that they are out of them, well, that places her in a different light, doesn't it? For the narrator to request an item and discover that it is not available is a different scenario than one in which she recommends something that she knows is unavailable. She is being difficult, and the narrator is more than prepared for that challenge. After reporting the egg situation, the battle ensues in the tenth verse. She identifies him to be an artist and immediately requests that he draw a picture of her. The narrator declines by saying he does not draw from memory. I guess this gets her dander up, she barks out that she is standing in front of him, and he replies that he realizes that, but he does not have his drawing pad. She produces a napkin and demands that he draw on it. He rejects her again, this time saying that he does not have a pencil (all of this occurs in the busy eleventh verse). She reaches behind her ear, provides a pencil, and advances her demand. Our patient narrator throws a few lines on the napkin and submits it for her review. She promptly rejects the rendering since she fails to notice the resemblance (the busy twelfth verse). The narrator is up for this charge. He stands his ground. She insists he is joking. He adds fuel to the fire by saying he wishes that were true. She countercharges that he does not read women authors (where does *that* come from?). He inquires as to how she reached that conclusion and its relevance. She responds that he just looks that way, he reports that he has read Erica Jong, and she walks away long enough for our narrator to ease out of his chair for a quiet exit. He returns to the busy street, and that's that.

What a strange segment.

The third portion of "Highlands" opens with a return to nostalgia and a wistful account of the horses, dogs, and isolated beauty of that treasured location (verse 15). We then pause for a flash for personal testimony in the sixteenth and seventeenth stanzas:

> Every day is the same thing out the door
> Feel further away then ever before
> Some things in life, it gets too late to learn
> Well, I'm lost somewhere
> I must have made a few bad turns

> I see people in the park forgetting their troubles and woes
> They're drinking and dancing, wearing bright colored clothes
> All the young men with their young women looking so good
> Well, I'd trade places with any of them
> In a minute, if I could

What a sad scene. He continues his walking—dodging ratty dogs and talking to himself (verse 18). He feels the end drawing nearer, and he is tired of talking (verse 19). We close with a personal pledge to take his body where his heart and mind have already gone: those beautiful highlands. He ends on a patient note. He believes he will make it one day. Until then, he has his nostalgia and his newfound avoidance of Boston waitresses to occupy his time.

"Highlands" is a rounder's capstone commentary. I'm going out on a limb, but not too far, to suggest that the waitress scene was a metaphor for various relational frustrations. Not romantic or spiritual frustrations, but for the kinds of hassles the auteur endured at the hands of audiences, journalists, and industry operatives. All of these groups of people wreaked their own type of havoc at varying points in the artist's career. The interpersonal teasing (telling you that you want something that you think they have only to discover you've been misled), the artistic demands (asking you to do something that you don't want to do and then getting angry with your response), and the empty personal attack that followed (substitute the attack about women authors with a charge about the folk or protest movements) all fall into patterns that we've seen before. Wrap the scenes of wistful nostalgia around that frustrating scenario, and, indeed, the voice of his generation eased out of his chair, left the building, and entertained his hopes of a better place—a serene, inspiring, contemplative place where you marvel at God's work in the leaves on the trees and the sand around the lake. The more reflective qualities of the third segment seal that interpretative deal for me. This is a classic capstone moment. Like "Buckets Of Rain" or "Restless Farewell," this track captures a sentiment and rides it home. Jack's script reports that there is a better place out there, and, by God, he is going there, one way or another. Besides, he has to since there are few alternatives.

Time Out Of Mind is a powerful moment in the oeuvre. It is not that Zimmerman explores the intensity of loving relations and builds a script for Jack based on those observations. No. I think it's the way in which those sentiments are presented that's the news here. There is a decided shift in tone. This is an older man reflecting on these situations through the advantages—and disadvantages—of his vast experience. Unlike younger Dylan and his penchant to rant and rave about something without regard for that scenario's resolution, Jack is consumed by the need for relational resolve. He wants to get closer than twenty miles away from his love. He wants to dismiss the sickness that love brings and return to his woman—even if such an act goes against the grain of every rule in the love manual. He wants to penetrate that relational darkness and, somehow or another, discover that ray of love's light that leads to a positive resolution. There is no "Idiot Wind" or "Dirge" here. There are no statements of recrimination presented for the sake of mounting an aggressive, perhaps heartless, attack. To the contrary, Jack Fate is building bridges, not burning them. And that, my friends, is an act of relational maturity. Unfortunately, the desperation portrayed in these songs leads me to the conclusion I advanced at the outset. For Bob Dylan, if these relational matters do not work out, so be it, he is moving to greener pastures. For Jack Fate, if these relational matters do not work out, so be it, he is moving beyond a low-carb diet toward something far more satisfying—for him. Yes, Zimmerman gave Jack something to say, and a lot of it is downright disturbing.

What would be nice right now would be something like a knock-knock joke, or some silly remark about the drummer or guitarist to lighten the emotional downturn generated by *Time Out Of Mind*. Our wish is Bob Zimmerman's command. Welcome, then, to part 2 of Jack's script and 2001's *Love And Theft*. I shall never forget the anticipation that surrounded this record's release. The auteur's official website offered snippets of the new record's contents. Dylan was scheduled to appear on national television to promote his new record. The buzz was that this is really a special record. *Everybody* associated with the wonderful world of Dylanology was ecstatic for that special release day that was September 11, 2001. That day forever changed the world, and *Love And Theft* had nothing to do with it. When a group of madmen rammed passenger planes into New York's twin towers, into the Pentagon in Washington, D.C., and into an open Pennsylvania field, Bob Dylan's new album did not mean very much to very many people. I remember the day well. I stood in my home in utter disbelief and, somehow or another, mustered the energy to go to my local record store to purchase the new album. It sat on my desk for close to a month. I couldn't open it, no matter how much I longed for the experience. What timing. What devastation. What a world gone wrong.

A few months prior to *Love And Theft*'s release, Bob Dylan turned sixty years old, and that contributed to the excitement surrounding the new record. With his birthday on May 24, 2001, journalists paused to consider Dylan's impact on the art form he pioneered forty years ago. Please allow a moment to review some of those statements as a preface to the new album. CNN's Jamie Allen said Dylan "is to modern rock music what Michelangelo or Leonardo Da Vinci was to the Italian Renaissance." The *Washington Post*'s Tim Page wrote that "ultimately, Dylan is likely to be remembered as one of those defiant American originals, like Philip Glass or Georgia O'Keeffe, who follow one central vision through myriad guises with single-minded intensity." The *Philadelphia Inquirer*'s Tom Moon reported that Dylan "has undergone complete job retraining" and now "aims to be a literate Little Richard" who embraces "the musical attitudes of the blues demons he idolized." The *New York Times*' Ann Powers claimed the auteur is "the Devil's Triangle of rock 'n' roll" and wisely quoted Pete Townshend's poignant opinion that assessing Dylan's impact on his life is "like asking how I was influenced by being born." What a great line! And on the day of his birth, the *Minneapolis Star-Tribune*'s editors declared, "Happy birthday, man, from all your friends back home." Correspondingly, the magazine that he played some role in naming solicited comments from a variety of artists for "an appreciation of Dylan at 60." *Rolling Stone* cites U2's Bono: "No matter where you are in your life, there's a Dylan record that helps you map out the locale"; Joni Mitchell: "no one has come close to being as good a writer as Dylan"; Tom Petty: "I think he really is a kind of roving-minstrel type, like from the medieval period. . . . I most value Bob's honesty—he's a very upfront person and a true gentleman"; and Camille Paglia: "Dylan is a perfect role model to present to aspiring artists. As a young man, he had blazing vision and tenacity. He rejected creature comforts and lived on pure will and instinct. He catered to no one but preserved his testy eccentricity and defiance. And his best work shows how the creative imagination operates—in a hallucinatory stream of sensations and emotions that perhaps even the embattled artist does not fully understand." Dylan, of course, remained silent—no interviews, no comments, no public celebrations. The musical world took note, though. These slices of that commentary demonstrate its appreciation for the Iron Range's original biker-poet. Bob Dylan never wanted to be called the voice of his generation, and he spent a lot of his *Chronicles* commentary debunking that phrase and its ancillary, the Archbishop of Anarchy moniker. Yet, he did want to influence the world of music in a lasting way. As our previous comments from *Chronicles* indicate, he was aware of his moment in history. How fitting that the world's media offered commentary in celebration of a landmark birthday that suggests his work achieved that goal.

When I opened *Love And Theft*, I discovered something that I didn't expect to find. The swamp dried up and in its place was some of the most inspiring music anyone will ever hear. I submit, dear readers, that you could read the phone book to *Love And Theft*'s instrumental track and win a Grammy for the recording. The music is astounding. Dylan described the artistic evolution that facilitated the new album to *USA Today*:

> In the early '90s, the media lost track of me, and that was the best thing that could happen. . . . It was crucial, because you can't achieve greatness under media scrutiny. You're never allowed to be less than your legend. When the media picked up on me again five or six years later, I'd fully developed into the performer I needed to be and was in a position to go any which way I wanted. The media will never catch up again. Once they let you go, they cannot get you back. It's metaphysical. And it's not good enough to retreat. You have to be considered irrelevant.

I must say that with statements like this, his commentary in *Chronicles* and in interviews supporting the autobiography's publication, and the clear-cut evolution in the NEST bands, Bob Zimmerman did, in fact, have a coherent plan for his career's revitalization. This artist *orchestrates* his art. Thus, with artistic peace of mind, a road-tested group of musical comrades (Larry Campbell [guitars, violin, banjo, and mandolin—the man is amazing], Tony Garnier [bass], David Kemper [drums], and Charlie Sexton [guitar] joined by famed organist Augie Meyers), and the creative momentum those two conditions generated, Bob Dylan and his band rendered a historical tribute that has to make Jack Fate smile from ear to ear. Jack's script took one heck of a turn! Musically, the auteur deployed the various instrumental styles of American song to his creative ends. He explained to Robert Hilburn how the new work differed from its award-winning predecessor: "I sort of blueprinted it this time to make sure I didn't get caught without up-tempo songs. If you hear any difference on this record—why it might flow better—it's because as soon as an up-tempo song comes over, then it's slowed down, then back up again. There's more pacing." The record features rockabilly, country, blues, show tune, Tin Pan Alley pop, romantic ballad, and rock 'n' roll sounds—all presented through that Texas musical vernacular that made this version of the NEST bands so distinctive. In many respects, as I suggested in *American Song*, it is as if famed musicologist Harry Smith collected his songs, hired the tightest band he could find, and recorded their versions of his acquisitions in a quiet Austin, Texas, studio. That Dylan described the album to Edna Gundersen as a "greatest-hits album . . . without the hits" demonstrates his evocation of the Basement Strategy philosophy in yet another creative context (remember, this is a recording strategy Dylan unveiled in *New Morning* and revisited in *Knocked Out Loaded*).

When Augie Meyers was asked about the *Love And Theft* recording sessions, he told *Rolling Stone*, Dylan would "fool around for a while with a song, then we'd cut it. And he'd say, 'I think I'm gonna write a couple more verses,' sit down and write five more verses. Each verse had six or eight lines. It's complicated stuff, and he was doing it right there." Not only did Dylan return to his beloved style of record production, but he also rediscovered the spontaneous approach to writing that rendered some of his finest work. The impressionistic portrait that is "Tweedle Dee & Tweedle Dum" complements the sermonic impressionism that controls "Floater (Too Much To Ask)," "High Water (For Charlie Patton)," and "Po' Boy" in a way that signals the author's return to the songwriting days of yore. Moreover, the life complaints that involve *Time Out Of Mind* holdover "Mississippi," "Summer Days," and "Lonesome Day Blues" join the relational complaints ("Honest With Me," "Cry A While," and "Sugar Baby") and the personal-relational pledges ("Bye And Bye" and "Moonlight") to add powerful additions to Jack's new script. All of these songs demonstrate the extent to which the auteur was in his element, free to explore his mental impulses while anchoring his impressions by way of the songs' musical structures. How rare to observe an artist with a forty-year career reach back to his or her cumulative experience and generate a work that so fully represents the life's work. Bob Zimmerman devised a comprehensive plan and displayed the resolve to see it through.

We begin with the complaints. The life complaints follow strategies that enable their narrators to kill two narrative birds with one symbolic stone. On one hand, "Mississippi" and "Summer Days" use relational complaints as a springboard to broader, more encompassing life commentaries. "Lonesome Day Blues," on the other hand, complains about everything. Still, even though the complaints have at this or that, there is a hint of a smile here and there. Most assuredly, the heavy-handed imagery of *Time Out Of Mind* is absent here. The results are quite a relief for everybody—especially Jack.

Our analysis opens with the smooth, Texas-tinged, country sounds of "Mississippi" (a *Time* leftover that was also recorded by Sheryl Crow). The band marches through the twelve four-line verses of this sermonic diatribe in a systematic manner (e.g., no extended instrumental breaks). The song presents a seasoned rounder who admits to one major mistake (staying in Mississippi more than he should have) while he struggles with a loving relationship. Sermonic reflections abound in this far-reaching complaint in which the narrator claims to have been through it all, spent all of his resources, and ended up with nothing. Subsequently, he reaches out to his woman as his last avenue of hope. The story opens with a statement of struggle— an unavoidable, inescapable struggle. As a case in point, our narrator offers this assessment in the second stanza:

> City's just a jungle, more games to play
> Trapped in the heart of it, trying to get away
> I was raised in the country, I been workin' in the town
> I been in trouble ever since I set my suitcase down

All of this "trouble" reminds us of a song from days gone by, doesn't it? The narrator chronicles his various difficulties from there. The song charts the central character's relational struggles through powerful lines with depressing imagery. For instance, in the third verse, our rounder describes his situation in this manner: "Sky full of fire, pain pourin' down." In the sixth, he claims he is "Feeling like a stranger nobody sees" as he walks through fallen leaves and thinks about their mistakes. In the ninth stanza, he proclaims that his boat has been destroyed and is going under before announcing, "I'm drownin' in the poison, got no future, got no past." Afterward, our narrator pauses to express his affection for those who have "sailed" with him. He is certainly suffering, but he remains gracious. In the eleventh verse, he reports that his clothes are soaked and fit tightly before concluding, "Not as tight as the corner that I painted myself in." Finally, the closing stanza opens with this assessment: "Well, the emptiness is endless, cold as the clay." There is a resignation to this song that tempers the narrator's sentiments. Things are bad, that is for certain, but there is a tone that suggests that she offers hope. Where these characters end up is anybody's guess, but I'd monitor my visits to the Magnolia State if I were you.

"Summer Days" raises the intensity of the dual-complaint strategy through a swinging instrumental track that blends the raucous sounds of Sun Records with that famed Texas swing approach. This is one swinging number—until you listen to the narrator, that is. This track is a systematic relational complaint that uses that condition as a starting point for a series of life complaints about celebrity, businesspeople, marriage, journalists (I think), politicians, and, of course, the circumstances around the relationship. It unfolds in four segments. The first three segments contain three three-line verses and a four-line bridge each, and the final segment features two three-line verses and a reprise of the opening stanza to close the song. Each verse offers an opening statement, repeats it, and sums the sentiment in the final line. The respective bridges punctuate the segments and are followed by instrumental breaks. This is a methodical statement presented via a blues lyrical format. The opening verse notes the passing of summer and a belief that something is happening somewhere else. The second stanza describes the narrator's house, farm animal, and woman. The third verse proposes a toast to an unnamed king (with these Sun Records sounds, this has got to be Elvis, right?). After these seasonal comments, the personal descriptions, and a royal toast, we turn to the first bridge and its celebrity complaint:

> Well I'm drivin' in the flats in a Cadillac car
> The girls all say, "You're a worn out star"
> My pockets are loaded and I'm spending every dime
> How can you say you love someone else when you know it's me all the
> time?

Notice how the relational complaint follows the celebrity comments. It is almost an aside, and that is how this song operates. The track marches along in this fashion: Comments about a foggy day preface a complaint about business (verse 4), sounds of a wedding set up questions about perceived realities and their potential incongruities (verse 5), a romantic scene prefaces a metaphysical inquiry (verse 6), then the second bridge does its thing:

> Where do you come from? Where do you go?
> Sorry that's nothin' you would need to know
> Well, my back has been to the wall for so long, it seems like it's stuck
> Why don't you break my heart one more time just for good luck

Once more, notice the multiple complaints, this time with that Jack Fate twist. Times appear to be tough for our narrator, yet he manages a sly smile at it all with that last line. You'd never find that line on *Time Out Of Mind*. The song continues to bop along with automotive and construction metaphors (verses 7 and 8), the third bridge's attack on politicians, and the narrator's promise to burn his house down before he leaves town for a more prosperous destination. What a ride!

Not only is "Summer Days" laid out in a systematic manner, but it also offers a weird combination of words and music. The music is incongruent with the song's thematic emphasis. During his lengthy 2001 interview with Italian journalists (published in *La Repubblica*), Dylan was asked about his new record's sound and how, according to these writers, the music inspired dancing. The journalists carried on about how they could not remember another Dylan song that did that. I believe they are referring to "Summer Days" with those comments. The song moves you to get up and swing. Yet, the lyrics suggest anything but a celebration. This is like playing Chuck Berry's "Mabeline" and singing the words to the Beatles' "Let It Be." The song takes us back to Pete Townshend's advice about dancing all over your problems. The attention to pacing is in evidence here.

Those Texas-fueled sounds do not stop there, but they do experience a radical shift in style with our third life complaint, "Lonesome Day Blues." Throughout the eleven four-line verses of this track, we absorb the big sounds of Texas-style Delta blues as the narrator barks his way through a series of pretty serious life complaints. The song marches through sad and lonesome ruminations about the narrator leaving his lover (verse 2), his father and brother's deaths and his sister's flight (the busy third verse), and the town's inaccurate gossip (verse 4), and then we suddenly pause for this bit of wisdom in the fifth stanza:

> Well, the road's washed out—weather not fit for man or beast
> Yeah the road's washed out—weather not fit for man or beast
> Funny, how the things you have the hardest time parting with
> Are the things you need the least

Once more, notice how these complaints work. We hear about wasted roads, bad weather, and a sermonic reflection on life's ironic qualities all wrapped into one stanza. Suddenly, we return to the laundry list of hardships: He misses his dead mother (verse 6), he criticizes another woman's lover (verse 7), he attacks his former captain for his insincerity (verse 8), he parades his cynicism for all to see (verse 9), and then he pauses once more, this time, for a statement of personal conviction:

I'm gonna spare the defeated—I'm gonna speak to the crowd
I'm gonna spare the defeated, boys, I'm going to speak to the crowd
I am goin' to teach peace to the conquered
I'm gonna tame the proud

After all of those complaints, our narrator is still up for a challenge. He left his woman, his family is dead, his other woman cheats, his memories are all jaded, but he is prepared to reenter the fray, preaching peace and taming pride. This guy has a lot on his mind. The song ends with one last wisdom. After describing the leaves falling in the forest and unnamed items dropping off of some shelf somewhere, he warns his lover that she needs his help after all: she cannot have sex alone. We're left without any clue as to her response. This is a heavy song presented in a time-honored manner. Unlike "Summer Days" and its juxtaposition of words and music, these lyrics fall right in line with their mode of expression. The blues are in the house on this track, make no mistake about it. Hopefully, our narrator lightened his load through this relentless emotional release. I must admit, my friends, that I was disappointed by the absence of a train wreck in this particular song. With all of the death, bad weather, disloyalty, and cynicism, where is the train wreck? I guess that's probably too much to ask.

These life complaints use relational difficulties to set the scene for broader commentary. *Love And Theft* also features two songs that zero in on relational problems and concentrate on those conditions. Our first, "Honest With Me," represents a strong example of a 1950s-sounding rock-and-roll song presented through a Texas filter. The steady backbeat and slashing guitars provide a dynamic sonic platform for a structured blend of impressionistic scenes, relational complaint, and what appears to be a concluding pledge to correct this situation—one way or another. The song unfolds in five segments that feature two four-line verses each, with six of those eight lines offering an impressionistic vignette, followed by the closing two-line repeated refrain. The imagery leaps all over the place, but always manages to lodge the complaint before shifting scenes. The song opens with the narrator in a busy city with creepy women and his challenging circumstances (segment 1). The next segment offers an unapologetic stance on his relational situation and a description of a visit by crowd-attracting freaks. That segment is followed by a description of the narrator's woman, her tendency to wave a baseball bat around, the narrator's difficulty with what appears to be an exceptionally tough steak, an example of his poor driving skills (or his attempt to destroy his car!), and his willingness to sell his physical attributes (in this case, his eyes and smile). That is one busy segment! It also demonstrates this song's format. We next drift into the narrator's offer to depart if he is disturbing his love interest and a pun about being naked and heading into the forest to hunt "bare" (yuk-yuk). Mind you, each of these uneven, or surreal, vignettes concludes with the narrator's complaint. Let's consider the fifth segment as our case in point:

I'm here to create the new imperial empire
I'm going to do whatever circumstances require
I care so much for you—didn't think that I could
I can't tell my heart that you're no good

Well, my parents they warned me not to waste my years
And I still got their advice oozing out of my ears
You don't understand it—my feelings for you
Well, you'd be honest with me if only you knew

As you can see, the song focuses at this point. The relational complaint is consistently lodged throughout the song even though odd imagery floats here and there. In the closing segment, the narrator concentrates on his relational situation, his apparently difficult woman, his parents' advice, and his willingness to ignore it for her. "Honest With Me" is a busy song presented though a fast-paced style that keeps everything moving at a brisk rate. Even though the narrator's complaint is serious, his comments about circus freaks, his baseball bat-waving woman, and his hunting habits bring that familiar levity to the story. I sense Jack's happy to be out of those swamps.

While that may be true, Jack still has the relational blues. In "Cry A While," the band, the vocalist, and the lyrics work in harmony to convey a big dose of relational angst through a Delta blues sonic framework. The narrator is venting here, as the opening stanza demonstrates:

Well, I had to go down and see a guy named Mr. Goldsmith
A nasty, dirty, double-crossin', back-stabbin' phony I didn't wanna have to
    be dealin' with
But I did it for you and all you gave me was a smile
Well, I cried for you—now it's your turn to cry awhile

This guy is not a happy camper, but that is how this tune operates across its seven four-line verses (using the last line–ghost chorus tactic as well): A complaint of some sort is lodged—here, about Mr. Goldsmith—and followed by the closing line's reference to the emotional turn-taking that is now at hand. The song continues with cryptic comments about the narrator's labor background (verse 2); his zeal for life, traveling complications, and spiritual efforts (verse 3); and his frustrations with his lover—communicated via Jack's own unique style:

Last night 'cross the alley there was a pounding on the walls
It must have been Don Pasquale makin' a two a.m. booty call
To break a trusting heart like mine was just your style
Well, I cried for you—now it's your turn to cry awhile

There is Jack again. He pokes fun at his neighbors as a preface to a serious dig at his lover's method of operation and his appreciation for the turning tide. The complaints roll on from there. He questions people's humanity and contrasts them with his God-fearing ways (verse 5); he offers a confused statement about preachers, children, and fatty foods that includes a promise to drown himself in whiskey instead of dying of old age (verse 6); and the song closes with a humorous revenge sequence. After she wagered on a horse that, unfortunately, ran in the wrong direction, the narrator concludes that the relational tide has, in fact, turned. For this guy, this turn of luck may require him to obtain a strong legal defense while she seeks out a friendly mortician. It does not appear she will cry very long after all. Our narrator appears to have a plan.

Love And Theft turns the relational corner in the same manner as *Time Out Of Mind* when it pauses for its two songs of personal and relational pledges. The shift in the two albums' sonic frameworks gives "Bye And Bye" and "Moonlight" a lighter feel and, therefore, contributes to *Love*'s pacing in a fashion distinct from "Make You Feel My Love" and its swampy style. "Bye And Bye" offers a touch of Texas lounge music as a backdrop for a road-weary rounder's pun-filled reflections on life. Throughout the song's four four-line verses and two two-line bridges, our narrator presents a series of happy-go-lucky observations that convey his dedication to his woman and his vast experiences with life. The opening stanzas set this scene well:

> Bye and bye, I'm breathin' a lover's sigh
> I'm sittin' on my watch so I can be on time
> I'm singin' love's praises with sugar-coated rhyme
> Bye and bye, on you I'm casting my eye
>
> I'm paintin' the town—swinging my partner around
> I know who I can depend on, I know who to trust
> I'm watchin' the roads, I'm studying the dust
> I'm paintin' the town, making my last go-round

That Jack. Hey hey, sitting on his watch, is he? Yuk-yuk. Our seasoned rounder is making his last round, knowing life's lessons about trust and dependability, secure in his views on life. Or is he? When we shuffle into the first bridge, we witness a moment of self-analysis in which our narrator admits to his prickly situation and uncertain attitudes. Nonetheless, he is optimistic, and the third verse communicates his hope for genuine happiness. In the second bridge, our rounder once more relates that his days on the prowl are over; therefore, his hopes for love are sincere. The relational pledge occurs in the track's final verse, when the narrator promises to seize the moment and prove his worth to his lady. Let's wish him luck! This simple statement of understanding, hope, and conviction offers much promise for a man apparently in his declining years. He has grown thoughtful over time, and that maturity fuels his relational ambitions. I think this character is going to do just fine.

That tone carries over into our second relational pledge, the Texas-style show tune that is "Moonlight." With Campbell's violin and Jack's crooning creating a romantic backdrop for the song's six verses (with two six-line bridges), this song takes us back in time to the 1930s or 1940s—or further. This track is a sweet, Texas-tinged, impressionistic lullaby. Imaginative descriptions of the changing seasons, the time of day, the weather, and the foliage set the scene of the narrator's simple request for the apple of his eye to join him for a romantic rendezvous under the stars. He longs for love as the seasons turn, and he issues his request (verse 1). He describes the fading day, and issues his request (verse 2). He describes the riverside, and issues his request (verse 3). The plot thickens with the first bridge:

Well, I'm preachin' peace and harmony
The blessing of tranquility
Yet I know when the time is right to strike
I'll take you 'cross the river dear
You've no need to linger here
I know the kinds of things you like

Assuredly, there is no substitute for experience, and our narrator is banking on that adage to pull him through. After our bridge, we return to the scenic descriptions and their corresponding request for that magical moment under the heavens. Our rounder is a bit of a poet with his flowing accounts of colorful clouds, falling leaves, rows of trees, active wildlife, and pastel, windblown flowers. The second bridge features these descriptions as well as Jack's penchant to use borrowed lines to express himself:

The trailing moss and mystic glow
Purple blossoms soft as snow
My tears keep flowing to the sea
Doctor, lawyer, Indian chief
It takes a thief to catch a thief
For whom does the bell toll for, love? It tolls for you and me

You just don't hear enough from these romantic rounders, do you? There is nothing quite like this mixture of poetic imagery and silly throwaway lines. I guess you have to use whatever you have. The story ends with our old rounder worked into a lather as he admires hills and trees and—guess what? Yes, he issues that request one last time: an invitation for a Texas rendezvous with an experienced poet under those Lone Star skies. Jack's new script certainly yields its romantic moments.

We'll consider the final relational tune—the capstone statement that is "Sugar Baby"—at the end of this review since it seems to capture *Love And Theft*'s essence in that traditional fashion. Another tradition in the Dylan Canon is that of unrestrained impressionism. As we've seen, several of *Love*'s life complaints and romantic stories use impressionistic lines to color their stories. The following songs embellish that songwriting strategy for the first time in quite a while. Not since *Blonde On Blonde* have we heard songs such as "Tweedle Dee & Tweedle Dum" and its more sermonic colleagues. While the four impressionistic tracks take us back in time, they do so with a steady eye on the present. No song on *Highway 61* contains the seasoned observations that appear in these compositions. The songs may float about in their own symbolic wake, but they feature identifiable strokes that separate them from what floated by before them. We begin with the madness of the Tweedle boys.

Love And Theft issues another call to the dance floor with the album's opening track, "Tweedle Dee & Tweedle Dum." Throughout the twelve four-line verses of this swinging song, the urge to get up and shake builds and builds. Thus, from the record's outset, Jack's new script takes a marked turn from those murky days in Lanois's swamp. In the present case, we witness Jack Fate's version of the "Sunshine Boys" by way of this impressionistic account of two old coots messing with one another. Nothing ever happens in this song, just verse after verse of descriptions and sayings with an occasionally prescriptive statement. The song opens with our two hardworking characters throwing knives into trees and having some relationship to two bags of human skeletons. (I have no idea what's up with the bags of bones! It rhymes, though.) Next, we're told that they silently trust God (verse 2); we learn that they plan to retire in the country (off to the Highlands?), they ride famous streetcars, and they admire pecan pies (verse 3); and other fleeting images just continue to rush by. No idea is ever developed in any meaningful way. The characters complain about one another one moment (verse 6) and yet seem happy the next (verse 9). With the seventh stanza, the narrator backs off the Tweedle story for this announcement:

> Well, the rain beating down on my windowpane
> I got love for you and it's all in vain
> Brains in the pot, they're beginning to boil
> They're dripping with garlic and olive oil

From this snippet of relational complaint, we quickly return to Tweedleville and the chaotic activities therein. These guys are all over the place. They are licensed for a parade (verse 9), they own a brick company (verse 10), and they complain about one another some more in the closing verse. We hear from the narrator for the second time in the song's penultimate verse:

> Well a childish dream is a deathless need
> And a noble truth is a sacred creed
> My pretty baby, she's lookin' around
> She's wearin' a multi-thousand dollar gown

This song is a fast-paced series of impressions that say nothing on two levels. For some reason, the narrator recounts the story of the Tweedle boys with two pauses for personal comments. None of it makes any sense whatsoever; nonetheless, it is a fun ride. The music carries us along in an enjoyable way while Jack's script unfolds in its own idiosyncratic manner. More importantly, there is not one lovesick person in the lot. Jack has a new script.

The impressionism advances from here, albeit in a more sermonic tone. The light, airy 1930s sounds of "Floater" support one of the most appropriately named tunes in the oeuvre. That this baby floats is for certain. This track conveys a feeling that our narrator is an old rounder sitting in a rocking chair on the front porch saying whatever enters his mind in front of an eager young man awaiting his turn in that old saddle. Each verse changes topics, so there is no story or any form of plot progression. We jump from a lazy day gazing out the window (verse 1), to forbidden thoughts of familial love (verse 2), to fishing (verse 3), to sailing (verse 4), to our first life lesson, presented in verse 5:

> The old men 'round here, sometimes they get
> On bad terms with the younger men
> But old, young, age don't carry weight
> It doesn't matter in the end

Can't you see that young rounder just nodding his head off in response to the old guy's wisdom? OK, maybe you can't. Our topical joyride continues with office lessons (verse 6) and a description of local trees (verse 7), and pauses once more for another life lesson:

> They say times are hard, if you don't believe it
> You can just follow your nose
> It don't bother me—times are hard everywhere
> We'll just have to see how it goes

From this porch platitude, we turn to thoughts about the narrator's mom and dad and their loving ways (verse 9), to insights about how to prosper in school (verse 10), to a Romeo and Juliet joke (verse 11), to historic comments about rivers (verse 12), to a firm warning to not mess with our still-able narrator (verse 13), to thoughts about his grandparents and their quiet abilities (verse 14), to his abandonment of his personal dreams (verse 15), and, finally, we close with a few words about the difficulties of dealing with people and their demands. This song just goes on and on and on and on; all the while, these little nuggets of wisdom rise and fall. From visions of forbidden love, to sailing tips, to age discrimination, to office politics, to tree talk, to school lessons, to Shakespeare, to rebellious waterways, to the family and extended family, to personal reflections about life's ambitions, this song covers it all. I'm certain our thorough auteur deleted the stock tips in order to avoid the current hassles that accompany that sort of insight. Goodness, I think we should rename this monument to attention deficit disorder "Jack Fate's Sermon from the Porch."

But we're just getting warmed up here. With "High Water (For Charlie Patton)," Larry Campbell sets his violin to the side, picks up his banjo, and takes us into some old-fashioned Texas-style Delta blues. The impressionistic sermons just keep on rolling throughout the seven eight-line stanzas (with that ghost chorus) of this tribute to Charlie Patton. The song features three vignettes about Big Joe Turner, Bertha Mason, and George Lewis that are complemented by two sets of two-verse commentaries (of sorts). After describing Big Joe's trip to Kansas City and presenting Bertha's lesson on dancing etiquette, we have our first "reflection" by our narrator:

> I got a cravin' love for blazing speed
> Got a hopped up Mustang Ford
> Jump into the wagon, love, throw your panties overboard
> I can write you poems, make a strong man lose his mind
> I'm no pig without a wig
> I hope you treat me kind
> Things are breakin' up out there
> High water everywhere

Yes, the signal is breaking up. What can be said of these lines? Our songwriting rabbit is in his own unique symbolic briar patch? Does that work? I don't know, but there's not a swamp in sight. Still, if you strain your eyes, there is a famous highway lingering in the distance. After discussing George's lesson concerning unwanted metaphysical perspectives, the narrator turns to two more cloudy reflections. The first is straight out of the "Highway 61 Revisited" songwriting manual:

> The Cuckoo is a pretty bird, she warbles as she flies
> I'm preachin' the Word of God
> I'm puttin' out your eyes
> I asked Fat Nancy for something to eat, she said, "Take it off the shelf—
> As great as you are a man,
> You'll never be greater than yourself."
> I told her I didn't really care
> High water everywhere

After three totally unrelated lines, we turn to a wonderful Newport Mod–style character and her useful advice. Our narrator offers his polite response, and the song closes with another confused tip about how to maximize happiness by sharing it with someone special. In that last verse, the narrator states how he is staying away from women, then in the next breath he relates how happiness works best when shared with your love. I believe we have evidence of a seasoned rounder's flexible morals: He is staying away from women by focusing on a woman. Hmmmmm.

These are some crazy songs, aren't they? We haven't seen this type of song-writing in close to thirty-five years. We cap off our impressionistic tunes with a real keeper. Using the sonic style of a Texas version of a Tin Pan Alley or vaudeville song, "Po' Boy" is a real zinger. Jack's deadpan humor is on display with this chaotic, joke-filled series of takes on different, unconnected scenes. Here a scene with dialogue pops up, quickly unfolds, offers a word of encouragement to the "po' boy," and moves on from there. We open with a man at the door asking for the narrator's wife, he tells him where she is (she is cooking in the kitchen), we greet the "poor boy" (whoever or whatever he is), and we jump to the next scene. The narrator next offers a store clerk $4 for a $3 item and pauses for a word of encouragement for our boy (verse 2). The third verse features a vague reference to a game of interest to the police; we pause for a bridge about the poor boy making his rounds (traveling first class, of course), then witness two vignettes that capture this song's essence:

> Othello told Desdemona, "I'm cold, cover me with a blanket.
> By the way, what happened to that poison wine?"
> She says, "I gave it to you, you drank it."
> Poor boy, layin' 'em straight—pickin' up the cherries fallin' off the plate

> Time and love has branded me with its claws
> Had to go to Florida, dodgin' them Georgia laws
> Poor boy, in the hotel called the Palace of Gloom
> Calls down to room service, says, "Send up a room"

That Jack! Always one for a funny story, he is. I sense a new movie in the works: *The Poor Boy Chronicles*. It's about a guy . . . never mind. The song suddenly turns reflective as the narrator thinks about his mother and father, and his uncle's kindness upon his mother's passing (the second bridge). The sixth verse offers a statement of adoration for an unnamed lover. It just pops up and goes away. The song closes in that age-old style: a knock-knock joke. And a bad one at that. I think the narrator is in his cups enjoying a series of stream-of-consciousness reflections about the poor boy and life. I don't know, but this song is slightly ajar. The jug is probably empty. Ah yes, call room service and ask them to send up a room. There's an idea!

These impressionistic songs are a long way from *Time Out Of Mind*. Actually, all of *Love And Theft*'s songs are a "Million Miles" from the relational swamps. There is not one "Love Sick" person in sight. Oh sure, there are all sorts of injured parties in these songs. But they seem a step or two removed from that pain. Nobody is "Standing In The Doorway" in "Summer Days" or "Lonesome Day Blues." No. They have already walked through that door, taken their licks, gotten drunk, and moved passed that sad memory—most of the time. Instead of wallowing in their romantic angst, these characters think about their parents, wonder about their grandparents, and consider their relationship to both generations. While the character in "Not Dark Yet" was leaning over the edge of the relational abyss, these characters are much older yet considerably freer in their demeanors. They are far more likely to growl at their lovers than they are to bleed in front of them. They are far more likely to pause and note the color of the leaves, smell the flowers, watch the clouds pass by, or listen to the wind than they are to sulk about in a dirty one-room shack pining for some money-hungry, cheating opportunist. Yes, oh yes, the narrator in "Highlands" longed for a thoughtful, peaceful existence in a tranquil, beautiful location far away from the mayhem imposed by belligerent, delusional waitresses in empty restaurants. The narrator in "Highlands" longed for the serenity of *Love And Theft*. He longed to sit amongst the bluebonnets and listen to the soft sounds of a 1930s Texas swing band. A huge fish jumping in the adjoining pond might distract our old rounder from Larry Campbell's violin, but when Campbell joins Charlie Sexton on the guitars and they launch into "Summer Days," well, the old guy cannot help but get up and shake a tired leg to that mighty fine Texas beat. Jack's script is thorough, I'll give it that. There is no anarchist anywhere in sight. We're talking *consequences* in Jack's script.

Wouldn't you know it! What better way to drive home my point than to turn to that one telltale device that floats throughout the oeuvre: *Love And Theft*'s capstone statement, "Sugar Baby." "Sugar Baby" captures my argument and more across its five four-line verses and five standard four-line choruses. This is as close to the swamp as this Texas sound gets on this record, but the bright guitars and gentle playing keep the band on solid ground and the gators at bay. The song is loaded with relational wisdom. This is the same man who wrote "Positively 4th Street" and "Like A Rolling Stone." Now he tames his attack and advances a different weapon: the sermonic reflection. Whether he is in his Bob Dillon or Jack Fate mode, the auteur—Bob Dylan—has traveled down these relational roads, and now he shares the moral of the story. He drives those wisdoms home in the only *Love And Theft* composition to feature a repeated, fully developed, chorus. The voice of his generation brings his misty message forward in this compelling capstone statement.

We open with a pensive scene. The narrator has his back to the sun so he can see clearly: Life's challenges are demanding and require attention. Next, he praises the local bootlegger's fine product, mentions living with an aunt that is not his aunt, and frets over life's difficult memories. The sermonic treatise continues with this take on affairs of the heart:

> The ladies down in Darktown, they're doing the Darktown Strut
> You always got to be prepared but you never know for what
> There ain't no limit to the amount of trouble women bring
> Love is pleasing, love is teasing, love's not an evil thing

What a verse. The advice flows here, doesn't it? After talk about that Darktown crowd, we drift into three fairly substantial lines. We get a variation on the Boy Scout credo, a reflection on women, and wistful commentary on love. The moral is pretty darned clear: Prepare yourself for the unexpected difficulties that a wholesome experience brings. That is one compelling sermonic reflection. He casts a wider net and ponders life's risky nature in the fourth verse and chorus:

> Every moment of existence seems like some dirty trick
> Happiness can come suddenly and leave just as quick
> Any minute of the day the bubble could burst
> Try to make things better for someone, sometimes,
> You just end up making it a thousand times worse
>
> Sugar Baby, get on down the road
> You ain't got no brains no how
> You went years without me
> Might as well keep going now

The narrator's vast experiences have dealt some serious blows, it seems. He anticipates foul play, understands the tenuous qualities of happiness, and ponders the uncertainty of human relations. In the chorus, he seems to encourage love to move along and leave him alone since, after all, that is the way it has always worked. We close with the sad truth that she broke his heart (hence, the relational complaint) and has ripped her way through life, and how this may ultimately be less profitable than she imagined when that day of retribution arrives. He encourages her to seek salvation. He is not angry. He is not aggressive. He is resigned and resolute, and, ultimately, generous. He understands that counterattacks are frivolous because he has been there and done that. Yes, the auteur delivers once more in that capstone spot. Sonically and lyrically, "Sugar Baby" is a wistful look back. The author of "Ballad In Plain D," "Like A Rolling Stone," and "Positively 4th Street" has aged, mellowed, and grown wiser—and it shows throughout *Love And Theft*.

Evidence of that last point exists in the unusual practice of the auteur actually commenting on a work's thematic orientation. Dylan had quite a bit to say about *Love*'s themes. Consider these remarks to *Rolling Stone*'s Mikal Gilmore: "The whole album deals with power. If life teaches us anything, it's that there's nothing that men and women won't do to get power. The album deals with power, wealth, knowledge and salvation—the way I look at it." On another occasion, he told *USA Today*, "I've never recorded an album with more autobiographical songs. . . . This is the way I really feel about things. It's not me dragging around a bottle of absinthe and coming up with Baudelairian poems. It's me using everything I know to be true." That is a direct acknowledgment of the album's use of sermonic reflections as a songwriting tool, isn't it? In a preview interview with the same publication, he told Edna Gundersen that the "songs don't have any genetic history" in terms of his previous work; rather, the music "is an electronic grid, the lyrics being the substructure that holds it all together." The man clearly had a plan—he always does. Dylan's newfound comfort is evident in his music, the means through which it was created, and his public commentary. After years of struggle, the songs—a blend of a flexible electronic grid and structured lyrics—prevailed.

Yes, Bob Zimmerman did it again. He gave young Bob Dylan something to say to the folk music crowd. He gave the Newport Mod something to say to everybody. He gave Renaldo what he needed to do his job. He gave a reborn Dylan the testimonies required for that mission. Now he caps it all off with a new script for Jack Fate. These words also fit nicely within Jack's mission. Once more, these are not phases that an artist is passing through; these are missions that are undertaken in a systematic manner. Zimmerman plans these things. When he implements a plan, he brings to bear all that has passed before the mission at hand. A touch of topical writing, a bit of impressionism, a slice of a sermon, a relational wail, a hokey joke—whatever is available, the auteur reaches around him, selects what he needs, and shapes it in service of that moment's mission. As a result, when we pull back and examine Jack's script, the threads are there. This is the same man who wrote "Hollis Brown," *Highway 61 Revisited*, the Alabama Chronicles, and "Talkin' John Birch." The connection between "Chimes Of Freedom," "Ring Them Bells," and "Highlands" is direct. The writer's perspective shifts as time passes, but you can see and hear the connection. The same holds for "Highway 61" and "High Water" or "Ballad In Plain D" and "Sugar Baby." The guiding sentiment evolves over time, yet the penchant for crazy-named characters, emotionally driven expressions, and campy humor runs throughout the oeuvre. This is an impressive feat.

At the top of that list of admirable traits is Zimmerman's capacity to write for specific characters. Like the Newport Mod or Renaldo, Zimmerman gave Jack Fate his own voice in his new script. Let's close this review of Jack's script with some thoughts on this carefully tailored score. In my view, four traits stand out in this section of the lifework: Jack's sense of humor, his voice, his symbolism, and, last but not least, the script's sonic qualities. The use of humor directly complements the silly jokes that Dylan (read, Jack Fate) tells during band introductions at a NEST show's conclusion (this is not a nightly occurrence; many times he says nothing aside from introducing the band). Remarkably, there are even a few zingers present in the swampy portions of Jack's script. The encounter with the waitress in "Highlands" joins the janitor joke in "Million Miles" to provide a flash of humor in an otherwise extremely dark work. Of course, the humor is more evident in *Love And Theft*. It rivals the sermonic reflection as the principal means of expression in the second portion of Jack's script. "Summer Days" pauses to joke about our capacity to repeat the past and offers a wisecrack about breaking the narrator's heart once more for good luck. "Floater" offers a Romeo and Juliet joke amongst its many impressions. "Honest With Me" ceases its relational complaint long enough for a homonymic pun. "Cry

A While" stops its harangue long enough to joke about a neighbor's early-morning (or late-night) sexual encounters. "Bye And Bye" is pure Jack when the narrator sits on his timepiece in order to be on time (yuk-yuk). And "Po' Boy" is one big joke. I mean, c'mon, a knock-knock joke? Jack Fate is the kind of guy who stands around his mates and tells a stupid joke or two to pass the time. The jokes are more often than not silly puns or word games. What would you expect from our Glissendorf Master? He tips his hat back, gives a serious look, and offers a one-liner that makes you cringe. This is not a new thing. Zimmerman's other characters often paused for a joke or two. The young folk poseur told all sorts of jokes and wrote really funny songs. The Newport Mod went off the deep end more than once (see the 1966 *Playboy* interview cited earlier). Renaldo often dedicated "Romance In Durango" to Sam Peckinpah by lying, saying that Sam was in the audience tonight and wishing him good luck. Actually, the Rolling Thunder Revue was one big joke, wasn't it? One gets the impression that Zimmerman's state of mind plays a major role in his use of humor. The creative equilibrium he attained during the Jack Fate era is evident in the wittiness running through these songs.

Complementing the contents of Jack's script is the voice through which he delivers that material. If you've never heard a seasoned rounder speak, play *Time Out Of Mind* and *Love And Theft*. What is planted in the two cover albums gains roots in the swamps and flowers in *Love*. Jack's voice croaks, strains to stretch out words or syllables, and in general sounds like a wise old Mississippi bluesman talking late at night, well after the midnight show. It accents his humor as well, sounding like Robert Johnson imitating Jack Benny. Wisely, the recording studio manages to capture that voice in all of its majesty. By reducing the echo and allowing the voice to work on its own, the recording reflects what we hear in live performance. We may challenge young Bob Dylan's claim to sing as well as Caruso, but we'll never challenge older Bob Dylan's claim to be Jack Fate.

What comes through that voice is important as well. The sermonic reflections that appear throughout Jack's script represent a new songwriting trend within the lifework. All through the relational complaints, life complaints, personal testimony, and relational pledges that comprise this script, we hear subtle wisdoms, solemn platitudes, and prescriptive commentary. We're told how love works, not how revenge is sweet. We're told how business operates, not how revolution is required. We're told to accept and admire nature, to respect the generations that passed before us, and to practice humility whenever possible—not to oppose those who are older, different, or unfriendly toward our personal orientations. I think it's interesting to note the growth of this writing style within the script itself. Jack was too close to his injuries in *Time Out Of Mind*. With distance, he changed his views, relaxed his posture, and accepted his lot in a more seasoned, reflective manner. Hence, the prescriptive qualities of the songwriting moved to the forefront in *Love And Theft*. That movement facilitated the humor that was reinforced by the voice that yielded a sermonic style that befits an older, wiser man.

Finally, the lynchpin to the entire process may be the NEST band. Assuredly, the swamp sound stands on its own. Dylan followed up on *Oh Mercy* in a powerful way; however, "Highlands" brought closure to a trend that needed to end. Unleashing his Texas-based sound in support of *Love And Theft* was a deft move. I don't think the Tennessee-based or urban-oriented NEST bands could have managed what Campbell, Garnier, Kemper, and Sexton achieved. *Love And Theft* features an extraordinarily precise sonic framework. There is an "electronic grid" in place, and the band provides the power to fuel that structure. Just look at the musical strategies operating on *Love*: We have Texas swing, Texas-style rockabilly, Texas-style Delta blues, Texas-style vaudeville, Texas-style country, and Texas-style lounge music. I may overplay the Texas thing a hair, but I tell you there are shades of Bob Wills everywhere in this sound. No matter the genre, it *swings*. Zimmerman's eye toward pacing was a welcomed addition to Jack's script, and it directly manifests in NEST shows.

Bob Zimmerman's plan for revitalizing his art was a stroke of genius. In a career chock full of radical innovations, this reorientation may be his grandest plan. He bided his time, allowed his vocal and instrumental methods to evolve, and provided the space necessary for his audience to reorient itself and embrace a new act. When that plan reached fruition, the artist devised a new script for this new incarnation of his Bob Dylan character. With *Time Out Of Mind*'s songs in place, the NEST shows merged that material with the revisions of the older compositions, and, in doing so, they silenced critics who claimed the show lived in the past and they enthralled patrons longing for signs for artistic progress. With *Love And Theft*, that process received yet another—perhaps more powerful—boost that propelled the NEST into another gear, allowing it even more strength and flexibility. This was quite the plan. But we're not finished quite yet. Just as Zimmerman allowed his young folk apprentice, his Newport Mod, his country-tinged balladeer, Renaldo, and the pop icon to be captured on the big screen, he used that device to introduce Jack Fate to the world. Hence, we follow this discussion of Jack's script with his celluloid debut. When all of this is assembled, it creates quite a package.

Jack's Movie: *Masked And Anonymous*

Renaldo & Clara toys with the Dylan myth. From the "Who is Bob" T-shirts, to the Ronnie Hawkins–as–Bob Dylan charade, to David Blue's history lessons, the film fondles the celebrity's image in various ways—usually through underdeveloped scenes featuring campy humor. Well, what is an aside in *Renaldo & Clara* becomes a running gag in 2003's *Masked And Anonymous*. In *Masked*, the world is introduced to a man who looks exactly like Bob Dylan and sings Bob Dylan songs, but he dresses differently, abdicates anarchy, and uses another name, Jack Fate. The film was written by Sergei Petrov and Rene Fontaine (yuk-yuk, actually Larry Charles and Bob Dylan), produced by Nigel Sinclair and Jeff Rosen, and directed by Larry Charles. It features actors such as Jeff Bridges, Penelope Cruz, John Goodman, Jessica Lange, and Luke Wilson, with cameos by Angela Bassett, Steve Bauer, Bruce Dern, Ed Harris, Val Kilmer, Cheech Marin, Chris Penn, Giovanni Ribisi, Mickey Rourke, Richard Sarafian, Christian Slater, Fred Ward, and more. It also introduces Larry Campbell, Tony Garnier, George Recile, and Charlie Sexton as the Simple Twist of Fate band. All of the actors reportedly worked for union-scale wages (or, apparently, for free, according to Larry Charles's remarks in the director's commentary feature on the movie's DVD release). We have, then, a labor of love project. Charles makes it quite clear that most of the film's participants joined the project because of the opportunity to work with Dylan—an attitude that was reinforced, he reports, by reading the script. The film satirizes politics, show business, journalism, various forms of human relations, and, throughout the unfolding scenes, the Dylan Myth. Nothing in *Masked* should be taken seriously. As far as I can ascertain, *everybody* had a grand time doing this zany film—a point that Larry Charles reaffirms time and again.

The story takes place in the not-too-distant future and operates on multiple planes. The United States has been overthrown by a revolution that has transformed the nation into a Third World country. Charles describes this new country as an "Alternate America" or a "Third World America." This Alternate America features a racially diverse populace with different ethnic groups gaining control over different institutions. The film does not suggest integration or synthesis at all. It portrays how each racial or political group has staked its own claim in some fashion and is steadfastly protecting its turf. Everybody, it seems, is at odds with one another. A Hispanic is president, some type of Black mafia controls the television networks, an Asian fellow is leader of the revolutionaries, and everywhere we turn we note racial combinations (e.g., a White lady brings her Black child to sing for Fate, a White ventriloquist uses a Black dummy, the Hispanic president maintains a Black mistress and a White wife, and a White vaudeville star appears in blackface). Charles's commentary acknowledges that this racial theme was one of the film's principal motifs. Our Alternative America has devolved from a melting pot into a feudal system.

Violence dominates this Alternate America. Everyone, everywhere carries automatic weapons or powerful handguns. Video clips of violent confrontations open the film and reappear from time to time (these clips involve actual footage secured from the BBC). Everybody everywhere is completely distrusting of everyone and everything. Everybody everywhere drinks or does drugs all of the time—most of the characters in this story are constantly *wasted* (Fate is a major exception; he is a serious fellow). This America is a decadent and depraved place. It appears as though any notion of civil liberties has disappeared. Disagree with the authorities (or anybody, it seems), and go directly to jail—or be shot on the spot. All media are seemingly corrupt. People cannot tell who is on what side. This Third World America is a mess.

It is actually hard to determine whose idea this was, but the television network has decided to broadcast a benefit concert for medical relief, and that event is the film's centerpiece. An archetypical show business sleazeball (John Goodman's character, "Uncle Sweetheart") is responsible for obtaining the talent for the benefit that is being produced by Jessica Lange's character ("Nina Veronica"—a direct reprise of Fay Dunaway's *Network* role). The tension between Sweetheart and Veronica is an ever-present element in the film. She negotiates with the demanding thugs at the network, then battles with Sweetheart over the show's lineup and contents on their behalf, and Sweetheart attempts to manipulate the entire happening to his seedy financial ends in order to pay off his debtors (represented by two Caribbean-sounding thugs). Much to Veronica's and the network's chagrin, Sweetheart secures but one performer for the broadcast: music legend Jack Fate.

The plot certainly thickens with Jack Fate. Fate is the president's son. Years ago—when Fate was at the height of his fame as a rock star—he attempted to intervene between his father (Richard Sarafian) and his mistress (Angela Bassett) for a variety of reasons (to benefit his mother, to end the affair, and for his own pleasure).

The president catches Fate in a hotel room with Bassett and throws him in prison—presumably, forever. Sweetheart (or somebody) manages to secure Fate's release, and the story traces Fate's departure from prison, his travels across the country, and his arrival in Los Angeles for the benefit concert. On his way to Los Angeles, Fate chats with a friend (Cheech Marin), boards an old bus, encounters a deeply disturbed revolutionary (Giovanni Ribisi) who is gunned down by more revolutionaries after a night of sharing his nightmare existence with an expressionless Fate, and Fate reflects on his father and their situation. The dialogue is in turns hilarious, understated, overstated, choppy, and fluid. At some point in his travels, Fate contacts an old friend, "Bobby Cupid" (Luke Wilson), and invites him to meet him at the benefit concert. Fate eventually arrives in seedy Los Angeles, secures lodging (the room just happens to be the one in which he was caught with Bassett), and attempts to contact his dying father (to no avail).

The president is dying, apparently, rather slowly. His chief advisor, "Edmund" (Mickey Rourke), is a serious thug. He grew up with Fate, since he is the son of the presidential palace's gardener and housekeeper. He was once an illegal immigrant, he grew up around this seat of power, and now it is about to be thrust into his evil hands. Charles reports that Rourke worked to make his character a perverse version of Thomas Jefferson or Andrew Jackson. He did, and this Alternative America is in big trouble. Edmund—also known as "the pervert"—is biding his time, patiently awaiting the president's death, and preparing to assume his role as the new leader. He could care less about the benefit concert since Fate is its only performer, and he's certain Fate is harmless. Later in the film, when Fate visits his dying father, Edmund greets him and does nothing to interfere with the visit. He is a confident, dedicated, focused killer.

From the benefit concert and the new America's political environment, we turn to the film's third plane: the event's coverage by the press (or what is left of it). An unnamed newspaper editor (Bruce Dern) brings in a decorated reporter, "Tom Friend" (Jeff Bridges), to cover the benefit concert since the editor is convinced that the concert is rigged toward some dastardly end. Friend is totally uninterested in the assignment until he learns that the lone performer is Fate. He eagerly changes his mind and returns home to pack. Friend's lover, "Pagan Lace" (Penelope Cruz), is a freak who worships all sorts of candlelit objects in a weird fashion (doing *everything* in threes, and bearing a tattoo "333" on her hand—there's some symbolism for you, have at it). She's sweet, but she's nuts. Friend attempts to keep Lace from accompanying him, but she persuades him otherwise. Tom Friend's role is an important part of this story.

These are the story's three planes—the benefit, Fate's troubled past and its political ramifications, and the press's coverage of the concert—and they unfold in a busy fashion as the activities surrounding the benefit concert are blended with Tom Friend's encounters with Fate and Fate's attempt to make peace with his past. All sorts of scenes rush by. Some scenes are truly impressive. For example, Val Kilmer's cameo as a crazed animal trainer who loves the untainted animal kingdom and despises humankind is a showstopper. A scarred and disheveled Kilmer hates people in general, and their oppression of animals in particular. He derides people for pretending to be something they're not, pointing out how one animal never imitates another. The scene is intensely bizarre. Fate simply stares as Kilmer raves. The scenes portraying Sweetheart's relationship with Veronica are also well-done. Great lines go zinging by as these two hardened characters play off of one another. Sweetheart's motivations are made perfectly clear, yet we learn little about Veronica. She is certainly disturbed, but we never really know why. She pops pills, cries over absurd news reports, and masturbates in semiprivate locations. She is neurotic, distrusting, and seemingly dedicated. As Kilmer's character would conclude, she is a mystery.

Other scenes sort of float in and out. For instance, Slater and Penn appear as lazy stagehands who complain about everything and never do anything. Bobby Cupid is a hyperserious young man who seems to be angry with the world (Charles suggests he's modeled upon early Marlon Brando roles). He is also quite protective of Fate and, therefore, distrustful of Friend. He is always on intimate terms with Fate as he floats from scene to scene. Tom Friend—it appears—is at odds with everyone in every scene in which he is present. He is rude to a stubborn Cupid, boorish with an evasive Fate, condescending to a blathering Sweetheart, and uncertain about a confused Lace. Tom Friend is a bad guy. He is dressed in black. These characters reappear in a steady mix of busy storytelling. Multiple scenes—such as Kilmer's—are one-shot deals. There is a colorful scene at the hotel featuring Fate and a desk clerk. Fate's brief visit with Cheech Marin's character is genuinely funny. And the various-paced music montages (featuring "I Believe In You," "Drifter's Escape," and "Cold Irons Bound") are used effectively (much of the story unfolds during these dense segments). Again, this is a busy film.

The story pivots when Fate borrows Cupid's car, wrecks it, visits his mother's grave, visits Bassett, and travels to his father's side. Throughout these scenes, the president continues to fade, the concert is constantly threatened, Friend offends everybody, Lace is dazed and confused, and Fate and his band do the occasional song (the movie is not always linear). The movie, as you can see, is hectic—and, occasionally, quite goofy. For example, after another confrontation with Friend, Fate leaves his dressing room, strolls around the set, and enters a tent labeled "Man Eating Chicken." The tent contains a man sitting quietly, eating some chicken. *That* is *Masked And Anonymous* for you. Just before the show begins, Fate travels into the rafters, where he encounters the ghost of "Oscar Vogel" (Ed Harris), a blackface minstrel who was murdered by Fate's father for speaking against the government. These are the kinds of scenes that pop in and out of the movie.

Eventually, the benefit concert begins at the very moment the president dies. The network fades in and out of Fate's opening number and Edmund's announcement of the president's demise (Charles reports that the video fading between Fate and Edmund involves the movie's lone special effect). Edmund assumes control. Revolutionaries (I think!) attack the TV studio. The show, I suppose, comes to an abrupt end (I'm not certain). Afterward, as the set is being cleaned, Sweetheart tries to force Lace to drink with him, a fight ensues between Sweetheart and Friend, Fate intervenes on Sweetheart's behalf (Jack Fate is no Bruce Lee, but he gets the job done), Friend pulls a gun on the two men, and Cupid attacks Friend with an old guitar he gave Jack earlier. After disarming Friend, Cupid stabs him in the neck with the guitar and kills him. Fate tells Cupid to leave. When the "authorities" arrive, they seize Veronica and demand to know what happened, and she claims that Fate is responsible for the murder. Fate is seized and loaded into a van, and the film ends with him on his way back to prison. No one defends him. No one stands up for him. Meanwhile, Sweetheart is taken away by the Caribbean thugs as Lace drinks his ever-present Jack Daniels. The movie ends with a long, tight facial shot of Fate and his parting words about life, perception, and personal philosophy.

Central to the movie's story is its production design. The director's commentary feature is rich in its detail of how this Third World America was created and portrayed. Larry Charles applied his travels through Third World countries to design the set, securing a bus like you'd see in South America, placing pictures and posters of the president *everywhere* in the manner of many dictatorships, and creating the general sense of a violent police state. Charles also designed a new flag for this new America. Any art that existed in background shots was covered in order to signify the decline of artistic expression. Everything looks dirty and decayed. People are divided and defensive. Radio is a major source of information—such as it is. Remarkably—and unfortunately—the shots of Los Angeles involved no art direction. Scenes of street life, street people, filthy streets, homeless people's makeshift abodes, and the like were obtained by riding around Los Angeles with a camera held out of the window. Hence, we must conclude that we are, in fact, closer to this fictitious America than we might like to think!

The Dylan Myth is presented in a gamelike fashion. It requires multiple viewings to grasp the flash here, the gimmick there. Dylan's music is ubiquitous in this film. Scenes shot in Veronica's office/trailer feature Muzac playing in the background covering Dylan's "Blowin' In The Wind." As the movie shifts between scenes, we hear international or alternative versions of Dylan songs (e.g., the opening credits feature a Japanese version of "My Back Pages," one segue involves the Ramones doing the same number, during a Fate-Friend confrontation a Middle Eastern version of "Tangled Up In Blue" plays, an Italian version of "If You See Her, Say Hello" is used, and an Italian rap version of "Like A Rolling Stone" joins Grateful Dead covers, old Dylan performances, and more). The music is also featured in a straightforward manner through band rehearsals for the concert (playing "Dixie," "Diamond Joe," and more at different points) and the opening of the benefit concert. Mrs. Brown's daughter performs "The Times They Are A-Changin'." Other Dylan references are more subtle. For instance, Tom Friend is dressed like Dylan (Charles's commentary confirms this). He first appears in a hooded outfit that Dylan is known for wearing; moreover, in his appearances at the benefit and elsewhere, he wears Dylan's standard mid-1960s attire (black leather jacket, white shirt, wild hair, and dark sunglasses). Another Dylan reference involves a scene in which the band performs "Drifter's Escape" and Cupid and Sweetheart offer idiosyncratic interpretations of the song (another scene, which was deleted, involves a similar scenario, and I wished they hadn't cut it since it featured the ventriloquist and his dummy arguing over a song's interpretation—the dummy had the stronger point, what symbolism!). Finally, Charles reports in his commentary that the closing shot of Fate riding off to jail was designed to be a bookend to the ending of *Dont Look Back*. Thus, from the music, to Dylan's attire, to interpretations of his songs, to the faded rock legend theme, to the closing scene's relationship to another Dylan movie, the Dylan Myth creeps in and out of this energetic satire like a running gag. Jack Fate is surrounded by Bob Dylan in *Masked And Anonymous.*

I must pause for my favorite Dylan reference in the film. It is very quick and requires a pause button to be fully appreciated. Early in the film, Veronica meets with the network officials to discuss the benefit concert. As the discussion ensues, the network "leader" passes in front of the networks' prime-time broadcasting schedule. The shows listed there are a hoot. Various shows are entitled "Not Dark Yet," "Empire Burlesque," "Jokerman," "Day Of The Locust," "It's Alright Ma," "Masked & Anonymous," and "Hurricane." Other shows are featured as well: "Slave Trade," "Lava Flow," "The Presidential Hour," and more. One thrilling sequence involves a three-hour series of shows that are aired on a single channel: "I Love You," "I Hate You," and "I Kill You." I think the writers on this project enjoyed themselves.

While the film's plot is actually quite coherent and enjoyably paced (you have to love the ever-present sound of thunder, helicopters, and gunfire in the background—turmoil!), these characters embody the film's values and are, therefore, its narrative centerpiece. Uncle Sweetheart is such a swine. Nina Veronica is so neurotic. Tom Friend is so utterly pretentious. Pagan Lace is sweetly crazed and a genuine foil to Friend. Bobby Cupid is so ridiculously serious. Edmund is an unmitigated thug. Jack Fate is so laconic and imperturbable. Throughout the decadent and depraved scenes of this Alternative America, it is these characters who bring those images to life. Interestingly, their principal mode of communication is *preaching.* Everyone is so bloody sermonic! The movie opens with Charles's voice enacting a screaming radio preacher. Veronica's initial appearance involves her philosophy on the current war. Kilmer rails against humankind and its oppressive nature. Sweetheart preaches all the time, declaring this situation or that moment to be some earthshaking revelation. The guy even claims he has gained weight by eating from the tree of the knowledge of good and evil. There *that* hangs! When Edmund meets Fate, he preaches about the self-serving sociological perspective that fuels his ambitions and justifies his decision making. Cupid and Friend offer self-righteous or self-indulgent accounts of varied happenings. Cupid has a philosophical interpretation for every act. Friend applies some version of conspiracy theory to everything. Even Lace's chaotic mumblings are occasionally sermonic. Fate is not immune to this practice either. Many of his comments or responses are so laconically philosophical that they appear to be throwaways. Assuredly, his closing ride to the prison is chock full of his views on life's varied lessons. And there is not an anarchist in sight. These people are consumed by their answers, not motivated by their questions. That attribute drives this film's plot.

Larry Charles and Bob Dylan make a variety of "statements" about different topics in this film. Some are more serious than others, that is for certain. Yet, their comments on America's divisive society, neurotic media, corrupt leadership, morally bankrupt entertainment industry, inept political philosophies, and obsessive religious practices are the project's backbone. Amongst all of these commentaries, one stood above the rest in my view. Tom Friend's confrontational "interviews" with Jack Fate directly portrayed one of the major, long-running thorns in Bob Dylan's side. Friend is obnoxious beyond belief. He *never asks a question.* Instead, he tosses off some reference to Janis Joplin, Jimi Hendrix at Woodstock, Hugh Hefner, or some other person or event; pontificates on *his* point; and *then* turns to Fate for his views. Fate never, ever responds. This in no way dissuades Friend, so he merely changes topics and rants on and on. Occasionally, he pauses to confront Fate, saying that he is supposed to have all the answers; then Friend moves on to another pontification. Fate stands there, stone-faced. Friend continually states that he is on Fate's side (everybody says this time and again; Charles reports that this, too, was a motif), then attacks him again. How many times has Bob Dylan endured this! Larry Charles claims that he has witnessed this on multiple occasions. Someone confronts Dylan, spouts off some view on something, and seeks Dylan's confirmation of that opinion. Charles relates that Dylan just endures the experience, never responds, and the individual eventually leaves. Dear readers, read interviews with Dylan in various major publications and notice the frequency with which this occurs. Sometimes I become so angry with journalists when they ask a meaningful question, Dylan begins to answer it, and they interrupt him with another, usually unrelated, celebrity-based question. I cannot tell you how many times I've endured this. I think Bob Dylan shares a glimpse into his world with Tom Friend's character. I don't think it's a very pretty picture.

Masked And Anonymous is a fun film. It is not *Gone With The Wind*, *A Star Is Born*, or *Citizen Kane*; rather, it is a campy examination of sociological trends, political and religious practices, and the entertainment industry with comical asides. The DVD release contains a segment entitled *Masked And Anonymous Exposed*, which offers interviews with the actors, producers, and Larry Charles (it does *not* feature Dylan, however). Each of the participants interviewed conveys fond feelings for the experience. Charles—in particular—offers positive recollections concerning the twenty days required to shoot the film, the long hours associated with that experience, and the dedication the various actors and technicians displayed throughout the filming process. Charles states that he tried to capture "moments" more than anything else and that the actors facilitated that strategy. Rather than concentrate on plot development, precise readings of the script, or other details, he encouraged the actors to focus on each scene, its demands, and their responses to those perceived conditions. Obviously, Charles is pleased with the results—although I perceived that he's disappointed with the critical responses to the film. To cope with those feelings, I strongly recommend that he consult his coauthor for his views on dealing with critics. I think he has experience with that particular phenomenon, don't you?

This brings us to the end of an ongoing era. The recent appearance of *Chronicles*, the revision and reissue of Dylan's lyric compilation, the continuing *Bootleg Series*, and Dylan's media comments regarding new albums and new releases of old songs join the never-ending qualities of the NEST to suggest that this period has a way to go. His interview on CBS' *60 Minutes* (his first TV interview in close to twenty years) concluded with Ed Bradley's report that *Chronicles*' second and third installments are forthcoming. I'm confident that this is the final period of Zimmerman's career, however. His career, I hope, will continue, but it will follow the path established during the Jack Fate era. I think he applied himself in his most concentrated manner when he planned the career revisions that brought about the NEST, the Basement Strategy–fueled cover albums, Jack's two-album script, and Jack's movie. *Chronicles* makes this point oh-so-clearly. Dylan also made it *very* clear in the *60 Minutes* interview aired on December 5, 2004. When CBS correspondent Bradley noted that Dylan continues to prosper in his chosen field, Dylan answered, "I do but I don't take it for granted." When Bradley inquired why Dylan continues to work so hard, Dylan replied, "Well, it goes back to that destiny thing. I made a bargain with it . . . a long time ago and I'm holdin' up my end." When Bradley asked what he bargained for, Dylan calmly responded, "To get where I am now." Bradley pursued the thought by asking with whom he made this bargain, and Dylan shyly replied, "With the Chief Commander." Bradley asked, "On this Earth?" The auteur laughed as he replied, "In this Earth and in a world we can't see." Ultimately, it comes down to Bob Zimmerman's missions, doesn't it? They are always there. These are not phases of development or responses to particular or spontaneous urges. To the contrary, when Zimmerman wrote for Bob Dylan he pursued specific missions that required coordinated acts that served that cause. In the end, the two missions of "service" in Dylan's oeuvre—the moral and Jack Fate periods—merge into one sacred obligation. Bob Zimmerman takes his missions seriously, and we have the art to prove it.

Writing Dylan: The Songs of a Lonesome Traveler

Throughout this study, I've referred to Robert Shelton's biography of Bob Dylan as perhaps *the* definitive treatment of the celebrity's life. Shelton's unique access to his subject, his family, and his friends made his much-anticipated work one of a kind. He befriended Abe. Beatty talked freely to him. Both parents shared family treasures with him. He knows the sights and smells of the Zimmerman's home on Seventh Avenue in Hibbing. I bet Beatty cooked for him. I suspect Abe talked business with him. He walked the streets of Hibbing. His subject also granted unprecedented access after shows, between tours, or during late-night flights. Surprisingly, the Shelton project is the only book on his career that Dylan claims to have read. One of the most significant portions of the book involves a conversation that occurred late one night on a March 1966 flight from Lincoln, Nebraska, to Denver, Colorado. The interview was wide-ranging. The commentary was rich. Dylan shared his thoughts about his audience, his performing, the recording industry, his writing, and—ever so slightly—his life. Regarding the latter, he was more than clear: "Nobody knows about me." Dylan argued that people know his dad's name and understand his middle-class upbringing; otherwise, they are clueless. The world of celebrity can be a senseless challenge, and the man known as "Bob Dylan" was clearly frustrated. He obviously trusted Robert Shelton, though. While he did not want Shelton's book to be authorized by *Bob Dylan*, he wanted his friend to have his scoop *and* to report his story, telling Shelton that he wanted him to have insights that no one else will ever obtain. *That* is how close Bob Dylan was to Robert Shelton.

After the two men boarded the plane and as the rest of the entourage fell asleep, the conversation thickened. Dylan sat with page proofs of *Tarantula* on one knee and a package of poems a young fan gave him at the Lincoln airport on the other. According to the account, Dylan was extremely kind to the youngster who aspired to be a poet, taking his work and promising to read it and respond. But the auteur was in a mood to talk, not read. The results were a windfall for Shelton's project, as well as for all of us who followed him. First, Dylan discussed performance and how that inspired him, although he was working far too much. He assured Shelton that he was going to reduce that schedule next year (and did he ever!). While he loved the stage, he hated what awaited him backstage. Way back in 1966, we see evidence of the performer's need to perform, and that same performer's desire to avoid the trappings that surrounded that performance. That conflict sharpened when Shelton asked him about the music industry. Dylan replied, "Oh, if it's not the promoter cheating you, it's the box office cheating you. Somebody is always giving you a hard time. . . . Even the record company figures won't be right. Nobody's going to be straight with you because nobody wants the information out." He claimed that at one point he made more money writing for others than for himself. He concluded that his contract was simply "horrible." Yes, the youthful fantasies of celebrity had evaporated into the harsh realities of the commercial art world. He loved the stage. He hated the sycophancy that awaited him afterward. He loved his songs. He hated the industry that marketed them. What conflict! What frustrations. Nevertheless, he treasured his work. He described his art to his friend:

> I think of all that I do as my *writing*. It cheapens it to call it anything else but writing. But there is not a person on the earth who takes it less seriously than I do. . . . It's not going to extend my life any and it's not going to make me happy. . . . I sing honest stuff . . . and it's consistent. It's *all* I do. I don't give a damn what anybody says. . . . I never really read what people say about me. I'm just not interested.

Shelton proceeded by asking if Dylan purposefully broke the established rules of songwriting as an act of rebellion or defiance. The writer responded, "It's not a question of breaking the rules. . . . I don't break the rules, because I don't see any rules to break. As far as I'm concerned, there aren't any rules." He continued with this simple, but thorough, description of his creative orientation: "My thing is with colors. It's not black and white. It's always been with colors, whether with clothes or anything. Color . . . sometimes it gets fiery red . . . at times it gets very jet black." Fascinating.

Shelton pursued that line of inquiry by asking if our Archbishop of Anarchy considered himself to be a poet. Dylan offered this characteristically sharp response:

> I think a poet is anybody who wouldn't call himself a poet. Anybody who could possibly call himself a poet just cannot be a poet. . . . When people start calling me a poet, I say: "Oh, groovy, how groovy to be called a poet!" But it didn't do me any good. . . . It didn't make me any happier. Hey, I would love to say that I am a poet . . . but I just can't because of all the slobs who are called poets. . . . I wouldn't call myself a poet for any more reason than I would call myself a protest singer. All that would do would put me in a category with a whole lot of people who would just bother me. To tell anybody I'm a poet would just be fooling people.

What a revealing exchange. Dylan told Shelton about midway through the conversation that he was "trusting" him to get this right. That trust was not misplaced. The truth was told. The Glissendorf Master came clean: He plays his game his way (forget "rules") and judges his achievements by his standards. Critics? Never reads them (he is "just not interested"). Peers? Never acknowledges those slobs (they "just bother" him). But they are fun to put down—just great Glissendorf victims. Labels? Introduce one, and he will spend the next five years shattering your point, just for kicks. Bobby Zimmerman of Hibbing, Minnesota, invented a game with its own—

secret—rules, and he privately experienced its successes and failures for over forty

years. This, my friends, is a level of independence that Marlon Brando's and James

The music I heard was Frankie Lane, Rosemary Clooney, Dennis Day or the Mills Brothers . . . when I hear stuff like that it always strikes a different chord than all the rock and roll stuff does. The rock and roll stuff . . . I had a conscious mind at that time, but ten years before that . . . stuff like Mule Train . . . the old hillbilly stuff [influenced him]. . . . When rock and roll came in after Elvis . . . Carl Perkins, Buddy Holly . . . Chuck Berry, Little Richard . . . that stuff influenced me. Johnny Ray knocked me out. Johnny Ray was the first person actually to *really* knock me out. I ran into him in an elevator in Australia . . . he was like one of my idols. . . . I was speechless . . . and then I heard Woody Guthrie . . . and then it all came together for me.

In 1978, he discussed this topic with Robert Hilburn:

My music comes from two places: white hillbilly music—Roscoe Holcomb, stuff like that—and black blues—people like Son House, Charley Patton, Robert Johnson. These are the two elements I've always related to best, even now. Then, all of a sudden in the '60s, I heard Woody Guthrie, which just blew my mind—what he did with a lyric. So, I stopped everything and learned his songs. That's what kept me going. I wanted to see how far I could take those elements, how well I could blend them together. Sometimes my music has gone a little to one side, then it drifts back to the other, but I'm always headed in the same direction.

That conversation continued some six years later:

At a certain point, though, I realized I had found something musically that no one else had found. I just stumbled onto it because I had been doing the regular stuff for a long, long time. . . . When I started, I combined other people's styles unconsciously. . . . I crossed Sonny Terry with the Stanley Brothers with Roscoe Holcombe with Big Bill Broonzy with Woody Guthrie . . . all the stuff that was dear to me. Everybody else tried to do an exact replica of what they heard. I was doing it my own way because I wasn't as good technically as, say, Erik Darling or Tom Paley. So I had to take the songs and make them mine in a different way. It was the early folk music done in a rock way, which was the first kind of music I played. On the first album, I did "Highway 51" like an Everly Brothers tune because that was the only way I could relate to that stuff.

The key to this creative process involves Zimmerman's *assimilation* of all that he heard or read or saw. Not only did he use those materials to his creative ends, but he also sincerely values them. His comments about Johnny Ray reveal the extent to which he *maintains* respect for those original influences. *Chronicles* tips its hat to Guthrie, Robert Johnson, Hank Snow, Rimbaud, painters Red Grooms and Picasso, Harold Arlen, a song entitled "Pirate Jenny," and the man who taught him the "archetype rules of poetic songwriting," Hank Williams. That respect generated the "Basement

sure of his creative direction or in need of inspiration, he turns to the Jack Fate portion of the Dylan composite, and Fate's encyclopedic knowledge of music. That
music frees the writer's mind and liberates his artistic instincts. Remember the 2004
Newsweek interview and his meditations? These inspirations are, without question, his
creative foundation and his guiding light. Those inspirations do far more than initiate the art; they *sustain* it. With Jack Fate's help, Bob Dylan is "always headed in the
same direction."

His quiet bedroom in Hibbing, his brief stay in Dinkytown, and the nirvana of
Greenwich Village added another ingredient to this artistic formula. Zimmerman
wrote poems as a child and displayed an interest in poetry in high school, but Dinkytown's and New York's bohemian environments heightened the young wordsmith's
predilection for the art form. At times, the public Bob Dylan expands his list of influences to include poets and novelists, as these comments to *Melody Maker* indicate:
"Yes, Rimbaud has been a big influence on me. When I'm on the road and want to
read something that makes sense to me, I go to a bookstore and read his words.
Melville is somebody I can identify with because of how he looked at life. I also like
Joseph Conrad a lot, and I've loved what I've read of James Joyce. Allen Ginsberg is
always a great inspiration." At other times, he backs away from that stance, as these
comments to John Cohen and Happy Traum reveal: "My thoughts weren't about
reading, no . . . they were just about that feeling that was in the air. I tried to somehow get a hold of that, and write that down, and using my musical training to sort
of guide it by, and in the end, have something I could do for a living." Dylan is specific about that last point in the BBC program. There, he offers a *functional* view of
his songwriting's origins:

> I wanted . . . a song to sing. It came a certain point where I couldn't sing
> anything. I had to write what I wanted to sing because what I wanted to
> sing nobody else was writing. I couldn't find it anywhere . . . what I felt
> was going on . . . nobody was writing then . . . I couldn't find that song
> someplace . . . if I could've, I probably would never have started writing.

As we've observed, what he "needs to sing" is contingent upon that day's mission
and the public image associated with those creative objectives. The *image*—topical
troubadour, Newport Mod, paternal patriot, poetic preacher, celebrity icon, or professional musician—drives the application of a cultivated musical instinct—his
training—that seeks to satisfy a specific agenda. *Chronicles* confirms time and again that
everything is applied in service of a given moment's needs. In so doing, his approach
does not ignore logic or rationality, but it does accent the emotive realm as it probes
the feelings associated with the subject at hand. (Remember, Dylan's "Outlined Epitaph #4" speaks directly to his preference for the emotive over the logical, political,
or institutional "truths" associated with societal structures.) Dear readers, it comes
down to those *colors*.

When Zimmerman writes for Dylan and his corresponding missions, his artistic philosophy guides the application of his reservoir of influences. "Bob Dylan" has
been quite precise in his explanations of his artistic philosophy. In particular, he used

interviews for *Renaldo & Clara* to state his case. In March 1978 he told *Playboy*, "I want to be moved, because that's what art is supposed to do. . . . Art is supposed to take you out of your chair. It's supposed to move you from one space to another." He echoed that view in July, when *Melody Maker* cited Dylan's dictum, "The purpose of art is to inspire." Later that year, he told *Rolling Stone*, "Art is the perpetual motion of illusion. The highest purpose of art is to inspire. What else can you do? What else can you do for anyone but inspire them?" Dylan sharpened that argument with these 1983 remarks to the *Chicago Tribune*: "The purpose of music is to elevate the spirit and inspire. Not to help push some product down your throat." A year later he added another dimension to his argument for the *Los Angeles Times*: "It puts you in tune with your own existence. . . . Sometimes you really don't know how you feel, but really good music can define how you feel. It can make you feel not so much alone. That's what it has always done for me—people like Hank Williams, Bill Monroe, Muddy Waters, Robert Johnson. . . . I'm afraid roots music is going to be obsolete the way we're going. I hope people go back to it. But most people [who make records] don't care about feeling. They just want success." (So this is how the lonely narrator in "Joan Baez in Concert, Part 2" coped with his adolescent loneliness?) Finally, in 1993 Dylan added one last ingredient to his philosophy in these remarks to the *Boston Herald*: "Art to me doesn't mirror society. The very essence of art is subversive to society, and whatever society is putting out, art's got to do something else."

Now, my friends, *this* is a straightforward argument: Art is to challenge the status quo through emotional appeals that arouse audiences. Our auteur denounces art's commerciality, emphasizes its inspirational or spiritual potentials, and anchors his view in personal experience by stressing the significance of "roots music" and its *emotional* impact on his life. His position is compelling: Understand what has transpired before you, assimilate that information, and use it to generate your own work, art that endeavors to inspire—*and challenge*—its audience. I really don't think you could articulate this perspective any more clearly, do you?

This brings us to the artist's relationship with his audience. He explained his stance in unequivocal terms to Cohen and Traum: "The most you can do is satisfy yourself. If you satisfy yourself then you don't have to worry about remembering anything. If you don't satisfy yourself, and you don't know why you're doing what you do, you begin to lose contact. If you're doing it for *them* instead of you, you're likely not in contact with them. You can't pretend you're in contact with something you're not." In July 1978 he told *Melody Maker*, "I've always liked my stuff. All you really have to please is yourself, in *any* arena of life." We hear this once more in a 2001 *Rolling Stone* piece: "I have to impress myself *first*, and unless I'm speaking in a certain language to my own self, I don't feel anything less than that will do for the public, really." Bob Zimmerman's art pursues emotional inspiration through self-satisfaction: He probes *his* feelings, satisfies a *personal* ambition, and shares the results with *them*. His primary audience has not changed across his forty-year career. I believe it is the key to his creative longevity.

With an understanding of his creative influences and his artistic philosophy, we move to his means of production. The evidence reveals that Zimmerman's writing techniques have evolved throughout his protracted career. We chart that evolution by opening with definitional matters and the writer's perspective on songs, their functions, and their origins. His views are stated simply. He reports in *Chronicles* that a song is "like a dream" and the songwriter's objective is to make that dream "come true." He told Shelton that his songs "are just pictures of what I'm seeing" and reiterated that claim in his interview with Hentoff when he reported his "songs are pictures and the band makes the sound of the pictures" (he says the same thing in *Chronicles* as well). In 2001, he simplified his point to *Rolling Stone* by saying that a "song is just a mood that an artist is attempting to convey." I think all of this crystallizes in that marvelous statement we considered in the Newport Mod era, in which Dylan described the sound that supports his work as "that thin, wild mercury sound." Remember? He discussed that sound's "metallic and bright gold" qualities, its natural origins (i.e., "the sound of the street with the sunrays, the sun shining down at a particular time. . . . The sound of bells and distant railroad trains and arguments in apartments and the clinking of silverware and knives and forks and beating with leather straps"), and its imperfect manifestation on his recordings: "I'm not doing it to see how good I can sound, or how perfect the melody can be, or how intricate the details can be woven or how perfectly written something can be. I don't care about those things." What a colorful conceptualization. Yep. It sure sounds to me that Bob Dylan's songs are "pictures"—natural, everyday pictures—and that his band provides a soundtrack for the mood associated with that mental construction. When he told Shelton, "My thing is with colors," his aim was apparently true. The goal involves a raw—not refined—manifestation of that visual inspiration. These remarks to Cohen and Traum shed much light on this inventive strategy:

> It's like this painter who lives around here—he paints the area in a radius of twenty miles, he paints bright strong pictures. He might take a barn from twenty miles away, and hook it up with a brook right next door, then with a car ten miles away, and with the sky on some certain day, and the light on the trees from another certain day. A person passing by will be painted alongside someone ten miles away. And in the end he'll have this composite picture of something which you can't say exists in his mind. It's not that he started off willfully painting this picture from all his experience. . . . That's more or less what I do.

That is, Zimmerman may have a feel for the various elements—or thoughts—that go into a given expression, and that feel may be personally satisfying, however, the "composite" that emerges from these different images is audience dependent. To argue that the auteur's compositions are "musical Rorschach tests" is, assuredly, a defendable position. We have witnessed this phenomenon time and again as we moved through the lifework's various periods. Shelton's "Rorschach" analogy works. Zimmerman may write for himself, but the results are wide open for all sorts of interpretation—or folly.

Other interviews build directly on these starting points—often, in compelling ways. For example, Dylan told Bill Flanagan, "Well, songs are just thoughts. . . . To hear a song is to hear someone's thought. . . . I'm a messenger. I get it. It comes to me so I give it back in my particular style." When asked about the process through which these "messages" are harnessed, he claimed that "not a whole lot of real thought goes into this stuff" in that it is "more or less remembering things and taking it down." He continued, "A lot of people ask, 'What comes first, the words or melody?' I thought about that. It's very rare that they don't come together. Sometimes the words come first, sometimes the melody comes first, but that's the exception. Most of the time the words and melody come at the same time, usually with the first line." These remarks to Jann Wenner are helpful:

> Well, I try to get it when it comes. I play the guitar wherever I find one. But I try to write the song when it comes. I try to get it all . . . 'cause if you don't get it all, you're not gonna get it. So the best kinds of songs you can write are in motel rooms and cars . . . places which are all temporary. . . . You go into your kitchen and try to write a song, and you can't write a song—I know people who do this—I know some songwriters who go to work every day, at 8:30 and come home at 5:00. And usually bring something back . . . I mean, that's legal too. It just depends on . . . how you do it. Me, I don't have those kind of things known to me yet, so I just get 'em when they come. And when they don't come, I don't try for it.

Ah yes, Epitaph # 8: When it arrives, it arrives; when it doesn't, it doesn't. By the way, *Chronicles* reinforces Dylan's comments to Wenner when it notes that the writing process works best for the author when he's on the move.

For Bob Dylan's early work, songwriting was a spontaneous act ("not a whole lot of real thought") that captured a particular moment (or "thought") through that Little Richard–inspired "wild mercury" sound, as he told Flanagan: "The saddest thing about songwriting is when you get something really good and you put it down for a while, and you take for granted that you'll be able to get back to it with whatever inspired you to do it in the first place—well, whatever inspired you to do it in the first place is never there anymore." The spontaneous qualities of Zimmerman's writings through *Blonde On Blonde* may be their most prominent attribute. A film, a newspaper article, or some other stimulus generated a "thought," and he rode it from there. He told Paul Zollo, "The best songs to me—my best songs—are songs which were written very quickly. Yeah, very, very quickly. Just about as much time as it takes to write it down is about as long as it takes to write it." The process may be spontaneous, but he edits what flows through him, as he explained to Rosenbaum: "I reject a lot of inspiring lines. . . . I reject a lot. I kind of know myself well enough to know that the line might be good and it is the first line that gives you inspiration and then it's just like riding a bull. That is the rest of it. Either you just stick with it or you don't. And if you believe that what you are doing is important, then you will stick with it no matter what." When Rosenbaum inquired if the melody flows as naturally as the first line, he replied, "Sometimes, and sometimes I have to find it." Dylan's 1964 comments to *Melody Maker* are instructive:

> You ask if I have any difficulty producing songs. You know, they come up and stay in my mind sometimes—sometimes a long time. I just write

them out when the right time comes. The words come first. Then I fit a tune or just strum the chords. Really I'm not a tune writer. The songs for me are very confining, or something. I'm not writing that many songs. I've written a lot of things with no structure, written them only because I like to sing them. 'Hard rain's a-gonna fall' . . . I wrote the words of it on a piece of paper. But there was no tune that really fit to it, so I just sort of play chords without a tune. But all this comes under the heading of a definition, and I don't care really to define what I do. Other people seem to have a hard time doing that.

Ah yes, back to "definitions" and "Other Songs" poem #5. This process isn't about those dreaded definitions, as he related to David Fricke: "It's like a guy digging a ditch. It's hard to talk about how the dirt feels on the shovel." Nevertheless, notice the similarity between his 1964 comments and his 2004 *Newsweek* interview cited in chapter 7. Forty years later, the basic method remains constant. Bob Zimmerman has a plan.

This plan has magical qualities. When Kurt Loder inquired about the lyrics from several of his early songs, Dylan replied, "As I look back on it now, I am surprised that I came up with so many of them. At the time it seemed like a natural thing to do. Now I can look back and see that I must have written those songs 'in the spirit,' you know? Like 'Desolation Row'—I was just thinkin' about that the other night. There's no logical way that you can arrive at lyrics like that. I don't know how it was done. [Loder: "It just came to you?"] It just came out *through* me." Here we get to the crux of the matter: The 1960s Bob Dylan was—dare I say it—a messenger, a purveyor of existing "messages" or "thoughts" that traveled *through* him via his inventive method. Virtually all of the interviews cited above support this position, as the public Dylan consistently stated that he did not invent songs. To the contrary, he was a medium for the songs; the songs found him. Consider these comments to Flanagan: "A lot of times you'll just hear things and you'll know that these are the things that you want to put in your song. Whether you say them or not. . . . They just sound good, and *somebody* thinks them. . . . I didn't originate those kinds of thoughts. I've felt them, but I didn't originate them. They're out there, so I just use them." Zimmerman did not sit down with a notepad, a thesaurus, and a rhyming dictionary in order to chart out his message. He placed himself in a situation so that he may "receive" a thought, process that "message," and present it through his "particular style." Key to that process, as he told Paul Zollo, is the environment: "Now for me, the environment to write the song is extremely important. The environment has to bring something out in me that wants to be brought out. It's a contemplative, reflective thing."

The auteur's ideas about his craft crystallize in these 1978 remarks to *Melody Maker*: "I'm just the postman. I deliver the songs." The "postman" analogy is helpful. Dylan did not "originate" the letter; the "message" was not *from* him. He was merely the conduit, the channel, the medium. In 1968, he told *Newsweek*, "I used to think . . . that myself and my songs were the same thing. But I don't believe that any more. There's myself and there's my song, which I hope is everybody's song." Not only did Dylan desire to share a song's "ownership" (what the postman delivers is the receiver's property), but he also shied away from any detailed comprehension of the letter's contents. To that end, he told *Time* in 1985, "My songs are not for me to understand. I don't make that a part of it. While I'm doing them I have an understanding of them, but that's all."

All of which leads to the conclusion that the pre-accident songwriting was more intuitive than calculated. Anthony Scaduto quotes former companion Suze Rotolo: "Dylan was perceptive. He felt. He didn't read or clip the papers and refer to it later, as you would write a story, or as other songwriters might do it. With Dylan it was not that conscious journalistic approach. It was more poetical. It was all intuitive, on an emotional level. . . . It was more than just writing, it was like something flowing out of him." Scaduto's interview with Mikki Isaacson provides a strong example of the 1960s Dylan at work. She recalled a summer trip and how Dylan wrote songs while riding in the backseat: "He had a spiral notebook, a small steno book, and he must have had four different songs going at once. He would write a line in one and flip a couple of pages back and write a line in another one. A word here and a line there, just writing away." David Hajdu offers another example when he describes a writing session in which Dylan "laid out dozens of photographs torn from newspapers and magazines in a montage on the floor and sat down amidst them with his guitar." Hajdu continues,

> Bob would start with a simple musical framework, a blues pattern he could repeat indefinitely, and he would close his eyes—he would not draw from the pictures literally but would use the impression the faces left as a visual model for kaleidoscopic language. He appeared to sing whatever came to him, disconnected phrases with a poetic feeling. When something came out that he liked, he scrawled it down hurriedly, so as to stay in the moment, and he would do this until there were enough words for a song. . . . He was not pursuing refinement, sophistication, and clarity of expression, those ideals of the Cole Porter generation of songwriters, but their near opposites: kinetic energy, instinct, and ambiguity.

The Glissendorf Master toyed with rhythmic patterns of words until lightning struck, recorded the occurrence dutifully, and continued until he had "enough words" to stop (a revealing approach to closure). The visuals inspired a mood, Zimmerman tried to ride that "picture," and the rest was magic (remember, not all magic is *good* magic). Again, this is the *exact* process Dylan described in his 2004 *Newsweek* interview.

The missions—and their corresponding images—are central here. The impulse that drove the work involved a narrative imperative to move the audience through the story's emotional portrayals that were, in turn, fueled by the writer's projected image. Bob Dylan's celebrity status personalized—and framed—these inspirational messages. Dylan's image of *himself* is fascinating. His view that he was a "messenger" who merely received messages—that he was the "postman" who delivered somebody else's mail—and articulated that content through the style du jour provided the basis of the writer's stylistic decision making. Since the song already existed, and the author was the medium, he wrote and recorded in a spontaneous fashion. Lyrics were rarely edited (when the song was flowing, that is), melodies were freely borrowed, and recording involved uninhibited performance. The spontaneity—a literal casting of one's creative fate to the wind—was the centerpiece of the inventive process. The creative imperative (the mission) provided the narrative anchor. Each edit, each additional take, each compromise detracted from the intuitive qualities, and inspirational power, of the original message. Remember how he attempted to orchestrate the original *Blood On The Tracks* sessions? No one could follow him. Remember how he recorded *Desire*? It worked that time. As much as possible, Zimmerman aspired to keep it simple: Raise the antenna, be sensitive, receive, and deliver with passion ("Little Richard" to the end). In his first 1978 interview with Jonathan Cott, he described this orientation: "You must be vulnerable to be sensitive to reality. And to me being vulnerable is just another way of saying that one has nothing more to lose. I don't have anything but darkness to lose. I'm way beyond that." With nothing to lose, the artist has everything to gain.

A major turning point occurred in 1974 as Zimmerman's spontaneous art evolved into systematic craft. For an extended period, the method that Dylan describes so well in his 1960s and 2004 interviews disappears. Recall his interview with Cott that I mentioned after the review of *John Wesley Harding* and how the songwriter claimed he had "amnesia" for a period following *Blonde On Blonde*. There, Dylan explained that the *John Wesley Harding* and *Nashville Skyline* projects were, in a sense, writing lessons, as the former involved a precise use of language while the latter featured expressions placed "between the lines." The two cover albums that followed (*Self Portrait* and *Dylan*) indicate that the writer's "connection" with his muse was indeed strained (among other things). He admitted that he "was convinced" that he "wasn't going to do anything else" until he met a New York art teacher who taught him "how to see." Norman Raeben's instruction complemented his student's personal situation to enable the *Blood On The Tracks* project. Afterward, he turned to Jacques Levy for help with *Desire*. Things had most certainly changed. Not until the moral period did the auteur's pen return to its old mode of operation. For well over ten years, Zimmerman struggled. The postman ceased to *receive* his mail and had to devise ways to *produce* those letters. When heavenly inspiration repaired those natural antennas, the songwriting reverted to its old methods—until, that is, his mission was completed.

After the spiritual fervor faded, the creative imperative that supported the work experienced a loss of intensity as Raeben's techniques stimulated a craft while it stymied an instinct. Raeben may have taught the artist how to connect his eye, hand, and mind, but that technical connection had little to do with Zimmerman's inspiration. A period of narrative flippancy followed that would continue through the early 1990s. Zimmerman had always toyed with words, lines, and images; now he dallied with entire songs (and, occasionally, albums). Creatively, the songwriter resigned himself to a different standard as the artistic process—once again—reversed itself. The intuitive writings that were spontaneously recorded were replaced by deliberate statements that were systematically produced. As his piano lessons and college education revealed, Bob Zimmerman does *not* operate in this manner.

This creative quandary is evident in Paul Williams's account of 1985's *Empire Burlesque*'s songwriting. He claims many of the ideas and phrases from that project came from movies: *Maltese Falcon, Key Largo, The Big Sleep, To Have and Have Not, The Hustler*, and more (including *Star Trek*). Although this is not inconsistent with using newspapers, photographs, or gardening manuals for inspiration, the evidence indicates that Zimmerman was struggling during this particular period. One explanation may be that when he *tries* to write, the author experiences difficulty, as these comments to Flanagan indicate: "*Anything* I try to write about, I can't do it. If I try to write *about* something—'I want to write about horses' or 'I want to write about Central Park' or 'I want to write about the cocaine industry'—I can't get anywhere with that. . . . What's anything about? It's not about anything. It is what it is." *This* from one of music history's great topical songwriters? Is this to suggest that Zimmerman did not "try" when he wrote about the John Birch Society, Hattie Carroll, Woody Guthrie, or the Bear Mountain picnic?

I think not. What he means is that he does not write in the fashion of a professional—Brill Building or Nashville—songwriter. To sit down and chart a story's development or a project's structure is to "try" in Zimmerman's artistic vernacular. Remember, he said he was "trying" to be a "poet" when he wrote *John Wesley Harding*. The result? All those songs were articulated through identical structures (i.e., three eight-line verses). The auteur had resigned himself to cookie-cutter songwriting. Moreover, ventures that require structure in order to sustain any semblance of coherence (e.g., the *Renaldo & Clara* film or the *Tarantula* book) suffer in their delivery, and their inspirational impact is diluted. In the 1980s Dylan's recordings became more and more structured, the producer's role expanded, and the writing grew increasingly calculated. He was, in every respect, *trying* to write. Though he acknowledged that his creative peak had passed, he regularly entered the recording situation and, at times literally, forced albums out—many times, it appeared, with callous disregard for song selection. Adding to this creative confusion was our next topic: the artist's difficulties with the recording process.

Zimmerman *wants* to record the way he writes. He *wants* to harness an impulse and ride that thin, wild mercurial inspiration. He *wants* everybody to go to that special place with him. What "Dylan" *wants* in the studio he rarely receives. Nat Hentoff's 1964 *New Yorker* piece cites producer Tom Wilson's view regarding his artist's recording style: "You don't think in terms of orthodox recording techniques when you're dealing with Dylan. You have to learn to be as free on this side of the glass as he is out there." Unfortunately, the artist needed more than freedom. In an interview with Greg Kot, producer T-Bone Burnett characterized Dylan-in-the-studio as "unproduceable [*sic*], truly unmanageable," and described how he would record him: "If I were to produce a record with Bob, what I'd do is sneak next to his house and hang a microphone from the bedroom window while he was writing a song, and when I'd gotten enough songs I'd give it to the record company." The artist could do *that* himself. Outside of Daniel Lanois or Jerry Wexler, most of Dylan's producers brought nothing to the party. Eventually, the art suffered as a result.

Little doubt that the genesis of this "truly unmanageable" style involves Zimmerman's attitude toward the recording industry and its agenda—a perspective that was reinforced by these hands-off producers. During Flanagan's interview, Dylan admitted that "a lot of my records have been made because it's—quote—time to make a record. . . . Sometimes I've never done the songs before—I'll just write 'em and put 'em somewhere. Then when I'm making a record I'll need some songs, and I'll start digging through my pockets and drawers trying to find these songs." He continued,

"Sometimes great things happen, sometimes not-so-great things happen. But regardless of what happens, when I do it in the studio it's the first time I've ever done it." There's a cavalier attitude for you! That Dylan told Flanagan that producers "usually get in the way" and how producers are "fine for picking you up at the airport and making sure all the bills are paid at your hotel" indicates his attitude about the production process and the personnel involved. Perhaps Dylan's third producer, Bob Johnston, said it best in his interview with Robert Shelton. He described Dylan's intensity in the studio and his decision to back off, let the artist go, and do what he can to make him "smile" when the day is done. Johnston obviously thinks that is a good thing. I disagree.

Zimmerman fell into this recording method for two reasons. First, the postman/medium did not require ensemble recording techniques to capture and disseminate the messages/thoughts he received—the freer the flow, the cleaner the message; and second, the postman despised the approach. Biographers report how Bob Dylan's first recording session (for Harry Belafonte) featured countless takes that required everyone to play their respective parts over and over and over. Afterward, the apprentice declared "Never again," and his subsequent experiences with Big Joe Williams and John Hammond reinforced his position. He offered these views to the BBC's *The Bob Dylan Story*:

> Recording a song bores me. It's like working in a coal mine. Well, I mean, it's not really as serious as that. I mean you're not completely that far underground . . . in a literal sense. But . . . you could be indoors for months and never know it, you know. I mean, what you think is real, it's just not anymore. All you're listening to are sounds all the time and your whole world is . . . working with tapes and things and I've never liked that side of it. Plus, I never got into it on that level. When I recorded, I just went in and recorded a song I had. That's the way people recorded then. But the people don't record that way and I shouldn't record that way either because they can't even get it down that way anymore. To do what I used to do or to do what anybody used to do, you have to stay in the studio a longer time to even get that . . . because technology has messed everything up so much.

The "coal mine" analogy is revealing. By entering that coal mine, you lose touch with "what you think is real," and *that* is a serious distraction for our auteur. Consequently, he "never got into it on that level" and opted for different standards of technical expression. Remember what he stated earlier when he described his "wild mercury sound," its "natural" qualities, and his rejection of perfection? When a song is done, it is done; so, he enters his coal mine and exits as quickly as possible. This often places a strain on his supporting cast. To that end, Tim Riley describes Dylan's recording style in this fashion: "This is like learning how to drive during freeway rush hour—reaction is all, and every moment is charged with a sense of nervy anticipation. The musicians didn't know what the next line was, never mind what sort of sardonic topspin Dylan's delivery would give it. It's gut-charged music-making without a net." Perhaps *that* is the secret to that "thin wild mercury sound." With everyone on edge, the magic flows. Yet, had the producers risen to this challenge—as opposed to acquiescing to what was considered to be idiosyncrasy—they could have done much more with Bob Dylan. But they did not, and the results demonstrate their absence in many instances. Young Dylan certainly had the creative energy necessary to achieve his missions, that is for sure. As his career continued, I think he could have used some help. At times, he did. When Wexler rose to the occasion, it was frustrating. When Lanois rose to the occasion, it was very frustrating. Nevertheless, just listen to *Slow Train* and *Oh Mercy*. I think those frustrations paid off.

Just as Dylan's BBC remarks suggest, his negative attitude toward the production process was exacerbated by the technologies of the 1980s. In 1985, Dylan expressed his frustrations to David Fricke: "My difficulty in making a record . . . is that when I record something in a studio, it never sounds anything like it when I get the tapes back. Whatever kind of live sound I'm working for, it always gets lost in the machines. Years ago, I could go in, do it and it would translate onto tape. It gets so cleaned up today that anything wrong you do doesn't get onto the tape. And my stuff is based on wrong things." Throughout the 1980s, Dylan drifted from producer to producer (including producing himself), searching for someone who could capture the sound perfected "years ago." His 1993 comments to the *Chicago Tribune* elaborate on the problem:

> Modern recording technology never endeared itself to me. . . . My kind of sound is very simple, with a little bit of echo, and that's about all that's required to record it. I'm most disappointed when producers overlook the strength of my music. The way most records sound these days, everything is equalized. My kind of music is based on non-equalized parts, where one sound isn't necessarily supposed to be as loud as another. When producers try to equal everything out, it's to dismal effect on my records.

Once more, any attempt to edit the postman's mail detracts from the original message and hinders the delivery process. Electronic innovations are artistic distractions (digital, ensemble recording is the functional equivalent of e-mail for this postman). For a letter to arrive slightly crumpled with indecipherable handwriting is part of the message's beauty. Word processors or digital soundboards may clean up the final product, but they dilute the emotional impact of the original idea/thought. A talented producer could have easily rectified this difficulty.

After close to thirty-five years of struggle, the process reverted to its original approach with 2001's *Love And Theft*. There, the auteur reached the perfect compromise in that he was able to achieve a state of calculated spontaneity in the studio. With a road-tested band able to anticipate every musical move, the songwriter revisited his old, spontaneous writing technique (remember Augie Meyers's remarks about Dylan writing in the studio?). He explained the state of his writing to *Rolling Stone*:

> Well, I follow the dictates of my conscience to write a song, and I don't really have a time or place I set aside. I don't really preconceive it. I couldn't tell you when I could come up with something. It just happens at odd times, here and there. It's amazing to me that I'm still able to *do* it,

really.... When you're young, you're probably writing stronger and a lot quicker, but in my case, I just try to use the traditional values of logic and reason no matter what age I've ever written any of my songs.

He elaborated on this creative method for the *Los Angeles Times*: "Some things just come to me in dreams. But I can write a bunch of stuff down after you leave... about, say, the way you are dressed. I look at people as ideas. I don't look at them as people. I'm talking about general observation. Whoever I see, I look at them as ideas...what this person represents. That's the way I see life. I see life as a utilitarian thing. Then you strip things away until you get to the core of what's important." The quest for that thin, wild mercury sound—and the words that punctuate it—continues. A thirty-five-year creative search ends *exactly* where it began, almost. Like Dylan acknowledged in his 2004 *60 Minutes* interview, he may no longer receive songs such as "It's Alright, Ma" in that old magical way, but he can "do other things" now. The artist assimilated a host of influences and techniques, and they enable his creative work to continue.

Complementing the auteur's writing and recording methods are his performance techniques. Bob Dylan's performance orientation has, most assuredly, evolved throughout his forty-year career. Like his language use, narrative style, or production methods and their mission-oriented applications, Dylan's performances—onstage and offstage—vary according to the creative agenda. From the self-effacing young folk apprentice, to the combative Newport Mod, to the reclusive resident genius, to his commercially defiant vaudeville act, to his pious gospel show, to the confused indifference of his 1980s tours, to his heartfelt musical renaissance of the mid-1990s, Dylan's performance style has varied with the needs of the moment. Just think about these radical stylistic differences and what they say about the volatile qualities of Zimmerman's career. The laughing, playful, Chaplinesque entertainer from the Greenwich Village period suddenly turns cold, aloof, and mysterious. An aesthetic war ensues, artist-audience battles follow, the decadence of *Eat The Document* unfolds, and the motorcycle accident brings to a halt what surely had to end. Afterward, a warmer, but still mysterious, performer appears. He acquiesces to commercial pressures and returns to touring via a gigantic production that leaves him empty and disillusioned. He feels used. In response, he proposes anti–Tour '74, the Rolling Thunder Revue. This, too, plays out in its own—seemingly unfulfilling—way. To the rescue comes the Lord and a return to the confrontational style of the Jacket Jamboree and the Newport Mod era, except this time the Word fuels the performance. This, too, plays out, and Zimmerman is left at another artistic crossroads. Now, a long debilitating struggle follows. He tries different strategies, to no avail. He distorts, contorts, and vilifies his music, but he *never* stops trying. The media write him off as a relic, but he persists. He rediscovers old vocal techniques, dusts off Lonnie Johnson's guitar lessons, and develops yet another artistic plan. From it all comes the Never Ending Series of Tours starring Jack Fate and a peace of mind that, somehow and in some way, synthesizes all of his previous experiences into a positive outcome. What a story.

Throughout this musical maturation, we observe various mixtures of the Glissendorf, Basement Strategy, topicality creative cocktail. If Zimmerman is in a positive frame of mind, we may witness a cessation of the musical gamesmanship and earnest musicianship. Should he perceive the need to confront his circumstances, we may observe a variety of lyrical and musical revisions or innovations that distance the auteur from his oeuvre. And should he, for some reason, feel antagonistic toward the situation, we may see outright hostility. Always there is distance. It is merely a matter of degree: a warm disengagement, a cool aloofness, or a cold confrontation. The context dictates the act. But *never* does he engage an audience, *never* does he empower an audience. His distance enables him to control the situation. The Bob Dillon portion of the Dylan composite is always prepared to do his thing. Dillon is an essential part of this artistic operation. He provides a balance that enables Zimmerman to deploy Jack Fate in service of specific missions that are free from any audience, unless, that is, the mission involves rejecting or rebelling against that audience—or, perhaps, *saving* an audience.

One performance context that has not changed over the years is Bob Dylan's work offstage. Here, too, the auteur performs for his public in yet another clever manifestation of the Glissendorf strategy. From the outset, Dylan's performances before the media have pursued private agendas. What started with celebrity fabrications quickly evolved into combative confrontations. Such antics have inspired knowledgeable writers such as Robert Shelton to conclude that *everything* Dylan does is a performance, that there is, indeed, no time in which he removes his mask to engage the public (don't forget that burning question from *Eat The Document*: Are you ever not onstage?). Just as he obliterated his songs in their *Budokan* or *Hard Rain* incarnations, he may trivialize a crucial biographical point—or fabricate a replacement—in an interview. Of course, a favorite strategy is to merely turn the question around on the interviewer ("Well, how have *you* changed since the sixties?" Dylan often fires back in response to the question that refuses to go away). "Bob Dylan" is the poster boy for the "Trust the art, not the artist" critical philosophy.

Besides, from a performance perspective, it was all downhill after the Jacket Jamboree anyway. Bob Zimmerman knew *then* who he was playing for, and it has never, ever changed. Even when his creative motives seemed most obvious (during the moral period), he served a personal function (testimony). This loyalty to self—this commitment to the muse—is Zimmerman's saving grace as an artist. Had he allowed "outsiders" to dictate his writing or performing styles or had he endeavored to "communicate" with a specific audience, he could have fallen prey to their wishes—and, my friends, *that* is *not* how you play Glissendorf.

The most amazing aspect of Bob Zimmerman's creative impulse is its simplicity. No part of his inventive process is complicated; in fact, the more sophisticated the act, the less meaningful the expression is for the author. This is, in every respect, art—not craft. The instinctive, free-flowing qualities of Zimmerman's storytelling—whether the narrative appears in song or poetry—are their defining characteristics. He told Paul Zollo, "In my mind it's never really been seriously a profession. . . . It's been more confessional that professional. . . . Then again, everybody's in it for a different reason." True. And Dylan's "reasons" changed periodically. His creative mission directly influenced the content of these spontaneous confessions: An aspiring folksinger applies that genre's traditional vernacular, an emerging poet employs that art form's intuitive imagination, a celebration of Americana expands on that art form's history, a poetic preacher synthesizes art and morality, and a professional musician manages the tensions associated with a commercial process that involves art *and* craft. In many respects, it is as if a pure act is constantly threatened by impure influences. Although Paul Williams questions the content-context relationship in his work, Zimmerman's career indicates the extent to which that content *is shaped by its context*. Whether he is writing the words or music or is recording both, "Bob Dylan's" art is the product of intuitive powers that represent the heart and soul of Bob Zimmerman's talent. To interject his brain is to dilute the process. Zimmerman is a medium with a special talent for shaping the emotional messages that flow through him. He may convert that thought into a folk song, a poetic abstraction, a country tune, a hymn, or a pop song. In all cases, the writer *feels* the message or thought, articulates that intuition through the critical lens that is his creative mission, and renders a self-satisfying expression that, hopefully, arouses his audience's emotions in an inspiring fashion. That, dear readers, is the key to that thin, wild mercury sound: It is a product of Bob Zimmerman's talent—an ability that generated the various scripts from which Zimmerman's Dylan characters worked.

Writing Dylan: The Stylistic Tendencies

Bob Zimmerman is a remarkably consistent writer. For an artist who claims to be so spontaneous, his work bears specific stamps that clearly identify him. When we construe the individual songs, albums, and eras that comprise the lifework, five narrative strategies emerge that not only recur throughout the oeuvre, but also dominate it. The narrative strategies—the complaint, the celebration, the satire, narrative impressionism, and wordplay—duck and weave their way through the various songs and, at times, control certain projects. *Street-Legal* is a statement of unrelenting negativity. *Saved* is a celebratory revival and a call for personal salvation. *Bringing It All Back Home* and *Highway 61 Revisited* are monuments of artistic innovation that liberated songwriters and transformed their art form. Though no single project focuses on the satire, it is the only story form to evolve systematically over time. The writer's satirical tendencies often suggest his state of mind and yield evidence regarding his professional orientation.

When considered chronologically, the lifework assumes certain rhythms of expression that embrace their creative *contexts*. That is, the mission dominates the expression's articulation. The complaint controls the folk-posturing period as it solidifies its standing as the oeuvre's bedrock story form. Whether he complains about relational or societal matters, Zimmerman's intensity is the defining characteristic of this storytelling strategy. Impressionistic wordplay governs the Newport Mod era, as the rebellious Bob Dillon expands Bob Dylan's creative boundaries. In pushing his creativity, the author also challenged his physical well-being; thus, after the Woodstock respite and the transitional statements within *John Wesley Harding*, a reinvigorated writer explores affairs of the heart for an extended, seven-album period. There he celebrates as much as he complains (well, almost) about relationships and their consequences. *Legal's* negativity introduces the moral period's three-phase spiritual journey in which Dylan forewarns, celebrates, and, afterwards, resolves his public quest for ultimate knowledge. From that point on, his stories focus on relationships with occasional asides for social issues, celebrity portraits, or satirical commentaries.

Throughout the respective projects, we note the intensity and innovation, the adaptation and cultivation, as well as the assimilative powers of Bob Zimmerman's art. His songs complain, celebrate, satirize, and fondle the various emotions associated with life's experiences in an idiosyncratic, adventurous, and ultimately cumulative manner. While Zimmerman cultivates these feelings, he applies an American worldview that informs the content and style of his subsequent observations. To claim "Bob Dylan" is grounded firmly in Jack Fate's encyclopedic knowledge of American roots music—and that those traditions provided signposts for Bob Zimmerman's artistic journey—is supported by none other than the work itself. As Dylan told David Gates about the religious conversion controversy, he has "learned more from the songs" than anything else in life (a point he reinforced with the same reporter in 2004). Let us now turn to those songs and appreciate the consistency of Zimmerman's writing for his Dylan characters.

From *Bob Dylan* through *Love And Theft*, the auteur has complained. The principal variables involve the intensity of the emotion and the internal workings of the portrayal. The *Freewheelin'* project sets the pace for the entire oeuvre as it establishes the two domains of negativity: relational and societal issues. The romantic elegies "Down The Highway" and "Don't Think Twice, It's All Right" (and the three adaptations) complement the societal statements "Blowin' In The Wind," "Masters Of War," and "Oxford Town" to inaugurate a narrative rhythm that extends for over forty years. The momentum continues with *The Times They Are A-Changin'* except, this time, the emphasis is clearly on social topics. "Hollis Brown," "With God On Our Side," "Only A Pawn In Their Game," "North Country Blues," and "Hattie Carroll" constitute a hallmark of topical complaint (the relational elegies "One Too Many Mornings" and "Boots Of Spanish Leather" join in the fun as well). Throughout, we observe the *intensity* of Zimmerman's pen as he not only complains, but also passionately embraces the injustices depicted in his songs. *Another Side* reverses that topical trend and takes us into relational concerns as the songwriter redirects his "finger-pointing" genre (e.g., "It Ain't Me, Babe," "I Don't Believe You," and the devastating "Ballad In Plain D"). These grievances fade for the next few projects as Zimmerman's wordplay emerges and provides a much-needed respite from this rage of negativity.

The relational complaint returns with *Blonde*'s seven entries (e.g., "One Of Us Must Know," "Just Like A Woman," and "Most Likely You Go Your Way") and continues for seven albums (not including *Portrait* and *Dylan*). Many of these works feature a blend of complaint and celebration as "Bob Dylan" concentrates on the vacillating qualities of loving relationships throughout the 1970s. Of course, *Blood On The Tracks* takes the relational angst theme to new levels of intensity, with *Desire* and *Street-Legal* echoing those emotions—each in its own way. After *Legal*'s abject negativity, the complaint spawns a thematic variation with the rise of the "warning" strategy (a style that dominates *Slow Train*). These songs establish the negative as a preface to The Answer that flows from the conversion rhetoric. The "warning" theme returns in *Saved*'s "Are You Ready?" and reappears via *Infidels*' "Man Of Peace," *Burlesque*'s "Trust Yourself," and *Mercy*'s "Ring Them Bells" and "Disease Of Conceit." Once the spiritual shot has been fired across the worldly bow, the pop icon phase concentrates on relational concerns with dashes of societal complaint appearing from time to time (e.g., *Infidels'* "Neighborhood Bully" and "Union Sundown" along with *Mercy's* "Political World" and "Everything Is Broken"). *Time Out Of Mind* addresses the dark side of human relationships in a particularly relentless, moody fashion. Finally, *Love And Theft's* "Honest With Me," "Cry A While," and "Sugar Baby" hammer their relational complaints home, while "Mississippi," "Summer Days," and "Lonesome Day Blues" blend the relational grievances that control *Time Out Of Mind* with life complaints and provide stellar examples of this foundational storytelling tactic. There is no question that the complaint is the most frequently deployed narrative strategy in Bob Dylan's oeuvre.

Our second strategy, the celebration, first appears in Dylan's debut album. "Talking New York" and "Song To Woody" initiate the "In praise of thee I sing" approach through two songs that complain about the difficulties the traveling musician endures before celebrating "the road" and its rewards in the stories' resolutions. The tactic returns briefly with "Bob Dylan's Blues" on *Freewheelin'* before shifting thematic gears from personal to societal topics in *The Times They Are A-Changin'*. There, the title cut and "When The Ship Comes In" celebrate the ultimate victory achieved by the acceptance of a change in social consciousness and the benefits of perseverance, respectively. *Times* also celebrates a personal transition in "Restless Farewell" when the author bids goodbye to the folk-posturing period. After the Newport Mod's word games, the celebration strategy returns with a force. Beginning with *Harding's* two songs of relational veneration ("Down Along The Cove" and "I'll Be Your Baby Tonight"), the Americana period contains a level of relational revelry unlike any other portion of the oeuvre. *Skyline's* five songs of loving observance (e.g., "To Be Alone With You," "Peggy Day," and "Tonight I'll Be Staying Here With You"), *Morning's* six songs of romantic bliss (e.g., "If Not For You," "New Morning," and "The Man In Me"), *Waves'* six accounts of relational joy (e.g., "Tough Mama," "You Angel You," and "Wedding Song"), and, later, *Desire's* "Mozambique" convey sentiments that represent a striking balance to the relational negativity interspersed throughout those albums.

The celebration strategy reaches its peak in *Saved*. *Saved* is a testament to spiritual contentment as the auteur declares his devotion ("Saved"), praises his "Covenant Woman," and relishes his commitment to Christ ("Solid Rock" and "Pressing On"). The celebrations end with *Saved*. Although we pause for brief moments of relational veneration from time to time (*Infidels'* "Sweetheart Like You," *Burlesque's* "Emotionally Yours," *Groove's* "Had A Dream About You, Baby" and "Ugliest Girl In The World," and *Red Sky's* "God Knows"), the celebration story form gives way to other matters.

While songs of celebration do not enjoy the narrative status that the complaints occupy, Zimmerman's capacity to weave positive songs of heartfelt emotion demonstrates that his narrative sword does, in fact, cut two ways. That this narrative strategy wanes in the latter portions of the oeuvre is unfortunate and, perhaps, suggestive of the control Zimmerman's creative context exerts over his pen. *Saved* and the relational celebrations on *Skyline*, *Morning*, and *Waves* relate how this attention to detail may highlight the subtle nuances of positive situations just as the writer uses that trait to explore the dark sides of life. The author's joy—like his humor—is a welcome addition to the lifework—especially when we consider the intensity of the negativity.

Our third narrative strategy is the oeuvre's most complicated and is the only approach to systematically evolve across the lifework. Zimmerman's satires never dominate his pen as the complaints, celebrations, or impressionism do; nevertheless, they convey his sense of humor, his moralistic storytelling, and a narrative precision unlike any other strategy. The humor first appears in the celebratory "Talking New York," as the auteur establishes the presentational rhythm that fuels many of the satires from the folk-posturing phase. With "Talkin' World War III," "Talkin' John Birch," and "Talking Bear Mountain," the writer perfects a fun, crazy examination of life's recurrent situations with each entry stressing a particular moral. For example, Zimmerman portrays the paranoid dreams of the Cold War mentality ("WWIII"), the stupidity of bigotry ("Birch"), and the silliness of greed ("Bear") through narratives with similar structures: The songs feature rich descriptive statements that are followed by short bursts of humorous commentary. After *Another Side*'s "Motorpsycho Nightmare" (an adaptation of the traveling salesman tale) and *Back Home*'s "Bob Dylan's 115th Dream" (a revisionist view of American history), the strategy disappears amongst the Newport Mod's wordplay.

When the satire returns with *Harding*'s "Frankie Lee and Judas Priest," we note a difference in the strategy's application as the comical asides (i.e., the short bursts of comments) are replaced by more detailed scenic descriptions and characterizations. At this point, the satire begins to split into two new manifestations: the portrait and the saga. *Harding*'s two portraits—the title cut and "I Dreamed I Saw St. Augustine"—introduce the shift away from campfire tomfoolery; nonetheless, the stories continue with their detail and moralistic messages. The transition advances with "Lily, Rosemary" from *Tracks* and its lighthearted invocation of the album's betrayal theme. With *Desire*, Dylan and Levy extend the evolution through the two portraits ("Joey" and "Hurricane") and the two sagas ("Durango" and "Diamond Bay"). Here, narrative detail replaces satirical humor as the story form's prime mover; in short, more precision, less passion. The satire disappears during the moral period and returns ever so slightly with *Shot Of Love*'s uneven portrait, "Lenny Bruce." While 1997's "Highlands" relates the satire's rich detail and moral overtones, this narrative strategy joins the relational-societal celebration in retirement. Too bad. Zimmerman does an excellent job with this narrative style.

The recordings of early performances indicate that the satire was an important part of young Bob Dylan's act. The humor, the topicality, and the rhythm of expression involved in these often elaborate stories were well suited to his emerging persona. Later on, when the wordplay controlled the oeuvre, the strategy gave way to a different—yet related—narrative game. With the satire's evolution into the saga and portrait, its driving force, the humor, dissipated drastically and, in many respects, detracted significantly from the storytelling strategy. The Traveling Wilburys' "Tweeter And The Monkey Man" (supposedly a spoof on Bruce Springsteen's narrative style), "Highlands," and the marvelous epic " 'Cross The Green Mountain" (from the soundtrack for the film *Gods And Generals*) indicate that Zimmerman maintains the capacity to write in this fashion, but—for whatever reason—this narrative strategy continues, by and large, to rest in peace.

From *stories* that complain, celebrate, and satirize, we move to Bob Zimmerman's pioneering achievements in lyrical impressionism. These nonstories appear in two basic forms: organized and disorganized wordplay. We begin with the former, and the narrative impressionism. Here we witness free verse poetry married to lyrical refrains and recurrent musical structures. That is, a line or two of lyric may accompany a recurring musical figure to create the illusion of narrative coherence, when in actuality the structure merely frames the wordplay contained within. The strategy first appeared on *Freewheelin'* via "A Hard Rain's A-Gonna Fall." The writer previewed the strategy once more on *Another Side* by way of "My Back Pages" and "Chimes Of Freedom" and their direct invocation of the "Hard Rain" strategy. Here, though, the individual stanzas begin to assume more internal coherence, although any relationship between the vignettes (i.e., the respective verses) is thematic in the loose sense of the term. The impressionistic strategy explodes with *Back Home* and *Highway 61*. At this point, the impressionism follows the complaint and celebration in its application to relational and societal contexts. *Back Home* features impressionistic accounts of societal issues ("Gates Of Eden" and "It's Alright, Ma [I'm Only Bleeding]") and relational matters ("She Belongs To Me" and "Love Minus Zero/No Limit") as well as the fantasy-filled, escapist self-exploration, "Mr. Tambourine Man." The fun continues with *Highway 61* and its impressionistic portrayal of relationships ("Like A Rolling Stone," "It Takes A Lot To Laugh," and "From A Buick 6") and that crazy harbinger of evil, "Highway 61." It sounds like an overwhelming overstatement to say these songs changed the musical world. I mean, how could a few songs on *any* set of albums change that much? How, indeed.

The narrative impressionism continues on one half of *Blonde* with the song of oppression (the much misread "Rainy Day Women #12 & 35") and four accounts of relational matters (e.g., "Leopard-Skin Pill-Box Hat" and "Sad Eyed Lady Of the Lowlands"). At that point, the adventurous pioneering ceased. *Harding* issues a pale version of the strategy via "All Along The Watchtower," just as *Infidels* and *Burlesque* return to adaptations with "Jokerman" and "Tight Connection," respectively. Whatever prompted Zimmerman's rebellion toward his chosen profession—and I sense Bob Dillon's rejection of the Western Union mentality here—it rendered a marvelous era of lyrical innovation. An impressionistic renaissance occurred with 2001's *Love And Theft* by way of "Tweedle Dee & Tweedle Dum" and the sermonic impressions in "Floater," "High Water," and "Po Boy." *Love And Theft*'s impressionism reveals the essential role this songwriting strategy performs within the auteur's musical repertoire. When musical confidence facilitates spontaneity, the words flow freely and imaginatively. *Love And Theft*'s humor also signaled Zimmerman's all-important creative state of mind.

The auteur's narrative impressionism is but one part of the innovative songwriting that characterized the Newport Mod phase. The playful, free-form metaphors that were framed by recurring tag lines or musical phrases enjoyed even more freedom through songs of unadulterated wordplay. Beginning with *Freewheelin'* and "I Shall Be Free" as well as the follow-up, *Another Side*'s "I Shall Be Free #10," Zimmerman initiated a songwriting style free of narrative structures. *Nothing* holds this surreal imagery and free association wordplay together. Celebrity names or recurrent lines may repeat a phrase or image, but Zimmerman's wordplay genre, in one extreme, deploys an antilogic that invokes an antilanguage to articulate antinarratives (see *Tarantula*, in which the writing subverts the basic principles of communication—in other words, a righteous game of Glissendorf); in another extreme, it releases an energy with an unrestrained commitment to the author's personal objective, whatever that might be. In both cases, it abdicates any responsibility for author-audience communication. A Western Union boy would be a character—not a carrier—in these expressions.

After introducing the tactic with the "I Shall Be Free" entries, the Newport Mod drives it home with *Back Home* and *Highway 61*. *Back Home* offers five examples of the wordplay strategy (e.g., "Subterranean Homesick Blues," "Maggie's Farm," and "It's All Over Now, Baby Blue"), *Highway 61* another five (e.g., "Tombstone Blues," "Ballad Of A Thin Man," "Just Like Tom Thumb's Blues," and "Desolation Row"), and *Blonde* our final two installments ("Visions Of Johanna" and "Stuck Inside Of Mobile With the Memphis Blues Again"). Nobody had ever written *songs* like these before, and they rippled throughout the musical world.

Rest assured, not all of Zimmerman's work falls neatly into these five narrative orientations; however, it is remarkable how many songs fit firmly into the respective categories. There is a continuity of expression that is, in every respect, the hallmark of the auteur. There *are* stylistic tendencies that are systematically applied. There *is* a rhythm of expression within the writings. When Zimmerman steps outside these structures for songs such as *Waves*' prayers (the two versions of "Forever Young"), *Slow Train*'s statement of "commitment" ("I Believe In You"), *Time Out Of Mind*'s loving pledge ("Make You Feel My Love"), *Love And Theft*'s personal proclamations ("Bye And Bye" and "Moonlight"), the nostalgia on *Freewheelin'* ("Bob Dylan's Dream"), or the nonsensical ditties on *Red Sky*, he uses language in idiosyncratic ways that also indicate his authorship. When we pause to consider that this is *forty years* of work, well, the continuity evident within the lifework offers powerful evidence of Dylan-the-auteur, doesn't it?

To conclude this study of Bob Dylan's oeuvre, I think we should return to this chapter's "creative impulse" section and the auteur's discussion of art's function, his artistic influences, and his creative objectives. The public "Dylan"—a man who can be more than evasive—was clear in his explanations of art's purpose and his ambitions within that framework. He relates that art's purpose is to inspire audiences through emotional expressions that challenge the status quo. To achieve that end, he employs Jack Fate's knowledge of music tradition (his "roots") in an effort to generate art that pleases him. For Zimmerman, if the work pleases *him*, if it challenges *him*, if it inspires *him* to assess *his* situation, then his creative goal is achieved. Dylan told *Melody Maker*, "My songs are just me talking to myself. . . . I have no responsibility to anybody except myself. If people like me—fine. If they don't, then maybe I'll do something else." This is not an audience-dependent artist. He neither labors over expressions nor longs for audience approval. In point of fact, he is *exactly* the opposite. If an album sounds *too* pleasing, then he shifts it around. If audiences oppose a particular innovation or idea, he confronts them and forces them to endure his perspective. He has perpetuated this attitude his entire life. Bob Zimmerman—true to the culture that spawned him—is as rebellious as any artist who has ever worked. The Bob Dillon dimension of the Dylan composite is a vital element of this creative orientation—an inventive process that is fiercely independent and decidedly, if not overwhelmingly, self-centered.

Zimmerman's artistic philosophy manifests directly in his work. His emphasis on emotional inspiration is evident in his rejection of logic and, occasionally, facts. The writer will, at any time, convolute factual evidence for the desired dramatic effect. Since he endeavors to challenge the establishment (whatever that may be; it could be an ongoing relationship or musical tradition), he willfully subverts whatever principles are before him in service of his goal. Who cares if he misrepresents his arrival in New York, or the facts surrounding Hattie Carroll's death, or the details pertaining to Rubin Carter's case, or Joey Gallo's biography, or any aspect of American history? If anyone looks to "Bob Dylan" to separate fact from fiction in his stories or to persuade them toward a particular end, that individual is *using* the work in a fashion inconsistent with its creation. While in his youth, Zimmerman wrote topical songs as he would have written advertising jingles. He did what he felt he had to do to enter his chosen profession. Only during his spiritual conversion did he use his art in a persuasive manner (for *one* album), but that application was so straightforward as to raise no questions regarding his creative agenda. If he has ever been a spokesperson for anything, it has been for himself—the rebel's lifelong cause.

Zimmerman has remained remarkably consistent in his pursuit of his creative goals. He has successfully expressed himself and served his inspirational roots. His steadfast dedication to his musical heritage is his guiding beacon. His rededication to performance in the 1990s and his relentless commitment to touring demonstrate his complete allegiance to his *music*. His innovative songwriting clearly complements that orientation. For most of "Bob Dylan's" work, he dutifully subscribed to the songwriting prescriptions of specific genres. His country, folk, gospel, pop, and rock-and-roll songs all stay within the expectations of that particular branch of traditional American music. For a brief period in the mid-1960s, he took that craft into another realm. He allowed his muse to have its way, and the art flowed *through* him. It was his greatest game of Glissendorf. (He won!) The satisfaction gleaned from the successful manipulation of an international audience must have been wonderfully rewarding for the Iron Range's most famous biker-poet. The postman's deliveries assumed a new, free-flowing form, and the mail would never be the same again—regardless of the carrier. This postman walked specific routes that displayed their own unique characteristics. To be sure, that route dictated the content and style of the subsequent work. Hence, we now turn to those "missions" one last time as we contemplate their impact on the auteur's oeuvre.

Writing Dylan: The Missions

The October 10, 2004, edition of the television program *CBS Morning* featured a segment celebrating Bob Dylan's art and contemplating its historic value. Noted scholar and Dylanologist Christopher Ricks was a guest on that show. Ricks was so articulate. He conveyed great confidence in his conclusions about the Archbishop of Anarchy's lifework. Amongst his many comments, he argued that Dylan's work—like the famed painter Picasso's art—passed through a series of phases as it unfolded over time. I have tremendous respect for Ricks's ideas, but I fear he missed the boat with that particular claim. Dylan's lifework did not unfold by way of a series of developmental phases; to the contrary, the artist systematically pursued a number of strategic missions that emerged as his career progressed. Yes, in some respects, each mission benefited from what had passed before it. Yes, in some cases, a mission responded to what had transpired earlier. But the respective eras operated under their own imperatives. They followed an artistic logic—not a personal ambition or a developmental progression—that responded to a creative exigency. Bob Zimmerman seems to be able to set himself aside when he writes for his Dylan characters (remember, these are *attitudes*, not *autobiography*). The professional ambitions of the folk-posturing period, the artistic response of the Newport Mod era, the required recovery of the Americana period, the professional reorientation of the crystallization era, the mandated service of the moral period, the second professional reorientation demanded by the pop icon era, and the joy of service associated with Jack Fate's mission demonstrate how Zimmerman embraced specific tasks that served his perceived artistic needs in a systematic manner. This is not a developmental phenomenon. Bob Zimmerman has told stories all of his life. The Jack Fate dimension of the Dylan composite has always adored performance and worshiped the music. The Bob Dillon dimension of Dylan's persona has always been rebellious. The difference is in the application of these lifelong qualities. That application was driven by that moment's creative needs.

In *Pete Townshend: The Minstrel's Dilemma*, I argue how Townshend actively *negotiated* his art across his thirty-year career. When he wrote *Tommy* and presented those demos to a friend (journalist Nik Cohn), he readily changed his initial approach and its emphasis on the central character's spiritual quest, added the song "Pinball Wizard" to enliven the story, and shifted the project's spiritual metaphors to accommodate that revision. In other words, he negotiated the content and style of his art in order to appeal to what Cohn believed to be a larger, more receptive audience. Bob Dylan would *never* do that. He does not *negotiate* his art as much as he *orchestrates* it. As we've seen, he enters the studio with his blueprint in mind and then spontaneously records that material (or at least tries to). *Negotiation* is nowhere to be found. He *orchestrates* the sessions, and his producers do their best to make him "smile" once the session is complete (good luck!). When "Bob Dylan" smiles, his entire audience smiles with him, since he *is* his audience. When he shifted the content and style of *Blood On The Tracks*, it was because he wanted the change—I mean, the record was already in production. That many people prefer the original version of that album means nothing to our auteur. Similarly, when he removed "Blind Willie McTell" from *Infidels*, it was because he believed the album was too strong. He is as independent as any artist at any time. Bob Dillon is as active a member of the Bob Dylan composite as Jack Fate.

This yields a functional approach to songwriting that I've characterized in terms of specific songwriting missions. During the folk-posturing period, he labored to obtain an audience and, afterward, to serve its needs. Once he achieved that goal, he entered a new era (the Newport Mod) with a new objective: to reject that audience and to serve his needs. When the demands of his profession and lifestyle crashed with his motorcycle, he pursued another goal: recovery. Here he formally developed the Basement Strategy and wrote songs that flowed from that spring well. A new mission emerged after Tour '74 and his lessons with Norman Raeben, in which he labored to reorient his muse and refine his songwriting strategies. Such efforts rendered the oeuvre's first coauthored songs—a most unlikely development in Bob Dylan's creative world. Suddenly the old fire returned via a new mission: service. When Dylan accepted Christ, his songwriting function changed and the quality of his work returned to the standards we observed during his protest days. Afterward, another reorientation period followed as the auteur struggled with the technologies of the day in his search for those wild mercury sounds of yesteryear. Finally, with the public appearance of Jack Fate, a new function emerged and this, too, involved service. This time, the writer served his songs. He used musical platforms that satisfied his instincts and generated words to fit his new character. In every case, a specific creative function guided the work, and he orchestrated the production process with that objective in mind. How ironic that Bob Zimmerman's songwriting prospers best when it *serves* some purpose or cause. He may write for himself (not personally, mind you, but professionally), but those writings enjoyed their finest moments when they *served* the protest movement (the benefactor of his mission of discovery), his rebellion, his God, and his muse.

Zimmerman's early storytelling involved a concentrated application of the folk process. His legitimate use of previously established song structures and lyrics fits firmly within the folk music songwriting tradition. Consequently, we observed the writer's evolution from Guthrie jukebox, to Greenwich Village magpie, to king of American protest music during this timeframe. From his initial album's covers of traditional death songs and musical tributes; his second album's blend of romance, protest, and satire; and his third record's total concentration on the protest genre, the auteur's march toward self-expression progressed. What began with Little Richard–inspired versions of a standard coffeehouse folk repertoire assumed a distinctive quality as the simplicity of "Blowin' In The Wind" evolved into the stark vitriol of "Masters Of War" and the cryptic "verbal binge" (in Tim Riley's words) of "A Hard Rain's A-Gonna Fall" quite quickly. Throughout that rapid progression, the writer's playful satires floated in and out of the musical framework, enlivening live performances while largely remaining off record. The storytelling from this era demonstrates the writer's emotional range. The anger of "Masters" is a real contrast to the playful sarcasm of "John Birch." The imagery, the simplicity of expression, and, of course, the intensity of both stories capture Zimmerman's unique co-optation of the folk narrative style. Simply, this period features a talented wordsmith in pursuit of a job. This "mission" required the Jack Fate dimension of the emerging Dylan composite to absorb every possible influence, allow that contribution to assimilate itself, and subsequently emerge via Robert Shelton's "distinctive song stylist" that was the budding auteur. At this point, no doubt, Zimmerman's artistic philosophy of writing for himself took a backseat to writing for the market.

All of this soon changed. With acceptance came expectation, and for Bob Dylan, with expectation comes Bob Dillon's rebellion. The songs that followed contain some of his most defiant songwriting, as Zimmerman not only shied away from message music but also avoided communication altogether. The subsequent wordplay parades about unrestrained, free to dash here and there, following inspirational whims that often have no relationship to one another. The muse is at rebellious play, and everything else is irrelevant. This journey into abstraction officially opened with Bob Dylan's public announcement that he no longer wished to write for "others" and that he would now write only for himself. That is exactly what he did with the spontaneous production that was *Another Side* as the writer's finger-pointing shifted contexts from the societal to the personal. *Another Side*'s blend of sharp personal attack, satire, and impressionism not only closed an era; it is also a fine bookend to its companion piece, the narrative portion of *Blonde On Blonde*. In between we witness the anticommunication of *Back Home* and *Highway 61*, in which Dillon's rebellion runs wild through interesting mixtures of Basement musicality and Glissendorf folly. The results were original, unprecedented, and the perfect response to his pugnacious quest to reject the constricting demands that surrounded him. That Bob Zimmerman could have easily hired those Western Union boys and filled the airwaves with messages is certain. That Bob Zimmerman refused to do so is historic.

The rebellion was costly. The celebrity histrionics that accompanied his Newport Mod persona exacted a serious toll on the young wordsmith's health. Through it all, the muse, too, suffered. The "accident" provided the opportunity, and a new mission emerged: recovery. Here the Basement Strategy guided the way as the auteur immersed himself in American song for his creative convalescence. From the basements themselves, to the countrified tales of loving relationships (i.e., *Harding* and *Skyline*), to his reunion with The Band, Zimmerman explored roots music's narrative traditions as he recovered from the various abuses of celebrity. Gone were the cryptic wordplay, the evasive imagery, and the cavalier attitude that characterized the Newport Mod. In its place came lyrical sincerity, traditional musicality, and homespun wisdom about love, life, and, gradually, worldly deterioration. Although there were pauses in Zimmerman's creative rehabilitation to deal with irresponsible fanatics and irrepressible executives, the writer's pursuit of revitalization was steady and determined.

After *Planet Waves*, the songwriter's tactics shifted from the more spontaneous style that characterized his best work to date to a foreign, strange approach that typifies how most songwriters work. From Day 1, it seems, our auteur has decried the Brill Building/Tin Pan Alley method of songwriting; yet in the mid-1970s he stepped firmly in that creative path. His lessons with Norman Raeben demonstrate the enormity of Zimmerman's struggle with his instincts and his intellect as he sought to do consciously what had heretofore been an unconscious process. That he enlisted Jacques Levy to assist with *Desire*'s development says even more. When we pull back to examine this period, it appears as though Zimmerman lost his instincts and endeavored to replace that spontaneous impulse with systematic craft. *That* is not how Bob Zimmerman writes for "Bob Dylan," and the results were predictable. One senses that struggle when listening to *Desire*'s songs and their seemingly forced attention to detail. Though *Street-Legal*'s "end times" rhetoric suggested a return to form, it, too, seemed strained. During the late 1970s, the mission became muddled, and the art communicated that lack of focus.

The converted take missions seriously. The drive associated with a spiritually inspired quest to use one's talent to serve is, in every way, unrelenting. The selection of Jerry Wexler said everything about his narrative commission: Present The Message through The Sound, and serve The Lord. Zimmerman's writing at this juncture—foreshadowed via the much-overlooked *New Morning*—is clear, purposeful, and stylistically grounded in an established American musical genre, gospel music. Stories focus on the two-pronged tale of warning and celebration. Trusting the audience to do the right thing and accept Christ, the warning wasted little time on condemnations and quickly yielded to celebration. The gospel show that accompanied *Slow Train* and *Saved* contained an orchestrated blend of the warning-celebration thematic with pauses for testimony and invitation. The King of American Protest experienced little difficulty in his evolution into a messenger for the Prince of Peace, as the auteur's topicality merely shifted subjects and musical genres. With *Shot Of Love*'s look back, Bob Dylan judged what is not to be judged, his detractors (here the sparks fly); and in so doing, he completed his mission by returning to the *Street-Legal* rhetoric. His public commentary is straightforward on this matter: He said what he had to say and moved on—even though the issues that seemingly warranted the conversion returned unresolved. Such is not the stuff of a developmental phase or a personal idiosyncrasy. Not all missions are as successful as others.

Zimmerman's 1980s quest for professional equilibrium—and artistic prosperity—was a long, winding search for creative security. Unable to record the treasured sound in his head, he compromised his creative method, accepted the compositional strategies of the 1980s recording industry, and lost his bearings. The more he wrote, the less he said. The first Lanois production was a productive compromise, but it failed to satisfy the auteur's principal audience, himself. Arthur Baker, Don Was, or whomever assumed the producer's chair (including Dylan) was, for some inexplicable reason, unable to record that wild mercury sound. Subsequently, Zimmerman's stories ran hot and cold, ranging from the sublime to the ridiculous. The *sound* evaded him, and only *it* could unleash the words (remember, the words "punctuate" the sound). Those all-important colors faded or—worse yet—washed each other out from the hot-cold extremes into bland pastels. There were flashes of brilliance during this musical expedition, but the writer's ultimate dissatisfaction is evident in his ever-changing modes of operation. *Infidels*' vigor was followed by *Burlesque*'s tired return to the Bob Dylan Revue. *Loaded* and *Groove* limped along in a songwriting malaise that seemed to cease with *Mercy*, only to return with *Red Sky*. It was as if Bob Zimmerman became tired of writing for Bob Dylan. The songwriting mission lost its focus and, in turn, its vigor. Much like the late 1970s, the late 1980s found Zimmerman at a creative crossroads: He could either accept his rock icon role *or* develop another plan. Operating a factory that manufactures wooden legs *could* be a welcome reprieve.

In an admirable demonstration of determination, Bob Dylan remained on tour, refining his act and rediscovering his rhythm. That dedication yielded yet another mission of service. This time, the artist served his muse and its principal manifestation, his *songs*. His love of traditional American music, his commitment to his songs, and his realization of his impermanence generated a new public character, Jack Fate. From the supporting shadows, the Jack Fate portion of the Bob Dylan composite stepped forward to receive his due, reinvigorate Bob Zimmerman's pen, and revive Bob Dylan's art by recommitting to service. The two cover albums of roots music invoked the Basement Strategy and, once more, placed him in the proper frame of mind. With time and perseverance, Zimmerman found the rhythm that had evaded him for so long. "Jack Fate" is the quintessential bluesman—on the road for interminable periods, taking his band around the world, playing 100 shows a year. Through the Never Ending Series of Tours, a voice reemerged—a voice that had been quiet since the folk-posturing period. It was Jack Fate's voice. Listen to *Time Out Of Mind* and *Love And Theft*. Listen to the wisdom. Listen to the echoes from Woody and Bob Dylan's first album. Fate's reflections on life, love, and waitresses unveil the wily character who dances all through the varied musical platforms that appear on *Love And Theft*. Fate's heart aches, but he musters the resources to laugh at it. Fate loves the music, and that attitude is oh-so-evident in the songs. Zimmerman responded to a new imperative, and Jack Fate serves that mission very, very well.

Love And Theft also uses the band's rhythmic dexterity to provide musical platforms for Bob Dylan's heralded impressionism. Until this point, rare indeed was that flash of Glissendorf that characterized the auteur's more rebellious writings. Not until the musical camaraderie of his road-tested ensemble provided the creative safety net of the basements did the postman cut loose and allow the mail to once again flow through him. He focused on the tried-and-true topic of relational issues, and the Basement musicality and instinctive wordplay responded. This mission carries on to this day. *Time Out Of Mind* and *Love And Theft* provide a solid complement to the revisions of Bob Dylan songs that are featured in contemporary NEST shows. Yes, Jack Fate enjoys a strong repertoire of material, and he dutifully carries that catalog around the world. If the artist's comments in his *Chronicles* interviews are accurate, we may expect more new music in the near future. The voice of his generation made his pact, and he is not backing off any time soon. It is his destiny.

The auteur's celebrations, complaints, satires, and wordplay weave their way in and out of the respective missions depending upon the storytelling needs of that day. The narrative strategies used to organize Bob Dylan's language, and convey his moods, were subject to his creative context since some moods require articulation and others do not. As the mission changed, the impulse responded. To be sure, Zimmerman's pen functions best "in service." When he used the protest movement to serve his professional ambitions, the work prospered. When he rejected all that he had achieved in order to serve himself, the work exploded. When he applied his talents in the service of his Lord, his writing returned to the fertile topicality that birthed Bob Dylan. When he unveiled Jack Fate and his art served his beloved songs, that commitment to service saved his career.

Correspondingly, when his pen was not "in service," it floundered. Obviously, it purposefully disappeared during the *Self Portrait* and *Dylan* follies. By his own admission, it was "half-stepping" during the writing of *Harding* and *Skyline*. What is widely interpreted to be the intensely personal mission associated with *Blood On The Tracks* demonstrated how our agenda-driven auteur could still rise to the occasion, yet his follow-ups to that supposedly private statement were often wanting. (Again, I qualify remarks about *Blood* since these songs' autobiographical qualities may be way overstated.) Finally, the 1980s rock icon ran the songwriting gamut from the strength of *Infidels*'s outtakes to the vacuity of *Red Sky*'s fun-loving pop songs. With the two cover albums and Jack Fate's public arrival, a compromise appears to have been achieved that enables a peerless longevity. *Chronicles* most certainly confirms this observation. The artist fought for his survival.

Throughout it all, the auteur has *orchestrated* his art's content and style. His creative process is not one of *negotiation*; to the contrary, specific creative agendas dictate what emerges from Bobby Zimmerman's pen. He orchestrates his words, his sounds, and his performances in steadfast service of his lifelong audience: himself. If he wants to take his best songs off of an album, he does. If he wants to dump a hard-earned audience, he will. If he wants to change his sound in the face of intense public pressure, he relishes the opportunity. The list goes on and on. Bob Dillon's rebellion knows no boundaries. It may very well be that Bobby Zimmerman of Hibbing, Minnesota, is that proverbial one of a kind. It may very well be that *no commercial artist* has confronted the industry that supports him or her to the extent of this auteur. The norm involves the type of negotiation that Townshend experienced with *Tommy*. The norm involves the type of negotiation that required Bruce Springsteen to create *Born In The U.S.A.* The norm involves the types of deals that yield all of Elvis Costello's "greatest hits" packages and catalog reissues. But those norms are nowhere in sight within Bob Dylan's career. He may issue "greatest hits" packages. He may release old outtakes or shows through his *Bootleg* series. Or he may allow his record company to reissue his back catalog in light of new technologies. In every case, however, he *orchestrates* the venture. Bobby Zimmerman is a fearless artist, and his career is a testament to that strength.

Writing Dylan: *Songs of a Lonesome Traveler*

When young Bobby Zimmerman sat up late at night on Seventh Avenue in Hibbing listening to Gatemouth Page's radio program and dreaming of the character that the world would know as "Bob Dylan," I imagine he concocted all sorts of stories that he planned to use as Dylan's biography. I believe that a large part of that plan involved his character's travels across America. I suspect that riding the rails, hitchhiking, traveling with circuses and rodeos—and more—were steady staples in this fictional account of unrestrained wanderlust. The guy wandered here and there, never staying in one location for long. I bet Bobby's fictitious character was to be a real rounder. He would know music from every region of the country. He would know women of all stripes. He would have friends in every town. He would know the circus geeks by their real names. He would know the law, too. He would owe money to everybody. He would take what he could where he could, then he would wander on down that lost highway. Yes, I suspect that was the story young Bobby Zimmerman envisioned for his legendary character. Somehow, I just *know* that this is true. Oh yeah, I bet this guy was supposed to die young, too. Methinks Bobby wanted to build a *legend*, not the celebrity-drenched voice of his generation or the forever-hounded Archbishop of Anarchy.

Bob Dylan's career was not like that at all. You see, Dylan is a traveler, not a wanderer. Travelers have *destinations* in mind. Travelers go to specific locations and do certain things. Afterward, they move on to the next trip and its challenges. Some travels may be more focused than others. Some trips may be related to previous travels in some manner. In all cases, a plan is in place, and the traveler's activities respond to that imperative in one way or another. *This* was Bob Zimmerman's career with his Bob Dylan characters. These characters pursued specific missions that involved strategic activities that were selected to do precise jobs. An agenda guided those practices the way a tourist map charts a voyage to a foreign land. The extent to which Zimmerman was actually a "lonesome traveler" is uncertain. I hope that he wasn't, but I just don't know. All that we know about this man's private life is a product of gossip, and that's a *bad*—check that, *horrible*—source. There is no doubt that his Dylan characters fit that description, though. Zimmerman wrote for characters that blazed their own trails as they made their way to their respective destinations. Only once did a Dylan character genuinely submit to an external agenda—and *that* was a fleeting experience, as religion soon crowded the preacher's pantheism and prompted a trip to another locale. Bob Dillon's rebellion fueled an idiosyncratic restlessness that was corralled and used by Bob Dylan through Jack Fate's encyclopedic knowledge of— and unyielding dedication to—the wonderful world of American song. When missions emerged with their specific requirements, Zimmerman wrote for that day's Bob Dylan character. Those writings display five master signatures—artistic imprints that signal authorship. Yes, dear readers, our Bob Dylan is an auteur. To his master signatures, we now turn.

I've said this throughout this closing chapter, and I must say it again here since it's the most prominent master signature: Zimmerman orchestrated his mission-oriented approach to art. It is as if he were a production designer dressing his movie set. From the outset, Zimmerman dressed his art to meet his mission's needs. He carefully crafted his characters' appearance, language, props, sonic strategy, method of presentation, and public relations tactics in light of the creative imperative steering the mission. The list of examples is simply overwhelming. They are also a lot of fun.

After Elston Gunn and Bob Dillon warmed up the act, the young Dylan *became* Woody Guthrie. This conversion left no characterological stone unturned: Dylan looked like Woody (he held that cigarette the very same way in the corner of his mouth), talked like Woody, and, very soon, thought like Woody. Dylan deserves an Oscar for that production design. When WoodyBob ascertained that the folk movement was hungry for the medicine that flowed from his brand of topical song, he filled their prescriptions with a state-of-the-art remedy, *The Times They Are A-Changin'*. That set was perfectly coordinated, don't you think? When Dylan wanted to shift away from the folkies, he initiated the move by orchestrating an all-night recording session to introduce the new Dylan's new subject matter (complete with a reporter standing by to capture it all for posterity). It must have been one hell of a show. It certainly was well-planned.

The Newport Mod was a masterful invention. His attire complemented his words, mannerisms, and demeanor. He was as antifolk as imaginable. He was from another planet. Multiple Oscars are in order here: The set design, special effects, sound design, and script all deserve the highest praise. When that show ran its course, and his motorcycle ran out of road (*there's* a story line for you!), Dylan recuperated by redesigning his set once more. The Newport Mod moved to the country. I doubt he's ever seen a forest before (Central Park doesn't count). The countrified family man was a splendid alternative to all that had traveled before him, and his music, public appearances, and reclusive nature worked in harmony to achieve this crucial mission. On another plane, the artist's thoughtful coordination of Big Pink's musicology exercises is another defining characteristic from this era. Perhaps a Golden Globe is appropriate here, since the subtleties associated with this production design probably flew below the Academy's radar.

The list goes on and on. Hey, I'm just getting warmed up! OK, you asked for it: How about that Bob Dylan Revue? The Bob Dylan Revue is a monument to artistic orchestration. The musical arrangements, the Bobettes, the selection of cover songs (my life changed when I heard "Mr. Bojangles" and "Big Yellow Bulldozer"), and the many Voices of Bob set the scene for the lifework's second longest running act. The Revue proved to be one flexible troupe. When the Revue went on a vacation and packed away the Las Vegas set until the next season, the artist's mission-oriented approach to art took a dive off the deep end. But first, we should pause and hand out that "People's Choice" award to the Revue. Goodness, the voice of his generation looks sharp in lavender lamé!

The musical world will only know one Rolling Thunder Revue. I love reading Sam Shepard's account of those crazy days traversing across New England. These people were nuts. Crazy or not, the RTR's attention to detail was its quintessence. Every aspect of Rolling Thunder was orchestrated to maximize its creative yield. Unannounced appearances, vaudeville-style scripts, outrageous but professional staging, and melodramatic performances were the RTR's signature ingredients. The auteur dressed that set like no other. The scene from *Renaldo & Clara* in which the crew sets up for a show demonstrated the enormity of this undertaking—and its professionalism. Oh yeah, that reminds me: How about that *Renaldo & Clara*? Can you image what it was like running around making a never-ending, unpredictable, chaotic movie during the day or late at night while pausing to do a madcap vaudeville show that evening? The RTR package transcends the Academy. The electors just stand there, mouths open, basking in the glow of a creative moment that will *never* return. Ever.

The list goes on and on. The Revue returns when the Thunder quiets. This time, the troupe toured the world with its special brand of *Dylan*'s music. Though I think they made an egregious error when they dropped "Mr. Bojangles" from the set list, the Revue compensated with its revision of "Blowin' In The Wind." To be sure, the gamblers turned their heads when they heard *that* bellowing throughout the casino. What a sound. The Bobettes are the best. This mission failed to receive any official accolades; however, there is a reality show on the drawing board in which contestants have to "Name that tune" or be put to death. I bet it works!

When The Call came, the artist secured Jerry Wexler's services for the Alabama Chronicles. That, my friends, is the test of a professional set designer. You've got to know what it takes to do a job properly in order to succeed. Zimmerman's Dylan wrote the script, assembled the actors, choreographed the movements, and designed the set that enabled the Bob Dylan Crusade to take the Alabama Chronicles on the road in His name. This was some serious stuff. Honestly, I don't think that this was a phase. It may have been a major disappointment, though. Whichever, the Bob Dylan Crusade signaled the preacher's respect for time-honored rituals. The Academy does not acknowledge acts like this—but it should. Once that mission played out, the artist wandered a bit through the most haphazard of the oeuvre's missions. The authenticity of the Woody-based production, the edgy qualities of the Newport Mod's act, the superstaging of Tour '74, the madness of the RTR's holistic approach to art, the sublimity of the Bob Dylan Revue's theatrics, and the divinity of the Bob Dylan Crusade's staging all disappear during the pop icon era. When he perceived his image was in decline, the artist piggybacked on tours with successful acts, sharing time with bands who designed their own sets. When you're accustomed to dressing your show to meet your theatrical needs, you probably lose some of your intensity when you're sharing somebody else's stage. I mean, it's just not the same. It's like wearing somebody's clothes; they don't quite fit—in fact, they may be downright uncomfortable. When you're in this situation, you need a new plan, don't you?

Academy Award–winning production designers have skills, or they would not have received that kind of recognition. Hence, when Bob Zimmerman realized that his current Dylan character had run its course, he oh-so-carefully plotted Jack Fate's emergence. *This* was no moment's task. We're talking moving from Technicolor to 3-D here. Your audience needs new glasses. The set requires additional considerations. The lighting and sound have to be revamped. The costuming becomes critical. And you have to determine which theaters are capable of handling the show. This takes a lot of work! Bob Zimmerman, it appears, is a planning fool.

I told you this guy orchestrates his art! Whatever the mission needs, he seems to be able to supply it. Obviously, there is more than a little bit of rebellion here. Sometimes all of this seems like a Broadway show that is breaking box office records and decides to suddenly shut down while people are waiting in line to purchase tickets. Or a movie that has spent a fortune to devise different endings for different days of the week without regard for critical or audience-based responses. There is a level of independence here that is, at times, unimaginable—maybe even reckless. It is like Frank Sinatra dropping everything to become a Rasta. Or Bob Marley giving up everything to perform for the pope. Or James Dean returning from the grave to play Richard Nixon's ghost on *West Wing*. Things get weird in Bob Dylan's world. In all cases, however, it is magical and, usually, original.

Central to this orchestration of these creative missions is our second master signature: Zimmerman's successful adaptation of the folk process. Just as he borrowed a line from Guthrie's "Pretty Boy Floyd" or lifted a melody for "Masters Of War," the artist deployed all sorts of "found objects" in service of his art. He may lift a line from a movie, an image from a short story, a character from a novel, a scene from a play, or a plot from the most famous book in the history of the world. Whatever it takes, the Archbishop of Anarchy will do. Remember his comment about that painter who assembles his painting? *That's* our auteur. Our "postman" accepts mail from diverse locations and delivers it via his own, strategically selected style. His emphasis may be on color. His focus may be on emotional exposition. His objectives may vary with the moment. In all cases, Bob Zimmerman uses his powers of assimilation to build and build and build his reservoir of resource material. He then systematically applies that knowledge to the specific task at hand.

Just look at the objects he deployed in his various missions. The whole Woody act involved opening the Oklahoma bard's footlocker and pulling out whatever was there to dress the folk-posturing set. Woody's words, his look, his attitude, his friends—whatever was needed was used. That trend carried on in its own way with the Newport Mod. Here Dylan selected what he needed from the Mods and left behind what he did not want. He wore Mod clothes, displayed Mod attitudes, and thoroughly dismissed Mod solidarity. But we're not done yet. Dylan did the same thing with Nashville. He may not have worn a Nudie suit, but he took what he needed to dress his country set. Nashville musicians, Nashville songwriting structures, Nashville producers, and, ultimately, Nashville music were the order of that creative day. But we're not done yet. Just look at Rolling Thunder! What's *not* pulled out of this magical grab bag! The movie used all sorts of previously established ideas and spun them on their head. The poetry readings, the old songs, the vaudeville staging—goodness. Rolling Thunder was the folk process gone mad. But we're not done yet. How about the Bob Dylan Revue, or the Bob Dylan Crusade, or the Never Ending Series of Tours? Everywhere, the folk process is in evidence. The Revue's sounds and appearance, the Crusade's application of time-honored rituals (not to mention its use of, shall we say, famous literature), and the NEST's staging, sound, and look all flowed from a convergence of ideas that were used to do a specific job. You know something? I suspect we're not done yet.

The remaining master signatures are important, but they are not as prominent as Zimmerman's orchestrations or his use of the folk process. These first two signatures involve what the artist used and how he used it to generate his art. These final attributes demonstrate his public stance on that work and how he arranged it. Turning to our third master signature, I realize that the voice of his generation was taken aback at the close of *Dont Look Back* when his manager informed him that the British press had labeled him an anarchist, but the Archbishop of Anarchy is just that: an anarchist. From the outset, it seems, answers have blown about in winds that do not visit Bob Dylan's house. The times may change in the world around him, but he offers not a clue as to the results of those changes. Oh sure, the weak may become strong, but what will they do afterward (I wager that they'll beat up on their oppressors, by the way)? He may decry racism, elitism, escapism, and imperialism, or poke fun at Communism, but our auteur rarely proposes a solution to the problems he portrays. What was the guy in "John Birch" going to do with a Commie once he caught one? How are we to stop elites from using poor people as their pawns or as target practice? What do we do with those greedy immigrants, those untrustworthy hobos, or those abusive landlords? There may be a "Jokerman" in the deck of life, but what are we to do about this guy? Burn the deck? How do you stop everything from breaking? What do you do to a politicized world to turn it around? Is anybody going to help our "Neighborhood Bully"? Is anybody going to do anything about all of those wasted "Clean–Cut Kid" types? Should we disband the unions? We just don't have a clue. It is not that Dylan advocates revolution or terror. He just rejects all of these conditions. Yes, just when you thought the English press was bonkers.

In these societal and political scenarios, Dylan seems to toy with his anarchistic worldview. He gets down to *business* in his songs of relational anarchy. He may wail about a relational situation, yet, odds are, he will propose nothing that remedies that sad or ugly condition. He may not propose revolution in societal or political situations, but he unabashedly endorses the practice in human relations. He wants to terrorize the former snob–turned–bum in "Like A Rolling Stone." When he asks her how it feels to be her now, there is a sneering smile accompanying that inquiry. Burn, baby, burn. He wants the world to know that his so-called friends are evil opportunists in "Positively 4th Street." Yes sir, somebody has a quite a bit of nerve. You know, it's a special moment when you wish someone could stand in your shoes and comprehend the dread of seeing them. He turns away from his old friends in "Restless Farewell" and issues a kiss-off as a parting shot. What can you say about "Dirge"? I guess we have to accept relational disloyalty, right? That's the message I get from "Shelter From The Storm." What is the character going to do in "Sara"? Sit on the beach and cry? The poor guy in "Señor"—what can we do for him? This relational anarchy reaches a point where characters no longer trust themselves and argue internally ("Heart Of Mine" and more). And *Time Out Of Mind*—oh my! Forget the low-carb diet; we're going for zero calories in this relational diet. I wish the characters on this record *would* rise up and terrorize these women, but they won't because we're in the aftermath of anarchy here. There is nothing to do but stand in the doorway of that one-room shack and throw up. "Love Sick," indeed. Only in Zimmerman's last incarnation of his Bob Dylan characters does he back away from this relational anarchy and offer sermonic prescriptions that comfort life's recurring problems. Yes, Bob Dylan is an anarchist. He may not tell you to burn down the mission, but he sure damns the people lounging inside. Those "finger-pointing" songs deploy a host of fingers to do their jobs, and the archbishop is more than up for that truth attack.

It stands to reason that an anarchist would rarely, if ever, endorse a remedy for the ills he reports. I mean, that is what an anarchist is—right? Still, it happened once, somehow. This is our fourth master signature: Dylan's avoidance of advocacy. This is why the man rejects that "voice of his generation" label so vigorously. It is flat-out inaccurate. No, young Dylan never openly endorsed all of those folk platitudes he sang about in his career's infancy. He seized that audience's complaint, colorized it in his own way, and gave it back to them for their edification. Sure, he appeared at public events like the March on Washington or the voter rallies in Mississippi, but he never said anything. He sang his song and yielded the microphone. The one time he did speak—at the Tom Paine Award dinner—well, that didn't work out so well, did it? So, he quickly distanced himself from those polemics. His liner notes brought forward all sorts of questions about definitions, slogans, scenes, organizations, and their manipulative ways. This artist is an anarchist, not an advocate.

Yes, he did call attention to Rubin Carter's plight. The song written on his behalf does more than "Union Sundown" or "Political World," but not that much more. Nevertheless, as that particular timeframe continued to unfold, the auteur chronicled the world's dastardly ways in more and more graphic terms. Ultimately, this inspired his lone moment of advocacy. Only during the moral period did Dylan step forward and place himself in an advocate's role. He dutifully faced disbelieving audiences with the fire and intensity of the Newport Mod, or Renaldo's blistering RTR performances, or perhaps even the quiet resolve of a teenage Bobby Zimmerman performing before his high school classmates. He stood up for God. He carried his Crusade to the people. He did a fine job until those old definitions, organizations, and scene-makers did what they always do. As a result, Dylan departed that scene with a vengeance. Just listen to the disappointment in *Shot Of Love*. Never more, cried the anarchist, never more.

I suppose Dylan (read, Jack Fate) is assuming a position of advocacy with the NEST, though. This time, he supports his art. Through the NEST, he fulfills his destiny, pursues his Heavenly obligations, and nurtures his gifts. It is, however, a quiet advocacy. The great production designer dresses a simple set. The reverence for the songs is made compellingly clear. The anarchist may have left the building, but he left his script behind. The NEST is a wonderful tribute to the art it supports.

That script leads me to our final master signature: the auteur's prolonged use of the capstone statement to close projects. In many respects, this is a simple trait. In other ways, it is a powerful attribute that signifies the mission-oriented nature of Zimmerman's work. On multiple occasions, our various Dylan characters have returned to the studio to cut that capstone track. These songs, more often than not, symbolize all that passes before them as they encapsulate the logic and emotion of the stories told via that particular project. Even the debut album deploys this signature with "See That My Grave Is Kept Clean," as it seems to resolve all of those songs about death. Just look at the list of capstone statements: "Restless Farewell" (*The Times They Are A-Changin'*), "It Ain't Me, Babe" (*Another Side*), "It's All Over Now, Baby Blue" (*Bringing It All Back Home*), "Desolation Row" (*Highway 61*), the incredible "Sad-Eyed Lady Of The Lowlands" (*Blonde*), "I'll Be Your Baby Tonight" (*John Wesley Harding*), the telltale "Tonight I'll Be Staying Here With You" (*Nashville Skyline*), the majestic combination of "Wigwam" and "Alberta #2" (*Self Portrait*), "Father Of Night" (*New Morning*), "Wedding Song" (*Planet Waves*), "Buckets Of Rain" (*Blood On The Tracks*), "Sara" (*Desire*), "Where Are You Tonight?" (*Street-Legal*), the incredible "When He Returns" (*Slow Train*), "Are You Ready?" (*Saved*), the mother of all capstone statements that is "Every Grain Of Sand" (*Shot Of Love*), the "Don't Fall Apart On Me Tonight" substitution for "Foot Of Pride" (*Infidels*), the requested "Dark Eyes" (*Empire Burlesque*), the swampy "Shooting Star" (*Oh Mercy*), the yuk-yuk perfection of "Cat's In The Well" (*Red Sky*), the cinematic "Highlands" (*Time Out Of Mind*), and the dreamy "Sugar Baby" (*Love And Theft*). So you wonder if Bob Zimmerman of Hibbing, Minnesota, orchestrates his art, do you?

As we pull back and consider over forty years of art, these are our master signatures. Our auteur responds to the missions before him in systematic ways. He uses all the things he has seen, heard, read, observed, imagined, and suspected to meet the creative needs of that particular moment. When he shapes those materials in pursuit of a given mission, he assumes an anarchist's stance, disavows solutions, and stresses the colors associated with the emotions he portrays in his pictures. Therefore, he eschews endorsements. Perhaps, it is a sign of weakness to enter the fray from a position of advocacy. It's better to keep your distance, maintain your objectivity, and allow your audience to exercise their will with your wonderfully colored musical Rorschach tests. Yet, these are missions. The presence of those precious capstone statements indicates that our artist is, in fact, a man with a plan. When he dresses his work, he does what all great productions do: He leaves you with something. Yes, a stance is taken, the materials needed to shape that position are secured, and a systematic process ensues. Just as Professor Ricks said way back yonder in chapter 5, the artist may not be consciously aware of all that is happening as he plies his trade, but that makes him "not less the artist but more." I guess when all is said and done, I agree with Dylan: A planet or something must have "bumped into" the land that evolved into that 1,600-acre strip mine in Hibbing—there's most definitely magic in that thin, wild "metallic" air.

As I close, I wonder about the extent to which the artist has enjoyed his historic career. When you watch him during his 2004 *60 Minutes* interview, he conveys a sense of duty more than joy. When Ed Bradley searches for a response to the fact that one of his songs has been voted the number one rock-and-roll song of all time, Bob Dylan just shrugs it off. We're in Jack Fate mode here. This guy has seen it all and trusts none of it. I wonder if that's how Bob Zimmerman of Hibbing, Minnesota, truly feels. I just don't know. So much seems to come down to questions of identity. And why shouldn't it? This has, after all, been the lynchpin to this entire phenomenon. It seems as though Dylan's 1987 interview with Kurt Loder puts much of this in perspective. When Loder asks where his subject might feel most "at home," the man the world calls Bob Dylan responded,

> I'm comfortable wherever people don't remind me of who I am. Anytime somebody reminds me of who I am, that kills it for me. If I wanted to wonder about who I am, I could start dissecting my own stuff. I don't have to go on other people's trips of who *they* think I am. A person doesn't like to feel self-conscious, you know? Now, Little Richard says if you don't want your picture taken, you got no business being a star. And he's right, he's absolutely right. But I don't like my picture being taken by people I don't know. [Loder: "But you are a star. . . ."] Yeah, well, I guess so. But, uh . . . I feel like I'm a star, but I can shine for who I want to shine for. You know what I mean?

How I wish that were true for him. I wish he *could* select his audience in that way. But that is not the way it is. Not for the voice of his generation, the Archbishop of Anarchy. You see, much like his hero Robert Johnson, Bob Zimmerman—the man behind it all, call him what you will—made a pact a long time ago. Part of that pact he discussed on *60 Minutes*. That was the good side of that arrangement. There is, though, another side—there always is, isn't there? That side deals with all of these folks who torment Bob Dylan. All those people who propagate the Dylan Myth. Those people who the auteur does not want to shine for. They are the Devil in this man's life, and he discussed that role in *Playboy* in 1978:

> The Devil is everything false, the Devil will go as deep as you let the Devil go. You can leave yourself open to that. If you understand what that whole scene is about, you can easily step aside. But if you want the confrontation to begin with, well, there's plenty of it. But then again, if you believe you have a purpose and a mission, and not much time to carry it out, you don't bother about those things. . . . You must have a purpose. . . . You must know why you're doing what you're doing.

When Rosenbaum inquired as to the nature of his mission, Dylan replied, "Henry Miller said it: The role of an artist is to inoculate the world with disillusionment."

You still wondering if this guy is an anarchist? His mission is, what's that, to promote disenchantment? He aspires to free us of our false beliefs? Of course, I forgot. "Art" is not supposed to "mirror society," is it? Oh yeah, the "very essence of art" is—how does it go—that it is "subversive to society." Yes, that's right: "Whatever society is putting out, art's got to do something else." My friends, this man is very clear on this matter. Notice that he does not aspire to replace those beliefs with something better. His mission is not to overhaul those illusions. He just wants to tear them down and leave you there, begging for a drumstick. That is a tall order. Zimmerman is game, though. He most certainly deployed his Bob Dylan characters with a purpose. He understood *exactly* what he was doing and why (well . . . most of the time). He sacrificed for his various missions, and that left him with the discomforts he articulated to Loder. I suppose it's unavoidable. I guess success has to have some sort of price. That stands to reason, I suppose. Perhaps the auteur said it best in "Silvio," when he reported that you have to pay for what you achieve.

I must admit I was saddened when I first saw that scene in *Renaldo & Clara* in which Ginsberg and Dylan walked around in the graveyard, checking out the tombstones. When they came upon Jack Kerouac's grave and Ginsberg asked his friend if that was how he wanted to be laid to rest, my heart sank when the guy answered that he wanted to be buried in an unmarked grave. Did it all come down to that? Did he spend his entire life building this massive identity, splitting it into strategic incarnations, and, in so doing, creating a historic lifework just to be placed in some unmarked grave in some unknown place? Has this identity thing gone that far? Is that Devil celebrity going to win that Final Round? There certainly would not be anybody around reminding him who he is in that scenario. There would be nobody to shine for, then. How sad. How unbelievably sad. I've always wondered about that scene. I've never felt good about it. Then I reread his 1978 interview with Jonathan Cott, and they actually discussed that moment in the film. My heart filled with joy when Dylan recalled the scene, his remarks to Ginsberg ("I want an unmarked grave"), and reported, "But of course I'm saying this as Renaldo."

But of course.

Acknowledgments

References

Allen, J. May 23, 2001. Bob Dylan at 60: Timeless and transcendent. www.CNN.com.

Anderson, S. January 1994. *Bob Dylan: World gone wrong*. *Spin*, 77–78.

Back to the roots. April 11, 1969. *Time*, 70–71.

Barker, D. 2001. Apathy for the devil. In Derek Barker, ed., *Isis: A Bob Dylan anthology*, 134–43. London: Helter Skelter.

———. 2001. A chat with Cesar Diaz. In Derek Barker, ed., *Isis: A Bob Dylan anthology*, 189–97. London: Helter Skelter.

Basic Dylan. January 12, 1968. *Time*, 50.

Bauder, D. June 21, 1985. Two '60s legends who won't fade away. *(Stamford, CT) Advocate* (NEWSBANK).

Bauldie. J. 1991. Liner notes to *Bootleg Series*, vols. 1–3. New York: Sony Music Entertainment.

Bernstein, J., and S. Daly. December 1990. Platter du jour. *Spin*, 83.

"Bob Dylan." May 3, 1963. *Studs Terkel's Wax Museum*. Chicago: WFMT.

"Bob Dylan." October 10, 2004. *CBS Morning*. New York: CBS.

"Bob Dylan." December 5, 2004. *60 Minutes*. New York: CBS.

"Bob Dylan: The 1965 Interview." 1997. *The Baktabak interview collection*. London: Baktabak Recordings.

"Bob Dylan: The American Troubadour." 2000. *Biography*. New York: A&E Television Networks.

Bob Dylan Story, The. 2002. BBC2. London: Smooth Operations.

Bowden, B. 1982. *Performed literature: Words and music by Bob Dylan*. Bloomington: Indiana University Press.

Bream, J. January 19, 1986. Bob Dylan. *Minneapolis Star Tribune* (NEWSBANK).

Buskin, R. 1999. *Inside tracks*. New York: Avon.

Carlin, P. November 3, 1997. Song: Time out of mind. *People*, 25.

Catlin, R. October 24, 1993. Dylan's other side plays others' songs. *Hartford Courant* (NEWSBANK).

———. September 11, 2001. Dylan plumbs depths of heart and soul in new gem. *Hartford Courant*, www.ctnow.com.

Champlin, C. January 25, 1978. Two views of Dylan's 'Renaldo & Clara.' *Los Angeles Times*, sec. IV, 1, 12.

Charles, L. 2003. Director's comments from *Masked and Anonymous*. Culver City, CA: Columbia TriStar Home Entertainment.

Cocks, J. June 10, 1985. Here's what's happening, Mr. Jones. *Time*, 84.

———. November 25, 1985. Hellhound on the loose. *Time*, 122.

———. October 26, 1992. Bringing folk back home. *Time*, 73.

Cohen, J., and H. Traum. 1972. Conversations with Bob Dylan. In Craig McGregor, ed., *Bob Dylan: A retrospective*, 263–92. New York: William Morrow.

Cohn, N. 1996. *Awopbopaloobop alopbamboom: The golden age of rock*. New York: Da Capo.

Coleman, R. January 9, 1965. Beatles say—Dylan shows the way. *Melody Maker*, 3.

Connelly, C. November 24, 1983. Dylan makes another stunning comeback. *Rolling Stone*, 65–66, 69.

Considine, J. D. March 27, 1991. 'Bootleg Series' plays out the bluesy, rough-edged steps of Dylan's development. (Baltimore) *Sun* (NEWSBANK).

Cott, J. March 13, 1975. *Blood on the Tracks*: Back inside the rain. *Rolling Stone*, 43, 45–46.

———. January 26, 1978. Standing naked: Bob Dylan. *Rolling Stone*, 38–44.

———. November 16, 1978. Bob Dylan: The 'Rolling Stone' interview, part II. *Rolling Stone*, 56–62.

Crenshaw, H. July 2, 1988. Dylan's 'Down in the Groove' entertaining, not innovative. *Atlanta Journal* (NEWSBANK).

Crowe, C. 1985. Interview with Bob Dylan. *Biograph*. New York: CBS.

Cusimano, J. April 1975. Records: Dylan comes back to the wars. *Crawdaddy*, 67–68.

Damsker, M. April 7, 1994. Books: The way we were. *Rolling Stone*, 25.

Davis, A. 2001. Arriving where he started. In Derek Barker, ed., *Isis: A Bob Dylan anthology*, 242–44. London: Helter Skelter.

Davis, F. 1995. *The history of the blues: The roots, the music, the people from Charley Patton to Robert Cray*. New York: Hyperion.

———. May 1999. Napoleon in rags. *Atlantic Monthly*, 108–17.

Day, A. 1988. *Jokerman: Reading the lyrics of Bob Dylan*. Oxford: Basil Blackwell.

DeCurtis, A. September 11, 1986. Records: *Knocked Out Loaded. Rolling Stone*, 92–93.

———. September 21, 1989. Dylan and the Stones: The shock of the old. *Rolling Stone*, 115–16.

———. April 4, 1991. Bob Dylan's blue highway. *Rolling Stone*, 53–55.

DiMartino, D. February 1993. History lessons. *Musician*, 89–90.

Dr. Bob sums up. June 22, 1970. *Time*, 61.

Dylan. February 11, 1974. *New Yorker*, 32–33.

Dylan, B. 1973. *Lyrics, 1962–1985*. New York: Alfred A. Knopf.

———. 1993. Liner notes to *World Gone Wrong*. New York: Sony Music Entertainment.

———. 1994. *Drawn blank*. New York: Random House.

———. 1994. *Tarantula*. New York: St. Martin's Press.

———. 2004. *Chronicles*, vol. 1. New York: Simon & Schuster.

———. 2004. *Lyrics, 1962–2001*. New York: Simon & Schuster.

Dylan in conference: I just hope to have enough boots to be able to change them. January 20, 1968. *Melody Maker*, 9.

The Dylanologist. April 12, 1971. *Newsweek*, 123.

Ebert, R. May 1, 1998. Blood on the tracks: Documentary shows Dylan as cruel twirp. *Chicago Sun-Times*, 37.

Eig, J., and S. Moffett. July 8, 2003. Did Bob Dylan lift lines from Dr. Saga? Author is flattered. *Wall Street Journal*, A1, 8.

Elder, R. September 13, 2001. Bob Dylan plays a winning hand. *Dallas Morning News*, www.DallasNews.com.

Emerson, K. May 27, 2001. Songs of ourselves. www.LATimes.com.

Erlewine, S. 1997. *All music guide to rock*. San Francisco: Miller Freeman.

Evans, P. October 4, 1990. Records: *Under the Red Sky. Rolling Stone*, 160–61.

Evearitt, D. December 3, 1976. Bob Dylan: Still blowin' in the wind. *Christianity Today*, 29–30.

Ewen, D. 1972. *Great men of American popular song*. Englewood Cliffs, NJ: Prentice Hall.

Faris, M. June 22, 1980. What's Bob Dylan up to of late? Just ask A.J. *Chicago Tribune*, sec. 6, 30.

Farley, C. September 29, 1997. Dylan's lost highway. *Time*, 87.

Favorite son: Birthday wishes to Bob Dylan. May 24, 2001. (Minneapolis) *Star Tribune*, www.Startribune.com.

Flanagan, B. 1986. *Written in my soul: Rock's great songwriters talk about creating their music*. New York: Contemporary.

———. February 1986. Record reviews: Two decades of poetry and hard truth. *Musician*, 114–16.

———. September 1988. Reviews: Bob Dylan: *Down in the Groove. Musician*, 110–12.

———. December 1993. My back pages. *Musician*, 85–86.

The folk and the rock. September 20, 1965. *Newsweek*, 88–90.

Folk singers. May 31, 1963. *Time*, 40.

Fong-Torres, B. February 14, 1974. Knockin' on Dylan's door. *Rolling Stone*, 36–41, 44.

Fricke, D. August 8, 1981. And what makes Bob sick. *Melody Maker*, 3.

———. December 5, 1985. Dylan's dilemma. *Rolling Stone*, 51–53.

———. July 14, 1988. Records: *Down in the Groove. Rolling Stone*, 142.

————. February 3, 1990. The tour of no return: Dylan on the road in the eighties. *Melody Maker*, 36.

————. December 25, 1997. The year in recordings: *Time Out of Mind. Rolling Stone*, 156.

————. September 27, 2001. The making of Dylan's "Love and Theft." *Rolling Stone*, 11–12.

Furia, P. 1992. *The poets of Tin Pan Alley: A history of America's great lyricists.* New York: Oxford University Press.

Fusilli, J. October 9, 1997. Bob Dylan: Never out of mind. *Wall Street Journal*, 4.

Futterman, E. April 7, 1994. Times they are a changin' . . . Dylan speaks. *St. Louis Post-Dispatch*, 1G.

Gates, D. March 13, 1989. Bob Dylan. *Newsweek*, 67.

————. April 8, 1991. Notes from underground. *Newsweek*, 63.

————. October 6, 1997. Dylan revisited. *Newsweek*, 62–68.

————. October 4, 2004. The book of Bob. *Newsweek*, 48–51.

Gill, A. September 6, 2001. Bob Dylan: Love and theft. *Independent*, www.independent.co.uk.

Gill, A., and K. Odegard. 2004. *A simple twist of fate: Bob Dylan and the making of* Blood on the Tracks. Cambridge, MA: Da Capo Press.

Gillett, C. 1996. *The sound of the city: The rise of rock and roll.* New York: Da Capo.

Gilmore, M. November 10, 1985. Behind the glasses, Dylan at 44 looking scruffy but ready. *Chicago Tribune*, sec. 13, 5, 8.

————. July 17, 1986. Positively Dylan. *Rolling Stone*, 31–34, 135–36.

————. May 30, 1991. Bob Dylan at fifty. *Rolling Stone*, 56–60.

————. 1998. *Night beat: A shadow history of rock & roll.* New York: Doubleday.

————. November 22, 2001. The *Rolling Stone* interview: Bob Dylan. *Rolling Stone*, 56–69.

Gleason, R. December 1968. Bob Dylan: Poet to a generation. *Jazz & Pop*, 36–37.

————. March 13, 1975. The blood of a poet. *Rolling Stone*, 22.

Glover, T. October 1975. Records: The ultimate underground record sees the light of day. *Creem*, 64–65.

Goldberg, J. September 1979. Dylan digs the diamond mine. *Creem*, 52.

Graustark, B. December 17, 1979. The (new) word according to Dylan. *Newsweek*, 90.

Gray, M. 2000. *Song & dance man III: The art of Bob Dylan.* London: Cassell.

Gundersen. E. 1998. Dylan on Dylan: "Unplugged" and the birth of a song. In C. Benson, ed., *The Bob Dylan companion: Four decades of commentary*, 223–25. New York: Schirmer.

————. May 18, 2001. Forever Dylan. *USA Today*, 1–3E.

————. May 18, 2001. Times change, but Dylan leaves a lasting imprint. *USA Today*, 1–4A.

————. July 16, 2001. 'Love' takes Dylan in different direction. *USA Today*, 1D.

————. September 10, 2001. Dylan is positively on top of his game. www.USAToday.com.

Hajdu, D. 2001. *Positively 4th street: The lives and times of Joan Baez, Bob Dylan, Mimi Baez Farina and Richard Farina.* New York: Farrar, Straus & Giroux.

Hampton, W. 1986. *Guerrilla minstrels.* Knoxville: University of Tennessee.

Hansson, N. September 2001. The Rome interview. *La Repubblica.* www.Expectingrain.com.

Happy birthday Bob: An appreciation of Dylan at 60. June 7, 2001. *Rolling Stone*, 48–52, 122.

Harrington, R. June 28, 1985. Dylan finally sheds himself of old religious trappings. *Cleveland Plain Dealer* (NEWSBANK).

————. September 16, 2001. Dylan's American gamut. www.Washingtonpost.com.

Henahan, D. September 7, 1967. The screen: Bob Dylan and company. *New York Times*, 50.

Helm, L. 2000. *This wheel's on fire: Levon Helm and the story of The Band.* Chicago: Acappella.

Hentoff, N. October 24, 1964. Profiles: The crackin', shakin', breakin' sounds. *New Yorker*, 64–90.

————. March 1966. Playboy interview: Bob Dylan. *Playboy*, 41–44, 138–42.

Heylin, C. 1995. *Bob Dylan: The recording sessions [1960–1994].* New York: St. Martin's Griffin.

————. 2001. *Bob Dylan: Behind the shades revisited.* New York: William Morrow.

Hickey, N. October 16, 1976. Dylan today. *Melody Maker*, 32–33.

————. 1998. Bob Dylan (1976). In C. Benson, ed., *The Bob Dylan companion: Four decades of commentary*, 150–56. New York: Schirmer.

Hilburn, R. January 25, 1978. Two views of Dylan's 'Renaldo & Clara.' *Los Angeles Times*, sec. IV, 1, 12.

————. May 28, 1978. Bob Dylan opens up on Bob Dylan. *Los Angeles Times*, sec. C, 1, 66.

————. November 17, 1978. Dylan returns to the Forum. *Los Angeles Times*, sec. IV, 1, 26.

————. August 18, 1979. Dylan's stirring 'Slow Train.' *Los Angeles Times*, sec. II, 10.

————. November 6, 1979. Bob Dylan: Fundamental light still shineth. *Los Angeles Times*, sec. V, 1, 16.

————. November 18, 1979. Dylan's new furor: Rock 'n' religion. *Los Angeles Times*, sec. C, 82.

————. November 20, 1979. Dylan's evangelicalism goes on. *Los Angeles Times*, sec. V, 1, 14.

————. November 11, 1980. Bob Dylan on his own terms. *Los Angeles Times*, sec. C, 1, 4.

————. August 30, 1981. 'Shot of Love': Buried gems. *Los Angeles Times*, sec. C, 73.

————. March 13, 1983. Looking back: Dylan at pop storm center. *Los Angeles Times*, sec. C, 54.

————. October 30, 1983. Bob Dylan at 42—rolling down highway 61 again. *Los Angeles Times*, sec. C, 3–4.

————. August 5, 1984. Dylan: The view from route '84. *Los Angeles Times*, sec. C, 54.

————. June 9, 1985. Dylan brings it all back home again. *Los Angeles Times*, sec. C, 57.

————. November 17, 1985. Bob Dylan—still a-changin'. *Los Angeles Times*, sec. C, 56, 62–63.

————. April 12, 1992. With no direction known: Dylan on tour. *Chicago Sun Times* (NEWSBANK).

————. 1998. "I learned that Jesus is real and I wanted that." In C. Benson, ed., *The Bob Dylan companion: Four decades of commentary*, 161–67. New York: Schirmer.

————. September 9, 2001. This year's Dylan is a sonic dynamo. www.LATimes.com.

————. September 16, 2001. How does it feel? Don't ask. www.LATimes.com.

————. April 4, 2004. Rock's enigmatic poet opens a long-private door. www.LATimes.com.

Hill, G. October 18, 1993. Dylan: Fans an inspiration for 'World Gone Wrong.' *Boston Herald* (NEWSBANK).

Himes, G. September 19, 1979. Self-righteous Dylan. *Washington Post*, C4.

Hinckley, D. May 29, 1985. Bob Dylan's 'Empire Burlesque.' *New York Daily News* (NEWSBANK).

————. November 3, 1992. 'Good' old Bob. *New York Daily News* (NEWSBANK).

The history of rock 'n' roll. 1995. Time-Life Video.

Holden, S. October 1, 1989. A 'new Dylan' crosses paths with the old. *New York Times*, H29.

Holmes, T. January 16, 1986. Dylan: A life in music. *Rolling Stone*, 43–45.

————. September 1988. Bob Dylan: *Down in the Groove*. *Spin*, 86.

Hubbard, R. March 11, 2004. Bob Dylan puts songs, band at center stage. www.TwinCities.com.

Humphries, P. 1995. *The complete guide to the music of Bob Dylan*. New York: Omnibus.

Infusino, D. July 30, 1986. Less than top Dylan is still very good. *San Diego Union* (NEWSBANK).

Jacobson, M. April 1995. Hero with 1,000 (gnarly) faces. *Esquire*, 147.

————. April 12, 2001. Tangled up in Bob. *Rolling Stone*, 64–74, 151.

Jennings, D. October 1974. Records: *Before the Flood*. *Creem*, 64–65.

Jeske, L. September 10, 1990. Bob Dylan revisited. *New York Post* (NEWSBANK).

Jones, A. February 3, 1990. Blood on the tracks: The legend of Bob Dylan. *Melody Maker*, 29–36.

Jones, M. May 23, 1964. If you want to do it—then do it! *Melody Maker*, 12.

————. March 20, 1995. A primitive's portfolio. *Newsweek*, 60–61.

Joyce, M. September 20, 1989. Bob Dylan, brooding but clear. *Washington Post*, D7.

————. September 16, 1990. The times keep on a-changin'. *Washington Post*, G1, 9.

Katz, L. March 25, 1991. New 'Bootleg Series' tracks musician from folk to rock. *Boston Herald* (NEWSBANK).

————. November 1, 1992. Dylan's new release is as 'Good as' it gets. *Boston Herald* (NEWSBANK).

————. October 26, 1993. Album gives insight into Dylan's 'World.' *Boston Herald* (NEWSBANK).

Keller, M. September 11, 1983. Religion, politics, a new record: What's up with Bob Dylan. *Chicago Tribune*, sec. 12, 5–6.

Kilday, G. January 22, 1978. Film-maker Dylan: A peek behind the mask. *Los Angeles Times*, sec. C, 1, 43.

King, P. June 26, 1988. 'Groove' is a downer for Bob Dylan. *Pittsburgh Press* (NEWSBANK).

————. October 8, 1989. Dylan, newcomer turn out fine albums. *Pittsburgh Press* (NEWSBANK).

Klein, J. 1980. *Woody Guthrie: A life*. New York: Delta.

————. March 11, 2004. Live reviews: Bob Dylan. www.Billboard.com.

Kleinman, B. 1998. Dylan on Dylan (1984). In C. Benson, ed., *The Bob Dylan companion: Four decades of commentary*, 30–40. New York: Schirmer.

Kot, G. September 24, 1989. Dylan delivers. *Chicago Tribune*, sec. 5, 3.

————. October 25, 1992. He may not have all the answers, but he always asks the right questions. *Chicago Tribune*, sec. 13, 16, 21.

————. August 15, 1993. Casting giant shadows. *Chicago Tribune*, sec. 13, 6–7.

————. September 28, 1997. Like a rolling stone. *Chicago Tribune*, sec. 7, 17.

Kotkin, J. January 20, 1978. Bob Dylan, alone. *Washington Post*, D1, 2.

Landau, J. May 1968. *John Wesley Harding*. *Crawdaddy*, 11–17.

————. March 13, 1975. *Blood on the Tracks*: After the flood. *Rolling Stone*, 43, 47–51.

Levy, J. October 1989. Bob Dylan: *Oh Mercy*. *Spin*, 98.

Lewis, G. 1970. The pop artist and his product: Mixed-up confusion. *Journal of Popular Culture* 2: 327–38.

Lingeman, R. June 25, 1971. Bob Dylan, I'm writing to you. *New York Times*, 32.

Loder, K. September 18, 1980. God and man at Columbia. *Rolling Stone*, 48.

————. June 21, 1984. The Rolling Stone interview: Bob Dylan. *Rolling Stone*, 14–18, 23–24, 78.

————. February 14, 1985. Records: Bob Dylan: *Real Live*. *Rolling Stone*, 46–47.

————. July 4, 1985. Records: Bob Dylan rocks again. *Rolling Stone*, 48–49.

————. November 5, 1987. Bob Dylan. *Rolling Stone*, 301–3.

————. October 15, 1992. The Rolling Stone interview: Bob Dylan. *Rolling Stone*, 110–13.

MacDonald, P. July 25, 1986. Tried true confessions. *Seattle Times* (NEWSBANK).

Malone, B. 1985. *Country music USA*. Austin: University of Texas Press.

Marcus, G. August 24, 1978. Records: 'Street Legal' a misdemeanor. *Rolling Stone*, 51–53.

————. 1997. *Invisible republic: Bob Dylan's basement tapes*. New York: Henry Holt.

————. 2004. Self portrait no. 25. In B. Hedin, ed., *Studio A: The Bob Dylan reader*, 73–91. New York: W. W. Norton.

Marin, P. February 20, 1972. With the help of electricity the young could hear themselves speak. *New York Times Book Review*, 4–5.

Marine, C. October 28, 1993. Bob Dylan revisited. *San Francisco Examiner* (NEWSBANK).

Marsh, D. March 11, 1976. Records: Desire under fire: Mythic images of women and outlaws. *Rolling Stone*, 55–59.

————. October 21, 1976. 'Hard Rain,' hard rock, hard sell. *Rolling Stone*, 39.

Maslin, J. July 12, 1979. Bob Dylan: Brave new world at Budokan. *Rolling Stone*, 72.

Mayer, I. July 16, 1986. Dylan's new disc only a partial knockout. *New York Post* (NEWSBANK).

McClure, M. March 14, 1974. The poet's poet. *Rolling Stone*, 33–34.

McGregor, C. 1972. *Bob Dylan: A retrospective*. New York: William Morrow.

————. May 7, 1972. Dylan: Reluctant hero of the pop generation. *New York Times*, 15.

McKeen, W. 1993. *Bob Dylan: A bio-bibliography*. Westport, CT: Greenwood.

McLeese, D. June 6, 1988. Dylan album offers a bit of everything. *Chicago Sun Times* (NEWSBANK).

————. October 1, 1989. Dylan finds 'Mercy' in Louisiana. *Chicago Sun Times* (NEWSBANK).

————. November 29, 1990. Recordings: Traveling Wilburys, vol. 3. *Rolling Stone*, 105–6.

Meehan, T. December 12, 1965. Public writer No. 1? *New York Times*, 44–45.

Milano, B. December 1997. Positively Bob Dylan. *Stereo Review*, 106.

Miller, J. December 9, 1985. The two lives of Bob Dylan. *Newsweek*, 93–94.

————. June 23, 1986. The minstrel in middle age. *Newsweek*, 80.

Mitchell, G. October 1975. Records: *The Basement Tapes*. *Crawdaddy*, 65–66.

Mitchell, R. September 27, 1989. Mercy, Dylan LP is good. *Houston Chronicle* (NEWSBANK).

Moon, T. June 13, 1988. The latest from Dylan: An easy, bluesy album. *Miami Herald* (NEWSBANK).

————. September 19, 1989. Dylan album reflects New Orleans sojourn. *Philadelphia Inquirer* (NEWS-BANK).

————. April 4, 1991. *Bootleg* adds luster to the Dylan myth. *Miami Herald* (NEWSBANK).

————. May 20, 2001. If it's a milestone time for Dylan, 60 isn't why. *(Philadelphia) Inquirer*, www.Inquirer.com.

Morgan, J. April 1985. Bob Dylan: *Real Live*. *Creem*, 50.

Morley, J. July 1991. Blue Light Special: Bob Dylan (Or, what Bob Dylan can teach you about the unfinished war in Iraq). *Spin*, 84–85.

Morse, S. October 24, 1993. 'World Gone Wrong' is Dylan gone right. *Boston Globe* (NEWSBANK).

———. September 26, 1997. Dylan explores his dark side. *Boston Globe*, D15.

———. September 7, 2001. King of hearts. *Boston Globe*, www.boston.com.

Muir, A. 2001. *Razor's edge: Bob Dylan & the never ending tour.* London: Helter Skelter.

Nelson, P. September 11, 1975. Records: The basement tapes caper: A new/old mystery. *Rolling Stone*, 50–54.

———. October 15, 1981. Records: The politics of sin. *Rolling Stone*, 59–61.

———. October 1990. Bob Dylan: *Under the Red Sky. Musician*, 121.

Nelson, P., and J. Pankake. 1998. Flat tire. In C. Benson, ed., *The Bob Dylan companion: Four decades of commentary*, 20–23. New York: Schirmer.

Nesin, J. February 1984. Keep the faith, Bobby! *Creem*, 51.

Nicholaus, C. April 1975. Dreck in the groove. *Creem*, 60–61.

O'Hare, K. March 24, 1991. New bootleg Dylan recalls the genius. *(Springfield, MA) Sunday Republican* (NEWSBANK).

Olsen, B. September 17, 2001. Bob Dylan, joker. *New Zealand Herald*, www.nzherald.co.nz.

Orth, M. January 14, 1974. Dylan—rolling again. *Newsweek*, 46–49.

———. February 10, 1975. Constant lover. *Newsweek*, 65–66.

———. November 17, 1975. It's me, babe. *Newsweek*, 94.

Page, T. May 24, 2001. Bob Dylan, not ready for to fade. www.Washingtonpost.com.

Palmer, R. 1978. *Baby, that was rock & roll: The legendary Leiber & Stoller.* New York: Harcourt Brace Jovanovich.

Pareles, J. September 1978. Untangling from the blues. *Crawdaddy*, 65.

———. July 17, 1986. Music: Bob Dylan and Tom Petty. *New York Times*, 15.

———. August 10, 1986. Bob Dylan and Neil Young face life in the 80's. *New York Times*, 20, 30.

———. January 29, 1989. With concert disks, is it live or memories? *New York Times*, 28.

———. September 28, 1997. A wiser voice blowin' in the autumn wind. *New York Times*, 1, 28.

———. July 27, 2003. Bob Dylan plays Bob Dylan, whoever that is. www.nytimes.com.

Pennebaker, D., and B. Neuwirth. 1999. Director's commentary from *Dont Look Back.* New York: New Video.

Perry, C. April 3, 1991. Dylan in rare form. *Houston Post* (NEWSBANK).

———. October 26, 1993. Dylan's irritating brilliance shines on edges of album. *Houston Post* (NEWSBANK).

Petkovic, J. September 11, 2001. You won't be cheated by Bob Dylan's latest. *(Cleveland) Plain Dealer*, www.Cleveland.com.

Poet's return: "It's what I do." September 12, 1969. *Time*, 80–81.

Pollock, B. 1975. *In their own words.* New York: Macmillan.

Pond, S. May 13, 1979. Dylan: Still a mystery. *Los Angeles Times*, sec. C, 83.

Pousner, H. November 30, 1985. Almost definitive Dylan. *Atlanta Journal* (NEWSBANK).

Powers, A. May 11, 2001. Dylan keeps a-changin', making him a hard act to follow. www.nytimes.com.

Puterbaugh, P. January 1990. Dylan's vision. *Stereo Review*, 111.

———. February 1993. Bob Dylan: *Good As I Been To You. Stereo Review*, 120.

Rachlis, K. December 2, 1976. Records: Rolling Thunder's downpour. *Rolling Stone*, 91–92.

Ransom, K. November 17, 1990. Dylan's new hard edge may surprise old fans. *Ann Arbor News* (NEWSBANK).

Richardson, S. September 16, 1993. Bob Dylan: The 30th Anniversary Concert Celebration. *Rolling Stone*, 72.

———. May–June 1994. Dylan's folk revival. *Acoustic Guitar*, 91–93.

———. December 15, 1994. Performance: Bob Dylan. *Rolling Stone*, 38.

———. May 4, 1995. Recordings: His back pages. *Rolling Stone*, 63, 65.

Ricks, C. 2003. *Dylan's visions of sin.* New York: HarperCollins.

Riegel, R. March 1982. More of an outlaw that you ever were? *Creem*, 42–43, 57–58.

Riley, J. July 9, 2001. Dylan talks pops. *Liverpool Echo*, www.icLiverpool.com.

Riley, T. 1999. *Hard rain: A Dylan commentary.* New York: Da Capo.

Robbins, P. 1998. Bob Dylan in his own words (1965). In C. Benson, ed., *The Bob Dylan companion: Four decades of commentary*, 48–57. New York: Schirmer.

Rock 'n' Roll. 1995. Public Broadcasting System. Boston: WGBH.

Rockwell, J. January 25, 1976. Are the times a-changin' too much for Dylan? *New York Times*, D1, 17.

———. November 24, 1985. Bob Dylan sums up a life in music. *New York Times*, B1.

Rodnitzky, J. 1976. *Minstrels of the dawn: The folk-protest singer as a cultural hero.* Chicago: Nelson-Hall.

Rohter, L. January 5, 1976. Dylan's 'Desire': Baring his soul after all these years. *Washington Post*, D1, 3.

Rose, D. December 1975. For whom the tribute tolls. *Crawdaddy*, 26–27.

Rosenbaum, R. March 1978. Playboy interview: Bob Dylan. *Playboy*, 61–90.

———. 2001. Born-again Bob: Four theories. In E. Thomson and D. Gutman, eds., *The Dylan companion*, 233–37. New York: Da Capo.

Ross, A. 2004. The wanderer. In B. Hedin, ed., *Studio A: The Bob Dylan reader*, 291–312. New York: W. W. Norton.

Rowland, M. December 1983. Record reviews: Bob Dylan: *Infidels*. *Musician*, 104.

Saal, H. February 26, 1968. Dylan is back. *Newsweek*, 92–93.

———. April 14, 1969. Dylan's country pie. *Newsweek*, 102–4.

Samuels, L. July 30, 1986. This time, the music's the message from Dylan. *Dallas Morning News* (NEWSBANK).

Santelli, R., H. George-Warren, and J. Brown, eds. 2001. *American roots music.* New York: Abrams.

Santoro, G. 2004. *Highway 61 revisited: The tangled roots of American jazz, blues, rock, & country music.* New York: Oxford University Press.

Scaduto, A. 1971. *Bob Dylan.* New York: Grosset & Dunlap.

———. November 28, 1971. 'Won't you listen to the lambs, Bob Dylan?' *New York Times Magazine*, 34–40.

Scheck, F. November 7, 1997. Bob Dylan, rock's preeminent wordsmith, makes a comeback. *Christian Science Monitor*, 15.

Schoemer, K. December 6, 1992. Bob Dylan revisits his roots and finds a gift for the young. *New York Times*, sec. 2, 26.

Selvin, J. September 28, 1997. Dylan's best new songs in ages. *San Francisco Chronicle*, 46.

———. September 9, 2001. Dylan is brilliant on 'Love and Theft.' *San Francisco Chronicle*, www.sfgate.com.

Seay, D. September 23, 1979. Dylan and the musical ministry. *Los Angeles Times*, sec. C, 82, 84.

Sheffield, R. September 27, 2001. Recordings: *Love and Theft. Rolling Stone*, 65–67.

Shelton, R. August 27, 1965. Pop singers and song writers racing down Bob Dylan's road. *New York Times*, 34.

———. August 30, 1965. Dylan conquers unruly audience. *New York Times*, 20.

———. July 29, 1978. How does it feel to be on your own? *Melody Maker*, 27–30.

———. 1986. *No direction home: The life and music of Bob Dylan.* New York: Ballantine.

———. 2001. Interview with Abe and Beatty Zimmerman. In D. Barker, ed., *Isis: A Bob Dylan anthology*, 12–25. London: Helter Skelter.

———. 2004. One foot on the highway. In *Younger than that now* (71–90). New York: Thunder's Mouth.

Shepard, S. 2004. *The rolling thunder logbook.* New York: Da Capo.

Shuster, F. May 16, 1992. A night with Dylan? What did he say? *Los Angeles Daily News* (NEWSBANK).

Simels, S. January 1984. Dylan lives! *Stereo Review*, 80.

Singer, D. January 4, 1980. Not buying into subculture. *Christianity Today*, 33.

Sloman, L. 1978. *On the road with Bob Dylan.* New York: Three Rivers Press.

Smith, A. May 5, 1991. Dylan's buried treasures. *(Providence, RI) Journal-Bulletin* (NEWSBANK).

Smith, L. 1999. *Pete Townshend: The minstrel's dilemma.* Westport, CT: Praeger.

———. 2002. *Bob Dylan, Bruce Springsteen, & American song.* Westport, CT: Praeger.

———. 2004. *Elvis Costello, Joni Mitchell, & the torch song tradition.* Westport, CT: Praeger.

Smith, R. J. October 21, 1997. Sick of it all. *Village Voice*, 69–70.

Snyder, M. October 22, 1989. Bob gives a peek at real Dylan. *San Francisco Examiner* (NEWSBANK).

Sounes, H. 2001. *Down the highway: The life of Bob Dylan.* New York: Grove.

Spitz, B. 1989. *Dylan: A biography.* New York: W. W. Norton.

Spitz, R. June 28, 1978. 'Street Legal' Magic. *Washington Post*, E4.

Steinberg, B. April 2, 2004. Bob Dylan gets tangled up in pink. *Wall Street Journal*, B3.

Stone, A. October 24, 1965. Interview with Bob Dylan. Detroit: WDTM.

Stookey, N. January 4, 1980. Bob Dylan finds his source. *Christianity Today*, 32.

Sumrall, H. July 18, 1986. Dylan cooks like a summer day. *San Jose Mercury News* (NEWSBANK).

Taylor, G. 1989. *Reinventing Shakespeare: A cultural history from restoration to the present.* New York: Oxford University Press.

Tempest, M. September 11, 2001. If music be the food of love, play on. *Guardian,* www.guardian.co.uk.

Thomson, E., and D. Gutman, eds. 2001. *The Dylan companion.* New York: Da Capo.

Trakin, R. September 1986. Record reviews: Bob Dylan: *Knocked Out Loaded. Musician,* 104–6.

Tucker, K. June 8, 1988. Bob Dylan's new album: Perverse and pretty good. *Philadelphia Inquirer* (NEWS-BANK).

———. October 3, 1997. Tombstone blues. *Entertainment Weekly,* 80–82.

Van Matre, L. February 3, 1974. Mellow Dylan makes a few weak 'Waves.' *Chicago Tribune,* 11.

———. November 10, 1985. Still compelling: A long look back at two decades of Dylan. *Chicago Tribune,* sec. 13, 4–5, 8.

———. July 22, 1986. Dylan back again, but latest album is no KO. *Chicago Tribune,* sec. 5, 3.

Varesi, A. 2002. *The Bob Dylan albums: A critical study.* Toronto: Guernica.

Varga, G. September 20, 1989. 'Mercy!' Dylan in top form. *San Diego Union* (NEWSBANK).

———. March 25, 1991. A look back at Dylan's best years. *San Diego Union* (NEWSBANK).

Verna, P. October 4, 1997. Reviews & previews: *Time Out of Mind. Billboard,* 89.

Vowell, S. December 1997. Bob Dylan: *Time Out of Mind. Spin,* 154.

Wagner, V. March 13, 2004. Dylan's famous, but he's no celeb. www.thestar.com.

Walls, R. October 1988. Bob Dylan: *Down in the Groove. Creem,* 26–27.

Webb, J. 1998. *Tunesmith: Inside the art of songwriting.* New York: Hyperion.

Welles, C. April 10, 1964. The angry young folk singer. *Life,* 109–14.

Wenner, J. November 29, 1969. The Rolling Stone interview: Dylan. *Rolling Stone,* 22–33.

———. September 20, 1979. Bob Dylan and our times: The slow train is coming. *Rolling Stone,* 94–99.

Wild, D. November 26, 1992. Come gather round, people. *Rolling Stone,* 17, 19.

———. January 7, 1993. Recordings: *Good As I Been To You. Rolling Stone,* 45.

Wilentz, S. 2004. Liner notes for *Bob Dylan: Live 1964.* New York: Sony Music Entertainment.

Williams, P. 1991. *Bob Dylan performing artist: The early years 1960–1973.* Novato, CA: Underwood-Miller.

———. 1992. *Bob Dylan performing artist: The middle years 1974–1986.* Novato, CA: Underwood-Miller.

———. 1996. *Bob Dylan: Watching the river flow.* New York: Omnibus.

———. 2004. *Bob Dylan performing artist: 1986–1990 & beyond, mind out of time.* New York: Omnibus.

Williams, R. September 23, 1990. The calm after the storm. *New York Times,* H28.

———. 1992. *Dylan: A man called alias.* New York: Henry Holt.

Willis, E. February 18, 1974. Rock, etc.: Dylan and fans: Looking back, going on. *New Yorker,* 108–10.

———. April 7, 1975. Rock, etc.: After the flood. *New Yorker,* 130–32.

Wilonsky, R. September 6, 2001. Bob Dylan: *Love and Theft.* www.Dallasobserver.com.

Wissolik, R., and S. McGrath. 1994. *Bob Dylan's words: A critical dictionary and commentary.* New York: Eadmer.

Worrell, D. November 25, 1985. "It's all right in front." *Time,* 123.

Worthington, R. July 31, 1988. The town of Bob Dylan's youth leaves his past blowing in the wind. *Chicago Tribune,* sec. 5, 5.

Young, C. August 1985. Record reviews: Bob Dylan: *Empire Burlesque. Musician,* 96–97.

Zito, T. January 16, 1974. Greeting the guarded voice of a generation. *Washington Post,* B1, 10.

Zollo, P. 1997. *Songwriters on songwriting.* New York: Da Capo.

Index

About the Author

LARRY DAVID SMITH is an independent writer and lecturer who specializes in narrative critiques of popular media. His work includes *Elvis Costello, Joni Mitchell, and the Torch Song Tradition* (Praeger, 2004), *Bob Dylan, Bruce Springsteen, and American Song* (Praeger, 2002), and *Pete Townshend: The Minstrel's Dilemma* (Praeger, 1999).